I0817453

MAGIC ARCHITECTURE

HIGHER PRODUCTIVITY
AFFECTS
CHANGES IN
SOCIAL STRUCTURE
CULTURAL ATTITUDE
AND POPULAR IDEOLOGY
RE-ACTION TOWARDS
NEW STANDARDS
IN LIFE ACTIVITIES

MAGIC ARCHITECTURE
THE STORY OF HUMAN HOUSING

FREDERICK KIESLER

EDITED BY

SPYROS PAPAPETROS AND GERD ZILLNER

The MIT Press   Cambridge, Massachusetts   London, England

fig. A.01

Sun, June 28, 1946

Atomic Blue Glow Kills Scientists

Army Reports Accidents Caused No Blast, Debris or Noise.

Los Alamos, N. M., June 28 (A. P.).—The Army today described an atomic chain reaction set up on May 21 at the Los Alamos atomic laboratory, which burned a scientist fatally, as a blue glow with "no explosion in the sense that there were no mechanical effects, no debris, no noise."

The detailed report also disclosed that the accident, which cost the life of another scientist, Harry K. Daglian, 24 years old, of New London, Conn., in September, was almost identical with the one in May which proved fatal to Dr. Louis B. Slotin, 35, of Winnipeg, Canada.

In both cases equipment slipped, allowing fissionable materials of the type used in atom bombs to come together swiftly instead of under control as had been done safely many times at the laboratory.

Seven others working with Slotin were burned, but recovered. Daglian was working alone.

The Army report gave this description of the accident:

"An accident occurred when a piece of equipment slipped. This brought the material swiftly together beyond the critical point. This resulted in a tremendous energy release within millionths of a second, which was evidenced to the persons present through a sensation of heat and visual perception of a blue glow around the material.

"In the words of one of the men present, 'It was as if you were standing near an arc welder when he struck the arc.'

No Blast or Noise.

"The blue glow resulted from the ionization of air particles by radiation emanating from the fissionable material. There was no explosion in the sense that there were no mechanical effects, no debris, no noise.

"In the millionths of a second in which this occurred, the immediate area and all in it were bombarded by intense high energy gamma rays and neutrons of all energies—fast, intermediate and slow. There were no beta and no alpha radiation.

"Dr. Slotin, at the instant of the mishap, knocked the equipment apart, thus halting the intensifying radiation and averting serious consequences, possibly death to his companions. He was grasping part of the equipment with his left hand at the moment of the accident."

The report told of immediate removal to the Los Alamos Hospital of the eight men, and the wait of several days before effects of radiation were apparent. Slotin died in nine days.

"The medical men began to treat the accident victims as soon as they were admitted to the hospital," the report said. "This treatment, in general, consisted of many transfusions of whole blood and plasma and fluids, principally glucose and saline."

The report said that the burns suffered by Slotin were comparable to a "three-dimensional sunburn," explaining: "The skin burns from the radiation are superficial, but as the rays penetrate the body they burn deep, resulting in injury and destruction of tissue and blood cells."

Daglian, whose burns were less severe, died in twenty-six days after the accident.

"Atomic Blue Glow Kills Scientists," *The Sun* (New York, NY), June 28, 1946: Press clipping with Kiesler's markings for transcription. ÖFLKS, CLP_6463/0

MAGIC ARCHITECTURE
SOURCES, DISCIPLINES, AND OBJECTS

SPYROS PAPAPETROS

Among the journal and newspaper clippings that make up the extensive research files compiled by the Austrian-American architect Frederick Kiesler for his book project *Magic Architecture* is a brief article titled "Atomic Blue Glow Kills Scientists." Published in the June 28, 1946, issue of *The Sun*, around the same time Kiesler was working on his manuscript, the article is based on an army report prompted by "an atomic chain reaction" that occurred one month prior in Los Alamos, New Mexico. (fig. A.01) In addition, the article discloses an "accident" from August of the previous year that was "almost identical" to the more recent event.[1] The most striking aspect of the incidents was that both were entirely silent, producing "No Blast, Debris, or Noise"–as announced in bold in the article's subtitle and echoed in a headline and main text. The "accident occurred when a piece of equipment slipped" while being handled by a scientist who was demonstrating an experiment to colleagues in the same room. The slip brought the radioactive material "beyond a critical point" and "resulted in a tremendous energy release within millionths of a second ... evidenced by the persons present by the bodily sensation of heat and the visual perception of a blue glow." In the words of one witness, "it was as if you were standing next to an arc welder, when he struck the arc," drawing a comparison with a manually activated electromagnetic technique used to join metal surfaces that produces a similar optical and thermal sensation.[2] As the report explained, "the blue glow resulted from the ionization of air particles by radiation emanating from the fissionable material." Within "millionths of a second, the immediate area and all in it were bombarded" by multiple energies, "fast, intermediate, and slow."

The temporal layering of mechanical energies was replicated in their damaging effects on the operator's body. The reaction caused "a three-dimensional sunburn"–an affliction that initially resembles a superficial irritation of the skin but gradually moves deeper, causing "destruction of tissue blood cells" that can prove fatal. While those present at the scene were immediately removed to the Los Alamos hospital to undergo several blood, plasma, and other fluid transfusions, the effects of radiation did not become apparent until "several days" later: Dr. Louis Slotin died on the ninth day following the June incident, while Harry Daglian had died twenty-six days after the first failed experiment in August 1945. It was only following Slotin's death that information on the two lethal events was made public.

The *Sun* clipping is one of the first published reports of the two previously unknown "accidents" that occurred in the Los Alamos National Laboratory for nuclear energy related to the secret federal program developed by the United States during War World II, known as the Manhattan Project. Although Kiesler's numerous drafts of *Magic Architecture* include two copies of a typed transcription with selections from the same article marked in pencil, no part of the report is quoted in the assembled book manuscript.[3] But like the chain reaction described in the army report, despite its inaudible impact, the piece continues to propagate, permeating not only the content, but also the *context* in which *Magic Architecture* was enveloped, beyond the physical limits of its leather binder.

Compiled at the end of World War II with the assistance of Kiesler's wife Stefi and submitted to editors soon after, *Magic Architecture* ultimately went unpublished. However, the 300-page manuscript, illustrated by more than seventy composite plates, would form the architect's most ambitious book project. It is also Kiesler's most interdisciplinary writing, elaborately planned as a Neo-Vitruvian Renaissance treatise divided into ten "parts" or books, each of which is further subdivided into multiple chapters that narrate an alternative history and theory of architecture. The side-product of two exhibition projects that remained largely unrealized (a "Hall of Ecology" planned for the Museum of Natural History in New York and the exhibition on American architecture that traveled to the USSR), the book demonstrates the architect's ability to curate physical as well as textual space and combine a verbal and visual demonstration of his arguments and ideas. As a whole, the assembled manuscript of *Magic Architecture* reflects the correspondence between Kiesler's anthropological projections into the cultural history (or prehistory) of architecture and its current socio-political predicament following the events of the Second World War. In his apospasmatic history of housing, Kiesler combines the comparative exploration of the "magic" practices associated with cave drawings and protohistoric subterranean settlements as reconstructed by mid-century archaeologists and paleoanthropologists with the alternative epistemology of the quasi-"magical" effects of atomic technology.

Kiesler's research files contain multiple clippings on atomic experiments before and after the Second World War, including an illustrated article from *Life* on the Bikini Atoll explosions on the Pacific Marshall Islands in July 1946.[4] In files of his ongoing studies of Correalism is a 1947 *New York Times* report on the research of two Columbia University physicists on atom-enhanced radar waves.[5] The same files contain three articles from David Dietz's syndicated series "Smashing the Atom," published in the *New York World Telegram* in November 1936. One heralds the "useful dividends" to be paid by "atomic theory" for the building and engineering industries, with a focus on the field of metallurgy through the improvement of aluminum construction resulting in "taller skyscrapers, larger bridges, faster trains, and stronger aircraft."[6] (fig. A.02)

The association between contemporary scientific technology and "ancient" magic is not fortuitous: design and its purported genealogies served as the medium of diachronic "correlation." Alongside his *Telegram* column, in 1938 Dietz published *Medical Magic*, a book musing on the resemblance of devices and processes used by "modern medical science" and those of "ancient magicians."[7] Apart from *Magic Architecture*'s own interest in the revelations of contemporary science, the deepest affinity between Kiesler's book and wartime science is an implicit similarity in *method*–a common operational technique used to amalgamate practices of nuclear energy and atomic radiation with anthropological theories of magic. In several paragraphs of his manuscript, the architect employs the term "sympathetic magic"–a supernatural form of association coined by the British comparative anthropologist James Frazer in *The Golden Bough*, a notorious turn-of-the-century compendium of European folklore and colonial ethnography.[8]

Although the two-volume edition of *The Golden Bough* in Kiesler's personal library carries no notes, its sympathetic influence travels across the architect's "correalist" projects.[9] Frazer's book, in its development of narratives about energy renewal and the circular distribution of power, compares the rules of sympathetic magic where things act upon each other by way of an "invisible ether" to the principles of modern science, in which "things can physically affect each other through an empty space."[10] Frazer further distinguishes sympathetic magic into "imitative or homeopathic" and "contagious," the former based on the laws of "similarity" acting over a distance and the latter by "contact" and physical immediacy (even if the armchair anthropologist never actually experienced physical proximity with the magical objects and electrifying subjects he was studying).[11]

Both of these contrasting forms of sympathetic magic are reactivated in the Los Alamos incident, linking, quite literally, as Michael Taussig in his contemporary reading of Frazer would propose, "similarity" and "contact":[12] first, via the contagious immediacy of the atomic chain reaction and second by the homeopathic reverberation of this event occurring *twice* in New Mexico, the first silently unfolding a few weeks after the shuddering bomb dropping in Japan. But it was the faint echo of this cataclysmic event at

Fair Enough

By WESTBROOK PEGLER

College Football Wages Need Revision Upward, Schools Heartless Bosses, Gate Receipts Pay Bills.

New York World-Telegram

SECTION TWO. NEW YORK, WEDNESDAY, NOVEMBER 18, 1936.

EDITORIALS—BOOKS—COMICS FASHION—SOCIETY—DRAMA

SMASHING THE ATOM

Atomic Theory Paying Useful Dividends in Taller Skyscrapers, Longer Bridges, Faster Trains, Stronger Aircraft—Work of Sir William Bragg Important in This.

By DAVID DIETZ, Scripps-Howard Science Editor.

Recovery Partly on Unsound Basis, Johnson Warning

Roosevelt Luck, International Madness and Other Dubious Factors Seen in Stock Market's Rise.

By HUGH S. JOHNSON.

My Day By Eleanor Roosevelt

BARGAIN DAYS

New Glands, New Man.

an infinitesimally smaller scale, moving from enemy territory on the other side of the planet to the interior of its "home" base in the United States, which made the repetition of these "accidents" uncannily overpowering. The "home" could now be assaulted from within by the inscrutable devices mishandled by its domestic operators. No shelter could ever be entirely insulated from the "blue glow" spilling from the Los Alamos laboratory.

If Frazer's ethnographic narratives of animist magic in *The Golden Bough* mirrored the technical applications of electro-physics in late-nineteenth-century industrialized economies, then Kiesler's *Magic Architecture* updates a similarly spiritualized technology for the radioactive environments of the Atomic Age (a term coined by Laurence). By correlating modern techniques with the anthropological origins of housing, Kiesler's manuscript recalibrates human habitation for an environment in constant war. Like an automaton, housing ventriloquizes its own fictional "story" at the very moment that its mechanisms start unraveling and human dwelling's planetary future becomes forebodingly imbalanced.

"Omnivorous all eating: that is man." This phrase opens one of *Magic Architecture*'s first chapters, "The Fear of the Unseen." Starting from the indiscriminate diet of the "all devouring" humans as opposed to the more focused nutrition of all other species, the chapter quickly shifts to the ways that humans strive to overcome their physical "inferiority" against larger animals:

> **His strength has retired to one corner of his brain. Here in the mold of his forehead he speculates on how to overcome his inferiority. He does not dare to combat any of the animals with his own hand. His cowardice is so great that his main occupation is to contrive instruments that will keep any other species of this earth away from him. He will not meet his enemy breast to breast; he will try to kill from a distance and remain unseen. And the greater his civilization the further away will he take his stand for the kill. His pride grows bigger with the distance of his hiding. His ultimate dream of safety is to be able to shoot from interstellar space—unseen, unheard with nothing of his scent coming downwind.** (I.2)

Here, the protective architecture of the brain is the eccentric seat of human power striving to compensate bodily deficiency by means of mental projection, a notion that was also explored by the physical anthropologist Ashley Montagu in "The Skillful Skull" (another article in Kiesler's offcuts and clippings), published in MIT's *Technology Review* and which analyzed the human "braincase" as "a noteworthy example of efficient architecture"; as Montagu argues, the brain is "architecturally" similar to the Gothic style because of the "buttressing" properties of its "series of arches."[13] (figs. A.03a-b) In his own prehistory of design, Kiesler moves from the "mold" of human foreheads to the offensive architecture of ballistic devices as an extension of power beyond the envelope of

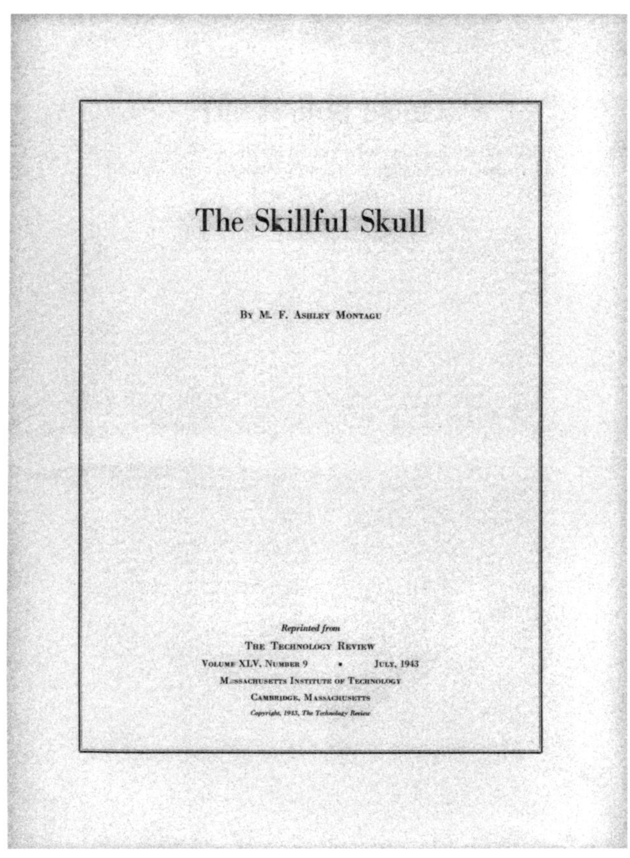

The Skillful Skull

By M. F. Ashley Montagu

Reprinted from
The Technology Review
Volume XLV, Number 9 • July, 1943
Massachusetts Institute of Technology
Cambridge, Massachusetts
Copyright, 1943, The Technology Review

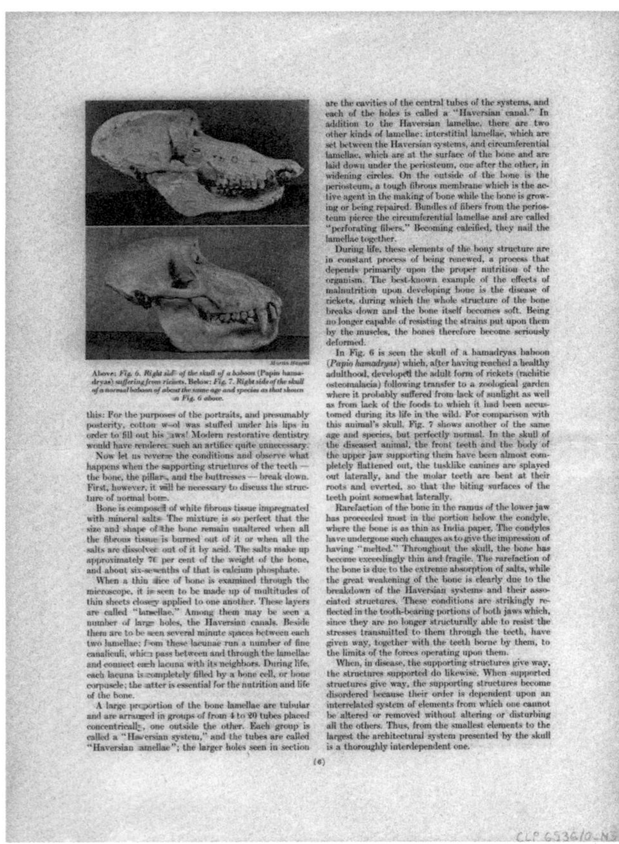

Above: Fig. 6. Right side of the skull of a baboon (Papio hamadryas) suffering from rickets. Below: Fig. 7. Right side of the skull of a normal baboon of about the same age and species as that shown in Fig. 6 above.

this: For the purposes of the portraits, and presumably posterity, cotton wool was stuffed under his lips in order to fill out his jaws! Modern restorative dentistry would have rendered such an artifice quite unnecessary.

Now let us reverse the conditions and observe what happens when the supporting structures of the teeth — the bone, the pillars, and the buttresses — break down. First, however, it will be necessary to discuss the structure of normal bone.

Bone is composed of white fibrous tissue impregnated with mineral salts. The mixture is so perfect that the size and shape of the bone remain unaltered when all the fibrous tissue is burned out of it or when all the salts are dissolved out of it by acid. The salts make up approximately 70 per cent of the weight of the bone, and about six-sevenths of that is calcium phosphate.

When a thin slice of bone is examined through the microscope, it is seen to be made up of multitudes of thin sheets closely applied to one another. These layers are called "lamellae." Among them may be seen a number of large holes, the Haversian canals. Beside them are to be seen several minute spaces between each two lamellae; from these lacunae run a number of fine canaliculi, which pass between and through the lamellae and connect each lacuna with its neighbors. During life, each lacuna is completely filled by a bone cell, or bone corpuscle; the latter is essential for the nutrition and life of the bone.

A large proportion of the bone lamellae are tubular and are arranged in groups of from 4 to 20 tubes placed concentrically, one outside the other. Each group is called a "Haversian system," and the tubes are called "Haversian lamellae"; the larger holes seen in section are the cavities of the central tubes of the systems, and each of the holes is called a "Haversian canal." In addition to the Haversian lamellae, there are two other kinds of lamellae: interstitial lamellae, which are set between the Haversian systems, and circumferential lamellae, which are at the surface of the bone and are laid down under the periosteum, one after the other, in widening circles. On the outside of the bone is the periosteum, a tough fibrous membrane which is the active agent in the making of bone while the bone is growing or being repaired. Bundles of fibers from the periosteum pierce the circumferential lamellae and are called "perforating fibers." Becoming calcified, they nail the lamellae together.

During life, these elements of the bony structure are in constant process of being renewed, a process that depends primarily upon the proper nutrition of the organism. The best-known example of the effects of malnutrition upon developing bone is the disease of rickets, during which the whole structure of the bone breaks down and the bone itself becomes soft. Being no longer capable of resisting the strains put upon them by the muscles, the bones therefore become seriously deformed.

In Fig. 6 is seen the skull of a hamadryas baboon (*Papio hamadryas*) which, after having reached a healthy adulthood, developed the adult form of rickets (rachitic osteomalacia) following transfer to a zoological garden where it probably suffered from lack of sunlight as well as from lack of the foods to which it had been accustomed during its life in the wild. For comparison with this animal's skull, Fig. 7 shows another of the same age and species, but perfectly normal. In the skull of the diseased animal, the front teeth and the body of the upper jaw supporting them have been almost completely flattened out, the tusklike canines are splayed out laterally, and the molar teeth are bent at their roots and everted, so that the biting surfaces of the teeth point somewhat laterally.

Rarefaction of the bone in the ramus of the lower jaw has proceeded most in the portion below the condyle, where the bone is as thin as India paper. The condyles have undergone such changes as to give the impression of having "melted." Throughout the skull, the bone has become exceedingly thin and fragile. The rarefaction of the bone is due to the extreme absorption of salts, while the great weakening of the bone is clearly due to the breakdown of the Haversian systems and their associated structures. These conditions are strikingly reflected in the tooth-bearing portions of both jaws which, since they are no longer structurally able to resist the stresses transmitted to them through the teeth, have given way, together with the teeth borne by them, to the limits of the forces operating upon them.

When, in disease, the supporting structures give way, the structures supported do likewise. When supported structures give way, the supporting structures become disordered because their order is dependent upon an interrelated system of elements from which one cannot be altered or removed without altering or disturbing all the others. Thus, from the smallest elements to the largest the architectural system presented by the skull is a thoroughly interdependent one.

(6)

CLP 6536/0-N3

Previous
fig. A.02 David Dietz, "Smashing the Atom," *New York World Telegram*, November 18, 1936. Research press clipping. ÖFLKS TXT_6418/0

Above
figs. A.03a-b Ashley Montagu, "The Skillful Skull," *Technology Review* 45, no. 9 (July 1943), separate reprint, 5. ÖFLKS, CLP_6536/0

Opposite, above
fig. A.04 Leigh White, "Buck Fuller and the Dymaxion World," *Saturday Evening Post* (Philadelphia), October 14, 1944, 22.

Opposite, below
fig. A.05 "Design's Bad Boy," *Architectural Forum*, 86/2, February 1947 (article offprint in Frederick Kiesler's collection) ÖFLKS, CLP_902/0

the warrior body. From the antiquity of Vitruvius and the *ballistae* described in the tenth book of his *De Architectura*, to the industrial modernity of Gottfried Semper and his mathematical treatise on the shape of ancient lead projectiles, architectural practices are informed by projective technologies that find their twentieth-century endpoints in the reterritorializing techniques marked by nuclear weapons.[14]

As Kiesler states in a handwritten draft, there are "tools for defense" and "tools for attack"[15] (see Addenda, fig. C.07a). Historically, architecture has been employed as a repository of design technologies that serve both operations. Yet among all other human designs, "[h]ouses," he writes, are "defense mechanisms"[16] (see Addenda, fig. C.07b)—a Freudian term that links human housing to the psychoanalyst's own composite design imbricating psychological structures with military formations.[17] From the draft of his "Story of Housing" in *Magic Architecture* to the plaster model of his *Endless House*, a quasi-intrauterine structure that was never built at full-scale, Kiesler's own architecture could be reconstrued as such a "defense mechanism." Nevertheless, the global histories of architecture and politics and in particular the five centuries of settler colonialism that inform *Magic Architecture*'s anthropological and ethnographic sources amply demonstrate that houses can also operate as *offense* mechanisms in support of globalizing territorial expansion. But this is another chapter in the history of housing which, in Kiesler's book, remains unwritten.

HOUSING TECHNOLOGIES (FROM FULLER TO LE CORBUSIER)

Magic Architecture is essentially structured by distance, as both physical space and epistemological medium informing the architect's intermittent writing. The unfinished manuscript is a transhistorical montage of disparate geographies and temporal eras that makes use of the comparative anthropological categories of magic: *contagion* facilitated by contiguity and *similarity* aided by distance. Eclectic and often spurious cross-disciplinary research attempts to amalgamate the epistemological faculties of human and natural sciences, including paleoarchaeology, cultural anthropology, and animal psychology with alternative genealogies of art, architecture, and design. The architect's "story of human housing" is a universalizing yet highly fragmented history that spans from the habitations of animals and cave "shelters" of earliest humans to the city "slums" of the twentieth-century's war-torn subjects.

In the opening paragraph of Part I, Kiesler criticizes the conversion of architecture into a "diver's suit, within which man could air-condition the climate at will" and whose material "in case of attack ... could be impregnated to emanate an aura of deadly radiation" (I.1). A handwritten draft with Kiesler's notes on the same passage reads: **"an aura of ~~automatic~~ deadly radiation would take care of deadly enemies of any form. Impregnation of the material would ~~radiate~~ emanate the security of an aura of deadly radiation."**[18] Conflating the genetic metaphor of "impregnation" (also present among Frazer's processes of "sympathetic magic")[19] with terms from atomic science and electro-physics like "radiation,"[20] Kiesler's rhetoric biologizes and at the same time militarizes the use of technology in house design.

Disparaging a "push-button civilization carried to absurdum" promoted by the commodified forms of contemporary housing (including provisional accommodation), one of Kiesler's rare manuscript annotations calls for additional illustrations featuring "advertisements from the New Yorker Hotel,"[21] an Art Deco tower that during its opening in midtown Manhattan in 1930 had offered the latest advances in automated telecommunications and sanitation technologies in "every room."[22] The main object of the author's critique of contemporary housing, however, is the prefabricated home: "light in weight, mobile … delivered by mail, low in cost and highly economic to operate" (I.1).[23]

Kiesler's criticism centers on the designs of Buckminster Fuller, whose Dymaxion House is featured in *Magic Architecture*'s first pair of plate illustrations.[24] His text also attributes to his "friend Buckminster Fuller" (mentioned by name only in a manuscript annotation and a couple of excised references that never made it to the typed text) the claim that "man *cannot* arrive at a high degree of culture until he has managed to dwell solely in the Arctic; thus, only the nation which conquered the Arctic can and will *dominate* the world" (I.1).[25] Such a controversial geopolitical claim would have sounded even more dubious at the end of World War II, when myths of the cultural superiority of northern peoples, bolstered by the adversity of cold temperatures, infamously imploded.[26] Nevertheless, the confidence placed on climate in techniques of "dwelling" as well as the construction of both "culture" and "civilization" abides in several of the ethnological sources of *Magic Architecture*, and informs Kiesler's own theoretical prehistory as well as the future history of house design.[27]

While deleting instances of Fuller's name from later versions of his text, Kiesler inserted an "annotation" at the end of his reference to the conquering of the Arctic: "Quote from an interview with Buckminster Fuller, Evening Post, New York"–a rare source in *Magic Architecture* that has not been possible to locate.[28] A popular article (not an interview) with a sarcastic portrait of Fuller was published in the Philadelphia *Saturday Evening Post* in 1944 but makes no direct reference to the Arctic or its climate other than a brief mention of Fuller's "Dymaxion Deployment Units" produced with the collaboration of the Butler company during World War II, "which soldiers call[ed] the Butler igloos."[29] A more implicit citation of the misattributed article exists, although rather iconographic in form: the main illustration of the *Evening Post* is a photographic portrait of Fuller laying on a carpeted floor assembling his "Dymaxion jig-saw world map." (fig. A.04) Kiesler himself would assume a similar recumbent posture in a 1947 *Architectural Forum* profile, "Design's Bad Boy." Here, the designer lies on the floor of his 7th Avenue Manhattan penthouse, on top of his large Chart of Metabolism rolled out like a carpet weaved by the (im)material correlations of "new standards" and across the binder containing the semi-completed manuscript of *Magic Architecture* (fig. A.05; for a different take from the same photo shoot, see the frontispiece of this volume).[30] Notably, the first pages of the manuscript have been removed and placed on top of the chart, in between the columns on "Social Structure" and "Cultural Attitude and Popular Ideology." The photograph of Bucky is shot from above as if to replicate a "bird's eye-view" of his Dymaxion earth map from outer space, while Kiesler's portrait as "the artist in his studio" (sketchbook in hand) copies the earthly vision of a symmetrical Renaissance perspective. Compared to the geopolitical cartography of the Dymaxion, Kiesler's Metabolism chart is an abstract delineation of "new standards" and life processes with no references to any specific location on earth. But perhaps the global geography missing from Kiesler's chart is recovered in the book manuscript of *Magic Architecture*, whose "story" and accompanying portfolio aimed to sample housing as well as building monuments across continents and eras. The world models of the two "visionary designers"[31] may be equally cosmic in territorial ambition, yet both emerge and are photographically broadcast from the limited enclosure of a domestic interior.

Housing was one of the themes of the exhibition on American Architecture by the National Council of American-Soviet Friendship, planned to travel to the USSR between 1944 and 1945 with Kiesler's involvement in the design and other aspects of the project.[32] Prefabrication, including reproductions of the Dymaxion House and other designs by Fuller, was also a thematic component of the exhibition by the time it ultimately arrived in Moscow in 1945.

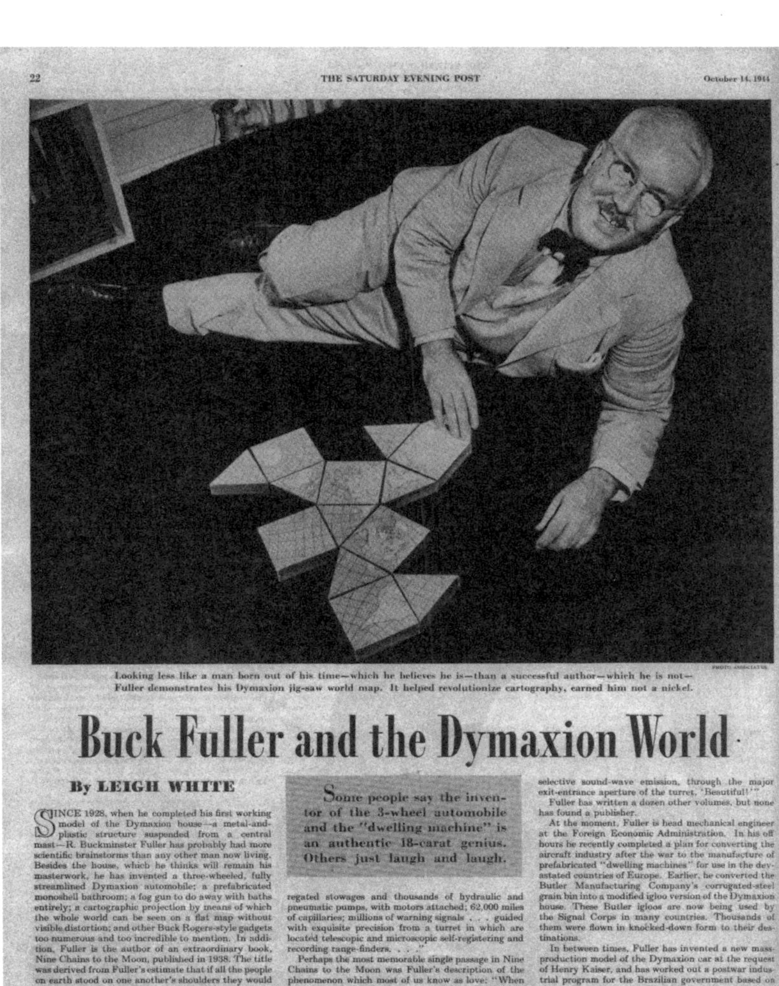

22 THE SATURDAY EVENING POST October 14, 1944

Looking less like a man born out of his time—which he believes he is—than a successful author—which he is not—Fuller demonstrates his Dymaxion jig-saw world map. It helped revolutionize cartography, earned him not a nickel.

Buck Fuller and the Dymaxion World

By LEIGH WHITE

Some people say the inventor of the 3-wheel automobile and the "dwelling machine" is an authentic 18-carat genius. Others just laugh and laugh.

SINCE 1928, when he completed his first working model of the Dymaxion house—a metal-and-plastic structure suspended from a central mast—R. Buckminster Fuller has probably had more scientific brainstorms than any other man now living. Besides the house, which he thinks will remain his masterwork, he has invented a three-wheeled, fully streamlined Dymaxion automobile; a prefabricated monoshell bathroom; a fog gun to do away with baths entirely; a cartographic projection by means of which the whole world can be seen on a flat map without visible distortion; and other Buck Rogers-style gadgets too numerous and too incredible to mention. In addition, Fuller is the author of an extraordinary book, Nine Chains to the Moon, published in 1938. The title was derived from Fuller's estimate that if all the people on earth stood on one another's shoulders they would make a human chain long enough to reach from the earth to the moon nine times.

The book was chiefly an effort to make men conscious of their scientific potentialities. Indeed, Fuller was so intent on explaining everything in scientific terminology that he described man himself as "a self-balancing, twenty-eight-jointed adapter-base biped; an electrochemical reduction plant, integral with segregated stowages and thousands of hydraulic and pneumatic pumps, with motors attached; 62,000 miles of capillaries; millions of warning signals . . . guided with exquisite precision from a turret in which are located telescopic and microscopic self-registering and recording range-finders. . . ."

Perhaps the most memorable single passage in Nine Chains to the Moon was Fuller's description of the phenomenon which most of us know as love: "When one phantom captain seeks a mechanism of the complementary type to join with his in the manufacture of an improvised-model replica of their mutual custody mechanisms, he misinterprets his unself-conscious appraisal of the adequacy of the observed complement to his 'own' half-plant as constituting suitable hook-up conditions in terms of superficial or sensorial-surface satisfactions. The result is often the peculiarly amusing selective sound-wave emission, through the major exit-entrance aperture of the turret, 'Beautiful!'"

Fuller has written a dozen other volumes, but none has found a publisher.

At the moment, Fuller is head mechanical engineer at the Foreign Economic Administration. In his off hours he recently completed a plan for converting the aircraft industry after the war to the manufacture of prefabricated "dwelling machines" for use in the devastated countries of Europe. Earlier, he converted the Butler Manufacturing Company's corrugated-steel grain bin into a modified igloo version of the Dymaxion house. These Butler igloos are now being used by the Signal Corps in many countries. Thousands of them were flown in knocked-down form to their destinations.

In between times, Fuller has invented a new mass-production model of the Dymaxion car at the request of Henry Kaiser, and has worked out a postwar industrial program for the Brazilian government based on the priority principles of the Russian five-year plans. At present, he is toying with a scheme for rebuilding Greece according to Dymaxion principles.

Actually, few of Fuller's inventions have won him the acclaim of the established leaders of his many professions, and none of them has earned him any money. Fuller views these facts philosophically, serene in his belief that he is a man born ahead of his time. He does

DESIGN'S BAD BOY

FREDERICK JOHN KIESLER, architect, stage designer and structural theorist, is a tiny (5 ft. 1 in.), 51-year-old Viennese who looks like a cross between a mischievous elf and a rather pompous troll. His strut, charm, wit and warm human understanding, coupled with a brilliant intellect and fantastic imagination, should already have made him a successful and famous man. But F. J. Kiesler has lived and worked in America for the past twenty years in comparative obscurity. Except for the group of architects and artists who comprise the forefront of the modern movement, his name is unknown even to members of his own profession. Here is a man whom experts rank with Walter Gropius and the late Moholy-Nagy as a pioneer in contemporary design, and some even place next to Wright and Le Corbusier. But, unlike the ideas of his famous contemporaries, Kiesler's best mental images have seldom been translated into actuality. Those which did break through the blueprint prison have been erected with a running accompaniment of difficulties which would have turned a less resilient man into a santorium case.

Kiesler's U. S. history is that of the avant-garde European astray in the American commercial woods. He came to the U. S. in 1926, 10 years before his famous colleagues, proudly wearing a brilliant continental reputation. There was only one drawback: Kiesler was so far ahead of America that nobody knew what he was talking about. In Europe, in spite of the postwar economic chaos, the twenties were a period of hope, of intense creative activity, of social and artistic experimentation. In America these years comprised the lush pre-depression era of stock market tips, bathtub gin and imported Italian palaces. Into this gaudy and slightly cockeyed age, Kiesler's ideas of scientific design and planning had about as much chance of being heard as Bach's cantatas in Texas Guinan's speakeasy.

Kiesler's architectural career had begun in the office of Adolf Loos, working on the slum clearance and rehousing projects which were to make Vienna a model for public housing developments all over the world. In the early twenties, he startled theatrical conservatives with his sets for the Berlin Productions of "R.U.R." and "Emperor Jones," using for the first time in the history of stagecraft a combination of real construction and motion picture projection. As Director and Architect for Vienna's International Music Festival in 1924, he transformed the staid *Konzerthaus* into a fairylike "space stage" and unveiled a model of his "Endless Theater," the first radically new approach to theater design since the burgeoning of the Italian opera house. He became an influential member of the *de Stijl* group,* which included architects Von Does-

* Forerunner of the Bauhaus.

Ben Schnall

L'ARCHITECTURE
VIVANTE

DOCUMENTS SUR L'ACTIVITÉ CONSTRUCTIVE DANS TOUS LES PAYS PUBLIÉS SOUS LA DIRECTION DE JEAN BADOVICI, ARCHITECTE

ÉDITIONS ALBERT MORANCÉ

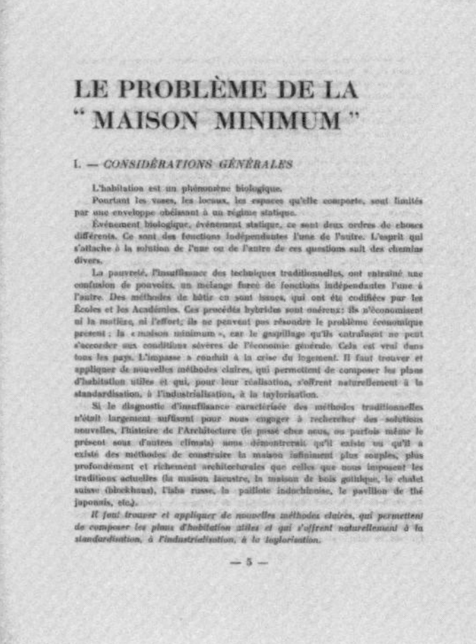
LE PROBLÈME DE LA "MAISON MINIMUM"

I. — CONSIDÉRATIONS GÉNÉRALES

— 9 —

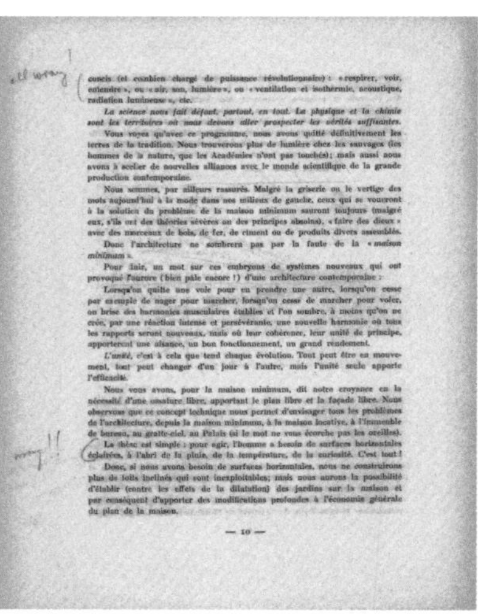
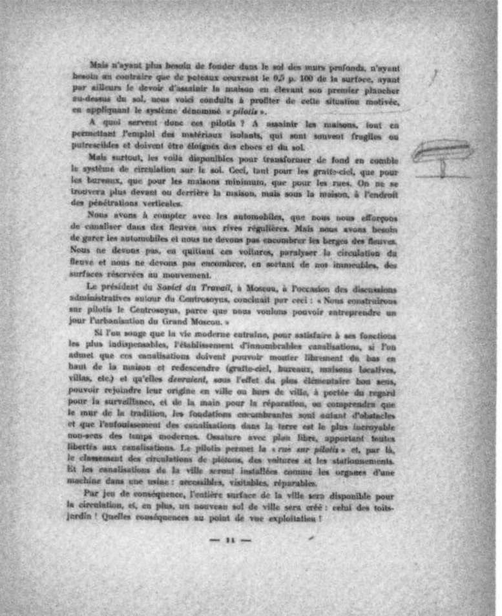

But as was the case with a number of Kiesler's exhibition projects, the display mechanism outweighed the objects constituting the "content" of the show. An intricately designed exhibition armature was meant to narrate the "story of housing" much more authentically (and even viscerally) than any of the photographic reproductions illustrating the same "story." Envisioned as a series of highly sculptural panels with overt anthropomorphic and zoomorphic forms, Kiesler's first proposal was promptly dismissed by the organizers. (figs. A.32a–b) An animated wall display was ultimately reduced to a series of interconnected orthogonal flat panels—his animal design becoming the unwarranted sacrificial victim of the kind of prefabrication its author had criticized. But despite his stance against prefabrication, the organizing logic of Kiesler's curatorial method informs the structure of *Magic Architecture*, a book assembled as its own kind of kit of parts with a series of panel-like plates, even if its contents chart a very different story.

*

Kiesler's denunciation of automation and prefabrication techniques is part of a postwar critique of mechanization in terms of its practical and ideological uses in modern architecture, and in particular, serial housing. In a proposal sent to publishers after the war, Kiesler presents *Magic Architecture* as "a book that fills a need in education"—an urgent need given the increasing demand for housing. In his "Note to the Publisher," Kiesler draws a comparison between the ambitions of *Magic Architecture* and those of Le Corbusier's *Vers une architecture*, which when it was published after the First World War "filled the need of that period."[33] Most of what was published in the following years, Kiesler explains, were "volumes of imitations and adaptations of [Le Corbusier's] work." But by the mid- to late-1940s, Le Corbusier's house design had become "outmoded" due to its "glorification of the machine age," an era that had been "eradicated by the experience" of the "new world war."[34] *Magic Architecture* was therefore conceived of and pitched as a new paradigm in architecture book publishing that could promote a truly "new architecture" after 1945—even if the majority of Kiesler's anthropological and scientific sources date from the interwar or even the pre-First World War period.[35]

In a further attempt to cast his book as the successor to Le Corbusier's *Vers une architecture*, Kiesler handwrote the word "Towards" to precede a section titled "Magic Architecture."[36] (See Main Text, fig. B.26b.) At the same time several sentences in the text and plate captions of *Magic Architecture* strongly voice Kiesler's criticism of Le Corbusier's "functionalist," "Machine Age" or "Business-City" ideas about housing.[37] The critique is more explicitly disparaging in notes found in the margins of Kiesler's copy of an issue of *Architecture Vivante* featuring Le Corbusier and Pierre Jeanneret's report on "the problem of the 'minimum-house,'" originally presented at the second CIAM conference of 1929.[38] Next to the authors' proclamation "precise, economical, and rapid circulation is the key to contemporary architecture," Kiesler retorts: "all wrong. It is right for city planning but not for the house."[39] And when the two architects resolutely declare that "industry ... demands a total revision of the functions of the dwelling" under the "revolutionary power charge" of, among others, "ventilation, isothermics, acoustics, and light radiation," Kiesler once again cries "all wrong!"[40] (figs. A.06a–d) Equally withering side comments are reiterated in French (*ridicule*!) and German (*falsch*!), including Kiesler's perennial claim that Le Corbusier's typology of the house on piloti was lifted *aus meinem Manifest!* (from my manifesto!), a reference to *Raumstadt* (*City of Space*), first published in 1925 and reproduced in English in *Magic Architecture* (X.5).[41]

But even in his repudiation of the Swiss architects' ideas, there is an implicit mirroring of Kiesler's theoretical project on housing with Le Corbusier's. Such correspondence moves beyond the elevated structure of the house on piloti, as well as the call by both architects for the interaction between architecture and the arts of painting and sculpture, which could inform a new *model* of house design.[42] To be sure, Kiesler's research on anthropology and prehistoric archaeology echoes Le Corbusier's own references to *l'homme primitif* and his geometric reconstruction of *la hutte primitife*[43] as well as an interest in the lakeside pile dwellings in Ireland and Switzerland that featured in subsequent publications of the 1920s, and whose sources have been analytically studied by Adolf Max Vogt.[44] Yet perhaps the most essential underlying connection between the transhistorical projects of the two architects lies in their implicit agenda of constructing a new human type by redesigning their dwelling conditions through an integrated form of architectural science. While for Le Corbusier this science was buttressed by functionalist biology and theories of eugenics following an earlier encounter with ethnography and prehistoric archaeology,[45] Kiesler's own evolutionary view of design in his earlier articles on Correalism draws from discourses of social and technological heredity.[46]

figs. A.06a–d Le Corbusier and Pierre Jeanneret, "Le probléme de la 'maison minimum'," *L'Architectrue vivante* 27 (Spring 1930), cover and pages with margin annotations and sketch by Kiesler. Kiesler estate library). ÖFLKS, ARCH ZEIT 090

An illustration of a project by Le Corbusier and Jeanneret included among the plates for *Magic Architecture* shows that Kiesler's criticism of the French architects' standards of mass housing lasted well into the 1940s and further illustrates the differences in their application of bodily physiology and biological organicism. The plate juxtaposes a group of Peruvian clay vessels shaped as building models with a 1924 drawing by Le Corbusier and Jeanneret of a "series of houses for artisans" (reproduced from the German edition of *Towards an Architecture*).[47] (See plates 25a*–25b* and photostats in figs. A.09a–b) The juxtaposition is not arbitrary: in their CIAM report reprinted in *Architecture Vivante*, the housing spaces are described as "vessels,"[48] echoing Le Corbusier's preoccupation with pottery (Serbian or other) since the years of his journey through the Balkans.[49]

In the plate caption, Kiesler describes these architectural vessels as "an ideo-plastic imaginative expression of an everyday tool," while Le Corbusier and Jeanneret's mass houses are scorned as "barren houses of our Machine Age" and as "physio-plastic expression[s]," caring only "for the physically organic."[50] Kiesler appropriates the distinction between "ideo-plastic" and "physio-plastic" art drawn by the German physiologist and psychologist Max Verworn in *Magic Architecture* (IV.6),[51] transcribing excerpts from one of his lectures. According to Verworn, physio-plastic art renders an object based on physiological perception; ideo-plastic representations gradually substitute physiological appearance with an associative "memory image."[52] Kiesler's caption appears to exchange image with function by pointing at the overvaluation of "physically organic" (meaning biological) performance in the Corbusian dwelling. On the other hand, he praises the Peruvian vessels for their capacity to carry not simply a depiction but the ideogram of "building art" embodying an "organic" model that moves beyond the "physical" towards the cultural, the symbolic, and the social. Kiesler's description of the Peruvian pots as "imaginative tools" echoes views of contemporary archaeologists, who describe these artifacts both as building models and liquid containers used in ritual libations.[53]

But the montage of the pre-Columbian architectural vessels against the houses of Le Corbusier and Jeanneret is only one instance among many where *Magic Architecture* stages a contrast between contemporary building technologies and "physical" and cultural anthropologies of housing. Instead of an automated building technology that Kiesler dismisses as mere "gadgeteering" and likens to the illusionist artistry of the "prestidigitator," the text is oriented towards an anthropological definition of both technology and magic in terms of handheld tools and techniques that foreground the development of social structures.

The drawings of the Peruvian architectural models on Kiesler's plate are reproduced from the 1931 book *Ancient Civilization of the Andes* by the American anthropologist Philip Ainsworth Means, from which Kiesler had two photostats made at the NYPL.[54] (fig. A.07a) The same clay models are also cited in one of the outlines for *Magic Architecture* as "[u]tilitarian household objects of Trujillo in [sic] form of houses, and temple pyramids (Inca, Peru)." Kiesler envisions them as "picture No. 1" in a chapter presenting "samples of architecture" from aboriginal cultures, which demonstrate a "harmonious unity" between people and their environment and whose "houses and artifacts are an undivided expression of physical and spiritual necessities."[55] The several "pictures" of ethnological artifacts mentioned in this preliminary outline can be traced to the revised edition of a German *Illustrierte Völkerkunde* (Illustrated Ethnology) published in 1922, whose first volume offers a "comparative" study of America and Africa (for Kiesler's handwritten notes and sketches from this publication see

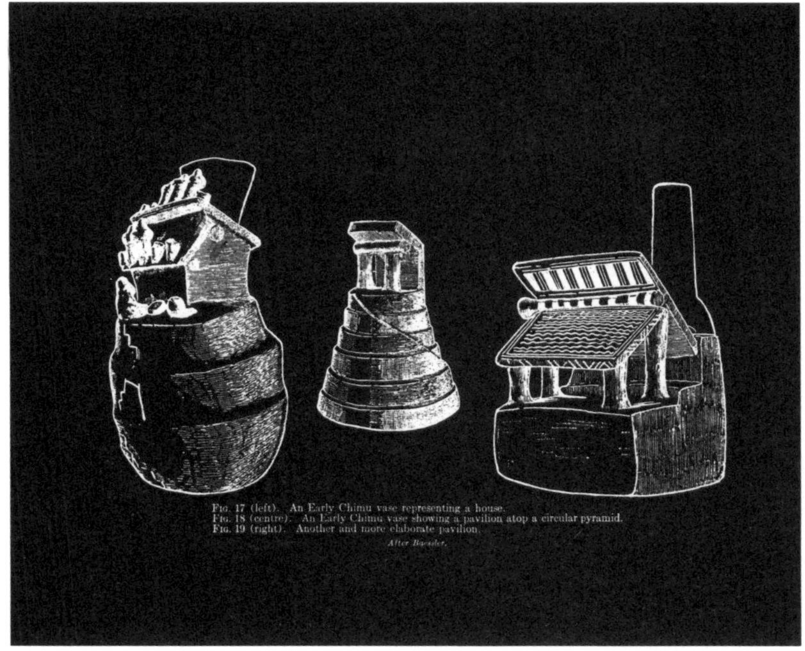

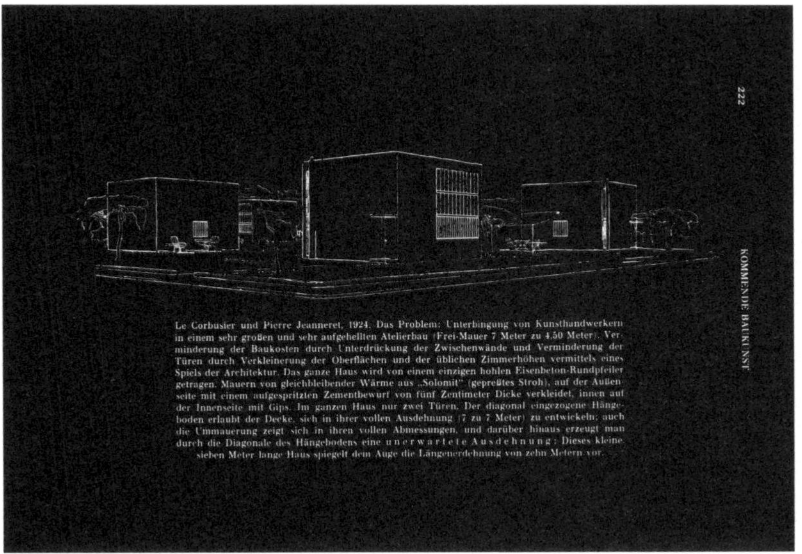
222

KOMMENDE BAUKUNST

Le Corbusier und Pierre Jeanneret, 1924. Das Problem: Unterbingung von Kunsthandwerkern in einem sehr großen und sehr aufgehellten Atelierbau (Frei-Mauer 7 Meter zu 4.50 Meter). Verminderung der Baukosten durch Unterdrückung der Zwischenwände und Verminderung der Türen durch Verkleinerung der Oberflächen und der üblichen Zimmerhöhen vermittels eines Spiels der Architektur. Das ganze Haus wird von einem einzigen hohlen Eisenbeton-Rundpfeiler getragen. Mauern von gleichbleibender Wärme aus „Solomit" (gepreßtes Stroh), auf der Außenseite mit einem aufgespritzten Zementbewurf von fünf Zentimeter Dicke verkleidet, innen auf der Innenseite mit Gips. Im ganzen Haus nur zwei Türen. Der diagonal eingezogene Hängeboden erlaubt der Decke, sich in ihrer vollen Ausdehnung (7 zu 7 Meter) zu entwickeln; auch die Ummauerung zeigt sich in ihren vollen Abmessungen, und darüber hinaus erzeugt man durch die Diagonale des Hängebodens eine unerwartete Ausdehnung: Dieses kleine, sieben Meter lange Haus spiegelt dem Auge die Längenerdehnung von zehn Metern vor.

Above

fig. A.07a Photostat for plate 25a*: "Peruvian pottery in the form of houses and temples," reproduced from Philip Ainsworth Means, *Ancient Civilizations of the Andes* (New York and London: Charles Scribner's Sons, 1931), 82. ÖFLKS, PHO_7159/0

fig. A.07b Photostat for plate 25b*: "Barren Houses of our machine-age," reproduced from Le Corbusier, *Kommende Baukunst* (Stuttgart: Deutsche Verlags-Anstalt, 1926), 222. ÖFLKS, PHO_7249/0

Overleaf

figs. A.08a–d Cover and pages from issues of *Koralle. Wochenzeitschrift für Unterhaltung, Wissen, Lebensfreude* (1938–1939). Research press clippings (see Bibliographies for full publication details). ÖFLKS, CLP_6581/0, CLP_6573/0, CLP_6569/0, CLP_6572/0

Addenda, figs. c.03a–b).[53] Kiesler also copies the main figure of the frontispiece of the same compendium—a reproduction of the well-known painting of the "Sioux" (Lakota) chief Black Rock by George Catlin held in the Berlin Ethnological Museum—in two of his preliminary drawings for *Magic Architecture* illustrating the differences in attire between an aboriginal and a modern "magic man" (see Addenda, figs. c.04a–b. In the text of his preliminary outline, Kiesler intended to juxtapose "Black Rock in full ornament" as a "war chief" with a "modern commander-in-chief (Eisenhower) in field uniform."[57] In his drawings, the first appears in the guise of Catlin's chief in battle gear, while the second wears a suit and a tall hat—indeed reminiscent of Eisenhower, Chief Commander of Allied Forces during World War II. The coy substitution of the field uniform with a business suit augurs not simply General Eisenhower's subsequent advancement into the US presidency, but also the imbrication of military force with governmental bureaucracy and business administration, the new unassuming and unornamented *mask* of "modern magic."

But this is also just one of Kiesler's frequent iconographic uses of anthropological and ethnographic documents as "pictures" conflating cultural and racial stereotypes from European ethnology and American folklore, as well as current US history and politics. This pictorial browsing is evident in the anthropological sources among Kiesler's research materials, and in particular his collection of illustrated journal and magazine clippings from European (mostly German or Austrian) and American publications including an extensive collection of *National Geographic* articles that range geographically from Kashmir and Mexico to South Africa and New Guinea and date from 1929 to 1946, the year Kiesler first sent his book manuscript to publishers.[58] More than several perpetuate stereotypical and racist assumptions about the cultural customs of each place, including their architectures. Kiesler used the articles primarily for their photographs, selecting those depicting bodily adornment and built structures—the latter often problematically identified in their captions with animal constructions and natural landscape formations, which the architect then montaged in his plates along with illustrations from other published sources. Even if no *National Geographic* article is quoted at length in Kiesler's manuscript, several of the ideas, concepts, and stereotypes about architectural and cultural construction found throughout the magazine appear in the uncritically rehearsed terminology of *Magic Architecture*.

A similar yet more variegated source is Kiesler's pile of clippings of brief articles from the German illustrated weekly *Koralle*, which focused on issues ranging from contemporary architecture to natural history and ethnography from the former German colonies and other distant territories.[59] (figs. A.08a–d) Notably the architect's selection is limited to articles from issues dating between 1938 and 1939 during a period when the German publication's combination of ethnographic exoticism and natural history as part of "entertainment, knowledge, and the joy of life" (as was the weekly's subtitle) intertwined with the politics of National Socialist cultural and ideological propaganda.[60] Again Kiesler mainly draws visual material from these articles for his plates while using more scholarly anthropological or historical sources for the text of *Magic Architecture*. A telling example is the chapter "Aztec Pyramid and Dwellings" (V.3), whose text consists of a long excerpt from the extensive monograph on the Aztecs by the French Americanist archaeologist Lucien Biart, while the corresponding plate (plate 31) reproduces the illustrations (and layout) of a brief article on Aztec "human sacrifices" by the German Americanist Walter Krickeberg published in *Koralle*.[61] (fig. A.08c)

*

Beyond journal compilations, more prominent in *Magic Architecture* is a series of books by anthropologists, ethnologists, and archaeologists not simply montaged in the illustrated plates but quoted at length. Other than a few references to the late-nineteenth-century comparative anthropology of James Frazer, mentioned earlier,[62] most of this literature was fairly new, published in the three decades before the manuscript was sent to publishers in 1946. Kiesler's sources reflect (with some delay) some of the major shifts in anthropological discourses in Europe and North America during the interwar era reflecting methodological differences among various schools: from the philosophical ethnosociology of Lucien Lévy-Bruhl (through its translation into German in the 1920s) to the paleoarchaeology of Henri Breuil and the speleology of Norbert Casteret; and from the physical and racial anthropology of Hermann Klaatsch, to the ethnology and cultural morphology of Leo Frobenius, as well as the social anthropology of Bronisław Malinowski and his mentee in Britain and America, anthropologist and popular author Ashley Montagu, whom Kiesler knew personally.

A common presupposition among most of the paleoarchaeological and ethnographic discourses present in *Magic Architecture* is the alleged similarity of "prehistoric man" with members of contemporary Indigenous societies treated as subjects of knowledge, particularly for areas where no prehistoric evidence appeared to exist.[63] Such conflation becomes strongly evident in the field of human dwelling concerning Indigenous structures built from perishable materials, such as tents made of animal skins or huts made of tree branches—the latter serving as an origin in Kiesler's "story of housing" following the ethnographic descriptions of such constructions in Oceania and Africa. The conflation of the prehistoric and the Indigenous partly originates in the distinction between historic

and "non-historic" peoples in nineteenth-century world histories and later ethnological descriptions of first societies in Africa, Oceania, and America living under colonial rule.[64] As soon as the field of prehistory was invented after the mid-nineteenth century, "non-historical" peoples known in the west by earlier ethnographic descriptions became the model for "prehistoric" humans subsumed under the general category of "primitive man"–a term persisting in anthropological, ethnosociological, and paleoarchaeological texts well into the twentieth century, and rehearsed persistently in Kiesler's narrative, partly inspired by Lévy-Bruhl.[65] Kiesler's arsenal of primitivizing terms is also defined by the primary evidence informing his sources, meaning the colonial descriptions by Jesuit missionaries and other travelers, some dating from the early modern period quoted by twentieth-century comparative ethnologists. For example, the first chapters of *Magic Architecture* contain long excerpts from the *Journal of a Voyage to South America* (1744) by the Jesuit priest and historian Pierre François Xavier de Charlevoix as quoted by Lévy-Bruhl alongside nineteenth- and twentieth-century ethnographic and anthropological reports (1.3). In a singular footnote in the same chapter, Kiesler mentions "[r]eference material very rich" and cites the names of anthropologists like John Roscoe and Robert Hertz among others, all names copied from Lévy-Bruhl's footnotes.[66] But other than a single illustration from Spencer and Gillen used in his plates there is no indication that Kiesler ever consulted the individual texts of these authors, beyond what was quoted by the French ethnologist.[67]

Kiesler's idiosyncratic use of images and texts from anthropological and ethnological sources resembles the indiscriminate "attitude" associated by James Clifford with "the ethnographic turn" in French surrealism.[68] In his critique of "ethnographic surrealism," Clifford summarized the disparate methodological approaches towards Indigenous cultures during the interwar era under "ethnography," less as a singular scientific discipline but rather as "a more general cultural predisposition that cuts through modern anthropology and what this science shares with twentieth-century art and writing."[69] Even if Kiesler was close to Tristan Tzara and Yvan Goll while in Europe in the 1920s, he only became intimately affiliated with the chief surrealists, such as Breton and Duchamp following their transplantation in America in the early 1940s, and his participation in their group exhibitions and publications remained very active until 1947.[70] Clifford's version of "ethnography" is another mystic link among Kiesler's surrealist affiliations, whose threads would later include magic; even if his encounter with ethnography (through the work of Frobenius and Montagu) predates his surrealist encounters in New York.[71] In addition to the countless articles on ethnographic material Kiesler clipped from German and American journals, his library includes issues of *Documents* and *Minotaure*, the French surrealist journals whose own displays of ethnographic documents illustrate, according to Clifford, the decontextualizing attitude towards non-European cultures practiced in surrealist circles. [72]

In his overview, Clifford distinguishes between the "ethnographic surrealism" of the 1920s and the "anthropological humanism" of the late 30s: the first craves and collects the shocking, the bizarre, and the uncanny following the legacy of the ethnographic displays of the old Trocadéro museum, while the second attempts to foreground what is "common" among cultures embraced by the new Musée de l'Homme a few years before the Second World War.[73] Both attitudes are present in *Magic Architecture*, yet Kiesler's indiscriminate mixture of ethnography and anthropology is beyond midpoint in this transition. While a great part of the material compiled in the architect's research files and illustrations looks back at the ethnographic exoticism and bizarrerie of the 1920s and 30s, the global "story of housing" unfolding in *Magic Architecture* with its catholic emphasis on "Man" is closer to the anthropological humanism that shapes postwar universalist and proto-structuralist discourses. Nevertheless, the remnants of a developmental logic persists in the anthropological sources of *Magic Architecture*, most of which come from texts written in the earlier part of the twentieth century describing a world living in distinct "civilizational stages." While *Magic Architecture* outlines a postwar vision of "unity," its epistemological foundations are plagued by a prewar image of humanity that racially divides its transcontinental participants.. An architecture already exists, then, within the ethnological sciences employed by Kiesler, whose spatial imprint traces the diachronic building of inequalities. Housing accommodates Kiesler's own "anthropological humanism" even if his narrative has overt anti-humanist tones, and his "story" implicitly narrativizes not the prehistoric origin but the contemporary endpoint of a humanity, whose modes of "dwelling" in the world are vastly inequitable.[74]

Kiesler's architectural "translations" of Bruhl and Frobenius disclose ethnology's own engagement with architectural concepts and their investment in architectonic hierarchies, now read, translated, and transposed by an architect-theorist. But Kiesler's primitivist architectural narrative also taps into the long fascination with "the primitive," from Vitruvius to Le Corbusier, that underlies western histories of architecture.[75] It further points to the transition of primitivism as a recognizable building "style" promoted by colonial ethnography into a form of "structuralism" that, as Ginger Nolan argues, emerged in postwar decolonial contexts shaped by the language and politics of "development."[76] When it was submitted to publishers in the immediate postwar era, *Magic Architecture* may have been foreshowing the transition from primitivism to structuralism, even if, like the unpublished manuscript, such a shift was outlined but not yet materialized. The text ends up reproducing a "graphic" traceable in its charts and diagrammatically arranged illustrations, yet best illustrated in the gaps, deletions, and paralyzing incompleteness of the manuscript.

ANTHROPOLOGIES OF HOUSING II: PARTITIONS AND CONSTRUCTION STYLES (FROBENIUS)

An entry in Stefi Kiesler's calendar lists a lecture delivered by Leo Frobenius at the Dalton School on April 29 of 1937,[77] one of several presentations delivered in English by the German ethnologist while in New York for the opening of the *Prehistoric Rock Pictures in Europe and Africa* exhibition at the Museum of Modern Art, which featured copies of rock paintings from his personal collection at the Institute of Cultural Morphology at Frankfurt.[78] In the very first chapter of Part I in *Magic Architecture*, Kiesler includes an excerpt of Frobenius's catalogue text that describes the contemporary practice of rock painting among Indigenous people in Congo (characterized by Frobenius as "pygmies") as a magic ritual performance related to animal hunting.[79] Kiesler's quotations also include a sentence (marked in italics in the catalogue text), which intimates the genetic connections between Africa and Europe manifested by rock art: "that which existed once in Europe lives on among its epigones in Africa today."[80] Such diachronic "epigonism" was purportedly manifested in the broad similarities in "style" that Frobenius projected among prehistoric rock paintings in Spain or the South of France and several areas in Africa, including Libya, Sudan, and South Africa, where rock painting was still practiced.

Kiesler also quotes extensively from Frobenius's *Kulturgeschichte Afrikas* (Cultural History of Africa), published in 1933 and translated in French soon after, which summarizes and revises the author's previous publications on Africa as well as his theory of cultural morphology.[81] The book is in Kiesler's library (with a dedication dated Christmas 1937) and several parts were transcribed and quoted in the text of *Magic Architecture*. Kiesler also used drawings and photographs from Frobenius's collection for many of the plates prepared for *Magic Architecture* depicting African building types.[82]

These architectural drawings appear in a section of *Kulturgeschichte Afrikas* that describes architecture as an expression of what Frobenius perceived to be the two dominant cultural approaches subsumed under the polarity of the "Ethiopian" and the "Hamitic" worldviews or "types," which also correspond to two contrasting *Baustile* (building styles). [83] This contrast is mentioned twice by Kiesler in his drafts.[84] In his own book, Frobenius associates the Hamites with two *Grundformen* (basic forms) of building construction, one fixed and "connected to the earth ground" and the other "mobile," which the ethnologist likens to the "winter and summer residences of North-Asiatic peoples."[85] The fixed "winter-dwelling" of the Hamites is a *Kreuzkellerbau*, or "cross-cellar building" tacked under the ground inside the slope of a hill and communicating with the outer world through a central "vertical shaft."[86] Included in *Magic Architecture*'s plates are the plan and section of this building type represented by an underground dwelling from West Sudan and described by Frobenius as a *Grottenbau* or cavern construction (plate 20).[87] (figs. A.09, A.11b)

Yet the earliest and "most original" mobile residence of the Hamites–also described by Frobenius as a *Wanderhütte* (wandering hut)–is a *Kuppelhütte*, a "simple round copula hut" in a "semi-spherical form" built by Indigenous people whom Frobenius describes as "forest pygmies" with a few "stacked branches." The same building type can also expand into a larger structure with interior partitions.[88] Kiesler sketches a similar hut made of tree branches in two charts of animal and human building tools and structures and, following Frobenius, associates both with "pygmies" (see Addenda, figs. C.06b, C.07b).[89] While the "cruciform cellar construction" of "Hamitic culture" expresses a "tendency to live inside the earth," "Ethiopian culture," according to Frobenius, demonstrates a will "to let the dwelling grow up above the surface of the earth," as in *Pfahlnbau*–"pile construction"–which, the ethnologist admits, "is no longer common in any part of Africa today, perhaps with the exception of a few tribes" in a single area of Congo.[90] Since the constitutive structural element of pile dwellings is the elevated "platform" consisting of a beam deck made of straight tree trunks, "its nature" is to be a four-cornered rectangular structure, reasons Frobenius. According to the ethnologist, circular pile dwellings in Africa or Oceania impose the "influence" of the round hut on an altogether different building type–essentially a hybrid construction imbricating the gestalt of a certain psychological mentality and building type upon the structural frame of another.[91] (fig. A.10)

Kiesler's very first plate reproduces a drawing of such a "round hut on stilts" by Frobenius along with the construction plan of its circular platform, followed by Buckminster Fuller's Dymaxion House in the second plate. The seemingly aberrant yet strategic mobilization of these building types across temporal and geographic contexts reverberates the shifting associations charted in the ethnologist's world maps representing the transcontinental distribution of these "types." (figs. A.11a–b) According to Frobenius, neither the Hamitic and Ethiopian human types nor their corresponding building forms are limited to Africa (he points at the presence of similar building types in other parts of the world including Australia or South America)

Scholars have remarked that at some point in Frobenius's conjectural ethnologies, a number of transpositions occur where Germanic peoples appear to be the "new" vigorous Ethiopians, while the Hamites are identified with the Semites.[92] To return to "architectonic" classifications, these double-profiled human types correspond not only to concrete building structures but also intangible predispositions about space, which were "constitutive" for their cultures.[93] In his studies of "cultural physiognomy,"

fig. A.09 Photostat used in plate 20: "Cavern construction [*Grottenbau*] near Mopti [West Sudan]. Earth-dwelling [*Erdwohnung*]. Above: plan. Below: section, Leo Frobenius, *Kulturgeschichte Afrikas* (Frankfurt am Main: Phaidon Verlag, 1933), 219, fig. 169. ÖFLKS, PHO_7231/0

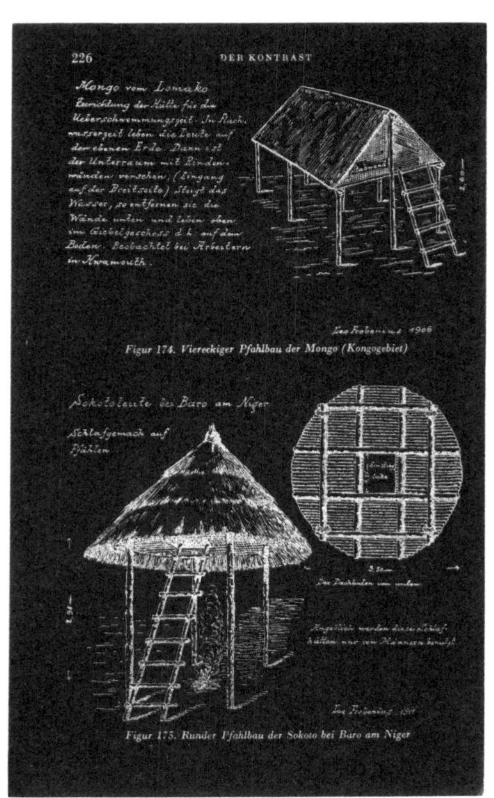

fig. A.10 Photostat partly used in plate 1: "Four-cornered pile house [*Viereckiger Pfahlhaus*] of the Mongo in the Congo area," and "Round pile house [*Runder Pfahlbau*] of the people of Sokoto, near Baro on the Niger river," Leo Frobenius, *Kulturgeschichte Afrikas: Prolegomena zu einer historischen Gestaltslehre*, 226. ÖFLKS, PHO_7237/0

Opposite
fig. A.11a (left) "Map 29. African Architecture. 1. Cellar construction and flat construction risen from it"; (right): Plan and vertical section of "Earthdwelling of the Gurunsi slaves" near Wagadugu, West Sudan [see Ouagadougou, Burkina Faso], Leo Frobenius, *Kulturgeschichte Afrikas*, 1933, 216–217, fig. 168.

fig. A.11b (right) "Map 30. African Architecture. 2. Dome or spherical constructions [*Kuppel- oder Kugelbauten*]"; (right): "Cavern construction [*Grottenbau*] near Mopti," from Leo Frobenius, *Kulturgeschichte Afrikas*, 1933, 218–219, fig. 169.

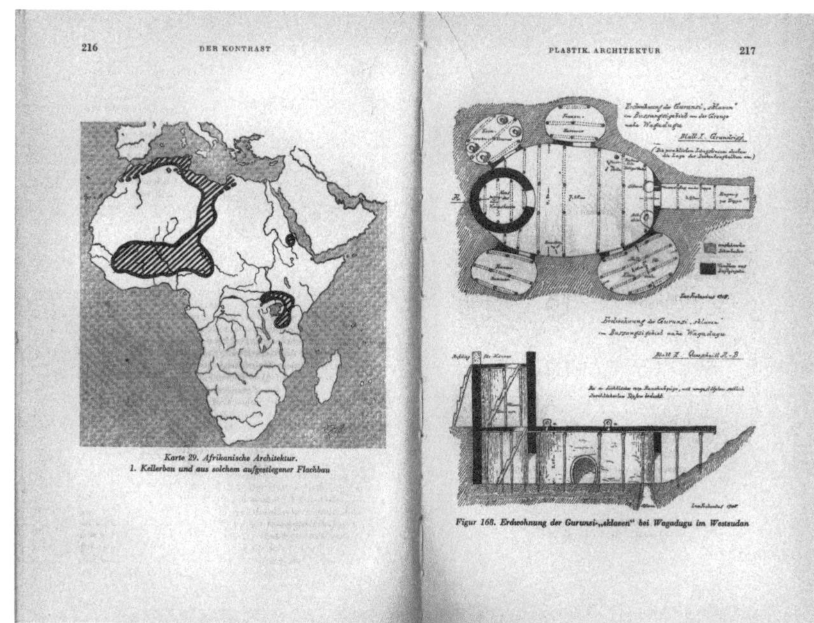

216 DER KONTRAST

Karte 29. Afrikanische Architektur.
1. Kellerbau und aus solchem aufgestiegener Flachbau

PLASTIK. ARCHITEKTUR 217

Figur 168. Erdwohnung der Gurunsi-„sklaven" bei Wagadugu im Westsudan

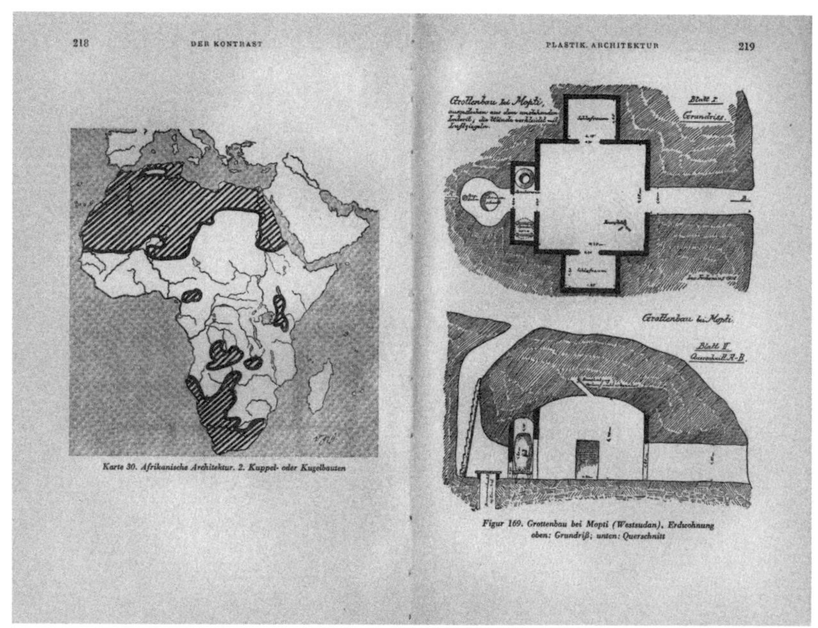

218 DER KONTRAST

Karte 30. Afrikanische Architektur. 2. Kuppel- oder Kugelbauten

PLASTIK. ARCHITEKTUR 219

Figur 169. Grottenbau bei Mopti (Westsudan). Erdwohnung
oben: Grundriß; unten: Querschnitt

Frobenius splits the *Raumgefühl* (space feeling) of "old cultures" into a penchant for *begrenzte* (limited) space, as in *Höhlengefühl* (caves), and a feeling for *Weitengefühl* (open space) corresponding to movement and creativity, as well as a desire for the *Unendliche* (endless) and conquering an *undurchgreiflische Weite* (impenetrable expanse) such as that of the sea.[94] As Suzanne Marchand points out, "[t]he former belonged to the Hamitic, and also Semitic people of the Orient; the latter to the Ethiopian and Germanic peoples."[95] While disguised as a psychological polarity, such an ethnological partition discloses a racial bias in favor of the space-conquering "Ethiopian" Germans over the cave-hunkering "Hamitic" Semites. In a later study by Frobenius (published a year after his visit to New York), the Hamites were identified in gender terms with a female "matriarchal" culture motivated by a "nomadic" impulse and a "centripetal" "space feeling," while the Ethiopians were defined by a male "patriarchal" organization and a "radial" or "centrifugal" *Raumgefühl* that disclosed a strong attachment to the ground.[96] It is not certain which side of the Hamitic-Ethiopian cleavage Kiesler might have envisioned himself inhabiting. His manuscripts, art, and architectural designs retrace all three of the building types outlined by Frobenius–the cavernous cellar, the round hut, and the house on stilts–as distinct stages of a composite developmental model, which he recombines at will.

Perhaps Kiesler's clearest theoretical projection–as well as *introjection*–of Frobenius's developmental typology of construction is found in the conceptual scheme placed immediately after the first two plates of building structures on stilts, and which illustrates the developmental process from "Myth" to "Architecture through the acquisition of technical 'skills'" (see plate 2a). The figurative substratum of the geometric diagram is a drawing in the MoMA exhibition catalogue by Frobenius and Fox from a rock painting in the former British colony of Southern Rhodesia (today Zimbabwe) depicting a "rain ceremony" based on a story describing the ritual sacrifice of a princess "buried alive" under a tree, after a high priest had a "vision" that this was "the only way to end the drought."[97] (fig. A.12) Following the theoretical interment of all of the painting's figures (the princess, the priest, the goddess, the tree, and the rain) below and above the ground, Kiesler stratifies his chart in a series of zones, depicted as circles which expand "within," "on," "above," and "beyond" the earth, and which further correspond with a series of building constructions: from spirit "tombs" to human "shelters," religious "temples" and the atmospheric "dwellings of the gods." (see Main Text, fig. B.04) In a more abstract version of the chart, this vertical progression is combined with the horizontal evolution from "Myth" to technical "Skill" and finally "Architecture" via the design techniques of "construction," "sculpture," "implementation," (tool-making) and "painting."

Note that the MoMA catalogue by Frobenius contains other earth fertility stories and depictions in rock paintings of similar "regicides" involving male "kings"–the narrative iconography that inundates the sacrificial economy of Frazer's *Golden Bough*. Yet Kiesler chooses the one story that reverberates brutal myths of female "foundation sacrifice" underlying the origin of momentous buildings in European folklore, yet here extracted from a rock in Africa, as the "substratum" for his theoretical construction charting the transhistorical emergence of "Architecture."[98]

Stratigraphic organization is then the main methodological parallel between the techniques of the architect and the ethnologist, whose composite historical project reacquires the form of an expanded geology–the original discipline (along with zoology) that informed the origins of colonialist anthropological research, as well as the first "world histories" of architecture. Ethnology's "architectonic" aim (large enough for the term *architektonisches* to occupy a separate, page-long section in Frobenius' index) was to convert cultural morphology's "surface" similarities of exterior forms into a tectonic system based on deep interior structures solidifying racial, sexual, and ethnic divisions on a global scale.[99] Frobenius' racialized building typologies are converted by Kiesler into a fictional chart that redraws the ethnologist's "culture circles" into a composite theory and (hi)story of architecture, whose postwar "anthropological humanism" unearths the rudiments of a prewar colonial mentality.

ANTHROPOLOGIES OF HOUSING III: TECHNIQUES OF "SHELTER" (KLAATSCH)

Kiesler's main references to "shelter" structures among Indigenous peoples are drawn from the evolutionist study *Der Werdegang der Menschheit und die Entstehung der Kultur* (Development of Humanity and the Origin of Culture) by the German physical anthropologist Hermann Klaatsch, professor of anatomy, anthropology, and ethnography at the University of Breslau.[100] The book was based on a number of Klaatsch's earlier studies, combining his research on hominid fossils found in prehistoric sites in Europe with observations made during his years living with Indigenous groups in Australia (1904–1907) in search of "the origins of humankind."[101] Klaatsch's dual geographic area of research was meant to support his disputed polygenist theory, which placed Australian aboriginals at the "lowest stage" of a human racial path that led to modern Europeans as opposed to a different group emerging

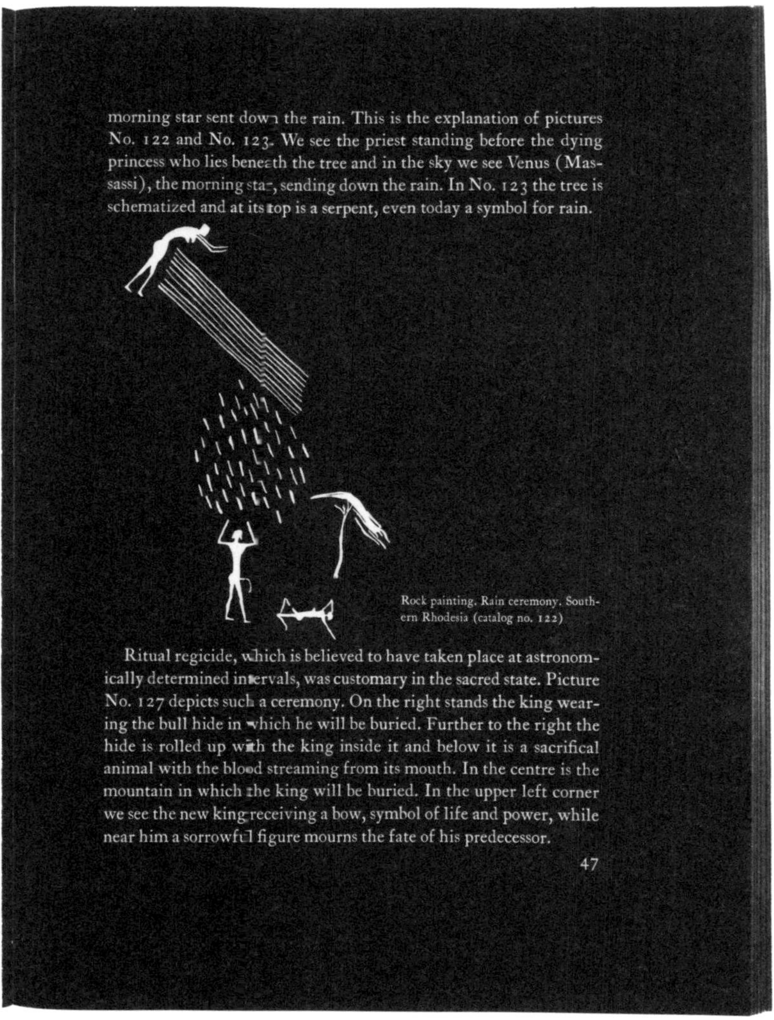

morning star sent down the rain. This is the explanation of pictures No. 122 and No. 123. We see the priest standing before the dying princess who lies beneath the tree and in the sky we see Venus (Massassi), the morning star, sending down the rain. In No. 123 the tree is schematized and at its top is a serpent, even today a symbol for rain.

Rock painting. Rain ceremony. Southern Rhodesia (catalog no. 122)

Ritual regicide, which is believed to have taken place at astronomically determined intervals, was customary in the sacred state. Picture No. 127 depicts such a ceremony. On the right stands the king wearing the bull hide in which he will be buried. Further to the right the hide is rolled up with the king inside it and below it is a sacrifical animal with the blood streaming from its mouth. In the centre is the mountain in which the king will be buried. In the upper left corner we see the new king receiving a bow, symbol of life and power, while near him a sorrowful figure mourns the fate of his predecessor.

47

in Africa.[102] He became infamous for his abhorrent treatment of human remains, including the mummy of an Indigenous Australian who he described as a "great warrior" and "King," and whose remains he procured by deceit during his expedition,[103] along with thousands of Indigenous artifacts (including a tree-bark hut) which were transported to Europe and kept in his private collection.[104]

The publication of Klaatsch's book was delayed by the outbreak of the Great War and following his death in 1916, it was edited by the German physician, journalist, and popular author Adolf Heilborn, who also contributed articles on natural history and ethnology to *Koralle*.[105] Following the theory of evolution by Darwin, on whom both Klaatsch and Heilborn published popular monographs, the book's three main sections correlate shifts in the evolutionary *Werdegang*, or pathway, of human anatomy with the developmental "stages" of human culture.[106] Both author and editor recruit the methods and categories of physical anthropology in the typological study and classification of weapons, implements, ornaments, and finally built shelters—the latter being the focus of Kiesler's notes from the book transferred almost verbatim to the manuscript sent to publishers after World War II. By that point more than a decade had passed since Klaatsch's anthropological compendium had been re-edited (or rather "continued and supplemented" as indicated on the title page of the 1936 edition) by a group of National Socialist scientists—an archaeologist, a prehistorian, and an anthropologist, with expertise in Germanic history, race theory, and eugenics—who, after expunging additions by the Jewish-born (yet later "atheist scientist") Heilborn, had reforged Klaatsch's comparative "developmental trajectory" into the prehistoric pathway of the Germanic race towards world expansion.[107]

This was not the edition read by Kiesler, and in fact none of the three editions of Klaatsch's study exists in his library. The transcriptions of excerpts typed by Stefi Kiesler, as well as numerous photostats from the New York Public Library, are from the second edition of 1922 with an appendix on "the latest findings on human paleontology" added by Heilborn.[108] Even if Klaatsch's book appeared in English in 1923 as *The Evolution and Progress of Mankind* (and Stefi Kiesler also transcribed parts of this translation), Kiesler used his own liberal rendition of the German text in his manuscript, producing a number of revealing (mis)translations.[109]

For example, Kiesler renders the effect of a belligerent power attacking from a distance—*böswillige Fernwirkung* in the original, which the English edition translates periphrastically "as a hostile force not in the immediate neighborhood but of deadly effect"—with the more striking "malicious telekinesis" (I.2).[110] The term telekinesis suggests the magic powers of influencing or moving things from a distance, also known as psychokinesis describing the supernatural levitation of objects with no hand contact and by the powers of the mind alone, one of the several parapsychological phenomena that drew the attention of the surrealists. Telekinesis is also present among Lévy-Bruhl's forms of "mystic influence" in processes and techniques of "participation," along with contact, sympathy, and transference.[111] In a passage from his *Cultural History of Antiquity* transcribed by the Kieslers for (but ultimately not included in) *Magic Architecture*, the Viennese cultural historian Egon Friedell argued (after his reading of Lévy-Bruhl) that among the mythical Atlanteans, the ability for "telepathy increased to telekinesis and teleplasticity to the power of remote movement (*Fernbewegung*) [and] remote radiation (*Fernstrahlung*)."[112] But in the context of Kiesler's postwar translation, the same lethal "effect from a distance" and propensity for the remote control of objects, persons, and spaces also bears an association to military technology, including the long-range ballistic missile weapons controlled and guided from afar first used by German forces in World War II during aerial attacks against Britain.[113]

Klaatsch, whether describing the elongation or contraction of a bone in animal and human appendages or tracing the movements performed by feet and hands while climbing a tree, walking on earth, handling a tool, or throwing a weapon, analyzes both culture and anatomy as spatially projective operations, whose endpoint is territorial dominance. The image embossed on the cover of the first editions of the book is based on a highly racialized depiction painted by Wilhelm Kranz of an Indigenous "Australian ascending a tree" with the use of hands and feet, as well as an elastic branch looped around the trunk as a "sling."[114] According to Klaatsch, this peculiar manner of vertical locomotion, which is distinct from the climbing habits of primates, had a defining impact on the physiology of the human species, as well as its cultural and later urban development. One of the long-term benefits of the "old tree climbing days" was, for Klaatsch, the "extension of vision," as well as the "practice of building on heights," which the physical anthropologist also associated with the "pleasures" and "practical advantages" of "mountain-climbing" in later cultures, including the "towers and forts ... raised on top of hills" among the Romans.[115] The "military advantages" of such walled "summits" also inform the first "agglomerations of houses we call towns," the earliest layers of which go "back as far as the Stone Age."[116] Klaatsch essentially converts the phylogenetic tree of nineteenth-century evolutionist science into a material support and ideational axis for human and urban development, which in the physical anthropologist's account, become genetically interdependent. In reconfiguring the "stories" of humanity and urbanity on a "genetic" level, Kiesler's biological narrative of housing is less concerned with the ambiguity of "origins" and more invested on the ideological and (pseudo-)scientific precision of the "first-born."[117]

The transcriptions and quotations from Klaatsch in *Magic Architecture* mainly concentrate on the emergence of dwelling (*Behausung*), from the third part of Klaatsch's book, as "the earliest beginnings of culture."[118] The description of housing follows remarks on the development of cladding (*Bekleidung*) identified with bodily adornment (*Schmuck*), and precedes the section on the evolution of society and religion, which come into being only after the emergence of collective dwelling.[119] Klaatsch recognizes dwelling as "one of the most important moments in the progress of humans from an entirely savage condition [*ganz wilde Zustande*] to the earliest stages of culture [*früheste Kulturstufe*]."[120] In his developmental and highly racialized account progressing from hominids to hominins, housing is not an aftereffect but a *precondition* for the gradual emergence of humanity. This evolutionist logic informs Kiesler's own "story of housing" where "cave" and "nest" appear as active agents that *buttress* the not-entirely erect hominid subjects that construct them and thus redefine both their anatomy and territorial expansion.

Klaatsch's section on dwelling starts with a discussion of protected shelters (*abri*) at the entrances of caves based on the German scientist's exploration of prehistoric sites in Europe and continues with *Künstliche Wohnstätte*–artificial dwellings such as round huts, wind and fire screens, as well as pile-houses in the Pacific and other parts of the world, also described among Heilborn's previous ethnological publications.[121] Both author and editor offer an evolutionist view of housing structures unfolding in stages and punctuated by certain building types, which are ostensibly common among first societies across continents. Following the description of temporary sleeping nests built by primates, the first human structures mentioned are round huts made of tree branches bent and tangled to create a semi-spherical dome covered with palm leaves.[122] In the book these wooden structures are called *Käfighütte*, or "cage huts," a term also used for "cage-houses" made by humans for birds or other animals. These dome-shaped "cage-type" (*Käfigartige*) structures are followed by round huts with conical roofs (*Kegelhüte*) also documented in Africa and finally pile-huts (*Pfalhütte*) common in the "South Sea islands" and the Malaysian archipelago, which Klaatsch also traces in Europe during prehistoric times. Like Frobenius, Klaatsch and Heilborn consider the typology of the four-cornered pile dwelling an important "point of connection" between prehistoric Europe and the South Seas, whose "deeply rooted memory" also pervades (following the theories of the Swiss naturalist and ethnologist Paul Sarasin) the origins of the Greek temple, as well as later on, the stone house, which is a "repetition," Klaatsch argues, of the wood construction of the "Ur-house."[123] A color plate as well as the final figure in the last section of Klaatsch's book on "the culture of prehistoric humanity" show "reconstructions" of Neolithic pile dwellings in Switzerland; in an earlier publication by Klaatsch, the first of these plates was juxtaposed with a "modern pile village in New Guinea."[124]

Among the photostats prepared by Kiesler for the plates of *Magic Architecture* is a page from Klaatsch's book that includes the photograph of a round "cupola," as Kiesler (after Frobenius) calls the semi-spherical "cage-type hut" made of tree branches.[125] (fig. A.13) In addition to montaging this photograph into one of his plates (plate 10), the architect reproduces a similar round hut in a miniscule sketch scribbled on a draft typescript for his chapter on "the nest" (I.7).[126] A similar circular hut appears in the two preliminary charts juxtaposing primate- and "pygmy"-built structures mentioned earlier in connection to Frobenius's *Kuppelhütte* (see Addenda, figs. C.06b, C.07b). Finally, in the following plate of *Magic Architecture* and next to a reproduction from Klaatsch showing the "elevated sleeping nests" of orangutans perched high up on trees, Kiesler adds two photographs of Indigenous "elevated shelters" resting on a series of tall stilts from an article on the Papua in New Guinea published in *National Geographic*, in which the author further animalizes Indigenous dwellings by likening them to "birdhouses" in one of his captions (plate 9 and fig. A.14).[127] Kiesler's conflation of textual and iconographic sources produces the montage of images and geographies traversing his plate atlas. But if in the ethnological research of the earlier part of the

Heimatsempfinden und Ortssinn. 195

Europäer, allein gelassen, rettungslos verloren ist. Man hat die Wilden vielfach zum Aufspüren der Fährten von Flüchtlingen benützt, sie im Dienst der Kriminalpolizei in ähnlicher Weise verwendend wie wir die Polizeihunde. Bei den letzteren ist es ja zweifellos der

Abb. 166. Beim Bau der käfigartigen Rundhütte (Nordqueensland).

Geruchssinn, der sie leitet; beim Naturmenschen ist es die feine Beobachtungsfähigkeit, die einen teilweisen Ersatz für den Geruchssinn bildet. Der Wilde unterscheidet die Fußspuren zahlreicher Individuen voneinander; leichte Knickungen im Gesträuch verraten ihm den Weg, den ein flüchtender Mensch genommen hat. Bei den meisten Wanderungen, die primitive Menschenhorden vollzogen, dürfte der Ortssinn wohl manchmal auf eine harte Probe gestellt worden sein; nicht unwichtig mag vielleicht das Erklettern der Bäume gewesen sein, um beim Vordringen in neue Gegenden auszuspähen nach alten Wegen der Rückkehr oder neuen Möglichkeiten des Wanderns in neue Jagdreviere.

Die berechtigte Vorstellung einer Art von Nomadentum des primitiven Menschen darf nicht in dem Sinne ausgedeutet werden, daß die Wilden keine Empfindung für die Heimat hätten. Wir haben schon oben darauf hingewiesen, daß das Umherwandern der Horden australischer Eingeborener nicht sinn- und regellos geschieht, sondern mit Rücksicht auf die Schonung von Wild und Beute. Die genauere Betrachtung zeigt, daß jeder Stamm sein Gebiet hat, und daß er die Grenzen des andern streng respektiert, wie er das gleiche auch für die eigenen verlangt. Er ist nicht seßhaft, aber darum ist er doch nicht heimatlos.

Langsam erst hat sich beim Menschen die Ansässigkeit an bestimmten Punkten ausgebildet. Fern von sozialen festen Einrichtungen, von den Begriffen „Dorf" und „Stadt", die mit Viehzucht und Ackerbau in Zusammenhang stehen, hauste die Urmenschheit in kleinen Verbänden oder Familien bei-

15*

Sept. 1929

INTO PRIMEVAL PAPUA BY SEAPLANE 309

Photograph by R. K. Peck

AN UPPER FLY RIVER NATIVE PERCHES HIS HOUSE HIGH IN AIR

Behind the man is a notched-pole ladder, by which he climbs to his home. Surrounding trees, felled in a confused jumble, form a sort of *chevaux-de-frise*, preventing enemies from rushing the tree dweller's home (see text, page 311).

houses were not empty, for men began to of our half-grown children, were by this

Opposite
fig. A.12 Photostat used in plate 2a: "Myth, Skills and Architecture" of "Rock painting. Rain Ceremony. Southern Rhodesia [see Zimbabwe]," reproduced from Leo Frobenius and Douglas C. Fox, *Prehistoric Rock Pictures in Europe and Africa: From Material in the Archives of the Research Institute for the Morphology of Civilization* (Frankfort-on-Main, New York: Museum of Modern Art, 1937), 47. ÖFLKS, PHO_7216/0

Above
fig. A.13 Photostat used in plate 10 (above, right) with markings by Kiesler, reproduced from Hermann Klaatsch, *Der Werdegang der Menschheit und die Entstehung der Kultur* (Berlin: Deutsches Verlagshaus Bong & Co., 1922), 195. ÖFLKS, PHO_7197/0

fig. A.14 Photostat used in plate 9 (below and right) reproduced from E. W. Brandes, "Into Primeval Papua by Seaplane," *National Geographic*, September 1929, 309. ÖFLKS, PHO_7195/0

twentieth century represented by Klaatsch and Frobenius such artificial alignment aimed to reconstruct the "origins of humanity" along the outlines of a fixed set of "building types" that would consolidate the hierarchy of "stages" in evolutionary histories of both humanity and architecture, what does Kiesler's regurgitation and realignment of the same anthropological models and housing types in the context of a postwar humanism aim to (re)construct?

THE PORTABLE CAVE: SPELEOLOGY, ARCHAEOLOGY, AND MAGIC DESIGN (BREUIL, CASTERET)

Following the research on the origins of the physiological and cultural development of "humankind" in Klaatsch's physical anthropology and Frobenius's ethnological science, Kiesler draws a series of paradigmatic objects that serve as the corresponding origins in the evolution of building construction and eventually "Architecture." These primary structures appear as permanent yet flexible psychological enclosures, rather than concrete building types. The first is the "cave" followed by the "nest"– the former treated as an archaeological site replete with human and nonhuman traces charting a speculative prehistory of "housing." Reimagined as a spatial "tool," the cave essentially functions as a "defense mechanism" triggering Kiesler's mental projection from the belligerent environment of postwar modernity to an equally hostile yet more malleable prehistoric landscape gradually molded by the human species.

Our collective memory of sheltering caves dates back to the time of the ice ages and, in truth, to earlier times when man, or so-called man (pre-paleolithic) was not yet entirely erect. He had crawled on four legs into his habitat with more ease than his later erect stance would permit. After he became upright he had to bend down to get through his door, and once inside he remained crouched. Finally he raised the roof of his new home to the full height of his stature. (I.6)

Kiesler's evolutionary description of the cave is informed by Klaatsch's history of humankind, quoted extensively in *Magic Architecture*'s cave chapter, observations on protected shelters with signs of human habitation found at the entrances of caverns in the south of France.[128] However, Kiesler appears to merge Klaatsch's description of the cave with his observations on the evolution of the human species. If for Klaatsch, the tree aided humans in their singular quest for "vertical locomotion" and visual control of territory, then the cave in Kiesler's "story," provides a similar technical support in the conquest of verticality and the creation of habitable space. The evolution of the architectural enclosure follows the development of vertical posture marking the geological origins of human bipedalism. Similar to the *trotte-bébé* described by Jacques Lacan in his "mirror stage" essay, the cave transforms into an orthopedic mechanism propping the individually insufficient subject to an illusory construction of uprightness and specular navigation of space.[129] In Kiesler's reconstruction of building's "primal scene," the cave is by no means a "ready-made" natural enclosure. It is actively shaped by the human occupier. The human shapes the cave as much as the cave informs the human. At the other end of this evolutionary perspective lies Georges Bataille's view of "Architecture" as the "culmination of the evolution of earthly forms" and the "passage from simian to human forms" ultimately crowned by architectural edifices.[130]

In one of the preliminary illustrations for *Magic Architecture*, Kiesler sketches a cave with an exposed interior space as well as exterior geological shell emulating a multiple axonometric section of the irregular rock surface of a cave gallery (Main Text, fig. B.18).[131] The mineral structure appears almost foldable or even reversible, collapsing the limits between interior and exterior. Representations of humans and animals shown as hollow, fossilized remains or dark outlines drawn among geometric symbols gradually detach themselves from the gallery walls on which they are immured and start to mobilize towards an exit. The dark tongue of an alluvial stream also juts out from the cave's mouth as if retracing the progress of the water stream that had originally eroded the cavern. Mobility and expansion are the inner qualities of Kiesler's retroactive design of the cave, normatively portrayed as an immobile, dark, and limiting enclosure. Occupying both sides of Frobenius's polarity between the safety of "cave feeling" and the audacious territoriality of *Weitengefühl*, the cave is eventually redrawn as the fulcrum of an endlessly expanding yet always split and dichotomous "universe."

In a chapter that follows those on the cave and the nest, titled "The Universe as Architecture," Kiesler writes: "The cave is extensive ... far beyond the actual need of a shelter. It extends its stony 'range' almost to the horizon, where sky and ocean meet; and above it reaches to the sun" (I.8). Kiesler delineates this cosmological model in a hand-drawn illustration reproduced among the plates of *Magic Architecture* that depicts the cave "shelter" as the "innermost cell" of a succession of concentric layers (plate 13 and Main Text, fig. B.06b).[132] The semi-circular zones of the upper half include the mineral enclosure of the cave (with an erect human figure standing in front of its entrance), the vegetal realm of trees, the aerial domain of birds, clouds, stars, and the sun, and finally the ethereal region of anthropomorphic gods and animal deities, all organized in layers "below," "on," "above" and "beyond" the earth, similar to Kiesler's geometric chart based on one of Frobenius's drawings of Ethiopian rock paintings seen earlier (plate 2a). The lower half consists of a series of symmetrically inverted layers populated by horizontally placed human figures ("the dead") surrounded by the nocturnal region of the moon and a gigantic serpent enclosing the subterranean universe whose outer region is populated by the masks of infernal "spirits." Terrestrial and subterranean areas appear to mirror one another as inverted realities or in Kiesler's terms "correalities." In a preliminary sketch for the same illustration, Kiesler draws this symmetrical universe as a handheld mirror turned into a horizontal position (see Main Text, fig. B.06c).[133] The world is an object and every object is a handheld model of the world–essentially a control "tool" manipulating "known" and "unknown" territories. Physical extension into planetary space originates in subjective mental projection, which (in the manner of a western Renaissance perspective), is reified into a mirror image of "self" and the "world"–reflecting another of Frobenius's polarities.[134]

A number of passages from Frobenius's *Kulturgeschichte Afrikas* transcribed in *Magic Architecture* detail this cosmological organization as well as the function of animal symbols in world religions.[135] Kiesler includes among his plates a comparative grouping of animal masks from ancient Egypt, Crete, and Greece to Africa, India, and Northern Guinea, which he (bringing Verworn into the mix) characterizes as "psycho-plastic expressions" aiming to enhance human power by animal masking (plate 26).[136] The sun and the moon magic symbols appearing repeatedly in Kiesler's cosmic diagrams evoke Frobenius's descriptions of the "sun- and the moon-worshipping generations" the former are associated with the aforementioned "feeling for open spaces," while the latter with the "cave-space-feeling," which create contrasting building constructions and territorial attitudes.[137]

But what would the regurgitation of Frobenius's contrast signify in a postwar environment striving to turn away from polarizing mythologies? In its projection of a unified world, Kiesler's cave proposes a tenuous synthesis of Frobenius's oppositions, yet it remains split by distinct significations. Sliding from prehistory to recent colonial history, Kiesler describes his preliminary ink drawing of the cave as "Light [and] shadow of the mirror of A.[rchitecture]/

of primitive man" (see Main Text, fig. B.06c). On the exterior, the cave projects an idyllic pre-civilizational landscape of trees, animals, and exotic birds. This is a familiar iconography that perhaps owes less to the fictional painted representations of prehistoric nature by German landscape painters, such as Wilhelm Kranz or Heinrich Harder inserted in Klaatsch's early twentieth-century publications, as to the photographic documentation of colonized Indigenous peoples in the exoticizing depictions contained in Kiesler's clippings from ethnographic articles in *Koralle* and the *National Geographic*. Yet, in terms of fictional prehistoric and modern colonial image-making, there is a distinct undercurrent of violence and death imprinted in Kiesler's own split-representation of the universe as a radially expanding cave. On the one hand his pencil drawing appears to unite the dead and the living in an ouroboric circle (see Main Text, fig. B.06b),[138] based presumably on the social contiguity between the spirits of the dead and the bodies of the living described in the ethnosociological visions of Lévy-Bruhl read and transcribed by the Kieslers.[139] But on the other, the architect's ink drawing of the "Universe as Architecture" as a mirror (see Main Text, fig. B.06c) appears to strive to keep the living and the dead neatly apart in two symmetrical yet inverted regions. This tectonic division is ostensibly the architectural legacy of the cave engraved prominently at the center of Kiesler's radially expanding "universe." In disciplinary terms, this is also the contribution of architecture to ethnology—a modern design technique aiming to create partitions against animist indigenous epistemologies and the alarming presence of *their* dead.

The prospect of violence also gives rise to eschatological visions associated with the cave inundated by fears of an inhospitable environment and relentless assault by inscrutable forces, once more arriving from a distance.

Timid man and the most powerful primates have one fear in common, namely the spontaneous savagery of climatic conditions: wind-storms, rain-squalls, lightning-fires, heat-drought, cold, and ice. That these onslaughts might mean death is not so frightening as the fact that the blows are delivered from a distance and are struck by an unseen enemy. Man and primates alike, flee; they make for caves above and below the ground; they look for thickets, for rich tropical foliage; they hide in hollow trees (I.2).

While planted in the prehistorical or ahistorical ethnosociological literature from the earlier part of the twentieth century he was sampling, Kiesler's text also reflects the climatological motivations and biases that inform colonial and gradually postcolonial architectural discourses of the postwar era. His description of extreme weather phenomena in "tropical" settings attests to the proliferating nature of fear caused by "unseen" climatic agents, but also to the multiplicity of protective solutions such unlocatable threat necessitates, of which the cave is only one option.

The first artificial shelter illustrated in the plates for *Magic Architecture* before the cave appears in the text of the book, are the African "umbrella type" huts schematically represented in Frobenius's studies, which Kiesler juxtaposes with Fuller's design for his Dymaxion House (plates 1, 2). While Frobenius would view the subterranean cellar and the portable tent as two alternate housing solutions adopted by the nomadic Hamites, Kiesler again attempts to merge these two building types into one, as his own version of the cave is paradoxically portable. The emergence of social nomadism appears continuous with architecture's portability. As soon as the first human groups are mobilized, writes Kiesler: "The cave, too, detaches itself from its natural adherence. It leaves the mountainside. It begins to stand alone, and is built artificially" (I.9). Architecture and society are mobilized concurrently—a coincidence that implies not a dissolution but a permanent transference of the cave. The cave for Kiesler is not a singular object, type, or space, but a recurring "condition," akin to a psychological state, which is then reenacted in a variety of future habitations shaped around a void, gap, or crevice. Against Plato's allegory, we never exit the cave, but keep carrying it with us. The architect's ongoing theoretical model of the *Endless House* "houses" such pre-condition.

Contrary to Sigfried Giedion, who after visiting the caves of southern France and Spain for several years emphatically declared that caverns lack "a clear concept of space" (which, according to Giedion, only emerges with the discovery of verticality in Egyptian monuments),[140] for Kiesler the cave represents a precondition for the development of the first independent "shelters" and consequently all other interior spaces. Following the cave's detachment from the mountainside, Kiesler describes that "[f]urther development of this individuation causes his cave to evolve into the character of a shelter: a newly erected structure. The vault of the cave is raised on walls and becomes an elevated roof"(I.9). In his handwritten manuscript of the same passage Kiesler adds on the margin: "Potentials."[141]

These "potentials" address not only building construction but the entire gamut of technical skills. While humans ostensibly reshape the cave's interior, the cave reciprocally "forms" human subjects by providing the material substrate for their first design efforts via painting and sculpture—the two "skills" which, according to Kiesler's stratigraphic diagram after Frobenius, precede the development of "Architecture."

In addition to Frobenius's texts in the MoMA catalogue on *Prehistoric Rock Pictures*, Kiesler also quotes extensively from a publication on the rock paintings of southern Andalusia authored (among others) by the paleoarchaeologist Abbé Henri Breuil,[142] whose "account of [a] cave [quoted] in Frobenius" Kiesler notes

TRANSLATOR'S NOTE

in G 1 and 2, and the longer zigzags, such as G 5, from Palomas I, have been shown by M. Breuil to be an exaggeration of this symbol.[1]

Fig. 8. Series H.

The next series, H, shows some 'ramiform' figures. The transition from the undoubtedly human symbol, H 1, to H 3 is easy, the three pairs of branches representing head, arms, and legs. In H 4 and those that follow the number of branches increases indefinitely and all resemblance to the human form is lost; except that in H 7 we seem to recognize in the lowest pair of branches the flexed legs of H 1. Though these many-branched figures may all be of human origin, it is difficult not to see in some of them, particularly in H 6, the representation of a tree or other vegetable growth. H 8, according to M. Breuil, is certainly human. H 9, 10, and 11 are probably female. M. Breuil suggests that the multiplication of arms in the last two figures (as in the case of certain Indian deities) may signify some supernormal power.

Fig. 9. Series I.

Series I consists also of female symbols. It will be noticed that nearly all have the arms raised. The circular base common to many of these conventional figures of women (e.g. Nos. 1, 3 to 6, also F 2) is in M. Breuil's view derived from a triangular base and represents a skirt or other garment. The typical bitriangular or hour-glass sign is shown in Nos. 9 and 10 (in the

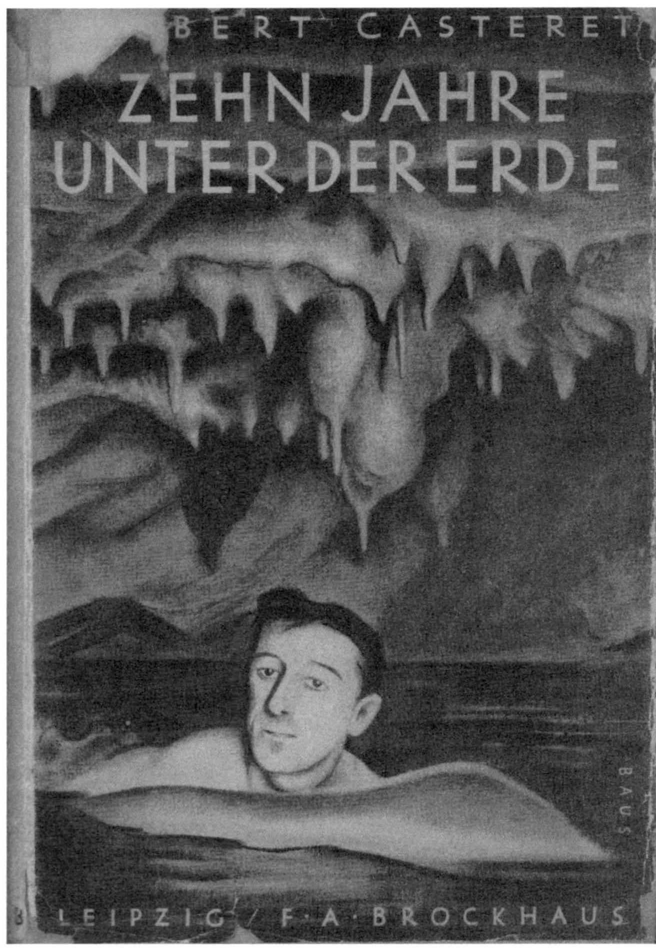

Previous
fig. A15 Frederick Kiesler, scrap note "Breuil – account of cave in Frobenius" ÖFLKS, TXT_6825/0_N5

fig. A.16 Photostat used in plate 24 (first row and lower rows), "Typical human symbols" reproduced from Henri Breuil and Miles Crawford Burkitt, *Rock Paintings of Southern Andalusia: A Description of a Neolithic and Copper Age Art Group* (Oxford: The Clarendon Press, 1929), 8. ÖFLKS, PHO_7192/0

fig. A.17 Norbert Casteret, *Zehn Jahre unter der Erde: Höhlenforschungen eines Einzelgängers* (Leipzig: Brockhaus, 1936).

in a paper scrap clipped to his drafts (fig. A.15).[143] The transcribed excerpts deal with the placement of the drawings inside the cave, as well as the use of color and symbolism, including pectiform, stelliform, and tectiform patterns, a number of which (mentioned in Kiesler's transcriptions) ostensibly represent "round huts on piles."[144] While Kiesler ultimately uses only a fraction of the excerpts he transcribed from the archaeological volume, he reproduces several of the illustrations showing "abstractions" of the human figure as well as symbols of a "house on stilts" (plates 24, 25). In a handwritten addendum to his transcription of the description of a series of rock drawings with schematic human forms, Kiesler recognizes in three star- or flower-like radiating patterns, "one of [Neolithic Man's] two homes, namely, the wooden hut in stilts (the other being the stony cave)"[145]–a contiguity between the two original forms of habitation that rehearses the genealogies of dwelling traced by Klaatsch and Frobenius (fig. A.16). The hypothetical transformation of the human figure to a heavenly body and/or pile dwelling in this "comparative" display of symbols supports Kiesler's grounding of the origins of housing in a preanimist force-field comprised indiscriminately from animate corporeal and inorganic sources.

Following his references to rock painting and their tectonic as well as "tectiform" extensions, Kiesler's manuscript expands on prehistoric "sculpture," which allows him to sketch a larger theory of spatially oriented design. References to cave "sculpture" are quoted from the autobiographical memoir *Ten Years Under the Earth* (*Dix ans sus la terre*, 1933) by the well-known French speleologist and popular author Norbert Casteret, which Kiesler read in German and then translated excerpts into English (even if an English translation already existed) (fig. A.17).[146] Famous for his discovery of a headless bear shaped on a rock of the Montespan cave in the French Pyrenees, acclaimed as the "first prehistoric sculpture" to be found in modern times, Casteret supports the so-called "magical" theory of the origins of human design. Observing the violent mutilations inflicted on the body of animal likenesses like the one in Montespan, the speleologist concurs with anthropologists who argue that the first human drawings aimed to *kill* rather than merely represent living creatures.[147] In their original performances, painting and sculpture were parts of the human arsenal producing what Kiesler described as "tools for attack." The target of such an attack by tools of human design was not simply the animal bodies living inside or outside the cave but the cave itself and its contested space of habitation.

As Casteret's speleological memoir discloses, humans were not the original inhabitants of caves. In his writings, he divides such occupants into two classes: "cavernicolous, born, living and dying underground, and cavernophilous, temporarily or accidentally living in caves."[148] Cave bears are the largest members of the former and hyenas of the latter, while bats "bridge the gap" in between.[149] Humans, even as temporary dwellers, as Casteret notes, often had to "battle" with the cave bears for an "underground refuge" space.[150] Casteret deciphers this "struggle for possession" in the traces of superimposition between bear feet and "naked human footprints" covered by "claw-marks."[151] The sculpture and few paintings of *ursus spelaeus* found in caverns offer for the speleologist additional links to the spatial contestations among the two species. The ultimate objective of magic design was not merely the procurement of material sustenance, but territorial control–the conquest of space by the elimination of the animal. Perhaps a (human) "concept" of space, as Giedion argued, was missing from the cave because their spaces were originally navigated and molded by nonhuman bodies. Painting and sculpture were projective spatial techniques aiming to expand human dominance inside animal territory. Space design originates in this physical as well as ontological space-setting operation that haunts the cave's human-animal prehistory.[152]

"ANIMAL ARCHITECTURE" I: TERMITARIES, BUILDING LABOR, AND INSECT SOCIETIES (MARAIS, BÖLSCHE)

From painting to sculpture, Kiesler redraws the cave as the mineralogical enclosure of human and animal space-altering activity, eventually, the geological substratum of design. While design retroactively mobilizes the cave, its virtual movement as a portable psychological enclosure animalizes it. Kiesler reconfigures the cave as an evolving organism that not only supports but participates in the growth of its occupants be they human, animal, or mineral. The cave's animal deportment is no stranger to architecture. On the contrary, it *foregrounds* architecture through the cultivation of building techniques originally developed by species other than the human. While animals first appear in Kiesler's diagrams as paintings or fossilized reliefs on cave surfaces, the same creatures gradually leap out from the cavern's mineral background to construct their own organic enclosures.

Like caves, animal habitations emerge to preserve life, yet they are haunted by the prospect of death. In an early section of the first chapter of *Magic Architecture*, "Man's House is Animal Architecture," Kiesler writes: "This death consciousness (*Todesbewußtsein*) of animals affects the mechanism of the entire body; not only the hands, the whole nervous system is constantly on the alert ... The individual animal improvises emergency solutions and robs nature from foliage to work them into defense masks (*Schutz-masken*): nests, houses" (II.1).[153] As if wearing a detachable animal mask, Kiesler's humans ultimately appear to refurbish the shield of animal housing into their own composite attire.

*

While mainly interested in the animals' building methods, the architect's research files contain a sizeable number of clippings with photographs of animals, from tigers to giraffes, iguanas and ants, only few of whom build, torn from a popular book on animal photography and science, containing two articles by Heilborn, himself the author of several interwar publications on animal photography that remained widely popular even after the Second World War (figs. A.18a–c).[154] The juxtaposition of powerful non-building animals like tigers, versus the small and vulnerable yet intricately equipped bodies of builders such as the ant, shows Kiesler's general interest in external animal morphology, as well as his more specific interest in the transformation of animal appendages, particularly in species that employ parts of their body as building tools. The same book of animal photography perused by Kiesler contains an article by German medical doctor and zoological author Walter Bernhard Sachs, on animals as "master craftsmen [*Handwerkmeister*] and technicians [*Techniker*]" analyzing the use of paws, front legs, teeth or beaks in mammals, birds, ants, and spiders engaging in a constructive operation "led by a dark instinct ... less the creation of reason [*Verstand*], rather an unconscious talent given to them by nature."[155] Sachs's article drew heavily from the first publications on animal dwellings by the natural historian and evangelical preacher Adolf Müller and his brother Karl, a senior forestry official, examining construction by mammals and birds above or below earth and water as part of the German "habitat."[156]

*

While Kiesler's research material includes extensive literature on a variety of animal species who build nests, such as bees and birds,[157] the chapters of *Magic Architecture's* Part II on "Animal Architecture" concern only two species: termites and beavers, the first providing a prototype for a socially organized building activity sustained by communal labor, the second a model for ecological design and environmental engineering.

KÖNIGSTIGER
Die Eigenschaften eines großen Räubers, List und Verwegenheit, sprechen aus der Physiognomie des Tigers.

FISCHOTTER
Soviel Verdruß der Fischotter dem Fischer bereitet, soviel Freude macht er dem Naturfreund durch sein lustiges, anziehendes Wesen.

WALDAMEISE
Ins Riesenhafte vergrößert, steht unsere nur 4 bis 9 mm lange Waldameise wie ein Ungeheuer der Saurierzeit vor uns.

Why start with termites? Once more, the answer lies in the threat of annihilation. From the moment the miniscule insect comes out of its abode, every other animal wants to eat it, therefore "nature produces them in … millions." "Every pair is necessary because the slaughter is immense," quotes Kiesler, echoing mass slayings of humans by their own species in recent atrocities (II.1).[158] Unlike the large black ant or the bee, the termite is essentially defenseless. What it lacks in terms of bodily means of defense, it compensates with building capacity. Building is its main protective weapon and therefore the termite builds incessantly: from the moment it is born until it expires. Rather than merely containing, building construction here consumes and ultimately replaces living.

Kiesler draws his description of the termitary primarily from *The Soul of the White Ant*, a study by the South African jurist and naturalist Eugène Marais originally published as a series of journal articles (1923–1931), and later as a book in Afrikaans (1934) before its translation into English (1937), one year after the author's death.[159] In this sociological study of insect colonies, produced after years of observing the building habits of these insects, Marais describes the termitary as an animate social structure akin to an "animal made of hundreds of thousands of animals" (as was the title of one of the German articles found among Kiesler's research clippings that summarizes Marais's studies).[160] (fig. A.19) The termitary's quasi-animist organization is based on the "soul" not of the individual ant, but the termite colony as a whole, organized around the hyperinflated body of the queen. The queen secretly communicates with the bodies of the guardians, who feed and care for her, as well as the workers who build the termitary that houses the queen, following a strict division of labor. While surrounded by this buzzing, animated activity, the queen herself is immovable in her chamber, but such immobility is productive, as it allows her to reproduce thousands of eggs every hour with industrious efficacy. Marais calls the queen not only the "soul" but also the "brain" of the termitary, without which the termitary and all of its animal inhabitants as well as building components would be unable to operate and eventually cease to exist.

What initially appears as the monarchic system of a hierarchic form of governance turns out to be a reversible condition, in which the queen is merely the disposable container of the material substance she is fed with by her guardians. Towards the concluding chapter of Marais's book, an accident happens during a dissection of the termitary opened up by the scientists to observe the queen and her attendants in her chamber, when the queen is seriously injured. Instead of trying to save their queen, her attendants immediately start sucking from her body the valuable substance they have been feeding her in order to preserve it in their stomachs before transferring it to another queen, if there is a neighboring nest. Otherwise, they and the termitary "die."[161]

This recyclable energy, only temporarily contained in the body of the ruler, is again reminiscent of the animist economy and the laws of sympathetic magic of Frazer's *Golden Bough* unfolding in the rituals of the decapitation of the Divine King the moment his power starts waning. But if in Frazer, the king's variable potency extends to all objects of nature secretly associated with his body, in the insect colony, the queen's force is mediated and limited by the "artificial" closed system of the termitary. Even if built by organic materials, the termitary's artifice has essentially substituted nature to a point that there is no distinction between the two. This is a similar feat to what human industriousness has achieved in its own building enterprises. In its emphasis on the storage and preservation of vital nourishment via tectonic construction, the termitary foregrounds the foundation of human economy evolving concurrently with its building methods. This line of socio-economic development from "social insects" to humans provides the theoretical scaffold supporting the main narrative of *Magic Architecture*.[162]

Paul Karlson:

Ein TIER aus hunderttausend TIEREN

Das rätselhafte Wesen TERMITE

Was ist Seele? Was ist das Leben? Wo ist der Sinn, wo ein Anfang oder Ende in unserer kurzen Fahrt auf dem ewigen Strom der Zeit? Soviel Fragen, soviel Rätsel. Solange es Menschen gibt, haben sie versucht, Klarheit zu erlangen — jenen gleitenden Fluchtpunkt zu fassen, in dem unsere eigene ungewisse Existenz sich deckt mit dem Wesen des ganzen Universums, jenen Brennpunkt, in dem das Licht der Klarheit, der Erkenntnis zusammenläuft und wieder auseinander strebt. Der Traum des Künstlers und die begnadete Vision des Gottgesandten, der eine neue Religion verkündet, die klare ordnende Ueberlegung des Wissenschaftlers — sie alle sind nichts als immer wiederholte, verzweifelte, unbegreiflich kühne Anstrengungen des Verstandes und des Gemüts, das ewig Unbegreifliche zu begreifen.

Was ist die Welt? Oh — hier sind wir eher in unserem Element. Das bunte Bild ist rasch geschildert, in tausend Aspekten bietet es sich dar, und jeder Erzähler hält seine Version für richtig. Und wenn es um Klassifikation geht, um Einordnen und Beschreiben — nun, Schemata lassen sich mit leichter Mühe finden, und freundliche Worte helfen aus, um die dunklen Stellen zu überbrücken. Bald scheint alles in schönster Ordnung — bis plötzlich ein Mann daherkommt und das Bild mit unbefangenen, prüfenden Augen betrachtet: da zerrinnt es, und schauernd stehen wir aufs neue vor dem Unbekannten, dem Wunder.

Das unbekannte Tier

Seine Heimat? An vielen Orten der Erde kann man es finden — in Afrika und Australien, auf Ceylon oder in Südamerika. Sein Aussehen? Das weiß niemand. Denn soweit wir es zu sehen bekommen, ist es fast jeder Gestalt fähig. Es kann wie ein Turmbau erscheinen, doppelt mannshoch, mit unregelmäßigen Buckeln und Wellen, graubraun von Farbe. Es kann langgestreckt, niedrig über der Erde liegen, streng von Norden nach Süden, dem magnetischen Meridian folgend, so genau wie ein guter Kompaß. Es kann wie ein breiter Buckel sich über die dürre Erde wölben — aber all das will nicht viel besagen, weil immer nur ein winziger Teil des Tierkörpers sichtbar wird. Unterirdisch erstreckt er sich, verlaufend und von ganz willkürlicher Gestalt, in große Tiefen, zwanzig, vielleicht dreißig Meter weit, und er breitet sich ins Erdreich seitlich aus, wie das Wurzelgeflecht eines Baumes. Seine Körpertemperatur? Ein, zwei oder ein halb Grad mehr als der Mensch. Und sein Name? Sein Name — einen passenden hat die Wissenschaft noch nicht gefunden — sein Name lautet „Termitarium", Termitenstaat. N i c h t Termite, nein, aber darauf kommen wir gleich. Der Entdecker endlich dieses wundersamsten aller Tiere heißt Eugène N. Marais. Und er will, daß seine Entdeckung in äußerster Strenge wörtlich genommen wird: der Termitenstaat, das Termitarium, wie wir von jetzt an sagen wollen, ist ein lebendiges Tier.

Ein paar Worte über Marais vorweg. Ein Journalist und Schriftsteller, zu den bekanntesten Südafrikas zählend; ein Mann, der vier Jahre Medizin studiert hat, daneben Jura, und englischer Rechtsanwalt ist. Endlich ein unermüdlicher, von fanatischer Geduld und Hingabe erfüllter Naturliebhaber, ein Mann, der „niemals ohne zahme Affen, Schlangen oder Skorpione und dergleichen war", der sich mit größter Freiheit in einer Pavianherde bewegen kann. Ein Mann, der wieder und wieder die Nacht auf dem „veld" verbringt, um den gleichmäßigen Zug der Termiten oder der Wanderameisen zu studieren, der viele Nächte die Leuchtkäfer beobachtet hat und dem jede Kreatur gleich willkommen ist. Ein Tierpsychologe von Rang und erstaunlicher Originalität. Vor zwei Jahren ist er gestorben. Er hat uns ein Buch hinterlassen: „Die Seele der weißen Ameise", im wesentlichen eine Bearbeitung früherer Zeitungsaufsätze, die — das wollen wir ausdrücklich betonen — 6 Jahre vor Maeterlincks Buch über die Termiten erschienen sind.

Dies Buch gehört zu den erstaunlichsten Schriften, die je erschienen sind. Hier ist sein Inhalt.

Ein Staat aus einem einzigen Leib

Wir sagten es schon: Marais betrachtet das Termitarium als ein lebendiges Tier. Er will ganz ernst damit genommen werden; keine Spur von Vorbehalt, von Symbolismus, von Mystik oder gar dichterischer Freiheit ist dabei. Es ist eine klare These — sehen wir zu, was ein Mann für Gründe dafür hat, der mehr als zehn Jahre seines Lebens nichts anderes tat, als Termiten beobachten.

Ein paar kurze Worte zur Einführung: trocken und lehrbuchhaft, der Kürze wegen. Termiten — fälschlich weiße Ameisen genannt — leben in „wohlorganisierten Staaten", wie man zu sagen pflegt. Es gibt wesentlich drei Arten: männliche und weibliche geflügelte Geschlechtstiere — König und Königin —, und Arbeiter und Soldaten, diese beiden geschlechtslos, blind, flügellos. Gleich nach dem Hochzeitsflug werfen König und Königin ihre Flügel ab, graben sich in die Erde ein und legen den Grundstock zu dem mächtigen Termitenbau, der

Toter Stein — oder lebendiges Wesen? Ein typischer übermannshoher Termitenbau aus der afrikanischen Steppe. Marais stellt die These auf, dies sei kein lebloser Bau — wie etwa ein Vogelnest oder ein Ameisenhaufen — sondern der Körper eines „Gruppentiers", eben des Termitenstaates.

Zentrum des Lebens. Die Termitenkönigin in ihrer Höhle — umgeben von dem König, von ihrer Leibwache, und umpflegt von Hunderten kleiner Arbeiter. „Wenn man die Königin tötet, zerfällt sofort und automatisch der ganze Termitenstaat."

Previous

figs. A.18a–c Photographs of "royal tiger," "beaver," and "wood-ant" extracted from Lola Kreuzberg, ed., *Wir Tiere: Erlebnisse und Begebenheiten aus der Welt der Tiere* (Berlin: Neufeld & Henius, 1930), 189, 235, 236. Research clippings. ÖFLKS, CLP_6506/0verso, CLP_6540/0_N10verso CLP_6506/0recto.

Above

fig. A.19 Paul Karlson, "Ein Tier aus hunderttausend Tieren: Das rätselhafte Wesen Termite," *Koralle* 6, no. 42 (October 23, 1938). Research press clipping. ÖFLKS, CLP_6607/0

Opposite

fig. A.20 Wilhelm Bölsche, *Der Termitenstaat: Schilderung eines geheimnisvollen Volkes* (Stuttgart: Kosmos, 1931).

fig. A.21 Comparative time-chart on the egg production of the termite queen, Wilhelm Bölsche, *Der Termitenstaat: Schilderung eines geheimnisvollen Volkes* (Stuttgart: Kosmos, 1931), 31.

Equally ample in socio-political associations, is a study of "the termite colony" (*Der Termitenstaat*) by the popular natural history writer Wilhelm Bölsche, included in Kiesler's research material but not quoted in the manuscript of *Magic Architecture*.[163] (fig. A.20) In excerpted passages transcribed by the Kieslers, Bölsche describes the termite workers' building material as a "form of concrete" used to build structures that are "comparable to the Cathedral of Cologne or an Egyptian pyramid, pasted together from the salvia or gastric juice of their builders."[164] The termitary is not an arbitrary pile of these digested morsels, but a "unitary construction" based on a "regular plan"–a product of "construction method" and "building design."[165] The supersized body of the queen surrounded by its attendants figuring prominently in the pamphlet's cover and in several of its illustrations, is eventually abstracted into the graphic chart of a "birth machine" producing million eggs in the time span of a year, "as many as the citizens of the states of Bavaria and Württemberg together" or ten million every ten years "almost as many as the combined populations of Germany and France," notes Bölsche.[166] (fig. A.21) The geopolitical analogies of this chart extend much further in some of the photographic illustrations reproduced in Bölsche's small book, which showcase the growth of termitaries in the tropical climate of the German and other European colonies in Africa as well as other parts of world, where the bulk of such entomological research was conducted.[167] This could explain why in Bölsche's pamphlet as well as Kiesler's plates, termitaries are shown next to the bodies of Indigenous African people, employed as anthropometric measures, yet only to demonstrate that termitaries tower above them (plate 16b).[168] In one of Bölsche's photographic illustrations showing a "broad massive termitary with a tower" in the Maasai Steppe, this indexing of Indigenous presence is provided by a male figure armed with a western rifle, the measure of a further asymmetry and disproportion of power in the colonial landscape of East Africa.[169] The termitary itself is enlisted as a model of not only physical, but primarily social and political organizational structure based on a hierarchical redistribution of labor and power control that expands among several territories of the globe.

In his plates, Kiesler juxtaposes a photograph of the RCA tower in New York with the drawing of a termitary, which in comparison with the body-height of the termite is "relatively four times as high as the Empire State Building, and six times as high as the Rockefeller Center" (plate 16d–e). The illustration on the left is from a London newspaper of 1929 that shows the termitary across a shoreline with an imaginary line-up of the tallest skyscrapers of New York, including the Larkin, Chrysler, and Woolworth towers, proportionately "toppled" by the ant structure. [170] (fig. A.22) The newspaper image appears as a montage that juxtaposes a typical colonial landscape with New York's metropolitan skyline surrounded by a transoceanic body of water. The juxtaposition between termitaries and American skyscrapers rehearses a proportional analogy between insect and human towers reproduced in Bölsche (and other textual sources consulted by Kiesler), in which a termitary (analogically as high as the Matterhorn mountain in the Swiss Alps) towers over the outlines of the Cheops Pyramid in Egypt, the Ulm Minster church, the Eiffel Tower in Paris, and the Chrysler Building in New York (all with the exception of the Ulm church illustrated among Kiesler's plates and drawings).[171] Following the expert German entomologist Karl Escherich quoted by Bölsche, the termite colony "represents the culmination-point of the social life of insects."[172] But what would such apex state in insect sociality signify for human economy and social organization, and in particular, the coordinated tectonics syncing the sites of human labor neighboring the termitaries of the African colonies, including plantations and mines, with the cathedrals of labor and other towering structures of European and American metropolises? Kiesler's composite plates reproduce not simply a morphological but a societal disproportion in the

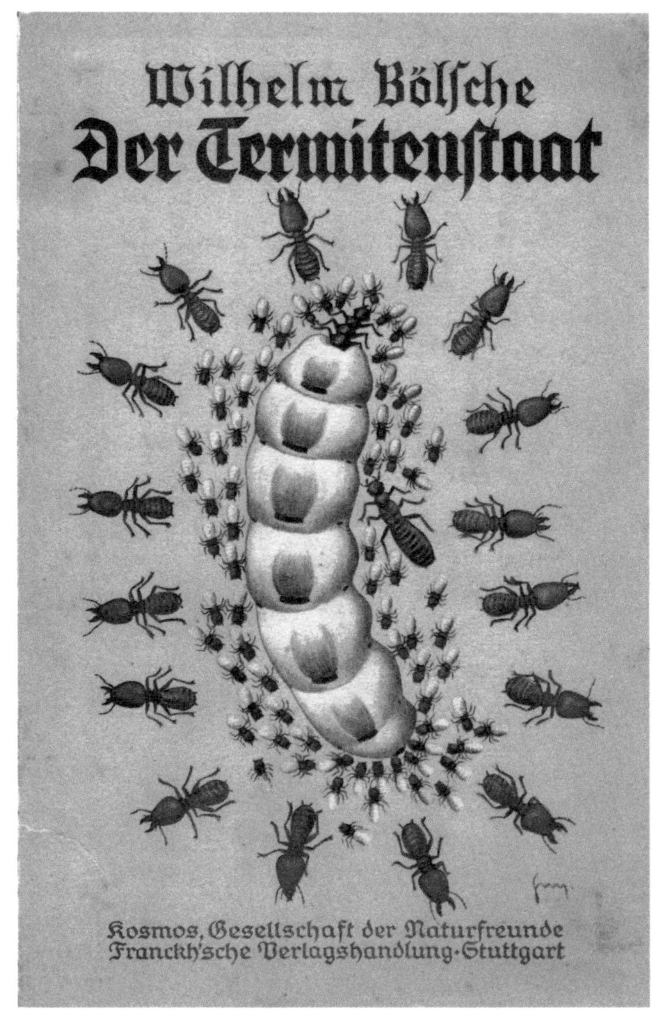

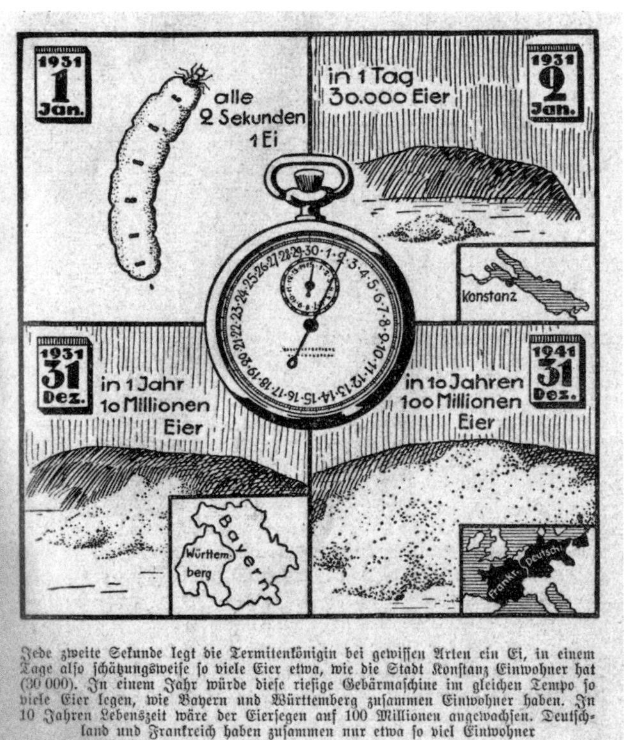

A MIRACLE OF BUILDING! ANT-MADE "SKY-SCRAPERS."

Insects. – Ant.

NEW YORK'S HIGHEST BUILDINGS DWARFED (RELATIVELY) BY AN ANT-HILL: (INSET) TYPES OF TERMITES (WHITE ANTS).

The wonderful architecture of the termites, or white ants, of which we illustrated some examples in our issue of March 2, is truly stupendous when considered in relation to the tiny proportions of the insects, and the "termitaries," as they are called, far outsoar the loftiest human efforts. Let us put it thus. The white ant, which is only 3-16th of an inch high, builds structures that rise to 20 ft. Man, whose average stature is six feet, has so far reached in his building a maximum height of 1208 ft. In proportion to their size, therefore, white ants build structures seven times higher than the highest built by man. Our illustration shows an interesting comparison on this ratio, between a 20-ft. tower constructed by termites, and five of New York's tallest sky-scrapers, built, or in building—the Larkin Tower (1208 ft.), and the Chrysler, Woolworth, Chanin, and Ritz Tower buildings, whose respective heights are given above. The larger photograph of the termitary was taken by Mr. Leon Bayer, M.D., and is reproduced by courtesy of the New York "Zoological Society Bulletin." In "The Ant People," by Dr. H. H. Ewers, an English translation [illegible] published by Messrs. Lane, we read: "The cubic contents of an ant building [illegible] hold a million times more inhabitants than the largest human habitation. S[illegible]ts of an entire Ant People have been found in which stood over sevent[illegible]dred of these mighty houses!"

Full size B. (6×8)

fig. A.22 Template for plate 16d: "A skyscraper for a hundred thousand inhabitants" reproduced from "A Miracle of Building! Ant-Made 'Sky-Scrapers'," *Illustrated London News*, March 16, 1929. Press clipping mounted on paper. ÖFLKS, CLP_6597/0

redistribution of power among human and animal species in different parts of the globe as it transmogrifies into building.

"ANIMAL ARCHITECTURE" II: INSTINCT, DRIVE, AND AUTOMATISM (WUNDT)

Central in the discussions of the parallels between termite and human labor is the potential overlap between social and building "instinct." The title of the introduction in Kiesler's section on "Animal Architecture" is "Instinct, Memory, and the Drive to Create," which implies a development from "instinct" to "drive" and from animal to human building activity. Throughout his English and (more rare) German drafts, Kiesler uses both instinct (*Instinkt*) and drive (*Trieb*) almost interchangeably, yet there is a clear sense in both his work and Marais that building activity in animals and humans moves beyond mere "instinct." The termite "worker" is not conscious of a building plan, yet it unfailingly brings all building tasks to completion. "The builders on one side of the breach know nothing of those on the other side," quotes Kiesler from Marais: "In spite of this the termites build a similar arch or tower on each side of the plate, the two halves match perfectly after the dividing cut has been repaired" (II.2) (plate 15). In fact Marais, quoted by Kiesler, rejects the individual autonomy of an inherited building instinct in the worker: "It is the instinct and design of a separate soul situated outside the individual termite"—a concept that resituates design and building technique into the territory of an unconscious participatory activity. The same communal building process invokes the notion of "participation" as a symbiotic communication among humans, animals, and natural elements described by Lévy-Bruhl in Kiesler's transcriptions from the French ethnologist's writings, even if in Marais, it is apparently limited among the members of a single species of insects.[173]

As noted in one of Kiesler's preliminary drafts (originally written in German and including a number of deletions), building activity ultimately appears as an attribute or gift that humans owe to animals, and functions, originally, as a defense mechanism:

> **This talent for building is not an exclusive prerogative of humans; it seems to be nothing else but ~~an automatically acquired~~ the extended ~~protection~~ movement of defense ~~of the body~~ of the animal-psyche: ~~the anxiety for~~ protection against pain, ~~paralysation~~, hunger and death, ~~contrives~~ forced from living conditions.**[174]

In the chapter on "The Building Tools of Animals" (II.4), Kiesler expands on the method of "inheritance" of building techniques from animal parents to their offspring, as such constructional methods become "part of the species:" "Through experience parents learn of the inefficiency of the defense powers and mechanisms of their own bodies, and eventually add to them automatically."[175] The word "automatically" at the end of the phrase seems to function as an afterthought or even as a contradiction in relation to methodical learning from "experience." If we examine Kiesler's original draft manuscript, the word is indeed an insertion that hovers in between three lines of text, two of which, like the word "automatically," are apparently additions written in smaller font than the rest of the text. (fig. A.23) In a closer look, "automatically" is written below the words "add eventually to it" (which later becomes "them," referring to "mechanisms") and above the following sentence: "This experience is taught to the offspring," with the bracket of the insertion in-between the words "is" and "taught."[176] The original sentence could then also read: "This experience is *automatically* taught to the offspring." Both of these options reveal the increasingly generalized applicability of the term "automatic" from skills that are "inherited" to those that are taught from "experience." The acts of teaching and learning could also be automatic processes, part of an instinct (or even a drive) that perpetuates the act of building in the species. While animals are born with a "natural talent," they, too, have to be taught how to build by their parents who are compelled to teach them "automatically"—similar to a process of automated machine learning. Design tools become part of cultural inheritance and therefore are subject to the laws of what early twentieth-century evolutionist theorists of cultural eugenics described as "social heredity"—a concept that was previously fleshed out in Kiesler's essay on "Architecture and Biotechnique."[177]

Similar to its hovering inscription on Kiesler's handwritten page, the very process of automatism is itinerantly mobilized in other parts of the manuscript. For example, an emphatic albeit gratuitous use of the term "automatically" in relation to learning appears in Kiesler's translation of Wundt's lectures on human and animal psychology quoted in his "Introduction" to the section on "Animal Architecture:" "It is now clear that the instinctive ability of the pianist to play automatically or of man in general to build and to wear clothing has a dual root; a physiological as well as a psychological one" (II.Intro).[178] The term "automatically" does not exist in Wundt's original text (nor the published English translation of his lectures) but is added by Kiesler. Eventually automatism becomes a mechanical insertion that pops up almost automatically in the architect's theoretical constructions, as in this other section of his chapter on the termitary: "All members of the enormous family work automatically through the will of the queen, whose role is compared by Marais to that of our brain" (II.2). Once again, no written trace of automatism exists in Marais's text.[179] Kiesler understands what Marais animistically describes as the "soul" of the termitary located in the body of the queen as an automatic brain, the origin of an artificial form of intelligence.

The persistent insertion of automatic processes in the text of *Magic Architecture* may echo theories of "automatism" associated with Dada and surrealist writers and thinkers like Tristan Tzara and André Breton, with whom Kiesler was intimately connected yet at different periods of his career.[180] But automatism could also point back to Kiesler's earlier involvement with nascent "robotic" technology, extensively documented by Stephen Phillips, who also underlines automatism's reliance on "magical promises of technological progress to create a posthuman fantasy of primordial unity"—a "unity" that bookends the main narrative of *Magic Architecture*.[181] Eventually Kiesler's research on the automatism of termite building techniques also looks forward, presaging more recent debates among postwar biological theorists and animal scientists as well as contemporary evolutionary biologists of the last decades on the genetic and ontogenetic processes of "animal architecture."[182]

At the core of this anthropological and epistemological inquiry lies the subject of agency, heredity, and cultural transmission in techniques of habitation among animals and humans. Perhaps, the "chance" character of Kiesler's psychological automatism refutes the functionalist determinism that Kiesler excoriated in the gadgetry of Fuller's prefabricated metal "shelter" and Corbusier's "machine-to-live-in" housing type. In one of the final sections of *Magic Architecture* referring to surrealism, the architect lays out the prospect of a self-perpetuated design process, where "[i]n truth, Vision should create out of itself, automatically" (X.9).

A decade or more later, in a series of notes with the headline "Animal Rex" written in the mid-1950s and included in his posthumously published memoir *Inside the Endless House*, Kiesler would return to the animist idea of the "soul" in animals, plants, and crystals, and in extension to painting, sculpture, and architecture, based on the discoveries of modern physiology and science. The same discussion culminates, as if by "objective chance," to a description of the collective building action of termites, yet via a new terminological framework:

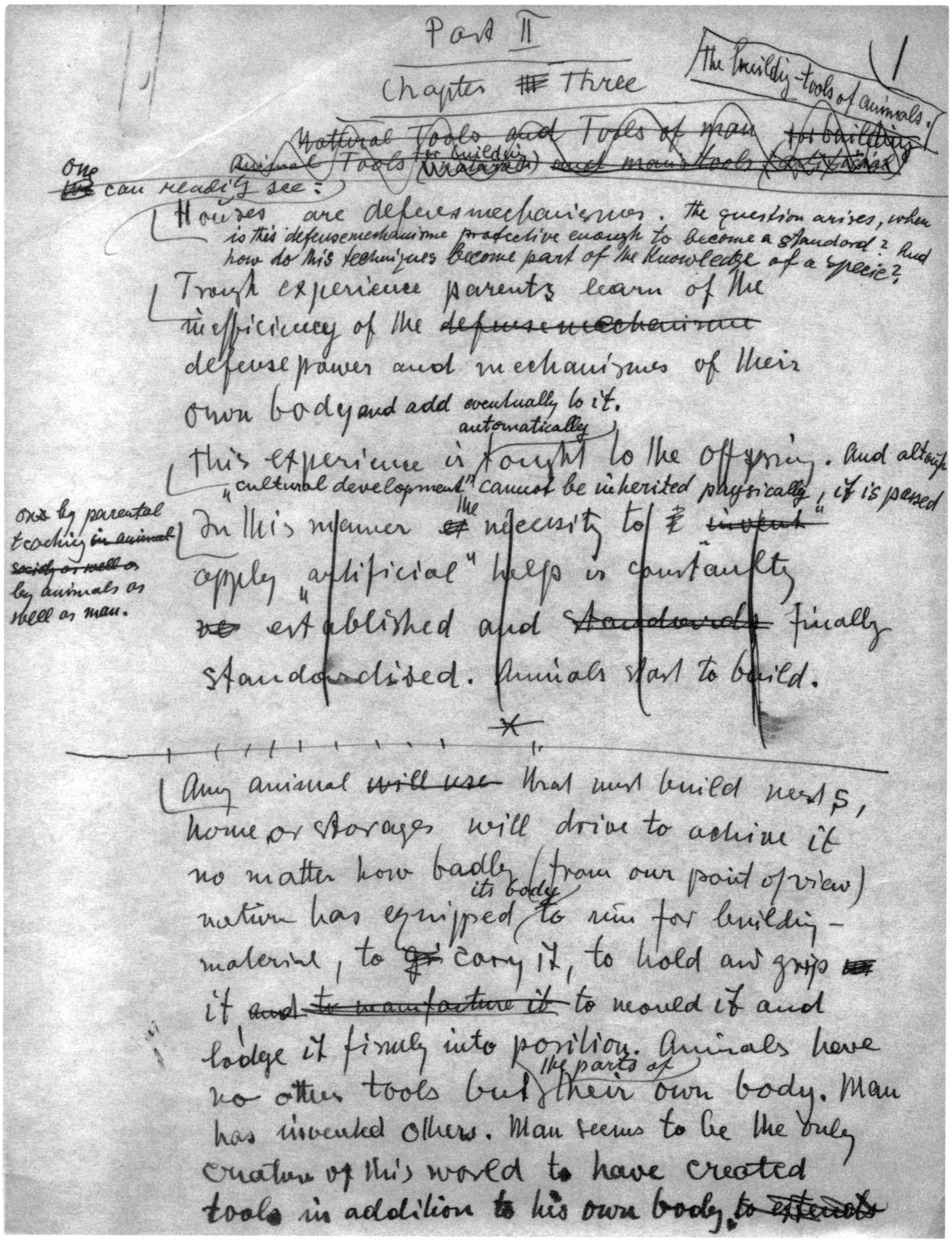

Part II

Chapter Three

The building-tools of animals. 1

One can readily see:

Houses are defensemechanisms. The question arises, when is this defensemechanisme protective enough to become a standard? And how do this techniques become part of the knowledge of a specie?

Trough experience parents learn of the insufficiency of the defensepower and mechanismes of their own body and add eventually to it.

This experience is automatically taught to the offspring. And although "cultural development" cannot be inherited physically, it is passed on by parental teaching by animals as well as man.

In this manner the necessity to "apply "artificial" helps is constantly established and finally standardised. Animals start to build.

*

Any animal that must build nests, home or storages will drive to achieve it no matter how badly (from our point of view) nature has equipped its body to run for building-material, to carry it, to hold and grip it to mould it and lodge it firmly into position. Animals have no other tools but the parts of their own body. Man has invented others. Man seems to be the only creature of this world to have created tools in addition to his own body.

fig. A.23 Frederick Kiesler, Part II, chapter 4 ("Chapter Three" reflects earlier book structure), "The Building Tools of Animals," MS draft with emendations. ÖFLKS, TXT_6699/0_N1

They, scientists and curio-seekers of natural laws of chance, have explained that termites have a language of their own apparently: otherwise how could they communicate through solid walls without knocking at them? Two million termites, inhabitants of a giant concrete home building in which they live, act simultaneously, most of them not seeing one another, separated by walls, floors and barricades of solid concrete construction of their home edifice, yet think, feel together, know, communicate, wireless, touchless, without earphones and alphabets or Morse codes.[183]

Even if partly based on the "old" discussion of the "soul" in Marais, the new description of the termitary makes full use of the language of wireless communication technologies informing postwar biological discussions, as in the writings of Ludwig von Bertalanffy.[184] Such language essentially renders the solid material walls of the termitary obsolete, which now appear as a demountable scaffolding for the unveiling of the termites' brainwave architecture.

"ANIMAL ARCHITECTURE" III: BEAVER DAMS AND ENVIRONMENTAL DELUGE

Following termites, the second species examined in more detail in *Magic Architecture* are beavers—a shift in example that allows Kiesler to redirect the discussion of "animal architecture" from the "automatic" building instinct of insects to the prescient ecological impulse of amphibious mammals. While the termite lives in a closed building colony, the beaver is an animal of open territory that crosses borders between land and water. If the termite was fighting to preserve its species against other animal predators, the beaver is a builder with a pronounced environmental awareness: he strives to avert ecological disasters such as the "mortal danger" of "seasonal drought" via the construction of dams that aim to preserve constant water levels (II.3). The bulk of Kiesler's description of the beaver dam is quoted from a nineteenth-century source, the British reverend and naturalist John George Wood's *Homes Without Hands*, one of the first monographs on animal habitations written in English, contemporary to the German studies of the Müller brothers, which reclassifies animal species according to the "principles" of their respective building constructions.[185] Wood claims to offer a methodical and true to nature description of the construction of the beaver dam as opposed to those of "romantic engravings" equating these animal dams with the aquatic blocks of humans, such as mill dams. (fig. A.24)

While the termite uses instantly any morsel of nature found in its path, the beaver is more selective in its building material. Kiesler provides a photograph from an illustrated journal, which according to the original caption "is the first of its kind" and for which the photographer had to wait two weeks until the animal woodcutter appeared at night, yet never to come again after being caught by the flash of the camera. (fig. A.25) But when the beaver continues its work and reaches a state where the circular cut is so deep that the trunk looks like "an hour glass" as Wood (quoted by Kiesler) describes, the animal operator "looks anxiously around" as if trying to predict on which side the tree is about to fall, then moves quickly to the opposite side and with "three powerful bites" offers the final blow to the lower trunk, which then falls on the ground (II.3).[186] Unlike the termite which seems to keep building unthinkingly, the beaver appears to act with a greater degree of precision, prediction, and premeditation as when it repairs the material of his dam structure with sticks, mud, and branches the moment it starts thinning.

The beaver's interventions to the natural landscape upgrade his construction skills from the mechanical activities of the builder

fig. A.24 "The beaver and its home," John George Wood, *Homes Without Hands: Being a Description of the Habitation of Animals Classed According to the Principles of Construction* (New York: Harper, 1866), 434.

Photograph by George Shiras, 3d

BEAVER CUTTING DOWN A BLACK ASH AT NIGHT: THE FIRST PICTURE OF ITS KIND

For two weeks the camera and flashlight faced this partly cut tree without result. Then one night the beaver came, leaving his picture as well as the tree, for it stands today unfelled, proof that a single animal does the work (see page 197). He was too frightened by the flash to return that season.

fig. A.25 Template for plate 18: "Beaver cutting down a black ash at night: the first picture of its kind," reproduced from photo captioned "Beaver cutting down a black ash at night: the first picture of its kind," by George Shiras III from "The Wild Life of Lake Superior, Past and Present," *National Geographic*, August 1921, 178. Press clipping mounted on paper. ÖFLKS, CLP_6502/0_N1

to the premeditated operations of a "modern engineer," as Kiesler characterizes the mammal, belonging to a class of "engineers, without college degrees," as was the title of one of the architect's research clippings on animal building, foregoing the requirements of professional education.[187] (fig. A.26a) The building work performed by beavers is further extended by nature, as when the river dam they have constructed becomes fertilized with seeds and trees start to grow "whose roots" add to "the general stability by binding together the materials" and thus uniting the animal structure with the natural landscape of the forest (II.3).[188] The beaver still then uses the interior of the damn for storage and opens up holes in the structure so that it can come in and out by swimming. (fig. A.26b) The storage function of the damn signals the confluence between animal economy and an expansive natural ecology, whose limits far exceed the beaver's physical territory.

Even more powerful than the actual structure of the beaver's dam is the natural element it resists–that is, water, which has a tectonic capacity of its own, as in the creation of caverns and other mineral formations by erosion. Yet, the massive influx of water is also associated with catastrophic global events such as the primeval deluge, which entirely changed the face of the earth, leaving behind a metamorphic earthly landscape, reminiscent of the new "pre-" or "post-historic" cartography of Europe envisioned by Max Ernst in his two versions of *Europe After the Rain* painted before and during the war.[189] If in the first part of *Magic Architecture*, threat arrived "from a distance," pointing towards land and sky, in the second part mortal danger emerges from a body of water. In its invocation of caves, nests, and water dams, *Magic Architecture* is also a post-cataclysmic document–a testament on the state of architecture after the deluge of World War II. The dam of the beaver, and in analogy, the termitary of termites, perform not only as physical but also symbolic barriers against the watershed of current historical events.

Drawing from the consequences of the recent global pandemic, Bruno Latour compares the building model of the termitary to human abodes in modern metropolitan environments, in which there is essentially no partition between interior and exterior or differentiation between "city-" and "country-dwell[ing]."[190] Building on Kafka's *Metamorphosis*, Latour describes the process of becoming an insect not as an evolutionary regression but as a new form of extensibility into the environment provoked by the conditions of confinement necessitated by the recent global pandemic. In Part IX of *Magic Architecture*, Kiesler intended to include a chapter on Kafka's posthumously published story "The Burrow"–another model of subterranean living mingling animals with humans–possibly prompted by the extensive usage of bomb-shelters during and after WWII in Europe, which the architect would learn of but never experienced.[191] Invoking the infinitely extensible interior enclosure of termites, who build a new fortified "exoskeleton" for themselves via the clay mound of the termitary and by means of which are able to "go anywhere,"[192] Latour envisions a condition in which there is no distinction between the body (animal or human) and its building carapace.

Similarly in Kiesler, the termites' "automatically" ingrained building mechanisms create a composite environmental and ontological condition in which there is no solid distinction between animal life and building structure. In his study, Marais refers several times to the termitary as a "composite animal," which Karlson in his *Koralle* article renders as a "group-animal [*Gruppentier*]" and a "multicellular compound."[193] The termitary is not simply a frame that houses animals but is itself an animal composed of several organic and inorganic layers that function as a "community" of collaborative organs.

Marais also refers to higher mammals as composite animals, yet the ultimate composite animal according to Kiesler is "Man." But what is the human being a composite of? If for Marais

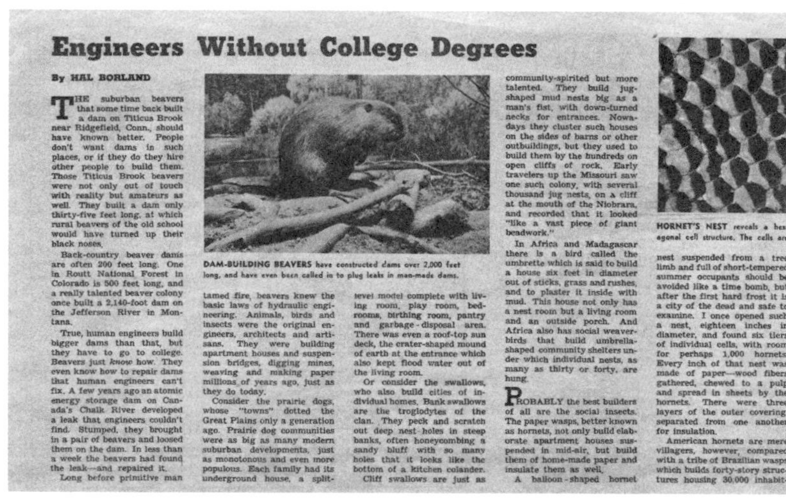

Engineers Without College Degrees

By HAL BORLAND

THE suburban beavers that some time back built a dam on Titicus Brook near Ridgefield, Conn., should have known better. People don't want dams in such places, or if they do they hire other people to build them. Those Titicus Brook beavers were not only out of touch with reality but amateurs as well. They built a dam only thirty-five feet long, at which rural beavers of the old school would have turned up their black noses.

Back-country beaver dams are often 200 feet long. One in Routt National Forest in Colorado is 500 feet long, and a really talented beaver colony once built a 2,140-foot dam on the Jefferson River in Montana.

True, human engineers build bigger dams than that, but they have to go to college. Beavers just *know* how. They even know how to repair dams that human engineers can't fix. A few years ago an atomic energy storage dam on Canada's Chalk River developed a leak that engineers couldn't find. Stumped, they brought in a pair of beavers and loosed them on the dam. In less than a week the beavers had found the leak—and repaired it.

Long before primitive man tamed fire, beavers knew the basic laws of hydraulic engineering. Animals, birds and insects were the original engineers, architects and artisans. They were building apartment houses and suspension bridges, digging mines, weaving and making paper millions of years ago, just as they do today.

Consider the prairie dogs, whose "towns" dotted the Great Plains only a generation ago. Prairie dog communities were as big as many modern suburban developments, just as monotonous and even more populous. Each family had its underground house, a split-level model complete with living room, play room, bedrooms, birthing room, pantry and garbage-disposal area. There was even a roof-top sun deck, the crater-shaped mound of earth at the entrance which also kept flood water out of the living room.

Or consider the swallows, who also build cities of individual homes. Bank swallows are the troglodytes of the clan. They peck and scratch out deep nest-holes in steep banks, often honeycombing a sandy bluff with so many holes that it looks like the bottom of a kitchen colander.

Cliff swallows are just as community-spirited but more talented. They build jug-shaped mud nests big as a man's fist, with down-turned necks for entrances. Nowadays they cluster such houses on the sides of barns or other outbuildings, but they used to build them by the hundreds on open cliffs of rock. Early travelers up the Missouri saw one such colony, with several thousand jug nests, on a cliff at the mouth of the Niobrara, and recorded that it looked "like a vast piece of giant beadwork."

In Africa and Madagascar there is a bird called the umbrette which is said to build a house six feet in diameter out of sticks, grass and rushes, and to plaster it inside with mud. This house not only has a nest room but a living room and an outside porch. And Africa also has social weaver-birds that build umbrella-shaped community shelters under which individual nests, as many as thirty or forty, are hung.

PROBABLY the best builders of all are the social insects. The paper wasps, better known as hornets, not only build elaborate apartment houses suspended in mid-air, but build them of home-made paper and insulate them as well.

A balloon-shaped hornet nest suspended from a tree limb and full of short-tempered summer occupants should be avoided like a time bomb, but after the first hard frost it is a city of the dead and safe to examine. I once opened such a nest, eighteen inches in diameter, and found six tiers of individual cells, with room for perhaps 1,000 hornets. Every inch of that nest was made of paper—wood fibers gathered, chewed to a pulp and spread in sheets by the hornets. There were three layers of the outer covering, separated from one another for insulation.

American hornets are mere villagers, however, compared with a tribe of Brazilian wasps which builds forty-story structures housing 30,000 inhabit-

DAM-BUILDING BEAVERS have constructed dams over 2,000 feet long, and have even been called in to plug leaks in man-made dams.

HORNET'S NEST reveals a hexagonal cell structure. The cells are

fig. A.26a Hal Borland, "Engineers Without College Degrees," *New York Times*, January 24, 1960, 56. Research press clipping. CLP_6596/0_N1

fig. A.26b Template for plate 19: "A Habitation built by nature's wonderful little 'architects'," from "A Canadian 'St. Francis': The Beaver's Friend– 'Grey Owl' and His 'Little Brothers' of the Wild," *Illustrated London News*, August 22, 1931, 279. Press clipping mounted on paper. ÖFLKS, CLP_6484/0

and other physiological and biological thinkers, humans are composite mosaics of various organic functions and previous ontological states, for Kiesler "[m]an is a composite animal of building materials and building techniques"—a phrase that synopsizes the evolutionary story of humans and their house design methods in the first half of *Magic Architecture* (II.5).[194] Humans for Kiesler are essentially mosaics of former material in/organic states and the building methods they use to construct their extended building carapace, all of which are previously invented by animals. These material methods include: "the Thatched roof and walls of birds; the Concrete of termites; the Earthmounds of the mole; the Timber of the beaver; the Netting of the spider," and finally "weaving" via "the use of fluids which become adhesive through drying, practices common to an infinity of creatures" (II.5). (Main Text, figs. B.08, B.09)

In this evolutionary construction, humans correlate not only to primates, which following Darwin's theory of evolution would be their closest animal predecessor, but also to a variety of other species, from insects like spiders to amphibian and aquatic mammals like beavers, all of which, morphologically, are very distant in scale and form from human bodies. Suddenly, the construction of the "human" appears to explode into a host of alternate animal prehistories and multi-species genealogies that may question hierarchical stratifications in established evolutionist narratives. At the same time, building technique normalizes the monstrosity of the human animal "composite" into the standardized pattern of an iterative production process of automated construction and the insularity of a military technical compound.[195]

"ANIMAL ARCHITECTURE" IV: THE NEST

In *Magic Architecture*, these animal building techniques lead to the "first" independent human structures that follow the (detachable) enclosure of the cave and are also made of natural materials. The chapter following Kiesler's narrative of the cave as a "natural shelter" preceding (and in a way introducing) the discussion of "animal architecture" is devoted to the nest as "the first artificial shelter" (I.7). The nest is primarily an animal structure introduced in Kiesler's "story of housing" by an account of the orangutan's temporary sleeping abode perched high on trees and made of fresh twigs and leaves described in a report from Sumatra by the Swiss zoologist Gustav Schneider transcribed and translated by Kiesler in the text of *Magic Architecture* from Klaatsch's *Werdegang*.[196] Kiesler's plates contain an illustration from the book by Klaatsch and Heilborn with a distant photographic view of a large tree mentioning an orangutan's tree nest in the caption, which is hard to see (plate 9). As if to compensate for the lack of visibility, the image editors of *Werdegang* have included what is purportedly a "detail" of the same illustration. Yet this close view of an orangutan sitting on top of a bed of leafy branches is obviously not excerpted from the previous image. In the 1920 first edition of Klaatsch's book, such view is a crudely assembled montage of the photographs of an orangutan and a nest, as well as the painting of a tree, cut and pasted together albeit in incongruous scales. (figs. A.27a–b) In the book's second edition of 1922 (consulted by Kiesler), both illustrations are substituted by paintings made "after" the "nature-photographs" of the original edition.[197] (figs. A.28a–b) In his plates for *Magic Architecture*, Kiesler reproduces the far view of the orangutan tree nest from the 1922 edition (plate 9), yet sensing perhaps the contradictions of their painted closeups, he opts to reproduce the close view of an "orangutan constructing his nest" (plate 8) from a completely different source—an engraving accompanying the entry on "animal dwellings [*Tierwohnungen*]" of the popular German encyclopedia *Meyers Großes Konversations-Lexikon* often used by the architect as a source for his plate illustrations on various subjects.[198] (fig. A.29)

figs. A.27a–b Hermann Klaatsch, *Der Werdegang der Menschheit* (1920), plate 10 "Nests of Orangutans"; plate 9 "Orangutan in his nest (detail of plate 10)."

The reason for zooming in on the details of these image-editing techniques by Kiesler and the evolutionist authors, whose narratives and pictorial representations the architect montages, is to document the effort, involving both precision and randomness, invested in constructing the phantasmatic body of a primate *constructeur* that escapes being captured by photography, as well as an equally phantasmatic argument about the indebtedness of human housing to animal habitation, which can also be construed as a "montage," albeit in a narrative and iconographic form that is deeply racialized. While the illustrations of the orangutan's nest are inserted in the very first pages of Klaatsch and Heilborn's section on "the manifestation of human characteristics and the earliest beginnings of culture" (juxtaposed with photographs of the incompatible dwellings of gorillas constructed by humans in contemporary European zoos like the one in Berlin), Schneider's analytic description of the construction of the orangutan's nest is not quoted until several dozens of pages later so as to form a parallel to the description of the origins of human building technique in the hemispherical structures of Indigenous peoples presumably put together by a similar tree-branch plaiting process.[199] Kiesler exploits such invisible similarity to bring side-by-side in his plate illustrations and hand-drawn diagrams the "shelters" of primates and humans in terms of material structure by montaging images from Klaatsch, *National Geographic*, and the aforementioned *Lexikon* (plates 8–10).[200]

These constructed correspondences allow Kiesler to make the portentous claim that: "If there were no other fact to determine the descent of homo sapiens [*sic*], the building methods of the primates and anthropoid apes wood betray his origin" (1.6). In other words, architecture and its foundation on (animal) building construction disclose previously unacknowledged evidence of human evolution. Under this architectural evolutionist perspective, the tree branches and other natural components of built constructions by Indigenous builders have a similar function as that of skeletal bones in early twentieth century physical anthropology, constructing lines of human and animal descent by means of anatomical organization. Skeletal structure is here substituted by building construction culminating in a racialized building type that is purportedly "universal," signaling the convergence among the working methods of evolutionary anatomists like Klaatsch and ethnologists like Frobenius rehashed by an architectural theorist-designer like Kiesler into a "composite" history of human housing.[201] While the human and animal skeleton provided evidence on the external morphology of animate organisms, living or extinct, built constructions purportedly disclosed elements of the interior psychology and mental patterns of their human builders, as for example in Frobenius's ethnological types, each of whom had a distinctive mode of building under or over the earth–an alleged psychognostic capacity of architectural construction that informs the interior structure of Kiesler's evolutionary narrative from "Animal" to "Magic Architecture."[202]

figs. A.28a–b Hermann Klaatsch, *Der Werdegang der Menschheit* (1922), plate 10 "Nests of Orangutans" "After nature photography"; plate 9 "Orangutan in his nest (detail of plate 10)."

fig. A.29 Research clipping with pencil markings used in plates 8 and 20 of *Magic Architecture*, "Tierwohnungen," in *Meyers Großes Konversations-Lexikon*, vol. 19, 6th ed. (Leipzig and Vienna: Bibliographisches Institut, 1908), 547–548. ÖFLKS, CLP_6501/0

"Building is not an invention of man" states Kiesler "but Architecture is" (II.1). Note that here and in other instances in the manuscript, "Architecture" is purposefully capitalized. Architecture with a small "a" addresses the area of building construction including elementary shelter types like the nest, which originate in the animal world but expand into human dwellings. As Kiesler states: "Architecture starts at a point beyond this animal [nest] function, and that is why animals never have Architecture, but they do build perfect shelters" (II.1). Architecture with a capital "A" belongs to and defines the human in distinction to the animal, yet what such "Architecture" would entail is not yet clearly defined at this point other than it moves beyond mere "building." But then how can Kiesler emphatically proclaim in the title of the same chapter: "Man's house-building is nothing else but Animal-Architecture?" (II.1)[203] The term "Animal Architecture" initially appears to be a contradiction–a composite of two asymptotic ontological states artificially conjoined by the authority of construction techniques. Several of the building techniques present throughout histories of architecture represent yet another trace of the animal condition deeply embedded in the racialized construction of the human. Within this framework, the term may not be a contradiction at all. The coining of "Animal Architecture" affirms that there are still different hierarchies and stratifications within architecture underpinning its associations with humanity and animality albeit in an inequitable and highly fractioning scale.

While Kiesler attempts to mark a distinction between animal and human architecture, he also traces a pronounced similarity between the dwellings of animals and those of a particular "type" of humanity. For example, in his text Kiesler quotes a comparison between beaver damn structures and Inuit abodes (II.3), and then in one of his plates, he juxtaposes a beaver dam structure with the so-called "primitive shelter" of a "Hindu" in India, anticipating, perhaps inadvertently, a similar flooding of the human structure (plate 19). These highly offensive photographic juxtapositions of the structures of animals with those of Indigenous and poor or lower-caste people in colonized territories of the Global South are supported by the strongly racialized discipline of nineteenth-century natural history in its close associations with both anthropological and animal science.

As mentioned earlier, the original textual source for *Magic Architecture*'s chapter on the beaver is Reverend John George Wood's *Homes Without Hands*, from whose text Kiesler quotes the comparison between the beaver damn and the Inuit igloo.[204] A priest and a naturalist, Wood wrote a number of popular books on the wondrous constructions of animals and plants that are remarkably similar to those of humans. These constructed and supposedly instructive similarities confirm according to Wood that "human invention," from "nautical" to "hunting" and "war" instruments to "architecture," is "anticipated by nature"–a principle that is in line with the precedent of animal construction in human architecture supported by Kiesler.[205] Following the tradition of other "men of science" who were equally invested in Christian religion, such as Adolf Müller in Germany mentioned earlier for his writings on animal habitations, animal structures in Wood's writings corroborate the intelligence and glory of God. For Wood the ingenuity of animal structures serves as physical proof not only of Divine intelligence in the "design" of natural organisms, but also the hierarchical order of human groups in terms of racial stratification, presented as God ordered. The author of a two-volume *Natural History* of the "uncivilized races of men,"[206] Wood includes in his book on "nature's teachings" a pictorial parallel between an illustration captioned "slave-capturing ants" depicting an egg-stealing operation from the nest of a foreign insect "colony" next to the drawing of an "African slave gang" marching in chains in front of a white master, whip in hand. Wood describes the adult ants that had previously hatched from the stolen eggs as "perfectly happy and contended" working "because told so by their own instinct."[207] Looking at the pair of illustrations, Wood's caption presents "instinct" as a force that internalizes the authorial voice of the master in the captive body of "stolen" and enslaved body. Wood's graphic parallel leads to a very different idea of the origin of what Kiesler calls "the building instinct in animals," and implicitly what Marais names the "soul" of the white ant termitary—a state not unaffected by the political and racial fractures of South Africa.[208]

While the image of "homes without [human] hands" is reminiscent of a quasi-effortless or miraculous manner of construction, as in the Greek term *acheiropoieitos* (made without hands), the book is haunted by images of animal and occasionally human manual labor, which make the alleged absence and intermittent presence of hands in the very foundation of these "homes" part of the nineteenth and early twentieth century's "architectural uncanny."[209] The immense quantity and incessant activity of construction labor along with techniques, of animals and insects, like silk-producing moths and spiders brought from other parts of the world to work for the benefit of European industrialists, is in fact one of the main underlying themes of books on "natural histories" of architecture, whose publication is contemporary with histories of animal and human labor violently extracted from the colonies.[210]

It may be that in Kiesler's plates the termitary is juxtaposed to the towering structures of New York and in Bölsche's *Termitenstaat* to modern Germany's national demographics, yet the original scene of the African colony is never far away. The British newspaper's illustration pasted on Kiesler's plate (plate 16d and fig. A.22), not only transposes the tallest towers of the Manhattan Skyline, but also transports the habitat of the colonial termitary upon the edge of a shore on the East Coast of the United States.

"ANIMAL ARCHITECTURE" VI: HOUSING EXHIBITIONS, BOVINE HOOVES, AND FELINE PAWS

In one of his Design Correlation articles centered on "animals and architecture" published in the *Architectural Record* in 1937, Kiesler had sharply criticized the formal application of "modern architecture" in the design of "houses" for several animal species in the London Zoo, from elephants to penguins, designed by Tekton.[211] In the section on "Animal Architecture" of the *Magic Architecture* manuscript, the architect presented instead the dwellings that animals build for themselves by using "techniques" that are later on re-employed by humans. Animals that build, unknowingly and unobtrusively, the "houses" of humans, rather than the other way around. For architecture to be truly modern it had to return to a pre-anthropic state.

In his unrealized proposal for an exhibition on ecology at the American Museum of Natural History in New York (ca. 1944), centered on the design of walkthrough diorama structured as a geological section representing the creation of life on earth, Kiesler also included a series of charts with an equally geological stratification of plant and animal species according to their proximity or distance from the surface of the earth: from seaweed and algae at the bottom of the ocean to the first polyps and multi-leg organisms crawling on the ground, to the first quadrupeds and bipeds (represented by kangaroos), as well as primates, which as he learned from Klaatsch, climb on trees to distance themselves from the ground and survey their territory (fig. A.30a). At the top of this evolutionary stratigraphy was the human being in its ideal state as a flying "man machine" (reminiscent of the analogous designs by Leonardo) entirely disengaged from the ground and capable of attacking all life on earth from the air.[212] This was another chart of "animal architecture" designed by the architect with an ontological as well as epistemological grid in mind—both figurative and numerical data copied from a textbook of historical geology by the paleogeologist expert Charles Schuchert as shown in one of the photostats in Kiesler's research material for his proposal.[213] (cf. figs. A.30b, A.31) While resolutely vertical in orientation, Kiesler's rectangular table is essentially circular in outlook by uniting the origin with the imminent end of earthly life. *Magic Architecture* essentially narrates the (after)story of the creation and destruction of the world by means of building construction and the development of animal and human settlement.

Through this perspective, the architect's preliminary designs the exhibition on American architecture, including aspects of housing culture, scheduled to travel to Moscow around the same period (1944-45) and with their seemingly bizarre and inexplicable zoomorphic forms, make perfect sense. Exhibition walls with their bovine hooves and tails represent the story of human housing through the greater story of human evolution and its inextricable connection to the animal. The domesticated figure of the cow perhaps signals the moment when previously nomadic animals are confined adjacently to human housing. (figs. A.32a-b) From the curvilinear animal wall of the unrealized exhibition proposal to the flat pages of the animal chapters in *Magic Architecture*'s bound manuscript, there was only a change in the exhibition format, but not the form of the architect's vision.

We could then go back to one of the alternate photographs taken in Frederick and Stefi Kiesler's penthouse on the occasion of the *Architectural Forum* article "Design's Bad Boy," which depicts the architect laying on the floor across atop a large sheet of paper with his chart of Correalism and across the binder containing the manuscript of *Magic Architecture*, mentioned earlier (see the frontispiece to this book).[214] The architect himself holds a small sketch pad, always the designing animal. But at the origin of this interior perspective is the architect's cat (rhythmically named Sing Sing), a faithful companion during his design process, reminiscent of Saint Jerome's lion that rests in the scholar's studiolo—Kiesler's primary model for his Mobile Home Library project.[215] While much smaller in size, Kiesler's cat is more alert than the lion, her paws are parallel with the limbs of the architect and the long paper sheet of his universal chart. Note the parallel alignment of the limbs of the non-building animal with those of the human designer, as if the two are coordinated in the creative process—whether drawing or writing. On top of the paper roll, Sing Sing is also near the assembled book manuscript, which at this point would contain a section on "Animal Architecture"—a type of activity in which cats, even if they have a very pronounced sense of territoriality and property of space, do not participate.[216] The book manuscript, architect, and cat enact a triangular "correlation" but it is markedly the cat's protruding paw that points towards the metabolist chart's goals of "higher productivity" and "new standards" in "life activities." Domesticated animals no longer need to build anymore and yet it is their latent automatic skills that drive human production.

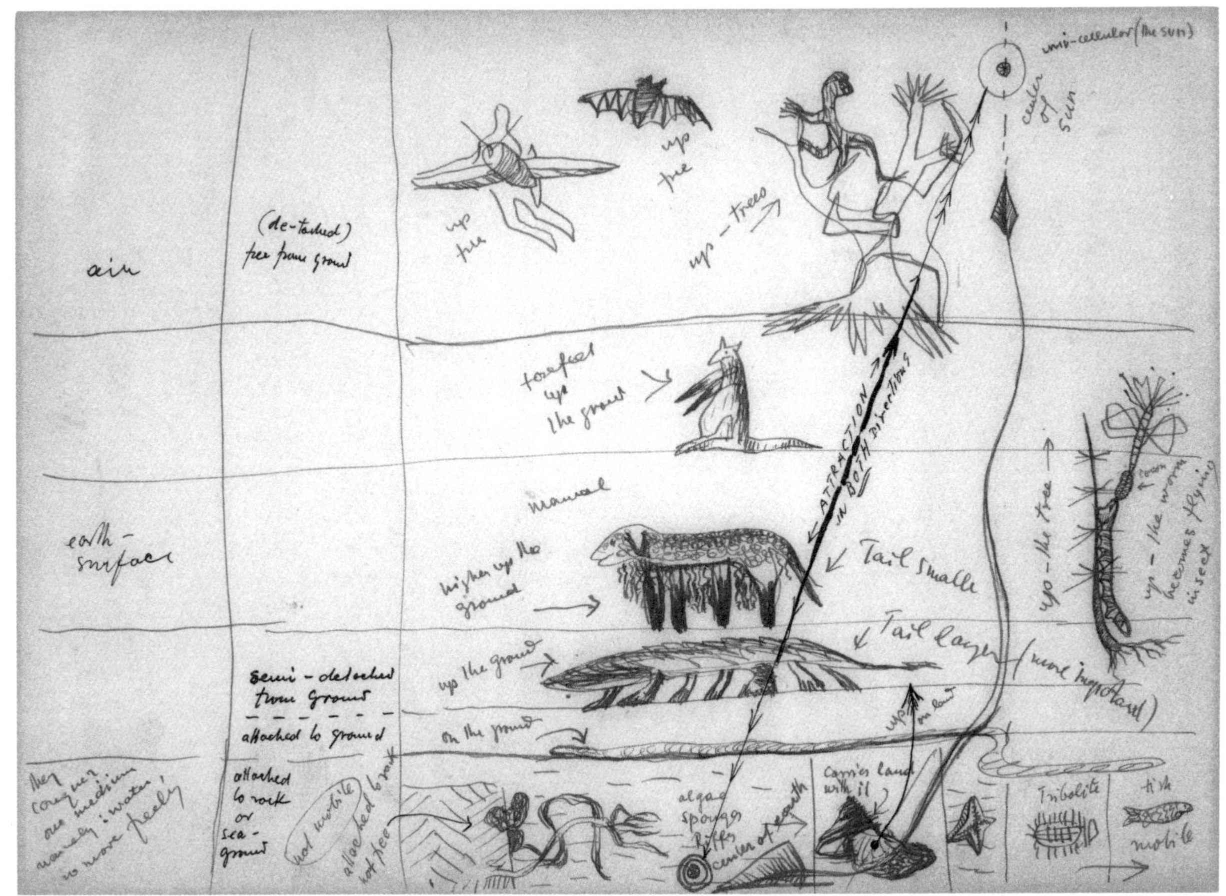

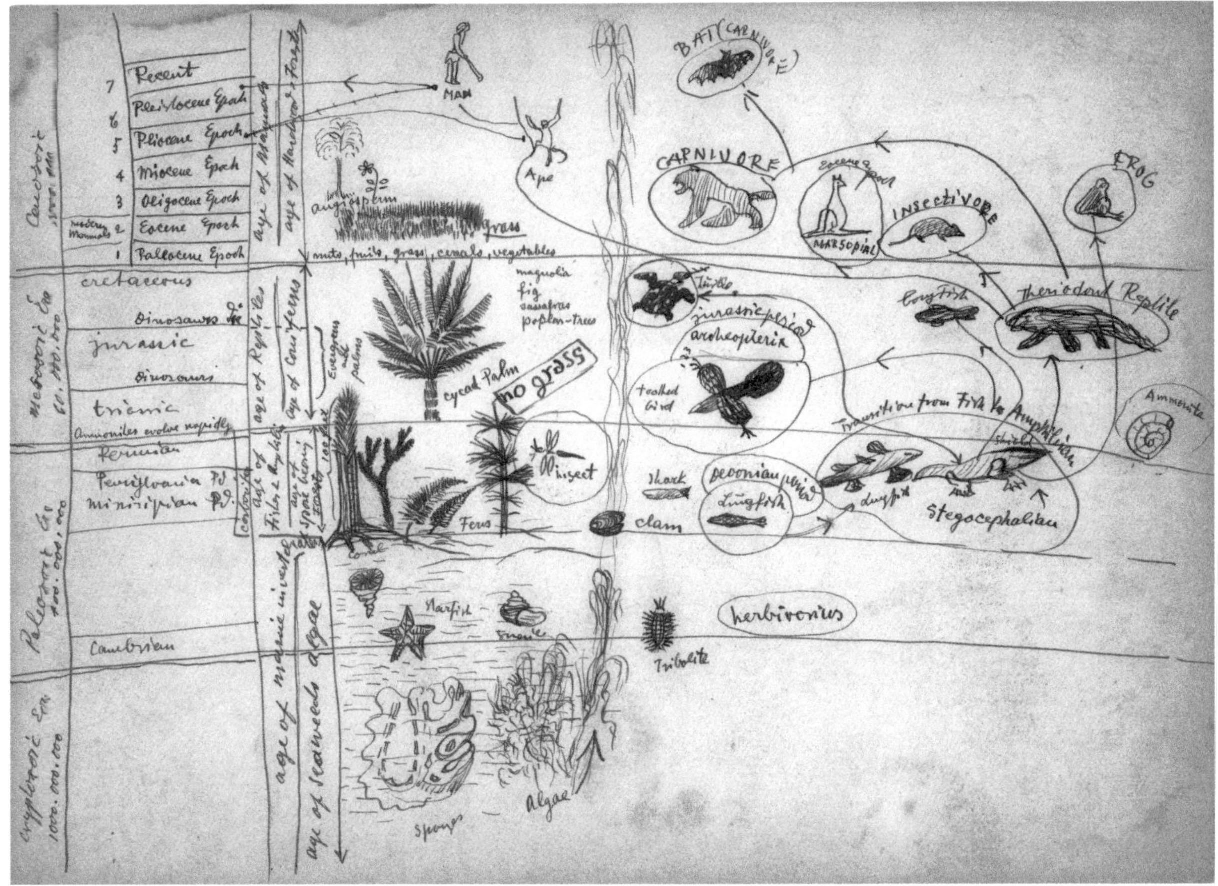

fig. A.30a Frederick Kiesler, chart on the classification of living beings according to their distance from the earth ground. Exhibition proposal for a "Hall of Ecology," American Museum of Natural History, New York, ca. 1944. ÖFLKS, SFP_6615/0

fig. A.30b Frederick Kiesler, time chart with classification of vegetal and animal species according to geological life eras, after Schuchert and Dunbar, *Outlines of Historical Geology*. Exhibition proposal for a "Hall of Ecology," American Museum of Natural History, New York (ca. 1944). ÖFLKS, SFP_6614/0

fig. A.31a Frederick Kiesler, geological time chart with classification of earliest life eras, after Schuchert and Dunbar, *Outlines of Historical Geology* Exhibition proposal for a "Hall of Ecology," American Museum of Natural History, New York (ca. 1944). ÖFLKS, TXT_6659/0

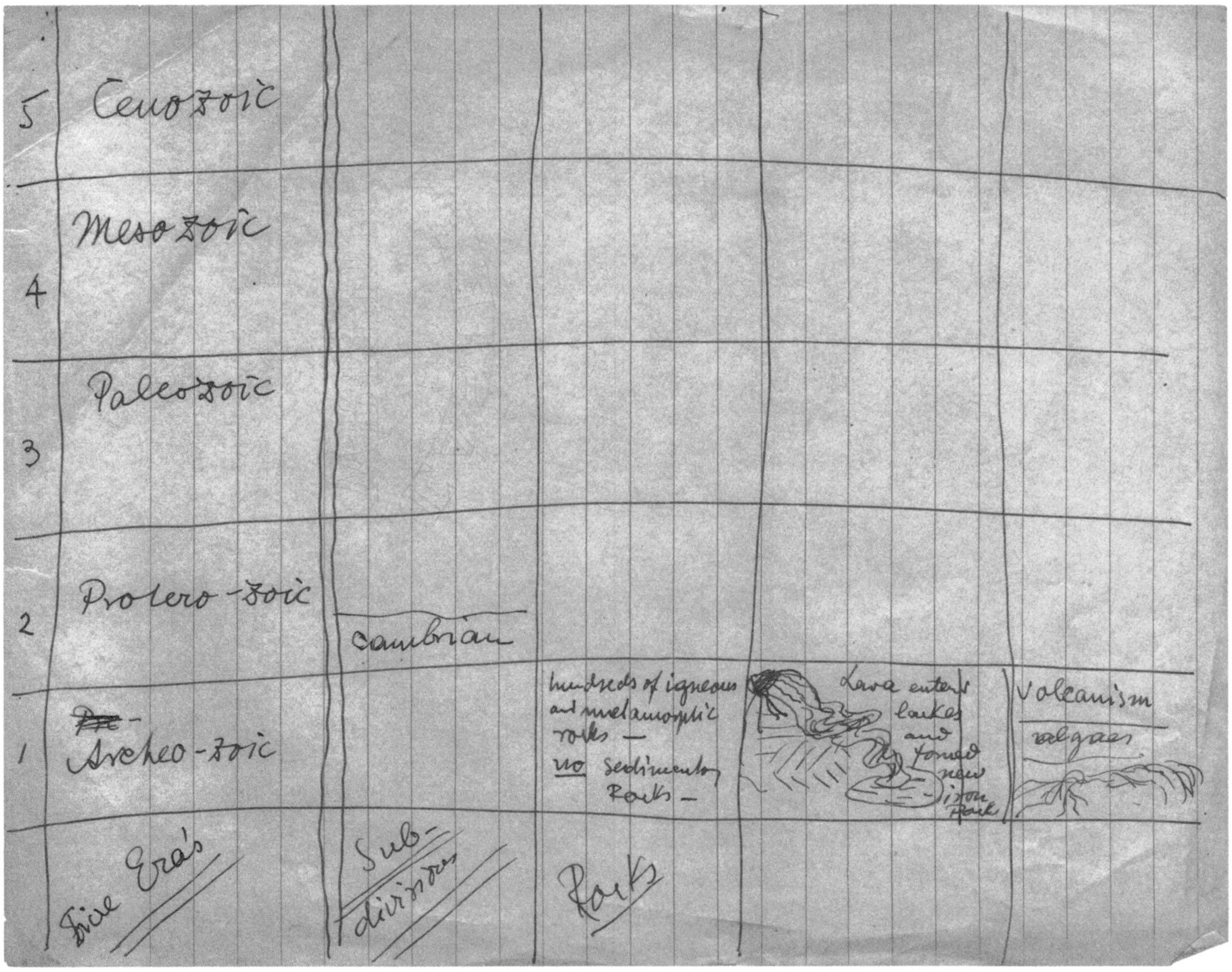

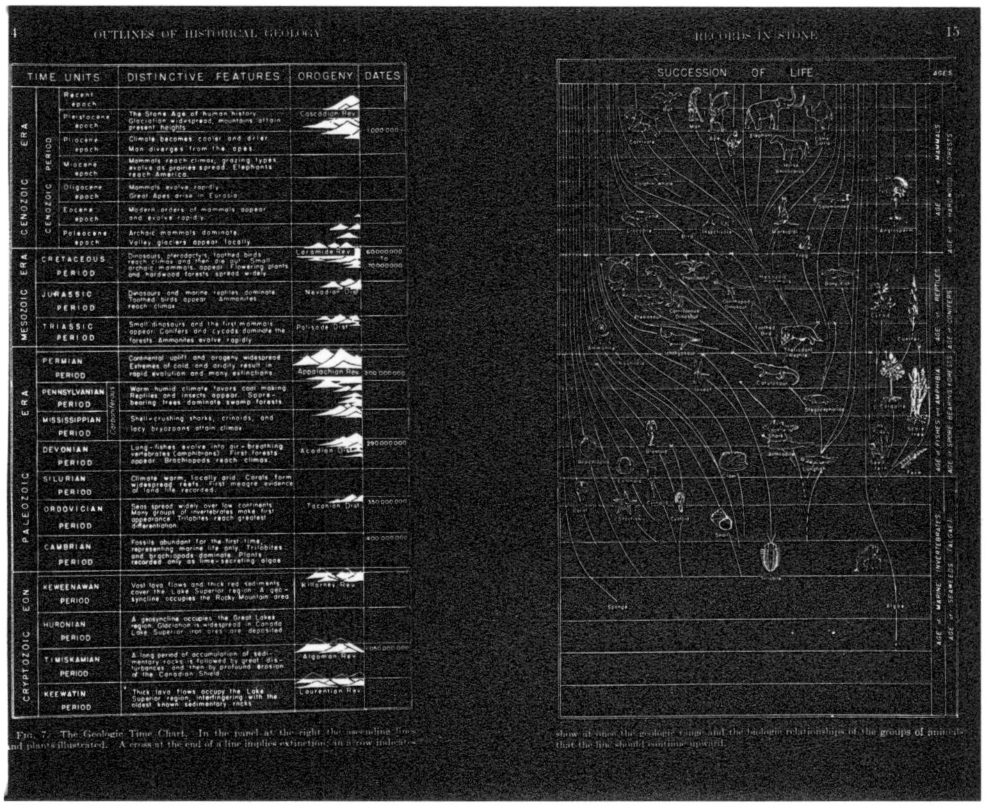

fig. A.31b Photostat of "Geological Time Chart" of earliest life eras from Charles Schuchert and Carl O. Dunbar, *Outlines of Historical Geology* (New York: John Wiley & Sons, 1937), 14–15. ÖFLKS, CLP_6462/0_N1_N2

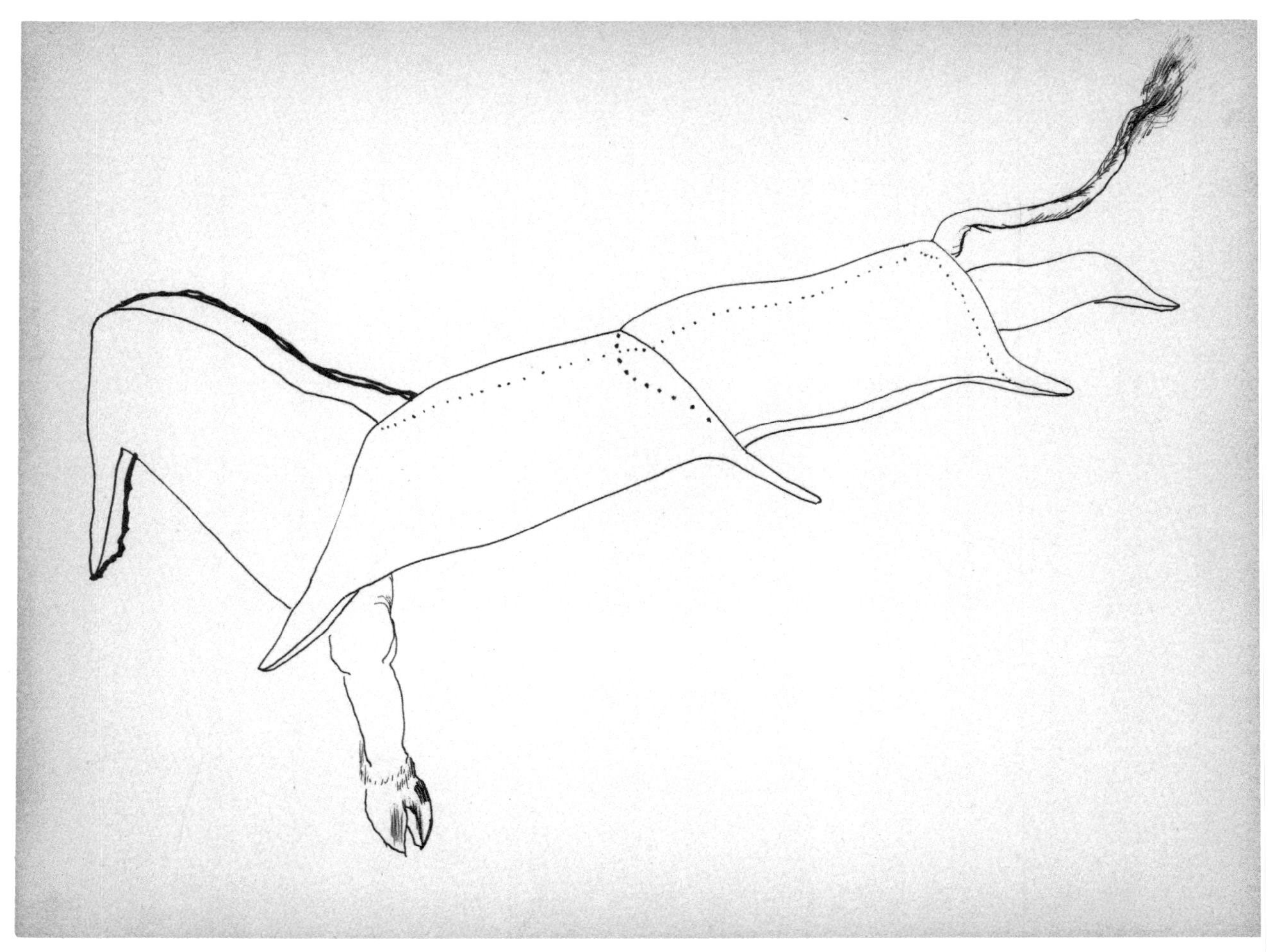

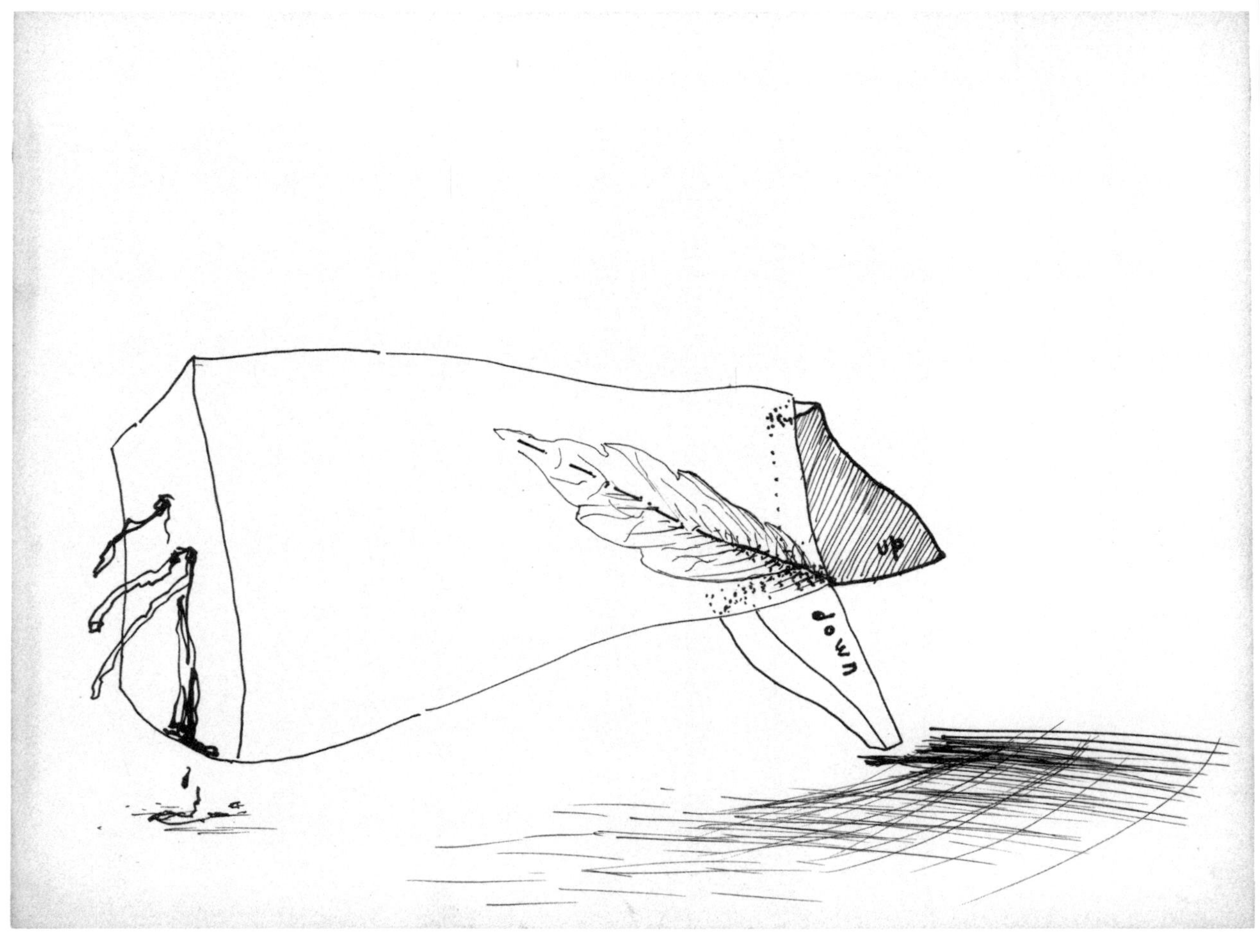

figs. A.32a–b Preliminary design proposal for the exhibition on American architecture planned to travel to the USSR by the National Council of American-Soviet Friendship, 1944–45. ÖFLKS, SFP_1034/0, SFP_1035/0

HUMAN TECHNOLOGY AND DESIGN TECHNIQUE I: TOOLS, BONES, AND STONES

Following his remarks on the origin of building techniques in animal construction, Kiesler's "story" shifts to the development of human tools and the acquiring of skills in painting, plastic relief, and design. The house for Kiesler is primarily a tool, the very medium of animal architecture. Animals have no other tools than the appendages of their own bodies, as opposed to humans who must manufacture their own tools, which they fashion as prosthetic extensions of their body to further its strength (II.4). A series of charts titled "the building tools of animals" drawn by the architect but not included in the assembled manuscript of *Magic Architecture*, contain detailed sketches of the tongue, satchel, and other parts of the mouth of the working bee, as well as the teeth, hind feet, hands, and tail of the beaver (see Addenda, figs. C.06a–b). The drawings illustrate the primacy of the mouth and jaw which precedes in building effectiveness the development of feet and hands (as in the case of the beaver). Man is still "teething" via industrial mechanisms, writes Kiesler, as the animal supports and ultimately substitutes the jaw with the more articulate members of the forefoot, and finally the hand. The endpoint of the chart, drawn on a separate sheet, is the hand of primates, with which the orangutan constructs his nest, and which Kiesler, in an offensive authorial gesture of his own, juxtaposes with the hand of the "aborigine," as instances of builders, who use only "bodily mechanisms" to construct their dwellings. In this racially charged association of "hands," the body of the "aborigine" is reduced into a tool, just like the instrumentalized body of the enslaved worker in colonialist production settings.

"Tools are extensions of the body; as extension of the hand, they further its reach, dexterity and power to provide physical protection. Nothing really apart from man, tools are his outer self," writes Kiesler in the first chapter of "Animal Architecture" (II.1). The description of tools as bodily extensions echoes the psychological interpretation of tool-making as "organ projection" by the nineteenth-century philosopher of technology Ernst Kapp attempting a fusion of organicist epistemologies with mechanist production modes.[217]

One of the charts included in *Magic Architecture* illustrates the "transformation of useless materials of nature into useful tools," depicting a series of stone flints, jaw or other animal bones, including fish vertebrae, all "dead" materials that acquire a new life by being used as "practical tools"–a process described by the architect as a "transfunctioning of service" from "nature" to "man" (II.7, Main Text, fig. B.10). As shown more clearly in a preliminary set of drawings for the same chart Kiesler's sketches of artifacts made of organic materials are copied from several photographs of implements reproduced in one of the final sections of Klaatsch's *Development of Humankind* titled "Prehistoric Humanity and its Culture." The section edited by Heilborn includes a wide assortment of artifacts from different geographies and eras, such as a "bone harpoon" and "arrowhead" from the Magdalenian era, an engraved bone "dagger" and "axe" made of stone and wood from New Guinea, and a tomahawk made of similar materials from Mesa Verde in Colorado, conflating, once again, prehistoric with indigenous "technology (*Technik*)."[218] (cf. figs. A.33a and Main Text, fig. B.11)

In a subsequent line-diagram Kiesler draws an overtly hairy human hand holding what appears to be a human jaw that serves as a "'practical' functional tool" (See Main Text, fig. B.12). Kiesler then illustrates how this "practical tool" can become an object of "adornment," "beautification," and "humanization" by turning into a "decorated relic." Here the human jaw, "removed" from the dead body after "ritual … exhumation," appears attached on a string necklace and is perforated by threads with rows of "areca nuts" hanging as oscillating pendants (II.8). Kiesler's diagram conflates a number of anthropological sources. First, the image of the handheld jaw converted into a "practical tool" draws from a similar illustration in Karl Weule's *Cultural Elements of Humankind*, part of the popular *Kosmos* series of small books on anthropology and natural history, which exists in Kiesler's library (fig. A.34). However, Weule's illustration depicts the "jaw of a cave bear" and not of a human, as evidence of prehistoric technics.[219] Paleoarchaeologists have studied the extent that splintered animal bones could be used as "practical tools."[220] However dubious, Kiesler's intimate association between tools and human bones is portentous of a line of argument that depicts technology not simply as an instrumentalized extension of the human body, as in Kapp's theory of organ projection, but as a covert cannibalizing process tracing the regurgitation and ejection of the human body's own anatomical form and structural substance.

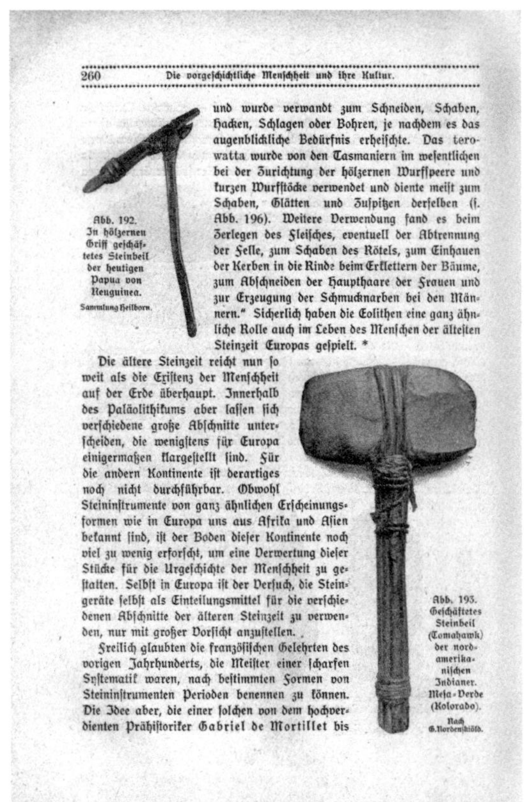

260 Die vorgeschichtliche Menschheit und ihre Kultur.

und wurde verwandt zum Schneiden, Schaben, Hacken, Schlagen oder Bohren, je nachdem es das augenblickliche Bedürfnis erheischte. Das terowatta wurde von den Tasmaniern im wesentlichen bei der Zurichtung der hölzernen Wurfspeere und kurzen Wurfstöcke verwendet und diente meist zum Schaben, Glätten und Zuspitzen derselben (s. Abb. 196). Weitere Verwendung fand es beim Zerlegen des Fleisches, eventuell der Abtrennung der Felle, zum Schaben des Rötels, zum Einhauen der Kerben in die Rinde beim Erklettern der Bäume, zum Abschneiden der Haupthaare der Frauen und zur Erzeugung der Schmucknarben bei den Männern." Sicherlich haben die Eolithen eine ganz ähnliche Rolle auch im Leben des Menschen der ältesten Steinzeit Europas gespielt. *

Abb. 192. In hölzernen Griff geschäftetes Steinbeil der heutigen Papua von Neuguinea. Sammlung Heilborn.

Die ältere Steinzeit reicht nun so weit als die Existenz der Menschheit auf der Erde überhaupt. Innerhalb des Paläolithikums aber lassen sich verschiedene große Abschnitte unterscheiden, die wenigstens für Europa einigermaßen klargestellt sind. Für die andern Kontinente ist derartiges noch nicht durchführbar. Obwohl Steininstrumente von ganz ähnlichen Erscheinungsformen wie in Europa uns aus Afrika und Asien bekannt sind, ist der Boden dieser Kontinente noch viel zu wenig erforscht, um eine Verwertung dieser Stücke für die Urgeschichte der Menschheit zu gestatten. Selbst in Europa ist der Versuch, die Steingeräte selbst als Einteilungsmittel für die verschiedenen Abschnitte der älteren Steinzeit zu verwenden, nur mit großer Vorsicht anzustellen.

Freilich glaubten die französischen Gelehrten des vorigen Jahrhunderts, die Meister einer scharfen Systematik waren, nach bestimmten Formen von Steininstrumenten Perioden benennen zu können. Die Idee aber, die einer solchen von dem hochverdienten Prähistoriker Gabriel de Mortillet bis

Abb. 193. Geschäftetes Steinbeil (Tomahawk) der nordamerikanischen Indianer. Mesa-Verde (Kolorado). Nach G. Nordenskiöld.

274 Die vorgeschichtliche Menschheit und ihre Kultur.

Eintönigkeit gewisse rohe Typen von Schabern, Bohrern, Kratzern usw. wiedergeben, wie sie offenbar dem niedrigsten Bedürfnis wilder Jäger entsprachen. Wo kein Grund und kein Antrieb zu höherer Entwicklung vorlag, da blieb dieses einfache Inventar bestehen und hat sich mit großer Zähigkeit seit der Tertiärperiode und durch die ganze Eiszeit hindurch neben technisch entwickelten Werkzeugen erhalten. In dem Streit darüber, ob die Eolithen ein Werk der Menschenhand oder lediglich Naturprodukte seien, wurde vielfach gerade die Konstanz der Typen als eben gegen Menschen-

O. Hauser phot.

Abb. 210. Knöcherne Harpunen- und Pfeilspitzen der Magdalénienstufe.

werk sprechend angeführt. Mit Unrecht: haben sich doch diese Eolithen bei manchen Naturvölkern, wie den Australiern und Tasmaniern, dauernd erhalten (vgl. auch Tafel 2 auf S. XXV und 35 auf S. 279, ferner Abb. 100 auf S. 105).

Die Betrachtung der Steininstrumente der Eiszeit Europas drängt zu der Annahme, daß zum mindesten zwei verschiedene Arten von Menschen uns hier ihre Werke hinterlassen haben: ein Menschentypus, der in stetiger Vervollkommnung es während der Eiszeit zu großen Fortschritten und sogar zu künstlerischen Leistungen brachte, und ein andrer, rückständigerer, der auf der niederen Stufe einer voreiszeitlichen Primitivkultur verharrte.

Wir haben diese beiden Menschentypen durch die Skelettfunde der letzten Jahrzehnte kennengelernt: der rückständige Menschentypus ist die Neandertalrasse, die vollkommenere Menschenart ist die Aurignacrasse. Von

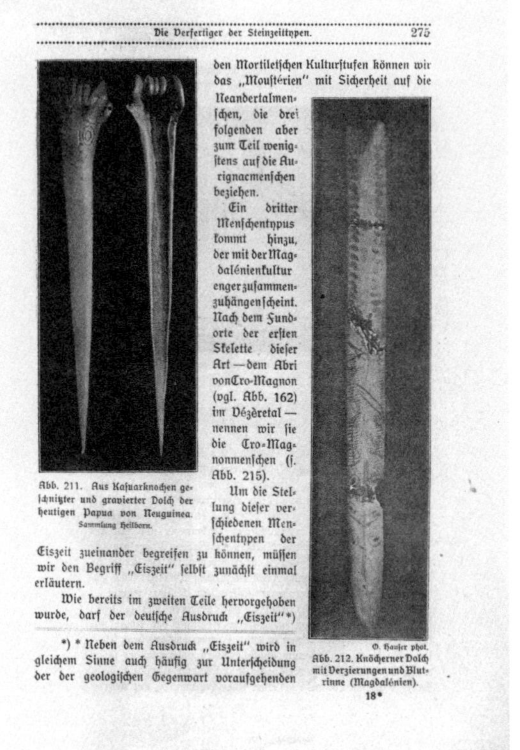

Die Verfertiger der Steinzeittypen. 275

den Mortilletschen Kulturstufen können wir das „Moustérien" mit Sicherheit auf die Neandertalmenschen, die drei folgenden aber zum Teil wenigstens auf die Aurignacmenschen beziehen. Ein dritter Menschentypus kommt hinzu, der mit der Magdalénienkultur enger zusammenzuhängen scheint. Nach dem Fundorte der ersten Skelette dieser Art — dem Abri von Cro-Magnon (vgl. Abb. 162) im Vézèretal — nennen wir sie die Cro-Magnonmenschen (s. Abb. 215). Um die Stellung dieser verschiedenen Menschentypen der Eiszeit zueinander begreifen zu können, müssen wir den Begriff „Eiszeit" selbst zunächst einmal erläutern.

Wie bereits im zweiten Teile hervorgehoben wurde, darf der deutsche Ausdruck „Eiszeit"*)

Abb. 211. Aus Kasuarknochen geschnitzter und gravierter Dolch der heutigen Papua von Neuguinea. Sammlung Heilborn.

O. Hauser phot.

Abb. 212. Knöcherner Dolch mit Verzierungen und Blutrinne (Magdalénien).

*) Neben dem Ausdruck „Eiszeit" wird in gleichem Sinne auch häufig zur Unterscheidung der der geologischen Gegenwart voraufgehenden

18*

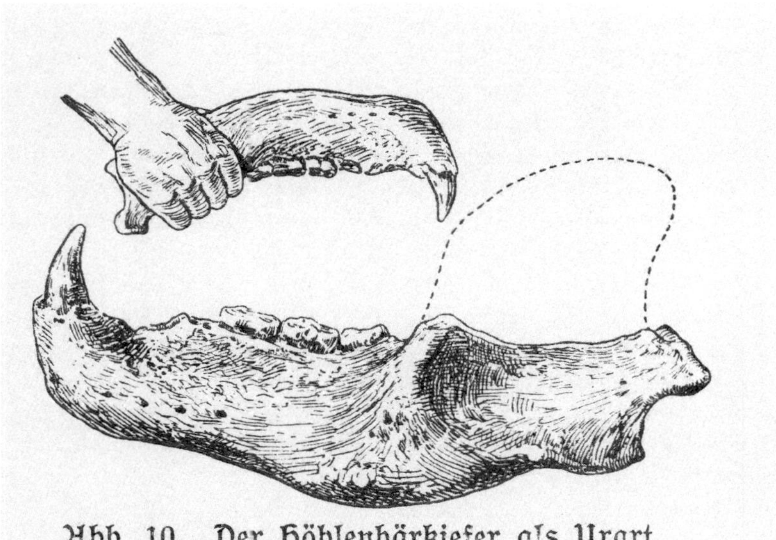

Abb. 10. Der Höhlenbärkiefer als Uraxt.

The material transition of human tool-making from bones to stones—essentially the "bones" of the soil—signals the expansion of this cyclical technical process to the geological body of the earth, from which these organic artifacts had been exhumed or excavated.

Kiesler's drawing at the bottom of the same chart showing the "decorated ... relic" of a human jaw is copied from a photographic illustration of a similar object in Bronisław Malinowski's well-known 1929 anthropological study of *The Sexual Lives of Savages*, which also exists in the Kieslers' library.[221] But as shown in the book, both the anthropologist's text (gravely misquoted in Kiesler's description) and his ethnographic photographs refer to a pendant with the human jaw of a person worn by his widow after the man's death and ritual exhumation.[222] The woman has to wear the jawbone pendant during a period of mourning as a sign of sexual unavailability. The bone necklace does not then perform as a tool for "beautification," as Kiesler argues, but instead as an apotropaic device for a deliberate absence from sociality. The palindromic movement of the pendant traces the periodic entry and withdrawal from society prescribed by human intervention on the body, be it "dead" or "alive." The manipulated human relic has a symbolic function yet it evades the unmediated instrumentality of the "tool."

Images of human hands holding the first tools of humankind, as *media* traversing the living and the dead, summon the photograph of the churned hand of the first US scientist, who died due to the effects of atomic energy during one of the accidents in the Los Alamos nuclear laboratory. While the actual "equipment" that contained the radioactive material is not visible in the picture, the effects of its accidental misuse are horrifically discernible on the victim's body. Acting as the conceptual pendant to Kiesler's drawing of the hand confidently holding its first instrument, this newspaper photograph depicts the uncanny moment when the increasingly powerful handheld tool turns against the hand that created it and can no longer withhold it.

Previous
figs. A.33a–c Photographic illustrations of "wood," "stone," and "bone tools" in Hermann Klaatsch and Adolf Heilborn, *Der Werdegang der Menschheit* (1922), 260, 274–275, figs. 192–193, 210–211.

Above
fig. A.34 "The jaw of a cave bear as a primeval ax," in Karl Weule, *Kulturelemente der Menschheit: Anfaenge und Urformen der materiellen Kultur* (Stuttgart: Kosmos, 1910), 35, fig. 10.

One of Kiesler's preliminary hand-drawn charts (not included in the assembled manuscript) diagrams the development of human design via a "direct abstraction" from nature (see Addenda, fig. C.09b). The chart's table is structured into two columns headlined "Design" and "Metal," and four horizontal rows. The "Design" sequence starts with the naturalistic depiction of a crocodile—a reptile caged inside the architect's chart next to an analogously circumscribed large piece of unprocessed "ore," first on the column of "Metal-wiring." Were it not for the vertical line dividing the two figures, one could picture the crocodile snapping the hard rock with its open jaws and swallowing, slowly but steadily, the mineral specimen. Design, Kiesler implies, is born by the omnivorous appetite of living beings seeking to assimilate the most indigestible objects, including inorganic substances by a transgressive territorial act of cross-species incorporation.

The second row of the evolutionary table displays the first offspring of the crocodile which is another crocodile—an "abstract" animal-machine that is also larger and smoother than the one of "nature." Just like the slab in the "Metal" column is a different object from the ore above it, so is this "abstract" crocodile a different animal from its natural progenitor: its atrophied feet having turned into pliers, its tail into an airplane's metal end, and the winding texture of the reptile's scaly skin solidified into an undulating line of welding seams connecting patches of metal cladding. The croc appears to have devoured the rock and is now ready to snatch the metal slab as well—the rectangular formation of its belly anticipating the homophagic inception. Design for Kiesler is birthed by such a sequence of an unlikely homophagy between animate figures and inanimate materials. The "abstracted" crocodile is the original "product design" of both the rock and the croc, suggesting that the lines of descent in this table are more diagonal than vertical, reminiscent of Roger Caillois' "diagonal correspondences," and the zigzag lines of the stylized crocodile's texture.

A preliminary handwritten draft accompanying the previous chart explains the architect's theoretical premise: "Design is abstracted from nature (animals, plants, rocks), as metals are abstracted from nature (ore)." (fig. C.9a) Design, then, is the combined product of mental abstraction and material "extraction"—a physical pulling from the surfaces of the earth and the bodies of animals and living beings. A series of enumerated steps in the same draft trace the stages of such extraction: from the "natural" figure of the crocodile (step "1"), a patch of its skin is extracted by being drawn inside an orthogonal frame during the act of "painting" (step "2") until this irregular bundle of painted lines "final[ly]" turns into a rhythmic geometric "ornament," (step "3") which is the origin of design, proper.

So far, the architect's process appears to rehearse previous twentieth-century narratives of abstraction, a number of them related to an extractive reading of so called "primitive art." It may come as no surprise that Kiesler's stylized figure of the crocodile draws from related images in an article from a 1939 issue of *Koralle* purporting to explain "how people of nature see the animal," found among Kiesler's research clippings.[223] Among several pairs of images of animals juxtaposed with their sculpted depictions by "indigenous artists" from colonized territories in the Global South, the article includes the photographs of a "strongly stylized" wood sculpture of a crocodile from a "ceremonial house by the Sepik River in the former Kaiser Wilhelm's land on New Guinea," as well as a rhinoceros "toy [*Spielzeug*]" sculpture from South Africa, which the author unabashedly compares with the drawing of a (western) "child" after seeing a rhinoceros in a zoo.[224] In a closer look, Kiesler's chart drawing of the "abstract" crocodile appears to conflate the forms of the crocodile sculpture from New Guinea with the diagonal patterns of the rhinoceros "toy" from South Africa. The chart's correlation of "abstraction" in painting with mineral extraction from "nature" sites in colonized territories mirrors Kiesler's own "extractive" reading of images of Indigenous artifacts from *Koralle*'s pseudo-ethnographic article. The synergies between material extraction and iconographic appropriation may reveal more of the invisible "wiring" in the circuitry of images and preconceptions that provides the epistemological scaffolding of the chart.

Finally in Kiesler's chart (fig. C.09b), we see that the body of the crocodile is replaced by an ornamental swatch bearing a pattern that further abstracts the diagonal lines previously crisscrossing the "abstract" crocodile depicting the transformation from sculpture and painting to ornament and the "applied arts." Design emerges when these ornamental patterns become applied to the human body, which is what happens in the fourth and final stage of Kiesler's diagram through textile art and metallurgy, represented, respectively, by a fabric skirt and a metal earring worn by intensely racialized cartoon-like female figures. These offensive depictions are similar to a series of sketches of Indigenous female "clothing" in another one of Kiesler's charts, this time depicting "the conversion of corporeality into dream images through painting and sculpting" (fig. B.14). Kiesler's sketches of Indigenous "clothing" are copied from photographs of "waist aprons" worn by "Ma[n]kon women in central East Africa" and a similar apron skirt made of "painted palm tree and reed" parts worn by a "Papua woman from Bogadjim in Astrolable Bay in Kaiser Wilhelm's Land in New Guinea," both reproduced in Klaatsch's *Development of Humankind*.[225]

This added "extraction" of ethnographic material allows Kiesler to move from the abstraction of nature to that of "applied arts" and what he describes as the "supernature" [*Übernatur*] of the design-enhanced human species. If in the chart's first two levels, abstraction equals a physical extraction from the colonized earth and the animal skin, in the lower two, the design of bodily clothing and ornament affixes the sample of an artificial ground onto the surface of the body, whose own image is entirely restructured by its artificial envelope. In that, the architect's chart depicts not simply the birth of design but also the birth of the human by design.

The chart itself is the architect's ultimate theoretical design. The spiral earring posing in the middle of the chart is not simply another product of design, but the ideogram of an evolutionary process, following which, the culminating point of human design also signals a return to its mineral origin and a gradual deviation from it by an increasing margin. That this spiral is made of metal "wiring" opens up another perspective onto the affinities of this 'original' design or technical artifact with the technological extension of modern infrastructural networks in the "atomic" era inhabited by Kiesler.

Returning to the preliminary draft illustrating the process of design abstraction (fig. C.09a), we see at the bottom of the page another rectangular table crowned by the hypothetical title "Ideology of building?" The question mark is repeated inside the table with a theoretical outline divided into three chronological eras: "eolithic," "neolithic," and, finally, the "atomic" era.[226] These three phases correspond to sources of design "abstracted" from "rocks," "animals," and "birds," respectively. Kiesler's later table-chart (fig. C.09b) illustrates the connection between design extractions from the rocks and animals of the colonies–but where do the "birds" of the "atomic" era fly from?

Perhaps a clue can be found in Kiesler's evolutionary chart of the development of life on Earth, part of his unrealized proposal for an exhibition on ecology at the American Museum of Natural History developed around 1944 (see fig. A.30a). At the top of that chart and right next to a bat, flies a human bird-like creature superimposed upon the image of a military airplane from which humans can now control both the aerial and the earthly domain. In the Atomic era, the sky constitutes humans' new effective milieu and the endpoint of their endlessly expansive design orientation. Superimposed with the metal-insulated body of the aircraft, Kiesler's "birdman" is reminiscent of the stylized figure of the crocodile and its metallic tail in his "Abstraction" chart (fig. C.09b). The flying "man-machine" condenses all three developmental periods of Kiesler's diagram of the "Ideology of Building" and their corresponding nature models–rock, animal, and bird–into what Marais would have called a "composite" figure. The "wiring" figures extracted from Kiesler's chart essentially diagram the reorientation of "design" from life's mineral and animal "birth" to its (super) human extinction.[227]

HUMAN TECHNOLOGY AND DESIGN TECHNIQUE III: "MAGIC DESIGN" AND SEXUAL SELECTION

Kiesler's description of the "birth" or invention of "design" in Parts III and IV describe the passage from "Animal" to "Magic Architecture," an architecture that surpasses mere "shelter" and incorporates human "imagination" yet has the capacity to unite "vision and fact" by staying in contact with "reality" (see chart in Addenda, fig. C.11).[228] These parts also narrate how the cultivation of specific "skills" and "techniques," such as (body) painting and engraving of relief sculpture lead to a grasping of architecture that becomes "psychoplastic" and ultimately "ideoplastic" (following the terminology of Max Verworn) (II.5 and II.6), and Kiesler's previous chart on the development from "Myth" to "Architecture" (plate 2a and Main Text, fig. B.04).

The "birth of magic design," states Kiesler in the first chapter of Part III ("Awareness of the Miraculous"), describes the moment when "man discovers his capacity to convert his own body into a dream image through painting or make-up" (III.1). The screen of the human skin is the first canvas of human design. While other (pre)histories of design present the flint and the hand-axe, stone tools detached from the body, as the first products of human culture, Kiesler prioritizes a form of design that derives from and is directly applied on the body itself. Moreover such "magic" design transcends functional need to respond to psychological impetus and desire. "Being able to change natural bodies and even his own at times, how much more desirable would it be to lift his own technological man-made ornaments, tools, and houses out of functional limitations into the realm of exuberant affirmation of his self!" [III. Introduction][229]

Kiesler describes facial "make-up" that imitates animal skin as an attempt to endow the wearer with an image of more-than-human strength. The painted skin in this case is an implement (used either for defense or attack), as well as an article of bodily adornment that enhances its carrier and performs symbolically in magic rituals. In this case, there is essentially no ontological distinction between implement and ornament–two object categories that are rigorously differentiated in late nineteenth-century museological classifications, as well as histories of modern architecture and design. Kiesler describes the function of body paint in shaman initiation rituals by quoting a passage from a German translation of Lévy-Bruhl's 1910 study of mentality in indigenous societies that draws from the well-known ethnographic studies of indigenous Australians by Spencer and Gillen.[230] Lévy-Bruhl's ethnosociological studies had no illustrations so for a particular image used in one of his plates (with an offensive juxtaposition of the painted face of an indigenous "medicine man" with the photograph of a tiger) Kiesler uses an enlarged cropped-up detail from a photograph reproduced in one of the later editions of Gillen and Spencer's study of the "Arunta" (see Arrernte) Indigenous Australians–one of the rare occasions that the Kieslers, thanks to the position of Stefi at the NYPL, engaged in more scrupulous image research.[231] There is a wide assortment of anthropological, ethnographic, and

Hochzeitskleider I.

Fig. 1a. b. Gehörnter Glockenvogel. 1/3. — 2a. b. Rotsterniges Blaukehlchen. 2/3. — 3a. b. Dominikaner-Witwe. 2/5. — 4a. b. Krikente. 1/4. — 5a. b. Kampfläufer. 1/4. — 6. Goldschnepfe (Weibchen). 1/4. — 7a. Balzendes Präriehuhn. 1/6. — 8a. b. Federbusch-Alk. 2/5. — 9a. b. Haubensteißfuß. 1/3. — 10a. Temmincks Tragopan mit aufgeblasenem Kehlsack und aufgerichteten Hörnern. 1/3. — (a Hochzeitskleid, b gewöhnliches Gefieder des Männchens.)

Meyers Konv.-Lexikon, 6. Aufl. Bibliogr. Institut in Leipzig Zum Artikel „Hochzeitskleid".

fig. A.35 "Wedding-gowns" of bird species from the article "Hochzeitskleid" in *Meyers Großes Konversations-Lexikon*, 6th ed. (Leipzig and Vienna: Bibliographisches Institut, 1908–1909), 406–407, plate I. The article was partly transcribed in Kiesler's research materials.

Opposite
figs. A.36a–b Ashley Montagu, *Coming into Being Among the Australian Aborigines* (New York: Dutton & Company, 1938). Personal copy in the Kiesler library (title page and flyleaf with author's handwritten dedication to Stefi and Frederick Kiesler). ÖFLKS, ANTHRO 009

archeological literature, including long excerpts from Lévy-Bruhl, Frobenius, Breuil, and Casteret among others used in the multiple quotations extending Kiesler's own rather sparse text for the sections on prehistoric painting and design. And then there are authors who are only indirectly cited, such as Charles Darwin, mentioned once in relation to the "erotic, sexual stimulus" of the beard in humans and primates, which Kiesler apparently draws from a similar reference in Klaatsch's *Werdegang* yet without acknowledgment by the architect.[232] However Darwin is implicitly central in Kiesler's foundation of adornment as well as the practices of human design on the laws of sexual selection: "Standards of preference are fundamental in sexual selection. This judgment is automatic. Male and female become aware of the reasons for being chosen. Both try to come near 'the ideal' and in this way to find security in success. Deficiencies of the body (which demonstrate themselves by comparison) urge corrections and alignment with preferred standards" (II.7). Such "corrections" and enhancements of the body take place through "design" such as the aggrandizement of its stature by the wearing of animal skins, or the alteration of its surface by scarification and tattooing. (II.7)

Notably Kiesler's references to adornment and design in relation to sexual selection belong to one of the final chapters of *Magic Architecture*'s second part on "Animal Architecture" and not the following two parts on the (super)human dimensions of "Magic Design." Indeed, following a quotation from Malinowski with an ethnographic description of "the ritual of adornment" of a male body during a "marriage ceremony,"[233] Kiesler expands his references to the role of "physical appeal" by describing the ability of "birds, reptiles, fish," to "often change their colors or even forms," which "in times of courtship" are "so … splendid that one speaks of 'wedding gowns.'" Among Kiesler's research material, is a transcription of an entry on animal "wedding dress [*Hochzeitkleid*]" copied from an illustrated German encyclopedic dictionary referring, among many other examples from birds and mammalians, to the instant color change in the "ornate plumage" of the male tragopan.[234] (fig. A.35) Kiesler then comments that "[w]ith the exception of blushing, man has lost, if he ever had it, the capacity to transform his skin and body, automatically." Therefore "[h]e had to invent tools and methods to do it. But the drive for it, the instinct, to produce it he shares with the animal kingdom." (II.7)

Human tools and other technical "methods," are then substitutes of the "automatically" transforming bodies of animals. While building techniques like weaving and piling are directly transmitted from animals to humans, design and the art of bodily transformation is motivated by a constitutional loss. This lack turns instinct into the drive that guides design production, which keeps reproducing tools that amplify instead of covering such loss.

Similar to Adolf Loos, whose "Ornament and Crime" Kiesler had presented in a lecture, ornament is associated with the "erotic" and the Indigenous.[235] Ornament and Architecture exist in different civilizational tiers, and therefore reciprocally exclude one another. Following Loos, societies that practice ornament have not yet advanced to Architecture, and those that have stepped on an architectural stage should not be returning to ornamentation. The textual structure of *Magic Architecture*, with separate "parts" for ornament, design, and architecture, affirms these distinctions even if its critique of Architecture (with a capital A) disturbs them.

HUMAN TECHNOLOGY AND DESIGN TECHNIQUE IV: TOWARDS A SOCIAL ANTHROPOLOGY OF DESIGN—SEX, SOCIETY, RACE (MONTAGU)

Following Kiesler's quotation of an extract from Malinowski on ritual adornment during a wedding ceremony, the architect closes his chapter on bodily "beautification" with two lengthy theoretical

COMING INTO BEING
AMONG THE
AUSTRALIAN ABORIGINES

A Study of the Procreative Beliefs
of the Native Tribes of Australia

By

M. F. ASHLEY-MONTAGU, PH.D.
Assistant-Professor of Anatomy, New York University

With a Foreword by

B. MALINOWSKI
Ph.D. (Cracow), D.Sc. (London), Hon. D.Sc. (Harvard);
Professor of Anthropology in the University of London;
Member of the Royal Academy of Holland

NEW YORK
E. P. DUTTON & COMPANY
1938

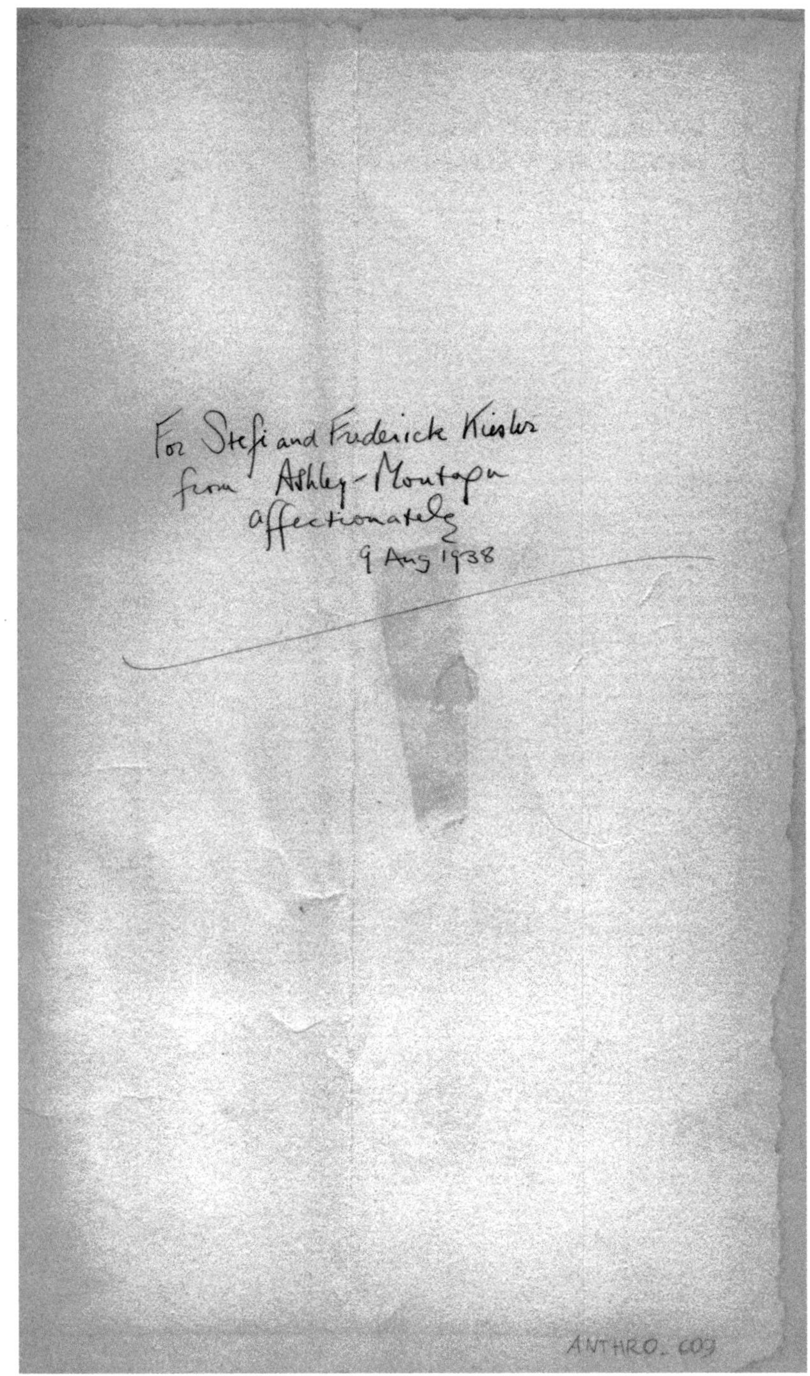

paragraphs from the first pages of Malinowski's book on the methodological significance of "sex" and "attraction"—meaning sexual attraction, not only as a seminal process in the creation of life but also as a "fundamental factor in the scientific treatment of human society" by the sociologist, who must analyze sexual relations within the legal framework of courtship and marriage (II.7).[236] Kiesler further collected a series of thematically related notes from Klaatsch's book on "family" and the "social" through "sex," "marriage," and the "home" in addition to his multiple other notes from the same volume on the creation of the earliest known forms of habitation and Indigenous shelters.[237]

In his introduction to *Magic Architecture's* tenth and final part and while drawing on the continuity between mental, social, and material patterns in Lévy-Bruhl, Kiesler describes "structures of the intellect" as "methods of protection" that can shelter "just as well as buildings of brick." (x. Intro) He then expands the notion of shelter into social and political systems, including the institution of the family: "The social structures, such as the family, the clan, tribe, a monarchy or a socialist community - they all are meant as: sheltering means; and in that respect they are more direct, more realistic, more "touchable" than philosophy or poetry although not as much as houses; they are social edifices, an outer layer or the nucleus of philosophy or poetry, and that is why we are at greater ease when we come in contact with them - naturally." (x.Intro) Instead of a monolithic idea of "shelter," *Magic Architecture* describes a sequence of "protective means" that traverse the mind and body of a person, the social circle of the family, and finally the "house," being the culminating material enclosure of all previous mental and social layers.

Additionally, among Kiesler's marginalia that were not included in the final text, there is a set of hastily written pencil notes in German in which the architect formulates "two forms of society," the first based on the "sex drive [*Sexualtrieb*]" leading to the union of "man and wife" and the creation of the "family, kinship, horde, tribe" though the "partly social, partly economic establishment of marriage," and the second on the "sociability drive [*Geselligkeitstrieb*]" between "same-sex individuals," which through "play instinct [*Spieltrieb*]" leads to the "unification" of different "age classes."[238] While highly incomplete, *Magic Architecture* does entail a "vision" or even a glimpse of a sociological interpretation of architecture based on the laws of kinship and social structuration, yet such a model was based predominantly, and by the mid-1940s parochially, on the ethno-sociological models of Malinowski and Lévy-Bruhl, whose theories were being challenged by a younger generation of structural anthropologists.[239]

Malinowski represents an important link for Kiesler's anthropological interests as the mentor of the anthropologist with whom the architect had a personal connection while in the United States, and who may have facilitated Kiesler's foray into anthropological literature. I refer to the physical anthropologist and popular author Ashley Montagu (of Jewish heritage born Israel Ehrenberg in London), who became a close acquaintance of the Kieslers in the late 1930s in New York. Stefi Kiesler's diary mentions the name "Montagu" for the first time ten days after her entry on Frobenius's lecture at the Dalton School in New York in late April of 1937.[240] By that time Montagu would have completed his dissertation in the Department of Anthropology at Columbia University under Franz Boas and Ruth Benedict. In 1939 Kiesler invited Montagu to present a lecture at his Laboratory for Design Correlation at Columbia on "Construction in Nature" with an emphasis on the creation of eyes in animal and human organisms and the development of "vision."[241] In addition to a number of offprints with Montagu's articles on physical anthropology, war, Malinowski, and the "domestication of the dog" among Kiesler's research files,[242] his personal library includes a copy of Montagu's dissertation published in 1938 under the title *Coming into Being among Australian Aborigines* with a preface by Malinowski.[243] Kiesler's copy contains an "affectionate" dedication to Frederick and Stefi Kiesler written by the author. (figs. A.36a–b)

Kiesler quotes from Montagu's book in the chapter "Enigma of Birth," in Part I of *Magic Architecture*, drawing directly from the anthropologist's ethnographic observations on the apparent lack of a causal connection between birth and sexual intercourse in the belief systems of several Indigenous Australian societies. Montagu had interpreted the "nescience of paternity" as part of a more expansive view of kinship and family structure in Indigenous epistemologies, advocating for a social rather than a biological understanding of parenthood.[244]

But there is also an essential difference between Montagu and the rest of the anthropological researchers consulted by Kiesler in terms of their theorization of race. Unlike Frobenius, whose racialized distinction between the "Hamitic" and "Ethiopian" human types and corresponding building typologies were fundamental for his "cultural morphology" system, Montagu was a strong opponent of all racial divisions, and even refuted the very idea of "race." In 1942, and at the height of Jewish persecution in Europe, he published *Man's Most Dangerous Myth: The Fallacy of Race*, following publications and radio appearances on the same subject.[245] Employing his expertise on anatomy and physical anthropology, Montagu refuted theories of the superiority of certain races put forward by Nazi race scientists. When the war ended, Montagu would become the rapporteur of UNESCO's' first official statement on "the race question," published in 1950 following a general conference the previous year and revised in 1952.[246] Montagu also wrote extensively on social and cultural issues, including the feminist classic *The Natural Superiority of Women*.[247] Even his dissertation *Coming into Being*, read and quoted by Kiesler, advances a larger equanimity of being among persons and things–one of the central, even if unattained, social objectives that underlie the "story of housing" in *Magic Architecture*.

THE "PREANIMIST" HYPOTHESIS: NATURE, RELIGION, AND PREARCHITECTURE (LÉVY-BRUHL)

The chapter preceding the "Enigma of Birth" that draws from Montagu's anthropological theories of "nescience" is symmetrically titled the "Enigma of Death" and quotes extensively from the work of the French philosopher and ethnosociologist of an earlier generation, Lucien Lévy-Bruhl, whose name figures prominently among Kiesler's drafts for *Magic Architecture*. Kiesler transcribes a number of excerpts from Lévy-Bruhl's 1910 *Les Fonctions mentales* in its German edition, *Das Denken der Naturvölker* edited by the Austrian Jewish scholar Wilhelm Jerusalem in 1921 (republished in 1926), which he then translates into English (even if an English edition of Lévy-Bruhl's book had existed since 1926).[248] Although strongly criticized by later anthropologists for his distinction between "logical" and "prelogical" mentalities, Lévy-Bruhl and the broad impact of his sociological ideas on art and literary circles were still points of reference in the 1940s, when Kiesler's text was compiled.[249] Kiesler's extensive quotations and transcriptions from his works reveal a rare attempt to pair Lévy-Bruhl's theories on mental and social "structures" with the domain of architecture.[250]

Chapter 2 of Part IV, rhythmically titled "Man Part of the Cosmos and Man Apart from the Cosmos," contains only a single note describing the chapter's transitional content: "pertaining to the transformation from the mystic (image-less) belief to visual objectivations: Idols, shrines"; and yet the content of this chapter is actually missing from the final manuscript. Looking at earlier drafts we discover why. Initially Kiesler intended to quote a lengthy excerpt from Lévy-Bruhl's study of mental structures, transcribed in German (in two different copies), which was ultimately not translated by Stefi and not included in later drafts.[251] (fig. A.37) The Kieslers quote from the second section of the ninth and final chapter of Lévy-Bruhl's study, in which the French sociologist mentions a distinction between animist and "preanimist" periods in the "evolution of society" according to Dutch ethnographer Albert Christian Kruijt:

> … one in which individual spirits are reputed to inhabit and animate [*bewohnen und beleben*] every being and every object (animals, plants, boulders, stars, weapons, tools, and so forth), and another and earlier one, in which individualization [*Individualisierung*] has not yet taken place, in which there is a diffused principle capable of penetrating everywhere, a kind of universal and widespread force [*verbreiteter Kraft*] which seems to animate [*beseelen*] persons and things, to act in them and to endow them with life [*Leben zu verleihen*].[252]

In the concluding section of his study and just before he transitions to modern scientific forms of thought, Lévy-Bruhl reflects on a "preanimist period," challenging the tenets of "individuation" that characterized Edward Tylor's nineteenth-century doctrine of animism by foregrounding a belief in a generalized and impersonal distribution of agency in nature and human societies. In addition to Kruijt, Lévy Bruhl mentions the importance of a "preanimist" state in the work of British ethnologist Robert Ranulph Marett, as well as French ethnographers and sociologists including Émile Durkheim and Marcel Mauss.

To take things from the beginning, preanimism was coined at the turn of the century by Marett as a response or amendment to Tylor's theory of animism, which prevailed over anthropological descriptions of Non-Western religions in the late nineteenth century.[253] Marett was reacting to Tylor's evident reliance to concepts of souls and spirits that appeared too closely associated with familiar ideas from Western theology and philosophy applied indiscriminately from ancient European to Indigenous religions. Following Marett, there had to be a state where natural forces were not individualized or personified and anthropomorphic gods or spirits did not exist. Marett proposed instead the generalized influence of a vital force similar to the Melanesian "mana" by quoting from the ethnographic descriptions of R. H. Codrington, a British missionary in the region.

A more extensive ethnographic description influenced by Marett's preanimist ideas is found in the ethnographic work of Kruijt, a Calvinist missionary in the Dutch colonies of southeast Asia,

(.87

Chapter ~~one~~ 2: ~~Introduction I~~ PART IV: ~~Introduction~~: Man part of ~~the~~ the Cosmos and man apart from the cosmos.

(do not type

Transl.

Levy-Bruhl:

IXth Chapter:

Uebergang zu höheren Typen der Gesitesbetätigung.

See Excerpt.

page 326

"In seiner letzten Arbeit über den "Animismus im indischen Archipel" hält es Kruijt für notwendig in der Entwicklung der Gesellschaften, die auf niedriger Stufe stehen, zwei aufeinander folgende Perioden zu unterscheiden: die eine, in der man glaubt, dass individuelle Geister jedes Wesen und jeden Gegenstand (Tiere, Pflanzen, Felsen, Gestirne, Waffen, Geräte etc.) bewohnen und beleben, und eine andere, frühere, in der die Individualisierung noch nicht stattegfunden hat, wo man an ein unbestimmtes Prinzip glaubt, das fähig ist, alles zu durchdringen, an eine Art überall verbreiteter Kraft, die die Wesen und die Gegenstände zu beseelen, in ihnen zu wirken und ihnen Leben zu verleihen scheint. Man erkennt hier die "präanimistische" Periode von Marrett wieder, deren Existenz Durckheim und Mauss gleichfalls betont haben. Kruijt fügt hinzu - und die Bemerkung ist für den Gegenstand, der uns beschäftigt, sehr wichtig -- dass die Einteilung in diese beiden

fig. A.37 Frederick and Stefi Kiesler, transcription of excerpts from the ninth chapter of Lucien Lévy-Bruhl, *Das Denken der Naturvölker* (1926). ÖFLKS, TXT_6744/0_N2

describing "animism in the Indian Archipelago," who is mentioned in Levy-Bruhl's 1910 study in the passage transcribed by the Kieslers. In the first chapters of his voluminous book written in Dutch, Kruijt distinguishes the belief on an "impersonal soul-matter" (*onpersoonlijke zielestof*) preserved in certain parts of the body, like hair and nails, or in bodily excretions, like urine and feces.[254] Kruijt also underscores "a strong communistic clan bond" (*sterk communistisch stamverband*) in societies sharing these "impersonal" beliefs.[255] The reference to a prevalent form of communalism, where no individual group member owns anything signaled the existence of a world without personal property of either material things or immaterial beings, like souls, gods, and spirits. These "impersonal" qualities may explain the attraction, as well as the reaction against preanimist ideas foreboding a post-theist condition in a world without religion or property, as some of Marett's critics feared.[256] For philosophers and folk-psychologists like Wilhelm Wundt, preanimism remained a theoretical "hypothesis," and in the fourth volume of his *Völkerpsychologie* Wundt described "preanimistic theory [*preanimistische Theorie*]" as following and even complementing the "animistic theory [*animistische Theorie*]" as part of a "constructive mythological system" that is intimately associated by Marett with a "theory of Magic [*Zaubertheorie*]."[257]

As Lévy-Bruhl noted in the excerpt transcribed by the Kieslers, Marett's preanimist ideas enjoyed recognition by turn-of-the-century French ethnosociologists, like Marcel Mauss, whose *esquisse* for a "general theory of magic," co-authored with Henri Hubert, expanded on the magical practices associated with the impersonal qualities of *mana*.[258] For Mauss's uncle and mentor, the sociologist Émile Durkheim (also mentioned by Lévy-Bruhl in the excerpt transcribed by the Kieslers), preanimist impersonal agencies were not merely a "theory" but a social conviction. In his *Elementary Forms of Religious Life*, the socialist theorist offered a powerful description of *mana* as an intergenerational impersonal force that animated the societies of today "as it animated those of yesterday and as it will animate those of tomorrow"—a formulation that reverberates the sociologist's theories of "organic solidarity" in his earlier work, *The Division of Labor in Society*.[259] The enduring solidarity of forces that transcend individual persons and generations in Durkheim disclose the covert correspondences of "preanimist" magic with the redistribution of power in modern European societies experiencing a turmoil towards communal and anarchic forms of governance promoting the abolition of religion and personal property.

But what would the preanimist hypothesis and its redistribution of power have to offer to Kiesler's "story of housing" written more than four decades after preanimist theories were invented and which by that time had been refuted by historians of religion, who, based on actual ethnographic observations of Melanesian societies, claimed that the presumably "impersonal force" of *mana* was in fact always attached to individual gods and human figures? The same interwar critics argued that preanimist theories betrayed the lingering presence of evolutionism in histories of religion dividing eras into "pre" and "post."[260]

Nevertheless, the belief in "mana" as an "impersonal force" shows up in a recent article on "the study of myth" by Richard (Volney) Chase, English professor at Columbia, published in *Partisan Review* in 1946, which Kiesler excerpts at length in Part IV of *Magic Architecture* describing "Myth and Magic." (IV.4) There Chase describes "*mana* or preternatural power" as "impersonal" and "apprehend[ed]" "as an immediate quality of things, just as color, sound, size, shape and motion."[261] The description of this "impersonal force" in visual, formal, and spatial terms may suggest some of the unexplored affinities of these impersonal epistemologies with contemporary practices and theories of art, particularly abstract art, where color, shape, and volume appear as vibrant "qualities" unmediated by the presence of figures and objects.

Moreover, Kiesler's copy of the anthropological study *Early Civilization* by the Ukrainian-born American anthropologist Alexander Goldenweiser contains passages underlined by Kiesler in the sections on "Magic and Religion" that also emphasize the connection of *mana* to magical practices: "It indicates power which is supernatural and impersonal. *Mana* itself is not an animal or human being, nor a ghost or spirit, it is just power, magical potency."[262] But what impact could this "impersonal force" have in the architecture that Kiesler designated as "magic"?

A deleted reference to "preanimistic periods" in one of Kiesler's preliminary manuscripts that does not appear in the final text may offer a clue on the architectural ramifications of the impersonal forms of matter as well as non-individualized being in the world ascribed to these periods. In a heavily amended handwritten draft of the fourth chapter of Part I, Kiesler describes an earlier time, when myths were an integral part of "everyday life" outside the frame of "causal logic" (fig. A.38):

> **I speak of the time when the boundaries of logic were practically non-existent and mystic relationships ~~of pre-animistic periods~~[263] could reign free. The symbiosis of man, family, and natural surrounding was complete, the cycle of emotional unity of all beings had not been broken. Emancipation had not yet taken the reigns from participation. Shelter could therefore be found everywhere. There was no need for artificially constructed protectives; nature provided everything.** (I.4)

Even if deleted from the manuscript, the notion of a "preanimistic period" persists in the architect's text, through the "mystic" and "symbiotic" relationships of "participation" present in the passages from Lévy-Bruhl's text describing Kruijt's "preanimist" principles of non-individuation and "collective consciousness" that were transcribed by the Kieslers but not included in the typescript of *Magic Architecture*.[264] It is as if the "mystic" impersonal power described in the ethnosociologist's text takes hold of the architect's writing the moment that its presence in his manuscript is elided. Yet the same obscure reference also reveals the absence of architecture in this non-individualized state of being, where "shelter" can be found everywhere within the domain of nature. There is no need for "constructed" or any other artificial "protection," Kiesler argues, because humans live united with their surroundings.

The idea of an unidentified period in which no built architecture exists is also sketched in one of Kiesler's preliminary book outlines describing "people [who] live in harmonious unity with their environment":

> **They live mostly an outdoor life... and no attempt at "Architecture" is formed. The house is no more than the nucleus of a wider shell, which is nature itself, her earth, rocks, bushes, forests, and the skies above. The building material which is taken directly from the environment makes the house so much part of nature.**[265]

Elsewhere in *Magic Architecture* Kiesler unequivocally states that "Nature *is* architecture." (I.8) He rejects analogy and metaphor in favor of identification, reminiscent of processes of sympathetic magic. Yet in the unitary state he describes above, architecture is not needed. It oscillates between absence and omnipresence, as in the environmental expansion of the housing "nucleus" into the "wider shell" of its surrounding elements in nature.

This idealized image of primordial unity between humans and their natural setting reverberates enlightenment ideals of "primitive" plenitude in Rousseau echoed in Laugier's invention of the "primitive hut" as the architectonic conversion of nature in the late eighteenth century—an era that Kiesler momentarily turns his attention to in the tenth and final part of *Magic Architecture* as a

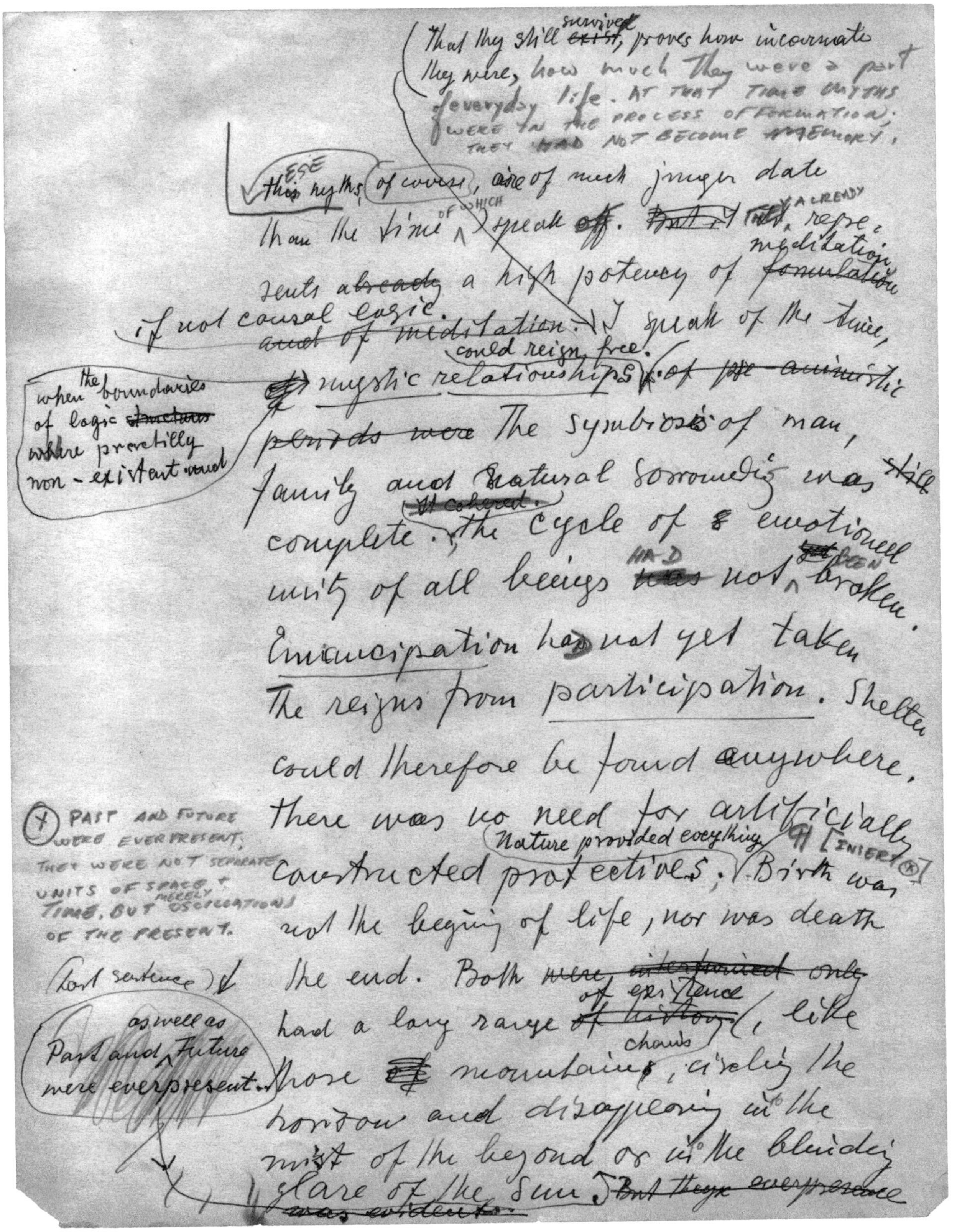

That they still survived, proves how incarnate they were, how much they were a part of everyday life. AT THAT TIME MYTHS WERE IN THE PROCESS OF FORMATION; THEY HAD NOT BECOME A MEMORY.

These myths, of course, are of much younger date than the time of which I speak. They already represent a high potency of meditation, if not causal logic. I speak of the time, when the boundaries of logic were practically non-existent and mystic relationships could reign free. The symbiosis of man, family and natural surroundings was complete. It cohered. The cycle of emotional unity of all beings had not been broken. Emancipation had not yet taken the reigns from participation. Shelter could therefore be found anywhere. There was no need for artificially constructed protectives; Nature provided everything. [INSERT ⊗] Birth was not the begining of life, nor was death the end. Both had a long range of existence, like those chains of mountains, circling the horizon and disappearing into the mist of the beyond or into the blinding glare of the sun.

⊗ PAST AND FUTURE WERE EVERPRESENT; THEY WERE NOT SEPARATE UNITS OF SPACE + TIME, BUT MERELY OSCILLATIONS OF THE PRESENT.

(Last sentence)

Past and, as well as, Future were everpresent.

fig. A.38 Frederick Kiesler, MS draft with emendations of Part 1, chapter 4, "The Enigma of Birth." ÖFLKS, TXT_6725/0_N10

preamble to the modern architecture of his own era.[266] Meanwhile nineteenth century's celebration of architecture *in* nature and the discovery or invention of human "prehistory" coincided with the coining of a "prearchitectonic" era by the preeminent architectural theorist of that century Gottfried Semper, who used the term to describe cultures that appear to lack monumental architecture and yet share a number of "pre-architectonic techniques" in their textile and pottery industries.[267] A century later, the term would reappear in the postwar writings of architectural historian Sigfried Giedion (also an acquaintance of Kiesler), who, based on his experience of space in prehistoric caves in the south of France employed the term to describe prehistory as "the prearchitectonic state of human development."[268]

Finally Kiesler himself in an article on architecture and sculpture published posthumously and written towards the end of his life, employs the same term in one of the architect's photo captions describing a Dolmen in Carnac (Brittany) as a "pre-architectural sculpture building."[269] Here the "pre-architectural" unites with the "sculptural" as if sculpture was the "pre-architectural" state of building (a statement that Hegel in his *Lectures on Aesthetics* on the subject of "symbolic" architecture would agree).[270] In the same caption, Kiesler describes the French Dolmen as "the beginning of the post and lintel construction." This orthogonal construction was in fact the antipode of Kiesler's own sculptural structural system of "continuous tension" uniting floor, wall, and ceiling without the use of beams or columns. Here the "pre-architectural" is directly connected with the architectural in its most conventional and established version. And yet the similarity of the same Dolmen with some of Kiesler's own cavernous spaces by contrast demonstrates what the same "pre-architectural" object could have become had it developed all of its sculptural capacities. The "pre-architectural" object transmogrifies all of these historically unfulfilled possibilities. Like preanimism, prearchitecture and prehistory are essentially *post* conditions that emerge after the dissolution of the forms they are supposed to precede.

The preliminary proposals for *Magic Architecture* contain a visual representation of such preanimist and post-theist vision of the world in one of the architect's hand-drawn charts with a cartoon version of the evolution of religion, which may also give us an insight into a post-architectural condition.[271] (see chart in Addenda, fig. C.02b) Arranged in individual frames moving from left to right, Kiesler's table describes the evolving relations between gods and humans in six enumerated steps or stages, starting from the preanimist belief in the ethereal forces of the firmament (1), followed by the worship of imposing earthly elements like a high mountain (2), and personified in the adoration of an equally mountainous divine "superman" (3), which is then shrunken in size and put on an Ancient Greek pedestal (4), before being flattened onto a "lower" pedestal (5) until finally all gods are knocked down from their pedestals by "Everyman," the generic stick figure of a human being, who puts his hand on the shoulder of a fellow human (of equal height) and shakes their hand in a gesture of solidarity (6).

The cartoon's end frame discloses that *Everyman's Architecture*, Kiesler's alternative title for his *Magic Architecture* project, is an architecture of equitable social relations.[272] Architecture subsists in social bonding, even if "participation" in such bonds remains unequal and can at times become violently coercive. Perhaps the greatest affinity between Magic Architecture and a theory of "preanimist periods" and/or "prearchitectonic times" is that the latter were and remain a theory, an unfulfilled hypothesis, perhaps too radical in its social potential. Histories of architectural theory, or in fact histories of architecture in general, are replete with such unfulfilled theoretical hypotheses. Could this radically homogeneous social structuration implied in the "preanimist" and the "prearchitectural" coincide not with the origins but the end of 'architecture' as an individualizing process? And what would the deletion and reappearance of these terms in the architect's writings suggest?

What follows the "prearchitectural" mélange of prehistoric and indigenous "participatory" design in the first half of *Magic Architecture*, is a process that takes us halfway back in the trajectory of Kiesler's cartoon on religious (d)evolution. *Magic Architecture*'s "time-machine" moves back to the protohistorical beginnings of Western civilizations, when, as Kiesler's contemporary historians would attest, conditions of social stratification and inequality correlate with the origins of monumental Architecture.

(PROTO-)ARCHITECTURES OF INEQUALITY

Following the description of caves, animal dwellings, tools, and the first traces of human design in bodily adornment, Kiesler's story performs a precipitous turn to the domain of Architecture, with a capital "A." Often in Kiesler's handwritten manuscripts, we witness the transition from the *architecture* of human and animal dwelling to the *Architecture* of religious and/or courtly monuments marking a split between private and public realms of building activity.

Towards the end of Part IV, Kiesler had described the formation of specially decorated "meeting houses" inside "villages" built alongside individual family "shelters" for the hosting of communal rituals formerly performed in "nature." (IV.6) Such "meeting houses" mark an overlap between domestic space and communal ritual, yet in the following chapter Kiesler abruptly transitions into an unspecified protohistoric era, in which "[t]he division into dwellings, ritual-building and state palaces has become very marked."[273] (IV.7) Architecture with a capital "A" is then solidified by a "division" between domestic and communal space marked by a gap in the architect's narrative disclosing the inconsistencies between the ethnosociological theories on the organization of space he had absorbed from Lévy-Bruhl and the archeological evidence he was confronted with as soon as he performed the passage from prehistory to history and "Architecture."[274]

Indeed, following the anthropological exploration of an architectural "prehistory" in parts I–IV, the second half of *Magic Architecture* (parts V–IX) is essentially a critique of the history of the built environment in terms of the social inequalities it perpetuates from protohistoric civilizations to the present. This highly peculiar and apospasmatic history starts with an attack on religious architecture in Part V, titled "Slums for the Body, Dream-Architecture for Rituals," describing the ancient habit of devoting a disproportionate amount of building effort to the housing of gods and dead rulers as opposed to the domiciles of the many more living who built those grandiose monuments. A deleted and barely legible (sub) title reads: "The Unity of Vision and Fact. Reality / led [in/to?] / Nothing but Dreams,"[275] invoking the "unity" described in the first half of *Magic Architecture*, which appears broken throughout the history of human civilization in the second half and yet will return as a prospective correalist resolution in the tenth and final part of the symmetrically laid out manuscript.[276]

Since Kiesler never finished writing the text for the chapters of this fifth section, most of them consist merely of a title and an image-plate. The iconography of each appears to be more or less the same: a gigantic funerary or religious monument towering over a row of low building structures housing the people who have ostensibly constructed the same monuments. This pattern of inequality in building scale and socio-economic status persists, according to Kiesler, from Ancient Egypt to the Gothic Middle Ages and from ancient Greece to colonial India.

The list starts with a plate captioned "The people of Cairo living in the shadow of the great Tomb-pyramid of Gizeh," with the reproduction of a photograph showing the shadow of the Pyramid of Cheops eclipsing part of the modern settlement of Kafr-el-Samman

fig. A.39 Frederick Kiesler, template montaged in plate 33, "Athens, Acropolis, view from southwest" from Ferdinand Noack, *Die Baukunst des Altertums* (Berlin: Fischer & Franke: 1910), plate 99.
ÖFLKS, CLP_6508/0

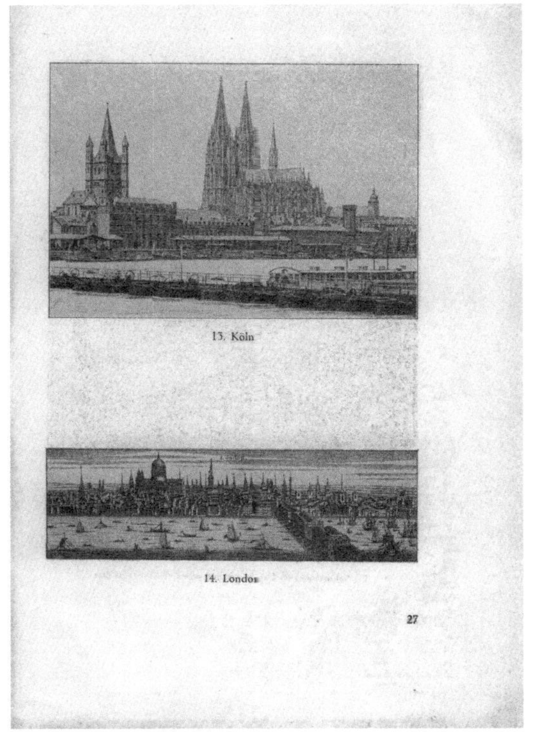

(plate 30).[277] A few plates later, Kiesler reproduces a photograph of the Parthenon on top of the rock of the Athenian Acropolis that does not show the neoclassical and vernacular houses that surround the archaeological site in modern day Athens. Therefore Kiesler inserts inside the larger photograph a small image of the vernacular home of a traditionally dressed Greek family, adding the caption "Great Architecture for the Gods, Slums for the people who built it" (plate 34 and fig. A.39).[278] Obviously neither the people of modern-day Egypt nor those of early twentieth-century Greece could have built these ancient monuments, yet the very temporal incongruity of Kiesler's montaged building components underlines the diachronic perseverance of Architecture's inequalities in labor distribution.

The pictorial survey ends with photographs of Gothic temples in European villages and cities, starting with the cathedral of Tournai in Belgium, captioned: "To appease the Gods, a populace easily sacrifices its wealth and health. It builds cathedrals for Gods they never saw; but mere shelter for themselves" (plate 35).[279] The same gallery of urban images includes photographs from non-Western historical monuments, such as an Aztec Pyramid with a detailed description of the spaces and instruments involved in the ritual of human sacrifices (plate 31)[280] and a gopuram gateway tower from Madurai, India, reproduced with the caption: "The people who built this magic monument live in slum-shelter" (plate 32).[281]

There seems to be something awkwardly "off" in the scaling of both high and low, opulent and modestly constructed buildings in these plates. They appear as if cut-and-pasted on top of one another, rhetorically enhancing their socio-economic disparity in spite of their spatial proximity. Whether the photographs reproduced by Kiesler are a montage (as is obviously the case in his plate on the Athenian Acropolis) or not, his abbreviated historiographic survey certainly *is* a montage of both text and image. Indeed, Part v amalgamates a series of textual descriptions of the same types of monuments by historians and other authors, including the account of the Aztec pyramids in Central America by French colonial researcher and Americanist Lucien Biart,[282] and the description of the Egyptian pyramid by the Viennese cultural historian and theater artist Egon Friedell, excerpted from his *Kulturgeschichte des Altertums* (*Cultural History of Antiquity*).[283] The excerpts transcribed by the Kieslers examine all monuments mainly from a socio-political perspective with an emphasis on quantities of human labor and building materials involved in construction. The architect's historiographic montage ultimately fails to counter inequality on account of the generic sameness with which it treats the very different architectural monuments it selectively surveys. And yet such generalized typological and iconographic consistency across histories of architecture may also stage a polemical claim. Equality does not have a building iconography, Kiesler inadvertently claims, yet systems of autocratic institutional hierarchy certainly do; they *are* Architecture.

*

The process of working through established architectural iconographies links *Magic Architecture* with one of its unacknowledged historiographic precedents. Architectural readers may recognize in Kiesler's photographic survey, an obvious iconographic correspondence between the towering monuments reproduced in his plates and the collection of forty "old crown building" monuments in the historical section of Bruno Taut's anthology *Die Stadtkrone* (*The City Crown*, 1919, containing contributions by Paul Scheerbart, Erich Baron, and Adolf Behne), mentioned later in Kiesler's manuscript along with Taut's other urban manifesto *Die Auflösung der Städte* (*The Dissolution of Cities*, 1920), but with no further commentary for either publication.[284] In certain cases, the urban monuments and settings depicted in *Magic Architecture* and *Stadtkrone* are the same, such as the Parthenon above the houses of modern Athens, the Piazza del Duomo in Pisa, and one of the Mandurai temples in India. (figs. A.40a-b) However, the photographs used by the two architects are different, as are the drawings and photographs of Gothic cathedrals in German city centers that are the centerpiece of Taut's "historical" section. (fig. A.40c)

Taut's central text in his anthology on "City Crowns," echoes some of the anti-functionalist housing debates motivating *Magic Architecture*. In the text's first section, titled simply "Architecture," Taut describes architecture as "fulfill[ing] the needs of humankind for protection from inclement weather and the manifold dangers they are exposed, since they cannot face nature without 'shelter' [*Behausung*]." Yet he also adds that "[o]nly when human desire goes beyond the satisfaction of simple functional needs, where people seek an abundance of luxury [*Luxus*], does architecture become more noticeable and reveal more of itself."[285] Later on Taut praises the religious structure of the cathedral of the "old

and beautiful city," with its purpose-undriven nave [*unzweckmässigen Schiff*] and even less purpose-driven tower [*noch unzweckmässigeren Turm*]" set "in powerful contrast to the simple dwellings of common people" particularly in "impressive temples from Antiquity or in the temples and pagodas of Asia."[286] Taut's characterization of the tower crown as *unzweckmässig* echoes Kiesler's idea of the necessity of the superfluous, which the Austrian perhaps in contrast to the German architect, would like to see redistributed from the religious tower to the workers' housing below.[287]

Based on the long history of the selectively international examples of religious monuments displayed in his book, Taut appends his own designs for the "city crown" of the future while confronted with the catastrophes of the Great War, when a number of Europe's grand Medieval cathedrals, like those celebrated in Taut's book, were gravely injured. Depicted in a number of elevations and bird's-eye perspectives analogous to his reproductions of past monuments, Taut's future city is organized around a modern "city crown," which is no longer a religious, but a cultural center, and whose central glass tower can accommodate large masses of people yet has no fixed program. (fig. A.41) It may appear paradoxical that Taut employs the ultimate monarchic symbol of the "crown" to delineate a collective urban vision of the future. The writing of the book was completed in 1917 while Taut was working for the German military, yet it was published in 1919, less than one year after the collapse of the Habsburg monarchy and its colonial empire.[288] Repurposing Semper's idea of metabolism (*Stoffwechsel*), Taut's reinvention of the urban "crown," aspires to convert the same centripetal pattern into the fulcrum of a more egalitarian society based on socialist principles.[289]

In terms of their socially driven content, Kiesler's intentions may align with Taut's, yet unlike Taut, Kiesler does not yet have an alternative design solution that would be comparable in scope to these historical monuments. To him, these powerful monuments remain irredeemable for producing building iterations of inequality between "everyman" and the state. The only equivalent he sees between the towers of the past and modern times are the ornate "pseudo-magic crowns" of the commercialized skyscrapers of New York, styled after historical monuments like the Great Pyramid or the Dome of St. Peter's, and which the architect castigates in the tenth and final part of his book project while bemoaning the commodification of architecture in the modern age (x.6). Since the resort to the pre-architectural condition and its preanimist radical redistribution of power is not historically viable, Kiesler's only other solution is the reinvention of the "home" veering away from preexisting historical models. Yet such an alternative would appear in the first iterations of his *Endless House* project in 1947, the year when the compilation of his "story of housing" essentially folded.[290] Additionally, the only mass-family housing design by Kiesler (repurposed from an earlier building scheme) appearing in one of the final plates of *Magic Architecture* (next to skyscraper projects by Le Corbusier and Frank Lloyd Wright) is a perspectival rendering of a "so-called 'horizontal skyscraper'"–a "tower" that in contrast with the religious towers of the past and the commercialized towers of the present is decisively non-vertical (plate 54).

Opposite
figs. A.40a–c Illustrations of "Ancient City Crowns" (Selinunte, Athens, Madurai Great Temple (India), Cologne, London), Bruno Taut, *Die Stadtkrone* (Jena: Diederichs, 1919), 28, 25, 27.

fig. A.41 Bruno Taut, "Perspectival view of City Crown," *Die Stadtkrone* (1919), 74.

Unlike prehistory, history acts appositionally and not synergistically in *Magic Architecture*. Therefore, Kiesler has to invent his own version of history for his "story of housing" to continue. Following Part v, *Magic Architecture* shifts from a speculative prehistory and abridged world history to an equally hypothetical "story" of what housing and architecture in general could potentially become but never did. Parts vi to ix include mainly literary architectures often described as "utopian," from Filarete's City of Sforzinda to Campanella's *City of the Sun* (vii.2–3), as well as imagined and unexecuted buildings by artists with whom Kiesler (presenting himself as an artist-designer with no realized buildings at that time) would identify: from Dürer's "Super-Arc of Triumph" (for Emperor Maximilian) to Leonardo's "concept" drawings of cathedrals (vi.1–2 and plates 37, 38) and from Michelangelo's project for the Dome of Saint-Peter's to Raphael's garden designs for the Villa Madama (vi.3,7). This heterogeneous assortment of unexecuted projects in the second half of the manuscript essentially constitutes another prehistory that is even more fragmentary than that of the first half. This "second" prehistory is one of the innovative architectural developments that ought to have emerged in the twentieth century but did not because it was impeded by the functionalist and hygienic inclinations of modernist architects, such as Le Corbusier. Kiesler's alternative history-in-the-making is closer to the "prehistory" described in the first half rather than anything that had factually happened in architectural history in the past five hundred years. The architect is simply not willing to succumb to the prescriptions of history and therefore feels compelled to invent his own. The ultimate aim of *Magic Architecture* was to correct or even *reverse* the course of history of twentieth-century architecture towards a design trajectory informed by Kiesler's correalist principles, even if finally, the same gesture served to secure a place for the architect's projects in the long genealogy of architectural projects that would never be built.

For his list of unrealized projects, Kiesler draws extensively from the 1925 book *Architektur die nicht gebaut wurde* (Architecture that was not built), by Josef Ponten. The publication is also advertised in the German edition of Le Corbusier's book, *Kommende Baukunst*.[291] (fig. a.42) Ponten's two-volume publication reconstructs a history of unbuilt architecture by assembling evidence from literary and pictorial descriptions dating from Antiquity to the early twentieth century. A former student of architecture and art history, Ponten was a popular writer and novelist, who wrote the book with the assistance of two young art and architectural historians, Heinz Rosemann and Hedwig Schmelz, both of whom are described as students of Heinrich Wölfflin, who, as noted by the author in his afterword, referred them to Ponten.[292] Heinz Rosemann would later become a well-established historian of Northern Renaissance and baroque architecture. Ponten's own reputation would later be marred by his involvement with National Socialism. The book was probably first discovered in the New York Public Library by Stefi Kiesler, who made a number of handwritten notes in its table of contents regarding some of the individual featured projects (figs. a.44a–b).[293] Some of Ponten's project descriptions are transcribed by Kiesler in his own manuscript, while a number of Photostat reproductions were ordered from the nypl and used in the plates for *Magic Architecture* (figs. a.45a–b).[294]

There is also a preliminary list that catalogues unbuilt projects from the twentieth century and earlier, which do not register in Ponten's survey. Included among them is Vladimir Tatlin's Tower for the Third International as well as a list of recent architectural projects, such as Le Corbusier's Voisin redevelopment plan, Buckminster Fuller's Dymaxion House as well as Kiesler's own "Horizontal Skyscraper" and his "Endless House" (see Addenda, fig. c.05a).[295] On the same page and next to the typewritten catalogue of unbuilt projects is an additional handwritten list mentioning

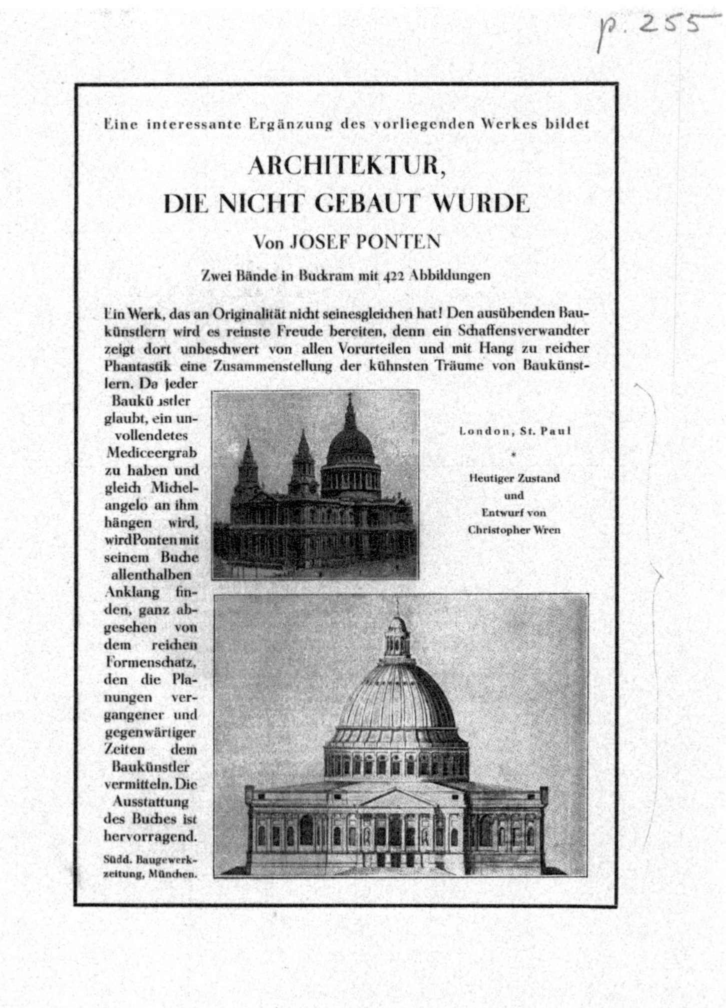
p. 255

Eine interessante Ergänzung des vorliegenden Werkes bildet

ARCHITEKTUR,
DIE NICHT GEBAUT WURDE

Von JOSEF PONTEN

Zwei Bände in Buckram mit 422 Abbildungen

Ein Werk, das an Originalität nicht seinesgleichen hat! Den ausübenden Baukünstlern wird es reinste Freude bereiten, denn ein Schaffensverwandter zeigt dort unbeschwert von allen Vorurteilen und mit Hang zu reicher Phantastik eine Zusammenstellung der kühnsten Träume von Baukünstlern. Da jeder Baukünstler glaubt, ein unvollendetes Mediceergrab zu haben und gleich Michelangelo an ihm hängen wird, wird Ponten mit seinem Buche allenthalben Anklang finden, ganz abgesehen von dem reichen Formenschatz, den die Planungen vergangener und gegenwärtiger Zeiten dem Baukünstler vermitteln. Die Ausstattung des Buches ist hervorragend.

Südd. Baugewerkzeitung, München.

London, St. Paul

*

Heutiger Zustand und Entwurf von Christopher Wren

"Brueghel: tower," "El Greco: Toledo" and "Wren–St. Paulus-Cathedral" followed by the names of "Scheerbart" and "Hüysmans." Kiesler would indeed complement Ponten's historical compendium of unbuilt architecture with his own additional selections, including buildings by painters such as Bruegel, Bosch, and El Greco in Part vi (vi.4–6, plates 40–41a), and "poets" (or, rather, literary authors) including Victorien Sardou, Joris-Karl Huysmans, Paul Scheerbart, and Franz Kafka in Part ix (ix.1–4, plate 50).

Indeed, just as the buildings of Ponten's and Kiesler's lists were never built, the majority of the chapters in *Magic Architecture* that were meant to analyze those very buildings were never written. Similar to the chapters of Part v, those of Parts vi to ix contain titles and plate illustrations, as well as brief descriptions mostly transcribed and translated from Ponten and a few other more unorthodox sources. While Kiesler's assembled typescript has no footnotes and his list of plates contains no credits, preliminary drafts and photostats have helped identifying some of his unacknowledged sources. These inadvertently disclose a string of historical accidents inscribed in the making of *Magic Architecture's* incomplete history.

For example, the reference to "Brueghel's tower" in Kiesler's draft project list obviously refers to Pieter Bruegel's *Tower of Babel* (1653), found in Vienna's Kunsthistorisches Museum. Like the biblical tower itself, Kiesler's chapter on the Flemish artist's painting remained incomplete with the exception of a single poetic paragraph describing the tower as "a circular pyramid in setbacks" that mediates between the earth and the sky (vi.4). The source for the reproduction of the painting which Kiesler used for the plate can be found among his journal clippings. (See plate 40 and fig. a.43.)[296] The text on the reverse of the clipping reveals that it had been torn from an issue of *Faust*, a monthly journal on literature, art, and music published in Berlin in the 1920s. Specifically, Bruegel's *Tower* was reproduced as an illustration for an article titled "Das Wesen der Sprache," or "The Essence of Language," by the Jewish German language scientist

Ernst Lewy.[297] While Lewy refers neither to the biblical tower nor to Bruegel's seventeenth-century painting, he presents language in spatial terms as a means of "communication" with the environment (*Umwelt*) and as "an expression of our mental being in its widest circumference" (*Umfang*).[298] "Linguistic construction styles," or *sprachliche Baustile*, he writes, are particularized by individual "peoples, nations, classes, and races." Lewy worries about the loss of linguistic peculiarities in peoples unrooted from their land as well as "smaller nations" threatened by modernization.[299] Yet after lamenting the prevailing linguistic anarchy caused by the Reformation, the author ultimately strikes an optimistic tone by extolling the resilience of linguistic difference even in "capitalist Western Europe" preventing a "sinking into the gasoline cloud of pessimism" (*Benzinnebel des Pessimismus*) and the demons of the "merely technological progress of paper culture and pseudo-civilization."[300] Lewy's article speaks not simply of the architectural but also the larger territorial and geopolitical ramifications of language that extend the discord of the *Tower of Babel* in Kiesler's contemporary era.

The biblical architectural figure of the *Tower of Babel* is a recurring motif in the idiosyncratic historiography of Egon Friedell, the Viennese cultural historian, essayist, theater actor, and cabaret art director, whose books were read and transcribed by the Kieslers.[301] In his *Cultural History of Antiquity* (1936), excerpts of which were copied for quotation in *Magic Architecture* yet ultimately remained untranslated, Friedell presents the *Tower of Babel* as a monument that expressed discord not only in the domain of language, but also in the "religious sentiment" it reflected in the most prominent "oriental" cultures: "sacrilegious arrogance" for the "Israelites," "grave cover" for the Egyptians "building ever so high," and a mythological gesture clasping the "vault of heaven" (*Himmelsgewolbe*) for the Babylonians.[302] In his *Cultural History of the Modern Era* and in a section immediately following his discussion of surrealism, Friedell associates the Tower of Babel with "sound-film" (*Tonfilm*) decrying the lethal effect that the modern inventions of Radio and sound Kino have had on the expressive mediums of language and the human voice. "This is the Decline of the West" concludes the cultural historian transposing the Tower's biblical discord to myths of cultural degeneration in the modern era.[303]

Note that Kiesler's handwritten list of chapters for Part VI, shows that the architect initially intended to start the section, "Painters as Dream-Architects," with Bruegel's *Tower of Babel* but then changed the chapter order into a more or less chronological sequence where Bruegel appears fourth after Dürer, Leonardo, and Michelangelo. And yet this initial placement signals that the Tower of Babel, whether referring to the biblical monument or Bruegel's painted reconstruction, functions as the theoretical origin, even if an aborted or incomplete one, of "pre-magic" architecture.

Four decades after Kiesler's incomplete chapter on the biblical monument, the Tower of Babel resurfaces in the contemporary philosophy of Jacques Derrida as an oblique architectural origin. In an interview published in *Domus*, the philosopher reminds his interlocutors that the tower was originally constructed in order to dominate and "colonize" the world by means of a common language.[304] The "de/construction" of the tower represents the "foiling" of the same "plan" for "political and linguistic domination"; thus, the philosopher concludes: "If the tower had been completed, there would be no architecture. Only the incompletion of the tower makes it possible for architecture as well as the multitude of languages to have a history."[305] The interview was published in the era following the thunderous collapse of architectural modernism's presumably universal language and the emergence of a "poststructuralist babble"–the inchoate chatter auguring a host of architectural possibilities.[306] In *Magic Architecture*, Kiesler was confronted by the origin of this predicament in the years after the war and thus his incomplete manuscript is another Tower marking the postmodern dispersal of architectural languages.

Pieter Bruegel / Der Turmbau zu Babel (Wien)

9

fig. A.42 Le Corbusier, *Kommende Baukunst*, endpaper with publisher's announcement of Josef Ponten, *Architektur die nicht gebaut wurde* (1925) including pencil mark next to drawing of an unexecuted design by Christopher Wren for St. Paul's Cathedral, London. Kiesler estate library. ÖFLKS, ARCH THEO 027

fig. A.43 "Pieter Bruegel the Elder / Der Turmbau zu Babel (Wien)," illustration plate in Ernst Lewy, "Das Wesen der Sprache," *Faust - Monatsschrift für Kunst, Literatur und Musik* 4, no. 6 (1925/26): 3-12 (plate 9). reproduced in *Magic Architecture*, plate 33. ÖFLKS, CLP_6541/0

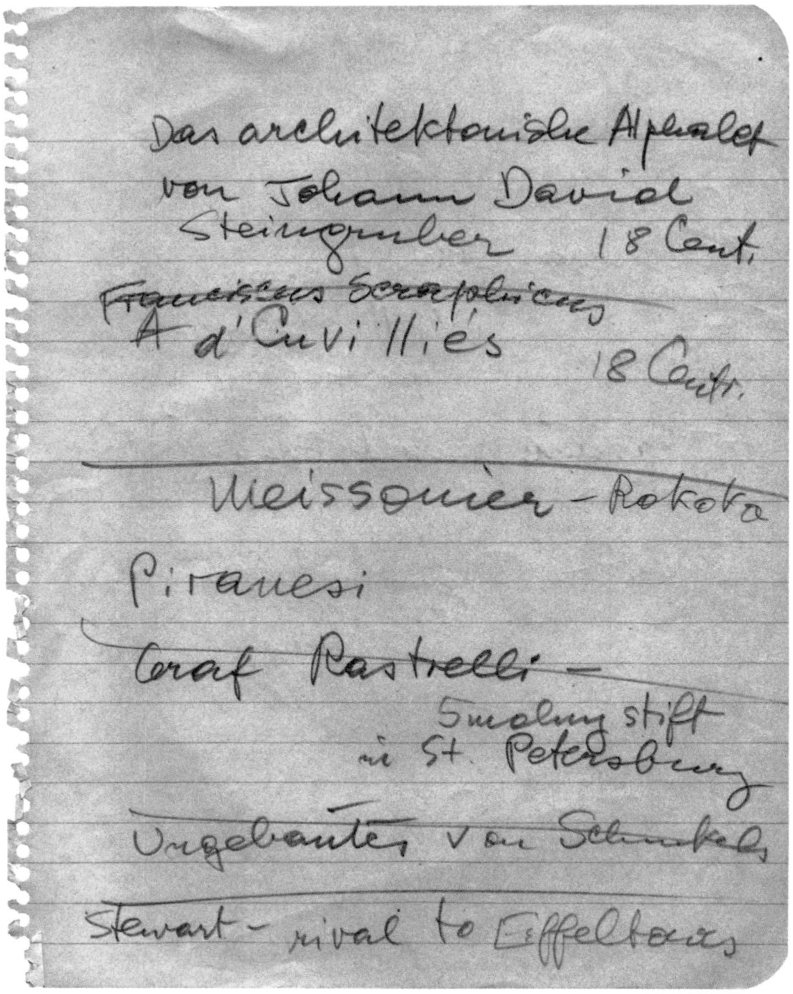

Das architektonische Alphabet
von Johann David
Steingruber 18 Cent.

~~Franciscus Seraphicus~~
A d'Cuvilliés 18 Cent.

Meissonier – Rokoko

Piranesi

~~Graf Rastrelli~~ –
Smolny stift
in St. Petersburg

~~Ungebautes von Schinkel~~

Stewart – rival to Eiffelturm

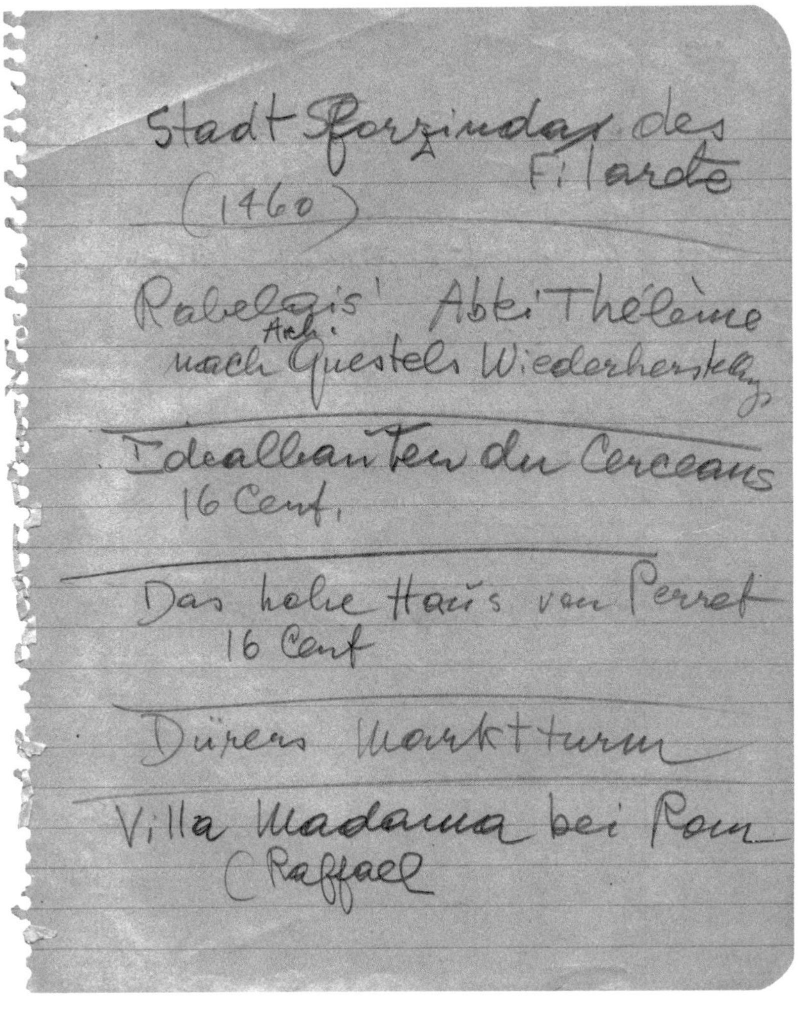

Stadt Sforzinda des
Filarete
(1460)

Rabelais' Abtei Thélème
nach Questels Wiederherstellung

Idealbauten du Cerceaus
16 Cent.

Das hohe Haus von Perret
16 Cent

Dürers Marktturm

Villa Madama bei Rom
(Raffael

figs. A.44a–b Stefi Kiesler, notes on unbuilt architectural projects transcribed from a copy of Josef Ponten, *Architektur die nicht gebaut wurde* (1925) at the New York Public Library. ÖFLKS, TXT_6878/0_N2verso and TXT_6878/0_N3verso

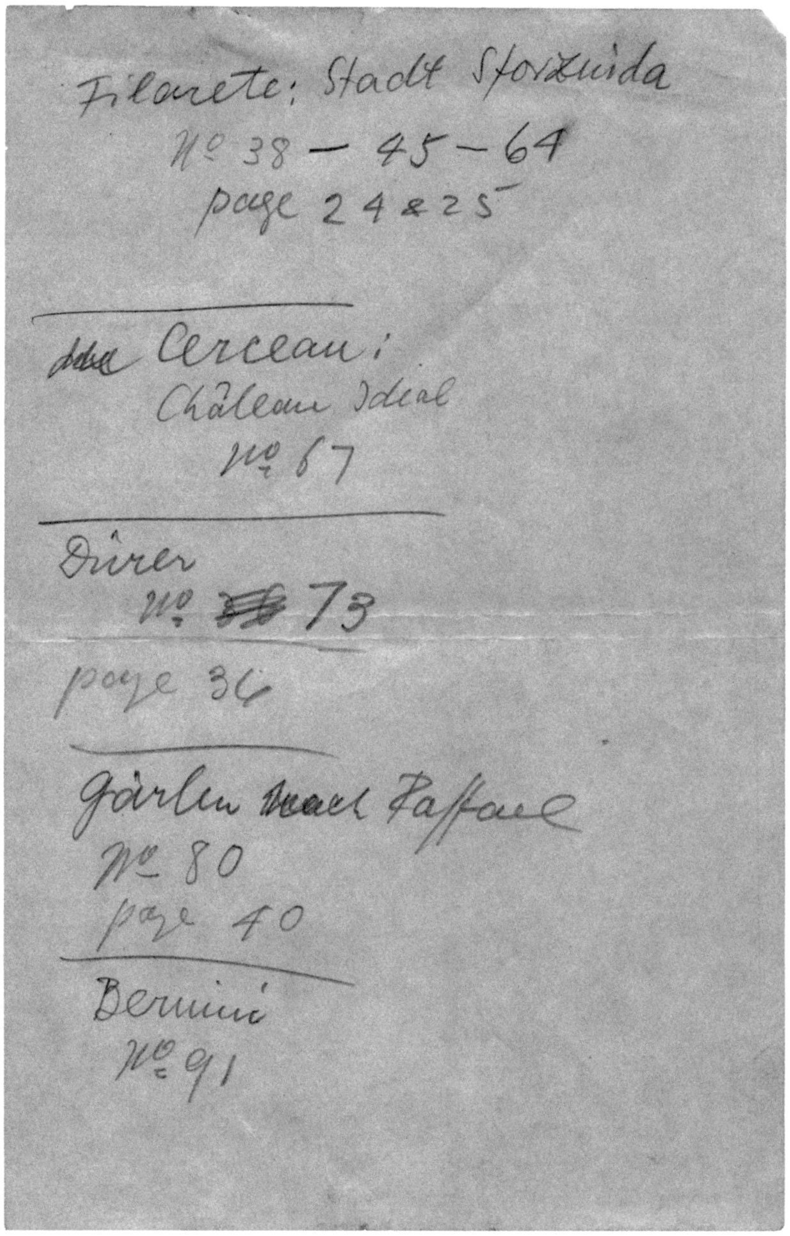

Filarete: Stadt Sforzinda
No 38 – 45 – 64
page 24 & 25

~~Idea~~ Cerceau:
Château Ideal
No 67

Dürer
No ~~[illegible]~~ 73
page 36

Gärten nach Raffael
No 80
page 40

Bernini
No 91

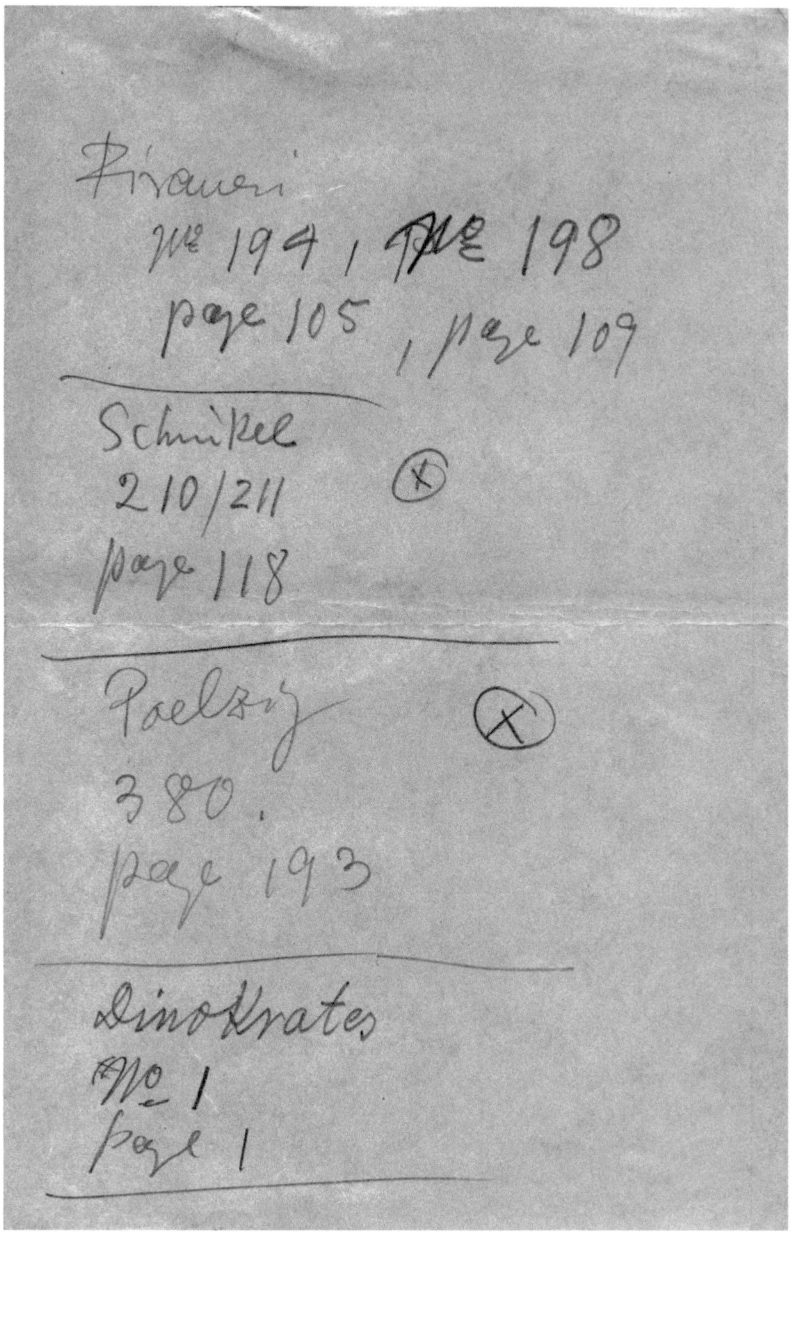

Piranesi
No 194, ~~No~~ 198
page 105, page 109

Schinkel
210/211 (x)
page 118

Poelzig (x)
380.
page 193

Dinokrates
No 1
page 1

figs. A.45a–b Frederick Kiesler, notes on unbuilt architectural projects selected for photostat reproduction from Josef Ponten, *Architektur die nicht gebaut wurde* (1925). ÖFLKS, TXT_6877/0_N1 and TXT_6877/0_N3

WHAT IS (FINALLY) MAGIC ARCHITECTURE? TOWARDS A DEFINITION

Kiesler's constant reshuffling and renumbering of his chapters, endlessly frustrating for Stefi's editorial guard, is indicative of not only the architect's personal indecision, but also suggestive of the tension between a theoretical and a historical treatment of architecture, "magic" or otherwise, and the multiple trajectories this "(hi)story" could have followed other than the one it did. Three quarters into his manuscript, and only in the introduction to the book's seventh part out of ten, he resolves to offer readers a definition of what is, finally, "Magic Architecture." The two brief paragraphs of this introduction included in the assembled typescript are only a stub of the much longer text titled "Definition" that survives in a series of manuscript and typescript drafts. This earlier text consists of a longer list of interrelated definitions formulated in short aphoristic statements separated by paragraph signs that evoke the format of a manifesto (see Main Text, figs. B.25, B.26a–b).[307] In his first statement, Kiesler boisterously declares: "*Magic Architecture* is the architecture of exuberant being."[308] Echoed in several of the architect's texts, the term "exuberance" describes a state of ontological plenitude affirming the proliferation of possibilities in the face of material adversity. One of the drafts titled "Economy and Exuberanz," written originally in German, describes Kiesler's ebullient tactics in his design for the well-known exhibition *Bloodflames 1947* at the Hugo Gallery in New York in early spring 1947–a period close to the editing phase of *Magic Architecture*.[309] Here, Kiesler associates "exuberance" with the profuse expenditure of design resources in his creation of a quasi-magical environment through the combination of architecture and painting, in spite of the constraints of the "small exhibition space" of the New York gallery: "I could transform flat walls in caves, allow low ceilings to fly upwards, stretch out room-corners and produce cavities and swellings as if by magic, where the box-lid-spirit wanted to remain stubbornly stiff."[310] Exuberance is the surrealists' response to spatial, material, and economic constraint, as is magic. Kiesler's *Magic Achitecture* formulates an equally exuberant, albeit irresolvable, response in the period after the war.

Tellingly, a similar exuberance applies to the architect's attempts towards a definition of Magic Architecture, as his statements proliferate: "Magic architecture is the expression of the creativeness of man. It is an architecture of contact; not of separation. It is the emphasis on participation, not on isolation."[311] Next to a series of "exuberant" affirmations, these brief sentences also contain an equal number of emphatic negations. The architect attempts to define *Magic Architecture* by what it is not, the architecture that it stands "in contrast to," as for example, the "dream architecture" of "temples and castles" (VII, Intro). Far from refuting the value of dreams, *Magic Architecture* attempts to rehabilitate them beyond fantasy and within the context of "reality," turning what earlier appeared as a stern refutation into a dialectical polarity. A series of even shorter aphoristic definitions scribbled by the architect on a piece of paper, perhaps the remnant of a first attempt towards a manifesto, strive precisely to bridge the space between "reality" and "dream" through architecture (see Main Text, fig. B.27):

> **Magic Architecture is the incarnation of the love for life.**
> **Magic architecture is the Reality of Dreams.**
> **Magic Architecture is Dream-Reality.**
> **Magic Architecture is the Embodiment of Dream-Reality.**
> **Magic Architecture is the Shelter of Dream-Reality.**
> **Magic Architecture is the Reality of Dreams.**
> **Magic Architecture is the Incarnation of Dream**
> **(in Reality).**[312]

The ritualistic repetition of the same two terms is no idle word play. It is as if architecture can be redefined by the magic of repetition and the variation it compels in the spatial positioning of its constitutive terms. Midway through this page, "Embodiment" is replaced by "Shelter," only to return in the end as "Incarnation." Similarly, in the fourth and middle sentence, "Dream" and "Reality" are united by a dash, even if in the final statement the "Dream" becomes disengaged from "Reality" by being placed inside brackets. Magic Architecture consists in mediated forms of contiguity and not direct material connections. The cumulative message of the variants in this inchoate manifesto is that ultimately Magic Architecture simply *is*; it marvels in the ontological exuberance of the transposable definitions of its Being.

While magic, such as the "sympathetic magic" described by Frazer, is based on a broad system of analogies and connections among distant things and persons, architecture introduces a structural division. Similar to the ontological disparities of "Animal Architecture," Magic Architecture is also a paradoxical composite attempting to amalgamate two different epistemological conditions. In the sociological terms of Kiesler's "Definition," it represents a mediation between the "isolation" of prestige granted by magic to its privileged artifacts and individual practitioners, and the inclusive right of "participation" that the architect confirms to human societies based on his reading of Lévy Bruhl, here solidified by the mediation of environmental design.

Indeed, a series of equally aphoristic statements jotted on two handwritten pages expand the definition of Magic Architecture from the domain of social ritual to an environmental process: "Magic architecture is a tool of realistic life. It performs wonders in the development of mankind, just like sunlight performs wonders in the development of plants–being a constant environmental companion. Magic architecture is a generator. It can originate on any scale. Any cell of habitation is a nucleus for a powerhouse of joyful living" (VII.Intro).[313] The "exuberance" of the initial definition now becomes spatialized and altogether reified into a powerful "tool" for vibrant living within the context of postwar biopolitics. The definition of magic discovers its architectural inscription in its diffusion into the cells of a vegetal and ultimately a housing organism. The ether of the "environment" is the most expedient medium for magic architecture's atmospheric expansion while confined in the territory of housing.

Instead of offering a definition of magic, Kiesler inadvertently offers an insight into the magical potency of "definitions," including the psychological tectonics of polarity and the epistemological analogies that support his textual structures. Kiesler affirms that Magic Architecture "holds the balance between two (human) extremes," namely, a "desire for the machine" and "the denial of science" (VII, Intro). Such magic "balance" is apparently based on a dialectic equilibrium between epistemological and "latent" psychological operations. The book is not about the "magic" of architecture, but the tectonics of thought processes behind the latent magical operations of twentieth century technologies that informed Kiesler's psycho-physiological projective designs.

Note that in at least one of the versions of the assembled manuscript, the complete text of the "Definition" appeared first in the book's front matter preceding Kiesler's prefatory "Synopsis" and his table of contents.[314] Here the "Definition" plays the role of an introductory statement, declaring in manifesto style what the "architecture" of this book is about. However, the (dis)placement of the same text in the Introduction of Part VII, now heavily truncated as well as rearranged, and having lost the word "Definition" from its title, may be even more declarative of the architect's plan. Could the insertion of a definition three quarters into the manuscript of *Magic Architecture*, mean that everything the author had been discussing for over two hundred pages was merely a preamble? Could it be that "Magic Architecture" proper is only about to start now, after the "Dream Architecture" of painters and before the literary architectures of Filarete and Campanella? Initially entitled simply "Magic Architecture," Kiesler later added the word "Towards" to the headline of his Part VII Introduction (see Main Text, fig. 36c), perhaps, in an attempt not only to mark a contrasting parallel between his book and Le Corbusier's *Vers une architecture*, but also to suggest that such a definition can only move "towards" its subject, yet never fully describe it.[315] A definition of magic is by necessity multiple and may only inscribe architecture by approximation. Yet the same "Towards" also connotes that "Magic Architecture" has not yet happened by this point, leaving the subject of its realization in this or in later parts open-ended.

In the end, the first sentence of the "Definition,"–"Magic Architecture is the architecture of exuberant being"–was crossed out by the author. Indeed, in a typescript version of his text the phrase appears barely legible behind a heavy cloud of graphite (see Main Text, fig. B.26a). Perhaps ultimately there were fewer reasons to be "exuberant" in the postwar environment of 1947 when the architect was assembling his text. And yet something of the obfuscated excitement of this original lost phrase remains, even if its presence in the typescript has turned "mystic."

UTOPIA, MYTH, AND MAGIC: REDEFINITIONS AFTER WWII

"The term magic architecture is not a utopian concept, as it might be misunderstood" forewarns Kiesler in a proposal explaining his project to publishers: "it is a natural development of technological inventions in the services of inner needs. Science and Art, Myth and Magic appear mutually interdependent in a social structure based on human rights."[316] In spite of *Magic Architecture*'s disidentification with utopia, the chapters of Part VII following the abridged text of the "Definition" transition from individual buildings to the urban scale by presenting a number of ideal cities that are at least partially identified with histories of utopia. These include the City of Dinocrates in Mount Athos (from a story told by Vitruvius, which Kiesler described after Ponten and illustrated from Fischer von Erlach), Filarete's Sforzinda, and Campanella's *City of the Sun*. Kiesler's excerpt from Campanella is transcribed from the edited anthology *Ideal Empires and Republics*, which in addition to Campanella, included Rousseau's "Social Contract" followed by Thomas More's *Utopia* and Francis Bacon's *New Atlantis*.[317] Yet Kiesler does not mention these two well-known "ideal republics."

The same list of ideal cities in Part VII initially included other imaginary urban sites by Piranesi, Scheerbart, and Taut but these were eventually crossed out. Kiesler's research material also includes a number of transcriptions from Egon Friedell's *Cultural History of Antiquity* that describe the mythological civilization of Atlantis.[318] Friedell reviews reconstructions of Atlantis from Plato onwards including a critique of Leo Frobenius's "African Atlantis." Interestingly Kiesler's transcriptions focus not on the built form of the lost city but on the epistemological architecture of its inhabitants, who had extraordinarily developed senses and, as noted previously, were able to communicate via *Telepathie* and remote radiation (*Fernstrahlung*)."[319] Friedell describes "sympathy" and "similarity," the distinguishing properties of Frazer's "sympathetic Magic," as primary powers informing the Atlantians' astonishing spatial sensibility and capacity for spatial projection:

> As we are able to grasp the exterior of everything with the greatest virtuosity, they were able to penetrate into its interior. Thus, by having truly experienced what was "happening on the inside," and how "social" relations are existing among us, similarities existed across the whole nature. Therefore, the parts of nature were almost the same to them as the limbs of our body are to us. We grasp reality by intelligence, they grasped it by "sympathy" [*Sympathie*].[320]

The Kieslers' transcriptions from Friedell on Atlantis were never translated and thus never made it into the manuscript of *Magic Architecture*. The omission of Friedell's description of Atlantis along a series of other ideal or lost cities becomes part of the modern history of Utopia that proliferates by its cancellation and historical erasure. For Kiesler, Utopia represents another prehistory of Magic Architecture among other precedents, yet it is not yet magic.

The text of the "Definition" is then strategically placed–it is not simply misplaced–in Part VII of *Magic Architecture*. It forms a new introduction to an architecture that expands into the twentieth century yet incorporates fragments from the ideal cities of Filarete, Campanella, and Taut reformed by the aesthetics of "participation" extracted from Lévy-Bruhl's primitivist sociology. The last and tenth part of *Magic Architecture* includes a plate titled "Utopias of the Machine Age" showcasing three skyscraper projects by Le Corbusier, Frank Lloyd Wright, and Kiesler in which the specter of utopia returns full circle, as in a time-machine (plate 54).

*

Among Kiesler's drafts, there is a page with miscellaneous notes containing a handwritten chart with an enumerated list of modern and ancient buildings: from the "Empire State" and the "Rockefeller, RCA" Towers to Kiesler's "Mobile Home Library" as well as a "floor-plan" from "Egypt" and "Greece" (underneath which lies the name of "Corbusier" crossed out next to Kiesler's "Space House" as another alternative) (fig. A.46).[321] The same page includes an additional definition of *Magic Architecture* written next to a preliminary version of Kiesler's previously mentioned diagram illustrating the development from "Myth to Architecture" and its cultural circles, "under," "on," "above," and "beyond" the earth, stratified by a mythological narrative Kiesler had discovered in Frobenius (cf. fig. A.46 with Main Text, fig. B.04 and plate 2a).[322] This alternative definition hastily scribbled at the bottom of the page expands the topological progression of the diagram to a psychological level: "Magic architecture is the omnipotence of desire and thought made real, built concrete." "Omnipotence" signals one of Kiesler's references to Freudian concepts, specifically the theoretical confluence of "Animism, Magic, and Omnipotence of Thought" in the homonymous third chapter of the psychoanalyst's *Totem and Taboo*.[323] Magic Architecture represents the moment when such magical "omnipotence" becomes not simply real, but "concrete," that is to say "built"–even if such "concrete" building is projected next to a geometric diagram, whose epistemological foundation relies on an Indigenous myth.

References to the history or practice of magic are relatively rare in *Magic Architecture*. Most are concentrated in Part IV with a study of myth. In the "Meaning of Magic" (IV.1), Kiesler discovers magic at the core of every human artifact, calling it "the mother of invention." In Part I, "Artificial power was Magic" (I.8). Just like Magic Architecture, magic is a powerful "tool," yet as Kiesler comments in Part IV, the word had partly fallen into "disrepute" because of its modern association with technological "gadgetry" and the architectural "thaumaturgy" of design "prestidigitators" from Buckminster Fuller back to Piranesi.[324] Kiesler further criticizes the "historians," "chroniclers," and "interpreters" of magic as "confusers" who usurp the work of the original "creators" of magic (IV. 1). Even if in his manuscript Kiesler acts as an idiosyncratic historian of Magic Architecture, he essentially thinks of himself as one of the initiated practitioners of magic, summoning his design skills to create "magical environments" like the one engineered at the Hugo Gallery.

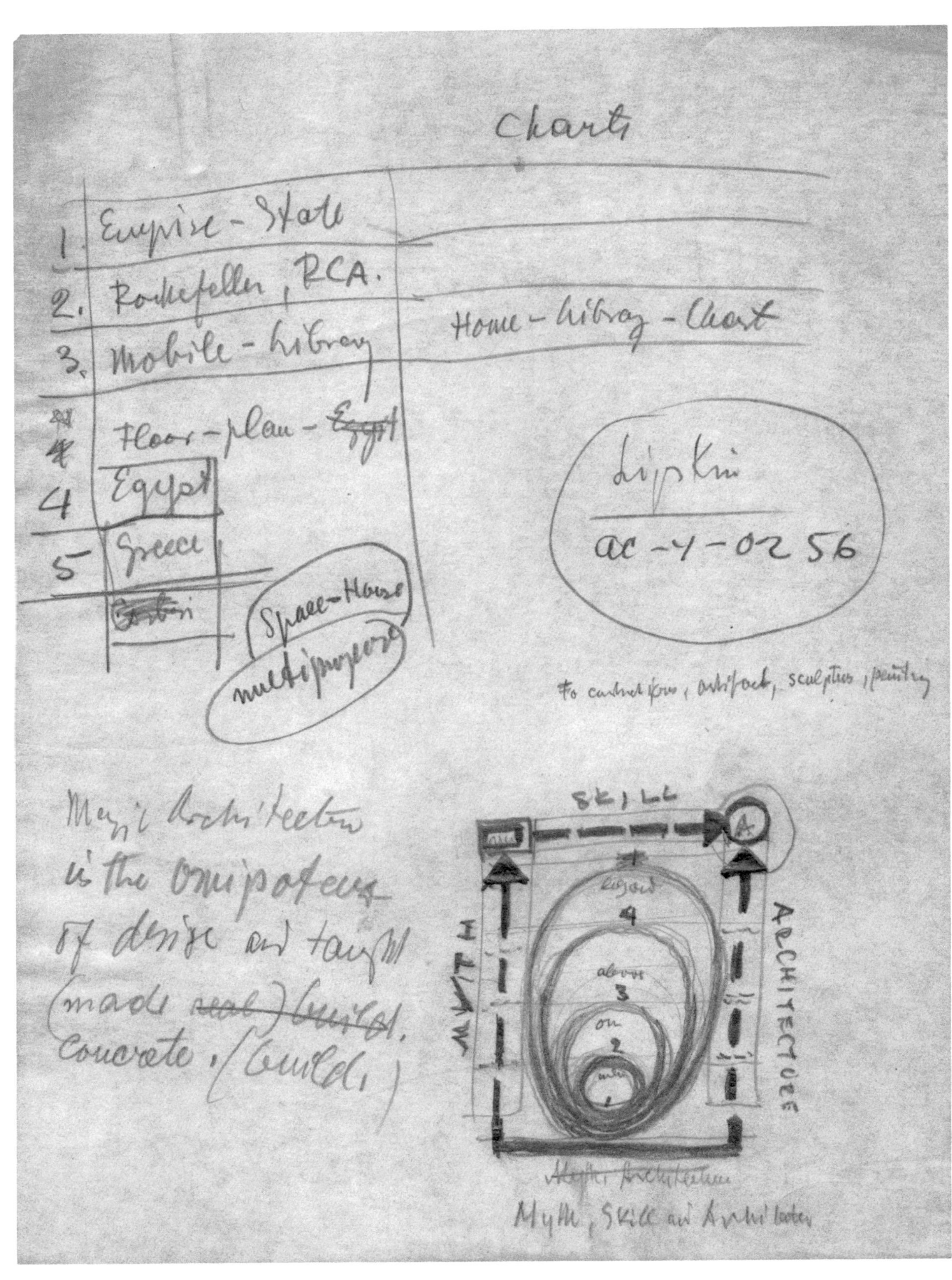

fig. A.46 Frederick Kiesler, MS draft with miscellaneous notes.
ÖFLKS, TXT_6749_0_N1

While criticizing the "historians," Kiesler quotes extensively from the work of the preeminent historian of medieval science and magic, Lynn Thorndike. In passages from the second volume of his *History of Magic and Experimental Science* transcribed by the Kieslers, Thorndike underscores the continuity of modern science and medieval magic with which histories of scientific practice remain inextricably connected.[325] In a later chapter of *Magic Architecture* titled "Myth and Magic" (IV.4), Kiesler includes an excerpt from an article by the English scholar Richard (Volney) Chase, "Notes on the Study of Myth" (the text is mentioned earlier in relation to Chase's references to mana and (pre)animism).[326] Other than a "compulsive technique or a pseudo-science as Frazer would say it," magic for Chase "is obviously an esthetic activity. Magic is immediately available to art, and art to magic." (IV.4) The contiguity between magic and art is key for Kiesler's description of the origins of Magic Architecture in practices of "sympathetic magic" informing bodily adornment in Part III. Chase further describes myth as "a blaze of reality"–a force that remains active in the world and not something "vaporous, abstract, or unreal." (IV.4) The emphasis on the "reality" of myth echoes Kiesler's definition of Magic Architecture as "the embodiment of dream-reality" in his handwritten manifesto. Yet such emphasis on "reality" also invokes the political repercussions of the study of myth in the interwar era, particularly the circle around Georges Bataille and the "College of Sociology" in Paris, aiming to deconstruct the association between myth and fascism–a project that would acquire renewed urgency after the collapse of totalitarian regimes at the end of World War II.[327] *Magic Architecture* is essentially an attempt towards a redefinition of both myth and magic in the areas of housing and architectural design, even if Kiesler's historiographic montage ends up remythologizing both.

The highly fragmented story of *Magic Architecture* appears in total contrast to the much more systematic attempt by Kiesler's fellow surrealist Kurt Seligmann in his *Mirror of Magic* published in 1948 by Pantheon Books–the publishing house founded by the close friend of the Kieslers, Kurt Wolff.[328] As described in its subtitle, Seligmann's book is an analytic "history of Magic in the Western world" describing magical techniques from the ancient Near East and Greco-Roman worlds to the Medieval and Renaissance eras and up to the eighteenth century in Europe. Critics noted that its chthonic iconography of tarot monsters and demons aimed to act apotropaicly in warding off the evil associations between magic and the fascist usurpation of power.[329] While Seligmann had previously published a multitude of essays on magic in the art journals *View* and *VVV*, to which Kiesler also contributed during the war, neither his studies nor his name are mentioned in *Magic Architecture*.[330] And yet such absence may connote the presence of a "history" that *Magic Architecture* did not want to become.

This is also the case with André Breton's references to magic and the occult before the 1947 International Exhibition of Surrealism in Paris spearheaded by Breton and Marcel Duchamp, in which Kiesler participated, and which was heavily invested in the ideas of "magic" and "superstition."[331] Kiesler and Breton shared an interest in the relation between magic and the "everyday," which the latter would formulate into the concept of "everyday magic [*magie quotidienne*]."[332] However Kiesler's *Magic Architecture* shares many correspondences with Breton's last large book, *L'Art Magique* first published in 1957.[333] *L'Art Magique* is a wide-ranging history of art from cave paintings to surrealism, as well as nineteenth-century symbolist and twentieth-century expressionist artworks. There are a few overlaps with Kiesler's magic gallery of paintings, such as Hieronymus Bosch's *The Garden of Earthly Delights*, a detail of which is featured in one of the plates of *Magic Architecture* (plate 40X).

L'Art Magique also cites the Tower of Babel twice, including a mention on its first paragraphs: "To enter even slightly into the heart of the controversy unleashed by the mere word magic, is to expose oneself to the oscillations of the last steps of the Tower of Babel." The author alludes to the "struggles" among the "supporters and contemptors" of magical power that "fight one another" while barricaded in their respective ideological "camps."[334] Breton's extensive introduction connects magic to animism though references to the "mistaking of the ideal for the real" in Tylor and the "law of sympathy" in Frazer including the distinction between the use of "similarity" in "imitative" and "contiguity in space and time" in "contagious" magic, as well as other theories of magic by Freud, Mauss, and Lévi-Strauss, who was one of the critical respondents in Breton's "questionnaire" appended at the end of the book.[335]

The second chapter (out of three) of *L'Art Magique* also contains a few pages on "the origins of architecture," which Breton associates with the "forest and the grotto." Breton describes architecture as "the most utilitarian of the arts" and which "one sees today subjected to the most hideous functionalism. Mimeticism had to play a role. The gigantic constructions of the termites, the floral galleries of some birds [...] testify that nature did not wait for humans to invent architecture."[336] Breton's textual and pictorial references to the magic properties of architecture skim through a wide array of buildings, from Stonehenge to Babylonian ziggurats and from prehistoric caves and picturesque grottos to the Theater of Bezançon by Claude-Nicolas (mistakenly mentioned as Pierre-Nicolas) Ledoux , echoing some of Kiesler's own assortment of (pre) magical architectures. In this section, the "mythical Tower of Babel" appears for a second time as an "accursed archetype" (*archetype maudit*),[337] contributing what Bataille would have described as an "accursed share" (*part maudite*) in the generalized discord of architectural languages after the war.

Following its publication, Breton's *L'Art Magique* was heavily criticized by contemporary reviewers, including several of the respondents to the questions of Breton's "survey" appended at the end of his book, for its "too grand elasticity" (as noted by Claude Lévi-Strauss) in the use of the terms "magic" and "art," as well as the haphazard assortment of images and theories from heterogeneous sources, authors, and eras.[338] In the words of Roger Caillois: "There is no Magic Art. The concept is contradictory: it does not reveal a decisive complicity, it introduces a factual unity in a scattering of subsidiary, evasive and supernumerary relations, which make it possible to find works of art of magical origin almost everywhere and in all epochs."[339]

A similar criticism could apply to Kiesler's *Magic Architecture*, had it been published. Following Caillois, one could also object that there is no Magic Architecture. Like "Animal Architecture," Kiesler's whole project is indeed a contradiction and reveals a manufactured "unity" between two asymmetrical terms. It may then almost appear as a relief that in some versions Kiesler's manuscript is titled *Everyman's Architecture*, and the term "magic" has been demoted to a subtitle–a demotion that is as equally mystifying as the word's original appearance on Kiesler's book project.[340]

POLITICS AT THE MARGINS: WAR AND COLONIALISM–TRANSCRIPTIONS AND DELETIONS

Magic may in fact reflect less the content of *Magic Architecture* in which explicit references to magic are sparse than the "sympathetic similarities" in *method* the text shares with the secretive operations of magic covertly embedded in its fabric. This structural secrecy applies to Kiesler's marginal references to contemporary politics and the events of the war, which, in spite of their blaring presence in the context of *Magic Architecture*, remain inaudible in its assembled manuscript.

Indeed, other than a few general observations on the state of world historical affairs in the first half of the twentieth century

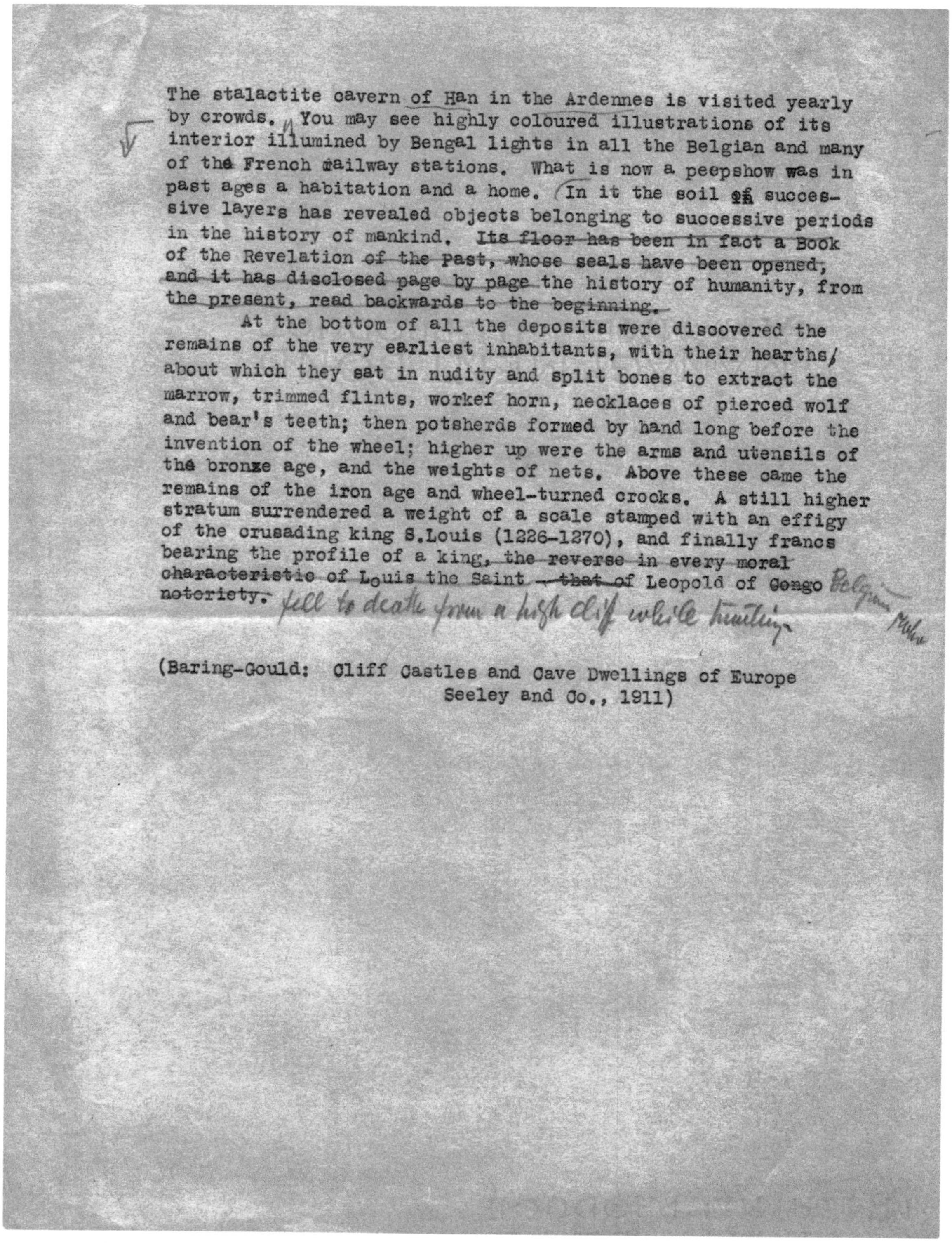

The stalactite cavern of Han in the Ardennes is visited yearly by crowds. You may see highly coloured illustrations of its interior illumined by Bengal lights in all the Belgian and many of the French railway stations. What is now a peepshow was in past ages a habitation and a home. In it the soil of successive layers has revealed objects belonging to successive periods in the history of mankind. ~~Its floor has been in fact a Book~~ of the Revelation ~~of the Past, whose seals have been opened, and it has disclosed page by page~~ the history of humanity, from ~~the present, read backwards to the beginning.~~

At the bottom of all the deposits were discovered the remains of the very earliest inhabitants, with their hearths, about which they sat in nudity and split bones to extract the marrow, trimmed flints, workef horn, necklaces of pierced wolf and bear's teeth; then potsherds formed by hand long before the invention of the wheel; higher up were the arms and utensils of the bronze age, and the weights of nets. Above these came the remains of the iron age and wheel-turned crocks. A still higher stratum surrendered a weight of a scale stamped with an effigy of the crusading king S.Louis (1226-1270), and finally francs bearing the profile of a king, ~~the reverse in every moral characteristic of~~ Louis the Saint ~~- that of~~ Leopold of ~~Congo~~ Belgian ~~notoriety.~~ fell to death from a high cliff while hunting

(Baring-Gould: Cliff Castles and Cave Dwellings of Europe
Seeley and Co., 1911)

fig. A.47 Frederick and Stefi Kiesler, transcription of *Sabine Baring-Gould, Cliff Castles and Cave Dwellings of Europe* (Philadelphia: Lippincott / London: Seeley and Co., 1911), 28–29, with handwritten emendations by Frederick Kiesler. TXT_6815/0_N2 synopsized in the last part of Kiesler's "story,"[341] politics appear rather clandestinely in *Magic Architecture* through a series of conscious deletions or inadvertent omissions found in the architect's own text and even more frequently in his transcriptions and quotations from the texts of other authors, who refer more explicitly to issues of historical context. "Refinding" this lost content requires careful exploration of the margins and the marginalia scribbled on the manuscript, as well as an archaeological descent into the historical layers that lay beyond its surface.

For example, in the last paragraph of his chapter on the cave (I.6) Kiesler shifts, rather unexpectedly, to a book on "cave dwellings" by the nineteenth-century British antiquarian Sabine Baring-Gould and to a brief excerpt on the "stalactite caverns of Han in the Ardennes" in Belgium.[342] Starting from their contemporary predicament as an artificially illuminated attraction for massive tourist crowds, the British author makes a stratigraphic section of the cave's subterranean layers based on the archaeological discovery of residues from several eras found in the underground sites of this network of caverns. In a phrase transcribed yet crossed out by Kiesler, Baring-Gould describes the caverns' "floor" as "a book of Revelation of the Past, whose seals have been opened" and which "has disclosed page by page the history of humanity, from the present, read backwards to the beginning."[343] (fig. A.47) This history spans from vestiges of "hearths" as well as "arms and utensils" from pre- and protohistoric "inhabitants" to the "weight of a scale" that bore "the effigy of the crusading king S. Louis" and "finally francs bearing the profile of a king, the reverse in every moral characteristic of Louis the Saint–that of Leopold of Congo notoriety." While the text of *Magic Architecture* preserves the rest of the transcribed paragraphs from Baring-Gould, Kiesler crosses out the words "Congo notoriety" and writes "Leopold, of Belgium, who fell to his death from a high cliff while hunting."[344] In a later typescript, the last phrase was revised to: "whose son [meaning Leopold's] fell to death from a cliff while hunting."[345] Both of these references are inaccurate. It was Leopold II's nephew, Albert I, who succeeded the infamous King on the Belgian throne in 1909, and who died while mountaineering on a cliff in the Ardennes, near Namur in Belgium, in 1934–a fatal royal accident sensationalized in the news across both sides of the Atlantic. Note that the same rough forest and mountain range of the Ardennes described by Baring-Gould in 1911, would later become the site of a series of ferocious battles in both world wars of the twentieth century, resulting in thousands of human casualties on both enemy sides. While erasing the colonial reference to the atrocities of Leopold's "Belgian Congo," Kiesler's doubly erroneous emendation also reburies a multitude of additional "remains" recovered from the first half of the twentieth century that were piled on top of the caverns' prehistoric and medieval geological strata.

And the same elision of historical references to war and colonialism happens a number of times during the process of transcription and transference from book to manuscript and to typescript. Kiesler's chapter on the "Aztec Pyramid and Dwellings" in Part V starts with a paragraph transcribed from *The Aztecs: History, Customs, and their Manners* (1887) by the French colonial author Lucien Biart, specifically the conclusion of the book's ninth chapter that refers to the inequitable social organization of the Aztecs torn between the "luxury" of the royal court and the misery of its "people," who were "oppressed [and] badly fed." The chapter's final paragraph ends with the phrase: "Oppressor and oppressed: do not these two words, unfortunately, sum up the history of man in all ages and in all countries?"[346] This last question could apply to the history not only of the ancient Mesoamerican empire, but also that of Modern France and its own colonial empire to which, Biart, as stated in his "necrology" published in the French *Journal of Americanists*, rendered "inestimable services" during the second French colonial invasion of Mexico in the 1860s.[347] But this exact question was omitted from the Kieslers' transcription and the manuscript of *Magic Architecture*.[348]

Nevertheless, Kiesler's Main Text acknowledges the effects of imperialism and colonialism particularly on architecture. In his general Introduction and in partial opposition to Biart, who situates the split between an architecture of resplendent courtly monuments and the "profane" homes for the common people in a precolonial era in the Americas, Kiesler describes the latter as an effect perpetuated by Western colonization:

> **Society consequently divided shelter into two main categories: one for the exercise of profane functions–the home; and the other for exercising spiritual functions–temples of worship. This split is so standardized, particularly in Western civilization, that it was imported into the Americas by the colonizing Spaniards as well as by the Pilgrims; and with it came the continual attempt to falsify the spiritual quality of architecture by the use of fashionable esthetic patterns - a decorative camouflage, it was and still is as short-lived as the business cycle from which it springs.** (Main Text, "Introduction")

Kiesler then attributes to colonialism the "importation" and simultaneous exportation not only of a certain building model of social and political hierarchy, but also the "decorative camouflage" applied on the same building type to conceal and enhance colonialism's "business cycle" via a heavy layer of stylized ornamentation. Both the building typology and its decorative cover exported to the colonies regurgitate an array of styles from Spanish baroque, British Neo-Palladianism, and French neoclassicism to twentieth-century American and European "decorativism," which Kiesler vociferously criticizes in several parts of his manuscript.[349] While widely associative, the transhistorical arc drawn by the architect traces the roots of nineteenth-century "ornamentalism" and twentieth-century "decorativism" to the colonial expansion of global commerce and capital, including its postcolonial circulation to and from "developing" countries, after the end of World War II.[350]

War itself does not explicitly appear in the architect's text other than in these few sentences in his epilogue as well as his book proposal sent to publishers. Yet a few marginal details in texts or documents omitted or "cropped out" from his presentation of the assembled manuscript disclose the presence of several recent wars preceding or following the end of World War II. For example, the brief article from a 1945 issue of the *Bulletin of the Metropolitan Museum of Art* quoted in Kiesler's chapter on El Greco's *View of Toledo* (VI.6) as the work of a "painter-architect" contains an additional sentence omitted from the Kieslers' transcription, which references the events of the Spanish Civil War in Toledo during the siege of Alcázar in 1936: "Foursquare beyond the cathedral stands the massive Alcazar, the stronghold which succumbed a few years ago only after months of continuous shelling."[351]

A similarly informative omission can be found in Kiesler's transcription of a partial republication of the "Essay on Theology" by the nineteenth-century agnostic biologist and evolutionist philosopher Thomas Henry Huxley in a 1944 issue of the literary journal *Encore*.[352] Kiesler selects only two paragraphs from Huxley's essay for the Introduction to Part V. They serve mainly as a polemical epigram for the following chapters that together describe the destructive role of religion and in particular Christian ritual based on pagan "image worship" as a source of power for terrifying and controlling people. Religious art and architecture play an essential role in the project of social control. The phrases by Huxley omitted from the assembled text of *Magic Architecture* make the case for the selection of his essay even stronger, as they disclose the power of images to capture the faithful by means of sublime terror: "Dante's 'Inferno' would be revolting if it were not so often sublime, so often exquisitely tender. The hideous pictures which cover a vast

HERALD TRIBUNE, FRIDAY, AUGUST

As Paris Celebrated the Surrender of Japan

Herald Tribune—Acme

The Eiffel Tower illuminated by searchlights following the officia[l] announcement of Japan's surrender to the Allies

fig. A.48 Template for plate 53, "The Eiffel Tower illuminated by searchlights following the official announcement of Japan's surrender to the Allies," from "As Paris Celebrated the Surrender of Japan," *New York Herald Tribune*, August 17, 1945. ÖFLKS, CLP_7179/0

space on the south wall of the Campo Santo of Pisa convey information, as terrible as it is indisputable, of the theological conceptions of Dante's countrymen in the fourteenth century, whose eyes were addressed by the painters of those disgusting scenes, and whose approbation they knew how to win."[353] The essay refers to the fourteenth-century frescoes of the *Last Judgment* and *Hell* (attributed to Buonamico Buffalmacco) on the south wall of the Camposanto monumental cemetery in Pisa, admired by Huxley's contemporary Pre-Raphaelite artists in Britain. As World War II came to an end, the Camposanto murals would appear again in the news at the end of July 1944 following a fire caused by a stray shell that caused extensive damage to the works. Images of the devastated site were featured in art history publications of that time documenting the restoration that started the following year.[354]

Moving closer to the end of the war, the image of an illuminated Eifel Tower at night in one of *Magic Architecture*'s last plates (see plate 53) was reproduced from a newspaper clipping of the August 17, 1945 edition of the *New York Herald Tribune* (fig. A.48). The newspaper section bears the heading: "As Paris Celebrated the Surrender of Japan," and the photo-caption: "The Eiffel Tower illuminated by searchlights following the official announcement of Japan's surrender to the allies."[355] In this clip, the history of the use of iron technology in nineteenth-century architecture, deemed pioneering and liberatory for twentieth-century historians of modern architecture like Sigfried Giedion, appears to spectacularly reverberate another form of liberation.[356] Kiesler offers an ambivalent celebration of the Tower as "a superfluous monument from a physio-functional point of view, but *the* very necessity for a link with the superfluous." (X.4) And yet the date of the newspaper photograph also discloses that it was published after a little more than a week following the second atomic bomb, and a week prior to the first atomic "accident" in the Los Alamos laboratory (also recorded among Kiesler's clippings).[357] Ultimately the most covert yet essential presence of magic in Kiesler *Magic Architecture* can be found in the latent presence of the political and historical omissions registered underneath the text attesting to the reverberative power of silence.

"DANCE OF DEATH": SPIRITUALIZED ECONOMY, ROCOCO DECORATION, AND THE PULVERIZATION OF MATERIALS

Similar to politics, certain references to economy are elided in *Magic Architecture*'s assembled manuscript. For example, the word "capital" is often substituted by other less charged economic terms, as in phrases in the final chapter of the manuscript commenting on the socio-economic transformations in France at the "end of the eighteenth century," when "the equal distribution of the fruits of the Revolution was transformed into profiteering" (X.10). In Kiesler's handwritten edits to Stefi's typescript, while revising the phrase "everywhere capital's profit was enormous," Kiesler crosses out "capital" and replaces it with "interest." He then crosses out "interest" and replaces it with "investment." Then he replaces the "It" in the beginning of the following sentence originally referring to "capital" with "Commerce" (fig. A.49). A few sentences earlier on the same page, Kiesler had also substituted "capital" with "commerce."[358] Neither "commerce" nor "investment," nor "interest" fit exactly the meaning of these sentences. Capital's deletions leave an awkward trace.

Another notable deletion occurs in the Kieslers' transcription from the preface to *The Empire of Dreamers*, a gloriously pessimist description of the cultural geography of Austria by the Germanophile Austrian author Hanns Sassmann published in 1932. Excerpted from the book's methodological preface, one of the paragraphs marked for transcription by Kiesler refers to the division of historiography into two historical systems (*Geschichtsysteme*)

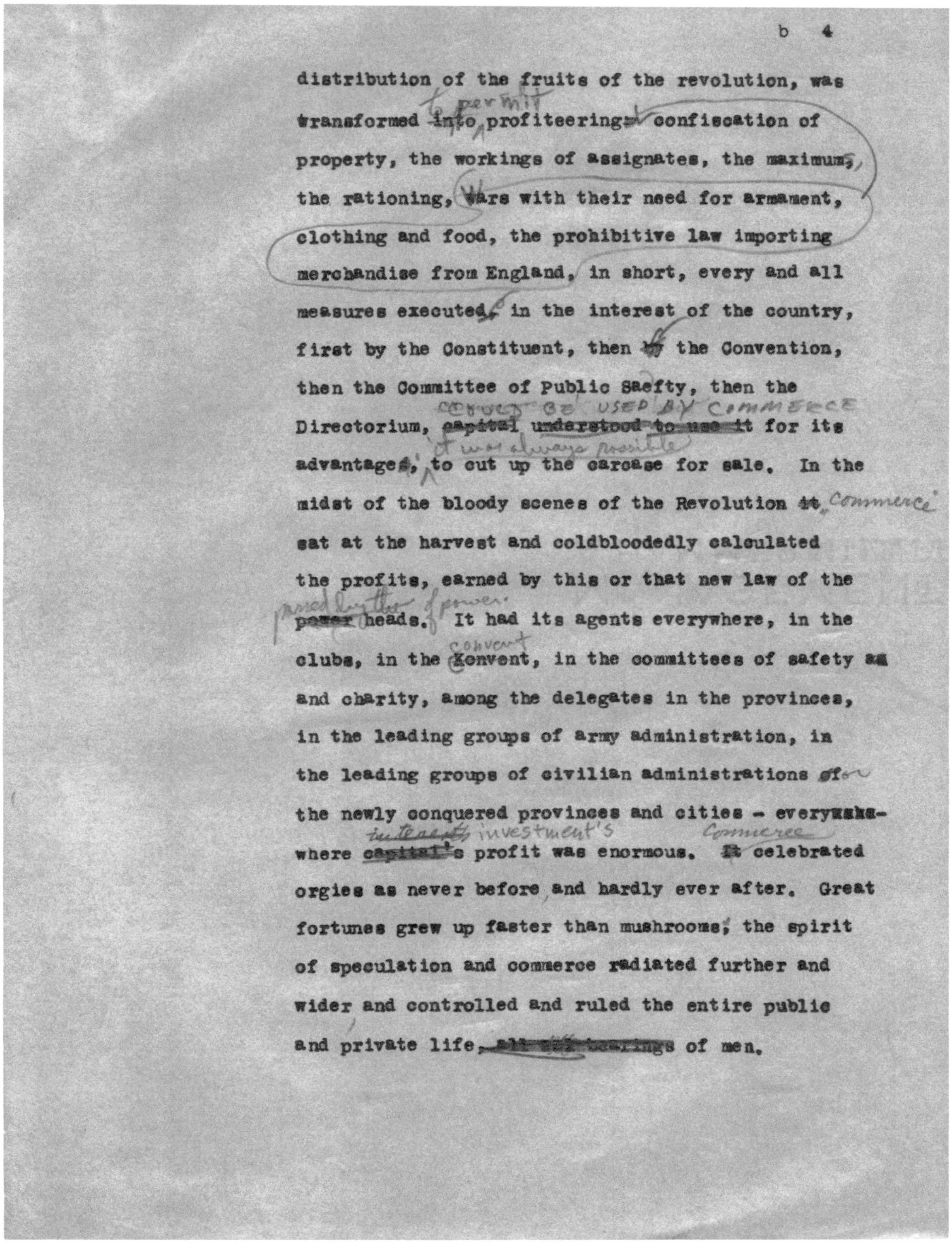

b 4

distribution of the fruits of the revolution, was transformed into profiteering: confiscation of property, the workings of assignates, the maximum, the rationing, wars with their need for armament, clothing and food, the prohibitive law importing merchandise from England, in short, every and all measures executed, in the interest of the country, first by the Constituent, then by the Convention, then the Committee of Public Saefty, then the Directorium, capital understood to use it for its advantages, to cut up the carcase for sale. In the midst of the bloody scenes of the Revolution it sat at the harvest and coldbloodedly calculated the profits, earned by this or that new law of the power heads. It had its agents everywhere, in the clubs, in the Konvent, in the committees of safety an and charity, among the delegates in the provinces, in the leading groups of army administration, in the leading groups of civilian administrations of the newly conquered provinces and cities - everywhere where capital's profit was enormous. It celebrated orgies as never before and hardly ever after. Great fortunes grew up faster than mushrooms; the spirit of speculation and commerce radiated further and wider and controlled and ruled the entire public and private life, all its bearings of men.

fig. A.49 Frederick and Stefi Kiesler, TS draft of Part X, "Epilogue and Prologue," with handwritten emendations by Frederick Kiesler (including deletion and substitution of the word "capital"—twice).
ÖFLKS, TXT_6720/0_N5

namely "the ideological and the materialistic conceptions of history [*ideologische und materialistische Geschichtsauffassung*], the latter also known as Marxist view of history according to its founder Karl Marx [*nach ihrem Begründer Karl Marx auch marxistische Geschichtsbetrachtung*]."[359] In the Kieslers' transcription (typed by Stefi), this last phrase on Marx and Marxist historiography is conspicuously missing—and in fact none of the excerpts from Sassmann's book were translated and thus never appended at the conclusion of the introduction to Part x as Kiesler originally intended.[360] Perhaps, then, the avoidance of the word "capital" was due not only to its association with capitalist and anti-capitalist (that is to say "communist") societies and economic systems, but also with a well-known homonymous book by an unnamable author.

Finally in the transcription and translation of a description of Filarete's Sforzinda from Ponten's *Architecture Never Built*, the text quoted in *Magic Architecture* omits one of Ponten's parenthetical remarks with a bitterly sardonic comparison between the merciless working conditions of Sforzinda's builders guarded by infantry and the military under the presence of the King (and where "disobedience [was] punished by death") and the contemporary state of building labor following the strives of the workers rights' movement in Weimar Germany: "The plagued master-builders of today see how easy it is to solve the issues of social welfare [*die Fragen der Sozialfürsorge*] of the right to strike and the right to organize [*des Streik- und Koalitionsrechtes*]."[361] This half-quoted passage is one of the few references to building labor in *Magic Architecture*, even if the main preoccupation of its author was the inequitable housing of "the people who build" history's luxurious "Dream Architectures."

The cryptic nature of some of these political and economic references could partly be interpreted by the political climate in the US with its public aversion of communism and workers' movements, particularly at the end of World War II and the beginning of the Cold War—a climate that was especially threatening for the Kieslers, considering their status as Jewish-Austrian émigrés (even if Kiesler became a US citizen in 1936), and Stefi's employment at a public institution In New York, the couple was close to left-wing intellectual circles, and Kiesler corresponded with the editors of the *Partisan Review* where he published two of his articles in the second half of the 1940s.[362]

More general references to systems of socio-economic distribution demonstrate an aversion to the effects of the accumulation of wealth on architecture through the ages, from the "plutocratic dwellings" of ancient Egypt (V.2) to the ornate interiors of European rococo and finally the "false capitalism" of modern economy and its "cathedrals of commerce," where the "ancient Religion of Gods was finally replaced by the religion of goods. The question was not: to be or not to be; the question was: to have or not to have" (X.6). But after the First World War, a "new revolutionary spirit" in Europe created a major shift: "Freed from imperialism, tzarism, and monarchism, the populace began to plan on a large scale for the realization of better social systems, and, logically, their every-day architects (in the past immune to progress) designed better architectural orders" (X.6).[363]

This correlation between "better social systems" and "better architectural orders" (meaning "systems" rather than styles) leading to general "progress" has its roots in an earlier set of theoretical charts. One titled "Progression-Chart of Architecture" was sketched in the early 1930s. Another of these diagrams titled "Morphology-Chart of Architecture" was appended to Kiesler's article with theoretical "annotations at random" on his *Space House* project published in 1934.[364] (figs. A.50a-b) Kiesler's table essentially constructs a complex set of relations which link the historical "progression" between forms of "continuity" in human creativity—from "craft," to "art," "applied art," "technique [mechanical art]" and culminating to "science"—and "typical" (meaning typological) "manifestation" of such "continuity" in architectural structures—from "shelters" and "temples," to "residences," "factories" or "[industrial] plants" and finally "community planning." These building types also correlate with the "social aspect" of "continuity" that describes a linear "development" of political and economic systems, from "patriarchy" to "monarchy," "plutocracy," "democracy," and finally "commonwealth" (replaced by "communalism" in the printed version of the chart).[365] Yet building typologies and social systems represent only two of the correlated factors in the architect's chart; five additional columns represent similarly abridged lineages of "function," "material," "plan method," "construction method," and "life span"—an entire constellation of factors, which synergistically inform a "progression" from prehistory to the present (and implicitly the future) of architecture as an all-encompassing "science." Like every genealogy, the column of the chart's "social aspects" progresses via both continuity and rupture.

There are at least ten different versions of the chart in which the terms occupying the squares are fluctuating, occasionally moving up or down on the chart grid.[366] For example, in the column of "social aspects", "patriarchate" alternates with "tribalism," "theocracy" with "deism," "monarchy" with "kingdom (probably from the German *Reich* meaning also empire)" and "slavery," "plutocracy" with "feudalism" and "oligarchy," "democracy" with "industrialism" and "capitalism," and finally "commonwealth" with "socialism" and "communalism." In the printed version of the chart, "Democracy" has been noticeably replaced by "Capitalism," which is further correlated with modern industrial "Plants" and "Mechanical Art" (perhaps a pointer to Le Corbusier's "house as a machine for living") juxtaposed with the "Communalism" of "Community Planning" and "Science"—pointing to Kiesler's own developing science of Correalist Design.

More than a decade later, Kiesler sketched another chart tabling the progression from "Animal" to "Magic Architecture" following "Dream Architecture" and the "Architecture of Imagination"—each of which corresponds to a building type: from "Shelters" to "Temples," "Palaces" and finally "Homes," meaning Kiesler's own version of "housing" from the *Space House* to the embryonic versions of his *Endless House* (see Addenda, fig. C.11).[367] Yet while this smaller and more compact chart in *Magic Architecture* includes columns outlining additional genealogies from "materialism" to "(created) Reality" and from "Facts" and "Vision" to the projected "Unity" between the two, it lacks the column on social systems that traversed the 1930s "Morphology" chart. Once again explicit references to politics and economy have been omitted, yet they implicitly mold the historical scaffolding that supports *Magic Architecture*.

Another correlation present in the 1930s yet absent in the 1940s chart was the correspondence between socio-political systems not only with building "types" but also with types of materials such as "natural," "artificial," "composite," "synthetic" or "diversely manufactured" along with corresponding material techniques such as "compression," "viscidity," "suspension," and "continuous tension" (fig. A.50b). This correlation between the (d)evolution of material forms and corresponding building techniques along with the transformation of socio-economic systems gives another spin to the Marxist "materialist conception of history" mentioned earlier in Kiesler's omitted quotation from Sassmann. Indeed while absent from his 1940s chart, Kiesler's concluding chapter in *Magic Architecture* describes a process in which materials like wood and stone become "domesticated" and then enslaved to the "human will" until finally "[t]o suppress the urge toward freedom of material—live or dead—man finally crushed it completely, destroyed its form and function, literally pulverized it." (X.10) In an illustrated diagram sketched at the margins of one of his preliminary book proposals, Kiesler illustrates through a series of miniscule drawings how building materials and architectural forms during the "*Dekadenz*"

Caps — follow copy

A R C H I T E C T U R E

PROGRESSION	ITS TYPICAL MANIFESTATION	ITS SOCIAL ASPECT	ITS BUILDING MATERIAL	ITS METHOD OF PLAN	ITS CONSTRUCTION METHOD	ITS ECONOMIC ASPECT	ITS PERIOD
CRAFT ↓	→ Shelter	Patriarchate	Natural Circumjacent	Direct Structural Simplification	Continuous-Compression, Tension	Utilitarian Solids, Frams and Skin	Temporary
ART ↓	→ Temples	Kingdom	Natural Interjacent	Indirect Architectural Basical	Compression and Tension	Super-function Blocks	Permanent
APPLIED ART ↓	→ Residences	Oligarchy	Natural and Artificial Domestic and Imported	Indirect Figurative Conglomeration	Viscidity ~~Compression and Tension~~	Shielding Function Multi-materialed piece-work	Accidental
TECHNIQUE ↓	→ Factories	Democracy	Natural and Compound Diverse Manufactured	Indirect Structural and Architectural Elimination	Compression and Suspension	Exposing Function Sheets, Tubing, Cables	Timed
SCIENCE ↓	→ Community Planning	Socialism	Synthetic Domestic Manufactured	Indirect Structural Unified Decen-tralization ~~Unification~~	Continuous Tension	New Functions Cast and Mould Units	Time-Space Mobile

italics. one page

Compositor — everything in script to be set up in italics. Everything in print — in regular type.

~~PROGRESSION — CHART OF ARCHITECTURE~~
MORPHOLOGY OF ARCHITECTURE

~~ITS CHARACTER~~ ~~EMPHASIS~~ ~~CONTINUITY~~	ITS TYPICAL MANIFESTATION	ITS SOCIAL ASPECT	ITS CONSTANT VARIABLE	ITS MATERIAL	~~ITS~~ METHOD OF PLAN (spiritual)	ITS CONSTRUCTION METHOD	ITS LIFE SPAN
CRAFT ↓	SHELTER	~~CHIEFTAINSHIP~~ ~~PATRIARCHATE~~ TRIBALISM	UTILITARIAN SKELETON & SKIN SOLIDS	NATURAL CIRCUMJACENT	~~IMPROVISE~~ DIRECT STRUCTURAL SIMPLIFICATION	CONTINUOUS-COMPRESSION, TENSION perched	TEMPORARY
ART ↓	TEMPLES	DEÏSM ~~KINGDOM~~ ~~THEOCRACY~~	SUPER-FUNCTION SINGLE-MATERIALED-BLOCKS	NATURAL INTERJACENT	~~AESTHETIC~~ GLORYFY INDIRECT ARCHITECTURAL COMPOSITION	COMPRESSION AND TENSION rooted	PERMANENT
APPLIED ART ↓	RESIDENCES	FEUDALISM ~~PLUTOCRACY~~	SHIELDING FUNCTION MULTI-MATERIALED-PIECE-WORK	NATURAL AND ARTIFICIAL DOMESTIC AND IMPORTED	~~SENSUOUS~~ SENSUALIZE INDIRECT FIGURATIVE CONGLOMERATION	VISCIDITY imbedded	INCIDENTAL
MECHANICAL ART ~~TECHNIQUE~~ ↓	PLANTS	~~CAPITALISM~~ ~~INDUSTRIALISM~~ ~~DEMOCRACY~~ 2 autocracy	EXPOSING FUNCTION SHEETING, TUBING, CABLES	NATURAL AND COMPOSITE DOMESTIC MANUFACTURED	FACTUALIZE INDIRECT STRUCTURAL AND ARCHITECTURAL ELIMINATION	COMPRESSION AND SUSPENSION subterranean	INTERIM
SCIENCE ↓	COMMUNITY PLANNING	~~COMMONWEALTH~~ Communalism	MULTI-PURPOSED FUNCTION CAST AND MOULD UNITS	NATURAL AND SYNTHETIC DIVERSE PRE-MANUFACTURED	INTEGRATE INDIRECT STRUCTURAL UNIFIED DECENTRALIZATION	CONTINUOUS TENSION anchored superterranean	TIME-SPACE-CONTINUITY

figs. A.50a-b Frederick Kiesler, two preliminary versions of the "Morphology-Chart of Architecture" published in "Notes on Architecture. The Space House. Annotations at Random," *Hound & Horn* 7, no. 2 (January-March 1934): 292-297. ÖFLKS, TXT_846/0; TXT_3587/0

of the baroque and rococo start to ornamentally twist and warp, so that ultimately stone is being "carved out of all its possibilities" and later "becomes pulverized into concrete" (see Addenda, figs. C.01a–b).[368] In fact "[e]very material," writes Kiesler, is "pulverized, even wood, into plastics for Artificial Architecture."[369]

Historical eras in Kiesler's charts and figurative diagrams are mobilized to serve the author's design. Past periods and styles are used almost interchangeably. Kiesler appears rather ambivalent towards the rococo, an architectural style particularly prominent in Austria and the historicist urban fabric of Vienna—a city that Kiesler never returned after his immigration to New York in 1926, even as he visited other European countries after World War II.

Part VIII of *Magic Architecture*, titled "Realism of Wealth" in the assembled manuscript, is alternatively titled "Dance of Death" or "Totentanz der Architecture" (in Kiesler's idiosyncratic *Denglish*) in preliminary drafts. Other than an (unwritten) introduction on "Fashion in Architecture," it includes only two chapters which are hardly written. The first, "Lust in Stone," offers a brief description of a "pleasure fountain" by Bayreuth court architect Paulus Decker excerpted and translated from Ponten. The second chapter, "The Rococo in France," was supposed to offer a "description of the Trianon," but this is absent from all drafts. (VIII.1–2) More suggestive though of the author's view of the rococo is an aphoristic statement written in Kiesler's preliminary notes for this last chapter added parenthetically under the alternative title: "A Project of the Rococo / (Every emotion ends in motion, and dies as a skeleton of mechanization)" (VIII.2).[370] The "skeleton of mechanization" alludes to architecture's "Dance of Death," or *Totentanz*, which reaches its climax in the following century: "The spiritual deflation of the Architecture of the nineteenth-century in Europe and elsewhere had naturally its inert expression in its plastic form with the Rokoko [sic]—only the rim remained. The firmness was gone," writes Kiesler in another draft.[371]

In the final chapter of *Magic Architecture* the same "spiritual deflation" is described as "a rapid decline from the low level of eighteenth-century rococo, which, at least, had retained the sensuousness of ornament" (X.10). During the period after the war, the study of eighteenth-century rococo experienced another Renaissance in architectural and design historiography, partly prompted by its pseudomorphic identification with the analogously ornate, curvilinear, and opulent art nouveau or *Jugendstil*, which until that point was equally marginalized in recent architectural histories as the eighteenth-century rococo.[372]

A decade after *Magic Architecture* was compiled and on the occasion of Mozart's bicentennial in 1956, also marked by an expansive rococo exhibition titled *The Century of Mozart*, Kiesler contributed an essay for *Art News*, which also included a rebuttal of rococo architecture, *particularly* in Austria: "Mozart's music is neither frivolous nor lecherous, it is Form through and through without décor. Rococo is décor: décor par excellence. But in 1789 all the curvilinear rococo frames were condensed into a single barren, raw wooden rectangle: the guillotine."[373] Staged at the William Rockhill Nelson Gallery of Art and the Atkins Museum of Fine Arts in Kansas City and accompanied by a program of concerts and opera dedicated to Mozart, the exhibition included a wide assortment of eighteenth-century artworks from "Europe and colonial America," as well as "Oriental" plates and platters from China.[374] Similar exhibitions with an "emphasis on the Rococo" took place in other cities in the United States during the 1955–56 season, including the Toledo Museum in Ohio, the Virginia Museum at Richmond, and the Wildenstein Gallery in New York, prompting the editor of *Art News* to note that "we are entering, as Frederick Kiesler has suggested, a Rococo phase of our own."[375] The "publicity release" for the Kansas City Nelson Gallery show stored among Kiesler's drafts explains the celebration of "the Century of Mozart" in America on account of "the special reason" that American people have for "celebrating this century, which witnessed the revolutionary birth of Modern France and of the United States, a time which fostered a democratic society and the concepts of liberty, equality and fraternity." This was also the year (1956) that marked "the 250th anniversary of the birth of Benjamin Franklin."[376] The same announcement mentions three additional shows "of German and Austrian Rococo at the University of Kansas Museum of Art."[377]

These references suggest that the 1956 Mozart celebration struck "home" for Kiesler. His current home in the US was staging lavish (Austrian) rococo shows across cities plagued by vast socio-economic inequities all while the menace of McCarthyism loomed over federal funding for the arts.[378] Tellingly, Kiesler makes one single reference to Mozart, in Part IX of *Magic Architecture*, on "The Poets' Architecture." Commenting on Victorien Sardou's etching *La Maison de Mozart* (*Ville basse*), a fantastic depiction of the composer's posthumous home on planet Jupiter first published in 1858 and which Kiesler included among the plates for *Magic Architecture* (plate 50),[379] he wrote: "A poet retreats from everyman's gold rush into the dream world of a habitat he considers worthy of a man of genius … who died in poverty."[380] Kiesler reproduces Sardou's drawing from his personal copy of a 1933 issue of *Minotaure*. The work preceded the article "Le message Automatique" by André Breton, who owned Sardou's original etching (fig. A.51).[381] The "automatic" drawing, which Sardou made while allegedly guided by the spirit of the seventeenth-century artist Bernard de Palissy, houses the eighteenth-century composer in a planetary habitation, whose disembodied architectural features, including columns and mirror frames suspended in mid-air, are made entirely by garlands of hybrid vegetal matter. Perhaps this ghostly architectural apparition of a house is another illustration of the architectural state of "pulverization," which even the communicating spirits of Mozart and Palissy reanimated in the publications and texts by Breton and Kiesler could not escape.

LA MAISON DE MOZART DANS JUPITER, EAU-FORTE AUTOMATIQUE EXÉCUTÉE EN NEUF HEURES PAR VICTORIEN SARDOU (*La revue spirite*, 1858)

«...C'est sur la rive droite de cette rivière, « dont l'eau, dit l'Esprit, t'offrirait la consistance d'une légère vapeur, » qu'est construite la maison de Mozart, que Palissy a bien voulu me faire dessiner sur cuivre. Je ne donne ici que la façade du midi. La grande entrée est à gauche, sur la plaine ; à droite est la rivière ; au nord et au midi sont les jardins. J'ai demandé à Mozart quels étaient ses voisins. — « Plus haut a-t-il dit, « et plus bas, deux Esprits que tu ne connais pas ; mais à gauche, je ne suis séparé « que par une grande prairie du jardin de Cervantès. »

La maison a donc quatre faces comme les nôtres, ce dont on aurait tort néanmoins de faire une règle générale. Elle est construite avec une certaine pierre que les animaux tirent des carrières du nord, et dont l'Esprit compare la couleur à ces tons verdâtre qu prend l'azur du ciel au moment où le soleil se couche. Quant à sa dureté, on peut s'en faire une idée par cette observation de Palissy, qu'elle fondrait sous nos doigts humains aussi vite qu'un flocon de neige : encore est-ce là une des matières les plus résistantes de la planète ! Sur ce mur les Esprits ont sculpté ou incrusté les étranges arabesques que notre dessin cherche à reproduire. Ce sont ou des ornements fouillés dans la pierre et colorés ensuite, ou des incrustations ramenées à la solidité de la pierre verte, par un procédé qui est en grande faveur maintenant et qui conserve aux végétaux toute la grâce de leurs contours, toute la finesse de leurs tissus, toute la richesse de leur coloris. « Une « découverte, ajoute l'Esprit, que vous ferez quelque jour et qui changera chez vous bien « des choses. »

La longue fenêtre de droite présente un exemple de ce genre d'ornementation ; l'un de ses bords n'est pas autre chose qu'un roseau énorme dont on a conservé les feuilles. Il en est de même du couronnement de la fenêtre principale, qui affecte la forme de clefs de sol : ce sont des plantes sarmenteuses enlacées et pétrifiées. C'est par ce procédé qu'ils obtiennent la plupart des couronnements d'édifices, des grilles, des balustres, etc. Souvent même la plante est placée dans le mur, avec ses racines et dans des conditions à croître librement. Elle grandit, se développe ; ses fleurs s'épanouissent au hasard, et l'artiste ne les fige sur place que lorsqu'elles ont acquis tout le développement voulu pour l'ornementation de l'édifice : la maison de Paliss est presque entièrement décorée de cette manière.

Destiné d'abord aux meubles seuls, puis aux châssis des portes et des fenêtres, ce genre d'ornements s'est perfectionné peu à peu et a fini par envahir toute l'architecture. Aujourd'hui ce n'est pas seulement la fleur et l'arbuste que l'on pétrifie de la sorte, mais l'arbre lui-même, de la racine au faîte ; et les palais comme les édifices sacrés n'ont plus guère d'autres colonnes.

Une pétrification de même nature sert aussi à la décoration des fenêtres. Des fleurs ou des feuilles très-amples sont habilement dépouillées de leur partie charnue : il ne reste plus que le réseau des fibres, aussi fin que la plus fine mousseline. On le cristallise ; et de ces feuilles assemblées avec art on construit tout une fenêtre, qui ne laisse filtrer à l'intérieur qu'une lumière très douce ; ou bien encore on les enduit d'une sorte de verre liquide et coloré de toute nuance, qui se durcit à l'air et qui transforme la feuille en une sorte de vitre. De l'assemblage de ces feuilles résultent, pour fenêtres, de charmants bosquets transparents et lumineux !

. . . .

Je ne finirai pourtant pas sans m'expliquer, en passant, sur le genre d'ornements que le grand artiste a choisis pour sa demeure. Il est facile d'y reconnaître le souvenir de notre musique terrestre : la clé de sol y est fréquemment répétée, et, chose bizarre, jamais la clé de fa ! Dans la décoration du rez-de-chaussée, nous retrouvons un archet, une sorte de téorbe ou de mandoline, une lyre et tout une portée musicale. Plus haut, c'est une grande fenêtre qui rappelle vaguement la forme d'un orgue ; les autres ont l'apparence de grandes notes, et des notes plus petites abondent sur toute la façade.

On aurait tort d'en conclure que la musique de Jupiter soit comparable à la nôtre, et qu'elle se note par les mêmes signes : Mozart s'est expliqué sur elle de manière à ne laisser aucun doute à cet égard ; mais les Esprits rappellent volontiers, dans la décoration de leurs maisons, la mission terrestre qui leur a mérité l'incarnation dans Jupiter et qui résume le mieux le caractère de leur intelligence. Ainsi, dans la maison de Zoroastre, ce sont les astres et la flamme qui font tous les frais de la décoration. »

VICTORIEN SARDOU.

54

Vienna had historical links not only with the development of the rococo, but also the racially biased revulsion against all ornamental cultures, European and Indigenous, through the textual and design rhetoric of Adolf Loos. Kiesler had presented Loos's seminal lecture "Ornament and Crime" of 1910 to an American audience in the 1930s in what must have been one of its first outings in English.[382] In addition to its association with criminality, primitivity, and femininity, ornament, according to Loos, was linked to wasteful economic production.[383] It is precisely this adverse economic effect of commercial "decorativism" and its material expenditure that Kiesler wished to counter and re-channel in his theory of Magic Architecture towards the "care for the superfluous" (I.1), which nourishes the "spiritual" creation of art and not the reproduction of fashionable yet unnecessary gadgets.

The economy of twentieth-century architecture is still "spiritualized," albeit differently as Kiesler states in a passage of his introduction to the book (noted earlier in relation to the "colonizing Spaniards") while "falsified" by "fashionable esthetic patterns." Kiesler knew fashion "from the inside"–if fashion has an inside. In addition to his well-known window displays for Saks Fifth Avenue and other similar commissions in New York in the 1930s, he also designed sets for the third edition of the *Fashion of the Times* exhibition, organized by the *New York Times* in October 1944 "for the benefit of the Greater New York Fund."[384] (fig. A.52) And while he never completed his introduction on "Fashion in Architecture" for Part VIII of *Magic Architecture*, he dully elaborated on the "fashionable aesthetics" and "decorative camouflage" of the architecture of the twentieth century with its "business cycle" and "cathedrals of commerce," in one of his final chapters commenting on the ornamental crowns of New York City skyscrapers that merged the sacred and profane: "The church wisely had planted the Cross on top of its structures to put a reverent stop to its spires and keep them from reaching too high; it was not so with the skyscraper. It borrowed the Church's ornateness but ended in a flat top" (X.4). "Flatness" is the result of exhaustion and the dispersal of the architectural languages of ornament, a linguistic form of "pulverization" that failed to produce any composite material or architectural form.

HISTORY, COMEDY, PSYCHOLOGY, AND DISEASE (GIEDION, FRIEDELL)

"The Dance of Death" and its skeletal figures were also featured in another World War II book project that described in detail the impact of mechanization in nineteenth-architecture and design: Sigfried Giedion's *Mechanization Takes Command*, written while the Swiss architectural historian was in exile on the East Coast of the US during the war and completed after its end (finally published in 1948).[385] Giedion argues that the nineteenth-century era of mechanization distances itself from death: "The greater the degree of mechanization, the further does contact with death become banished from life."[386] Commenting on a series of engravings by the "post-romantic" artist Alfred Rethel titled *Another Dance of Death*, an acerbic and "untrue" portrayal of the deadly battles of the 1848 revolution, Giedion claims that the dressed skeletal death figure from "the fifteenth century" inserted by Rethel in the modern street scene is a mere "literary" device amounting to a satirical "masquerade" that essentially transforms death into a mechanized image of the past.[387]

Giedion's references to mechanized iconographies and processes of death align his historical project with part of the general objectives as well as a few of the specific objects that show up in the drafts of *Magic Architecture*.[388] For example, among the contents of the last part of his book describing "purely imaginary buildings" sketched in a preliminary proposal, Kiesler includes the fantastical designs of "inventors and hobbyists" found at "the US Patent

Opposite
fig. A.51 Victorien Sardou, "La Maison de Mozart (Ville Basse)," etching reproduced in *Minotaure* 3-4 (December 1933): 54, with the description "La Maison de Mozart en Jupiter, eau-forte automatique exécutée en neuf heures par Victorien Sardou (*La revue Spirite*, 1858)" preceding the article by André Breton, "Le message automatique" (*Minotaure* 3-4: 55-65). Copy of the surrealist review in the Kiesler estate library with pencil marking for photo-reproduction in *Magic Architecture*, plate 50.

fig. A.52 Exhibition brochure, *Fashions of the Times 3rd Edition* ("Sets designed by Kiesler"). New York Times Hall, October 24-27, 1944, for the benefit of the greater New York Fund. MED_ 5984/0

Office" with "some of the most astounding dreams of 'practicability' in store." [389] As has been documented, the US Patent Office was Giedion's main site of archaeological research into the "anonymous history" of mechanized design inventions in America. Among his planned book contents in an earlier proposal, Kiesler lists the "[u]topian invention in furnishings, air-conditioning, Bathing, gadgets" including "the bathtubs of Benjamin Franklin." [390] In *Mechanization Takes Command*, Giedion devotes the final "part" of his book to the "Mechanization of the Bath," and while he does not mention Benjamin Franklin's "bathtubs" or his famous "air bathing" habits, he includes Franklin's "stove" as one of the most "efficient" designs of the eighteenth-century "mechanization of the hearth." [391] While sharing Giedion's interest in cultures of psycho-physiological "regeneration," Kiesler is not favorably predisposed towards mechanized design. He views the "mechanical hocus-pocus" of contemporary building culture and the "endless incantations of mechanical activities" as a retrospective atonement of modern humans against their loss of faith in the power of magic. [392] Unlike Giedion, he does not view mechanized household appliances as a core factor in the development of modern housing as it ought to become. Instead, Kiesler is more interested in the "utopian" aspect of some of the imaginative or even improbable design inventions of past centuries arguing that their ultimate "goal" is: "to improve the lot of mankind; to improve its physical and mental well-being; to make the dream an everyday reality," which represents the main "definition" of *Magic Architecture*. [393]

Returning to the distinction between idealist and materialist conceptions of history mentioned in Kiesler's quotation from Sassmann, both Giedion and Kiesler appear to oscillate between the two historical views, and yet their individual versions of idealism and materialism are markedly different. In *Mechanization Takes Command*, the objective goal placed at the end of Giedion's teleological and thus idealist perspective into the anonymous materialist history of nineteenth-century design is the advent and perseverance of "modern architecture" in the twentieth. *Magic Architecture* does not share this linear historiographic perspective and in its oscillation to and from prehistory and the present does not have a fixed beginning or end. Its exploration of utopian, unbuilt, or unbuildable architectures through the ages qualifies it as a hypothetical history of "as if." and thus a genuine, even if marginalized, component of modern architecture's epistemological foundations on an "objective" form of "idealism." [394]

In the paragraphs of his historiographic preface to *The Empire of Dreamers* transcribed by the Kieslers, Sassmann had singled out the "Viennese philosopher of history ... Egon Friedell and his epoch-making *Cultural History of the Modern Age*" as a transformative representative of the "idealistic conception of history." [395] As noted earlier, Friedell is present among Kiesler's drafts in his transcriptions from the Viennese author's *Cultural History of Antiquity* centering on the Egyptian pyramid and the lost city of Atlantis, yet the Kieslers' library also contains the first volume of Friedell's *Cultural History of the Modern Age*, describing the eras of "Renaissance and Reformation." [396] In his methodological introduction "What is Cultural History and to What End is it Studied?" Friedell sets up a series of irregular historiographic principles that are characteristic, as Sassmann had argued, of the "development of romantic experience" in idealist histories in the beginning of the twentieth century, and which may be echoed in Kiesler's own writing. First, that all history starts with (and derives from) illness (*Krankheit*). Friedell's *Cultural History of the Modern Age* commences with the pandemic of the Black Death in the fourteenth century and finishes with the Great War. Not only the worst but also "the best in human history comes from illness," writes Friedell after Novalis, as illness triggers a "heroic struggle for existence" (*Existenzkampf*) among humans turning periodic states of biological infirmity into vital dynamic conditions that lead to an effervescent "spiritualization" (*Vergeistigung*) that rise in periods when the physical body dwindles. [397] Thus, "health is a metabolism of disease" (*Stoffwechselerkrankung*). [398] Friedell employs illness not only as a powerful organic "metaphor" [399] but as a *method* for the writing of what he describes as a "genetic or developmental" (*genetische oder entwickelnde*) method of history "which aims at representing events as an organic ensemble [*Zusammenhang*] and course [*Verlauf*]" [400] and as expressions of an organic "morphology" and "physiology" of culture.

Disease and pathology become for Friedell departure points that not only describe historical events but delineate historiographic principles, and which further germinate into a series of methodological *symptoms*. These creatively pathological symptoms include the states of artistic "incompletion" and "professional dilettantism," meaning the lack of commitment or expertise into a single area of history when engaging the world: "a universal history can only be compiled out of a vast stock of dilettantish researches, incompetent judgements, and incomplete data." [401] These irreverent historiographic ethics extend to the cultural reinstatement of "the legitimate plagiarist (*der legitime Plagiator*): "strictly speaking, the whole of the world's literature consists of plagiarisms" announces Friedell. "The world is now so old" he argues, that "after millennia of so many important people that lived and thought in it there is little that is new to discover or say." [402] Expanding Proudhon's saying "La propriété c'est le vol"–property is theft– from its "doubtful" use in the field of economics to its "undoubtful" applicability in matters of intellectual property, Friedell proclaims that "the whole intellectual history of mankind is a history of thefts." Making a comment on the modern culture of commercial patents that preoccupied Giedion, he writes that "while the question of priority is important in the case of vacuum cleaners," "in the sphere of the intellect, [it] is of no importance." [403]

The impact of all three of Friedell's principles of world historical writing–incompletion, dilettantism, plagiarism–can be retraced in Kiesler's own writing. In the mid-1920s, Kiesler had to "file suit" to successfully defend the originality of his *Space-Stage* design against accusations of plagiarism by the designer of another round stage. [404] However, recent critical studies have attributed the authorship of several of his design projects to other artists and designers, [405] and the assembled manuscript of *Magic Architecture* contains a great number of extensive quotations from several authors, only a few of whom are mentioned by name. While quotation marks and page numbers are noted in the handwritten drafts and transcriptions, they gradually disappear in the typescript. [406] The unusual length of some of Kiesler's quotations may also suggest that at a certain point he might have been pondering the idea that his book project would include an anthology of texts by other authors who were experts on their subjects. This had been Stefi's approach to her own unpublished project, *Dream Book*, a large, edited anthology of texts by a variety of authors from antiquity to the present on the subject of dreams, and whose thematic outline shows a number of overlaps with Kiesler's selection of writers and texts quoted in *Magic Architecture*. [407]

The stratagem of the "part-anthology" also had a precedent in architectural literature. The first section of Bruno Taut's *Die Auflösung der Städte* (*The Dissolution of Cities*) contains a series of drawings with written statements by Taut and the second half, a compilation of excerpts from recent works by writers, philosophers, and political theorists (but no architects) including Tolstoy, Kropotkin, Nietzsche, Lenin, Engels, Scheerbart, and Walt Whitman. [408] These selections include the page numbers of the original publications on the left margin of the pages of Taut's book, similar to Stefi's typed transcriptions following Kiesler's guidelines for quotation.

Anthologizing is perhaps also Kiesler's response to his own "dilettantish" status researching and writing in scholarly areas where he had no formal training, from archaeology and anthropology to animal science, even if he could partly rely on the advice of colleagues at Columbia University and elsewhere in New York, some of whom visited and gave lectures at his Laboratory for Design Correlation, as, for example, Ashley Montagu.[409] The evident lack of expertise (and the incommensurate amount of time it takes to acquire it) may have been one of the many reasons that the manuscript of *Magic Architecture* remained in a dynamic state of perpetual "incompletion" and yet never died; even in the mid-1950s after several years of little or no writing progress, Kiesler resumed bibliographic research and continued to add transcriptions on the subject of animal physiology.[410]

While transcribing excerpts from Friedell's *Cultural History of Antiquity*, Kiesler essentially follows the methodological principles of his *Cultural History of the Modern Age. Magic Architecture* had the potential of uniting the histories of these two works in one volume with a focus on architecture. The intrinsic commonality between Kiesler and Friedell's projects is the extensive engagement of both authors with the theater—Friedell as an actor and theatrical art director and Kiesler as a theater architect and designer of theatrical and operatic stage sets. Friedell's *Cultural History of the Modern Age* is dedicated to director Max Reinhardt (Friedell had been part of his experimental theater group) as well as the owner of the Grosses Schauspielhaus in Berlin designed by Hans Poelzig. Kiesler also translated his theatrical experience in the design of the textual space of his book projects and dramatic representation of history.

In Friedell, this historical space is shaped by disease. This is partly true in Kiesler, in terms of the spatial psychopathological conditions that characterized modern environments after World War II, yet whose origins the architect traces in earlier periods. In the conclusion to his chapter on Piranesi, Kiesler points to a pathological transition in human history at "the end of the eighteenth century," when "man's beliefs have very much come down to earth." "He no longer worships the sun, the stars or giant mountains," writes Kiesler, "the *only thing he now fears is disease*" (VI.8, emphasis added). Use of the verb "fear," rather than "experience," also points to the ideational factors that do not simply anticipate but *become* the disease, as in the case of the several phobias emerging in the nineteenth century, including the urban psychopathology of agoraphobia, or *Platzangst*, essentially the fear of "the fear of space" that also creeps into contemporary forms of art and architectural historiography.[411]

Fear, then, is mobilized in the construction of a history where shifts in periodization occur not according to human desires but by following the changing object of fear. In the first chapter of *Magic Architecture*, Kiesler describes the entire development of religious architecture as a psychopathological phenomenon constructed by anxiety: "These graves, altars, and temples were the tools for healing the pain of anguish. This is an Architecture of Fear," which by "further specialization," gives birth to "monstrous creatures" such as "tumuli-species of architectural saurians, ammonites, and trilobites" (I.1). Animalization and fossilization, here applied to ornamented architectural species, are organic evolutionary processes that would fit Friedell's idea of a "genetic or developmental" type of history that studies the evolution of hybrid forms including the creation of historical monstrosities.

While referring to the historicist masquerade of religiously inspired revivalisms in the age of Ruskin and Morris and the "overstuffiness" of the "Victorian era," Kiesler uses a new medical metaphor: "The holy mask laid upon the cancerous growth [of building tissues] to assure healing was replaced by a knife which went beyond the skin, and cut the parasite out of hiding"(X.7). The impromptu comment is characteristic of the transition from an abstract pathological metaphor of "illness" in the nineteenth century to the concrete medical objects and clinical processes of the twentieth.[412] This medical objectification of fear of disease will also lead

LE PALAIS IDÉAL (HAUTERIVES, DRÔME), PAR LE FACTEUR CHEVAL.

l'expérimentation en cours serait de nature à démontrer que la perception et la représentation — qui semblent à l'adulte ordinaire s'opposer d'une manière si radicale — ne sont à tenir que pour les produits de dissociation d'une *faculté unique, originelle,* dont l'image eidétique rend compte et dont on retrouve trace chez le primitif et chez l'enfant. Cet état de grâce, tous ceux qui ont souci de définir la véritable condition humaine, plus ou moins confusément aspirent à le retrouver. Je dis que c'est l'automatisme seul qui y mène. On peut systématiquement, à l'abri de tout délire, travailler à ce que la distinction du subjectif et de l'objectif perde de sa nécessité et de sa valeur. « Il y a, disait Myers, une forme d'audition interne [si étrange]... Il existe des ensembles complexes et puissants de conceptions formées au dehors (certains disent au delà) du langage articulé et de la pensée raisonnée. Il y a une marche, une ascension à travers les espaces idéaux que certains regardent comme la seule véritable ascension ; il y a une architecture que certains regardent comme le seul séjour... »

Par le seul fait qu'elle voit sa croix de bois se transformer en crucifix de pierres précieuses, et qu'elle tient tout à la fois cette vision pour *imaginative et sensorielle,* Thérèse d'Avila peut passer pour commander cette ligne sur laquelle se situent les médiums et les poètes. Malheureusement ce n'est encore qu'une sainte.

ANDRÉ BRETON.

LES CHIMÈRES, PAR GUSTAVE MOREAU. (Fragment)

65

fig. A.53 "Ideal Palace by the postman Cheval," in André Breton, "Le Message Automatique," *Minotaure* 3–4 (December 1933), 65. Copy of the surrealist review in the Kiesler estate library with page marker for photo-reproduction in *Magic Architecture*, plate 7.

Following
fig. A.54 Hendrik Willem Van Loon, "An Animated Chronology. 500,000 B.C. - A.D.1922," in *The Story of Mankind* (New York: Garden City Publishing, 1921).

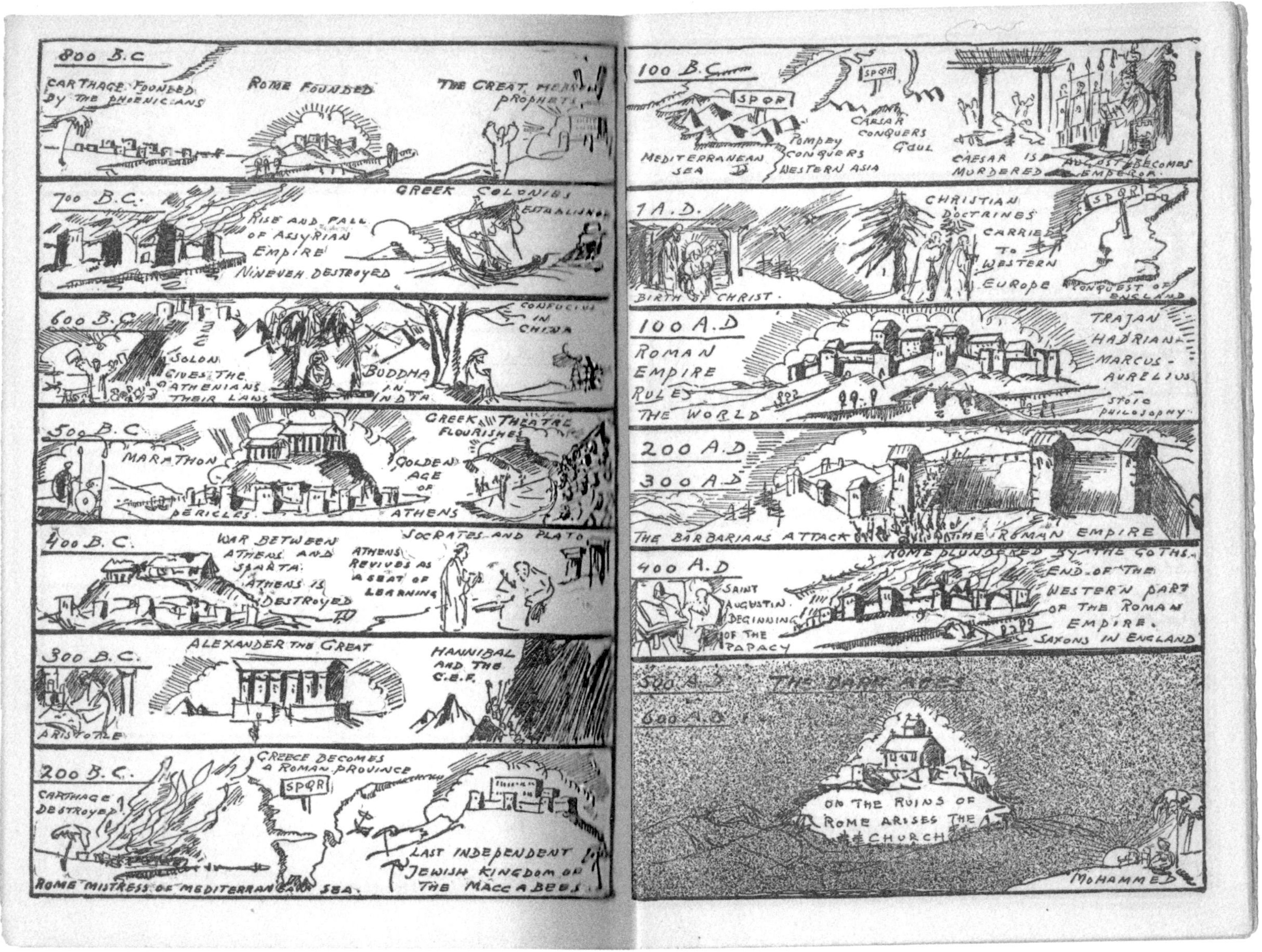

into the "hygienic" practices and forms of twentieth-century architecture, another "defense mechanism" criticized albeit very briefly in the handwritten outline for the final part of *Magic Architecture*: "Cleaning Architecture / Functional Architecture / (Architecture in Narcosis) / Hygiene / Architecture Ready to be operated on."[413] In the assembled manuscript, this outline ultimately corresponds with a brief chapter in Part x on "The Hygiene of Functional Architecture" (x.8). This single paragraph describes the "cleaning" of buildings "inside and outside of ornamental growths" following Loos's edict on ornament.

*

In its many alternate conclusions and various forms of irresolution, the text of *Magic Architecture* performs pathology manifested in its fluctuating structure. In one of his preliminary book proposals that was probably never sent to publishers, Kiesler envisions a fourth and final part, which "[s]hould account in a short chapter [about] ideas in buildings that are purely imaginary," and then he writes, "to the point of sheer insanity"–but crosses out this last phrase.[414] Ultimately, this architecture responding to Friedell's ideas of pathological "illness" does not have a separate chapter or place in *Magic Architecture*; it is spread throughout the text of the second half of the manuscript and the plates, as for example, the house of the French postmaster Cheval that Kiesler reproduced (among other sources) from Breton's article on "automatic writing" in his copy of *Minotaure*'s double 1933 issue that also contained Sardou's spirited "House of Mozart" on Jupiter. (fig. A.53) These extraordinary designs are not ahistorical; they are in fact dated by their very shielding from historical context, similar to the insulated housing structures in Huysmans' *Against Nature* and Kafka's "The Burrow," both planned for quotation in the final chapters of *Magic Architecture*, as well as Kiesler's own *Endless House*.[415]

This form of eccentricity is part of a reterritorializing project. As Kiesler states in a preliminary outline, the main goal of *Magic Architecture* is for societies "to abando[n] the buildings of the *psychic periphery*, namely the Temple and the Administration-center as the primary factor of attention" and set a new "architectural emphasis" for human history "on the house and the home."[416] If Kiesler's erstwhile friend Roberto Matta and other surrealists aspired to create a "psychological morphology" through painting, then in *Magic Architecture* Kiesler uses the history of housing to recreate a psychological *topography* that would reconstitute notions of "periphery" and (home-)center by reterritorializing architecture's "different spheres." Next then to the architect's diagrammatic method there's a topographic impulse, manifested in his tracing of circular areas, "below," "on," "above" or "beyond" the surface of the earth in his original diagram drawing from Frobenius (plate 2a) and his "morphological" charts.

The topographic impulse informs the design and mapping of *Magic Architecture*'s incomplete design. Next to unwritten chapters and deleted sentences, the book manuscript also had a number of alternative epilogues, including the poetic finale of the final chapter (x.10) which takes places in Heaven, as in a baroque operatic stage, where the ancient Greek "satiric" writer Aristophanes is inviting the "skepticist" seventeenth-century French philosopher Voltaire (also a frequent character in Friedell's *Cultural History of the Modern Age*) for a "fly-walk around the earth" that will eventually conclude with the "habitats of man across this island called *Magic Architecture*."[417] This imaginary "fly-walk," is reminiscent of a similar transhistoric "flight" by two imaginary architects in Viollet-le-Duc's *Histoire de l'Habitation Humaine*, also a narrativized world history of human housing "from prehistoric times to our days" published in the previous century.[418] Even if at the end of this final scene, Kiesler writes the word "Finis," this will not be the end of *Magic Architecture* as this satirical finale was never copied to the final manuscript and the word "finis" (*un mot interdit* for Kiesler) was deleted (x.10).[419] And yet the aborted finale of the Aristophanes-Voltaire air-flying tour aligns *Magic Architecture* with Friedell's satirical conception of History as an operatic world stage that turns into an operative historical platform.

And so turns *Magic Architecture's* alternate appendix, which is a "Chart" on the "Orbit of *Exstasy* (Addenda, figs. C.12a–b) with a cyclical diagram uniting stars, mountains, animals, and humans from previous eras to the origin of "Everyman" in the present—a human being who lives in solidarity with their fellow human beings as outlined in Kiesler's preliminary "storyboard" on world religion (see Addenda, fig. C.02b) and who is the nucleus of the "communalist" architecture Kiesler had first sketched in the culminating stage of his earlier morphological charts (figs. A.50a–b). Ultimately the "x" of the chart's "Exstacy" also predicted its excision from the assembled text and substitution by the non-figurative rectilinear chart of metabolism that outlines seemingly endless theoretical correspondences among all areas of world design production.

But even Kiesler's *Everyman* is a mere stick figure, as are so many of the historical figures and theoretical diagrams compiled in his book project. As noted in Kiesler's correspondence with publishers excerpted in the "Annotated Chronology," one of the editors, who politely rejected his proposal on account of considerations of "balance" between "quality" and popularity (meaning sales profit) in the publishing house's catalogue, mentions that "a book on the subject of architecture could sell extremely well if slanted for the popular market" before citing as an "example" the work of the Dutch American historian Hendrik van Loon, who wrote popular historical books "on a broader field."[420] Indeed van Loon was the author of a number of histories, which like Kiesler's *Magic Architecture*, were presented as "stories," such as *The Story of Mankind*, *The Story of the Arts*, and *The Story of the Bible* as well as a book titled *The Home of Mankind* (a world history of geography that traced, uncritically, the changing map of the earth under the impact of European colonialism).[421] The distinguishing property of van Loon's "stories" was that they were profusely illustrated with the author's own drawings. His most popular book *The Story of Mankind* contains several illustrations for each chapter showing large area maps or individual figures depicting scenes described in the text. It also included an "Animated Chronology, 500,000 B.C. – A.D. 1922," inserted at the end of the book as an illustrated appendix, which synopsized the most important events of human history via a sequence of table charts 'animating' a characteristic scene for each century—from the Egyptian pyramids and Greek colonies to the Great War and the founding of the League of Nations in the first decades of the twentieth century (fig. A.54).

It is striking that throughout this "Animated Chronology," each historical period or century is identified with monumental architectural objects, including temples, palaces, and castle fortifications—an identification that corroborates (yet again uncritically by van Loon) Kiesler's claim in Part V of *Magic Architecture* that human history starts and is identified with the power structures of its architectures. Yet this is not to suggest that Kiesler followed van Loon's "example" per the publisher's advice. The original proposal he sent to editors included a number of "line drawings" (which kept increasing with each new draft of his proposal) that would figuratively illustrate parts of his "Story of Housing." The very format of the illustrated chart, as for example, his aforementioned caricature of the world history of religion, which was divided in a series of cells reminiscent of a film storyboard and cartoon comics publications (see Addenda, fig. C.02b), rehearses Friedell's tragicomic view of world history. Yet it is perhaps Kiesler's list of plates that could be retrospectively reread as an "animated chronology," even if closer to a discontinuous and turbulent genealogy that traces the trajectory from human prehistory to the radioactive present.

AN "EPILOGUE AND PROLOGUE" FOR THE TWENTIETH CENTURY: UTOPIA'S RETURNS (FROM LEDOUX TO KIESLER)

Even if the title of *Magic Architecture's* tenth and final part is "Flares of a new unity between vision and fact," its structure is the very image of disunity and disorganization. While the ten chapters of Part X attempt to describe the architectural developments of the first half of the twentieth century, they unexpectedly veer back to episodes and figures from the late eighteenth and nineteenth centuries without following a chronological order. Kiesler's preliminary proposals and early chapter drafts show that most of the chapters of Part X were initially written for the third and final part of an earlier version of the manuscript with a tripartite structure that followed a more regular chronological order.[422] The third part of this early version started with developments in the architecture of the late eighteenth-century after the French Revolution and continued with a number of episodes, such as Fourier's "Ideal Phalanx," Schinkel's "Return to Classicism," the "Magic of Steel" of the Eiffel Tower, the "Reaction" that leads "Back to Handicraft" in late nineteenth-century Britain, and finally Bruno Taut's "Cities for a New Globe." The same preliminary drafts include initial sketches of chapters on "Garden Cities" in England and an "Ideal Sanatorium" by Tony Garnier, which are not present in the assembled manuscript.[423] It appears that both in its early and final state, the last part of *Magic Architecture* was structured as a progressive sequence of regressions or "returns" including the "decorative" historicism that lingered in Kiesler's contemporary commercialized architecture in the interwar era in the US, emblematized by the "pseudo-magic crowns" of New York skyscrapers (X.6).

The most current version of Part X in the assembled manuscript is even more bewilderingly *anacoluthic* as in its list of chapters, Schinkel follows Taut, and Ruskin or Morris follow Kiesler and New York's twentieth-century skyscrapers. Finally, while the tenth and last chapter of Part X and of *Magic Architecture* in general is supposed to describe "The Twentieth Century's Second Quarter," its last two pages go back to Claude-Nicolas Ledoux and the emergence of socio-architectural utopias during the late eighteenth century including the economic and social turmoil that followed the French Revolution (which is how this entire part should have started had it followed a chronological order). It is as if Kiesler reshuffles the cards of history and lets them drop on the table to form a new constellation of events that is both arbitrary and endlessly telling. This reshuffling is similar to an "objective chance" manifestation haunting the theoretical fictions of several surrealists including Breton and his writings on "everyday magic." This "chance" sequence of events is here converted into a historiographic tactic that redistributes the order and gravity of ideas versus "facts" in architectural histories.[424]

Whether the product of chance, the very (dis)order of the chapters *performs* the palimpsests that are described inside these chapters. For this reason, it is significant that Schinkel's unbuilt neoclassical palace on the Acropolis follows Taut's "new cities" for the twentieth century or that the socialist reaction back to handicraft in nineteenth-century Britain follows the capitalist regression to Egyptian or Italian Renaissance decorative revivals in 1930s New York. Whether deliberately planned or opportunistically

EMIL KAUFMANN

VON LEDOUX
BIS LE CORBUSIER

Ursprung und Entwicklung der Autonomen Architektur

„Avant toutes ces lois sont celles de la nature, ainsi nommées parce qu'elles dérivent uniquement de la constitution de notre être."
Montesquieu

WIEN 1933

VERLAG DR. ROLF PASSER
WIEN — LEIPZIG

fig. A.55a Emil Kaufmann *Von Ledoux bis Le Corbusier* (Vienna: Rolf Passer, 1933). Cover with handwritten partial title, Kiesler estate library. ÖFLKS, ARCH THEO 030

fig. A.55b Emil Kaufmann, *Von Ledoux bis Le Corbusier* (Vienna: Rolf Passer, 1933), title page with handwritten dedication by the author (above right). Kiesler estate library. ÖFLKS, ARCH THEO 030

improvised, the seemingly disorganized sequence of chapters in Part X accurately portrays the irrational sequence of events in the architecture of the past two centuries.

Kiesler's final anachronic move to end the main corpus of *Magic Architecture* with the late eighteenth century is revealing for an additional reason. The final part of this last chapter starts with the subheading "Claude-Nicolas Ledoux" (added in the typescript by hand), yet there is no mention of Ledoux in the text of these final pages.[425] There is however a plate, which according to Kiesler's caption shows "Two dream-houses of an architect in search for Magic Architecture but yet not found" (plate 55), alluding to Ledoux, whose spherical "House for a Forester" appears on Kiesler's plate in a perspective and small section drawing. The other "dream house" on the same plate, described in the caption as a "Villa with an Observation Tower" is by Jean-Jacques Lequeu, whose name is never mentioned either in the plate caption or the text of *Magic Architecture*. The source for both illustrations is unmistakably Emil Kaufmann's *Von Ledoux bis Le Corbusier: Ursprung und Entwicklung einer Autonomen Architektur* (*From Ledoux to Le Corbusier: Development of an Autonomous Architecture*), published in 1933.[426] Kiesler owned a copy of the book by the Austrian-US émigré architectural historian with a dedication by the author that included his address in Vienna (figs. A.55a–b). The copy in Kiesler's library has a blank cover on which the architect writes with a blue pen simply "Ledoux," excising the name of Le Corbusier from the book title. As Kaufmann's readers can attest, his slim book is mainly a study of Ledoux in the context of late eighteenth- and early nineteenth-century architecture until Durand and Schinkel's classicism. Only in the last couple of pages of Kaufmann's volume do representatives of twentieth-century architecture appear, among whom Le Corbusier figures as a "pioneer and leader of the young France." But just before Le Corbusier, Kaufmann mentions the "Austrian Adolf Loos" and "Dutch Berlage" while later quoting more extensively from the writings of Austrian-American émigré Richard J. Neutra.[427]

In one of his preliminary drafts for one of his final chapters that mentions the "overstuffed" decorativism of the Victorian era, Kiesler mentions "**3 small countries carried against this sensual trend, the burden of truth. Holland through Berlage, Austria through ~~Wagner, Loos~~**." The sentence stops with the deleted names of Wagner and Loos, but then Kiesler strikes out the entire paragraph. Yet the mention of Holland via Berlage and Austria via Loos is unmistakably a reference to Kaufmann's own text, which named these countries and architects before Le Corbusier as the "leader" in France (even if Le Corbusier was Swiss), and whose name Kiesler evidently does not want to mention as part of the same progressive "reaction."

The tactical deletion is implicitly crucial for the larger historiographic task of *Magic Architecture*, which was to alter the orientation of the historical arc projected by Kaufmann from the end of the eighteenth to the early twentieth century towards the direction of "Magic Architecture" and not the machinist architecture of Le Corbusier. Therefore, the Swiss-French architect's name had to be excised both from Kiesler's text and Kaufmann's book title, so that the arc of the architecture of the modern era is ultimately redrawn "Von Ledoux bis Kiesler" and *not* "bis Le Corbusier." The publication of *Magic Architecture* would serve precisely this goal by replacing Corbusier's *Vers une architecture* with an account of unrealized architectural precedents that pointed *Vers une architecture magique*—"towards" Magic Architecture. *Architecture Magique* was the French title of *Magic Architecture* in Kiesler's correspondence with the house of Gallimard in Paris that was considering publishing a French edition of his book.[428] It would have been a great success but also a great irony if the first publication had ever materialized in France; but it did not.

Cities seeking sheltering protection.
(left) The city "Bodda" in the Wadi Doan, Africa.
(right) Ruins of the ancient city Macchu-Picchou, in the Amazones, South America

fig. A.56a Alternate plate for *Magic Architecture*, not used in the assembled version: "Cities seeking sheltering protection," featuring Wadi Doan (Yemen) and Machu-Picchu (Peru). ÖFLKS, SCL_75/0

fig. A.56b Alternate plate for *Magic Architecture* not used in the assembled version: Hans Poelzig, Festival Theater for Salzburg, reproduction from Josef Ponten, *Architektur die nicht gebaut wurde* (1925), II:193 fig. 380. ÖFLKS, SCL_72510/0

*

The question of utopia also helps explain the relationship between the first and the second half of *Magic Architecture*, whose narratives appear to be disconnected: I refer to the portrayal of prehistoric construction and primitivist conflation with Indigenous forms of sociation (first four parts of the manuscript) and the chronologically incongruous review of "utopian" and "dream" architectures from the fifteenth to the eighteenth and nineteenth centuries preceding the apparition of Magic Architecture in the twentieth (the last five parts of the manuscript). The description of eighteenth-century utopias may further clarify the origins of Kiesler's sociological albeit primitivist view of prehistory and demonstrate how the two seemingly incongruent "halves" of his manuscript are essentially the two reversible sides of the same historical mirror sketched among the architect's cosmological diagrams (see Main Text, fig. B.06c). The first half is about an architecture that never existed and the second about one that could never be built.

Referring to the culture of the "unity of man, society, natural, and technological environment" "fostered" by "old and oldest social ideas" in the late eighteenth century, Kiesler notes that even in this idealized state, reminiscent of narratives of natural happiness in Rousseau (also mentioned in Kaufmann), fear creeps in again along with "guilt" yet projected back into prehistory: "It appeared that this happiness was based on sacrifice and fear, an aspect which linked this mentality very closely with the life of persecution, fear, and guilt of the cave-man."[429] The concatenation of "fear" and "guilt" attributed to the culturally and racially overdetermined prehistoric inhabitant of caverns discloses the role of projection and identification in Kiesler's ambivalent portrayal of prehistory, oscillating between paradise and hell on earth, as well as the Enlightenment and primitivist modernity. In other words, primitivism does not end in the first half of *Magic Architecture*; it returns in the final half, through the very psychological structure of fear that contaminates everything, including historical production. Yet whose fear and guilt and for what?

*

The diagrammatic conception of this projective history is not linear but circular, where the end also signals an origin that is not the same as the departure point from which a historical development had started. For example, the coda following the tenth chapter of Part X, is titled "Epilogue and Prologue" disclosing the reversible logic of organization in Kiesler's textual montage, where the end can also function as beginning creating an "endless" irresolvable structure.

The same text titled "Epilogue and Prologue" was initially placed as chapter 9 of Part X and had other preliminary titles or keywords mostly stricken out by Kiesler, including: "Introduction," "Modern Times," "Future," "Epilogue?" "Fuller," "Kiesler."[430] (see Main Text, fig. B 47) This epilogue-prologue is meant to describe how finally "shelter becomes Magic Architecture." It contains a few geopolitical remarks on the state of housing in the territories of the United States and Russia, echoing Kiesler's recent experience from his involvement in the exhibition on American architecture sent to Moscow by the National Council of American-Soviet Friendship (1944–45). The text does not make specific references to Kiesler's own work or Fuller's, but the subtitle of the text, "Shelter becomes Magic Architecture," where "shelter" stands obviously for Fuller and "Magic Architecture" for Kiesler, makes both architects implicitly present.

In a preliminary typescript of this text is a handwritten annotation at the margin: "Tatlin." His "Tower" or "Monument to the Third International" was among the list of projects to be included in *Magic Architecture* but like so many other "unbuilt" projects that Kiesler had even made photostats and plates for was not used. Others included Poelzig's unrealized *Festpielhaus* for Salzburg as well as a plate captioned "Cities seeking sheltering protection" and including photographs of Wadi Dawan in Africa and Machu Picchu.[431] (figs. A.56a–b) Not only the names of Poelzig and Tatlin, but also the "becoming" of "shelter" into "Magic Architecture" is ultimately demoted into an "Epilogue and Prologue," outside the regular chapter structure of the book, signaling its "out-of-bounds" or post-historical status as a "reality" that has not yet been reached.[432]

Furthermore, the title of Part X, "Flares of a new Unity of Vision and Fact," makes a cyclical reference to the title of the book's general introduction, "The Unity of Vision and Fact," while chapter 9 of Part I is titled "The Split of Unity and Fact" and an alternative title for Part V was "The Unity of Vision and Fact led in (sic) Nothing but Dreams." In his introduction and throughout the chapters of *Magic Architecture* Kiesler describes an original condition of "oneness" where there are no "separate worlds between vision and fact" as was the world experienced by (the defunct anthropological category of) "Eolithic man," yet such unity is "broken in modern man" (Main Text, Introduction). "Flares" of this unity now return in the epilogue of *Magic Architecture*, when almost miraculously, a new social "unity" is beginning to form lifting all barriers:

> **The effects of the social revolution in America and Europe, and the two world wars have *steadily* increased the radius of *contact* among different nations and races of this earth.[433] Just as social barriers between different economic groups begin to disappear, so it may be hoped that psychological barriers to understanding between different peoples of the world may be reduced to insignificance.** (X. Epilogue and Prologue)

Kiesler expands this "new social belief" spatially and temporally "from the confines of little Greece of 500 BC to the wide extent of all the nations of the globe (Ibid.)" This wishful resolution is reminiscent of the introductory panel that Kiesler had designed for the exhibition on American architecture by the National Council of American-Soviet Friendship (1944–45), in which photographic portraits of "People coming from the West" and "People coming from the East" represented the different ethnicities in the United States and would join together via sculpted figures of two human hands (figs. A.57a–b) The exhibition's portrait gallery is prophetic of similar images of racial inequity supposedly undone in UNESCO's "Statement on Race" drafted by Montagu in 1950.[434] Yet even the racially stereotyped photographs of the people included in Kiesler's exhibition design, reminiscent of earlier anthropological displays and similar to those that would appear ten years later, 1955, in the *Family of Man* exhibition at the Museum of Modern Art,[435] signal that such unity essentially betrays the intense fragmentation and division, social, racial, economic, and political that would still abide in the United States and the world in postwar decades, and which could not be undone by the expedient affordances of Frazer's "sympathetic magic" or the symbiotic principles of Lévy-Bruhl's "mystic participation."

While the demands for socio-political unity failed or became limited to the introverted insularity of the *Endless House*, similar calls and images of "unity" or "oneness" would be transferred to the domain of the arts, meaning painting and sculpture, and their unification with architecture in Kiesler's large-scale painting and sculptural projects, yet in a combination that is different from Le Corbusier's epidermic "synthesis of the arts" of murals, reliefs, and sculptures as decorative embellishments inside and outside modernist public buildings in Latin America and elsewhere.[436] In the first two paragraphs of his epigrammatic statement on "Magic Architecture for the Hall of Superstition," written on the occasion of the *International Exhibition of Surrealism* in Paris of 1947, Kiesler would explicitly correlate the effects of "unity" among the arts with a new form of "social conscience":

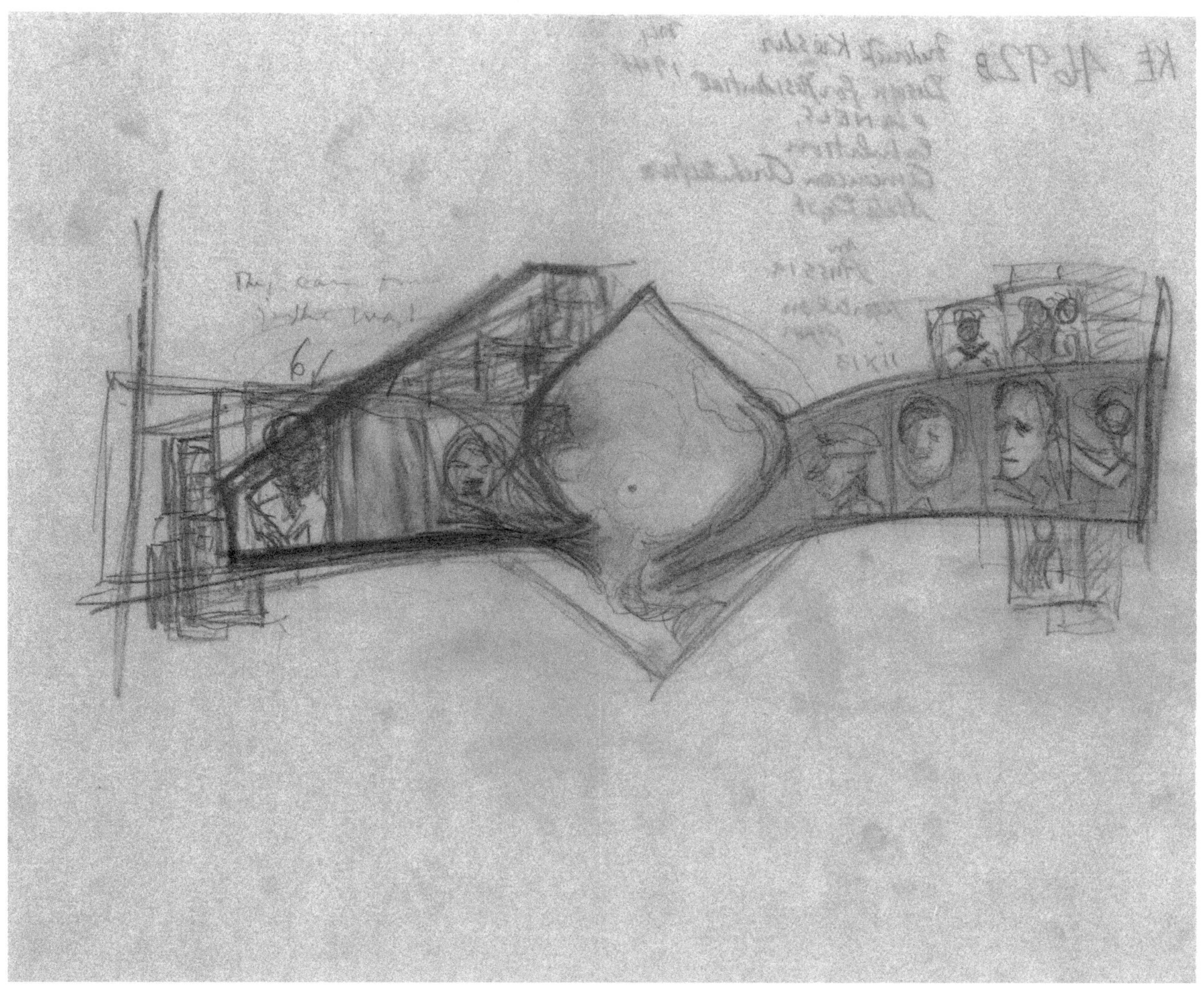

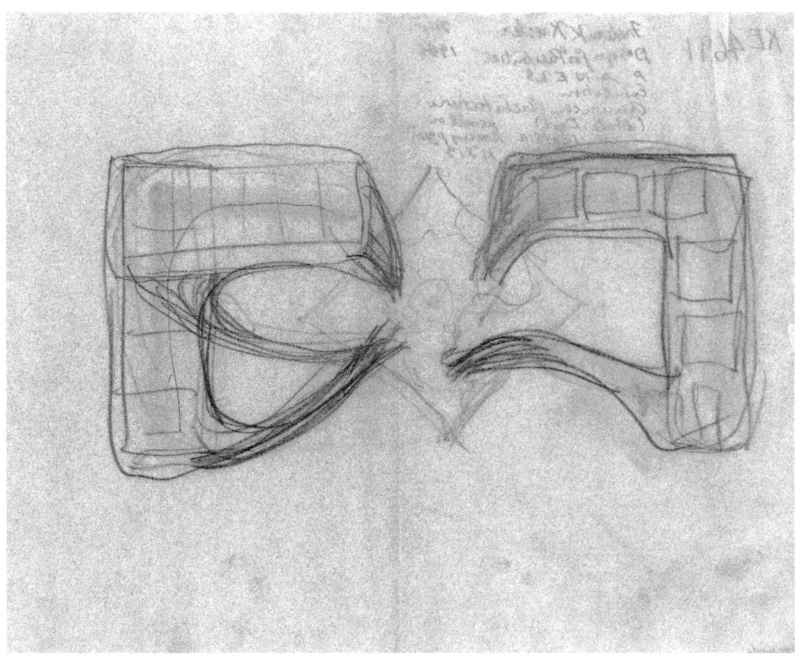

figs. A.57a–b Frederick Kiesler, design proposal for the introductory panel of the exhibition on American architecture sent to the USSR by the National Council of American-Soviet Friendship, 1944–1945. ÖFLKS, SFP_1012/0, SFP_1014/0

The nineteenth century saw the twilight and the first quarter of the twentieth century saw the dissolution of the unity Architecture-Painting-Sculpture. The Renaissance throve on this unity. The people's faith in the happiness of the beyond carried it on its wings. Our new period has rediscovered the social conscience. The instinctive need for a new unity has been reborn. The hope of this unity is no longer situated in the beyond, but in the HERE AND NOW.[437]

From his painted *Galaxies* to his last large group sculptures, Kiesler's unitary artworks share an environmental impetus to restore the social space set on a transhistorical perspective in *Magic Architecture*. The failed publication of Kiesler's book project echoes the failure of postwar architecture's social prospects. And yet the same failure also speaks of the unfulfilled possibilities that are now haunting this architectural history of magic.

AFTER MAGIC I: MANUSCRIPT AS TOOL

Like Ponten's history of "architecture that was not built," the manuscript of *Magic Architecture* became a history that was not published. As analytically described in this book's Annotated Chronology, a 1949 letter from Gallimard publishers in Paris, with whom Kiesler, after multiple rejections by American publishers, hoped to release a French edition of *Magic Architecture*, informs the architect that when the chief editor Raymond Queneau, with whom Kiesler was in correspondence since 1947, finally read a manuscript by the architect, he could not find the historical account of "architecture through the ages" that Kiesler had initially described.[438] Queneau, whose own literary work frequently engages

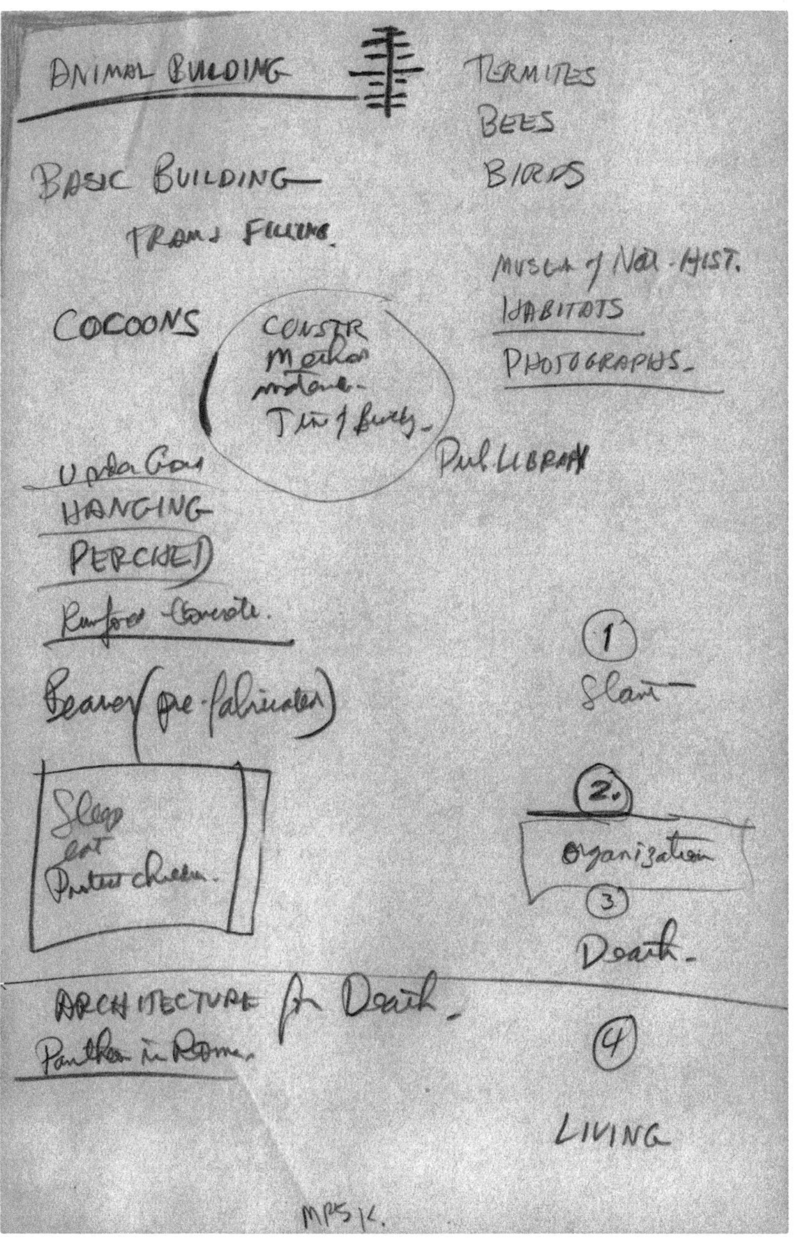

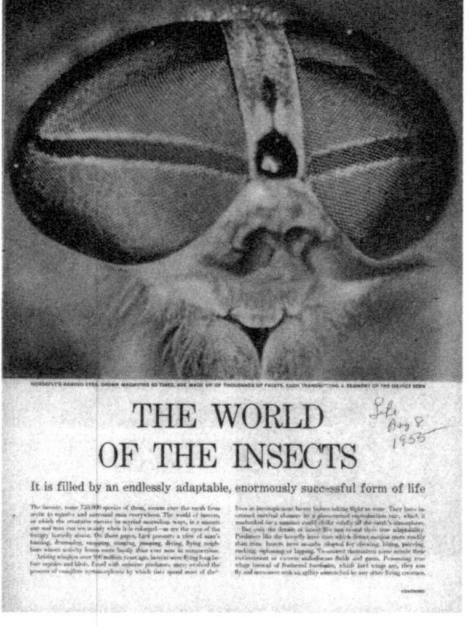
THE WORLD
OF THE INSECTS
It is filled by an endlessly adaptable, enormously successful form of life

fig. A.58 Frederick Kiesler, handwritten notes on "Animal Building." ÖFLKS, TXT_6885/0_N7

fig. A.59a "The World of the Insects," *Life*, August 8, 1955, 43–55. Research press clipping. ÖFLKS, CLP_6591/0

fig. A.59b "The Life of the Bee," *Life*, August 11, 1952, 62–69. Research press clipping. ÖFLKS, CLP_6592/0

with architectural structures and the city, was right.[439] Kiesler's project is not a diachronic history of architecture, but it is what a discombobulated architectural history could become if it incorporated an anthropological theory of social structures.

While publishing opportunities dwindled and Kiesler became preoccupied with other projects and a slew of exhibitions, the research on themes of *Magic Architecture* did sporadically continue, as evidenced in the 1955 correspondence with *Life* magazine and the American Museum of Natural History soliciting articles on "diverse construction of the nests, homes, and burrows of various insects, birds, and animals," as well as series of notes by Kiesler on "animal building" in the same species that dealt with life processes: "eat, sleep, partur[ition]" within the "organization" cycles of "death" and the "living."[440] (fig. A.58) In addition to clippings of articles on insects and bees from *Life* (figs. A.59a–b) and a set of library slips from NYPL related to books on bees (including titles published between 1948 and 1954, after the manuscript of *Magic Architecture* was compiled),[441] Kiesler's research included a lengthy transcription of excerpts from Karl von Frisch's 1950 study of the "vision, chemical sense, and language" of bees including the olfactory orientation signals related to their "round dance."[442] While still interested in issues of "general construction" among animal species, the architect's focus in the 1950s shifts towards sensorial perception and spatial communication via new technological means and its relationship to human habitation.

Seeds of this endless research were transplanted in future publications. As mentioned, the discussion of the "wireless" and "touchless" communication through a termitary's solid walls reappears in Kiesler's *Inside the Endless House*, a collection of his "journal" notes from 1956 onwards published posthumously in 1966.[443] While metabolizing morsels of previous research, the same "journal" becomes a record of personal and professional events, such as travels and design commissions, that prevented Kiesler from completing the writing of *Magic Architecture* and other manuscripts he had planned. The "journal" also includes trips to monuments described in *Magic Architecture* such as the Pantheon in Rome and the Parthenon in Athens, which Kiesler sketched repeatedly, just like Le Corbusier on his first trip to Athens. Kiesler reproduced his sketches of the Acropolis in his "journal" (fig. A.60a) echoing again Le Corbusier's publication of his own drawings of the ancient Greek site in *Vers une architecture*.[444]

Yet the references to the Pantheon and the Parthenon in Kiesler's journal contained no extensive descriptions, as opposed to the frescoes of Michelangelo in the Vatican and Giotto in Assisi. "Giotto treats people like architecture and architecture like people," writes Kiesler. He celebrates both Giotto and Michelangelo, whom he describes as a "space-man" and even a "space-computer," as "tri-partite artists" combining architecture, painting, and sculpture "all in one"–a quality to which Kiesler himself aspired, especially in the large "environmental" sculptural and painting projects made during the last decades of his career.[445] Kiesler would stop over in cities such as Rome and Athens in his trips to Israel (fig. A.60b), where he was commissioned to design (with his architecture firm partner Armand Bartos the Shrine of the Book, a large museum project in Jerusalem housing the Dead Sea Scrolls Biblical Manuscripts. The building opened in April 1965, a few months before Kiesler's death.[446] Tellingly both of Kiesler's most important architectural designs, The Shrine of the Book and the Mobile Home Library, partially constructed in his Columbia Laboratory and featured in the penultimate plate of *Magic Architecture*, were designed as enclosures that would "house" books (plate 59). Books are perhaps the ideal inhabitants of Kiesler's projects across scales. If he could not write them, his built work allowed books by other authors to reside in them. Kiesler's "libraries-as-homes" and vice versa signal the essential metabolism (*Stoffwechsel* in Semper's terms) that transpires across the architect's book, exhibition, and building or painting projects. The metabolic project produced by the incompletion of his "Story of Housing" was the *Endless House*, born in 1947 (or *reborn* according to Kiesler), just as the book manuscript of *Magic Architecture* would appear to die.

Invented as a "tool" for a new type of architecture for the twentieth century that would oppose the machine instrumentalism of Le Corbusier, Kiesler's *Magic Architecture* transforms into a rudiment or even a fossil of its former organic self. Not only does it contain a number of incomplete or unrealized architectural projects by other authors, but the manuscript itself becomes a monumental ruin. An initial proposal by Kiesler to publishers in the US written after the end of the war mentions five hundred pages of text and one hundred illustrations, while another note to editors promises six hundred pages of text and two hundred illustrations (half of them "line cut" drawings).[447] The composite manuscript assembled in the archive of the Kiesler Foundation today includes three hundred pages of text and over seventy plates (initially numbered to sixty) in addition to five line diagrams and drawings, which means that this archival fragment is about half of the book volume originally projected by the architect.

But perhaps *Magic Architecture* could never be anything other than a fragment, not only because of the enormity of the task (a book in ten parts, each up to ten chapters that expand into so many different areas of knowledge) but because "incompletion," according to Friedell, is an essential ingredient of "world" histories. This is also the historical process through which Kiesler's book project transitions from "unfinished" to "endless." Like the rest of the architect's "endless" designs, *Magic Architecture* memorializes itself through the same preservationist techniques that de-*organicize* all active tools into fossils buried under the ground and waiting to be rediscovered by archaeologists, while their rudimentary vestiges are already engraved on the surface of contemporary structures.

AFTER MAGIC II: VISIONARY, FANTASTIC, SCULPTURAL, AND EVERYMAN'S ARCHITECTURES

If *Magic Architecture* is a missing chapter in the history of twentieth-century architectural literature, then the book from which it is missing has already been published, and the rest of its chapters have been completed by other authors, both before and after Kiesler's passing.

Perhaps the first glimpse of such *post-histoire* appeared while Kiesler was still alive, in the exhibition *Visionary Architecture* organized at MoMA in the fall of 1960. According to the press release, the exhibition featured "twentieth-century projects considered too revolutionary to build" which would present a "second history of architecture" "prior its becoming real," that is "unhampered by technical details and uncompromised by the whims of patrons, or the exigencies of finance, politics, and custom."[448] Among a widely heterogeneous compilation of projects that expanded from the unrealized skyscraper projects of El Lissitzky and Theo van Doesburg in the 1920s to emerging biological and ecological architectures in the late 1950s, such as Noriaki Kurokawa's *Agricultural City* (1959) and William Katavolos's *Chemical Architecture* (1960), the exhibition included the work of well-known American designers such as Frank Lloyd Wright's *Mile High Skyscraper* (1956), Louis Kahn's *City-Tower* (1955), Buckminster Fuller's imperious "dome shelter" over Manhattan Island (1960), as well as Le Corbusier's neo-colonial plans for Rio de Janeiro and Algiers (1929 and 1930). Yet next to the twentieth-century visionaries, the exhibition, curated by Arthur Drexler, Director of MoMA's department of architecture and design, also included an "introductory historical section" with a small number of "visionary" precedents beginning in the Renaissance with Leonardo da Vinci's "ideal city" plan and the imaginary towers of Filarete's *Sforzinda* to the Enlightenment of Étienne-Louis Boullée's Cenotaph for Isaac Newton.[449] (fig. A.61a)

Among this cornucopia of "visions," the exhibition included a space dedicated to Kiesler that featured a model of the *Endless House* along with photographs and a "life-size photo-mural" of its interior next to Kiesler's plans and drawings for his *Endless Theater* (1925) retracing the origins of the idea of the "Endless" at the beginnings and throughout the architect's career.[450] (fig. A.61b) Beyond previous juxtapositions with Fuller and Le Corbusier, *Visionary Architecture* put Kiesler's work in dialogue with the architectural representatives of German expressionism, Hermann Finsterlin, Bruno Taut (with drawings from *Alpine Architecture*, 1917–18) and Hans Poelzig (including his unrealized Festspielhaus for Salzburg of 1920). The last two of these designers also appear in *Magic Architecture* (as do Leonardo and Filarete) yet what brings *Visionary Architecture* closer to Kiesler's unfinished book project is the historical reevaluation of these "unbuilt" projects as object lessons that, in the words of Drexler, could help establish "critical standards" after which "vision and reality might then coincide"[451]–a coincidence that was at the core of Kiesler's definition of Magic Architecture as "Dream-Reality" even if such correspondence remained tentative.

*

In 1960, the same year that *Visionary Architecture* opened at MoMA, the architectural critic Ulrich Conrads and art historian Hans-Günther Sperlich published *Phantastische Architektur*, an account of mostly unbuilt projects selected from the first six decades of the twentieth century that, according to the authors, merged "utopia" not with reality but with "fantasy."[452] The richly illustrated publication centered on the designs of architects within the circles of German expressionism and the *Arbeitsrat für Kunst* (Work Council for Art) showcasing material recently recovered from the estates of Adolf Behne and Wenzel Hablik. The book has multiple overlaps with Kiesler's unpublished *Magic Architecture*: its selection of architectural projects is arranged thematically, allowing the authors to juxtapose buildings from different decades or even centuries and create a circuitous genealogy of "fantasy" within histories of architecture that is equally "fantastic"–that is, the product of a historiographic fiction. A number of the works included also appear in Kiesler's plates or drafts: Ferdinand Cheval's "Ideal Palace" in Hauterives and Piranesi's engraving of via Appia,[453] building plans shaped as alphabet letters by Gobert, Steingruber, and Glonner (reproduced in Ponten), projects by Sant'Elia, Scharoun, Tatlin, and several designs by Bruno Taut. The volume also contained an anthology of literary "documents" with texts on architecture by Scheerbart, Behne, and many others including a selection of the "Utopian Correspondence" between Bruno Taut and his circle later exhibited and published as "The Crystal Chain Letters" from the Hablik archive.[454]

In the English edition, published as *The Architecture of Fantasy* in the United States and *Fantastic Architecture* in Britain in 1963, translators Christiane and George Collins acknowledge "Ponten's Architecture that was not built" as well as the *Visionary Architecture* exhibition at MoMA, which "has finally brought Bruno Taut, Finsterlin, and the *Frühlicht* projects to public attention."[455] Even if the editors of the English edition mention Reyner Banham's *Theory and Design in the First Machine Age* among the precedents of their volume (perhaps because of Banham's emphasis on the work of Italian Futurists like Sant'Elia), the *Architecture of Fantasy* was most harshly reviewed by Banham in an issue of *Art Bulletin* for its "opportunistic" and "occasional" treatment of the newly available material on German expressionism, but also for its use of the term "utopia" as a "catch all" phrase for "any bit of nut-architecture that comes along."[456]

fig. A.60a Frederick Kiesler, Views of the Parthenon, Athens, April 25, 1958. Ink sketches mounted on paper for reproduction as line drawings in Kiesler, *Inside the Endless House. Art, People and Architecture: A Journal* (1966). ÖFLKS, SFP_6864/0

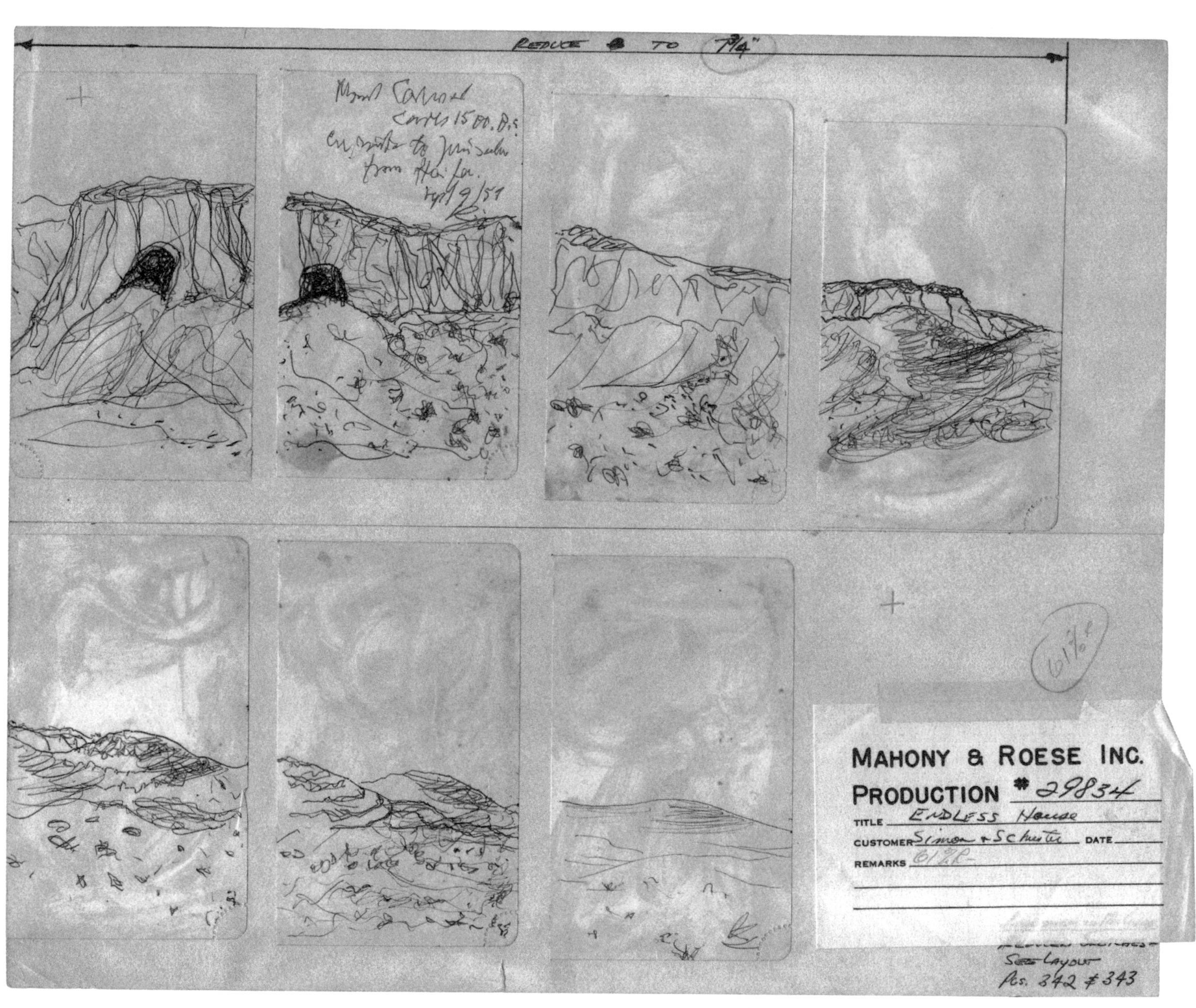

fig. A.60b Frederick Kiesler, “Mount Carmel caves 1500 B.C. Entrance to Jerusalem from Haifa Sept 9/57.” Maquette with ink drawings for reproduction as line drawings in Kiesler, *Inside the Endless House* (1966). ÖFLKS SFP_6851/0

While Kiesler was part of the *Visionary Architecture* show, he does not appear in the original edition of *Phantastische Architektur*. However, his library contains the first edition of Conrads and Sperlich's volume, which does not make any mention to his work. The expanded English editions rectified this omission with a spread on the *Endless House* (including photographs of the model exhibited at MoMA in 1960), and statements about the project by the architect.[457] The entry follows those on the expressionist designs of Poelzig and Finsterlin from the beginning of the twentieth century, as well as Gaudí and Hans Luckhardt (figs. A.62a–b). Sculptural architectural projects by Tekton and Luciano Baldessari from the 1940s and 1950s appear after Kiesler's work, as well as recent house projects by Bruce Goff in Oklahoma and California, and an egg-shaped "beach house" placed upon a rock designed by Sanford Hohauser. All, except for Kiesler, made the original cut. In a sense, Kiesler was present in *Fantastic Architecture* through the house designs of other architects before his own "house" model was added.

Tellingly, *Fantastic Architecture* did not contain Le Corbusier, perhaps because by 1960 most of his architecture was built, including some of his most "utopian" ideas. Kiesler may have not won the battle of the books with Corb, yet by the 1960s his "visionary" ideas about art, architecture, and the environment were gaining in popularity with a younger generation of practitioners and critics. Both architects died in 1965, signaling the end of their personal rivalry, yet the antagonism of their ideologies abides.

In 1964 Conrads published the first German edition of his popular anthology *Programs and Manifestoes of 20th-Century Architecture*, which included a brief excerpt from Kiesler's *Space City* manifesto first published in the mid-1920s (also translated in Part x of *Magic Architecture*), as well as a translation of Kiesler's brief "Magic Architecture for the Hall of Superstition," originally published in French in the catalogue of the *International Surrealism Exhibition* in Paris of 1947.[458] This was the only text with "Magic Architecture" in the title that was published during Kiesler's lifetime. And while not part of his book manuscript, its concluding paragraph entailed the "totality" of its message:

I oppose to the mysticism of Hygiene, which is the superstition of "Functional Architecture" the realities of a Magical Architecture rooted in the totality of the human being, and not in the blessed or accursed parts of this being.[459]

Even if the text originally published in 1947 was translated from Kiesler's English, the reference in its last statement on the "accursed parts" (*parties maudites*) of one's being has a prophetic Bataillian undertone.[460] It brings the characterization of "housing" as "magic and profane" in one of the general subtitles of the book manuscript of *Magic Architecture* or "holy and profane" in one of its chapter titles under a "general economic" perspective.[461] This perspective originates in the polarity between the pairing of capitalism and religion in the category of the "sacred," which the artist would abundantly experience while living in the US, and the illusive combination of art and the "everyday" in the "profane," which converts the "superfluous" into a "necessity" and leads to the "exuberant life" of *Magic Architecture*. The ultimate correlation produced by *Magic Architecture* would be that "magic and profane" would be unified into one state of being and housing type.

But if there is a published text written by Kiesler after 1947 that comes closest to the socio-economic principles of his unpublished *Magic Architecture*, then that would be the article "Notes on Architecture as Sculpture" that appeared in *Art in America* in May 1966, and whose "text and photo captions were completed," according to the journal editors, "one week before [the artist's] death" on December 27, 1965.[462] The article's content and illustrations rehearse part of the monumental iconography of the plates of *Magic Architecture*, including the Great Pyramid of Giza, the Parthenon, and Machu Pichu, as well as temples from India and Japan and a Gothic cathedral as diachronic examples of "architecture as sculpture." (see Annotated Chronology, figs. C.24a–d) But here the emphasis is on the "institutions" and "facts" that support these sacred monuments, whose long history includes, per Kiesler, religious buildings by twentieth-century architects such as Frank Lloyd Wright's Beth Sholom Synagogue in Philadelphia and Le Corbusier's catholic church in Ronchamp (for which Kiesler finally has a few good things to say).

The "facts" that determined the contemporary state of architecture correlate religion with economy, which by 1965 had become even more "profit" driven:

chiefly, a pursuit of fashions, an insidious by-product of our madness for the ever-changing new, a direct outgrowth of novelties sponsored at least twice a year by industry, be they womens' fashions, industrial design products–automobiles, refrigerators, washing machines, television sets--the whole range of a profit mentality, which truly builds in obsolescence as deliberately as nature makes everyone ultimately die–except that these manufactured objects have a much shorter range of life, some from season to season, others from showroom to junkyard.[463]

As Kiesler had stated in one of his preliminary drafts of *Magic Architecture*, "Modern man is [o]bsolete." This final article clarifies the reasons behind such "obsolescence" and the natural "death" it imposes on commodities and people (see Addenda, fig. C.05a).[464] The essay offers glimpses of what could have been Kiesler's introduction to "Fashion in Architecture" in Part VIII of *Magic Architecture* in its description of the ontological transformation of the "human being" while "bombarded hourly through newspapers, magazines, radio and television, to keep up with fashion." "To be is to sell yourself in style," Kiesler concludes.[465]

The last published article also redraws the socio-economic perspective that was launched in Kiesler's early chart on "Morphology" and expanded in *Magic Architecture* by reaffirming that "the most important impetus of any architecture is the vision of *a new social content*. Without that, we will go on building and building, constructing, *ad infinitum*, fooling ourselves with an ever-increasing amount of scientific equipment."[466] For the same reasons Kiesler castigates the endless "adaptations" of "cold-blooded glass boxes" by the "Bauhaus school" and the "imitators" of Mies van der Rohe, which have "unconditionally surrendered to air-conditioning. Their breathing is as artificial as the building's illusion of outside and inside, its extinction of privacy is a false adaptation of democracy."[467] Similar to the "Morphology" chart of thirty years earlier, here "democracy" is identified with capitalism and the industrialist aesthetic of contemporary commercial and/or residential towers.

The architect also diagnoses the symptoms of the reverse condition that had recently emerged against the loss of "privacy" in modern glass buildings, based on a solid "sculptural" exterior, as in Paul Rudolph's Art and Architecture building at Yale, which Kiesler compares to military uses of medieval fortresses echoing the building practices of the atomic era:

> **It is evident that the hermetic sealing of the interior from the outer world is a desirable protection against destruction by atomic weapons, which is on everyone's mind. Banning a direct hit, such buildings of concrete or stone or brick could constitute a fairly bombproof shelter. They could withstand powerful pressure by an explosion pretty well and resist fire. They could resist even better if they were built underground in a simple "Pelasgic" system of construction as in the treasury of Atreus in Mycenae.**[468]

For Kiesler, the atomic threat is as present in 1965 as it was two decades earlier when it suffused the writing of *Magic Architecture*.[469] There is no "postwar" era for the architect and given the ongoing wars and political tensions across the globe in the mid-1960s, the constancy of his anxiety was justified. Even the illusory "unity" emerging in the first years after the war within a climate of international collaboration that was recorded in the "Epilogue and Prologue" of *Magic Architecture* was eventually reduced to the formal rapport between architecture and sculpture. Yet Kiesler insists that the "evolution" of architecture as sculpture still entailed a radical revolutionary potential: "the difference between the glass houses of thirty years ago and the new approach of sculptural architecture," is "as violent, as the difference between powder-rifles and the principle of fission and fusion in atomic bombs and rockets."[470] Kiesler's renewed use of analogy with military technology discloses that sculptural architecture still hides a ballistic force that is furtively explosive. Yet such explosive impact is pacified and covered by the "fat" of technological gadgetry that softens the tissue of "skin and bones" glass houses by way of "meager interior furnishings equipped to disperse boredom with hi-fi, television with remote controls or telestar imagery with sound."[471] It is as if by 1965, TV sets and remote controls had domesticated the threat of telekinetic military technologies by transforming *Magic Architecture*'s "fear of the Unseen" into a comfortably domesticated spectacle.

While Wright and Le Corbusier build churches, the goal of "Everyman's home, is still to be achieved." But here Kiesler actually names some of the groups included in the category of "everyman,"

Opposite
figs. A.61a–b *Visionary Architecture* exhibition: (a) "Introductory Historical Section" (b) model and photomural of *The Endless House*, and model and drawings of *The Endless Theater* (1925), photos George Barrows. Historical Photographic Archive. Museum of Modern Art, September 29–December 4, 1960. The Museum of Modern Art Archives, New York. IN670.2.

Above
figs. A.62a–b Frederick Kiesler, *The Endless House*, "interior of living space," model, and plan in Ulrich Conrads and Hans Sperlich, *Fantastic Architecture*, translated, edited, and expanded by Christiane Crasemann Collins and George R. Collins (London: Architectural Press, 1963), 70–71.

including "the old, the young, the poet, the worker, the priest, jailbirds, thieves, money-changers, executives and truckers."[472] This reference brings us back to the change of the main title of Kiesler's book from *Magic Architecture* to *Everyman's Architecture* among existing typescripts, which is certainly telling, but we have no way of knowing which came first (fig. A.63).[473] "Everyman's" "everyday" architecture was a possibility within what Kiesler envisioned to be "Magic Architecture," or the two architectures could be combined into one as in Breton's discourse of *magique quotidienne*.[474] Kiesler's "magic" was instead meant to be grounded on "reality" and the subjective psychology, or following Freud, "psychopathology of everyday life."

The common objective of both *Magic* and *Everyman's Architecture* are the processes of life. Kiesler clarifies that the aim of his "research group" at the Columbia Laboratory for Design Correlation was primarily to "investigate the function of life-forces at their roots and not just modify or modernize old habits of living." He reaffirms his belief that "the study of the forces which make and maintain life is more important for schools of architecture than studies of past or present styles of design."[475] Histories of architecture ought then to transform into histories of life and the development of architectural processes designed to inform the living. Here, Friedell's grasp of "genetic" history ultimately generates in Kiesler an evolutionary architectural model for recreating life: "Nature creates bodies, but art creates life. Living in the *Endless House* is to live an exuberant life, not only the life of a digesting body or routine of social duties or the wind-up of functions of the four seasons, automatism of day and night, of high noon and midnight moon."[476] This supposedly new architectural form of life, which essentially regurgitates the evolutionist theories behind the architect's interwar writings on biotechnique, recreates not only life but time by breaking the "routine" cycle of natural periodicity, and, implicitly, a new type of history refusing to conform into the standardized periodicities of the "styles" and "fashions" of each era.

The reference to universal periodicity shows that "life forces" are also "cosmic forces," thus the ultimate environmental effect of Everyman's Architecture is a "cosmic" form of consciousness: "Thus, we will create a man-made cosmos around us, in which we will not have to depend on decorations to render our homes livable, but which will give us an awareness of belonging to a space center and of the ever-present cosmic forces which feed us continuously, nourish us physically, emotionally and spiritually, without end."[477] The infinite expansion of the house into outer space and the suffusion of individual "awareness" by a network of cosmic life forces had been previously described at length in the "The Universe as Architecture" chapter of *Magic Architecture* (I.8). Two decades later, this "universal" architecture acquires a new biopolitical content in the 1960s as science and technology transition away from the "atomic era" to a new "space age," during which humans appear to take control of the ethereal regions that previously threatened them. Kiesler's transformation of the house into a "space-center" signals a post-architectural condition that marks at once the dissolution and ultimate expansion of architecture and the self in the domain of a galactic "household." This cosmic expansion parallels the ambivalent development of Kiesler's projects in the last two decades of his career, from *Magic Architecture* to the *Endless House* and from the painted *Galaxies* to the corporeal 'space capsule' of *Bucephalus*, whose transient inhabitant can contemplate the universe while lying inside the emptied stomach of a dead horse, in preparation for an endless otherworldly encounter.

*

The final article also signals the dissolution of the self into a collectivity of authors, who will continue the environmental production of Endlessness after Kiesler. In "Architecture as Sculpture" Kiesler had cited the work of "a new group of designers and architects arising in the Unites States" whose experiments with new material technologies were informed by a programmatic merging of architecture and "science."[478] Similarly, the unfinished research of *Magic Architecture* was to be continued and published by others. Indeed, Kiesler's strictly bibliographic and often careless engagement with the Indigenous architecture of colonized territories in Africa, Oceania and the Americas was later extended by architect-researchers in the 1950s, 60s, and beyond.

This ambivalent lineage includes the research of Aldo van Eyck in collaboration with the ethnographer Hermann Hahn on the architecture of the Dogon in Africa published as journal articles in Dutch and English in the early 1960s.[479] It also addresses Bernard Rudofsky's well-known 1964 MoMA exhibition *Architecture without Architects* and accompanying catalogue that included a wide-ranging selection of "vernacular" architectures across the globe. [480] A preliminary list of photographs includes a section on "Amateur Architecture," whose sole representative is Ferdinand Cheval's "Ideal Palace," while another titled "Nature as architect, ruins, improved nature" comprised "rock cut dwellings in Cappadocia, Turkey," a volcano in Peru, an "ice grotto" in the South Pole, and the mineral formation known as the Enchanted City in Spain.[481] Another section on "Subterranean architecture, caves" reproduced present-day settlements, such as cave habitats in Cappadocia (again) and "troglodyte dwellings" in Tunisia" as well as the "Necropolis" in Pantalica in Sicily, and other similar sites in Italy.[482] The exhibition uncritically added the category of the "vernacular" next to the "Indigenous" and the "prehistoric" completing modernity's genealogy of architectural "others."

Rudofsky would later publish a "natural history of architecture" titled *The Prodigious Builders*, whose section on "Brute Architecture" describes the building structures of animal species, including the burrowing structures of beavers and the towers of termites, among other sections on the natural and human structures of caves, labyrinths, and "vernacular" dwellings. [483] Unlike Kiesler who essentially identifies "Animal Architecture" with the functional needs of "shelter," Rudofsky is interested in the built structures of animals such as beavers' dams that move beyond the sphere of "vital necessity," and similar to a "human trait," are in "excess" of one's "needs."[484] Rudofsky confirms to animal building, the "exuberance" of the "superfluous" that Kiesler aspires to affirm in human "everyday" structures. Even more than Kiesler's "Animal Architecture," Rudofsky's "Brute Architecture" was informed by the "ecological imbalance" of a world that was increasingly "shrinking" because of the extinction of vegetal, animal, and "architectural species."[485]

Evidently this genealogy continues with a more expressly utopian strand of pre-architectural schemes of the late 1960s and 70s in the work of Superstudio and other design collectives, who envisioned a post-apocalyptic desert landscape that appeared to be eerily prehistoric, yet reflected or *deflected* current emergencies during a period of ecological crisis and energy shortage. The indirect link here with *Magic Architecture* lies not only in the iconography of the pre-historicized landscape but rather in the format of the illustrated chart and its montage narrative, as in the "radical" group's film "storyboard" of world architecture from Stonehedge and the Egyptian pyramids to the "natural and artificial deserts" of the present, published in *Casabella* 1971, and which according to one of its editors summoned the pedagogical models of Bruno Taut's early twentieth-century utopias.[486] The post-catastrophic landscape of the mid-1970s created a mise-en-abyme with the atomic *cadrage* of the mid-1940s, when everything, including histories and practices of architecture, ought to start again from the beginning. In its "posthumous" publication, *Magic Architecture* records the origin, half-mythological and half-historical, of this ambivalent starting point.

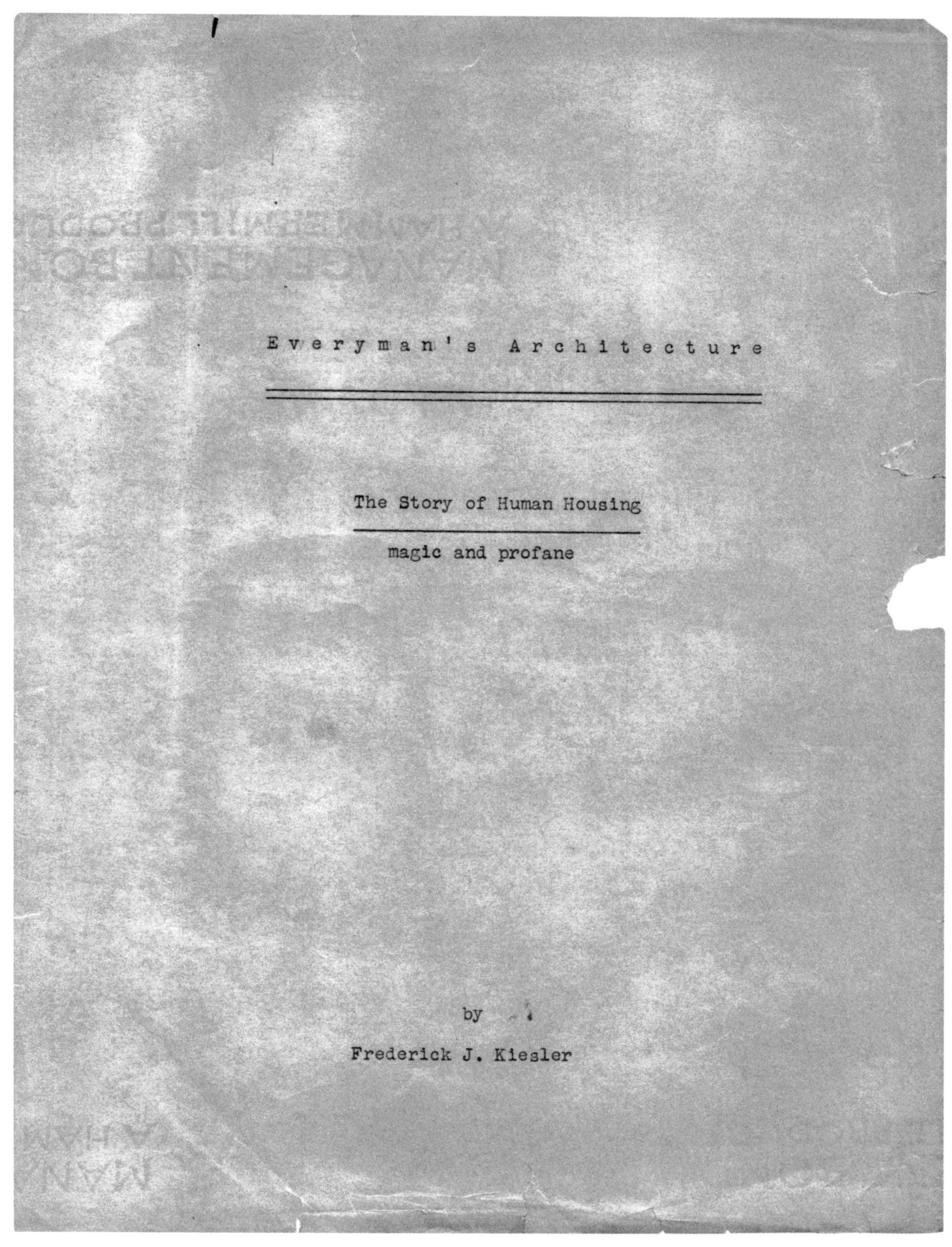
Everyman's Architecture

The Story of Human Housing

magic and profane

by

Frederick J. Kiesler

fig. A.63 Frederick Kiesler, "Everyman's Architecture/The Story of Human Housing/magic and profane," title page. ÖFLKS, TXT_6189/0_N3

1 "Atomic Blue Glow Kills Scientists / Army Reports Accidents Caused No Blast, Debris, or Noise," *The Sun* (New York, NY), June 28, 1946, 21. CLP 6463/0

2 Numerous manuals as well as instructional films from the 1940s document the operation of arc welding which produces a blue glow. See Lincoln Electric Company, *Procedure Handbook of Hand Welding Design and Practice* (Cleveland: Lincoln Electric Co., 1945). For the official account of the incident, see US Atomic Energy Commission, "A summary of accidents and incidents involving radiation in atomic energy activities–June 1945 through December 1955" (Washington, DC, 1956), 4-6. For a fictionalized account also published in the 1950s, see the novel by Dexter Masters, *The Accident* (New York: Alfred Knopf, 1955). On the career of the scientist who caused the accident, see Martin Zeilig, "Louis Slotin and 'the Invisible Killer,'" *The Beaver* 75, no. 4 (August-September 1995), 20-27.

3 For the text of these transcriptions see Addenda: Transcriptions and Translations, p. 360. TXT_6820/0; TXT_6820/1

4 "The Bomb Explodes: Photographs of Actual Detonation Show Blinding Flash and Firebal," *Life*, July 22, 1946, 52. CLP 65764/0

5 William L. Laurence, "Radar Waves find New Force in Atom," *New York Times*, September 21, 1947, 1-2. A prolific science journalist and Pulitzer winner, Laurence was the "appointed" historian of the Manhattan Project. He witnessed the dropping of the bomb in Japan as well as US nuclear tests elsewhere. He is the author of *Dawn Over Zero: The Story of the Atomic Bomb* (New York: Alfred A. Knopf, 1946) and other publications on atomic weapons.

6 David Dietz, "Smashing the Atom," *New York World Telegram*, November 17-19, 1936. Dietz was a science editor for the Scripps-Howard Newspapers (including the *New York World Telegram*) and author of *Atomic Energy in the Coming Era* (New York: Dodd, Mead & Co., 1945).

7 David Dietz, *Medical Magic* (New York: Dodd, Mead & Co., 1938). Dietz's bibliography lists only recent scientific literature, citing no references to histories or theories of magic.

8 For example: "By mimicking like with like man invents practical or sympathetic magic" (IV.5). Kiesler also quotes excerpts from the writings of Henri Breuil on prehistoric paintings (III.2) as well as Lynn Thorndike's *History of Magic* (IV.1) that refer to "sympathetic magic." The excerpts from Thorndike mention Frazer by name.

9 The edition in Kiesler's library is: James Frazer, *The Golden Bough: A Study in Magic and Religion*, 2 vols. (New York: The Book League of America, 1929).

10 Frazer, *The Golden Bough*, I.12. Extending the analogies between animist magic and the contemporary science of electrism, Frazer likens the functions of taboos to the performance of "electrical insulators" (I:225) and the body of the sacred man to "a Leyden jar charged with electricity" (II:594).

11 See "Sympathetic Magic" in Frazer, *The Golden Bough*, I:11-44, especially the first three paragraphs.

12 Michael Taussig, "*The Golden Bough*: The Magic of Mimesis," in *Mimesis and Alterity: A Particular History of the Senses* (London: Routledge, 1993), 44-58.

13 M. F. Ashley Montagu, "The Skillful Skull: Man's Braincase in its Ability to Resist and Dissipate Manifold Stresses is a Noteworthy Example of Efficient Architecture," *The Technology Review* XLV, no. 9 (July 1943): 3-7 included in Kiesler's research material. CLP_6536/0

14 On Semper's research on projectiles, see Gottfried Semper, *Über die bleiernen Schleudergeschosse der Alten* (Frankfurt: Verlag für Kunst und Wissenschaft, 1859).

15 Frederick Kiesler, research notes: SFP_6665/0_N3_verso See Addenda: Drafts.

16 Frederick Kiesler, research notes: SFP_6665/0_N3_recto See also Addenda: Drafts.

17 On the concept of "defense mechanism" and the problems of its "blanket use," see "Defense Mechanisms" Jean Laplanche and Jean-Bertrand Pontalis, *The Language of Psychoanalysis*, trans. Donald Nicholson-Smith (New York: Norton, 1973), 109-111.

18 See *MA* Main Text, I.1. TXT_6828/0_N5

19 See Taussig, *Mimesis and Alterity*, 55.

20 In addition to previous references to atomic technology, see sections on "Radiation" in the physics textbook included in Kiesler's library: Newton Henry Black and Harvey N. Davis, *Elementary Practical Physics* (New York: Macmillan, 1939).

21 See manuscript draft titled "Data and Annotations" with three annotations on Part I, chapter 1. TXT_6828/0_N1

22 In the first decades after it opened in 1930, the New Yorker Hotel was renowned for pioneering the latest technological advances, including telecommunication devices, such as radio, television, teletype services, and sanitation equipment, including portable bathroom cleaners with ultraviolet ray technology, all prominently advertised in the popular press.

23 Kiesler's research material for *Magic Architecture* includes the following articles on prefabricated structures: "Building for Defense ... 1,000 Houses a Day at $1,200 Each," *Architectural Forum* 74, no. 6 (June 1941): 425-429; and "The 8,000 LB. House: Fuller's $6,500 Four-Room Industrialized Unit is Round," *Architectural Forum* 84, no. 4 (April 1946): 129-137. The same 1946 issue of *Architectural Forum* includes several other articles and plenty of advertisements on prefabricated housing after the Second World War. See also Addenda: Bibliographies.

24 Kiesler clipped the photograph and plan of Fuller's Dymaxion from a page of the catalogue for *Art in Our Time* (New York: MoMA, 1939) and pasted it directly onto his plate without the use of a photostat, which is exceptional for his montage practices. For the source, see also List of Plates: Sources, and Addenda: Bibliographies.

25 Emphasis in the original. See deleted phrases in Kiesler's handwritten draft of the first chapter of Part I, which mentions Fuller as a "friend" (I.1). TXT_6801/0_N2

26 For Fuller's views on the role of climate in the migration and distribution of peoples around the globe, see his "Fluid Geography," first published as an article along with a "World map" in *American Neptune* IV, no. 2 (April 1944): 119-136. For his ideas on the higher state of "inventiveness" among humans living in colder climates, see his "Speculative Prehistory of Humanity" in Buckminster Fuller and Kiyoshi Kuromiya, *Critical Path* (New York: St. Martins, 1981), 3-24.

27 Note Kiesler's formulation, including a deleted phrase, in the following draft of Part I, chapter 1: **"Meanwhile, I hope, that man will find time–between moving from cold regions to colder ones, to exercise himself a little in the interests of culture, that is to give time to the Care of the Superfluous ~~(Civilization he will leave for each next colder region to invent into a higher and higher level.)~~"** TXT_6801/0_N3 Kiesler's identification between "civilization" and coldness becomes particularly poignant within persisting narratives of the importance of "cooling" in late-colonial and postcolonial discourses of "tropical architecture" after World War II.

28 See Main Text I.1. TXT_6828/0_N1 The *New York Evening Post* existed until 1934, when it became the *New York Post*. Fuller published a couple of short pieces in the *Evening Post* in 1932, and two other brief articles in the same paper by Elsa Maxwell and Harvey Wiley Corbett ran on the Dymaxion house design between 1945 and 1946. Unfortunately no interview or reference to the Arctic exist.

29 Leigh White, "Buck Fuller and the Dymaxion World," *Saturday Evening Post*, October 14, 1944, 22-23, 71-73.

30 For a different photograph of Kiesler on the floor of his apartment from the same shoot, see frontispiece of this book.

31 Both Kiesler and Fuller were later featured in MoMA's *Two Houses: New Ways to Build* exhibition in the fall of 1952 and the *Visionary Architecture* exhibition in the fall of 1960.

32 For a description of Kiesler's exhibition design proposals, including those not realized as well as those that traveled to Moscow, see Jean-Louis Cohen, "American Exhibits for Moscow," in *Building a New World: Amerikanizm in Modern Architecture* (New Haven: Yale University Press, 2020), 384-406.

33 "Note to the Editor," *Magic Architecture*, Main Text.

34 "Note to the Editor," *Magic Architecture*, Main Text.

35 Le Corbusier's book exists in Kiesler's library in its German edition, as *Kommende Baukunst*, trans. and ed. Hans Hildebrandt (Berlin: Deutsche Verlags-Anstalt, 1926). Kiesler's library also includes the original French edition of *The Radiant City* and the English edition of *When the Cathedrals Were White*, while one of his plates includes the reproduction of an illustration from the German edition of Le Corbusier's *Urbanisme*, again edited by Hildebrandt. Le Corbusier, *Quand les cathédrales étaient blanches; voyage aus pays des timides* (Paris: Librairie Plon, 1937); *La ville radieuse. Éléments d'une doctrine d'urbanisme pour l'équipement de la civilisation machiniste* (Boulogne-sur-Seine: Éditions L'architecture d'aujourd'hui, 1935); *Städtebau*, ed. and trans. Hans Hildebrandt (Berlin: Deutsche Verlags-Anstalt, 1929).

36 See also annotations in the Main Text (VII. Introduction). TXT_6755/0_N1

37 See for example Part X, chapter 8 ("The Hygiene of Functional Architecture") and plates 25b* and 54.

38 Le Corbusier and Pierre Jeanneret, "Le problème de la 'maison minimum,'" *Architecture Vivante* 8, no. 27 (Spring 1930): 5-15. The article draws from the architects' report for the second CIAM conference held in September 1929, which was republished in Le Corbusier's *La ville radieuse* (29-34). This is the only issue of *Architecture Vivante* in Kiesler's library, which contains several art and architecture journals from the US, France, and Germany.

39 Le Corbusier and Jeanneret, "Le problème de la 'maison minimum,'" 6. For Kiesler's comments, see copy of *Architecture Vivante* in the architect's library at the Kiesler Foundation.

40 Le Corbusier and Jeanneret, "Le problème de la 'maison minimum,'" 9-10. Kiesler also comments "wrong!!" next to a paragraph extolling the "need for horizontal surfaces that are [well] lit," and which offer "shelter from rain, temperature, and curiosity."

41 Le Corbusier and Jeanneret, "Le problème de la 'maison minimum,'" 7. Frederick Kiesler, "Manifest. Vitalbau-Raumstadt-Funktionelle Architektur," *De Stijl* no. 10-11 (1924-1925): 141-146. The English translation included in *Magic Architecture* was first published in Kiesler, *Contemporary Art in the Store and Its Display* (New York: Brentano's, 1930), 48.

42 See Kiesler's unpublished manuscript of 1947, "Menschen, Kunst und Architektur," described in Almut Grunewald, "People, Art and Architecture Versus Space, Time and Architecture," in *Frederick Kiesler: Face to Face with the Avant-Garde, Essays on Network and Impact*, ed. Peter Bogner and Gerd Zillner (Basel: Birkhäuser, 2020) 237-248.

43 Le Corbusier, *Vers une architecture*, 2nd ed. (Paris: Crès et Co., 1924), 53-56; Le Corbusier, *Kommende Baukunst*, 53-56; and Joseph Rykwert, *On Adam's House in Paradise: The Idea of the Primitive Hut in Architectural History* (New York: Museum of Modern Art, 1972), 14-16.

44 According to Vogt, there is a veiled reference to the Neolithic lake dwellings in Le Corbusier's *Urbanisme* alongside images of "savage huts" and more explicit descriptions in his *Une Maison, un Palais* as part of a typological genealogy of prehistoric structures that includes the Neolithic structures of Stonehenge and the Ġgantija megalithic complex on the island of Gozo. Adolf Max Vogt, *Le Corbusier, The Noble Savage: Toward an Archaeology of Modernism* (Cambridge, MA: The MIT Press, 1998), 183-224; see also page 222 where Vogt mentions how Hans Hildebrandt in the German edition of *Urbanisme* (*Städtebau*) makes clear that a map of "lake dwellings" included in the book's illustrations refers to Zurich before Roman occupation.

45 Fabiola López-Durán, "Picturing Evolution: Le Corbusier and the Remaking of Man," in *Eugenics in the Garden: Transatlantic Architecture and the Crafting of Modernity* (Austin: University of Texas Press, 2019), 144-188.

46 On Kiesler's references to genetics as well as "social and technological heredity," see Frederick Kiesler, "'On Correalism and Biotechnique': A Study on the Genetics of Building Design," *Architectural Record* 86, no. 3 (September 1939): 60-75. See also Herbert William Conn, *Social Heredity and Social Evolution: The Other Side of Eugenics* (New York: The Abingdon Press, 1914). And for a later study see Ashley Montagu, *Human Heredity* (New York: New American Library, 1960) included in Kiesler's library.

47 Le Corbusier, *Kommende Baukunst*, 222. In the original edition: "Maisons en série pour artisans," *Vers une architecture*, 224-225.

48 Le Corbusier, "Le problème de la "maison minimum,'" 5-6.

49 The architect describes his travels in Le Corbusier, *Journey to the East*, ed. and trans. Ivan Zaknic in collaboration with Nicole Pertuiset (Cambridge, MA: The MIT Press, 1989), 15-19.

50 See caption for plates 25a* and 25b* (there are two earlier pairs of plates with the exact same numbers, which may imply that these plates are later additions). In an outline of the projected "first part" of his book project, Kiesler uses the term "physio-functional" for the design of "shelter." See "Preliminary Outline of 'First Part'" in Addenda: Drafts.

51 Max Verworn, *Ideoplastische Kunst (Ein Vortrag)* (Jena: Gustav Fischer, 1914); and *Zur Psychologie der Primitiven Kunst (Ein Vortrag)* 2nd ed. (Jena: Gustav Fischer, 1917). Kiesler's library includes Verworn's *Allgemeine Physiologie* (Jena: Fischer, 1915) but not the two previous books.

52 Verworn, *Zur Psychologie der Primitiven Kunst*, 20-21. For the Kieslers' transcriptions of excerpts from Verworn's lecture "on the psychology of primitive art," including an annotated chart by Kiesler, see Addenda: Transcriptions and Translations, pp. 363-64.

53 On the function of these clay artifacts as spatial architectural models as well as drinking vessels, see Juliet B. Wiersema, *Architectural Vessels of the Moche: Ceramic Diagrams of Sacred Space in Ancient Peru* (Austin: University of Texas Press, 2015). And Joanne Pillsbury, "Building for the Beyond: Architectural Models from the Ancient Americas," in *Design for Eternity: Architectural Models from the Ancient Americas* (New York: Metropolitan Museum of Art, 2015), 3-29 (particularly 26-29).

54 Philip Ainsworth Means, *Ancient Civilizations of the Andes* (New York and London: Charles Scribner's Sons, 1931), 82, fig. 17-19. The Kieslers made photostats of two pages from the book–pages 80 (containing descriptions of these "house representations" by Means) and 82, at the New York Public Library–but only used the drawings from page 82 in plate 25a*. PHO_7157/0 and 7159/0 The images of the Peruvian architectural models in Means's book follow an earlier publication by the German anthropologist and archaeologist Arthur Baessler with drawings by the illustrator Wilhelm von den Steinen. Arthur Baessler, *Ancient Peruvian Art. Contributions to the Archaeology of the Empire of the Incas from his Collections*, vol. 1., trans. A. H. Keane (New York: Dodd, Mead & Co., 1902-1903), fig. 50 in plate 11 and figs. 55 and 58 in plate 13. See also List of Plates: Sources.

55 See outline for Part I transcribed in Addenda: Drafts. TXT_6807/0

56 See "Pottery Vessels from Trujillo in the Form of Houses and Temple-Pyramids," in Georg Buschan, ed., *Illustrierte Völkerkunde*, vol. 1., 2nd ed. (Stuttgart: Strecker und Schröder, 1922), 398, fig. 158. These drawings are also after Baessler. The section on America of this illustrated ethnology is authored by the German Americanist archaeologist Walter Krickeberg (also the author of an article in *Koralle* among Kiesler's research clippings. See Addenda: Bibliographies). TXT_6876/0_N1-N2 for Kiesler's handwritten notes and sketches of several images of ethnological artifacts and monuments from this volume.

57 See "Preliminary Outline of 'First Part,'" transcribed in Addenda: Drafts. TXT_6807/0

58 For a full list of *National Geographic* articles among Kiesler's clippings, see Addenda: Bibliographies. The same list includes articles from *Life* dating from 1945 to 1955.

59 For a full list of articles from *Koralle* among Kiesler's clippings, see Addenda: Bibliographies.

60 The full title of the weekly publication for the years 1938 and 1939 and during the period of National Socialism was *Koralle. Wochenschrift für Unterhaltung, Wissen, Lebensfreude*. In its earlier incarnation as a monthly in the 1920s it was titled *Die Koralle. Monatshefte für Alle Freunde von Natur und Technik* (Monthly for All Friends of Nature and Technology). For a study of the periodical, see Cora Bendig, *Die populärwissenschaftliche Zeitschrift Koralle im Ullstein und Deutschen Verlag 1925–1944* (PhD diss., Ludwig Maximilian University, 2014).

61 Lucien Biart, *The Aztecs: Their History, Manners and Customs*, trans. J. L. Garner (Chicago: McClurg & Co., 1887). Walter Krickeberg, "Menschenopfer für den Sonnengott: Wie die Azteken den Fortbestand der Welt sichern wollten" *Koralle* 6, no. 24 (June 19, 1938): 852–853.

62 See notes 9 and 10.

63 A crude example of such conflation is in a *National Geographic* article clipped and used by Kiesler in his plates, in which the author, a sugar plantation "pathologist" and geography lecturer sent on an expedition to New Guinea to explore new profitable avenues in sugar cane production, purports to have discovered "Neolithic man" in Indigenous societies on account of their use of stone tools. E. W. Brandes, "Into Primeval Papua by Seaplane: Seeking Disease-Resisting Sugar Cane, Scientists Find Neolithic Man in Unmapped Nooks of Sorcery and Cannibalism," *National Geographic* LVI, no. 3 September 1929, 253–332. Kiesler uses three illustrations from this article in plates 9 and 12a.

64 For an anthropological critique of such historiographic practice in parallel with the politics of colonialization and the globalization induced by capitalism, see the classic study of Eric R. Wolf, *Europe and the People Without History* (Berkeley: University of California Press, 1982).

65 On the history of the use of these terms in nineteenth- and twentieth-century contexts, see among many others: Elazar Barkan and Ronald Bush, ed., *Prehistories of the Future: The Primitivist Project and the Culture of Modernism* (Stanford: Stanford University Press, 1995). For a history of twentieth-century "primitivism" in German literature with particular reference to the impact of Lévy-Bruhl's ethnosociological theories, Nicola Gess, *Primitive Thinking: Figuring Alterity in German Modernity* (Berlin: De Gruyter, 2022).

66 See footnotes in the eighth chapter of Lévy-Bruhl's *Les fonctions mentales dans les societies inferieures* (Paris: Alcan, 1910). Kiesler read and transcribed excerpts from the German edition: Lucien Lévy-Bruhl, *Das Denken der Naturvölker*, ed. Wilhelm Jerusalem, trans. P. Friedlander, 2nd ed. (Vienna and Leipzig: Braumüller, 1926), 267–322.

67 Kiesler uses a photograph reprinted among Spencer and Gillen's published studies of the "Arunta" and other Indigenous Australians in his plates, which indicates that either he or his wife Stefi looked at their work while selecting images, as they did with publications not cited in his text. See sources in the list of captions for plate 11.

68 James Clifford, "On Ethnographic Surrealism," in *The Predicament of Culture: Twentieth-Century Ethnography, Literature, and Art* (Cambridge, MA: Harvard University Press, 1988), 117–148.

69 Clifford further adds: "The term *ethnography* as I am using it here is evidently different from the empirical research technique of a human science that in France was called ethnology, in England social anthropology, and in America cultural anthropology." *The Predicament of Culture*, 121.

70 See Annotated Chronology; and Bogner and Zillner, eds., "Biographical Miscellanea and Nodes in the Network," in *Face to Face with the Avant-Garde, Essays on Network and Impact* (Basel: Birkhäuser, 2020), 15–52 (for Kiesler's acquaintance and collaborations with Breton in the 1940s, 31–34).

71 For example, Kiesler's common interest with the surrealists in Pre-Columbian art and Aztec sacrifices documented in *Magic Architecture*. On Kiesler's first meeting with surrealist artists on an exposition about magic, see entry October 30, 1945, in Annotated Chronology.

72 Clifford, *The Predicament of Culture*, 129–134. The Kieslers' library includes one issue of *Documents* (1930) with articles and "chronicles" on "ethnographic" subjects by George Bataille, Michel Leiris, Georges-Henri Riviere, Carl Einstein, and others, as well as two issues of *Minotaure*: no. 3–4 (1933) and no. 7 (1935), which do not contain ethnographic material.

73 Clifford, *The Predicament of Culture*, 140, 145. On the differences of museological and anthropological approaches between the two French ethnographic museums, see Alice L. Conklin, *In The Museum of Man: Race, Anthropology, and Empire in France, 1850–1950* (Ithaca: Cornell University Press, 2013).

74 On a broader study of anti-humanism in early twentieth-century German anthropology, Andrew Zimmerman *Anthropology and Antihumanism in Imperial Germany* (Chicago: University of Chicago Press, 2001), particularly chapter 2 "*Kultur* and *Kulturkampf*: The *Studia Humanitas* and the People Without History," 38–61.

75 See Jo Odgers, Flora Samuel, and Adam Sharr, eds., *Primitive: Original Matters in Architecture* (London: Routledge, 2006).

76 Ginger Nolan, *Savage Mind to Savage Machine: Racial Science and Twentieth-Century Design* (Minneapolis: University of Minnesota Press, 2021), particularly 1–8, "Introduction: From Primitivism to Structuralism;" and 83–108, "Postwar European Modernism or What the Primitive Hut Really Said."

77 See Annotated Chronology.

78 In addition to lectures at MoMA and the Dalton School, Frobenius spoke at the Museum of Natural History, the Metropolitan Museum of Art, and Sarah Lawrence College. See Richard Kuba, "Leo Frobenius in New York. Felsbilder im Museum of Modern Art," in *Zwischen Aneignung und Verfremdung: ethnologische Gratwanderungen. Festschrift für Karl-Heinz Kohl*, ed. Volker Gottowik, Holger Jebens, and Editha Platte (Frankfurt: Campus Verlag, 2009), 139–155 (for Frobenius's New York lectures, 143–44). Reprinted in Karl-Heinz Kohl, Richard Kuba, and Hélène Ivanoff, eds., *Kunst der Vorzeit: Felsbilder aus der Sammlung Frobenius* (Munich: Prestel Verlag, 2016), 186–199.

79 Leo Frobenius, "The Story of Rock Picture Research," in Leo Frobenius and Douglas C. Fox, *Prehistoric Rock Pictures in Europe and Africa: From Material in the Archives of the Research Institute for the Morphology of Civilization, Frankfort-on-Main* (New York: The Museum of Modern Art, 1937), 13–28 (for the excerpts quoted by Kiesler, 22–23). Frobenius's essay was a translation of his introduction to his collection of rock paintings published the previous year: Leo Frobenius, "Unser Beitrag zur Felsbilderforschung" in *Das Urbild. Cicerone zür vorgeschichtliche Reichsbildergalerie* (Frankfurt am Main: Forschungsinstitut fur Kulturmorphologie, 1936), 4–22. See also Kuba, "Leo Frobenius in New York," 144. For a history of Frobenius's exhibitions on prehistoric art and their association with modern art institutions, see Kohl, Kuba, and Ivanoff, eds., *Kunst der Vorzeit: Felsbilder aus der Sammlung Frobenius*.

80 Frobenius, *Prehistoric Rock Pictures*, 22; quoted in *MA*, I.1.

81 Leo Frobenius, *Kulturgeschichte Afrikas. Prolegomena zu einer historischen Gestaltlehre* (Zurich: Phaidon-Verlag, 1933). French edition: Léo Frobenius, *Histoire de la civilisation africaine*, trans. Hanne Back and D. Ermont (Paris: Gallimard, 1936). Stefi and Frederick Kiesler's transcriptions include several passages from Frobenius's *Kulturgeschichte Afrikas*. For a translation of excerpts not included in the assembled manuscript of *Magic Architecture*, see Addenda: Transcriptions and Translations, pp. 360–61.

82 Kiesler's research clippings also include illustrations from Frobenius's book *Erythräa: Länder und Zeiten des heiligen Königsmordes* (Berlin: Atlantis Verlag, 1931), not mentioned in *MA*. See Addenda: Bibliographies.

83 See Frobenius, *Kulturgeschichte Afrikas*, 213–231, including figures with architectural drawings as well as maps of Africa marking the geographic distribution of each building style. See also the following section, 234–241.

84 See Kiesler's endnote 3 in Part I, chapter 1: "Extensive quote from Frobenius: Hystorie [sic] of the Culture Africa's. The Hamitic Type and the Aethiopean Type." TXT_6828/0_N1 On a different page, Kiesler adds the following notes in German: "Hamitische Kunst: 'Ich bin–die Welt sei.' / äthiopische Kunst: Tod-leben-gemeinschaft" ("Hamitic Art: 'I am–the world is.' / Ethiopian Art: Death-life-community"]. TXT_6828/0_N5 See *MA* annotated text, I.1. For an extensive critical analysis of Frobenius's theoretical descriptions of African architecture, along with the writings of his father Hermann, see Itohan Osayimwese, "On Architecture and the Myth of Authenticity During the German Colonial Period," *Traditional Dwellings and Settlements Review* 24, no. 2 (2013): 11–22; "Prolegomenon to an Alternative Genealogy of German Modernism: German Architects' Encounters with World Cultures c. 1900," *The Journal of Architecture* 18, no. 6 (December 2013): 835–874; and *Colonialism and Modern Architecture in Germany* (Pittsburgh: University of Pittsburg Press, 2017), 71–76.

85 Frobenius, *Kulturgeschichte Afrikas*, 214, 234. In Frobenius's earlier popular study on "the unknown Africa," Hamitic and Ethiopian cultures are associated with "chthonic" and "tellurian" *Kultursymptome* also manifested in architecture and construction tropes, or *Bauweise*. *Kulturgeschichte Afrikas* shares a number of architectural illustrations with this earlier book, which as originally noted by Fritz Neumeyer and recently analyzed in detail by Itohan Osayimwese was read by Mies van der Rohe. Leo Frobenius, *Das unbekannte Afrika: Aufhellung der Schicksale eines Erdteils* (Munich: C. H. Becksche Verlangsbuchhandlung, 1923), 69–77. See also Osayimwese, "On Architecture and the Myth of Authenticity," 15.

86 Frobenius, *Kulturgeschichte Afrikas*, 214.

87 Frobenius, *Kulturgeschichte Afrikas*, 219, fig. 169 (fig. A.11b) and NYPL photostat in the Kiesler collection (fig. A.09). PHO_7231/0 An earlier spread in Frobenius's book contains drawings of the plan and section of an "Earth-dwelling of the Gurunsi 'Slaves,'" 217, fig. 168. The oval shape and four similar side chambers are reminiscent of the form of Kiesler's (later) design of the *Endless House*, but the drawings are not reproduced in *Magic Architecture* or Kiesler's Photostats (fig. A.11a).

88 Frobenius, *Kulturgeschichte Afrikas*, 214.

89 Frederick Kiesler, charts on the building tools of animals and humans SFP_6664/0_N2; SFP_6665/0_N3 reproduced in Addenda: Charts. Here Kiesler regurgitates the racist myths and unscientific observations surrounding Pygmies, "drawing analogies between Pygmies and animals, or, …casting doubt on the status of Pygmies as humans"–biased preconceptions, which as Chris Ballard explains originate in western colonial travelers' accounts in the eighteenth century and persevered well into the first half of the twentieth and beyond. See Chris Ballard "Strange Alliance: Pygmies in the Colonial Imaginary," *World Archaeology* 38, no. 1 (2006): 133–151.

90 Frobenius, *Kulturgeschichte Afrikas*, 215.

91 Frobenius, *Kulturgeschichte Afrikas*. Drawings of the "four-cornered" and the "round pile hut" are reproduced on page 226, figs. 174 and 175. For the photostat of this page partly used in plate C.1, see fig. A.10. PHO_7237/0

92 Suzanne Marchand, "Leo Frobenius and the Revolt against the West," *Journal of Contemporary History*, 32, no. 2 (April 1997): 153–170; and Michael Spöttel, "German Ethnology and Antisemitism: The Hamitic Hypothesis," *Dialectical Anthropology* 23 (1998): 131–150.

93 Marchand, "Leo Frobenius," 165.

94 Leo Frobenius, *Vom Kulturreich des Festlandes (Dokumente zur Kulturphysiognomik)* (Berlin: Volksverband der Bücherfreund Wegweiser-Verlag, 1923), 96–97. Also cited in Marchand, "Leo Frobenius." On the political motivations of Frobenius's cultural morphology, see Renèe Sylvain, "Leo Frobenius: From '*Kulturkreis* to *Kulturmorphologie*,'" *Anthropos* 91 (1996): 483–494.

95 Marchand, "Leo Frobenius," 165.

96 See Leo Frobenius, *Schicksalskunde* (Weimar: Hermann Böhlaus Nachfolger, 1938), 76, 89–93, 128; also cited in Marchand, "Leo Frobenius."

97 Frobenius, *Prehistoric Rock Pictures*, 46–47.

98 On the European folklore of "foundation sacrifice," see Frazer, *The Golden Bough*. In her study of sacrificial narratives centered on Equatorial Africa, Florence Bernault argues that stories of human sacrifice occupying "the core of colonial imaginaries" in nineteenth- and early twentieth-century western literatures reflect the extensive violence affronting colonized bodies in these areas. Florence Bernault, "Body, Power and Sacrifice in Equatorial Africa," *Journal of African History* 47 (2006): 207–239.

99 See section E, "Architektonisches" in the register of subjects in Frobenius, *Kulturgeschichte Afrikas*, 646–647.

100 Hermann Klaatsch, *Der Werdegang der Menschheit und die Entstehung der Kultur*, ed. Adolf Heilborn, 2nd exp. ed. (Berlin: Deutsches Verlagshaus Bong & Co., 1922). The first edition was published by the same press in 1920. Klaatsch was previously a professor at the University of Heidelberg. On Klaatsch's studies and academic career, see the obituary by Bruno Oetteking, "Hermann Klaatsch," *American Anthropologist* 18, no. 3 (1916): 422–425.

101 On Klaatsch's earlier comprehensive study on the origins of human evolution preceding his Australian trip, see Hermann Klaatsch, "Entstehung und Entwickelung des Menschengeschlechtes," in *Weltall und Menschheit: Geschichte der Erforschung der Natur und der Verwertung der Naturkräfte im dienste der Völkern*, ed. Hans Kraemer (Berlin: Bong, 1902–1904), II:3–338. For a comparison between the cultures of prehistoric Europeans and Indigenous Australians, see Klaatsch's *Die Anfänge von Kunst und Religion in der Urmenschheit* (Leipzig: Verlag Unesma, 1913). For a complete and astutely critical study of Klaatsch's travel to Australia, see Corinna Erckenbrecht, *Auf der Suche nach den Ursprüngen. Die Australienreise des Anthropologen und Sammlers Hermann Klaatsch 1904–1907* (Cologne: Gesellschaft für Völkerkunde, Verein zur Förderung des Rautenstrauch-Joest-Museums der Stadt Köln, 2010). For an English translation of one of Klaatsch's reports from Australia, see Brigitte Stehlik, "Hermann Klaatsch and the Tiwi, 1906," *Aboriginal History*, 10 (1986): 59–78.

102 Matthew P. Fitzpatrick, "Indigenous Australians and German Anthropology in the era of Decolonization," *The Historical Journal* 63, no. 3 (2020), 686–709 (for references to Klaatsch's polygenist theory 694 and 704). See also, John Collette, "Hermann Klaatsch's Views on the Significance of the Australian Aborigines," *Aboriginal History* 11, no. 1/2 (1987): 98–99.

103 Klaatsch *Der Werdegang der Menschheit und die Entstehung der Kultur*, 237–238.

104 On Klaatsch's collection of artifacts and human remains as well as transcriptions of his letters from Australia documenting his illicit methods and practices for obtaining them, see the exhibition catalogue by Carsten Wergin and Corinna Erckenbrecht, *Der Ruf des Schneckenhorns. Hermann Klaatsch (1863–1916). Ein Heidelberger Wissenschaftler in Nordwestaustralien* (Heidelberg: heiBOOKS, Universität's Bibliothek Heidelberg, 2018). See also Erckenbrecht, *Auf der Suche nach den Ursprüngen*; and Fitzpatrick, "Indigenous Australians and German Anthropology." On the same subject, see Antje Kühnast, "Hermann Klaatsch's 'Australoid' common ancestors," in *Theorising Race and Evolution. German Anthropologie's Utilisation of Australian Aboriginal Skeletal Remains During the Long Nineteenth Century* (PhD diss., University of New South Wales, 2017), 236–268.

105 Adolf Heilborn, "Preface," in Klaatsch, *Der Werdegang*, iii. On Heilborn's articles for *Koralle*, see Bendig, *Die populärwissenschaftliche Zeitschrift Koralle*, 131–152 and 163–164. For a biography and list of books published by Heilborn (born Jewish but later dissociated from the Jewish community), see Archiv Bibliographia Judaica: *Lexikon deutsch-jüdischer Autoren*, vol. 10 (Munich: K. G. Saur, 2002), 311–325. Among his many publications on physical and cultural anthropology, natural history, art, and literature, Heilborn wrote a popular history of the German colonies: Adolf Heilborn, *Die Deutschen Kolonien (Land und Leuten)*, 3rd ed. (Leipzig: Teubner, 1912).

106 Hermann Klaatsch, *Grundzüge der Lehre Darwins. Allgemein verständlich dargestellt.* (Mannheim: J. Bensheimer, 1919); and Adolf Heilborn, *Darwin. Sein Leben und seine Lehre* (Berlin: Ullstein, 1927). Heilborn was also a follower of Ernst Haeckel.

107 Hermann Klaatsch, *Das Werden der Menschheit und die Anfänge der Kultur*, continued and supplemented [*fortgeführt und ergänzt*] by Julius Andree, Hans Weinert, and Jörg Lechler (Berlin and Leipzig: Deutsches Verlagshaus Bong & Co., 1936).

108 Adolf Heilborn, "Die neusten Ergebnisse der Paläontologie des Menschen." in Klaatsch, *Der Werdegang der Menschheit* (1922), 387–419. On the same subject, see Heilborn's earlier publication, which extensively covers the research of Klaatsch: Adolf Heilborn, *Der mensch der Urzeit. Vier Vorlesungen aus der Entwicklungsgeschichte des Menschengeschlechts* (Leipzig: Teubner, 1910).

109 Hermann Klaatsch and Adolf Heilborn, *The Evolution and Progress of Mankind*, trans. Joseph McCabe (New York: Frederick Stokes Company, 1923). For the Kieslers' transcriptions from the English edition of Klaatsch's book, see TXT_6844/0_N1-N5

110 Cf. MA I.1 with Klaatsch, *Der Werdegang der Menschheit* (1922), 223; and *The Evolution and Progress* (1923), 203.

111 The French ethnologist uses the term *action à distance*. Lévy-Bruhl, *Les fonctions mentales dans les sociétés inférieures*, 78. The German translation of Lévy Bruhl's book (which Kiesler read and quotes in MA) translates the same term as *Fernwirkung*. Lucien Lévy-Bruhl, *Das Denken der Naturvölker*, ed. Wilhelm Jerusalem, trans. P. Friedlander (Vienna-Leipzig: Braumüller, 1921), 58. The English edition uses the term "telekinesis": Lucien Lévy-Bruhl, *How Natives Think*, trans. Lilian A. Claire (London: Allen 1926), 77.

112 Egon Friedell, *Kulturgeschichte des Altertums: Leben und Legende der vorchristlichen Seele* (Zurich: Helicon Verlag, 1936), 44. For an English translation of the Kieslers' transcriptions from Friedell's history including this passage, see Addenda: Transcriptions and Translations, pp. 364–67.

113 Volkhard Bode and Gerhard Kaiser, *Building Hitler's Missiles: Traces of History in Peenemünde*, trans. Katy Derbyshire (Berlin: Ch. Links Verlag, 2008).

114 See cover in Klaatsch, *Der Werdegang der Menschheit*, editions of 1920 and 1922 and painting after Wilhelm Kranz "Australier ersteigt einen Baum," color plate IV and related photographs 88–89 (figs. 86–87).

115 Klaatsch, *The Evolution and Progress* (1923), 189–190.

116 Klaatsch, *The Evolution and Progress* (1923), 190.

117 In a handwritten version of Part I, chapter 1 of MA that refers to the earliest humans, Kiesler deletes and substitutes "Neanderthals" with the term "Homo primigenius," which appears several times in Klaatsch's book. Homo primigenius was originally used by Ernst Haeckel and the anatomical paleoanthropologist Gustav Schwalbe, who described Neanderthals as the "first-born humans" in relation with (yet distinct from) later humans. However, Klaatsch disagreed with such views and disputed the use of the term primigenius: "Certain scholars were also inclined towards the opinion that Neanderthals were the actual primeval humans (*Urmenschen*), the ancestors of at least all Europeans, and out of this error one can explain the inappropriate (*unzweckmässige*) description Homo Primigenius (that is, the first-born human) for the Neanderthal race, a description, which is just as unfortunate (*unglücklich*) as Elephas primigenius for the Mammoth, which, earlier on, was considered the oldest representative of elephants in Europe." See Klaatsch *Der Werdegang der Menschheit* (1922), 317; and *The Evolution and Progress* (1923), 271. Note that in his "Prehistory of Humans" of 1904, Schwalbe had precisely argued that the classificatory appellation Homo Primigenius should "perhaps most purposefully [*wohl am zweckmässigsten*] be attributed" to Neanderthals in order to reflect their "more primitive characters" [*primitivere Charaktere*], in distinction from those of the "human type living today, first appearing in the younger diluvium." Gustav Schwalbe, *Die Vorgeschichte des Menschen* (Braunschweig: Vieweg, 1904), 10. After World War II the term became obsolete. On the racial and nationalist controversies reflected in the use and disuse of the term, see Fred H. Smith, "The Naming of Neanderthals. William King, Ernst Haeckel and the rise and fall of 'Homo primigenius.'" Presentation abstract. American Association of Physical Anthropologists (2016).

118 Klaatsch, *Der Werdegang der Menschheit* (1922), 192–211. In the English edition, the section on "housing" forms a separate chapter titled "The Evolution of the Home," in *The Evolution and Progress* (1923), 177–190.

119 Klaatsch, *Der Werdegang der Menschheit* (1922), 169–192; and "The Evolution of Clothing," in *The Evolution and Progress*, 163–189. Heilborn also wrote extensively on the evolution of clothing and bodily adornment in his "general ethnological" studies: Adolf Heilborn, *Allgemeine Völkerkunde, Vol. I: Feuer, Nahrung, Wohnung, Schmuck, und Kleidung*, 2nd ed. (Leipzig: B. G. Teubner, 1915), 92–131. Both books by Klaatsch and Heilborn cite the anthropological study of "adornment" by the evolutionist primatologist and cultural anthropologist Emil Selenka, *Der Schmuck des Menschen* (Berlin: Vita Deutsches Verlagshaus, 1900), which is based on the classificatory categories of adornment theorized by Gottfried Semper.

120 Klaatsch, *Der Werdegang der Menschheit* (1922), 193. Cf. Klaatsch, *The Evolution and Progress* (1923), 177: "Housing is one of the chief features that indicate the advance of man from savagery to early civilisation."

121 See the chapter on housing (*Die Wohnung*) in Heilborn, *Allgemeine Völkerkunde*, I:60–92. Both Klaatsch's and Heilborn's remarks on Indigenous house construction draw from the ethnographic descriptions of Sumatra by the German medical scientist and traveler Max Moszkowski. See "Von der Entstehung des Wohnhauses" (The Origin of the Dwelling-House) in Max Moszkowski, *Auf neuen Wegen durch Sumatra: Forschungsreisen in Ost- und Zentral-Sumatra (1907)* (Berlin: Dietrich Reimer [Ernst Vohsen], 1909), 260–280.

122 Klaatsch, *Der Werdegang der Menschheit* (1922), 203; and *The Evolution and Progress* (1923), 183.

123 Klaatsch, *Der Werdegang der Menschheit* (1922), 206–207; and *The Evolution and Progress* (1923), 187. See also Heilborn, *Allgemeine Völkerkunde*, I:78. On Sarasin's analogies with the Greek temple: Paul Sarasin, "Über die Entwicklung des griechischen Tempels aus dem Pfahlhause," *Zeitschrift für Ethnologie* 39 (1907): 57–79.

124 See Wilhelm Kranz, "Pfahlbau-Dorf am Züricher See zur Steinzeit," in Klaatsch, *Der Werdegang der Menschheit* (1922), color plate VIII; and Eiffler, "Rekonstruierter Pfahlbau zu Schönenwerd (Soluthor, Sweiz)," op. cit., 385, plate 45. See also Klaatsch's remarks on pile dwellings in his earlier study "Entstehung und Entwickelung des Menschengeschlechtes," which reproduces the same color plate of a "pile dwelling village" by Kranz along a "modern pile building village from New Guinea [*Modernes Pfahlbaudorf von Neu-Guinea*]," in Jules Dumont d'Urville, *Voyages de la corvette l'Astrolabe* (1833). See Klaatsch, *Weltall und Menschheit* (1902–1904), II:311–312. On the appropriation of pile dwellings in the South Pacific as models for the reconstruction of prehistoric lakeside dwellings in Switzerland, see Vogt, "The Helvetian Appropriation of New Guinea Villages on Pile-Work above the Water," in *Le Corbusier, The Noble Savage*, 247–253.

125 "Beim Bau der käfigartigen Rundhütte (Nordqueensland) (during the construction of the cage-type round hut (North Queensland)." The image has no credit and is not included in the English edition of Klaatsch's book. Klaatsch, *Der Werdegang der Menschheit* (1922), 195, fig. 166; reproduced in Kiesler's photostat. PHO_7197/0

126 MA I.7 preliminary draft. TXT_6851/0_N3

127 "Like huge birdhouses on poles are these Pygmy dwellings." E. W. Brandes, "Into Primeval Papua by Seaplane," 289. CLP_6495_0

128 Cf. Klaatch, *Der Werdegang der Menschheit* (1922), 196–197; and. *The Evolution and Progress of Mankind* (1923), 179–180.

129 Jacques Lacan, "The Mirror Stage as Formative of the I Function as Revealed in Psychoanalytic Experience," in *Écrits*, trans. Bruce Fink (New York: W. W. Norton, 2006), 94.

130 Georges Bataille, "Architecture" first published in the "Dictionnaire Critique" of *Documents* (1929), 2: 117. For an English translation and commentary, see Denis Hollier, *Against Architecture: The Writings of Georges Bataille*, trans. Betsy Wing (Cambridge, MA: MIT Press, 1989), 46–56.

131 Drawing for a preliminary draft of the chapter titled "The Discovery of the Superfluous." PHO_6718/0

132 SFP_6662/0_N2 for the original drawing.

133 SFP_6664/0_N1 for the original drawing.

134 See Kiesler's speculations on "self" and "world" after Frobenius in note 84.

135 Frobenius, *Kulturgeschichte Afrikas*, 146, 168 (transcribed in TXT_6816/0_N1). For a translation, see Addenda: Transcriptions and Translations, pp. 360–61.

136 Frobenius, *Kulturgeschichte Afrikas*, 137, figs. 51–59.

137 Frobenius, *Kulturgeschichte Afrikas*, 151; and Marchand, "Leo Frobenius," 165.

138 A similar figure of the ourovoros (serpent devouring its own tail) is shown in a figure in Frobenius's *Cultural History of Africa* with the drawing of a "serpent on a round bronze shield" from Benin in West Africa. The same serpentine figure is described in his text as the *Weltmeerschlange* (world sea snake). *Kulturgeschichte Afrikas*, 170–171, fig. 117.

139 See later references to Kiesler's reading of Lévy-Bruhl in this introductory text and the Main Text of *Magic Architecture*.

140 Sigfried Giedion, *The Eternal Present: A Contribution on Constancy and Change, Vol. I: The Beginnings of Art* (Oxford: Oxford University Press, 1962), 526.

141 See Main Text MA, I.9. TXT 6783/0_N2

142 Henri Breuil and Miles Crawford Burkitt, *Rock Paintings of Southern Andalusia: A Description of a Neolithic and Copper Age Art Group* (Oxford: Clarendon Press, 1929). Quoted in MA, III.2.

143 TXT_6825/0_N5a

144 For Kiesler's transcriptions from the aforementioned publication by Breuil including excerpts planned for but ultimately not quoted in the assembled manuscript of MA: TXT_6828/0_N2-N4; TXT_6813/0_N1-N3verso TXT_6814/0 (the last document also contains additional excerpts from Frobenius's *Kulturgeschichte Afrikas*). For transcriptions from Breuil not included in MA, see Addenda: Transcriptions and Translations.

145 TXT_6828/0_N2 As the editors of the volume on the rock paintings of Southern Andalusia explain, the hypothesis that these radiating patterns (described in the original captions as "human figures") represent houses on stilts is indebted to the studies of the Polish Iberianist archaeologist Eugeniusz Frankowski, *Hórreos y palafitos de la Península ibérica* (Madrid: Museo nacional de ciencias naturales, 1918). Yet the authors also "surmise" that "these flower-like stars" could also be "intended for heavenly bodies." Cf. Breuil and Burkett, *Rock Paintings of Southern Andalusia*, 6, 14f. Kiesler copies both references to the identification of these symbols as houses on stilts, in his transcriptions TXT_6828/0_N2-N4

146 Norbert Casteret, *Zehn Jahre unter der Erde: Höhlenforschungen eines Einzelgängers*, trans. Friedrich von Oppeln-Bronikoskwi (Leipzig: Brockhaus, 1936). For the Kieslers' transcriptions of the German edition of Casteret's memoir, see TXT_6821/0 For the original French edition: Norbert Casteret, *Dix ans sous terre: Campagnes d'un explorateur solitaire* (Paris: Perrin, 1933). For the English edition (not used in MA): Norbert Casteret, *Ten Years Under the Earth*, ed. and trans. Barrows Mussey (New York: Greystone Press, 1938). This English edition is based on a compilation of Casteret's French edition and consequent memoir *Au Fond des Gouffres* (Paris: Perrin, 1936).

147 "Magic in Prehistoric Times," in Casteret, *Ten Years Under the Earth*, 41–50; and "Die Magie in vorgeschichtlicher Zeit," in *Zehn Jahre unter der Erde*, 55–63.

148 Casteret, *Ten Years Under the Earth*, 229. This passage is not included in the German edition.

149 Casteret, *Ten Years Under the Earth*, 233.

150 Casteret, *Ten Years Under the Earth*, 76; for a similar passage *Zehn Jahre unter der Erde*, 88.

151 Casteret, *Zehn Jahre unter der Erde*, 37; *Ten Years Under the Earth*, 21. See also editors' notes in annotated text (IV.5) for the passage transcribed by the Kieslers but omitted from the text of MA.

152 Casteret tends to employ problematic language in his descriptions, sometimes exacerbated in the Kieslers' translation of their transcriptions from the German edition of his work, as in this excerpt that was ultimately crossed out and not used in the assembled manuscript: "In the unexpected action of being portrayed the primitive shows not only anger and timidity, but also a well founded fear. He looks with awe at the white man whose innumerable inventions give him the supremacy (renders the German *Überlegenheit* [*Zehn Jahre unter der Erde*, 68], *supériorité* in the original French [*Dix ans sous terre*, 115]). But most of all primitive man fears that the stranger will take possession of his person. For, procuring the picture of a person, one possesses his double [*Doppelgänger*], in a magical sense; and one can charm the victim and exercise all sorts of sorcery." TXT_6752/0_N3 Cf. the published English translation of the same passage in *Ten Years Under the Earth* (1938): "According to circumstances the reaction is angry or timid, but the fear has a reason. The white man with his innumerable inventions is an alarming being anyway; but what the savage fears above everything is to have a stranger get possession of his picture. By getting your portrait I acquire your double, in the magical sense of the word, and I am then able to bewitch you, and work all sorts of mischief upon you."

153 Part of the original draft for this chapter was written by Kiesler in German. TXT_6705/0_N4recto and TXT_6730/0verso

154 Lola Kreuzberg ed., *Wir Tiere: Erlebnisse und Begebenheiten aus der Welt der Tiere* (Berlin: Neufeld & Henius, 1930). The book contained two articles by Adolf Heilborn, "Mensch und Tier" and "Schauspieler, Tänzer und Sänger," 13–30 and 237–259. See also Heilborn 's own edited animal photography publication series *Das Tier im Bild* in three volumes: *Kampf ums Dasein*; *Liebespiele der Tiere*; *Aus der Kinderstube der Tiere* (Berlin: Brehm Verlag, 1929–1930) republished in a number of editions before and after the Second World War.

155 Walter Bernhard Sachs, "Handwerkmeister und Techniker," in *Wir Tiere: Erlebnisse und Begebenheiten aus der Welt der Tiere*, ed. Lola Kreuzberg (Berlin: Neufeld & Henius, 1930), 279.

156 Adolf und Karl Müller, *Wohnungen, Leben und Eigenthümlichkeiten in höheren Thierwelt* (Leipzig: Otto Spamer, 1869); and *Thiere der Heimath: Deutschlands Säugethiere und Vögel* (Kassel and Berlin: 1882).

157 For a complete list of Kiesler's research on animal science, see Addenda: Bibliographies, Research Clippings.

158 See the chapter, "The building Instinct of Animals: The Termitary of the Termites," MA II.2. For the source of Kiesler's quotation see the following note.

159 Eugène Nielen Marais, *The Soul of the White Ant*, trans. Winifred De Kok (New York: Dodd, Mead & Co., 1937). For a critical history of the publication and translation, see Stephen Gray, "Soul-brother Eugène N. Marais: Some notes towards a re-edit of his works," *Tydskrif vir letterkunde* 50, no. 2 (2013): 63–80.

160 Paul Karlson, "Ein Tier aus hunderttausend Tieren: Das rätselhaft Wesen der Termite," *Koralle* 6, no. 42 (October 23, 1938): 1482–1486. Kiesler's clippings include only the first page of the article by Karlson, an author of popular books on physics and nature. His article offers a liberal interpretation of Marais's termitological observations, centered on the questions of the "soul." Marais's book was first published in German in 1936 as *Die Seele der weissen Ameise* (Berlin: Deutsche Buchhandlung, 1936). Notably, the second German edition (Berlin: Herbig, 1939) was in Mies van der Rohe's personal library among other German book publications on ants. See Fritz Neumeyer, *The Artless Word: Mies van der Rohe on the Building Art*, trans. Mark Jarzombek (Cambridge, MA: The MIT Press, 1991), 357 n27.

161 Marais, *The Soul of the White Ant*, 135. For the actual passage, see editors' note on Kiesler's remarks on the same issue in the Main Text, II.5.

162 Kiesler's research clippings include a newspaper report on the French ecologist Gaston Bonnier's remarks on the "socialist" organization of bees described as "collectivism without individuality." "Socialism among bees," *The Independent* 65 (1908): 833–839.

163 Wilhelm Bölsche, *Der Termitenstaat: Schilderung eines geheimnisvollen Volkes* (Stuttgart: Kosmos, 1931).

164 Bölsche, *Der Termitenstaat*, 65, 67. For the Kieslers' transcriptions from Bölsche's book, see TXT_6811/0_N3

165 Bölsche, *Der Termitenstaat*, 10, 68.

166 Bölsche, *Der Termitenstaat*, 31.

167 For example, Bölsche is drawing from Escherich's entomological study of termites in Ceylon: Karl Escherich, *Termitenleben auf Ceylon: neue Studien zur Soziologie der Tiere zugleich ein Kapitel kolonialer Forstentomologie* (Jena: G. Fischer, 1911).

168 The orthographic section of a termitary in Kiesler's plate 16b is reproduced from "Sky-Scrapers of the Termite World," in *Compton's Pictured Encyclopedia*, vol. 1 (Chicago: F. E. Compton & Co., 1922), 143, CLP_6543/0 See also List of Plates: Sources.

169 See photograph in Bölsche, *Termitenstaat*, 63.

170 "A Miracle of Building! Ant-Made 'Sky-Scrapers,'" *Illustrated London News*, 174, no. 4961, March 16, 1929, 455. For the clipping reproduced in Kiesler's plate: CLP_6597/0

171 See diagram in Bölsche, *Termitenstaat*, 9. In a passage on the Egyptian pyramid copied from Friedell's *Kulturgeschichte des Alterthums* found among the Kieslers' transcriptions, the Austrian cultural historian mentions the studies of the American entomologist McCook comparing the termitary of the Pennsylvanian ant with the Cheops' Pyramid in Giza, as well as the larger conglomerations of towers in termite colonies compared to which, the cities of London and New York are mere "villages." See Appendix: Transcriptions and Translations.

172 Bölsche, *Der Termitenstaat*, 74. See also Karl Escherich, *Die Termiten oder weissen Ameisen: Eine biologische Studie* (Leipzig: W. Klinkhardt, 1909). Bölsche's and Escherich's termite studies along with the Belgian essayist Maurice Maeterlinck's *La vie des termites* (Paris: Bibliothèque Charpentier, 1927), which overlaps with Marais's study, exist in the New York Public Library.

173 For Kiesler's transcriptions from Lévy-Bruhl's "Primitive Mentality," see later in this introductory text, as well as TXT_6815/0 and TXT_6810/0

174 "**Dieses Talent zu *bauen* ist nicht ein einzigartiges Vorrecht des Menschen; es scheint nicht anders zu sein ~~als~~ als ~~eine automatisch gewordene~~ eine erweiterte ~~Schu[tz]~~ Abwehrbewegung ~~des Körpers zu sein~~ der Tierpsyche ~~zu sein die Angst für~~ zu sein, Schutz vor Schmerz, ~~Lahmlegung~~ Hunger und Tod ~~erfindet~~ den Lebensbedingungen abzuzwingen.**" English translation by the editors. TXT_6705/0_N4recto

175 The original manuscript reads: "**add eventually to it. / automatically**" TXT_6699/0_N1 In consequent typescripts of the same chapter, the same phrase is transcribed as: "**add to it them automatically**" and "**add to them automatically**." TXT_6733/0_N1; TXT_6854/0_N1; TXT_5877/0_N86

176 TXT_6699/0_N1

177 Kiesler, "On Correalism and Biotechnique," 60–75. See note 46 of this introductory text. Also, Paul Karlson refers to the creative capacities of the termite as "instincts without heredity [*Instinkte ohne Vererbung*]," "Ein Tier aus hunderttausend Tieren," 1484, 1486.

178 In his lectures, Wundt connects instincts to actions and habits (here in the published English translation not used by the Kieslers): "Only two hypotheses remain, therefore, as really arguable. One of them makes instinctive action a mechanised intelligent action, which has been in whole or part reduced to the level of the reflex; the other makes instinct a matter of inherited habit, gradually acquired and modified under the influence of the external environment in the course of numberless generations. There is obviously no necessary antagonism between these two views. Instincts may be actions originally conscious but now become mechanical, and they may be inherited habits." Wilhelm Wundt, *Lectures in Human and Animal Psychology*, trans. J. E. Creighton and E. B. Tischener (New York: Macmillan, 1912), 393. Wundt continues: "[W]hat has been already said that all and each of them,– from the instinctive finger-movements of the practised pianist down to the instinct to build a shelter and wear clothes for protection against the weather,–spring from two conditions, one physiological and the other psychological. The former consists in the property of our nervous organisation gradually to mechanise complex voluntary movements; the second, in the operation of the mimetic impulse, which is probably natural to all animals that live in any kind of society, but is especially powerful in man." Wundt, *Lectures*, 397–398. On the transcription and translation of passages from Wundt's lectures on human and animal psychology in *Magic Architecture*, see editors' note in the Main Text Part II, Introduction.

179 Automatism is present in Karlson's *Koralle* article on the termitary, where the worker and soldier termite transforms "into an automaton and a robot [*zu einem Automaten und Roboten*] amenable to the psychological power of the queen." Karlson, "Ein Tier aus hunderttausend Tieren," 1484, 1486.

180 See André Breton, "Le Message Automatique" *Minotaure* 3–4 (1933): 55–65; and from the same issue Tristan Tzara, "D'un certain Automatisme du Goût," 81–84. Kiesler owned this issue of *Minotaure* and included Breton's article in the list of readings for his laboratory at Columbia University. For English translations of both texts, see: "The automatic message" and "Concerning a Certain Automatism of Taste" in *The Surrealists Look at Art* (Venice, CA: Lapis Press, 1990), 153–187, 193–213. On the expansive literature on surrealist theories of chance and automatism, see Abigail Susik, "Chance and Automatism: Genealogies of the Dissociative in Dada and Surrealism," in *A Companion to Dada and Surrealism*, ed. David Hopkins (London: Wiley, 2016), 242–257; and Stamos Metzidakis, "Automatic Writings and Authorial Egos," in *Forum for Modern Language Studies* 58, no. 1 (January 2022): 53–70.

181 Stephen J. Phillips, *Elastic Architecture: Frederick Kiesler and Design Research in the First Age of Robotic Culture* (Cambridge, MA: The MIT Press, 2017), 189–192.

182 Mike Hansell, *Animal Architecture* (Oxford: Oxford University Press, 2005). James L. Gould and Carol Grant Gould, *Animal Architects: Building and the Evolution of Intelligence* (New York: Basic Books, 2007).

183 Entry dated May 27, 1956. Frederick Kiesler, *Inside the Endless House. Art, People, and Architecture: A Journal* (New York: Simon and Schuster, 1966), 35.

184 The reference to "natural laws of chance" may be informed not only by the earlier interest of surrealists on chance and automatism, but also by the contemporary work of Ludwig von Bertalanffy, *Problems of Life: An Evaluation of Modern Biological Thought* (New York: Harper, 1952), which existed in Kiesler's library. For the sections on evolution and life processes of organisms as an outcome of "chance and law," see pages 92–105.

185 John George Wood, *Homes Without Hands; Being a Description of the Habitation of Animals Classed According to the Principles of Construction* (New York: Harper, 1866). Kiesler selects a few paragraphs on beaver structures from Wood's "Chapter XXI: Social Habitations. Social Mammalia," 431–438.

186 Cf. Wood, *Homes Without Hands*, 435.

187 Hal Borland, "Engineers Without College Degrees," *New York Times*, January 24, 1960, 56–57. See also Addenda: Bibliographies: Research Clippings.

188 Cf. Wood, *Homes Without Hands*, 436.

189 Ralph Ubl, *Prehistoric Future Max Ernst and the Return of Painting between the Wars*, trans. Elizabeth Tucker (Chicago: University of Chicago Press, 2013).

190 Bruno Latour, *After Lockdown: A Metamorphosis*, trans. Julie Rose (Cambridge: Polity, 2021), 20.

191 On the experience of underground bomb shelters during World War II, see the section on "Cave" in Penelope Curtis, *The Pliable Plane: The Wall as Surface in Sculpture and Architecture 1945–75* (London: Mack, 2022).

192 Latour, *After Lockdown*, 4.

193 One of Marais's central theoretical "theses" is that "[t]he termitary is a separate composite animal at a certain stage of development, and lack of auto mobility alone differentiate it from other such animals." See "Chapter 6: The Composite Animal," in *The Soul of the White Ant*, 53–65; and "Chapter 8: The Development of the Composite Animal," 76–81. See also Karlson, "Ein Tier aus hunderttausend Tieren," 1484.

194 For a contemporary view of the human species as a "mosaic" of evolutionary characters, see Georges Chapouthier, *L'Homme, ce Singe en Mosaique* (Paris: Odile Jacob, 2001).

195 On a contemporary view of the question of "technique" in animals and humans, see Marie-Hélène Parizeau and Georges Chapouthier, eds., *L'être humain, l'animal et la technique* (Quebec: Les Presses de l'Université Laval, 2007).

196 Klaatsch, *Der Werdegang der Menschheit* (1922), 202. For the original report by Schneider–which differs slightly from the transcription in Klaatsch's book–see Gustav Schneider, "Ergebnisse zoologischer Forschungsreisen in Sumatra. Erster Teil. Säugetiere (Mammalia)," *Zoologische Jahrbucher* 23 (1905): 1–172 (46 for this passage). The same description is heavily abbreviated in the published English edition of Klaatsch's book. Cf. Klaatsch, *The Evolution and Progress of Mankind* (1923), 182–183. See editors' notes in the Main Text (I.7).

197 Cf. Klaatsch, *Der Werdegang der Menschheit* (1920) and (1922), 69–71, plates 9–10. Note that these illustrations of the orangutan nest represent one of the very rare divergences between the two editions of 1920 and 1922, both assembled by Heilborn.

198 "Nest des Orang-Utan," illustration for the article "Tierwohnungen," in *Meyers Großes Konversations-Lexikon*, 6th ed. (Leipzig and Vienna: Bibliographisches Institut, 1908), vol. 19 (supplement), 547–548 (Plate, fig. 2).

199 Klaatsch also includes Captain Cook's eighteenth-century report of tree dwellings among the Tasmanians. Klaatsch, *Werdegang* (1922), 202–203.

200 See also Kiesler's drawings for his chart "The working tools of animals in comparison to human tools," included in Addenda: Charts. SFP_6664/0_N2

201 For the centrality of building "structure" in the conception of typology and style in nineteenth-century France and the legacy of such discussions in "modern architects" interests in racially charged conceptions of the primitive or of indigenous development" in the twentieth century, see Charles L. Davis II, "Viollet-le-Duc and the Body: The Metaphorical Integrations of Race and Style in Structural Rationalism" *arq* 14, no. 4 (2010): 341–347.

202 See Kiesler's table chart on the development from "Animal" to "Magic Architecture," included in Addenda: Charts.

203 In an earlier draft of the same chapter, the same term appears as "animal architecture" (non-capitalized). TXT_6739/0_N1

204 Wood, *Homes Without Hands*. For the Kieslers' transcribed excerpts from Wood's book, see TXT_6811/0

205 John George Wood, *Nature's Teachings: Human Invention Anticipated by Nature* (Boston: Roberts, 1885). First edition 1877.

206 John George Wood, *The Natural History of Man: Being an Account of the Manners and Customs of the Uncivilized Races of Men* (London: Routledge & Sons, 1868–1870).

207 Wood, *Nature's Teachings*, 410.

208 On the ambivalent legacy of Marais in the colonial history of South Africa, see Sandra Swart, "The Construction of Eugène Marais as an Afrikaner Hero," *Journal of Southern African Studies* 30, no. 4 (2004): 847–867.

209 Anthony Vidler, *The Architectural Uncanny* (Cambridge, MA: The MIT Press, 1992).

210 On a history of animals and animal labor during colonization, see Antoinette Burton and Renisa Mawani, eds., *Animalia: An Anti-Imperial Bestiary for Our Times* (Durham, NC: Duke University Press, 2020). On the role of "animal building art" in the creation of late nineteenth-century discourses of "world art" following the racialized presuppositions of contemporary anthropological science, see Susanne Leeb, "Die Baukunst der Tiere oder Die Anthropologische Differenz," in *Die Kunst der Anderen: "Weltkunst" und die anthropologische Konfiguration der Moderne* (Berlin: b-books Verlag, 2015), 34–66.

211 Frederick Kiesler, "Design Correlation: Animals and Architecture," *Architectural Record* 81 (April 1937): 87–92.

212 Frederick Kiesler, study for an exhibition project on "Ecology" in the American Museum of Natural History, New York, 1944. The Kiesler Foundation, Vienna, SFP_6614/0.

213 Charles Schuchert and Carl O. Dunbar, *Outlines of Historical Geology* (New York: John Wiley & Sons, 1937). Used as a textbook, the volume was distributed to the US Army during World War II as educational material.

214 "Design's Bad Boy: A Pint-Size Scrapper Who After Thirty Years Still Challenges All Comers," *Architectural Forum* 86, February 1947, 88–91. See also the frontispiece of this book and Annotated Chronology.

215 On the use of the iconographic theme of St Jerome in his study in Renaissance painting as a pictorial precedent for the "Mobile Home Library" system developed in Kiesler's Laboratory at Columbia University, see Phillips, *Elastic Architecture*, 137–138.

216 For an imaginative association of domesticated felines and modern economic theory, see Leigh Claire La Berge, *Marx for Cats: A Radical Bestiary* (Durham, NC: Duke University Press, 2023).

217 Ernst Kapp, *Grundlinien einer Philosophie der Technik, zur Entstehungsgeschichte der Cultur aus neuen Gesichtspunkten* (Braunschweig: G. Westermann, 1877). English edition: *Elements of a Philosophy of Technology: On the Evolutionary History of Culture*, ed. Jeffrey West Kirkwood and Leif Weatherby (Minneapolis: University of Minnesota Press, 2018).

218 "Die vorgeschichtliche Menschheit und ihre Kultur" in Klaatsch, *Der Werdegang der Menschheit* 1922), 253–386; specifically, figs. 192, 193, 210, 211. See also editors' notes in the Main Text, II.6.

219 Karl Weule, *Kulturelemente der Menscheit. Anfänge und Urformen der meteriellen Kultur* (Stuttgart: Kosmos, 1910), 35 (fig. 10). English edition: *Cultural Element in Mankind: Commencements and Primitive Forms of Material Culture* (London: Simpkin, Marshall, 1926).

220 On the study of prehistoric bone tools, see Karel Valoch, "Bone Tools from Předmostí in Moravia (Czechoslovakia)," *Anthropologie* 51, no. 1 (2013): 33–62.

221 Bronisław Malinowski, *The Sexual Lives of Savages*, vol. 1 (New York: Liveright; 1929), plates 34–36.

222 Malinowski, *The Sexual Lives of Savages*, 33

223 "Wie sehen die Naturvölker das Tier?" *Koralle*, vol. 6, no. 31 (August 7, 1938): 1094–1096.

224 "Wie sehen die Naturvölker das Tier?," 1094–95.

225 Klaatsch, *Der Werdegang der Menschheit* (1922), 164–65, figs. 140–141.

226 Kiesler derives the use of the term "Eolithic" used by archaeologists in the late nineteenth and early twentieth centuries to connote the earliest period of the Stone Age. From Klaatsch, *Der Werdegang der Menschheit* (1922), 105, fig. 100, 108, and plate 2. On Kiesler's problematic implementation of the term, no longer in use when *Magic Architecture* was written, see Maria Stavrinaki, *Transfixed by Prehistory: An Inquiry into Modern Art and Time*, trans. Jane Marie Todd (New York: Zone Books, 2022), 318.

227 For an earlier reading of these Kiesler charts, see Spyros Papapetros, "The Birth of Design" in *Superhumanity: Design of the Self*, ed. Nick Axel, Beatriz Colomina, Nikolaus Hirsch, Anton Vidokle, and Mark Wigley (Minneapolis: University of Minnesota Press, 2018), 221–230.

228 See Kiesler's Preliminary chart on the "progression" from "Animal" to "Magic Architecture" based on the "preponderance" of "origin," "form" and "aim," in Addenda: Charts. See also Kiesler's preliminary drafts for Part III, Chapter 1 titled "The Birth of Design," cited in the editors' notes.

229 For Kiesler's rebuttal of modern functionalism and affirmation of the input of psychological functions in design, see his article mentioned in his correspondence with publishers about *Magic Architecture*. Frederick Kiesler, "Pseudo-functional sm in Modern Architecture," *Partisan Review* 16, no. 7 (July 1949): 733–742.

230 Lévy-Bruhl, *Das Denken der Naturvölker* (1926), 318–319. In this passage, Lévy-Bruhl quotes from Baldwin Spencer and Francis James Gillen, *The Native Tribes of Central Australia* (London: Macmillan, 1899), 523–525. See editors' notes from Part III, Chapter 1.

231 See photograph in the same chapter of Spencer and Gillen, *The Native Tribes of Central Australia* excerpted by Lévy-Bruhl and quoted by Kiesler: page 527, fig. 105. The same photograph of the "medicine man" also appears in Spencer and Gillen, *The Arunta; A Study of a Stone Age People*, vol. 2 (New York: Humanities Press, 1927), fig. 118. This exists in the NYPL and might be a likely source for Kiesler's reproduction. See also List of Plates: Sources.

232 Klaatsch, *Der Werdegang der Menschheit* (1922), 186; *The Evolution and Progress* (1923), 172. See also editors' notes for chapter II.7 in the Main Text.

233 Malinowski, *The Sexual Lives of Savages*, vol. 2, 354–355.

234 For the original entry, see "Hochzeitskleid," in *Meyers Großes Konversations-Lexikon*, 6th rev. ed. (Leipzig and Vienna: Bibliographisches Institut, 1908–1909), 406–407 (407 for the excerpt transcribed by the Kieslers). For a transcription and English translation of the German text see editors' notes for chapter II.7 in the Main Text.

235 Kiesler delivered a lecture, presumably on January 31, 1932, at the Brooklyn Museum, which drew from Adolf Loos's lecture "Ornament and Crime," first delivered in 1910. Cf. newspaper report "Baubles Women Wear Likened to Those of Savages," *Brooklyn Daily Eagle*, February 1, 1932. For excerpts and transcripts from Loos's lecture, which may have served as the script for Kiesler's own, see TXT_892/0-4 Kiesler's library contains two copies of Adolf Loos' *Trotzdem 1900–1930* (Innsbruck: Brenner 1931), one of which bears many annotations, as well as a copy of the monograph on Loos by Heinrich Kulka: *Adolf Loos* (Vienna: Schroll 1931). For Kiesler's alleged working relationship to Loos see Annotated Chronology (1932).

236 Malinowski, *The Sexual Lives of Savages*, vol. 1, 1–2.

237 Cf. the Kieslers' transcriptions (TXT_6743/0_N7-N11; TXT_6844/0_N1-N5) with the published English edition of Klaatsch's book, *The Evolution and Progress of Mankind* (1923), 178–179 and 191–192.

238 See notes in TXT_6804/0 in German transcribed and translated in the editors' notes for chapter II.7.

239 In the context of these anthropological debates, see, among others, Lévy-Bruhl's late response to the critique of his ethnosociological models and mentality systems in his *Carnets* (Paris: Presses universitaires de France, 1949); English edition: *The Notebooks on Primitive Mentality* (New York: Harper & Row, 1975). There is no mention of this book in Kiesler's drafts or personal library.

240 See Annotated Chronology (1937) and note 78 of this introductory text.

241 See report by Alden Thompson on the lecture by Ashley Montagu "Construction in Nature" (January 13, 1939). TXT_5102/0_N1-N18

242 For a full list of offprints from Montagu's article publications in Kiesler's possession, see Addenda: Bibliographies: Offprints.

243 Ashley Montagu, *Coming into Being Among the Australian Aborigines: A Study of the Procreative Beliefs of the Native Tribes of Australia* (New York: E. P. Dutton & Company, 1938). Montagu's book mentions the physical anthropology of Klaatsch and also draws from the ethnographic work of Spencer and Gillen–two sources that are common with Kiesler's *Magic Architecture*.

244 See the chapter "Maternity and Paternity in Australia" in Montagu, *Coming into Being*, 307–330.

245 Ashley Montagu, *Man's Most Dangerous Myth: The Fallacy of Race* (New York: Columbia University Press, 1942).

246 *The Race Question* (Paris: UNESCO, 1950) and *The Race Question: Results of an Inquiry* (Paris: UNESCO, 1952). For a recent critical commentary of this statement compiled by numerous scientists and revised (after criticisms) by Montagu, see the chapter by Stefanos Geroulanos, "Darwin in the Age of UNESCO," in *The Invention of Prehistory: Empire, Violence, and Our Obsession with Human Origins* (New York: Liveright, 2024), 266–281.

247 Ashley Montagu, *The Natural Superiority of Women* (New York: Macmillan, 1953).

248 See Lévy-Bruhl, *Das Denken der Naturvölker* (1921 and 1926); Lévy-Bruhl, *Les fonctions mentales dans les sociétés inférieures* (1910); *How Natives Think*, trans. Lilian A. Claire (1926). See also notes 66 and 111 in this Introduction.

249 For an extensive study of Lévy-Bruhl's ideas on "primitive mentality in the context of European literary modernism, see Gess, *Primitive Thinking*, 51–60. On a brief history of criticism of his ideas of "prelogical" mentality, see S. A. Mousalimas, "The Concept of Participation in Lévy-Bruhl's 'Primitive Mentality,'" *Journal of the Anthropological Society of Oxford* 21, no. 1 (1990): 33–46.

250 Sigfried Giedion briefly discusses Lévy-Bruhl's theories of "primitive mentality" mainly through his late writings published in Lévy-Bruhl's *Carnets* (1949) in relation to prehistoric and contemporary art in *The Eternal Present: A Contribution to Constancy and Change* vol. 1: *The Beginnings of Art* (New York: Bollingen Foundation / Pantheon Books, 1962), 288–289.

251 See two different typed transcriptions of the same section of Lévy-Bruhl's *Das Denken der Naturvölker* TXT_6744/0_N1-N6 and TXT_6810/0_N1-N2

252 Lévy-Bruhl, *How Natives Think* (1926), 327 (translation modified); and *Das Denken der Naturvölker* (1921), 326.

253 Robert Ranulph Marett, "Preanimistic Religion," *Folk-Lore* 2 (June 1900): 162–182. Republished in R. R. Marett, *The Threshold of Religion*, 2nd rev. ed. (London: Methuen, 1914), 1–28.

254 Albert Christian Kruijt, *Het Animisme in dem indischen Archipel* (The Hague: Martinus Nijhoff, 1906), 16–49. For a writing by Kruijt in English on similar descriptions, see his article on "Indonesians" in *Encyclopedia of Religion and Ethics*, ed. James Hastings (New York: Scribner's, 1964), VII:232–250.

255 Kruijt, *Het Animisme in dem indischen Archipel* 3; see also "Indonesians," *Encyclopedia of Religion*, VII:232.

256 See Marett's own comments on the opinions of his critics in his "Preface" in *The Threshold of Religion*, xiii–xiv.

257 Wilhelm Wundt, *Völkerpsychologie*, 26–28.

258 Henri Hubert and Marcel Mauss, "Esquisse d'une théorie générale de la magie," *L'Anée Sociologique* 7 [ed. Émile Durkheim] (1902–1903): 1–146. For the English edition: Marcel Mauss, *A General Theory of Magic*, trans. Robert Brain (London: Routledge, 1972).

259 Émile Durkheim, *The Elementary Forms of the Religious Life*, trans. Joseph Ward Swain (London: Allen & Unwin, 1964), 189.

260 See Geo Widengren, "Evolutionism and the Problem of the Origin of Religion," *Ethnos*, 10, no. 2–3 (1945): 57–96. At the beginning of his article, Widengren draws extensively from Ukraine-born American anthropologist Alexander Goldenweiser's refutation of evolutionism in his *Anthropology, An Introduction to Primitive Culture* (New York: F. S. Crofts & Co., 1937). Kiesler owned and annotated a copy of Goldenweiser's *Early Civilization: An Introduction to Anthropology* (New York: Knopf, 1922) which he quoted in a preliminary draft of *Magic Architecture*. See Addenda: Charts.

261 Richard Chase, "Notes on the Study of Myth," *Partisan Review* 8, no. 3 (Summer 1946): 338–346 (quoted in *Magic Architecture*, IV.4). See also Chase's *Quest for Myth* (Baton Rouge: Louisiana State University Press, 1949).

262 These sections also refer to the studies of *mana* and magic in Codrington, Marett, Frazer, Mauss and Hubert, and Durkheim among others. See copy with pencil markings in Kiesler's library of Goldenweiser, *Early Civilization*, 197. For Kiesler's notes and sketches on tools from Goldenweiser's book, see Addenda: Charts.

263 See deleted text in manuscript TXT_6725/0_N10 and editors' notes for chapter I.4.

264 See typed transcriptions from Lévy-Bruhl TXT_6744/0_N1-N6 and TXT_6810/0_N1-N2 mentioned earlier in this section.

265 See preliminary book outline for Part I in Addenda: Drafts TXT_6807/0_N3 For a drawn representation of such unified world expanding around the nucleus of a cave see Main Text, figs. B.06b-c. SFP6666/0_N1-N2

266 Anthony Vidler, "Rebuilding the Primitive Hut: The Return to Origins from Lafitau to Laugier," in *The Writing of the Walls* (New York: Princeton Architectural Press, 1987) 7–21. And for the revival of architectural primitivism in the postwar era, Nolan, "Postwar European Modernism or What the Primitive Hut Really Said," in *Savage Mind to Savage Machine*, 83–108.

267 Gottfried Semper, *Style in the Technical and Tectonic Arts*, trans. H. F. Mallgrave and M. Robinson (Los Angeles: Getty Research Institute, 2004), 250, 468.

268 Giedion, *The Beginnings of Art*, 516.

269 Frederick Kiesler, "The Future: Notes on Architecture as Sculpture," *Art in America* 54, no. 3, May–June 1966, 57–68 (here 64).

270 See section on "Architectural works wavering between Architecture and Sculpture" in G. W. F. Hegel, "Architecture: Independent or Symbolic, Classical, Romantic," in *Hegel's Aesthetics: Lectures on Fine Art*, trans. T. M. Knox (Oxford: Oxford University Press, 1975), II:630–700 (here 640–644).

271 Frederick Kiesler, preliminary sketch for the chart on "The Orbit of Exstasy (sic)" in six stages. Part of preliminary book outline of *Magic Architecture* in four parts. TXT_6800/0_N5verso Kiesler's chart resembles some of the cartoon-like illustrations drawn by the popular author Hendrik Willem van Loon in *The Story of Mankind* (London: Harrap, 1922) and *The Story of the Bible* (New York: Boni & Liveright, 1923).

272 See alternate manuscript titles: "EVERYMAN'S ARCHITECTURE: Origin and Future of Magic Architecture. The Story of Human Housing" TXT_6685/0_N1 and "EVERYMAN'S ARCHITECTURE: The Story of Human Housing magic and profane" TXT_6189/0_N3; and unpaginated copy in the Archives of American Art.

273 Contrary to such division, the 1907 article of Swiss naturalist and ethnologist Paul Sarasin, "Über die Entwicklung des griechischen Tempels aus dem Pfahlhause," described the typological connections between the house on stilts and the Greek temple. Sarasin's study is mentioned in Klaatsch. See note 123 in this introductory text.

274 On new archeological evidence locating the origins of monumental architecture in prehistoric eras, which challenges the distinctions marked by Kiesler about "the origins of inequality" in the architecture of protohistoric civilizations, see David Graeber and David Wengrow, *The History of Everything: A New History of Humanity* (New York: Farrar, Strauss and Giroux, 2021) 85–106. On a history of domestic architectural space in contiguity with public space in early urban settlements, see Pier Vittorio Aureli and Maria Shéhérazade Giudici, "Familiar Horror: Toward a Critique of Domestic Space," *Log* 38 (Fall 2016): 105–129.

275 See editors' notes on alternative titles for Part V in the Main Text.

276 Cf. Main Text, title frontispieces for Parts V and X.

277 The photograph reproduced by Kiesler in this plate is by George Hoyningen-Huene: "Giza. Shadow of pyramid of Khufu and village of Kafr-el-Samman," in George Hoyningen-Huene and George Steindorff, *Egypt* (New York, J. J. Augustin, 1943), 38–39. See List of Plates: Sources. The American photographer Lee Miller made a similar photograph of the Great Pyramid and the village in 1938.

278 Montage by Frederick Kiesler. Main photo: "Athen, Akropolis, Ansicht von Südwesten" (Athens, Acropolis, view from southwest), from Ferdinand Noack, *Die Baukunst des Altertums* (Berlin: Fischer & Franke: 1910), plate. 99. Inside photo: unidentified.

279 Tournai Cathedral (Belgium). "Kathedrale von Tournai, Ansicht von Südwesten (Tournai Cathedral, southwest view)," from Max Hauttmann, *Die Kunst des frühen Mittelalters* (Berlin: Propyläen-Verlag, 1929), plate XVII.

280 The images in this plate come from the article by Walter Krickeberg, "Menschenopfer für den Sonnengott: Wie die Azteken den Fortbestand der Welt sichern wollten," (Human Sacrifices for the Sun God: How the Aztecs wanted to Secure the Survival of the World) *Koralle* 6, no. 24 (June 19, 1938): 852–853.

281 "Rameswaram, Strasse mit Torturm des Grossen Tempels" (Rameswaram, street with gate tower of the Great Temple). From: Martin, Hürlimann, *Indien: Baukunst, Landschaft und Volksleben* (Berlin: Ernst Wasmuth Verlag A.G., 1928); and *India: The Landscape, the Monuments and the People* (New York: B. Westermann, 1928), plate. 2. The NYPL owns both editions.

282 Biart, *The Aztecs*. See note 61 in this introductory text and editors' comments in the Main Text V.3.

283 Friedell, *Kulturgeschichte des Altertums*; see note 112 in this introductory text. For the text of Kiesler's transcriptions from Friedell, which were ultimately not included in the assembled book manuscript, see the English translation by the editors in Addenda: Transcriptions and Translations, pp. 364–67.

284 Bruno Taut, *Die Stadtkrone* with contributions by Paul Scheerbart, Erich Baron and Adolf Behne (Jena: Diederichs, 1919). English edition: *The City Crown*, ed. and trans. by Matthew Mindrup and Ulrike Altenmüller-Lewis (London: Ashgate, 2017).

285 Bruno Taut, *The City Crown*, 74 (translation modified); *Die Stadtkrone*, 50.

286 Bruno Taut, *The City Crown*, 77 (translation modified); *Die Stadtkrone*, 53.

287 In his text, Taut explains the use of the term "purpose" (*Zweck*) as "basic need" (*Notdurf*). Taut, *The City Crown*, 77 (translation modified); *Die Stadtkrone*, 53.

288 See the account of Taut's correspondence with his brother about the book manuscript in Matthew Mindrup, "Introduction," in Bruno Taut, *The City Crown*, ed. and trans. Matthew Mindrup and Ulrike Altenmüller-Lewis (London: Ashgate, 2017), 12–14.

289 See Taut's own remarks on "social thought" (*soziale Gedanke*) underpinning the design of cathedrals and other religious monuments for the people. *Die Stadtkrone*, 61; *The City Crown*, 84–85.

290 According to Kiesler the *Endless House* originates in his "Endless Theater" and other experimental projects of the mid-1920s, and while he had already designed a "Space House" exhibited as a model at 1:1 scale in 1934, the first exploratory drawings for the "Endless House" as a housing type-model appear in mid-1947. For an astutely documented history of its trajectory, see Gerd Zillner, "Frederick Kiesler's *Endless House*: An Attempt to Retrace an Endless Story," in *Endless Kiesler*, ed. Klaus Bollinger, Florian Medicus, and the Austrian Frederick and Lilian Kiesler Private Foundation (Basel: Birkhäuser, 2015), 98–168.

291 Josef Ponten, *Architektur die nicht gebaut wurde. Mit am Werke Heinz Rosemann, Hedwig Schmelz* (Berlin: Deutsche Verlags-Anstalt, 1925). See also the advertisement of Ponten's book in Kiesler's copy of Le Corbusier's *Kommende Baukunst*.

292 Ponten, *Architektur die nicht gebaut wurde*, I:161.

293 For Stefi Kiesler's handwritten notes on a number of projects from Ponten (mentioning the NYPL bookmark 3-MQA+ of the original edition) see TXT_6878/0_N1-N2

294 For Kiesler's handwritten list of illustrations from Ponten's second volume, see TXT_6877/0_N1-N2

295 Frederick Kiesler, preliminary list of unbuilt architectural projects with handwritten additions in Addenda: Drafts TXT_6800/0_N3recto

296 Frederick Kiesler, clipping in plate 33: "Pieter Bruegel the Elder, Der Turmbau von Babel (Wien) [The Tower of Babel (Vienna)]." CLP_6541/0

297 Ernst Lewy, "Das Wesen der Sprache," *Faust–Monatsschrift für Kunst, Literatur und Musik* 4, no. 6 (1925–1926): 3–12 (9 for the plate).

298 Lewy, "Das Wesen der Sprache," 6.

299 Lewy, "Das Wesen der Sprache," 7.

300 Lewy, "Das Wesen der Sprache," 11.

301 As noted earlier, apropos the chapter on the Egyptian Pyramid in Part V, the Kieslers transcribed excerpts from the first volume of Friedell's *Kulturgeschichte des Altherthums*, yet they also owned the first volume of his popular *Kulturgeschichte der Neuzeit: die Krisis der Europäischen Seele von der Schwarzen Pest bis zum Weltkrieg* (Munich: C. H. Beck, 1927).

302 Friedell, *Kulturgeschichte des Altherthums* (1936), 270–271.

303 Egon Friedell, *Kulturgeschichte der Neuzeit* III (Munich: Beck, 1931) 568–569. For the English edition: *Cultural History of the Modern Era: The Crisis of the European Soul from the Black Death to the Modern Era*, trans. Charles Francis Atkinson (New York: Knopf, 1932) III:475.

304 Jacques Derrida, "Architecture Where the Desire May Live," *Domus* 671 (1986), 17–25. Reprinted in Neal Leach ed., *Rethinking Architecture: A Reader in Cultural Theory* (New York: Routledge, 1997), 301–305.

305 Derrida, "Architecture Where the Desire May Live" 25 (and in Leach ed., *Rethinking Architecture*, 304). The same excerpt is quoted in Catherine Ingraham, *Architecture's Theory* (Cambridge, MA: The MIT Press, 2023), 19; and Mark Wigley, *The Architecture of Deconstruction: Derrida's Haunt* (Cambridge, MA: The MIT Press, 1993) 24–25, 224n.

306 Ingraham, *Architecture's Theory*, 19.

307 For the original text of this "Definition," including paragraphs excised in the assembled manuscript, see text and editors' notes in Main Text (VII, Intro).

308 See TXT_6695/0_N1 and editors' notes for Kiesler's Introduction to Part VII.

309 The exhibition was curated by the art critic Nicolas Calas for Alexander Iolas's Hugo Gallery in New York and included works by Arshile Gorky, David Hare, Wifredo Lam, Roberto Matta, Isamu Noguchi, and Helene Phillips, among others. For a description of Kiesler's exhibition design, see Michael Taylor, "Arshile Gorky and Frederick Kiesler: Elective Affinities," in *Frederick Kiesler: Face to Face with the Avant Garde*, 265–280 (here 269–270).

310 **In der Klein-Raum Ausstellung (Hugo) in New York, … mit der Illusion der Malerei konnte ich flache Wände in Höhlen, niedrige Decken auffliegen lassen, Zimmerecken ausstrecken und Löcher und Schwellungen dort hinzaubern, wo der Kastendeckelgeist trotzig steif verbleiben wollte.** Excerpt from Frederick Kiesler, "Ecomomie and *Exuberanz*." TXT_876/0

311 See TXT_6695/0_N1 and TXT_6718/0_N2, and editors' notes for Kiesler's introduction to Part VII.

312 See TXT_6803/0 and editors' notes for Kiesler's introduction to Part VII.

313 See manuscript draft TXT_6695/0_N1-N2. The text of this draft was excised from the assembled book manuscript but is restored in this edition.

314 See text titled "DEFINITION" TXT_6688/0_N1-N2 and editors' notes in Kiesler's introduction to Part VII.

315 See TXT_6755/0_N1 and editors' notes for Kiesler's introduction to Part VII.

316 Frederick Kiesler, "Note to the Publisher" (Main Text, Front Matter).

317 *Ideal Empires and Republics: Rousseau's Social Contract, More's Utopia, Bacon's New Atlantis, Campanella's City of the Sun* (New York, NY: Walter Dunne, 1901).

318 Transcribed passages from Friedell, *Kulturgeschichte des Alterthums*, 38, 40, 44–45, 95. For the original text of these transcriptions see TXT 6822/0_N1-N4 and for a translation by the editors, see Addenda: Transcriptions and Translations, pp. 366–67.

319 Friedell, *Kulturgeschichte des Alterthums*, 44.

320 Friedell, *Kulturgeschichte des Alterthums*, 44–45.

321 See draft with miscellaneous notes. TXT_6749_0_N1

322 See Part I and comments earlier in this introductory text.

323 Sigmund Freud, *Totem und Tabu: Einige Übereinstimmungen im Seelenleben der Wilden und der Neurotiker* (Vienna: Heller, 1913). The Kieslers' library includes an English translation: *Totem and Taboo*, in A.A. Brill, *The Basic Writings of Sigmund Freud* (New York: Random House, 1938), 807–930. Other books by Freud in the Kieslers' library include *A General Introduction to Psychoanalysis* (New York: Doubleday, 1953), and *Leonardo da Vinci: A Study in Psychosexuality* (New York: Random House, 1947), as a well as a few critical studies of Freud by other authors. While Freud does not appear by name in *Magic Architecture*, there are a number of references to Freudian concepts.

324 See Kiesler's remarks on magic "today" (Part IV, chapter 1). Kiesler also uses the term "prestidigious" in reference to Piranesi's projects (Part VI, chapter 8).

325 Thorndike, *A History of Magic*, II: 977–978.

326 Chase, "Notes on the Study of Myth." See earlier references to Chase's article in the section "The Preanimist Hypothesis" of this introductory text.

327 Denis Hollier, ed., *The College of Sociology (1937–39)* (Minneapolis: University of Minnesota Press, 1988).

328 Kurt Seligmann, *The Mirror of Magic: A History of Magic in the Western World* (New York: Pantheon Books, 1948). As noted in the Annotated Chronology, the Kieslers were present at a party hosted by Seligmann marking the completion of his book on the history of magic in March 1948.

329 Gražina Subelytė, "The Alchemy of Painting: Kurt Seligmann," in *Surrealism and Magic: Enchanted Modernity*, exhibition catalogue ed. Gražina Subelytė and Daniel Zamani (New York: Prestel, 2022), 191–195 (here 192).

330 For a list of articles on magic by Seligmann published in *View* and *VVV* from 1941–1946, see Bibliography in *Surrealism and Magic: Enchanted Modernity*, 266.

331 See André Breton, *Arcane 17* (New York: Brentano's, 1945). For the catalogue of the 1947 exhibition including a text by Kiesler, see André Breton, Marcel Duchamp, ed., *Le Surréalisme en 1947*, (Paris: Galerie Maeght, 1947).

332 Gavin Parkinson, "Towards *L'Art Magique*: Surrealism and Magic in the 1950s," in *Surrealism and Magic*, ed. Gražina Subelytė and Daniel Zamani, 83–97 (here 84–85).

333 André Breton, *L'Art Magique* (Paris: Club Français du Livre, 1957); new edition with the collaboration of Gérard Legrand (Paris: Phibus, 1991).

334 Breton, *L'Art Magique* (1957), 2.

335 Breton, *L'Art Magique* (1957), 8–9.

336 Breton, *L'Art Magique* (1957), 148.

337 Breton, *L'Art Magique* (1957), 149.

338 See the responses to the questions of Breton's *Enquête* by Claude Lévi-Strauss and Roger Caillois, Breton, *L'Art Magique* (1957), 56, 69–71. See also Parkinson, "Towards *L'Art Magique*," 93–95.

339 Roger Caillois, response in *L'Art Magique* (1957), 70.

340 On the various titles of Kiesler's book manuscript, see editors' comments on the title page in the Main Text.

341 See introduction to Part X and "Preliminary synopsis of last part" included in Addenda: Drafts.

342 Sabine Baring-Gould, *Cliff Castles and Cave Dwellings of Europe* (Philadelphia: J. B. Lippincott Company / London: Seeley & Co., 1911), 28–29. For the transcription from the book with Kiesler's handwritten corrections, see TXT_6815/0_N2

343 Baring-Gould, *Cliff Castles and Cave Dwellings*, 29; and hand-corrected transcription.

344 Baring-Gould, *Cliff Castles and Cave Dwellings*. See also editors' notes for Part I, chapter 6.

345 See assembled manuscript and preliminary typescript for Part I, chapter 6 TXT_6850/0_N3

346 Biart, *The Aztecs*, 195. For the original publication (not used by the Kieslers), see Lucien Biart, *Les Aztèques: histoire, moeurs, coutumes* (Paris: A. Hennuyer, 1885). For Kiesler's instructions for quotation from Biart's book, see TXT_6753/0_N5

347 Biart was a French author and Americanist specializing in Mexican archaeology and ethnography. Originally trained as a physician, he lived in Mexico in the 1860s conducting naturalist and anthropological research during the second French colonization effort. He was a "corresponding member" of the French Anthropological Society and the "scientific committee for the study of Mexico" appointed by the French Ministry for Public Education in 1864. He left Mexico after the withdrawal of the French from the country in 1867. See the "necrology" by Ernest-Théodore Hamy, "Lucien Biart," *Journal de la Société des Américanistes* 2 (1898): 196–97 (here 196). For a fictionalized account of part of his time in Mexico adapted as an illustrated children's novel, see Lucien Biart, *Adventures of a Young Naturalist*, trans. and adapted by Parker Gillmore (London: Sampson Low, Son & Marston, 1870).

348 For the text transcribed from Biart's book and used in the assembled manuscript of *Magic Architecture*, see TXT_5877/0_N146-N151 (here N146).

349 The link between territorial expansion and magical practices is also presented in one of the architect's preliminary outlines: "Thus the desire of both civilizations, aboriginal and modern, to prepare themselves for the conquest of more territory than their stomachs and minds can digest, has led to the preponderance of thaumaturgy in primitive and of the mechanical hocus pocus in modern man" (see Addenda: Drafts). Here, the appetite for territorial expansion is projected on both modern and Indigenous societies, reflecting racially biased views of human and animal "aggression" resulting in a "territorial imperative" in the work of animal ethologist Konrad Lorenz and popular evolutionist author Robert Ardrey in the 1950s and 60s. Theories of territorial aggression as intrinsic to humans were countered by the anthropologist Ashley Montagu, who (as mentioned earlier) was a friend of the Kieslers and lectured at Kiesler's Columbia Laboratory for Design Correlation. On the political repercussions of these ethological debates, see Erika Lorraine Milam, *Creatures of Cain: The Hunt for Human Nature in Cold War America* (Princeton: Princeton University Press, 2012), 79–112.

350 For the centrality of European and Indian heavily ornamentalized festival and building practices in the colonial British empire, see David Cannadine, *Ornamentalism: How the British Saw Their Empire* (Oxford: Oxford University Press, 2001). For the contemporary perseverance of these racialized cultural practices, see Anne Anlin Cheng, *Ornamentalism* (Oxford: Oxford University Press, 2019).

351 Harry B. Wehle, "Notes," *Metropolitan Museum of Art Bulletin* 3, no. 10, June 1945, n.p. (opposite 233). While the cover of this issue of the *Bulletin* featured a detail of El Greco's *View of Toledo*, Wehle's "Notes" featured a full illustration of the painting which Kiesler used in his plates (plate 41).

352 Thomas Henry Huxley, "The Stocks and the Stones: From the Evolution of Theology," *Encore* 3, no. 17 (June 1943): 704–708 (706–777 for Kiesler's selections). The original essay is published as: Thomas Henry Huxley, "The Evolution of Theology: An Anthropological Study," in *Nineteenth Century* (March-April 1886), 346–365 and 485–506. It was later republished in collections of Huxley's essays: T. H. Huxley, *Essays upon Some Controverted Questions* (London: Macmillan, 1892), 131–208; and *Collected Essays: Science and the Hebrew Tradition* (London: Macmillan, 1893), 4:287–372.

353 Huxley, "The Stocks and the Stones," 706–777. For Kiesler's instructions for transcription and the actual transcription, see TXT_6753/0_N1 as well as editors' notes for the introduction to Part V.

354 See "The Campo Santo of Pisa Now," *Burlington Magazine* 86, no. 503 (February 1945): 35–39.

355 "As Paris Celebrated the Surrender of Japan," *New York Herald Tribune*, August 17, 1945, 17; see also List of Plates: Sources.

356 Sigfried Giedion, *Building in France, Building in Iron, Building in Ferro-Concrete*, trans. J. Duncan Berry (Santa Monica, CA: Getty Research Institute, 1995), 143–145. English edition of *Bauen in Frankreich, Bauen in Eisen, Bauen in Eisenbeton* (Leipzig: Klinkhardt & Biermann, 1928).
357 See the beginning of this introductory text.
358 See Kiesler's handwritten edits in the typescript prepared by Stefi Kiesler. TXT_6720/0_N5
359 Hanns Sassmann, "Vorwort," in *Das Reich der Träumer. Eine Kulturgeschichte Österreichs vom Urzustand bis zur Republik* (Berlin: Verlag für Kulturpolitik, 1932), 7–18 (here 7). On Marxist historiography and the workers' movement, see Bernd Rabehl, *Geschichte und Klassenkampf; Einführung in die marxistische Geschichtsbetrachtung der Arbeiterbewegung* (Berlin: Rotbuch Verlag, 1973).
360 For Kiesler's instructions for quotation from Sassmann, see TXT_6723/0_N3. For the transcriptions from Sassmann with notes by Stefi Kiesler, see TXT_6710/0_N1-N3. See also Addenda: Transcriptions and Translations for an English translation, p. 368.
361 Ponten, *Architektur die nicht gebaut wurde* (1925), 1:33. For the Kieslers' transcription of Ponten's description of Sforzinda typed by Stefi Kiesler, see TXT_6863/0 and editors' notes for chapter 2 of Part VII.
362 For the early history of the *Partisan Review* and its affiliation with cultural Marxism in the 1930s and 40s, see James Gilbert, "Literature and Revolution in the United States: The Partisan Review," *Journal of Contemporary History* 2, no. 2 (April 1967): 161–176. Kiesler befriended and corresponded with one of the founding editors of the *Review*, literary critic Philip Rahv (born Fevel Greenberg, at Kupyn, [today] Ukraine).
363 The same phrase is repeated in a preliminary MS outline on "twentieth-century developments" with an overview of some of the projects mentioned in Part X. See Addenda: Drafts. TXT_6800/0_N1–N2 **"In der Klein-Raum Ausstellung (Hugo) in New York, … mit der Illusion der Malerei konnte ich flache Wände in Höhlen, niedrige Decken auffliegen lassen, Zimmerecken ausstrecken und Löcher und Schwellungen dort hinzaubern, wo der Kastendeckelgeist trotzig steif verbleiben wollte."**
364 Frederick Kiesler, "Notes on Architecture. The Space House. Annotations at Random," *Hound & Horn* 7, no. 2 (January–March 1934): 292–297 (see chart on page 297). For preliminary versions of the chart see TXT_845/0, TXT_846/0, and TXT_846/1.
365 "Notes on Architecture," 297. The British "Commonwealth of Nations" was formalized in 1931, yet the meaning of "Commonwealth" in Kiesler's preliminary charts probably alludes to the practice of collective economy in the political systems of "socialism" and "commun(al)ism" that appear in the rest of Kiesler's charts and is not related to the colonial and postcolonial economic alliances of the British Empire.
366 There are approximately ten different versions of the same "morphological" chart in Kiesler's archive–some handwritten, in either ink or pencil and filled with deletions, substitutions, and corrections, and others cleanly typed–all of which slightly differ with the one that was ultimately published. In addition to the versions mentioned in the previous note, see TXT_3582/0_N1, TXT_3583/0_N1-N2, and TXT_3537/0-3589/0.
367 Frederick Kiesler, Preliminary chart on the "progression" from "Animal" to "Magic Architecture" based on the "preponderance" of "origin," "form" and "aim" included in Addenda: Charts. TXT_6817/0_N2
368 Frederick Kiesler, preliminary book outline of *Magic Architecture* in four parts. Page with handwritten annotations and an addendum with sketches on baroque and the rococo for the third part (later Part VIII) (TS, pencil) transcribed in Addenda: Drafts. TXT_6800/0_N5recto
369 Frederick Kiesler, preliminary book outline of *Magic Architecture* in four parts; see Addenda: Drafts.
370 While not included in the assembled manuscript, this sentence is restored in the Main Text of this edition. See editors' notes for Part VIII, chapter 2. TXT_6830/0_N1 In the MS draft, the statement on the rococo follows a handwritten draft on Piranesi, which suggests that Kiesler was thinking of a chapter on the rococo immediately following the last chapter of Part VI on Piranesi. TXT_6781/0_N3
371 Page from Kiesler's notepad for Parts. VI–X TXT_6781/0_N4
372 See the section on "Neo-Rococo" in Stefan Tschudi Madsen, *Sources of Art Nouveau*, trans. Ragnar Christophersen (Oslo: H. Aschehoug, 1956), 102–112.
373 Frederick Kiesler, "Mozart: 1956–1756. A Modern Artist Appraises Mozart the Artist as his Bicentennial opens with a huge Rococo show at the Nelson Gallery, Kansas City," *Art News* 54, no. 9, January 1956, 22–25, 58 (here, 25). For Kiesler's original draft, see TXT_904/0; TXT_905/0
374 The museum is now known as the Nelson-Atkins Museum of Art. It was designed in "classical" style and completed in 1933. See the catalogue *The Century of Mozart–January 15 through March 4, 1956 The Nelson Gallery and Atkins Museum Bulletin* 1:1. The catalogue included articles on "Art and Decoration in the Eighteenth Century" and "Chinese Taste" written by the Museum staff.
375 "Editorial: The Coming Season," *Art News* 54, no. 6, October 1955, 17, 61 (here 17); see also "The Age of Versailles for Ohio," *Art News* 54, no. 7, November 1955, 30–31.
376 See "Publicity Release" containing pencil markings (archived among Kiesler's Mozart essay drafts TXT_904/0 and TXT_905/0), page 1.
377 "Publicity Release," 2.
378 See the editorial on the McCarthyist attacks on "modern sculpture" including "left wing" "accusations" also published in *Art News* six months prior to their announcement of the rococo shows: A. Frankfurter, "Editorial: Souls of Clay," *Art News*, 54, April 1955, 17.
379 Victorien Sardou, "Des habitations de la planète Jupiter," *Revue spirite: Journal d'études psychologiques* (August 1858): 222–232.
380 Cf. drafts TXT_6781/0, TXT_6833/0_N1, and TXT_6763/0_N1. See editors' notes for Part XI, chapter 1.
381 "La Maison de Mozart en Jupiter, eau-forte automatique exécutée en neuf heures par Victorien Sardou (*La revue Spirite*, 1858)," *Minotaure*, 3–4 (1933): 54. André Breton, "Le message automatique" *Minotaure* 3–4 (1933): 55–65.
382 On Loos, see note 235 in this introductory text.
383 For an English translation, Conrads, *Programs and Manifestoes on 20th-Century Architecture*, trans. Michael Bullock (Cambridge, MA: The MIT Press, 1970), 18–24. For a reappraisal in architectural debates for and against the return of ornamentation after World War II, see Reyner Banham, "Ornament and Crime: The Decisive Contribution of Adolf Loos," *Architectural Review* 121, February 1957, 85–88.
384 During this period Kiesler was also involved in the design of the Russian-American exhibition on housing. See exhibition brochure *Fashions of the Times, 3rd Edition* MED 5984/0
385 Sigfried Giedion, *Mechanization Takes Command: A Contribution to Anonymous History* (New York: Oxford University Press, 1948).
386 Giedion, *Mechanization Takes Command*, 242.
387 Giedion, *Mechanization Takes Command*, 241–243; figure 126 on 243 reproduces Rethel's engraving.
388 On the correspondences between Kiesler's and Giedion's writings, based on a different pair of book projects, see Amut Grunewald, "Frederick Kiesler and Sigfried Giedion: *People, Art, and Architecture* Versus *Space Time and Architecture*," in *Frederick Kiesler: Face to Face with the Avant-Garde*, 237–263.
389 See Addenda: Drafts.
390 In the same paragraph in his proposal, Kiesler also notes that "the American Congress forbids bathtubs by decree as immoral." See Addenda: Drafts.
391 Giedion, *Mechanization Takes Command*, 529–30.
392 See Addenda: Drafts.
393 See Addenda: Drafts.
394 This is a reference to the "objective idealism" of Hans Vaihinger's *Philosophy of "As If": A System of the Theoretical, Practical and Religious Fictions of Mankind*, trans. C. K. Ogden (London: Routledge & Kegan Paul, 1924).
395 Sassmann, *Das Reich der Träumer*, 7. For the Kieslers' transcription TXT_6710/0_N2, see Addenda: Transcriptions and Translations, p. 368.
396 Friedell, *Kulturgeschichte der Neuzeit* I (1927). For a recent English edition: *A Cultural History of the Modern Age: The Crisis of the European Soul from the Black Death to the World War*, vol. I: *Renaissance and Reformation* (London: Routledge, 2017). For a study of the development of Friedell's cultural histories and their publication and reception histories during the interwar era, see Roland Innerhofer, *Egon Friedell. Kulturgeschichte zwischen den beiden Weltkriegen* (Vienna: Böhlau, 1990).
397 Friedell, *Cultural History of the Modern Age* (2017) 57–58; *Kulturgeschichte der Neuzeit* (1927), 66–67.
398 Friedell, *Cultural History of the Modern Age* (2017) 60, *Kulturgeschichte der Neuzeit* (1927), 69.
399 In his 2008 introduction to the English edition, Allan Janik places Friedell in a long genealogy of studies, from Foucault's *Birth of the Clinic* to Susan Sontag's *Illness as a Metaphor.* See Janik, "Introduction," in *Cultural History of the Modern Age: The Crisis of the European Soul from the Black Death to the World War*, vol. I: *Renaissance and Reformation* (London: Routledge, 2017), xxi–xxii.
400 See section on the "Unscientific character of history" in Friedell's "Introduction," in *Cultural History of the Modern Age* (2017), 4, 7; *Kulturgeschichte der Neuzeit* (1927), I:4, 8.
401 See section on "the professional dilettante" / "der berufene Dilletant," *Cultural History of the Modern Age* (2017), 41–42 (here 42); *Kulturgeschichte der Neuzeit* (1927), I:47–49 (here 49).
402 See section of Friedell's introduction on the "legitimate plagiarist" / "der legitime Plagiator," *Cultural History of the Modern Age* (2017), 44–46 (here 44); *Kulturgeschichte der Neuzeit* (1927), I:50–53 (here 51).
403 Friedell, *Cultural History of the Modern Age* (2017), 44–46 (here 45); *Kulturgeschichte der Neuzeit* (1927), I:50–53 (here 51–52).
404 For an analytic account of the dispute, see Phillips, *Elastic Architecture*, 62–65.
405 For the reattribution of Kiesler's designs to Marcel Duchamp and others, see Marc Dessauce, *Machinations: Essai sur Frederick Kiesler, l'histoire de L'architecture moderne aux États-Unis et Marcel Duchamp* (Paris: Sens & Tonka, 1996). For an account of Kiesler's close study of and collaboration with Duchamp from the 1930s onwards, see Alex Kauffman, "Frederick Kiesler and Marcel Duchamp: The Marcel Imprint," in *Frederick Kiesler: Face to Face with the Avant-Garde*, 249–263.
406 More on the subject of quotations, see "Note by the Editors" following this introductory text.
407 See chapter outline by Stefi Kiesler, *Dreams in Literature (The Dream Book)* in the archive of the Kiesler Foundation and Annotated Chronology.
408 Bruno Taut, *Die Auflösung der Städte: oder die Erde eine gute Wohnung; oder auch Der Weg zur Alpinen Architektur* (Hagen im West: Folkwang, 1920)
409 For Montagu's visit, see earlier in this introductory text.
410 See bibliographic notes on bees on library slips from the mid-1950s included in Addenda: Bibliographies: Library Slips, and later in this introductory text.
411 In his well-known study of agoraphobia, Anthony Vidler analyses the work of turn-of-the-century art historians Alois Riegl, Wilhelm Worringer, and Aby Warburg in this spatio-pathological vain, "Agoraphobia: Psychopathologies of Urban Space," in *Warped Space: Art, Architecture, and Anxiety in Modern Culture* (Cambridge, MA: The MIT Press, 2000), 25–49.
412 In his posthumously published "journal," Kiesler would resume the use of "cancer" as a metaphor for money economy ("My father always used to tell me: 'Money is the cancer of society'") and museum culture: "Here we have the money cancer of art, money eating into the bodies of the societies of East and West alike, a cancer which cannot be cured any more by deeds or deals, but most likely only by the ruthless thrust of knives into the foul bodies of museums. those mummifiers of paintings and sculptures, cold-blooded and passionless money-changers." Kiesler, *Inside the Endless House*, 357, 450.
413 See TXT_6824/0_N3 and editors' notes on chapter 8 of Part X.
414 See Addenda: Drafts.
415 The chapters on Huysmans and Kafka remained largely unwritten; see editors' comments on chapters 2 and 4 of Part IX.
416 See Addenda: Drafts.
417 See handwritten draft TXT_6798/0_N6recto and verso and editors' comments on chapter 10 of Part X.
418 Eugène-Emmanuel Viollet-le-Duc, *Histoire de l'habitation humaine: Depuis les temps préhistoriques jusqu'a nos jours* (Paris: Bibliothèque d'éducation et de récréation, 1875). English edition: *The Habitations of Man in All Ages*, trans. Benjamin Bucknall (London: Sampson Low, Marston, Searle, & Rivington, 1876).
419 See editors' comments on chapter 10 of Part X.
420 See letter from Henry Rago to Frederick Kiesler, September 3, 1946, presented in Annotated Chronology.
421 Hendrik Willem Van Loon, *The Story of Mankind* (New York: Garden City Publishing, 1921); *The Story of the Bible* (New York: Boni & Liveright, 1923); *The Home of Mankind: The Story of the World we Live in* (London: G. Harrap, 1933).
422 See Kiesler's "Note to Publisher" where the contents of the book are to be divided into three sections: **1. Prehistory 2. From Egypt to the French Revolution 3. From the French Revolution to the Present Times**. Included in Addenda: Drafts.
423 See in particular preliminary descriptions of chapters sketched in Kiesler's notepad TXT_6781/0. On Garnier and "Garden Cities" in England see TXT_6824/0_N2-N3, and editors' notes on the title sheet of Part X.
424 On discussions of "objective chance" in the work of the surrealists, in particular Breton's writings on automatism, see Kerry Watson, "Surrealism, Chance and the Extended Mind," in *Distributed Cognition in Victorian Culture and Modernism*, ed. Miranda Anderson, Peter Garratt, and Mark Sprevak (Edinburgh: Edinburgh University Press, 2020), 171–188.
425 For the added subheading on Ledoux see TXT_5877/0_N216 and editors' notes for Part X, chapter 10.
426 Emil Kaufmann, *Von Ledoux bis Le Corbusier: Ursprung und Entwicklung einer Autonomen Architektur* (Vienna: Rolf Passer, 1933).
427 Kaufmann, *Von Ledoux bis Le Corbusier*, 61–62. See 64n33 for Kaufmann's quotes from Richard J. Neutra, *Wie baut Amerika?* (Stuttgart: Julius Hoffmann, 1927).
428 See Annotated Chronology.
429 See Addenda: Drafts.
430 See draft TXT_6720/0_N1 and editors' notes for "Epilogue and Prologue" in Part X.
431 See unused maquettes for plates SCL_72510/0 and SCL_75. The image source for the first plate is "Pölzig: Ideenskizze für ein Festspielhaus in Salzburg," in Ponten, *Architektur die nicht gebaut wurde*, 193 (fig. 380).
432 See text TXT_6861/0_N1 and editors' notes for "Epilogue and Prologue" in Part X.
433 Note that an earlier draft of the same passage from the "Epilogue" refers to the "social revolution" in "England and Russia" later changed to "Europe and America." See editors' comments in "Epilogue" and Kiesler's handwritten text in TXT_6798/0_N1-N2
434 Frederick Kiesler, pencil drawing of introductory panel design for the exhibition on American architecture sent to the USSR by the National Council of American-Soviet Friendship, 1944–1945. SFP_1012/0 See Annotated Chronology, p. 378.

435 See the catalogue for the "photographic exhibition created by Edward Steichen for the Museum of Modern Art," *The Family of Man* (New York: Simon and Schuster/MoMA, 1955).
436 On a reception history of the "synthesis of the arts, see Romy Golan, *Muralnomad: The Paradox of Wall Painting, Europe 1927–1957* (New Haven: Yale University Press, 2009).
437 Kiesler, "L'Architecture magique de la Salle de Superstition," André Breton, Marcel Duchamp, ed., *Le Surréalisme en 1947*, 131–134 (here 131). Translated in Conrads, *Programs and Manifestos on 20th-Century Architecture*, 151–152. On this text see also the last section of this Introduction.
438 Henri Parisot to Kiesler May 28, 1949 LET_1850/0. See Annotated Chronology.
439 Among the many architectural readings of Queneau's literary oeuvre, see D. Brian Munn, "Walled from the Wild: (Sub)urban Enclosure in Raymond Queneau's The Bark Tree and Other Novels," *International Fiction Review* 26, no. 1 (1999).
440 For the correspondence with *Life* and the American Museum of Natural History, see TXT_6885/0_N3-N4. For various notes on "animal building" in "termites, bees, birds, and beavers" and life processes, see TXT_6885/0_N5-N8.
441 See articles "The Life of the Bee," *Life*, August 11, 1952; and "The World of the Insects" *Life*, August 8, 1955. CLP_6592/0 and CLP_6591/0. For the library slips with book titles on bees, see Addenda: Bibliographies: Library Slips.
442 Karl von Frisch, *Bees: Their Vision, Chemical Senses and Language* (Ithaca: Cornell University Press, 1950); for Kiesler's transcriptions (with handwritten notes) see TXT_6882/0_N1-N6. The Kieslers also transcribed Maurice Maeterlinck's classic study *The Life of the Bee*, trans. Alfred Sutro (New York: Dodd, Mead & Co, 1901), TXT_6884/0_N1-N7. For other bibliographic notes on bees TXT_6883/0_N1-N2
443 Kiesler, *Inside the Endless House*, 35. See also earlier in this introductory text on the section on "Animal Architecture."
444 For Kiesler's published drawings of the Parthenon and the Acropolis, see Kiesler, *Inside the Endless House*, 447, 449. For Le Corbusier's drawings of the Parthenon, Propylaea, and the Acropolis environs, see *Vers une architecture* and *Kommende Baukunst*, 162–163, 177. See also Le Corbusier, *Voyage d'Orient: Carnets* (Milan: Electa, 2002). As if by "objective chance," Le Corbusier's full narrative of his "trip to the Orient," including an account of his first visit to the Athenian Acropolis, was published the year after his death in 1966, the same year as Kiesler's posthumous publication of his *Journal*. Le Corbusier, *Le Voyage d'Orient* (Paris: Éditions forces vives, 1966).
445 For a thorough study of these large-scale works, see Stephanie Buhmann, *Frederick Kiesler Galaxies: The Multipaneled Constellations* (Berlin: Green Box, 2022).
446 For a description of the discovery of the ancient scrolls and Kiesler's "vessel" building design, Buhmann, *Frederick Kiesler Galaxies*, 317–324.
447 See "Note to the Publisher" MA, TXT_6190/0_N3 and "Note to the Editor" MA, TXT_6711/0_N1.
448 Museum of Modern Art, "Visionary Architecture," press release (September 29–December 4, 1960).
449 See previous note for a "Note" on the exhibition "checklist." And Thomas S. Hines, *Architecture and Design at the Museum of Modern Art: The Arthur Drexler Years, 1951–1986* (Los Angeles: Getty Research Institute, 2019), 74–79.
450 For an analytic description of Kiesler's contribution to the 1960 MoMA show, see Gerd Zillner, "Frederick Kiesler's *Endless House*: An Attempt to Retrace an Endless Story," 145–149.
451 Museum of Modern Art, "Visionary Architecture," press release, 3.
452 Ulrich Conrads and Hans George Sperlich, *Phantastische Architektur* (Stuttgart: Gerd Hatje, 1960).
453 Conrads and Sperlich, *Phantastische Architektur*, 8
454 See the exhibition catalogue, *Die Gläserne Kette: visionäre Architekturen aus dem Kreis um Bruno Taut, 1919–1920: Ausstellung im Museum Leverkusen, Schloss Morsbroich, und in der Akademie der Künste, Berlin* (Leverkusen Museum, 1963); and Iain Boyd White, ed., *The Crystal Chain Letters: Architectural Fantasies by Bruno Taut and his Circle* [trans. Iain Boyd White] (Cambridge, MA: The MIT Press, 1985).
455 Conrads and Sperlich, *The Architecture of Fantasy: Utopian Building and Planning in Modern Times*, trans. and ed. Christiane Crasemann Collins and George R. Collins (New York: Praeger, 1962) and *Fantastic Architecture* (London: Architectural Press, 1963), 7. The translators also mention the work of Herman Scheffauer in this context; see Herman George Scheffauer, *The New Vision in the German Arts* (New York: Huebsch, 1924).
456 Reyner Banham, "The Architecture of Fantasy," *Art Bulletin* (March 1965): 47:1, 144–45 (here 145). Another reviewer read the book differently: "Architectural Freudians, the four authors [including authors and translators] of this richly documented book peeled the tidy skin of reason away from our twentieth-century minds to reveal an architectural snakepit. From Gaudí to Goff, the naïve, the sophisticated, the primitive, and the suave architectural phantasies are breathlessly urged on the reader." Theodore M. Brown, "The Architecture of Fantasy," *JSAH* 24, no. 4 (1965): 331.
457 Conrads and Sperlich, *Fantastic Architecture* (1963), 70–71, 171.
458 Frédérick Kiesler, "Raumstadtbau" and "Magische Architektur" in Ulrich Conrads ed., *Programme und Manifeste zur Architektur des 20. Jahrhunderts* (Berlin: Ullstein, 1964), 92, 142–143. English edition: "Space City Architecture" and "Magic Architecture," in *Programs and Manifestoes on 20th-Century Architecture*, trans. Michael Bullock (Cambridge, MA: The MIT Press, 1975), 98, 151–152. For the first publication of Kiesler's early manifesto, see Frederick Kiesler, "Manifest. Vitalbau-Raumstadt-Funktionelle Architektur," *De Stijl* 10/11 (1924–1925): 141–146 (Conrads's book contains the erroneous date 1926). Kiesler's manifesto first appeared in English in *Contemporary Art Applied to the Store and its Display*, 48. The "Magic Architecture" text was a translation of Kiesler's 1947 note "Architecture magique de la Salle de Superstition," in Breton and Duchamp, eds., *Le Surréalisme en 1947*, 131–134 (see also Annotated Chronology). The publication notes that Kiesler's text "was translated from English by H. P. Roche," yet no English draft of this text survives in the Kiesler archive. The German edition of Conrads's book also included a Kiesler drawing of the "Hall of Superstition" originally published in the 1947 exhibition catalogue (see Annotated Chronology).
459 Conrads, *Programs and Manifestoes*, 151.
460 *La Surréalismee en 1947*, 134. Georges Bataille, *La Part Maudite: Essai d'Économie Générale. La Consumation* (Paris: Editions de Minuit, 1949).
461 See alternative book title: "EVERYMAN'S ARCHITECTURE: The Story of Human Housing; magic and profane" TXT_6189/0_N3; and editors' comments on the book's title page. See also chapter title "Magic Architecture, Holy and Profane" in chapter 4 of Part VII describing "Michelangelo's Sistine Chapel" and "Houses in Pompeii." In the first chapter of the book, Kiesler distinguishes between "sacred ideoplastic structures," which serve "the ritual of the imagination" and "profane physioplastic structures" that serve "the physical functions of the body" (1.1). These two categories apparently correspond to Kiesler's own housing models versus those of Le Corbusier.
462 Kiesler, "Notes on Architecture as Sculpture." See note 269 in this introductory text.
463 Kiesler, "Notes on Architecture as Sculpture," 58.
464 In this impromptu aphorism, Kiesler actually writes "absolete," which is an interesting conflation between "obsolete" and "absolute" and even more suggestive of the terminal state of modern societies. The phrase is scribbled at the top of a list with Kiesler's selections from Ponten's *Architektur die nicht gebaut wurde*. See the list of architectural projects never built in Addenda: Drafts, TXT_6800/0_N3 (fig. C.05a).
465 Kiesler, "Notes on Architecture as Sculpture," 58.
466 Kiesler, "Notes on Architecture as Sculpture," 59.
467 Kiesler, "Notes on Architecture as Sculpture," 60.
468 Kiesler, "Notes on Architecture as Sculpture," 62.
469 For his final and rather ambivalent thoughts on the relation between the "atomic bomb" and architecture, see entry titled "The Atomic Bomb" dated November 16, 1960, in *Inside the Endless House*, 303–305.
470 Kiesler, "Notes on Architecture as Sculpture," 63.
471 Kiesler, "Notes on Architecture as Sculpture," 65.
472 Kiesler, "Notes on Architecture as Sculpture," 64.
473 On the various titles of Kiesler's book manuscript, see editors' comments (Main Text, Title Page).
474 André Breton, "Magie quotidienne," *La Tour Saint-Jacques* 1 (November-December 1955), 19–31, cited in Gavin Parkinson, "Surrealism and Everyday Magic in the 1950s: Between the Paranormal and 'Fantastic Realism'," *Papers of Surrealism* 11 (Spring 2015) (electronic publication). Parkinson also mentions Henri Lefebvre's criticism of the surrealists' introduction of magic in practices of everyday life in his *Critique of Everyday Life* first published in 1958.
475 Kiesler, "Notes on Architecture as Sculpture," 65.
476 Kiesler, "Notes on Architecture as Sculpture," 67. Cf. also Kiesler's text "The 'Endless House': A Man-Built Cosmos" in *Frederick Kiesler, Inside the Endless House*, 566–569.
477 Kiesler, "Notes on Architecture as Sculpture," 68.
478 Kiesler, "Notes on Architecture as Sculpture," 68.
479 Aldo van Eyck, "Architecture of the Dogon," *Architectural Forum* 115, no. 5, September 1961, 116–121, 186. For a thorough analysis of this collaborative exploration see Karin Jaschke, "Mythical Journeys: Ethnography, Archaeology, and the Attraction of Tribal Cultures in the Work of Aldo van Eyck and Herman Haan," PhD diss., School of Architecture, Princeton University, 2012.
480 Bernard Rudofsky, *Architecture without Architects: A Short Introduction to Non-Pedigreed Architecture* (Garden City, NY: Doubleday, 1964).
481 See "Photographs selected for *Architecture without Architects*," Museum of Modern Art Archives, New York, Collection: MoMA exhibitions. Series Folder: 752.3, 1. I am grateful to Guillermo Arsuaga for pointing out these documents. For the published photographs from the same section titled "Nature as Architecture," see *Architecture without Architects*, figs. 19–21.
482 "Photographs selected for *Architecture without Architects*," 6; and *Architecture without Architects*, fig. 13.
483 Bernard Rudofsky, "Brute Architecture," in *The Prodigious Builders: Notes Toward a Natural History of Architecture with Special Regard to Those Species that are Traditionally Neglected or Downright Ignored* (New York: Harcourt Brace Jovanovich, 1977), 48–83.
484 Rudofsky, *The Prodigious Builders*, 58.
485 Rudofsky, *The Prodigious Builders*, 13.
486 See "The continuous monument/story board for a film," in Superstudio, "deserti artificiali e naturali," *Casabella* 358 (1971), 18–22. In his prefatory notes, the editor Giovanni K. Koenig suggests that Bruno Taut's reconstruction of the world in his *Alpine Architecture* and *World Master Builder (Der Weltbaumeister)* offers a "brief pedagogical lesson," whose "syntactical structure is curiously equal to that of the designs of Superstudio."

In the beginning was the binder—a "spring leather" Elbe brand binder from the 1940s with an inner paper folder containing the loose sheets of Kiesler's book manuscript, visible in his photographic portrait reproduced as a frontispiece to this edition and emulated on its cover. The binder performed not only as a containing but also as a compositional device, allowing periodic substitution of typewritten pages with new chapter drafts that kept switching places as Kiesler repartitioned his manuscript. Like the typewriter or the pencil and paper that originally produced the text of *Magic Architecture*, the binder is equally a writing instrument and a delirious rewriting machine. It preserves the manuscript by maintaining the text in flux and thus endlessly deferring its completion. Transitioning from the flexible logic of the binder to the fixed format of the published book presented a challenge that the designer and editors of this volume had to constantly renegotiate.

This posthumous publication of Kiesler's *Magic Architecture* aspires to be different from other editions of previously unpublished architectural texts, foregrounding a quasi-geological method towards the reconstruction of the book manuscript. Such a stratigraphic approach is based on the restoration of the manuscript's anterior layers and the retrieval of previously discarded materials in an effort to retain the book's original character as a continuous research project. Our critical edition aims to present the full extent of all surviving versions of Kiesler's highly fragmented opus to document the development of his project from its initial and still inchoate conception to its later and more fully formed yet still unsettled stages, including alternative ideas about the book's structure and content that during the writing process were eventually abandoned. While this transcription is as complete as possible, it does not aim to establish a final text for a book its author never finished or published. It rather performs as the living document of an ongoing investigation that, even after publication, remains an "open work," or in Kiesler's own words, *endless*.

Our critical edition contains a complete transcription of Kiesler's original text divided into ten parts, each part containing two to ten individual brief chapters. In the edited transcription, each chapter includes the corpus of the Main Text supplemented by a "subtext" of the editors' notes that transcribe the most essential variants from the manuscript's earlier versions, and which are printed on the same page but in separate columns. That way, the architect's central narrative remains unbroken and is still comfortable for all readers to follow, while more inquisitive users can peer into earlier formulations of the same text without having to turn the page. The continuity between the architect's compiled typescript and the subtext of his early manuscript drafts is signaled by the use of black throughout the Main Text and in the sidenotes in all sections of our publication to indicate Kiesler's own writing, clearly separated from the editors' text, which is set in silver.

As analyzed in the Annotated Chronology, the bulk of the manuscript was assembled during the aftermath of the Second World War until the first months of 1947, during which period, Kiesler circulated his book proposal and kept discussing his project with editors from a number of publishing houses and while applying for research grants. Throughout this process, the architect's manuscript apparently went through several revisions documented in his early drafts, none of which bears a date. However, there are mainly three types of written documents surviving in the archive and used in this edition.

First are the manuscript drafts authored by the architect containing the first outlines, sketches, and initial pieces of text in Kiesler's hand. Several sections of these hastily written pages—such as some of the chapters ultimately included in Parts VI to X first sketched on a writing pad—never progressed beyond the state of an outline containing only the title of a chapter, later transcribed to a typescript prepared by Kiesler's wife Stefi. While rather rough in terms of writing and containing a great number of deleted words or sentences and other emendations, these "first" unedited manuscripts are precious, as they are closest to the architect's original ideas and therefore are duly listed in the textual variants compiled by the editors in the sidenotes of each chapter. Some of these early variants include words or sentences in which Kiesler abruptly switches from English to German, struggling to find the proper term to express what he had in mind. Often the English terms substituting the words originally written in German do not have the same meaning and tend to neutralize the signifying charge of the German text. Therefore, sections of the manuscript originally written in German are fully transcribed in the variants contained in the sidenotes, along with an English translation.

The second stage of Kiesler's writing contains the main bulk of typescript drafts transcribed by Stefi Kiesler from the architect's original handwritten manuscripts. Our transcription follows the original typescript and only occasionally corrects some of Kiesler's misspellings or German rendition of English words, while preserving others along with certain factual errors concerning names, titles, and dates. These typescript drafts also include handwritten emendations, deletions, or additions, as well as sidenotes and comments by Kiesler himself and editorial remarks or questions about the transcription by Stefi. Often a second or a third edited transcription of a chapter is needed to reach a clean typescript. Meanwhile sentences or entire paragraphs are omitted from one transcription to the next, either deliberately based on Kiesler's handwritten instructions to Stefi or by accident. Most of these deleted passages are restored in the sidenotes and in special cases in the Main Text of this edition. For instance, the concluding paragraphs in the final chapter (Part X, chapter 10) describing a dream flight by Voltaire and Aristophanes across the human habitations of the earth were crossed out in one of the typescripts and not transcribed in later drafts, but are restored in our edition, as an alternate conclusion to Kiesler's "story of housing."

The third and final stage of the original text consists of clean typescripts scrubbed of editorial markings (but still with a few handwritten corrections). These were compiled into what is referred to as the "assembled version" of the manuscript, which exists in three or more copies, one contained inside the black binder featured in Kiesler's photo-portrait reproduced as this book's frontispiece. Selected parts of this or later versions of the text were sent to publishers from 1946 to 1949, along with plates and other illustrations. Our edition's Main Text is based predominantly on transcriptions of assembled versions catalogued at the archive of the Kiesler Foundation in Vienna. However, all other extant versions including a Xeroxed copy from the Lillian Kiesler papers at the Archives of American Art at the Smithsonian Institution in Washington D.C. are consulted and quoted in this critical edition.

A warning for contemporary readers of this period text: When writing *Magic Architecture* in the 1940s, Kiesler made extensive use of terms such as "primitive man," "aboriginals," or "savages" referring to a universalizing yet highly discriminatory classification of Indigenous peoples. Such language uncritically replicates the vocabulary of late nineteenth- and early twentieth-century anthropological and ethno-sociological publications Kiesler was avidly perusing. Even if prevalent in popular and scientific texts of his time, these terms remain highly problematic today. These racialized perspectives become more overt in Kiesler's visual comparisons displayed in his charts and illustrations, as when he juxtaposes the tree structures of primates with the building constructions of Indigenous people in Oceania or Africa. Additionally, several of the photographs Kiesler selected for his plates, particularly those extracted from popular science journals, such as the American *National Geographic* or the German *Koralle*, contain graphic visual and textual material that is equally offensive. The introductory essay Sources, Disciplines, and Objects that precedes this Note by the Editors, and which presents the key themes and scientific disciplines enmeshed in *Magic Architecture*, critically analyzes the bibliographic sources of these highly charged descriptions transcribed by the Kieslers in the context of late nineteenth- and early twentieth-century epistemologies and their colonial mindset. To preserve the tone of the original English text, as well as to give an accurate picture of the biases of its author and the historical literature he is quoting, these terms have not been altered or omitted by the editors and the offensive visual material included in his plates, drawings, and research clippings has not been blurred or removed. The decision to leave the text and images unchanged requires readers to interpret Kiesler's use of language and imagery from a critical distance and retrace it in its historical and ideological context. Several problematic images and passages in Kiesler's own text, as well as the texts of the authors he and Stefi were transcribing, as for example the evolutionist history of human culture by the early twentieth-century physical anthropologist Hermann Klaatsch, are analyzed in detail in the introductory essay and editors' sidenotes.

As mentioned, *Magic Architecture* contains lengthy excerpts from texts by other authors. Such quotations become so extensive that they eventually make *Magic Architecture* appear an edited anthology, not unlike Stefi Kiesler's compilation of literary excerpts on dreams in her unpublished *Dream Book* project (which shares a number of common author names with *Magic Architecture*) or Bruno Taut's 1920 publication *The Dissolution of Cities*. While the earliest manuscript drafts by Kiesler contain quotation marks that bracket these excerpts as well as detailed requests for transcription to Stefi (containing exact passages and page numbers), later typescripts (including those in the assembled versions of the manuscript sent to publishers) mostly lack quotation signs, thus often failing to distinguish between Kiesler's own writing and texts by others. In our edition every effort has been made to identify all quoted passages, comparing them with the original published texts from which they are drawn. Since quoted excerpts are often liberally transcribed and translated by the Kieslers, these too are set in bold in our edition of the Main Text, like Kiesler's own writing, yet they are clearly marked either by the use of block quotes or quotation marks to indicate an alternate source, fully cited in the editors' notes and commentary.

Kiesler's often erroneous dates and name spellings of peoples and places are often substituted in the Main Text with contemporary spellings, yet his original (mis)spellings and other factual errors are mentioned in the sidenotes. The same strategy applies to his idiomatic spelling of certain words, particularly in his handwritten drafts, where his non-native knowledge of English and the use of German-English (*Denglish*) is on full display, as for example in his use of the neologism *architectur*–a mix of *Architektur* (German) and *architecture* (English, but without the final "e"). Even if inconsistent, Kiesler's capitalization of certain English nouns–as in the case of "Architecture" versus "architecture"–is also preserved in the Main Text and the editors' notes. In the variants transcribed from the manuscript's earlier drafts, close attention is given to deleted words in Kiesler's handwritten and/or typed text, which are often absent in later drafts. Several of Kiesler's deletions required particular effort to read behind the heavy cloud of graphite by which the architect tried to erase or hide them.

The critical edition of the Main Text is supplemented by a set of "composite" plates of illustrations, hand-numbered by the architect from one to sixty (yet with several duplicate numbers, for a total of over seventy plates), which Kiesler put together by cutting and pasting illustrations from German and English books as well as geography or other popular science journals. Kiesler clarified the plates' functional limitations in a note to a prospective publisher: **"The illustrations attached to the manuscript do not constitute the final selection. They also do not represent the type of print from which reproductions are to be made. These illustrations are solely to give an idea of how I intend to emphasize the story of the book through them, particularly in using parallels, juxtapositions or schematic drawings." (Re: Illustrations** TXT_6687/0_N1**)** He also wrote elaborate captions, sometimes with variants. Every effort was made to identify the original sources of the images reproduced in the photostats (ordered from the NYPL or Columbia University libraries), then cropped and glued on legal-size paper along with the typewritten text of the captions. The original image sources of these plates are included in individual lists at the end of each part. These sources encompass a great and often surprising array of publications, which the Kieslers scoured while collecting images for the plates of *Magic Architecture*. The figures added to the Main Text include a series of original line drawings and charts made by the architect specifically for *Magic Architecture* to illustrate his ideas schematically. Figures in the Main Text also contain a set of additional reproductions of Kiesler's original manuscripts and typescripts showing some of the deleted or inserted words and passages, as well as sketches he drew or scribbled on the margins of his drafts.

Following the transcription of the Main Text, this edition includes a series of Addenda containing supplementary textual and visual material assembled by the architect specifically for *Magic Architecture*. These include: First, a set of alternate textual drafts ultimately not included in the assembled manuscript of *Magic Architecture*, such as a number of alternate book proposals and preliminary outlines of the book content written by the architect with the aim of sending them to publishers in expectation of a book contract. Second, a set of preliminary charts and diagrams drawn by Kiesler that were ultimately not included in the book manuscript in its later stages yet contain a number of alternative ideas on his main formulations as well as the structure of his book. Third, a series of transcriptions or translations of texts by other authors (such as the ethno-sociologists Lucien Lévy-Bruhl and Leo Frobenius) selected by Kiesler and typed and/or translated by Stefi. Many of these transcriptions and translations were included in the Main Text; yet this section of the Addenda includes transcriptions and translations that were ultimately not incorporated in the Main Text. A number of these transcriptions were originally made in German, and wherever there is no translation either by the Kieslers or in a published English edition of the work (such as for the texts by Viennese intellectuals Egon Friedell and Hans Sussmann), an English translation of these excerpts by the editors is included. The fourth and final section of the Addenda contains a set of bibliographic lists that contain books and articles used by Kiesler in his text and plate illustrations, as well as the dozens of newspaper and journal articles he excerpted in his research clippings compiled while working on *Magic Architecture*.

The volume concludes with an Annotated Chronology documenting the production of Kiesler's book through correspondence with publishers, situating *Magic Architecture* within the broader historical and professional context of Kiesler's career on both sides of the Atlantic, before and after the Second World War.

M A G I C   A R C H I T E C T U R E

Origin and Future

The Story of Human Housing

by

Frederick J. Kiesler

MAGIC ARCHITECTURE
THE STORY OF HUMAN HOUSING

FREDERICK KIESLER

Alternative titles:

MAGIC ARCHITECTURE
ORIGIN AND FUTURE
THE STORY OF HUMAN HOUSING
TXT_6687/0_N2

EVERYMAN'S ARCHITECTURE
ORIGIN AND FUTURE OF MAGIC ARCHITECTURE
THE STORY OF HUMAN HOUSING
TXT_6685/0_N1

EVERYMAN'S ARCHITECTURE
THE STORY OF HUMAN HOUSING
MAGIC AND PROFANE
TXT_6189/0_N3; AAA N.P.

NOTE TO THE PUBLISHER [1]

This book fills an urgent need in education.[2]

Prosperity as well as poverty lie ahead of us after this Second World War.

Much undue profit will be taken of a situation which lacks economic equilibrium. Much more profit will be taken through lack of knowledge of the innermost need of home-design.

Already the idea of prefabricating homes and towns has started a race in pseudo-design and super-selling methods.

To counteract this drive for self-deceit of those who sell and those who buy, of those who teach and those who learn, a statement on the fundamental needs[3] of the human being with regard to housing his family and the social community is badly required.[4]

*

Twenty-five years ago—shortly after the First World War—a similar situation existed. The book of Le Corbusier, Towards a New Architecture, which appeared in Paris, filled the need of that period.[5] But there is no book to serve us as guide now.

What exists are volumes of imitations and adaptations of his work. But it is outmoded today. And the reason for that is its base,[6] namely the glorification of the machine age. This glorification is now eradicated by the experience of this new world war, and the end which it put to science for science's and manufacturing's sake.[7]

It is a fact of growing importance that the house of a family is not only a living machine (as Le Corbusier put it); it is also a nervous system.[8] The fallacy of Le Corbusier is that he accepts "Functions" as already defined and proceeds to express[9] them architecturally in the new dress of abstract art. That is why it so readily became just another fashion.

*

The purpose of my book is to re-examine the meaning of "function"; it then proceeds, by a comparative method, to establish human needs with regard to shelter and architecture. These needs appear to be primarily of psychological and not of a materialistic character. To satisfy the desires of his psyche, man uses all his physiological potentialities[10] for this aim—and not vice versa.[11]

*

My script, therefore, is a Morphology of architecture,[12] not a history of styles, materials and building methods, antique or modern fashions.[13] It traces the inner development of man in correlation to his physio-plastic achievements in Art and Shelter.[14]

The result is the possibility of a symbiosis of technological inventions (today fully possible) and psychological needs.[15] It leads to a reduction of pseudo-scientific gadgets in manufacturing and to an emphasis upon simplicity. This simplicity is not an escape into the primitive but an affirmation of primordial necessities.[16]

*

"Magic Architecture" is not a utopian concept as it might be misinterpreted; it is a natural development of technological as well as ideological inventions in the services of inner needs.[17] Science and Art, Myth and Magic, appear mutually interdependent in a social structure based on human rights.

Slums are just as much the result of faulty intellects as they are the result of inadequate construction and deflated maintenance.

* * *

1 This document appears at the beginning of the assembled book manuscript and serves as a prefatory note to Kiesler's synopsis and table of contents. It was included as part of the book proposal materials submitted to publishers after the end of World War II; for dates, see Annotated Chronology.

2 **This book fills a need in educating ~~new~~ professionals as well as the public at large as to the desired course of architecture in the time to come.** TXT_6724/0_N4

3 **simple need** TXT_6712/0_N1

4 **badly needed.** TXT_6712/0_N1

5 Kiesler refers to Le Corbusier, *Towards a New Architecture*, trans. Frederick Etchells (New York: Brewer & Warren, 1927), the first English translation of Le Corbusier, *Vers une architecture* (Paris: Les Éditions G. Crès, 1923). Kiesler's library includes the German edition of Le Corbusier's book; see Sources, Disciplines, and Objects.

6 **~~foundamental~~ base** TXT_6724/0_N4

7 **The experience of the Second World War has put an end to ~~the~~ science ~~per se~~, for science's sake.** TXT_6724/0_N4

8 **The House of a Family is not only a living-machine; it is also a nervous system, a fact of growing importance.** TXT_6724/0_N4 Here Kiesler is referring to Le Corbusier's well-known statement "A house is a machine for living in," Etchells, *Towards a New Architecture*, 4.

9 **~~clad~~** TXT_6724/0_N4

10 **physiological ~~mechanisms~~** TXT_6724/0_N5 **~~psycho~~physiological potentialities** TXT_6712/0_N2

11 For Kiesler on the psychological aspects of function in architecture, cf. Frederick Kiesler, "Pseudo Functionalism in Modern Architecture," *Partisan Review* 16, no. 7 (July 1949): 733-742.

12 **This script represents therefore a morphology of Architecture** TXT_6724/0_N5 Cf. Kiesler's earlier writings on morphology including "Morphology-Chart of Architecture." TXT_3588_0 Part of these writings including Kiesler's chart was published in his "Notes on Architecture. The Space House. Annotations at Random," *Hound & Horn* 37 (January-March 1934): 292-297. See also Sources, Disciplines, and Objects, pp. 64-65.

13 **~~old~~ antique or modernistic fashions.** TXT_6724/0_N5

14 **physio-plastic life in Art and ~~Arch~~ shelter.** TXT_6724/0_N5-N6

15 **The result is ~~a strife for to~~ the possible reality of symbiosis of technological facts (fully available to us today) in service primarily of inner need, not of materialistic securities.** TXT_6724/0_N6

16 **It leads to a reduction of pseudo-scientific gadgets in ~~produ~~ manufacturing and to an emphasis ~~to co-relation in~~ on simplicity, not as an escape into primitivity, but as of a necessity of freedom of action.** TXT_6724/0_N6 **but an affirmation of valid necessities.** TXT_6712/0_N3

17 **The term "Magic Architecture" appears then, not as usually interpreted as a phantastic exaggeration of wish-Dreams ~~Castles~~, but as a natural development of technological inventions in the services of inner needs.** TXT_6724/0_N6-N7

The last section of the book deals with the possible architectural solutions for future houses.[18] A thoroughly detailed analysis of the problem will be carried through. Plans and models of actual projects will be shown[19] and their validity scrutinized.

The script is written in a narrative style.[20] Although based on research in various scientific fields,[21] its language and pictorial material are not merely to appeal to the specialist.[22] It aims at the general public. The different professions involved in housing will naturally take to it. But my main interest is the public at large—the people, who are to be housed.

18 the possible architectural ~~problems and possible~~ solutions of the Future. TXT_6712/0_N4

19 actual ~~samples~~ projects will be given. TXT_6712/0_N4

20 The ~~book~~ is written in a simple, narration style. TXT_6724/0_N3

21 Although based on scientific research ~~and investigation into statements of contemporary p~~ TXT_6724/0_N3 The solitary "p" suggests Kiesler was thinking of "practice" or "production" before striking out the entire phrase.

22 are ~~specifically~~ intended to be straightforward and not appealing to the ~~specialized~~. It aims at the general public ~~at large~~ as well as the professions involved in ~~Architecture, and~~ Housing. ~~and the social science~~ TXT_6724/0_N3

EVERY HOUSE CONSTITUTES A NERVOUS SYSTEM; A HOUSE IS FAR MORE AN ARCHITECTURAL BODY THAN IT IS A LIVING MACHINE. Insert (A)

EVERYMAN'S HOME SHOULD GROW, NOT ONLY FROM PHYSIO-FUNCTIONAL DEMANDS, BUT ALSO FROM PSYCHO-LOGICAL NEEDS – THESE NEEDS CAN INSPIRE THE HOME, AND MUST BE SATISFIED BY THE HOME. THE IMAGINATION THAT MAN HAS DEVOTED TO HIS RELIGIOUS STRUCTURES MUST TRANSFORM THE POTENTIAL SLUMS IN WHICH HE HAS GROWN ACCUSTOMED TO LIVING.

THIS ENRICHED ARCHITECTURAL ENVIRONMENT WILL HAVE, AS ITS PRIMARY AIM: THE ENCOURAGEMENT OF THE INDIVIDUAL'S INHERENT CREATIVE CAPACITIES. WITHOUT THIS AIM, TALK OF "SOCIAL PROGRESS" IS SURELY EMPTY TALK.

###

IF MAGIC CAN BE DEFINED AS THE REALIZATION OF SUPRA-NORMAL BUT INBORN POWER IN MAN, THAN MAGIC ARCHITECTURE CAN MEAN A SHELTER OF IMAGINATIVE LIVING. I THEREFORE DO NOT CONSIDER MAGIC ARCHITECTURE AS A MYSTIC OR FANTASTIC CONCEPT, BUT AS AN EXTRA-ORDINARILY REALISTIC AIM – THE RESULT OF SCIENCE AT THE SERVICE OF INNER NEEDS.

IT WOULD SEEM THAT NO MATTER WHAT EQUIPMENT OR PLUMBING OUR HOUSES HAVE, PEACE OF MIND, INSIDE AND OUTSIDE OUR HOUSE, IS STILL THE CARDINAL FACTOR OF OUR EXISTENCE, AND MUST BE PLACED ABOVE ANY TECHNICAL CONSIDERATION.

NOW THAT WE HAVE FINALLY ACQUIRED A RICH FUND OF TECHNICAL KNOWLEDGE FOR THE REALIZATION OF ANY HUMAN WISH, OUR JOB is TO DEFINE A RELATIONSHIP BETWEEN THIS KNOWLEDGE AND OUR ~~WISHES~~ FUNDAMENTAL WISHES.

THE FORMULATION OF THESE PRINCIPLES AND THEIR PRACTICAL APPLICATION IS THE AIM OF THIS BOOK.

Practicality must be stripped of the traditional obstacles that have been allowed to encrust our attitude to this word — and, armed with science, we ~~must~~ will look freshly at the heart of our problem.

Frederick Kiesler, Final page of "Synopsis" with handwritten corrections and additional text (TS, pencil) ÖFLKS, TXT_5877/0 N12

SYNOPSIS[23]

This manuscript will trace, develop, and bring to a conclusion the origin and future possibilities of Architecture. Since[24] the early days of history, man has delegated imagination in architecture to religious (or sacral) buildings, while he himself has dwelt (up to now) in houses which can be, by comparison, very aptly described as: potential slums.

*

The split of his creative ability into works of vision and works of fact has thrown him as well as his work out of balance with his natural and social environment.

Through immeasurable sufferings men have become more and more aware of this "fissure" and the individual of today as well as his society are trying to not only mend this split but lay a new foundation for the growth of a wholesome and more "practical" reality.

*

In building a shelter for physical protection man performs a deed not different from that of any animal constructing a nest, a storage, or shelter. It is instinctive skill.

But to raise the standard of the home and house to that of Architecture is a privilege of man. Yet, we were unable to avail ourselves of this human capacity, although, today, we have finally acquired the necessary technical knowledge to achieve it. The lack of underlying principles has continuously prevented realization. To formulate these principles and their practical applications is the aim of this book.

In other words: Every house constitutes just as much a nervous system as does the human body. The house is not only a living machine (Corbusier).[25]

The house and home of everyman should not only be the result of physio-functional demands, but also an inspiration to and satisfaction of psycho-logical needs. Man's shelter may then become Architecture without resorting to the escape into religious buildings.

The impact of such an architectural environment should contribute very much to the development of the inherent creative capacities of an individual, rather than merely satisfy his routine-functions.[26]

*

If Magic is the realization of supra-normal but inborn power in man, then Magic Architecture is the shelter of imaginative living. And by Magic Architecture I therefore do not understand a mystic or fantastic concept, but an extra-ordinarily realistic one:[27] the result, of science in the service of inner needs.

It still seems, and very definitely so, that no matter what equipment or plumbing or else, our houses have (as long as they have some workable ones)–peace of mind, inside and outside our houses is still the cardinal factor of our existence, and must supersede[28] any technical consideration.[29]

Now that we have finally acquired a rich fund of technical knowledge for the realization of any human wish, our job is to define a relationship between this knowledge and our fundamental wishes.

The formulation of these principles and their practical application is the aim of this book.[30]

Practicality must be stripped of the traditional obstacles that have been allowed to encrust our attitude to this word–and, armed with science, we will[31] look freshly at the heart of our problem.

23 Here Kiesler provides a summary of the main programmatic positions of his project. The text appears in two different versions, one of which has a number of additional paragraphs. In assembled versions of the manuscript, this synopsis comes after his note to the publisher but before the table of contents.

24 **It will demonstrate, that since** TXT_6686/0_N1

25 **Every house constitutes a nervous system; a house is far more an architectural body than it is a living machine.** TXT_6686/0_N2; TXT_6845/0_N1-N2 Cf. Kiesler's Note to the Publisher.

26 Alternative text for the previous two paragraphs: **Everyman's house should grow, not only from physio-functional demands, but also from psycho-logical needs–these needs can inspire the home, and must be satisfied by the home. The imagination that man has devoted to his religious structures must transform the potential slums in which he has grown accustomed to living.**
This enriched architectural environment will have, as its primary aim: the encouragement of the individual's inherent creative capacities. Without this aim, talk of "social progress" is surely empty talk. TXT_6686/0_N2; TXT_6845/0_N1-N2

27 **I therefore do not consider Magic Architecture as a mystic or fantastic concept, but as an extra-ordinarily realistic aim** TXT_6686/0_N3; TXT_6845/0_N3-N4

28 **and must be placed above** TXT_6686/0_N3; TXT_6845/0_N3-N4

29 One version of the synopsis ends here. Another contains three additional one-sentence paragraphs. These are reproduced in the main text of this edition. See fig. B.01, cf. TXT_5877/0_N6; TXT_6686/0_N3

30 Cf. with the final sentence of the fifth paragraph in the synopsis: **To formulate these principles and their practical applications is the aim of this book.** TXT_6686/0_N3; TXT_6845/0_N3-N4

31 **we ~~must~~** TXT_5877/0_N12

fig. B.02

Blue Circle: suggests selected chapters for reading
Red Circle: indicates sample chapters of writing

grey circle: corresponding number with illustration

BOND
PRODUCT

MANAG
A HAMM

C O N T E N T

PART ONE

MANAGEMENT
A HAMMERMILL P

Frederick Kiesler, Table of "Content" with annotations and colored pencil markings (TS, ink, pencil) TXT_5877/0_N9

CONTENT*

Introduction: The Unity of Vision and Fact

PART I

Chapter 1 The Eternal Preamble to Architecture
Chapter 2 Fear of the Unseen
Chapter 3 The Enigma of Death
Chapter 4 The Enigma of Birth
Chapter 5 Birth Necessitates Shelter; Death Inspires Architecture
Chapter 6 The Cave, First Natural Shelter
Chapter 7 The Nest, First Artificial Shelter
Chapter 8 The Universe as Architecture
Chapter 9 The Split in the Unity of Vision and Fact

* See illustration (fig. B.03) accompanying the first page of the table of contents, with **selected chapters for reading** and **sample chapters for writing** marked by Kiesler in blue and red circles, as part of his book proposal submission to publishers. TXT_5877/0_N9

Kiesler went through several iterations when it came to titling any part of his book, from the table of contents—**Contents/ M.A.** TXT_6702/0_N1 and **Table of Contents** TXT_6189/0_N4—to the chapter titles, including the following changes:

Introduction: **The Unity of Vision and Fact** / ~~**Preamble to Architecture**~~ TXT_6702/0_N1

Chapter 1 In various drafts, the general title of Part I is **Eternal Preamble to Architecture**, also used to title the first chapter. TXT_6686/0_N22-23

Chapter 2 ~~**Omnivorous man**~~ TXT_6702/0_N1

Chapter 3 ~~**The conquest of death**~~ **Enigma Death** TXT_6702/0_N1 **The Enigma Death** TXT_6686/0_N4

Chapter 4 **Enigma Birth** TXT_6702/0_N1 **The Enigma Birth** TXT_6686/0_N4

Chapter 5 missing in Kiesler's handwritten list of contents; Part I has eight chapters. TXT_6702/0_N1

Chapter 8 **Chapter seven:** ~~**Man, the perfect imitator**~~ TXT_6702/0_N1

Chapter 9 **Chapter eight: The Unity Split** TXT_6702/0_N1

PART II*

ANIMAL ARCHITECTURE AND MAN'S ABILITY TO BUILD

Introduction: Instinct, Memory, and the Drive for Invention
Chapter 1 Man's House is Animal Architecture
Chapter 2 The Building Instinct of Animals: The Termitary of the Termites
Chapter 3 Animal Engineering: The Dam of the Beaver
Chapter 4 Building Tools of Animals
Chapter 5 Man, a Composite Animal of Building Techniques
Chapter 6 Man's First Invention: The (First) Transformation of Dead Material into Useful Tools
Chapter 7 The (Second) Transformation of Dead Material into Magic Tools of Physical Attraction
Chapter 8 The (Third) Transformation of Dead Material into Magic Tools of Spiritual Power

* Alternative titles:

Introduction: **Instinct, Memory and** ~~**Tools**~~ TXT_6702/0_N2

Chapter 4 **The Building Tools of Animals** TXT_6189/0_N2
In the handwritten list of contents, chapter 5 appears as an addendum to chapter 4, and chapters 6–8 are initially listed as chapters 5–7, respectively. TXT_6702/0_N2-N3

PART III*
AWARENESS OF THE MIRACULOUS

Introduction: From Animal Housing to Magic Architecture

Chapter 1 The Birth of Magic Design
Man discovers his capacity to convert his own body into a dream-image through make-up

Chapter 2 Man discovers that the fingers of his hand are magic wands for the transformation of surfaces into images through the application of paint

Chapter 3 Man discovers that by making grooves (engraving) hard stone objects held in his hand he can transform soft stone surfaces into images.

Chapter 4 Discovery and Affirmation of the Superfluous

* Alternative chapter titles:

Chapter 2 Man discovers that the fingers of his hand are magic wands for the transformation of stone surfaces TXT_6702/0_N4

Chapter 3 Man discovers that ~~stone~~ hard objects in his hand can transform less hard surfaces, like stone, into images through grooves (engraving) TXT_6702/0_N4

PART IV*
ART AND THE UNKNOWN

Introduction: The Superfluous Becomes a Necessity

Chapter 1 The Meaning of Magic
Chapter 2 Man Part of the Cosmos and Man Apart from the Cosmos
Chapter 3 Artifacts, Symbols, and Art
Chapter 4 Myth and Magic
Chapter 5 The Psycho–Plastic–Era
Chapter 6 The Ideo–Plastic–Era
Chapter 7 The Era of Metamorphosis
Chapter 8 The Era of Abstraction
Chapter 9 The Physio-plastic Era

* Part IV is untitled in Kiesler's handwritten list of contents. Chapters 1, 4, and 9 are also missing, and next to the title of chapter 2 is written: **(to be translated?)** TXT_6702/0_N5-N6
The TS for chapter 2 includes a handwritten annotation: **Note: (Pertaining to the transformation from the mystic [image-less] belief to visual objectivations: Idols, shrines.)** TXT_6189/0_N27; TXT_6702/0_N5

PART V*
SLUMS FOR THE BODY DREAM-ARCHITECTURE FOR RITUALS

Introduction: Image–Worship

Chapter 1 The Split in Vision and Fact Standardized
Chapter 2 Egyptian Pyramid and Town
Chapter 3 Aztec Pyramid and Dwellings
Chapter 4 Indian Temple and Street
Chapter 5 Parthenon and House
Chapter 6 Gothic Cathedral and Town
Chapter 7 Hagia Sophia and Houses
Chapter 8 Skyscraper and Street
Chapter 9 Cathedral and the Holy Grail
Chapter 10 The Gothic Arch

* The handwritten list of contents for Part v contains seven chapters, with chapters 8 and 10 appearing later in the TS. Chapter 1 is initially listed as the introduction to Part v. The following is also struck through in the handwritten list of contents: ~~**Introduction: nothing but Vision Dreams**~~.

Alternative chapter numbering and titles:

Chapter 2 **Chapter 1: Egyptian Pyramid and streets**

Chapters 3, 5-7, 9 appear as chapters 2, 3, 5-7 respectively:

Chapter 2 Aztec Pyramid and ~~street~~ Houses
Chapter 3 Parthenon and Street
Chapter 5 Gothic Cathedral and Street
Chapter 6 Hagia Sophia and Street
Chapter 7 Cathedral of the Holy Grail TXT_6702/0_N6-N7

PART VI*
PAINTERS AS DREAM—ARCHITECTS

Introduction: Construction without Chains

Chapter 1 Dürer's Super-Arch of Triumph
Chapter 2 Da Vinci: Concept of Cathedral
Chapter 3 Michelangelo: Concept of Cathedral
Chapter 4 Bruegel's Tower of Babel
Chapter 5 Hieronymus Bosch's Houses (a) and Tools (b)
Chapter 6 El Greco's Toledo
Chapter 7 Raphael's Gardens
Chapter 8 The Religious Development of the Roman Empire: Piranesi's Rome

* The handwritten list of contents for Part VI contains seven chapters in total.

Alternative chapter numbers and titles:

Chapter 1 **Dürer's:** (sic) **Super Arch de Triumph** TXT_6702/0_N8

Chapters 2-3 **Chapter 2: Da Vinci and Michelangelo: Concepts of Cathedrals** TXT_6702/0_N8

Chapter 5 **Hieronymus de Bosh's Houses** TXT_6702/0_N8 **Hieronymus de Bosch's Houses (a) and Tools (b)** [handwritten on the TS] TXT_6686/0_N9 Kiesler refers to the well-known Dutch painter Hieronymus Bosch (1450-1516) throughout his drafts as Hieronymus de Bosch, which today commonly describes the eighteenth-century Latin poet Jeronimo de Bosch (1740-1811), also from the Netherlands. Kiesler also referred to Marcel Duchamp, as H(ieronymus) Duchamp (a covert reference to Saint Jerome and his "study" juxtaposed with Duchamp's 14th street studio in New York). See text and montage by Frederick Kiesler, *Les Larves d'Imagie d'Henri Robert Marcel Duchamp*, *View. The Modern Magazine*, 1, March 1945, 24.

Chapters 7-8 are numbered 3 and 7, and respectively titled: **Raphael's Gardens** and **Piranesi's Rome** TXT_6702/0_N8

PART VII*
MAGIC ARCHITECTURE

Introduction: Towards Magic Architecture

Visions of Cities

Chapter 1 Mount Athos by Dinocrates
Chapter 2 Filarete's City Sforzinda
Chapter 3 The City of the Sun by Campanella
Chapter 4 Magic Architecture, Holy and Profane
a) Michelangelo's Sistine Chapel
b) Houses of Pompeii

* Alternative part and chapter titles:
Part VII: Magic Architecture / ~~Dream Cities of Vision~~
Introduction: Magic or the Belief in Life / Cities of Vision
Chapter 2 Sforzinda by Filarete
Chapter 4 was added later. Another draft reverses the order of its sub-chapters on Michelangelo and Pompeii. TXT_6702/0_N9

PART VIII*
REALISM OF WEALTH

Introduction: Fashion in Architecture

Chapter 1 Lust in Stone (Fountain by Paulus Decker)
Chapter 2 The Rococo in France (Trianon)

* Alternative part and chapter numbering and titles:
Part VIII Part VII 1/2: The Dance of Death ~~Death Dance of Architecture~~
Chapter 1 Lust in Stone (Brunnen by Paulus Decker)
Chapter 2 The Ornament of the Rococo TXT_6702/0_N10

PART IX*
THE POET'S ARCHITECTURE

Introduction: Castles in the Air

Chapter 1 Mozart's House by Victorien Sardou
Chapter 2 An Interior by Huysmans
Chapter 3 Glass Architecture by Paul Scheerbart
Chapter 4 The Building by Franz Kafka

* According to Kiesler's handwritten list of contents, Part IX was originally numbered Part VIII, and the introduction was untitled. TXT_6702/0_N11

PART X*
FLARES OF A NEW UNITY OF VISION AND FACT

Introduction: Socio-Architectural Utopia and the Reality of Industry

Chapter 1 Fourier's "Ideal Phalanx"
Chapter 2 "Cities of a New Globe" by Bruno Taut
Chapter 3 Reaction: Back to Classicism
Chapter 4 Magic in Steel: The Eiffel Tower
Chapter 5 The City in Space
Chapter 6 The Double-Personality of the Skyscraper: Business and Art (special illust.)
Chapter 7 Reaction: Back to Handicraft: The Victorian Era
Chapter 8 Hygiene of Functional Architecture

Chapter 9 Flight into the Dream World of Surrealism (Art without Architecture)
Chapter 10 The Twentieth Century's Second Quarter: Towards a New Reality (Claude-Nicolas Ledoux)

* Similar to the two previous parts, Kiesler changed his mind multiple times about the placement of this final section, listing it first as **Part VIII** and then as **Part IX**. Chapter 5 is missing from his handwritten list of contents, which still includes ten chapters, with the addition of an epilogue.

Alternative chapter titles and numbering:
Introduction ~~Design-Correlation Social~~ Socio-Architectural Utopias and the Reality of Industries TXT_6702/0_N12
Chapter 1 Fourier's "Phalanstère" TXT_6702/0_N12
Chapter 3 ~~Glass Architecture by Paul Sheerbarth~~; Chapter 3: Reaction: Schinkel's Project for the Acropolis TXT_6702/0_N12 Chapter Three / Reaction: Back to Classicism: Schinkel's Project (1781) for a Palace of King Otto of Greece on the Acropolis TXT_6189/0_N45 1781 was Schinkel's birth year, not the date of his Acropolis project. This mistake is repeated in the typescript.
Chapter 7 Chapter 6: Reaction: Back to Handicraft. (Ruskin, Morris, Thoreau) TXT_6189/0_N50
Chapter 8 Chapter 7: The Hygiene of Functional Architecture TXT_6702/0_N13
Chapter 10 Chapter 9: The Twentieth Century's Last Quarter: ~~The~~ Interdependence of Vision and Fact ~~(Kiesler, Fuller)~~ TXT_6702/0_N13 Chapter 10: ~~The Architectural Division in Homes, Temples, and Administration abolished. The Magic Architecture of the Home and Work~~ Epilogue: The Home as Nucleus of Magic Architecture Accomplished. A Chart "Orbit of Extasy" TXT_6702/0_N13. (Claude-Nicolas Ledoux) was added as a handwritten note to the TS after chapter 10. TXT_6686/0_N13; TXT_5877/0_N13

EPILOGUE AND PROLOGUE*
MAN'S SHELTER BECOMES MAGIC ARCHITECTURE

Section 1 As to Facts
Section 2 As to Materials
Section 3 As to Design
Section 4 As to Equipment
Section 5 Science and Architecture (Drawings of Types of Houses of the Future)

* The handwritten list of contents does not contain the above-mentioned sections of the epilogue and the appendices. For an alternate epilogue and accompanying chart in the handwritten list, see epilogue titling in previous note TXT_6702/0_N13

APPENDED:

A Metabolism Chart of the Mobile Home-Library

It analyzes the effects of technological environment upon man, particularly as a stimulant to higher productivity and as a factor in reducing fatigue moments.

Plan, Elevation, and Construction Details of the Mobile Home-Library

Chart of the Four Standard Types in Manufacturing Products

DATA, ANNOTATIONS, AND CURIOSA*

Referring to certain specialized details of historical and scientific content which would, if included in the main part, disturb the continuity of the text.

* * *

Index of Subjects
Index of Names
Charts
Acknowledgments

* Only a few "data" and "annotations" for Part I were drafted, but ultimately they were not included in the assembled text. None of the indexes materialized, and there is no draft of Kiesler's acknowledgments.

INTRODUCTION
THE UNITY OF VISION AND FACT[32]

When the species, Man, developed into the state of so-called homo sapiens, along with this ascent an additional need arose.[33] This need was something much more difficult for him to define than the sensual functions of the body; as man grew this new need became so much a part of him that he had to give it a name, and he called it–the Spirit.[34] Just as he sheltered his body, he found it imperative to give comfort to his new need, the Spirit.[35] His cave became ornate with drawings, which testified to the miraculous powers of nature, the force that made him successful in hunting and so enabled him to overcome the sufferings of hunger, fear, and death.[36]

Modern man's oneness of being is broken. Half his world shelters the frustrations of daily existence, the other half is filled[37] with the ghostly evaporations of his thwarted ego.[38] Happily, primitive man knew no separate worlds of vision and fact.[39] Eolithic man, that primordial creature of our dawn, born with his eyes wide open, but who chiefly saw with his inner sight, was a luckier being than contemporary man: he knew only one world, and in that world vision and fact were continually present within the pattern of everyday experience. When Dawn Man carved his tools with floral or animal imagery, no artificial frames or borders cut off his works of "Art" from the space of life–the same space, the same life that flowed around his animals, his demons, and himself.

This primordial unity, the unity between man's creative consciousness and his daily environment, has been lost. Today, Art is nothing more than a decorative cipher bare of meaning. We live in a world which is symbol and agent of an artificial duality of "vision" and "reality," "image" and "environment," or "projection" and "truth."[40] These two opposing spheres[41] must be seen once more as jointly indispensable forces in the same world. There must be a recreation of the ancient magic[42] by which the god and the mask of the god, the deer and the image of the deer existed, with equal potency, with the same immediate reality in one living universe; it must be recreated with the creative capacities of our own time.

Again and again, creative men have tried to re-establish that unity. In architecture we find testimony of that in plans for buildings that were never built; some rare structures that were built, despite every social and economic difficulty, bear living testimony to the magic power of man's craft in architecture.

Architecture is the one human skill which presents the greatest difficulty in coordinating physical functions with spiritual needs. Society consequently divided shelter into two main categories: one for the exercise of profane functions–the home; and the other for exercising spiritual functions–temples of worship. This split is so standardized, particularly in western civilization, that it was

32 In both the final list of contents and the assembled manuscript, this introductory text appears as a general introduction to Kiesler's book, but in an earlier draft, the text is used as the introduction to Part I. TXT_6717/0_N1 The same draft includes a hand-drawn "3D" frame with the title MAGIC ARCHITECTURE typed and then struck through, with the title of the introduction written above. See fig. B.03. TXT_6717/0_N2

33 ~~If architecture were only a matter of physical shelter it would be nothing more than sort of fox hole, a nest bowl, or a mole hill. It seems however that w~~hen the species TXT_6717/0_N2

34 he gave it a name: ~~the spirit, the soul.~~ he called it: the spirits TXT_6717/0_N2

35 The original TS shows "express" twice struck through, and "spirit" added as a handwritten annotation: ~~And h~~/He soon found it imperative to ~~express shelter that soul spirit too.~~ TXT_6717/0_N2

36 His cave became ornate with drawings, testimonies ~~of~~ to the ~~miracles of his powers in hunting, of forces~~ of nature that were unexplain~~able and with powerful symbols taken from his daily environment, the association with would help him~~ to overcome ~~the~~ sufferings ~~or even death.~~ TXT_6717/0_N2

37 is ~~empty with~~ TXT_6717/0_N5

38 ~~frustrated eyes~~ TXT_6717/0_N5

39 ~~And soon~~ primitive man knew no separate worlds of vision and fact. ~~He knew one world in which both were continually present within the pattern of everyday experience.~~ TXT_6717/0_N2 Cf. Frederick Kiesler, "Brief Note on Designing the Gallery" (1942): Primitive man knew no separate worlds of vision and of fact. He knew only one world in which both were continually present within the pattern of everyday experience. And when he carved and painted the walls of his cave or the side of a cliff, no frames or borders cut off his works of art from space or life–the same space, the same life flowed around his animals, his demons, and himself. TXT_188/0 For a reproduction of the typescript, see *Friedrich Kiesler: The Art of this Century* (Ostfilden, Germany: Hatje Cantz, 2002), 34–35.

40 Cf. with Kiesler, "Brief Note," 34: It is the principle of unity, primordial unity, the unity between man's creative consciousness and his daily environment which governs the presentation of paintings, sculptures, furnishings, and enclosures in these three galleries ... Today the framed painting on the wall has become a decorative cipher without life and meaning, or else, to the more susceptible observer, an object of interest existing in world distinct from his. Its frame is at once symbol and agent of an artificial duality of "vision" and "reality," or "image and environment," a plastic barrier across which man looks from the world he inhabits to the alien world in which the work of art has its being.

41 ~~worlds~~ TXT_6717/0_N3

42 ~~with the tools of our own spirit + with the means and meaning of our time,~~ TXT_6717/0_N3

fig. B.03

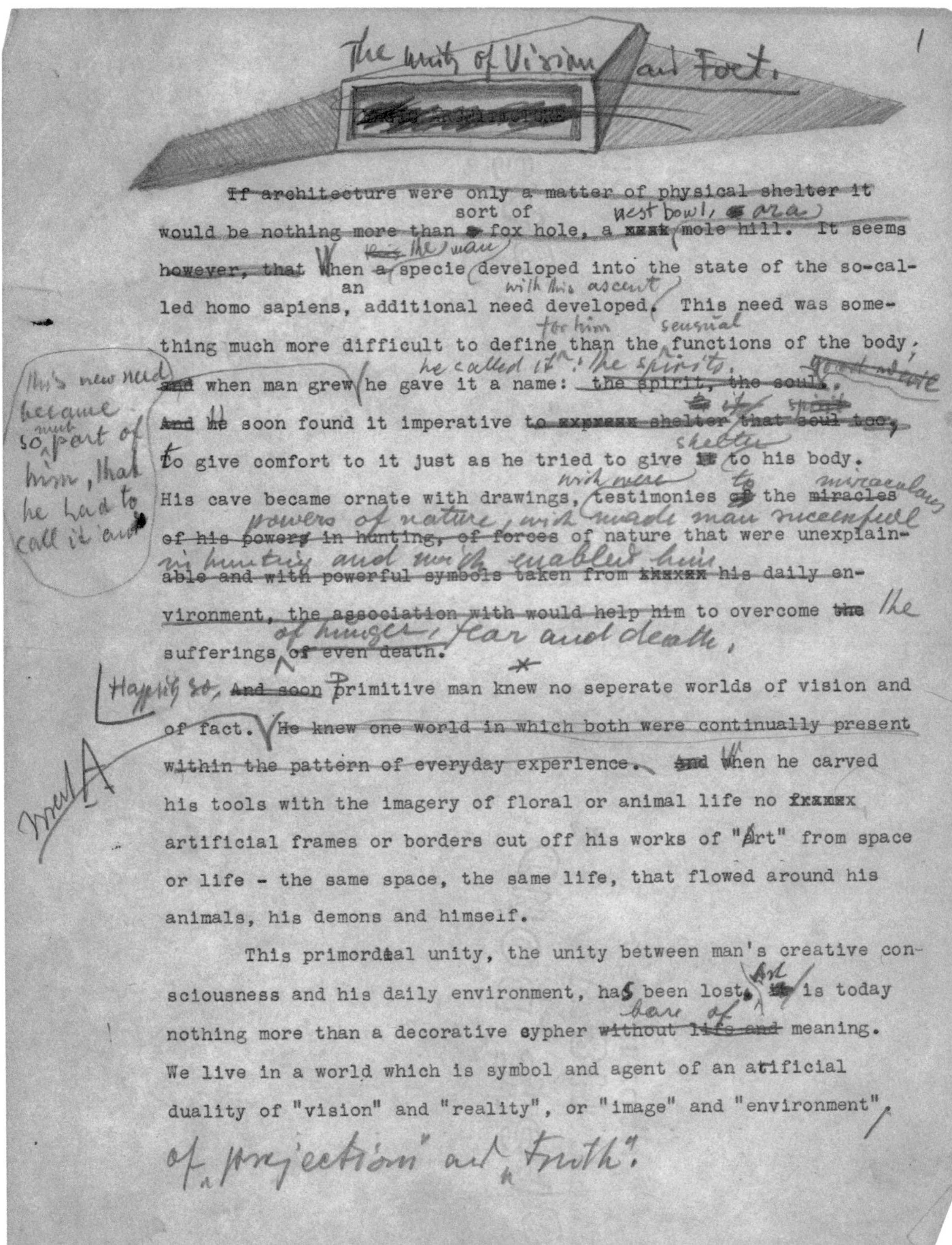

The Unity of Vision and Fact.

1

If architecture were only a matter of physical shelter it would be nothing more than a fox hole, a mole hill. It seems however, that when a specie developed into the state of the so-called homo sapiens, additional need developed. This need was something much more difficult to define than the functions of the body; and when man grew he gave it a name: the spirit, the soul. And he soon found it imperative to express shelter that soul too, to give comfort to it just as he tried to give it to his body. His cave became ornate with drawings, testimonies of the miracles of his powers in hunting, of forces of nature that were unexplainable and with powerful symbols taken from his daily environment, the association with would help him to overcome the sufferings of even death.

And soon primitive man knew no seperate worlds of vision and of fact. He knew one world in which both were continually present within the pattern of everyday experience. And when he carved his tools with the imagery of floral or animal life no artificial frames or borders cut off his works of "Art" from space or life - the same space, the same life, that flowed around his animals, his demons and himself.

This primordial unity, the unity between man's creative consciousness and his daily environment, has been lost. It is today nothing more than a decorative cypher without life and meaning. We live in a world which is symbol and agent of an atificial duality of "vision" and "reality", or "image" and "environment", of "projection" and "truth".

Frederick Kiesler, Draft of Introduction "The Unity of Vision and Fact" with corrections and hand-drawn title frame (TS, pencil) ÖFLKS, TXT_6717/0_N2

imported into the Americas by the colonizing Spaniards as well as by the Pilgrims; and with it came the continual attempt to falsify the spiritual quality of architecture by the use of fashionable aesthetic patterns—a decorative camouflage, it was and still is as short-lived as the business cycle from which it springs.

We, the inheritors of this duality, must try to re-establish the unity of vision and fact. This book will serve as a witness stand for certain projects and some realizations which demonstrate the urgent need and the actual possibility of such a living unity in architecture.[43]

With the twentieth century, the "average man" has come of age. He has learned to read,[44] and he has learned to read the events of history. Superstition has developed into an experimental science; handicrafts have become technological standards. The social sciences are developing into safeguards of man's physical and mental health. For the first time in the history of western civilization we have the chance[45] not only to "prefabricate" houses, but to provide "Architecture" for every man.[46]

The "dream home" must be neither a castle in the air—a monument to arrogant possessions, a scramble of fashionable styles—nor a sales product of gadgeteering. Contemporary man's home and his town must represent a conquest over technical difficulties with the aim of unfolding the inherent power of imaginative living, and there must no longer be a separation between the world of vision and fact.

43 ~~This book will try to bring to the fore those works of those leaders throughout man's history who have again and again attempted to demonstrate~~ in projects and in some realizations the urgent need and the actual possibility of such a living unity in architecture was demonstrated. This book will be their witness stand. TXT_6717/0_N2 Cf. Kiesler, "Brief Note," 35: "We the inheritors of chaos, must be the architects of a new unity."

44 ~~books~~ TXT_6717/0_N4

45 ~~the building industry has its~~ chance TXT_6717/0_N4

46 We have the chance ~~To eliminate the duality of homes and shelter for living and homes for worship and to create with the practical tools of the sciences, structures that are neither castles in the air nor products of engineering, but the expression of a realism that has conquered the practical necessities and harnessed magic.~~ TXT_6717/0_N4

Eternal Preamble to Architecture

Truthfully, Architecture without Poetry, is nothing else but ~~protection~~ a protective umbrella of straw, skin or stone against unfavorable climate conditions. If Architecture were essentially nothing but that, ~~then~~ it would follow, that a highly mechanistic civilization, (like ours) would arrive ultimately at a solution of climate-control in the form of a divers-suit, within wich ~~the~~ man could air-condition the climate at will. Houses would than be superflous, and Architecture unheard off. That would be the ideal state of „functional" ~~Architecture~~ design. It would be light in weight, mobil, prefabricated, delivered by mail, low in cost and highly economically to operate.

Man had apparently always a „yen" (there is

PART I
ETERNAL PREAMBLE TO ARCHITECTURE[1]

CHAPTER 1
ETERNAL PREAMBLE TO ARCHITECTURE

Architecture[2] without Poetry is nothing but a protective umbrella (of straw, skin, or stone) against unfavorable climatic conditions—and against attacks from[3] humans and other animals during sleep.[4] If (pl. 1) architecture were essentially nothing but that, it would follow that a highly mechanistic civilization (like ours) would arrive ultimately at a solution of climate control in the form of a diver's suit within which man could air-condition the climate at will. In case of attack, the material of the suit could be impregnated to emanate an aura of deadly radiation.[5] Houses would then be superfluous and architecture unheard of. That would be the ideal state of "functional" design.[6] It (pl. 2) would be light in weight, mobile, prefabricated, delivered by mail, low in cost, and highly economic to operate.[7]

Man apparently has always had a "yen" (there is no better word for it) to move from the naturally warm climates, where nature brought him into being, to colder regions; and there to create fires,[8] houses, and clothing to make the atmosphere[9] artificially comfortable so that he could survive the deadly animosity of the region of his choice.[10] And accordingly, it is said[11] man cannot arrive at a high degree of culture until he has managed to dwell solely in the Arctic; thus,[12] only the nation which conquered the Arctic can and will dominate the world.[13]

Meanwhile, I hope, that man will find time—between moving from cold regions to colder ones, to exercise himself a little in the interests of culture, that is to give time to the Care of the Superfluous.[14] Of course, that will be nothing new; for thousands of years[15] man has used the warm periods between ice ages[16] for such play. We have prehistoric rock paintings to prove that. The earliest have been found in the Aurignacian period, the last interglacial period of the four we count in Europe, lasting, according to the Swedish geologist de Geer,[17] from 30,000 B.C. till about 5,000 B.C. Homo primigenius, as of 250,000 years ago—this Neolithic Aurignacian of 10,000 years—seems historically speaking, almost like a recent ancestor of yesterday.[18]

But equally interesting is the fact that new rock paintings, seemingly in the same technique and apparently having the same meaning as the prehistoric ones, have been made as recently as 1905. We have proof of this from latter-day expeditions to Africa.[19] Traveler Frobenius reports:

> No one lives who can tell about their origin (rock paintings), and were it not for the thought which gave rise to the search for their like in Africa, their silence might well have been eternal. ... But our rich experience has enabled us to say: that which existed once in Europe lives on among its epigones in Africa today.[20] ... In the Homburi Mountains in the Sudan, Desplagnes found rock pictures which were made by novices in the course of their initiation rites, something which we ourselves were able to investigate further later. Southward, this time in the forest of Liberia, Dr. Germann[21] found more novice paintings which, since there were no rocks, had been made on mud walls erected for the purpose.[22]

The account continues:[23]

> In 1905 we obtained further evidence from a Congo race, hunting tribes, later famous as the "pygmies," who had been driven from the plateau to the refuge of the Congo. We met them in the jungle district between Kassai and Luebo. Several of their

1 In the list of contents, Part I is untitled and no hand-drawn title sheet exists. In later drafts, it is titled **Eternal Preamble to Architecture**, which also doubles as the title of the section's chapter 1. Cf. TXT_6686/0_N4, TXT_6686/0_N22–N23 For the front page of Kiesler's preliminary draft with this title, see reproduction on previous page. TXT_6801/0_N1

2 **Truthfully, architecture** TXT_6801/0_N1

3 **~~beasts~~** TXT_6741/0_N1

4 **—and against ~~the~~ attacks ~~of~~ from beasts human and animal during sleep.** / **—when asleep.** / **—during the helplessness of sleep.** TXT_6828/0_N5

5 **~~The impregnation of the material would automatically emanate the security of an aura of deadly~~ radiation** TXT_6741/0_N1 **an aura of ~~automatic~~ deadly radiation would take care of deadly enemies of any form.** / **Impregnation of the material would ~~radiate~~ emanate the security of an aura of deadly radiation.** TXT_6828/0_N5

6 **"functional" ~~Architecture~~ Design** TXT_6801/0_N1

7 For this first chapter, Kiesler originally drafted three annotations as endnotes. These do not appear in the assembled book manuscript. They are written on a page titled "Data and Annotations" and are part of a larger appendix listed in the table of contents as "Data, Annotations, and Curiosa," which never materialized. The first of these endnotes reads: **page ... (1) Here follows a technical description of an industrial housing dream in which the ideal of a push button-civilization is ~~advocated.~~ carried to absurdum based on Data from architectural, scientific and managerial magazines and from newspapers and from advertising. (See advertising of Hotel New Yorker.)** TXT_6828/0_N1 On The New Yorker Hotel and Kiesler's research on prefabrication, see Sources, Disciplines, and Objects, pp. 10–11.

8 **started to build fires.** TXT_6801/0_N2

9 **temperature** TXT_6801/0_N2

10 **in order to survive within the deadly cold of the regions of his choice.** TXT_6801/0_N2

11 **And according ~~to my friend Buckminster Fuller~~** TXT_6801/0_N2 In the place of the deleted name Kiesler eventually inserted the following endnote included in the aforementioned list of "Annotations and Data" (but not transcribed in the assembled book manuscript): **(2) Quote from an interview with Buckminster Fuller, Evening Post, New York.** TXT_6828/0_N1 On possible published sources for this "quote," see Sources, Disciplines, and Objects, pp. 11, 84.

12 **~~And according to my friend~~** meaning Fuller, see previous note TXT_6801/0_N2

13 For Fuller's ideas on Nordic climates, see Sources, Disciplines, and Objects, pp. 11, 84.

14 **find time for exercising a little culture, which is the Care of the Superfluous. ~~(Civilization he will leave for each next colder region to invent into a higher and higher level.)~~** TXT_6801/0_N3

15 **since ~~several hundred~~ dozens of thousands of years** TXT_6801/0_N3

16 **between the glacials** TXT_6801/0_N3

17 Gerard de Geer (1858–1943), Swedish geologist and geochronologist, whose theories of geological timescale were based on the melting of ice sheets. Kiesler draws the reference to de Geer and part of his chronologies (including his references to "ice ages" and "interglacial" periods) from the text of the exhibition catalogue by Leo Frobenius and Douglas C. Fox, *Prehistoric Rock Pictures in Europe and Africa; From Material in the Archives of the Research Institute for the Morphology of Civilization, Frankfort-on-Main* (New York: The Museum of Modern Art, 1937), 21.

18 See handwritten "insert" to an earlier TS: **~~Indeed a rather jungish race of man.~~ Considering the age of the ~~Neanderthal creature as of the~~ Homo primigenius, as of 250,000 years ago—this Neolithic Aurignacian of 10,000 years seems ~~morphologically~~ historically speaking—almost like a brother yesterday.** / **recent ancestor.** TXT_6741/0_N14 Kiesler's substitution of "Neanderthal" with the term "Homo primigenius" (first-born human) reflects his reading of Hermann Klaatsch. See Sources, Disciplines, and Objects, pp. 18, 86.

19 **~~Spain, France, Belgium, and Sweden.~~** TXT_6801/0_N4

20 **Quoted from Frobenius, page 22.** TXT_6801/0_N4 Kiesler quotes from Frobenius and Fox, *Prehistoric Rock Pictures*, 22. The underlining in this passage is by Kiesler.

21 A **Dr. Erman** appears in Kiesler's transcription, TXT_6686/0_N25 however, the 1937 MoMA exhibition catalogue (Frobenius and Fox, *Prehistoric Rock Pictures*, 22) mentions "Dr. German" (with one "n"). See Paul Germann, "Zeichnungen von Kindern und Jugendlichen aus dem Waldlande von Nord-Liberia," ed. Fritz Krause, *Ethnologische Studien* 1, nos. 1–2 (1929): 75–89 (with ten plates).

22 Frobenius and Fox, *Prehistoric Rock Pictures*, 22.

23 **~~And here is the account of the expedition~~** TXT_6801/0_N5

members, three men and a woman, guided the expedition for almost a week and were soon on friendly terms with us. One afternoon, finding our larder rather depleted, I asked one of them to shoot for me an antelope, surely an easy job for such an expert hunter. He and his fellows looked at me in astonishment and then burst out with the answer that, yes, they'd do it gladly, but that it was naturally out of the question for that day since no preparations had been made. After a long palaver they declared themselves ready to make these at sunrise. Then they went off as though searching for a good site and finally settled on a high lace on a nearby hill.

As I was eager to learn of what their preparations consisted, I left camp before dawn and crept through the bush to the open place which they had sought out the night before. The pygmies appeared in the twilight, the woman with them. The men crouched on the ground, plucked a small square free of weeds and smoothed it over with their hands. One of them drew something in the cleared space with his forefinger, while his companions murmured some kind of formula or incantation. Then a waiting silence. The sun rose on the horizon. One of the men, an arrow on his bowstring, took his place beside the square. A few minutes later the rays of the sun fell on the drawing at his feet. In that same second the woman stretched out her arms to the sun, shouting words I did not understand, the man shot his arrow and the woman cried out again. Then the three men bounded off through the bush while the woman stood for a few minutes and then went slowly towards our camp. As she disappeared I came forward and, looking down at the smoothed square of sand, saw the drawing of an antelope four hands long. From the antelope's neck protruded the pygmy's arrow.[24]

It would appear that in none of his daily actions does tribal man lose the consciousness of cosmic relationships. Not only is he guided by them, but he calls for their direct help, and relies on it. Be he the Nordic type that distinguishes between himself (the subject) as something different from the environment (the object), or the southern type, that sees no difference, but only variations of one and the same pl. 3 cosmos,[25] and identifies himself with it in all forms; he will strive for integration of vision[26] and reality. It is very probable that all forms of art spring from that desire; it is the eternal root of Architecture. There can be no other reason for man's activities than his need to sustain his unity with the cosmos, because in that he feels the only assurance[27] for survival, whether this survival be corporeal or imaginary. In this cycle Architecture is the spatial tool for bringing all spheres of the visible and invisible into contact with one another, while painting is the two-dimensional tool for visual coordination. As described by Frobenius, painting is a ritual; but so are all of primitive man's activities: the making of fire, the building of shelter, eating, marriage, birth, and the cremating or burying of the dead.[28]

Without a faith,[29] these actions[30] would be meaningless, lacking any link and life without continuity; but continuity is man's aim. Painting, sculpture–art in general is still something of a ritual with us (although grossly intertwined with economic considerations), but our daily activities are functional to the point of disillusionment in their quality of mechanical necessity.

Today, as Burton put it,[31] man, that Magnum miraculum, "the marvel of marvels; audacis naturae miraculum," nature's boldest and most marvelous stroke; "Imaginis imago," image of his own dream,[32]–this noble creature (as Plato calls him);[33]

Deo congruens, fitted for divinity, becomes miserabilis homuncio, a castaway, a caitiff, one of the most miserable creatures of the world, if he be considered in his own nature, an unregenerate man, and so much obscured by his fall that (some few relics excepted) he is inferior to the beast; a monster by stupendous

24 Frobenius and Fox, *Prehistoric rock pictures*, 22–23. For a discussion of "pygmies" in racial anthropological and ethnological discourses of that era, see editor's Sources, Disciplines, and Objects, pp. 15–16, 85.

25 Here Kiesler added the following endnote: **(3) Extensive quote from Frobenius: Hystorie of the Culture Africa's. The Hamitic Type and the Aethiopean Type.** TXT_6828/0_N1 Kiesler refers to the study of Leo Frobenius, *Kulturgeschichte Afrikas: Prolegomena zu einer historischen Gestaltlehre* (Zurich: Phaidon Verlag, 1933). The book exists in the Kiesler estate library. The Kieslers selected and transcribed several other passages from this work, although not all were included in the manuscript of *Magic Architecture*. TXT_6814/0_N1-N3, TXT_6816/0, TXT_6818/0 Kiesler's description of "Nordic" and "southern" human types in this passage of the main text reflect Frobenius's distinction between the "Hamitic" and the "Aethiopian type" mentioned in his endnote. The same polarity is rehearsed in a handwritten addendum written by Kiesler in German: **Hamitische Kunst: „Ich bin – die Welt sei." / äthiopische Kunst: Tod-leben-gemeinschaft** ("Hamitic Art: 'I am–the world is.' Ethiopian Art: Death-life-community"). TXT_6828/0_N5 For Frobenius's comparative description of Hamitic and Ethiopian "building styles," see *Kulturgeschichte Afrikas*, 214–215 and Sources, Disciplines, and Objects, pp. 16–17, 85.

26 **~~dream~~** TXT_6741/0_N4

27 **~~security.~~** TXT_6741/0_N4

28 **burying the dead ~~the erecting of Architecture–all his activities.~~** TXT_6741/0_N6

29 **Without ~~ritual~~** TXT_6741/0_N6

30 **these fictional activities** TXT_6741/0_N19

31 **Today, as Burton so aptly puts it.** TXT_6741/0_N6 In this paragraph, Kiesler quotes (liberally) from a well-known passage of Robert Burton, *The Anatomy of Melancholy*, specifically the opening paragraphs of the first "section" of the "First Partition," describing "Man's Excellency" and "Fall." The English rendering of the phrases in Latin shows that the passage is extracted from an edition in the Everyman's Library series, first published in 1932. See Robert Burton, *The Anatomy of Melancholy*, introduction by Holbrook Jackson (London: Dent; New York: Dutton, 1932), 1:130.

32 Here the published edition differs: "*Imaginis imago*, created to God's own image, to that immortal and incorporeal substance, with all the faculties and powers belonging unto it was at first pure, divine, perfect, happy, 'created after God in true holiness and righteousness.'" Burton, *The Anatomy of Melancholy*, 1:130.

33 **(as Plato calls him)** TXT_6741/0_N6 This handwritten addition is later transcribed in the wrong place. In Burton's original text, Plato's name is attached to the previous description of "man" as "the marvel of marvels," which follows "audacis naturae miraculum" (Nature's boldest and most marvelous stroke). Burton, *The Anatomy of Melancholy*, 1:130.

(1)

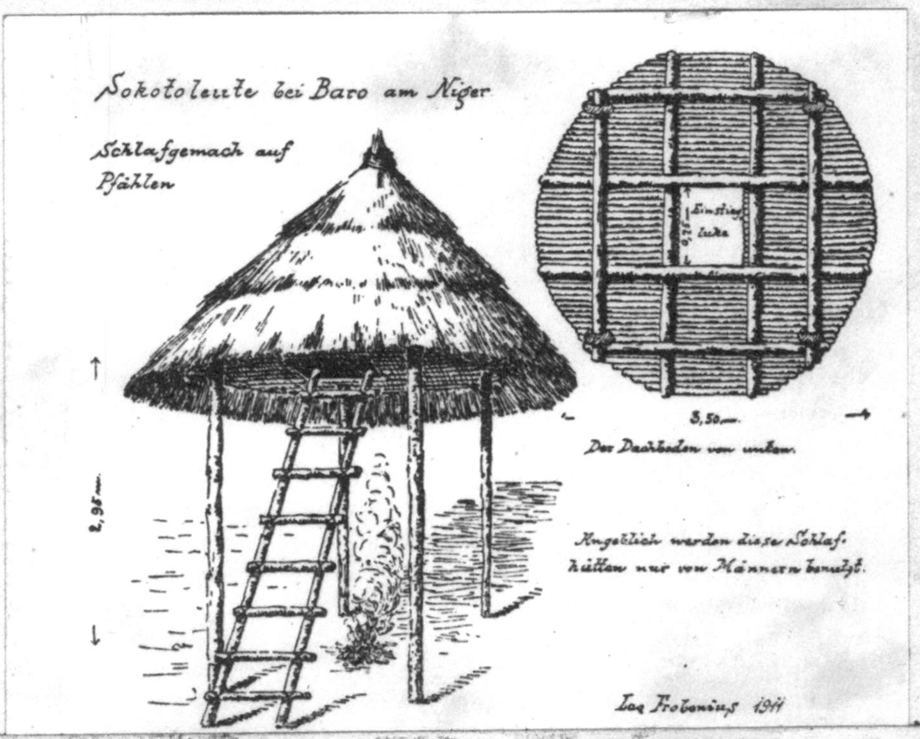

(1). Page 21

Earliest artificial shelter of man looked more or less like an umbrella; resting either directly on the floor or on stilts for better protection from animal attacks.
(below): aborigines also provide shelter for their spirits, and built the same types ~~xxxxxxx~~ of homes for them as for themselves, except somewhat bigger and more luxurious.

Shelter for Spirits

page 21

2

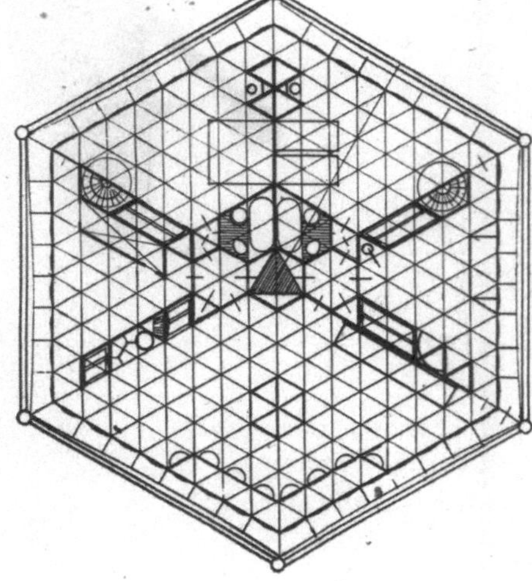

Shelter (20th century)

(2). Curiously enough, we find in our own time a similar elevated umbrella-shelter fostered as an ideal house and home.
(model for a pre-fabricated Dymaxion-house by Fuller, U.S.A.)

metamorphoses from participant to emancipated. Quantus mutatus[34] ab illo, how much altered from what he was!

Perhaps we can estimate him as he was.[35] And as a contrast to our behavior in exercising art, let us look at one of the murals of caveman; and let us hear the evidence of Frobenius, before I offer my own conclusion:

For instance, here is the myth which relates how the high priest had a vision in which he saw the only way to end the drought[36] would be to bury alive a virgin princess under a certain tree. There were no marriageable virgins available in the royal house, so he caught a young one and shut her up till she was of age. Then she was buried beneath the tree. Immediately the tree began to grow. It grew for three days and three nights and, as the morning star appeared at the end of the third night, the top of the tree touched the sky and the morning star sent down the rain.[37]

This rock painting permits the crystallization of a coordination system of four spheres of interest.[38] pl. 2a

Starting at the bottom of the picture:
the first sphere,[39] within the earth
the second, on the earth
the third, above the earth
the fourth, beyond the earth.[40]

Correspondingly, in ascending progression the stations of the myth may be called:[41]
the buried princess
the priest and the growing tree
Rain[42]
the vision of the star of Venus (morning star)[43]

* * *

Again in ascending progression we may establish a parallel to the stations of architecture:
first,[44] the sphere of the Tomb
second, the sphere of Shelter (the home)
third, the sphere of the Temple
fourth, the sphere of the dwellings of Gods.

* * *

These ascending columns of evolution represent ideological progressions. The link between Myth and Architecture is achieved through the technical evolution which starts with the ability:
first, to construct
second, to sculpt
third, to tool (to implement)
fourth, to paint.[45]

Of course, the stages in this progression do not follow the strict regularity of the steps in a ladder, but rather have the simultaneous existence of separate parts of one and the same organism.[46]

* * *

The correlation of Myth and the Present[47] seems always (unless there is a lack of sustained growth in one of these two fields) to develop in the following morphological Order[48]
Myth
Shelter
Artifacts
Sculpture
Painting
Architecture[49]

Architecture seems to be the sum-total of all the former states in this evolution.[50] But in times of mythological decay architecture does not

34 **mutandis** TXT_6741/0_N6; TXT_6686/0_N28 "Quantum mutatus ab illo!" Burton, *The Anatomy of Melancholy*, 1:130.

35 **we can approximate how he was** TXT_6741/0_N6

36 **draught** [in the TS] TXT_6686/0_N29

37 **(on opposite page illustration: Rain ceremony)** TXT_6787/0_N1recto; TXT_6741/0_N20 The note was later crossed out. This paragraph is also a quotation from Frobenius and Fox, *Prehistoric Rock Pictures*, 46–47. The book includes a drawing of the rock painting described by Frobenius and reproduced in Kiesler's diagram, plate 2a.

38 **This rock painting permits the crystallization of an interesting coordination system. We arrive at four spheres of interest of ~~the~~ prehistoric man** TXT_6787_N1recto

39 **may be** TXT_6741/0_N8

40 For the ink chart used in plate 2a, see TXT_6688_N11-N12; SFP_6739/0 Kiesler has drawn a number of similar charts in pencil in preparation for plate 2a. See fig. B.04. TXT_6749/0_N2-N4; TXT_6741/0_N7

41 **Correspondingly the stations of the Myth (from below up):** TXT_6787/0_N1recto

42 **The actual Rain** TXT_6787/0_N1recto

43 **and the star-Venus-Vision from beyond** TXT_6787/0_N1recto

44 **First (from below up):** TXT_6787/0_N1recto

45 **second, to make artifacts; third to mold or sculpt; fourth to ~~design~~ paint.** TXT_6741/0_N9

46 **But rather have the simultaneous organic existence of separate parts of the same plant.** TXT_6741/0_N9

47 **Actuality/presence (necessity).** TXT_6741/0_N10 **The correlation of Myth and ~~Presence (Actuality?) (necessity?)~~ the Present.** TXT_6741/0_N21 **Myth and Presence (necessity)** TXT_6787/0_N1verso

48 Cf. Kiesler's earlier charts on "Morphology" mentioned in "Note to the Publisher," p. 98) and Sources, Disciplines, and Objects, pp. 64–65.

49 In the MS, these "states" are numbered from "first" to "sixth." TXT_6787/0_N1verso Versions of the TS show a dash between architecture and all previous states. There is also an arrow between "Sculpture" and "Architecture." TXT_6741/0_N10; TXT_6686/0_N29

50 **And in this cycle, Architecture is ~~the shelter of / contact point~~ the spatial tool for the contact of all spheres and ~~the art of~~ painting the visual coordination.** In the handwritten draft, this last theoretical formulation precedes a preliminary version of Kiesler's chart **Myth, Skills, and Architecture**, reproduced in plate 2a. TXT_6749/0_N4 See fig. B.04.

fig. B.04

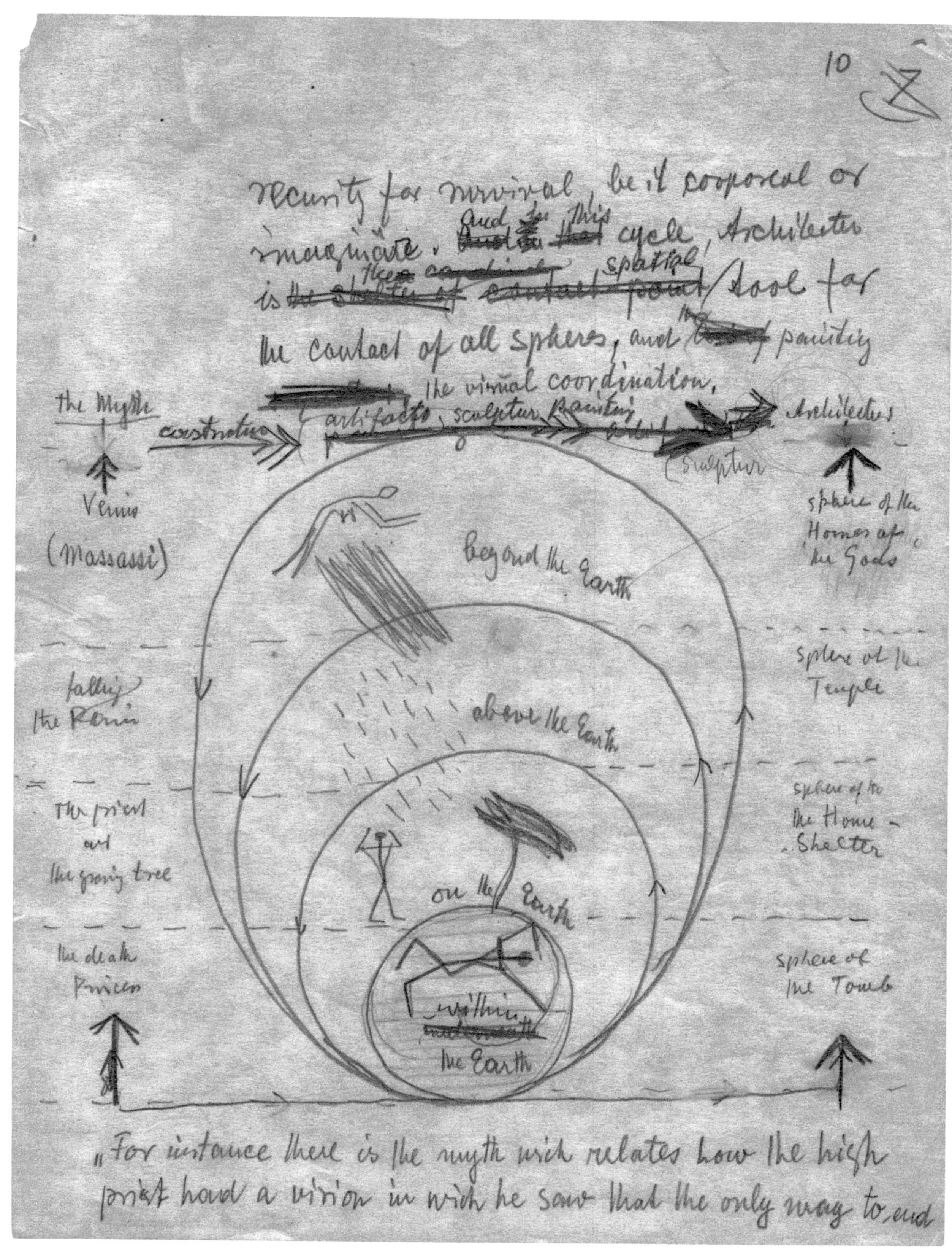

Frederick Kiesler, Part 1, Chapter 1, "Eternal Preamble of Architecture," preliminary draft and hand-drawn chart for plate 2a (MS, pencil)
ÖFLKS, TXT_6749/0_N4

2 A

(2a)

- 12 -

page 27

- 13 -

Myth, Skills and Architecture

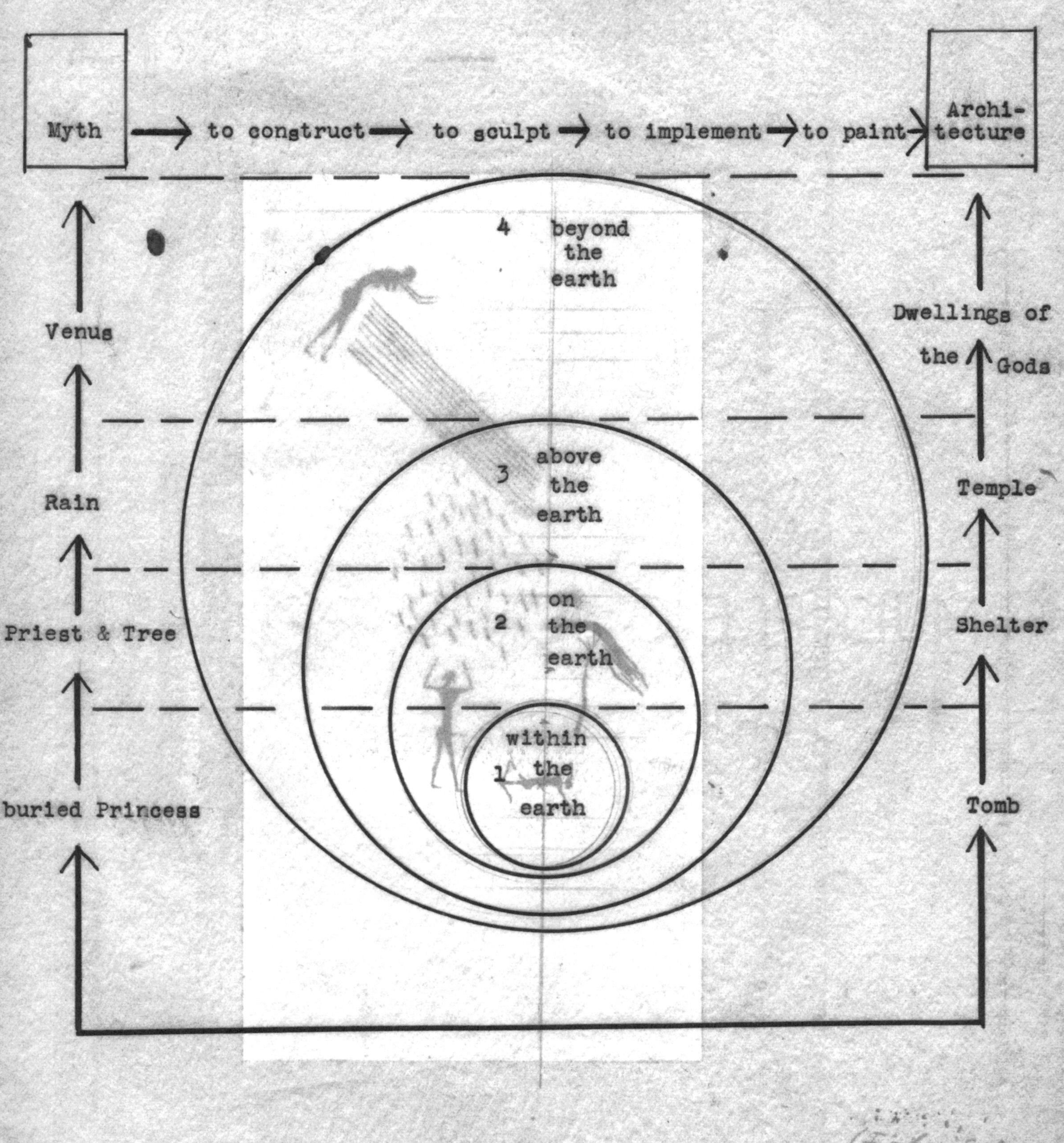

(Frobenius)

2a

connect with the state of shelter. Man sacrifices the home for the sake of special buildings, such as temples, into which he pours all his knowledge of configurative techniques and for which he forsakes all personal benefits. Architecture becomes a means for the performance of special Rituals.[51] The home remains nothing but Shelter. Here we have the cleavage in the building activity of man: on the one side, sacred ideo-plastic structures; and on the other side, profane physio-plastic structures.[52] One serves the ritual of the imagination; the other the physical functions of the body. The cycle of natural development is thus broken,[53] and any of the six spheres of the Order may be ejected, pushed into the background or forced into an artificial amalgamation.[54] Architecture then reaches a state of schizophrenia. It loses its identity and lives on in any combination of the spheres, but never in solid unity comprising all of them.

This seems always to have been the crucial moment in architectural development. At the height of the ascent in man's creativeness he has been unable to sustain the myth.[55] He has proved unable to make the flow of the ascent return and, like the waters of a beneficial source, flow down into the valleys and fertilize[56] all the land to the horizon. Had this been possible the Myth would then have penetrated every structure of man's activities.[57]

pl. 2a

But the old Myth produced only a highly specialized Architecture.[58] All the trends of life activities were forced into one outlet: the building of special shrines inspired by the fear of death. These graves, altars, and temples were the tools for healing the pain of anguish. This is an Architecture of Fear. Further specialization of this architecture brought monstrous structures[59] into being, pagodas, domes, tumuli-species of architectural saurians, ammonites, and trilobites.[60] Like malignant tumors, these hypertrophic structures absorbed all the vitality[61] of the body of the populace for their own sake, until finally there was nothing left to batten upon, and they too died.[62]

The remains of these monstrous[63] growths, found in all regions of human civilization, became the prey of archeologists, historians, and of traveling painters.[64] It was the painters, blinded by the dust of time, who drew and sold images of these monuments as "still lifes,"[65] and so helped to cover up the emptiness of fashionable new homes with death-masks of faille. The myth had become Décor.

CHAPTER 2
FEAR OF THE UNSEEN

Omnivorous, all-eating: that is man.[66]

He is not satisfied with being carnivorous, which is enough for the lion or condor; he is not satisfied with being herbivorous[67] like the buffalo; he also eats fruits[68] and honey; as a matter of fact, he eats minerals and drinks juices to no end; but in spite of devouring almost anything alive and many things dead, he is inferior in strength to the lion, which lives on meat only, or the buffalo which lives solely on grass.

His fear is far greater than that of any animal, which lived before his epoch or which lives now,[69] because it is manifold as the food he appropriates for himself and his breed.

His strength has retired to one corner of his brain. Here, in the mold[70] of his forehead, he speculates[71] on how to overcome his inferiority.[72] He does not dare to combat any of the animals with his own hand. His cowardice is so great that his main occupation is to contrive instruments that will keep any other species of this earth away from him.[73] He will not meet his enemy breast to breast; he will try to kill from a distance and remain unseen.[74] And the greater his civilization the farther away will he take his stand for the kill. His pride grows bigger with the distance of his hiding. His ultimate dream of safety is to be able to shoot from interstellar space—unseen, unheard, with nothing of his scent coming downwind.[75]

51 (Temples, Churches) TXT_6787/0_N1verso

52 The distinction between physio-plastic and ideo-plastic modes of representation was introduced by the physiologist and art theorist Max Verworn (see Sources, Disciplines, and Objects, pp. 13, 84). For Kiesler's use of the same two terms to describe building structures, see Part IV.

53 broken, split TXT_6787/0_N1verso

54 or lost altogether. TXT_6787/0_N1verso

55 He has been unable to develop a new myth or a transformation of the old. TXT_6787/0_N2

56 with ~~the attracted~~ rivers attracted and rivulets nearby TXT_6787/0_N3

57 The Myth would then penetrate every shelter of the people, every kind of structure of habitat and imagination. Nothing would be left out. The circulation forth and from the heart of faith, like that of the human blood, would have a continuous flow. The cycle closes. Its glow contacts all stations of the ~~body~~ Order, the minutest cell by cell, the giant crystal and the dwarf, tool and thought, ~~muscle and mechanism,~~ house and fire, ~~solitude and,~~ the melancholy and frenzy of man in architecture. Text added in MS, revised, and ultimately crossed out entirely in TS. TXT_6787/0_N3; TXT_6741/0_N11

58 altars, churches, Temples. TXT_6787/0_N2

59 gigantic structures TXT_6787_N3

60 species of architectural Sauriers, Amonites, and Trilobites. TXT_6686/0_N33 monuments, like the races of Sauriers, Ammonites, and Trilobites. TXT_6787/0_N2

61 all ~~forces~~ of the body TXT_6787/0_N3

62 and finally verdämmerten [vanished at dawn] ~~in their drunkenness of powers and overstuffidness~~ and ~~cracked~~ fell over, ~~like~~ overstuffed drunkards of selfish power. TXT_6787/0_N2

63 Monstrous growths TXT_6686/0_N33

64 The cadavers of this giant found in all regions of human civilization with the ~~dirt of centuries~~ iridescent pat[ina? (illegible)] of time resting on them become the prey of archaeologists, historians, and of traveling artists who paint and sell them as "nature morte" for the new walls of fashionable homes. TXT_6787/0_N4

65 (or more pointedly in French, as "nature morte") TXT_6741/0_N12; AAA n.p.

66 Omnivore—that is MAN—the all eating. TXT_6785/0_N1 In his handwritten list of contents, Kiesler had initially titled this chapter "Omnivorous man" but then crossed out this title. TXT_6702/0_N1 See Contents in the annotated text, p. 103.

67 with being a vegarious [sic] TXT_6785/0_N1

68 ~~eggs and~~ TXT_6785/0_N1

69 He is ~~more fearful~~ / His fear is far greater than any of any animal before or with him TXT_6785/0_N1

70 mould TXT_5877/0_N15; TXT_6785/0_N1 While Kiesler was consistent with this spelling throughout the TS, here, it has been changed to the American spelling.

71 ~~contrives~~ TXT_6785/0_N1

72 ~~physical~~ inferiority. TXT_6785/0_N1

73 ~~at a distance~~ TXT_6785/0_N2

74 he will try to kill ~~him~~ unseen. TXT_6785/0_N2

75 ~~unsuspected, unperceived~~ unseen, unheard, ungewittert [undetected by scent] TXT_6703/0_N1

If he feels that way when awake and in full control of his speculations, how much more terrified must he be during sleep? He lights fires to keep away other beasts;[76] he climbs trees to keep his body safe while he sleeps.[77]

He finally learns to imitate the security of these natural quarters[78] by constructing platforms which rest on high stilts, or by molding caverns[79] made of walls and roofs, erected out of fried mud.[80] Timid man and the most powerful primates have one fear in common, namely the spontaneous savagery of climatic conditions: windstorms, rain-squalls, lightning-fires, heat-drought, cold, and ice. That these onslaughts might mean death is not so frightening as the fact that the blows are delivered from a distance and are struck by an unseen enemy.[81] Man and primates alike, flee; they make for caves above and below the ground;[82] they look for thickets, for rich tropical foliage; they hide in hollow trees.

Not only, as we see, does man react to the same circumstances as animals do, that is, he runs for safety, but if he finds animals already occupying a shelter, he will chase them away, capture or kill them.[83] Through weakness his struggle for survival is merciless.[84]

> As among herd animals fright works itself up to completely mindless panic[85] and can bring about destruction, even when presence of mind would have made rescue possible, so among primitive man we find fear mounting to frenzy. Only in that way are we able to understand the strange trait, confirmed unanimously by observers of Australian and certain other natives, who actually die from fear of death; or, rather, that their fancy of a mysterious power endangering them, can actually result in death. This mental state is called death-craze or "Thanatomania."[86] The striking feature in this delusion is that the damaging injury is looked upon as coming from the remote, as a malicious telekinesis of an absolute effect. This[87] peculiarity of the cultural life of the Australian aborigine cannot be explained otherwise, as their uncertainty about the cause of death corresponds to their ignorance of the origin of birth.[88]

CHAPTER 3
THE ENIGMA OF DEATH

In his bewilderment regarding the causes of death, man takes the state of sleep—which also lacks motion and animation—to be a simile capable of explaining the phenomenon.[89] Furthermore, the fact that one awakens from sleep permits him two divinations: first that death is prolonged, more vigorous sleep which also retains the possibility of wakening some time no matter how far off; and second that dreams constitute a direct message from the unknown since in them man has visions and messages about people who are already dead.[90]

Both phenomena[91] plant in man early in his career the idea of immortality.[92] The technical process of eternal life is imagined as a continuous transformation[93] from birth to death and[94] from death to birth. Rebirth at this stage of the mind is not only a matter between humans but might also occur between any creations[95] of the world of fauna, flora, or the inorganic; the concept of the universe is a unified one and there is equality in rebirth. "The anxiety of explaining to himself the process of death leads the primitive even today to believe in immortality."[96] To keep power over the dead, they are mummified. In 1845 Sir George Grey[97] reported the following:

> When, due to putrefaction, the skin cracks, the body is left to dry. The opening of nose, mouth, and rectum are carefully closed, partly sewn, partly stopped up with feathers of the emu, as if striving to make it impossible for the soul to flee. Later the dried mummy is bent forward, the knees pulled up to the head, the arms pressed sidelong to the head and tied up with rope made from vegetable fibers. That a mummy receives treatment equal

76 **He lights fires to watch over him;** TXT_6785/0_N2

77 **he keeps into caverns and caves; he climbs on trees and sleeps there.** TXT_6785/0_N2

78 **the safety of these natural protections** TXT_6785/0_N2

79 **artificial caverns.** TXT_6785/0_N2

80 **or clay.** TXT 6703/0_N1

81 **but the more terrifying side of it is the fact: that it strikes from a distance, and by an unseen enemy.** TXT_6785/0_N3

82 **Caverns and caves ~~serve as protection for that too~~ / They make for caverns and caves above or underneath ground.** TXT_6785/0_N5

83 **He does the same as all animals: He runs for safety. And if he finds them already there, he'll ~~kill them chase them out, or kills them and~~ share the ~~habitat~~ shelter with them, chase them out or kill them in his struggle for survival or be killed.** TXT_6785/0_N5

84 This passage is followed by Kiesler's own English translation of an excerpt from the study of the physical anthropologist and paleo-evolutionist Hermann Klaatsch, *Der Werdegang der Menschheit und die Entstehung der Kultur*, ed. Adolf Heilborn 2nd expanded edition (Berlin: Deutsches Verlagshaus Bong & Co., 1922), 223. English edition: Hermann Klaatsch and Adolf Heilborn, *The Evolution and Progress of Mankind*, trans. Joseph McCabe (New York: Frederick Stokes Company, 1923), 201–203. The Kieslers selected and transcribed excerpts from both the German and the English edition of this book, yet in the text of *Magic Architecture* Kiesler is using his own liberal translation of the German text, often without acknowledgment. TXT_6844/0, TXT_6864/0 On Klaatsch and Kiesler's spurious use of his book, see Sources, Disciplines, and Objects, pp. 17–19, 32–33, 85–86.

85 **~~headless despair and chaotic dread~~** TXT_6703_N2

86 **~~W. E. Roth called~~ this mental state ~~the~~ death craze or "Thanatomania"** On "thanatomania," see Walter Edmund Roth, *Superstition, Magic, and Medicine*, North Queensland Ethnography Bulletin No. 5 (Brisbane: G. A. Vaughan, Government Printer, 1903), 28. TXT_6703_N3

87 **~~over and again confirmed~~** On Kiesler's coining of the term "malicious telekinesis," see Sources, Disciplines, and Objects, p. 18 TXT 6703_N3

88 **Ignorance ~~about~~ of the origin of ~~individual life~~ birth."** The closed quotation mark exists in this TS but is missing in later transcriptions. TXT 6703/0_N3

89 **~~Man, in his bewilderment over death, searches for instruments of divination, and finds them in the phenomenon of sleep, which is a little death, and in dreams, which are a link between the known and the unknown.~~** TXT_6707/0_N3

90 Cf. the following passage quoted and then crossed out in an earlier MS: **~~"The primitive is unable to draw a sharp border-line between unconsciousness, sleep, and death. Although conscious of the ceasing of life functions within the dead, he is not quite certain that the vanished "soul" will not return again into the body as it does when the sleep is over."~~** TXT_6707/0_N3 Another MS draft contains the same quotation in German, transcribed from Klaatsch, *Der Werdegang der Menschheit* (1922), 224. TXT_6780_N2recto Cf. the English translation: Klaatsch, *The Evolution and Progress* (1923), 203: "He sees no sharp distinction between unconsciousness, sleep, and death. Although he does not fail to notice the cessation of the vital functions at death, he is never quite sure whether the departed something will not return to the body, as he sees it do when a man awakens from sleep."

91 **~~both omen~~** TXT_6707/0_N1

92 **~~eternal continuity of existence~~** TXT_6707/0_N2

93 **~~interchange~~** TXT_6707/0_N2

94 **and ~~vice versa~~** TXT_6707/0_N2

95 **~~species, creatures~~** TXT_6707/0_N2

96 **The ~~impossibility~~ of explaining death...** TXT_6707/0_N2 A similar passage exists in German in an earlier MS. TXT_6780_N2recto Cf. Klaatsch, *Der Werdegang der Menschheit* (1922), 230; and *The Evolution and Progress* (1923), 211: "the Australian cannot understand death. From this comes directly one of the most important elements of all the higher religions, the belief in immortality; which is, therefore, not to be regarded, as is so often done, as the laborious outcome of philosophical speculation."

97 George Grey (1812–1898), British colonial administrator in Australia and New Zealand. For his travel memoirs, see George Grey, *Journals of Two Expeditions of Discovery in North-West and Western Australia* (London: T. & W. Boone, 1841), both volumes. Kiesler's drafts indicate different spellings of his last name: **Gray** TXT_6691/0_N2 and **Grey** TXT_5877/0_N2

> to that accorded the living is shown in the manner in which he is attended. In the evening he is placed next to the campfire, and ceremonials are arranged in his honor; he is seated in such a manner that he can see everything.[98]

We still find in China that the realm of the dead reflects exactly the systems and rites of the world of the living. There as here, life continues in clans. "Everyone has the rank and position he had in his lifetime. The dead have their armies, their battles, their cemeteries, their funerals and ceremonies."[99] Yes, the ghosts fear men as much as men fear the spirits. "One robs oneself of the most costly possessions to adorn the departed with them," reports Charlevoix. "From time to time coffins are opened to change the clothing, bits of food saved with great sacrifice are placed on graves and carried into regions esteemed as the abode of the soul. ... Great care is taken in covering the corpse and wrapping it in such a way that no earth can touch it; the dead rest in a cell that is completely covered with skins and fitted with jewelry and ornaments, much richer than a hut."[100]

It is no wonder that the first attempts at shelter, which did not spring solely from functional everyday necessities, but which derived from the imagination, are "graves." No matter how primitive they may be. The functions of such structures are imagined. No one knows what the dead need. But those who remain imagine the desires, the needs of the dead, as an image of their own needs and desires. The desire is to pacify the dead, to give him what were his own earthly possessions in order to equip him for a successful new life and in so doing, to avert his revenge.*

As we know from the further development of civilization almost up to the present time the homes of the dead are of greater importance to the living than their own. Graves are planned, constructed, and maintained with greater care than that devoted to the houses of the living. The design of graves is not only part of the concept of the immediate family, but also represents the collective idea of the group, or society; its proper execution and care is of public interest; its concept is an abstraction of the experiences of all living persons. Graves are Architecture in "abstracto," and give us more clues to the "ideals" of a populace than their huts.

> * Reference material very rich
> (Spencer and Gillen. De Groot. Roscoe. Charlevoix. R. Hertz. Hewitt.)[101]

CHAPTER 4
THE ENIGMA OF BIRTH

Motto:

> Before I was born out of my mother, generations guided me,
> My embryo has never been torpid, nothing could overlay it.
> For it the nebula cohered to an orb,
> The long slow strata piled to rest on it,
> Vast vegetables gave it substance,
> Monstrous sauroids transported it in their mouths and deposited it with care,
> All forces have been steadily employed to complete and delight me,
> Now on this spot I stand with my robust soul.
>
> Walt Whitman[102]

In the animal kingdom of which man is one of many vassals, one finds a strange attraction for the locality of birth.[103] This locality may be called the psychological shelter of man. We must not however think about shelter in the terms of today, but rather in the sense of a locality where members of a family group would meet for reasons of mutual security.[104] From that point of view, the place of birth carries

98 **~~well overlook it all~~.** TXT_6707/0_N4 This passage is originally written in German and contains Kiesler's liberal transcription of several excerpts from Klaatsch's book. TXT_6780_N2recto-verso Cf. Klaatsch, *Der Werdegang der Menschheit* (1922) 236; *The Evolution and Progress* (1923), 214-215: "The intestines are first removed. At least, I found this done in the north of Australia, though the first Australian mummy discovered, in 1845, and sent to Europe by Sir George Grey, had not had these organs removed. The apertures of the body (mouth, nose, etc.), had been carefully closed–partly sewn, and partly stopped up with emu feathers–as if to keep the soul inside the body. ... After a time the body is ready to be treated. It is bent forward, and the knees are brought up to the head. The arms are pressed to the side of the head and tied with cords made from plant-fibres. ... The method of dealing with it shows that the mummy is regarded as equivalent to a living person. It is put by the camp-fire at night, and there are little ceremonies in honour of the deceased, during which the body is so placed that it can see everything." For a more extensive description of the process of making and handling the mummy, including the Australian mummy sent by Grey to the Hunterian Museum of the Royal College of Surgeons in England in 1845 (described in Klaatsch's and Kiesler's texts), see Klaatsch's earlier article, "Die Todes-Psychologie der Uraustralier in ihrer volks- und religionsgeschichtlichen Bedeutung," in *Festschrift zur Jahrhundertfeier der Königlichen Universität zu Breslau* (Breslau: Marcus Kommissionsverlag, 1911): 401-440; 414 for the description of the mummy sent by Grey to England. For Klaatsch's own theft of the mummy of a "warrior" described as "King" of an Indigenous Australian group and transportation to Germany as well as his abhorrent treatment of human remains, see Sources, Disciplines, and Objects, pp. 18, 85.

99 Here Kiesler is quoting from Lévy-Bruhl, *Les fonctions mentales dans les sociétés inférieures* (Paris: Alcan, 1910), 356. English edition: *How Natives Think*, trans. Lilian A. Claire (London: Allen, 1926), 304. However, in his own draft he often fails to indicate quoted material. In this passage Lévy-Bruhl cites the study of J. J. De Groot, *The Religious System of China* (London: Brill, 1910), 1:48, 924. Kiesler is using a German edition of Lévy-Bruhl's text, excerpts of which are included in the transcriptions prepared for *Magic Architecture*: Lucien Lévy-Bruhl, *Das Denken der Naturvölker*, ed. Wilhelm Jerusalem, trans. P. Friedlander, 2nd ed. (Vienna-Leipzig: Braumüller, 1926), 271.

100 Kiesler is quoting this extract from the twenty-sixth letter of Charlevoix's *Journal d'un voyage dans l'Amérique septentrionale* (Paris: Ganeau, 1744), 3:372, from the 1926 German edition of Lévy-Bruhl, *Das Denken*, 268. An English translation of the original text by Charlevoix reads: "they strip themselves of everything most valuable about them, in order to adorn the deceased: they open their coffins from time to time, in order to change their habits; and they take victuals from their mouth, in order to carry them to their graves, and to the places where they imagine their souls resort. ... It appears to me that they carry the corpse to the place of burial without any ceremony, at least I have found nothing upon this head in any relation, but when they are once in the grave, they take care to cover them in such manner that the earth does not touch them: so that they lie as in a cell entirely covered with skins, much richer and better adorned than any of their cabins." Pierre Francois Xavier de Charlevoix, *Journal of a Voyage to South America* (London: Dodsley, 1770) 2:186-188.

101 All of these authors and their texts are cited in the eighth chapter of Lévy-Bruhl's *Les fonctions mentales dans les sociétiés inférieures*, which deals with the treatment and role of the dead in modes of sociation and participation in Indigenous societies. Works cited include: Baldwin Spencer and F. J. Gillen, *The Native Tribes of Central Australia* (London: Macmillan, 1899); J. J. De Groot, *The Religious System of China* (London: Brill, 1910); John Roscoe, "Further Notes on the Manners and Customs of the Baganda," *The Journal of the Anthropological Institute of Great Britain and Ireland* 32 (January-June 1902): 25-80; Robert Hertz, "*Contribution á une étude sur la représentation collective de la mort*," *Année sociologique* 10 (1907): 48-137; J. N. B. Hewitt, "Iroquoian Cosmology," in *Annual Report of the Bureau of American Ethnology to the Secretary of the Smithsonian Institution* (1899-1900) 21:127-339; and Charlevoix, *Journal d'un voyage dans l'Amérique septentrionale* (Paris: Ganeau, 1744).

102 This excerpt from Walt Whitman's "Song of Myself" (1892) was inserted with the note **~~as motto of chapter~~** on the front page of an early draft but is missing from later versions of the assembled manuscript. Cf. TXT_6725/0_N1; TXT_5877/0_N21 Kiesler quotes the passage from Ashley Montagu, *Coming into Being Among the Australian Aborigines: A Study of the Procreative Beliefs of the Native Tribes of Australia* (New York: E. P. Dutton & Company, 1938), 130. Quotation marks appear in the original manuscript. The excerpt from Whitman is used as an epigraph for the fifth chapter of Montagu's book, "The procreative beliefs of the native tribes of North-Eastern Australia, Queensland, and Cape York Peninsula" (130-168), and Kiesler's copy bears pencil marks above and below the passage. On Montagu and Kiesler, see Sources, Disciplines, and Objects, pp. 43-44, 84, 88-89.

103 **In the animal kingdom, and man is part of it, one finds a strange feeling for the locality of one's birth. ~~The aborigines of Australia show a marvelous sense of orientation~~.** TXT_6784/0_N1 Cf. Klaatsch, *Der Werdegang der Menschheit* (1922), 194; *The Evolution and Progress* (1923), 178: "A strong feeling of attachment to the place of birth is very common in the animal world, and it is associated with a sense of locality that is quite astonishing."

104 **We must think of it much more in terms of the inert desire for security, ~~for a~~ from a psychological aim.** TXT_6784/0_N1 Cf. Klaatsch, *Der Werdegang der Menschheit* (1922), 194; *The Evolution and Progress* (1923), 178: "We must, however, not think at once of houses in the modern sense, but of some centre at which the members of the primitive community foregathered, some common shelter from the storms of the early struggle for life."

with it the memory of the sheltering love of the mother, and the matriarchate is then the first form of social contract.[105]

Whatever evolution man has gone through, the attraction to the place of birth and to the actual house and home remains the same. Exactly like the animal, he is drawn to return home no matter how far away the search for the necessities of existence may have carried him. "It is well established that animals, carried away from their place of birth will find their way back with an uncanny sureness. Horses sold in Australia, so often run away to return to their birthplace that it is standard procedure to brand them in order to establish their ownership."[106] No doubt the ancestors of man had similar homing instincts forming part of an extrasensory capacity for topographical orientation which we possess today only in a rudimentary way. "It is not the sense of smell, which is so forceful a help to animals, but an extraordinary sense of orientation and an ability to observe automatically the details of the environment."[107]

The idea that primitive man led a nomadic life is justified, but his nomadism must not be interpreted as a lack of feeling for the home locale.[108] It was precisely this feeling that led to the logical end of nomadism and the fixing of the home locale, which laid the base of all architecture, from cave to apartment house.

Only slowly was a desire for settling developed in man. Still a long way from social order, from such concepts as "village" or "town," which were to derive from cattle-breeding and farming, primitive men lived together in small groups or families, partly camping in the open, partly seeking shelter under rock and caves, or in artificially erected dwellings.[109]

Primordial man was nomadic, and naturally so;[110] but his "regional" wanderings were dictated[111] by lack of food and the prospect of nourishment, his strong instincts guiding him unerringly in this respect. His hunger was more easily satisfied than ours. In his material strivings he was strengthened by a distinct consciousness of being one of the links in a chain of events which represented the very will of the universe.[112] His feeling of being part of everything organic as well as inorganic in his natural surroundings put him at ease–virtually at home–everywhere he went. A rock formation did not need to have (as it must for us of the twentieth century) the exact form of a human figure in order to give pre-logic man[113] a feeling of kinship to it, or to permit him to see and feel the stone as the image of a human being. He was able easily to evoke, if not automatically, an almost living reality from the slumbering form in the amorphous rock. For aboriginal man life springs from anything in nature. Birth is not restricted to the sexual mechanism of a man and a woman. Coming into being is rather a super-individual, cosmic event.[114]

"According to the tradition of the Arunta tribes in Australia," this is how man was born.[115] "In the early dream-time" of "the far distant past, or Alchera,[116]

> in that time when there were neither men nor women, there dwelt in the western sky two beings, of whom it is said that they were Numbakulla; that is, self-existing beings who came out of nothing. And it happened one day that they discerned, far away to the east, a number of Inapertwa: that is, rudimentary human beings or incomplete men, who possessed neither limbs nor senses, who did not eat, and who each presented the appearance of a somewhat amorphous human being, all doubled into a rounded mass in which just the vague outlines of the various parts of the body could be seen. These Inapertwa, who were destined to be transformed into men and women by the Numbakulla, represented the intermediate stage in the transformation of animals and plants into men, so that when Numbakulla came down to earth and fashioned the Inapertwa into men, each individual so fashioned naturally retained an intimate relationship with the animal, plant or other object, of which he was indirectly a transformation, and with which he was at one time identical.

105 **The matriarchal is also the first form of social rights.** TXT_6784/■_N1 Cf. Klaatsch, *Der Werdegang der Menschheit* (1922), 219; *The Evolution and Progress* (1923), 197: "Thus the matriarchate (or mother-right) is the oldest form and stage of the family, as we still find amongst many savages, even amongst some which have advanced culturally far above the Australian level."

106 **Even today horses which are sold in Australia, receive a mark of their birthplace, in case they run away, it will be known where they'll be found later.** TXT_6784/0_N1 Cf. Klaatsch, *Der Werdegang der Menschheit* (1922), 194; *The Evolution and Progress* (1923), 178: "It has been proved that animals taken far away from their homes find their way back with extraordinary sureness. Horses in Australia always remember their birth-place, and go back there whenever they run away."

107 **Indians distinguish with unfailing accuracy the difference of individuals in footprints.** TXT_6784/0_N1 Cf. Klaatsch, *Der Werdegang der Menschheit* (1922), 195; *The Evolution and Progress* (1923) 178: "The savage can distinguish between the footprints of several different individuals."

108 **The idea is justified that primitive man led a nomadic life, but that must not be misinterpreted as meaning he had no sense for the place of home. His wanderings are indeed not haphazard. The hordes of Australian Aborigines chose their respective region only with regard to hunting possibilities, and each tribal unit respects the others right to it.** TXT_6784/0_N1 Klaatsch, *Der Werdegang der Menschheit* (1922), 195; *The Evolution and Progress* (1923), 178: "When we speak of primitive man as a nomad, it must not be understood to mean that he had no sense of home. We have already pointed out that the wanderings of Australian tribes are not aimless and irregular, but are undertaken for the purpose of sparing the game. We find, on close inquiry, that each tribe has its own region: that it respects the limits of the regions of other tribes and demands the same respect for its own. It is not fixed, but it is not homeless." The same passage is included in the Kieslers' transcriptions of excerpts from the published English translation of Klaatsch's book but is not used in the text of *MA*. TXT_6844/0_N1

109 **Only slowly a desire of settledness was developing in ~~early~~ man. For him definite social orders, from which concepts as "village" or "town," which derived from cattle breeding and farming, primitive man lived ~~together~~ in small groups, or families, partly camping in the open, partly seeking shelter under rocks or in caves, or in artificially erected huts.** TXT_6784/0_N2 Cf. Klaatsch, *Der Werdegang der Menschheit* (1922), 195–196; *The Evolution and Progress* (1923), 178: "The settlement of a tribe in a particular spot was a long and gradual development. As they had no settled social institutions, no 'villages,' which begin with domestic cattle and agriculture, primitive men merely lived in small groups or families; sometimes camping in the open air, at other times huddling under a rock-shelter, or in a cavern, or in an artificial structure of some sort." This passage is also transcribed. TXT_6844/0_N1

110 **Primordial man was not nomadic, and naturally so** TXT_6691/0_N7 **Primordial man was nomadic, and naturally so** [correction of previous draft] TXT5877/0_N24; TXT_6725/0_N4

111 **were prompted** TXT_6725/0_N3

112 **will of ~~nature~~** TXT_6725/0_N3

113 **pre-logical man** TXT 6725/0_N4 The term derives from Kiesler's reading of Lévy-Bruhl, see earlier note 99 and Sources, Disciplines, and Objects, pp. 14–15.

114 This is the main argument presented by Montagu on the procreative beliefs of Indigenous people in Australia in *Coming into Being Among the Australian Aborigines* (quoted immediately after in this chapter but without acknowledgement in the assembled text).

115 **Ashley Montagu: Page 30. Insert A; According to the Arunta tradition, in the early dream-time of the far distant past...** TXT_6725/0_N5 Starting here Kiesler transcribes (with a few changes) a long excerpt from Montagu, *Coming into Being*, 30–32; see also 14–48, "The Arunta, the type pattern of Australian culture." In the opening paragraphs, Montagu acknowledges that his account of the Arunta "is for the most part based" on Baldwin Spencer's *The Arunta* (London: Macmillan, 1927). Kiesler's copy of Montagu's book bears pencil marks on pages 30–32, indicating excerpts to be transcribed.

116 All underlined words in Kiesler's TS are italicized in Montagu, *Coming into Being*, 30.

It is in this way that man came into being, and it is for this reason, that men necessarily possess totems, that is, an animal, plant, or other object or thing, such as water, wind, sun, fire, cloud, or whatnot, with which each individual is closely identified, since it is to that plant, animal, object, or thing that the native believes himself to owe his original creation. Spencer and Gillen write of the relationship between the individual and his totem: "At the present day a very definite relationship is supposed to exist between the individual and his totem. A man will eat only very sparingly of the latter, and even if he does eat a little of it, which is allowable to him, he is careful, in the case, for example, of an emu man, not to eat the best part, such as the fat. The totem of any man is regarded, just as it is elsewhere, as the same thing as himself; as a native once said to us when we were discussing the matter with him, 'That one,' pointing to his photograph which we had taken, 'is just the same as me; so is a kangaroo' (his totem)."[117]

The Alchera ancestors of the Arunta possessed powers far exceeding those of their living descendants; it is they, for example, who created the various natural features of the land inhabited by the tribe today, the gorges, the rivers, the gaps, and so forth.

The Alchera ancestors were originally banded together in totemic companies who wandered over the land in various directions, as recorded in the traditions associated with them. Each ancestor carried with him one or more sacred stones, which were associated with the Kuruna, that is, the spirit part of the individual, and which are called by the Arunta Churinga. Wherever the ancestors originated, and wherever they camped during their wanderings, there were formed Knanikilla, or local totem centres. At each of these spots—and they are well known to the old men, who pass the knowledge on from generation to generation—a certain number of the Alchera ancestors went into the ground, each leaving his Churinga behind. His body died, but some natural feature, such as a rock or tree, arose to mark the spot, while his spirit part remained in the Churinga. These Churinga, as well as others, which the wandering parties left behind them, were stored in Pertalchera, or sacred storehouses, which usually took the form of small caves or fissures in the rock, or even a hollow tree or carefully concealed hole in a sandbank. The result is that as we follow their wanderings, we find the whole country is dotted over with Knanikilla, or local totem centres.[118] Thus, for instance, in one locality there will be wild-cat spirit individuals, in another a group of emu, then a group of kangaroos, and in another a group of hakea flowers. At each of the spots at which a Churinga was deposited the natural object, which arose to make its site, such as a tree or a rock, became the abode of the Knanja, which also means totem. These were the first sacred shelters built not for man himself but for his totems.

It is this conception of spirit individuals associated with Churinga and resident in certain definite spots, determined by the situation of the Knanja, that lies, according to Spencer and Gillen, at the root of the Arunta totemic system.

Even the functional requisites for sexual intercourse are seen to be closely related to the procreative beliefs of primitive man. The following two myths stem from the native tribes of North Queensland:[119]

It was out of the local river whence men and women originally sprung, but on their first appearance there was no specialization or differentiation of sex: the stiff spear-grass gave the males their distinctive attribute while the two labia majors remind the girls of their early peregrinations along the two river banks. (Tully River.)

The moon (kakara) made the first man and woman, the former out of the same stone used for manufacturing tomahawks,

117 Quoted from Spencer, *The Arunta* (1:80), in (Montagu, *Coming into Being*, 31, n. 1).

118 TXT_6725/0_N7 Here Kiesler omits the following from Montagu: "or local totem centres, at each of which is deposited a number of Churinga with *Kuruna*, or spirit individuals, associated with them. Each totem centre is, of course, associated with a particular species of totem." Spencer, *The Arunta* (75-76), in Montagu, *Coming into Being*, 31, n. 2.

119 Kiesler's transcriptions from Montagu continue with another excerpt from the fifth chapter, "The procreative beliefs of the native tribes of North-Eastern Australia," which contained the introductory motto by Whitman. In the following two paragraphs, Montagu draws from Walter Edmund Roth, *Superstition, Magic, and Medicine*, 16 quoted in Montagu, *Coming into Being*, 130-131.

the latter out of box-tree. The man was completed by rubbing him all over with white and black ashes, and placing in his inside a stick of pandanus-root, which, when required, can be brought into prominence. The woman was rendered subtle and soft by rubbing her belly to produce her courses; to finish her distinctive features she was slit up with a sharp edge of a flat mangrove-root.

Of course, these myths are of much younger date than the time of which I speak. They already represent a high potency of meditation,[120] if not causal logic. That they still survive[121] proves how incarnate they were, how much they were a part of everyday life. At the time myths were in the process of formation; they had not become memory. I speak of the time when the boundaries of logic were practically non-existent and mystic relationships[122] could reign free. The symbiosis of man, family, and natural surrounding was complete,[123] the cycle of emotional unity of all beings had not been broken. Emancipation had not yet taken the reigns from participation. Shelter could therefore be found everywhere.[124] There was no need for artificially constructed protectives; nature provided everything. Past and Future were ever-present: they were not separate units of space and time, but merely oscillations of the present.[125] Birth was not the beginning of life, nor was death the end. Both had a long range of existence,[126] like those mountain chains, circling the horizon and disappearing in the mist of the beyond or into the blinding glare of the sun.

CHAPTER 5
BIRTH NECESSITATES SHELTER; DEATH INSPIRES ARCHITECTURE[127]

From his earliest beginning, man paid more attention to the houses of the dead, than to the houses of the living.[128] Not only were they decorated, but they were sturdier in construction, built for endurance, planned as companions for eternity.

The beginnings of architecture are, strangely enough, not connected with life necessities,[129] but with death. For the living,[130] a hut, pl. 2 a simple shelter, will do; for the same man dead, higher requirements arise. The inability to explain death logically has implanted such insecurity in man that he has to draw on his imagination to divine[131] reasons for it; and, at all times, he has suspected some Superman or Superpower behind this tragedy. The death houses he erects for the corpse, therefore, have also to serve[132] as a dwelling place for the unknown power of death. This dual purpose makes man go beyond the actual physical necessities of burial. Besides placing in the grave utensils for food as they are used during lifetime inside a shelter of the living, he invents rites, periodically re-enacted ceremonials and incantations to satisfy the superpower "beyond."[133] pl. 3 He does the same thing with the plan of the grave.[134] He, so to say, invents architectural incantations (ornamentation), plastic rites[135] (strictly geometrical plans and elevations) as well as elaborations of the surroundings of the house; these might very well be regarded as visual transformations of ceremonial reverence.[136]

Throughout the different parts of the globe we find greater uniformity[137] in grave architecture than among shelters for the living! While man will be satisfied with living in a simple shelter that barely pls. 4–7 protects him from bad climatic conditions or obvious attacks from enemies, he will not be satisfied with a similar impermanence[138] in his burial place. In this instance he will go beyond the concept of shelter;[139] the incident of death stimulates him to make contact with the beyond, and in so doing, he expresses the relationship in visual symbols[140] because that is one of his "legitimate ways" of reality.

Architecture seems to be the plastic (spatial) link between "the here and the beyond,"[141] between the tangible and the intangible.

Shelter connects with birth, Architecture with death.

120 high potency of ~~formulation and of~~ meditation TXT_6725/0_N10

121 still ~~exist~~ TXT_6725/0_N10

122 Relationships ~~of pre-animistic periods were ...~~. TXT_6725/0_N10 On the "pre-animistic period," see the Kieslers' transcription of an excerpt from Lévy-Bruhl, "Übergang zu höheren Typen der Geistesbetätigung," in *Das Denken der Naturvölker* (323–346; especially 326–329) TXT_6810/0_N1-N2. Kiesler's references to "mystic relationships," "symbiosis," and "participation" in the same paragraph can also be traced in his transcriptions of Lévy-Bruhl. On "pre-animistic periods," see Sources, Disciplines, and Objects, pp. 44–46, 88.

123 ~~It cohered.~~ TXT_6725/0_N10

124 found anywhere. TXT_6725/0_N10; TXT_5877/0_N30

125 ~~But their ever-presence was evident.~~ / ~~Past as well as Future were ever-present.~~ TXT_6725/0_N10

126 Both ~~were intertwined~~ had a long range of ~~history~~ TXT_6725/0_N10

127 Alternative chapter titles: Death ~~and~~ Architecture / Death, First Inspiration to Architecture: ~~Monuments to memory"~~ TXT_6696/0_N1; TXT_6849/0_N1

128 Other drafts show an alternative beginning: We only have to look at our own cemeteries to observe how carefully the grounds are taken care of and the stone memorials erected and kept; ~~in comparison to~~ most quarters of the living~~, with~~ are slums in comparison. TXT_6696/0_N1; TXT 6719/0_N1 For the second sentence, cf. Kiesler's references to the city and the cemetery in his early manifesto, "Vitalbau–Raumstadt–Funktionelle Architektur," *De Stijl* 10/11 (1924–1925): 141–146, especially 144, "Die Friedhöfe haben mehr Luft für die Gerippe der Toten, als unsere Städte für die Lungen der Lebenden" [Cemeteries have more air for the skeletons of their dead than our cities for the lungs of their living] See also Frederick Kiesler, *Contemporary Art Applied to the Store and its Display* (New York: Brentano's, 1930), 48.

129 life ~~impulses~~ TXT_6696/0_N1

130 For life TXT_6696/0_N1

131 ~~find~~ TXT_6696/0_N1

132 ~~at the same time~~ TXT_6696/0_N2

133 he invents incantations to satisfy the "superpower behind" rites and periodically re-enacted ceremonials. TXT_6696/0_N2

134 ~~as a house.~~ TXT_6696/0_N2

135 ~~accentuated~~ plastic ~~forms~~ rites TXT_6696/0_N2

136 which might very well be regarded as ~~purely ceremonial instinctive~~ visual transformation of ceremonial reverence. TXT_6696/0_N2

137 similarity TXT_6696/0_N2

138 temporeity [sic] TXT_6696/0_N3

139 minimal shelter TXT_6696/0_N3

140 and that of touch, TXT_6696/0_N3

141 between the known and the unknown TXT_6696/0_N3

CHAPTER 6
THE CAVE, FIRST NATURAL SHELTER[142]

Our collective memory of sheltering caves dates back to the time of the ice ages and, in truth, to earlier times when man, or so-called man (pre-paleolithic) was not yet entirely erect. He had crawled on four legs into his habitat with more ease than his later erect stance would permit. After he became upright he had to bend down to get through his door, and once inside he remained crouched. Finally he raised the roof of his new home to the full height of his stature.[143]

The collective memory of man[144] concerning shelter obtained through an armor of stone or any solid thing above and behind him—the safeguard against physical inferiority and fear—dates even further back than his own species. "Under every stone in a forest we find a rich life of animals seeking shelter there against rain, heat and enemies."[145] "In extreme danger caveman retires to deep hollows, but normally he lives in the open; and in mild climates invariably selects half-caves, cliffs that is, mountain-ledges with overhanging roofs."[146] "Many such 'abris' as the French called them, can still be seen in the valleys of the Dordogne."[147] They date back to the Aurignacian period. Belonging to this time is the Cro-Magnon man found near the valley of Vézère.[148] "There, where deep ledges (open towards a valley or the sea) shadowed by another layer of lime cantilevered above it, like the rock formations in the southeast of France or in Australia, particularly near Sydney," primitive man made his camp for rest, hunting and fishing.[149] "It is no wonder that one can find immense heaps of sea shells dating from the oldest period scattered along the coast of fjords and bays of southeast Australia. 'Wild' man liked this type of home: plenty of natural, sweet water sources,[150] endless forests abounding in kangaroos, a rich world of small marsupials[151] and finally the sea, with its inexhaustible[152] supply of fish and oysters."[153]

The same cliff dwellers can be found along the French sea coast, where even before the ice age the mountainous lava flows of the central plateau left natural caves in the Jurassic lime which made desirable refuges for man during the ice periods. It is interesting that he chose only such "abris" in the Vézère valley which were oriented toward the sunny south and the east. There were no interruptions in occupancy through the many thousands of years; layer upon layer of different "civilizations" can still be found.[154]

Today the stalactite cavern of Han in the Ardennes is visited yearly by crowds.[155] You may see high colored illustrations of its interior illumined by Bengal lights in all the Belgian and many of the French railway stations. What is now a peep-show was in past ages a habitation and a home. In it the soil of successive layers has revealed objects belonging to successive periods in the history of mankind.[156] At the bottom of all the deposits were discovered the remains of the very earliest inhabitants, with their hearths about which they sat in nudity and split bones to extract the marrow, trimmed flints, worked horn, necklaces of pierced wolf and bear's teeth; then herd-posts formed by hand long before the invention of the wheel; higher up were the arms and utensils of the bronze ages, and the weights of nets. Above these came the remains of the Iron Age and wheel-turned crocks. A still higher stratum surrendered a weight of a scale stamped with an effigy of the crusading King Louis (1226–1270), and finally francs bearing the profile of a king—

Leopold of Belgium, whose son fell to his death from a high cliff while hunting.[157]

142 **The cave as the first ~~natural~~ shelter** TXT_6735/0_N1

143 **He had crawled then much easier ~~(in sort of baby-fashion) on his four extremities~~ into his ~~home~~ habitat, than later when erect. Once upright he had to bend down for his door and mostly remained (seated, kauernd** [cowering] **covered?) inside. Later he had to look for higher ceilings and finally raised the roof of his new homes to the full height of his stature.** TXT_6786/0_N3

144 **collective memory of ~~the species~~** TXT_6786/0_N3

145 Cf. Klaatsch, *Der Werdegang der Menschheit* (1922), 196; *The Evolution and Progress* (1923), 179: "In the tropics we find a wealth of animal life under every stone, sheltering from the rain, heat, and enemies." As in other instances, Kiesler neglected to indicate the quoted material of this sentence and the passages that immediately follow. Quotation marks have been added by the editors.

146 Cf. Klaatsch, *Der Werdegang der Menschheit* (1922), 197; *The Evolution and Progress* (1923), 180: "It was only dire need that drove man into the darkness of the caverns. His general condition was, clearly, to use the overhanging rock-shelters—'half caverns,' one might call them—which must have been used at a much earlier date."

147 **Many such "abris" as the French call them can still be ~~found today~~ in the ~~departments~~ of the Dordogne.** TXT_6786/_N3-N4 Cf. Klaatsch, *Der Werdegang der Menschheit* (1922), 196; *The Evolution and Progress* (1923), 179: "Many districts in the south of France, especially the famous valleys of the Dordogne Department, have yielded remains of such settlements of the time of the Ice Age."

148 **The shelter of Cro-Magnon man was found near in the valley of Vézère.** TXT_6786/0_N4

149 Cf. Klaatsch, *Der Werdegang der Menschheit* (1922), 196; *The Evolution and Progress* (1923), 179: "Sea coasts with many and low limestone cliffs to provide shelter give us, in Australia to-day, particularly in the neighbourhood of Sydney, a picture of such settlements."

150 **water ~~fountains~~** TXT_6786/0_N4

151 **and small Beuteltiere** [marsupials] TXT_6786/_N4

152 **never-ending** TXT_6786/0_N4

153 Cf. Klaatsch, *Der Werdegang der Menschheit* (1922), 197; *The Evolution and Progress* (1923), 180: "We are, therefore, not surprised to find great heaps of shells in the idyllic stations which are scattered along the fiords of south-eastern Australia. Nothińg could be more pleasant than these creeks, where nature has provided a home, with everything that he needs, for the naked savage: rustling streams, noble woods with plenty of kangaroos and smaller marsupials, and the sea, with its large stores of oysters and fish."

154 Cf. Klaatsch, *Der Werdegang der Menschheit* (1922), 198; *The Evolution and Progress* (1923), 180: "The same picture is conveyed to our minds by the pleasant districts in the south of France where the remains of caveman are most numerous. Long before the Ice Age there had been mighty volcanic eruptions, and they had made many cavities in the Jurassic limestone of the region. It was these that provided man with a roof during the Ice Age. We find no interruption of the settlements. One layer of remains was heaped upon another, representing the successive generations, until at last the rock-shelters were filled up."

155 **"Today ~~year by year~~ the stalactite caverns of Han in the Ardennes are visited by crowds. You may see highly coloured" … Quote** TXT_6786/0_N5 Instruction to reproduce an excerpt from Sabine Baring-Gould, *Cliff Castles and Cave Dwellings of Europe* (London: Seeley & Co.; Philadelphia: J.B. Lippincott Co., 1911), 28–29, also included in the Kieslers' transcriptions. TXT_6815/0_N2

156 Kiesler omits the following from the Baring-Gould transcription: "Its floor has been in fact a book of the Revelation of the Past, whose seals have been opened, and it has disclosed page by page the history of humanity, from the present, read backwards to the beginning."Baring-Gould, *Cliff Castles*, 29.

157 **and finally francs bearing the profile of a king, ~~the reverse in every moral characteristic of Louis the Saint—that of~~ Leopold of ~~Congo notoriety.~~ Belgium, who fell to death from a high cliff while hunting.** TXT_6815/0_N2 Later, Kiesler revised the last phrase to: **whose son fell to death from a cliff while hunting**. TXT_6850/0_N3 Both of Kiesler's references are factually wrong. It was Leopold II's nephew, Albert I, who succeeded Leopold on the Belgian throne in 1909 and who died in 1934 while mountaineering on a cliff in the Ardennes. For the political repercussions of Kiesler's errors and erasures, see Sources, Disciplines, and Objects, p. 61.

a 

b 

c 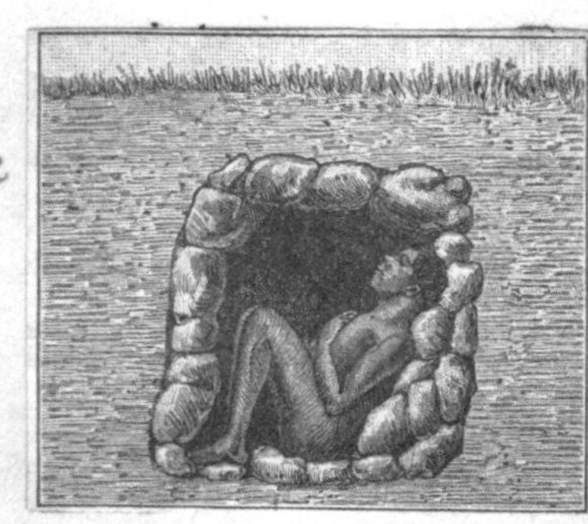

(3). Page 54.

(a,b,c) Shelter for the dead (Indians) are more elaborate than for the living.

(d) Great architectural monuments for communities of dead (China).

d 

Shelter for the living

(4). Page 55

(Above): Huts for the living
(below): Same type huts, but richer, for the dead. (Africa)

Shelter for the dead (ornamented)

(5). Largest Mausoleum for a single person in Bijapur, India.

6

(6). Largest Rotunda in Europe, (dedicated to the memory of martyrs.)
(Pantheon, Rome.)

(7). Mausoleum of a contemporary French postmaster built by himself for himself.

(Detail.)

CHAPTER 7

THE NEST, FIRST ARTIFICIAL SHELTER

If there were no other fact to determine the descent[158] of homo sapiens, the building methods[159] of the primates and anthropoid apes would betray his origin. Man has indeed added nothing to the fundamentals of shelter building.[160] pl. 8

Shortly before nightfall (fifteen minutes before six o'clock) the orang starts the making of his nest. He stands erect,–although in a slightly stooped natural position on a forked branch, using his left arm for support; while, with his right hand he pulls towards him branches that are further away; he breaks them with his hand and heaps them crosswise to left and right, in front and behind him, until he is surrounded by a wreath of broken branches, as high as forty-five centimeters or higher. This done, the orang starts preparing the ground by breaking smaller twigs and putting them in the middle of the nest. In this way the form of the nest is completed[161] and now he starts padding it. For this purpose he grasps long branches as far back as he can reach and slides his half closed hand down the entire length of the branch so that all the leaves strip off and fall directly into the nest or collect in his hand. If the latter is the case he throws them on a certain spot in the nest and presses them into the cracks with his fist. He fills out the framework. Then the orang lays himself down sidewise, pulls towards him the fine ends of the branches and weaves them into his nest to form a dome-like covering. Here and there he breaks off a few branches and pulls them over himself so that they cover him completely.[162] Apparently he does that to guard himself against the heavy[163] dew and the coldness of the night.[164]

An analysis of the material used by the orang utan "(orang–man, utan–forest; forestman)"[165] and the methods of construction and the continuity in procedure, would easily prove that in principle there is no difference between his shelter and ours: The frame-house of our time is erected in the same way as the orang erects his.[166] pl. 9

A state in shelter construction intermediate between the anthropoid and "homo-atomic" can still be found today among tribes of aborigines in North Queensland. (Moszkowski has photographed pl. 10 and described them.)[167] In these tropics the natives bend large palm leaves together[168] to form a dome, so providing shelter and mimicry at the same time. "Usually, interwoven and interlocked, bamboos (or branches) form a round cupola over which palm leaves are laid and attached. The same shelter-types are found among the Botocudo[169] of South America."[170]

We can see that laying a network of branches and filling in the holes with leaves or small twigs is one of the standard methods of building enclosures. In the case of the orang utan it is interesting to observe that he does not use dry wood or dry leaves (like most birds), but only fresh ones. Besides other considerations such as the necessity of using the green color of fresh leaves, live branches retain an elasticity which must be welcome to rest on or to use as cover, since they will more easily accommodate the movement of the body which they protect, when it turns or moves, than dry branches, which would slide and fall off.[171]

Whether it be for the protection of the outdoor fire, or, as it might well have been, for protection from wind, one of the earliest "buildings" is the so-called "Wind-shield."[172] In Sumatra it is still made today in this manner: four branches of equal length are stuck into the ground; over the "forked" end, other branches are laid until they form a floor-level; then, leaves, pieces of bark, or twigs, are filled into the holes so as to attain a flat surface. A similarly constructed rectangular, flat wall-piece is then attached to this elevated platform and inclined as a sort of roof; this is the original "Wind-umbrella."

158 **the "~~wherefrom~~"** TXT_6706/0_N1

159 **~~which modern man as well as prehistoric man~~** TXT 6785/0_N3

160 **Translation page 202 / Kurz vor eintretender Dunkelheit ... page 202 ... * from Gustav Schneider Report am Sumatra.** TXT 6785/0_N3 This is Kiesler's instruction for the translation of an excerpt from a report by the Swiss zoologist, collector, and custodian of the Zoological Institute in Basel, Gustav Schneider, quoted in Klaatsch's book. Cf. Klaatsch, *Der Werdegang der Menschheit* (1922), 202. For the original report by Schneider, which differs slightly from the Klaatsch transcription, see Gustav Schneider, "Ergebnisse zoologischer Forschungsreisen in Sumatra. Erster Teil. Säugetiere (Mammalia)," in *Zoologische Jahrbucher* 23 (1905): 1-172 (46 for this passage). The same description is heavily abbreviated in the published English translation of Klaatsch, *The Evolution and Progress* (1923), 182-183: "Gustav Schneider has recently studied the orang in Sumatra. He found the nests usually forty to seventy feet above the ground, and made in the fork of a tree. If the nest was on a free branch, it was higher above the ground–up to a hundred feet and more. The nests are generally in more or less inaccessible places, on cliffs or even in marshes, and are like storks' nests; except that the interior is well filled with leaves. The orang does not break off the twigs near its own nest, but plaits them together and forms a sort of evergreen natural roof, which conceals it. It begins to make its nest about quarter of an hour before sunset. The work takes about half an hour. The nests are, according to Schneider, only used for sleeping.

161 **~~concluded~~** TXT_6706/0_N1

162 **and ~~covers himself with them~~** TXT_6706/0_N2

163 **~~strong~~** TXT_6706/0_N2

164 The end of the quoted material is not indicated in the TS. **~~To prepare his nest the orang needs (as Schneider tested with watch in hand) thirty minutes."~~** TXT_6706/0_N2 Cf. Klaatsch, *Der Werdegang der Menschheit* (1922), 202; *The Evolution and Progress* (1923), 183, quoted in note 160.

165 Cf. Klaatsch, *Der Werdegang der Menschheit* (1922), 73; *The Evolution and Progress* (1923), 89: "The natives of Borneo regard the orang as a man, as the name itself indicates; for 'orang' means man and 'utan' wood, so the full name means 'man of the woods.'"

166 **particularly the methods of construction and the continuity ~~of his~~ in procedure, would easily prove that in principle nothing has been changed: the frame-houses of our ~~contemporary~~ time is ~~are exactly~~ in the same** [manner] **erected ~~and the function~~.** TXT_6785_N3-N4

167 See Max Moszkowski, *Auf Neuen Wegen durch Sumatra. Forschungsreisen in Ost- und Zentral-Sumatra (1907)* (Berlin: Dietrich Reimer [Ernst Vohsen], 1909).

168 **~~until they~~** TXT_6706/0_N3

169 **Botokudes** [sic] TXT_5877/0_N39; TXT_6706/0_N3

170 **Usually ~~a framework of~~ bamboos (or branches) ~~form a round~~ interwoven and interlocked form a round dome over which palm leaves are ~~placed~~ attached. The same shelter types are found at the ~~Rugendas~~ the Botokudos of South-Amerika.** TXT_6785/0_N3 Cf. Klaatsch, *Der Werdegang der Menschheit* (1922), 203; *The Evolution and Progress* (1923), 183: "Moszkowski tells us that in the thickets of Sumatra we find rudimentary huts made by putting a number of leaves together. In the beautiful woods of North Queensland palm-branches are bent together, in the rainy season, to make a sort of round hut; and the Botocudos of South America are said to do the same." The name "Rugendas," deleted in this earlier draft, is mentioned in the 1922 German edition of Klaatsch, 203. It refers to the ethnographic painter Johann Moritz Rugendas (1802-1858), who traveled to Brazil and made a series of well-known lithographs of the Botocudo. See Moritz Rugendas, *Malerische Reise in Brasilien* (Engelmann & Cie, 1835). Next to this paragraph in the TS is a manuscript annotation for a "picture" with a miniature hand-drawn sketch of a hut based on an illustration found on page 195 of Klaatsch's book (no. 166). TXT_6851/0_N3 See reproduction below the notes of this page. This book illustration is a photograph of two Indigenous people assembling a hut structure covered by palm leaves with the caption "Beim Bau der käfigartigen Rundhütte (Nordqueensland)–During the construction of the cage-type round hut (North Queensland)." The same illustration from Klaatsch is reproduced among Kiesler's plates for *Magic Architecture* (plate 10). The entire page 195 from Klaatsch, *Der Werdegang der Menschheit* (1922) (with handwritten markings) is included in Kiesler's photostats (see Sources, Disciplines, and Objects, fig. A.13). PHO_7197_0 Kiesler's sketch is similar to two other sketches he made of a hut in a draft describing the tools and habitations of animals. SFP_6664/0_N2 Reproduced in Addenda: Charts, fig. C.07b.

171 **Besides other considerations such as the necessity of using the green color of live leaves, ~~it provides~~ fresh branches retain an elasticity, which must be more welcome to rest on~~.~~ ~~Our construction we humans, put particular care in using wood well dried; our houses are not~~ or to cover with, since they will more easily accommodate the movement of the body, which they protect, when turning or moving, than dry branches which would ~~more easily simply side~~ slide off and fall.** TXT_6786/0_N1

172 **"Wind-~~umbrella~~"** TXT_6706/0_N4

Floor and umbrella together make the first square hut. On the elevated floor, which affords protection from the dampness of the ground, fire is kept burning on an underlay of earth-crumbs, or stones.[173]

The other method of building enclosures, which we still rely on, is that of piling stones upon each other. In doing so we are guided by our collective memory of sheltering caves, which, in truth, were nothing else but a continuous arch of stones about us.[174] We use the stone either raw, trimmed or cut to fit, or (when there is a lack of mud for making sun-dried brick) we pulverize stone and bring it back to life in a molded form by mixing its powder with liquids until it hardens again, this time to a size, weight, and trim we have decided upon.[175] In this way we pride ourselves on having controlled nature and made her, at least to a certain degree, obey our wishes. And we used to do that and still do it because caves and thick foliage are not always available when we need them; and leading a life which changes according to the availability of food, we had either to take our tents with us when moving, or we had artificially to erect caves and houses when nature failed[176] to provide them for us.

CHAPTER 8
THE UNIVERSE AS ARCHITECTURE[177]

It is important for us to observe the fact that from his earliest beginnings man has continued to be interested in houses primarily as physical shelter. The spiritual factor does not enter his house, and in later developments it comes in only as décor or make-up. When it does appear it is evidently the same desire for beautification of physical forms as he satisfied by painting his body, by ornamenting it with deep cuts, or by hanging various foreign objects on it, and by trimming his hair.[178]

This desire for beautification is, in the case of his own body, a substitute for something he apparently feels is lacking, be it a deficiency in sexual appeal, or a desire to equal those forces of nature which have the continual faculty of striking from above or below the earth with super-human power; and whose mercy and benevolence he tries to gain surreptitiously by imitating their image.[179]

For self-deceit and to deceive other tribes,[180] he masks him-
pl. 11 self with attributes and symbols of supernatural powers. He imitates the jungle with branches and leaves, he throws fire-spears; he mocks thunder with his own roaring, copies the snake's poison with the venomous cleft of his dart; he dons horns, feathers, and animal skins; he does not want anymore the traits of ordinary man; he is superman, an omni-being, an essence of jungle plus animal–animals of the day and night, animals of prairies and mountains, animals of water and
pl. 12 air. He is anything but just man.[181]

He likens himself to those natural powers that kill, and hopes either to achieve their potency by assuming this décor, or that his avowal of his own weakness will give him the gratification of leading a life without death. He finally develops these "artifices" into "art." Art becomes a symbol of the confessed weakness and a voluntary retirement into the realm of abstraction. In this mid-realm of Man-God, Earth-Heaven, he lives a life of humility.[182]

* * *

But at the beginning of his "domestication"[183] he still felt himself so much a part of the environment, that his masquerades appeared real to him. To look like something else was equal to being something else. These tricks of transformation, however, were not entirely imaginary;[184] they contained some truth. The bow and arrow[185] gave primitive man a far greater reach than he had without them. He could now kill at a distance, and remain unseen.[186] The poison which he appropriated from the snake for the tip of his spear was infallibly deadly. Fire, which he could produce by rubbing a wooden

173 A manuscript draft shows the final two paragraphs of this chapter are marked as "insert." TXT_6780/0_N1-N2 This section has been excerpted from Klaatsch, *Der Werdegang der Menschheit* (1922), 204; for an illustration of such a "wind-screen" after Moszkowski, see 196, fig. 167. Cf. Klaatsch, *The Evolution and Progress* (1923), 185: "Four equal-sized pieces of wood are stuck in the ground, as in the building of a round hut, and twigs are placed on the forked ends of these. The openings are covered with leaves, hides, or bunches of smaller twigs, so as to form a sort of 'platform.' The basis of the fire-place is made on this with stones or earth." TXT_6780/0_N1-N2

174 **Aztec Stones, / greek-stone / glass-Bricks ...** [handwritten annotation in margin of TS] TXT_6851/0_N4

175 **by mixing this powder with liquids until they harden again, ~~and obey our design~~ but according to our size, weight and trim.** TXT_6786/0_N2

176 **missed** TXT_6786/0_N2

177 **~~Man, the perfect imitator~~** TXT_6736/0_N1

178 **the same desire of beautification of physical forms, like those ~~he inherited~~ which he practiced on his own body~~: trimming of hair, teeth, nails, skin~~ by painting it, or producing ornaments by deep cuts, by trimmings of his hair and hangings of various foreign origins.** TXT_6786/0_N6

179 **This desire of beautification ~~of a house~~ is ~~like~~ in the case of his own body ~~not only~~ a substitute for something he apparently feels is lacking, be it a deficiency in ~~streng~~ sexual appeal, or a desire to equal those forces of nature, which have the continual faculty of striking from above or below the earth with super-human power, and whose Gnade und Wohlwollen, er zu erschleichen sucht, indem er ihr Bild an sich selbst nachahmt ~~und seine Schwäche eingesteht~~** [whose grace and benevolence he tries to gain by fraud while replicating their image on himself **and [thereby] admitting his weakness**]. Annotation in the margin: **camouflage** TXT_6786/0_N6

180 The following paragraphs of this MS are written in German, which is a singular instance among Kiesler's preliminary drafts for *Magic Architecture*. **Zu diesem Zwecke der Selbsttäuschung auch der anderen Sippe ~~zerstört er mit weißer und roter Farbe die Züge des Menschen an ihm~~ maskiert er sich selbst mit Attributen und Symbolen jener Mächte.** [For this purpose of self-delusion as well as of the other clan, **~~he wipes out the features of man in him with white and red paint~~** he masks himself with attributes and symbols of those powers.] TXT_6786/0_N6

181 **Er imitiert Urwald mit Ästen und Blättern, er wirft Feuerspeere, er äfft den Donner mit Gebrüll nach das Gift der Schlange mit dem Ritz des Pfeiles, er trägt Horner** [sic] **Feder, ~~Fel~~ Tierfelle, er ~~ist nicht mehr~~ will nicht mehr ~~die~~ Züge der Menschen haben, er ist Übermensch, ein All-Wesen, eine Essenz aus ~~Ur~~Wald Tier, ~~and Sonne, Mond, Feuer~~ der Tiere des Tages und der Nacht, Tiere der ~~Erde~~ Prairie ~~and Tier der~~ der Berge und ~~der~~ Wasser, Tiere der Lüfte ~~des Feuers eine Vereinigung aller Kräfte~~–alles, nur nicht Mensch allein.** [He imitates jungle with branches and leaves, he throws fire spears, he mimics thunder with a roar, the poison of the snake with the graze of the arrow, he wears horns, feathers, animal furs, he no longer wants to have the features of man, he is Superhuman, an All-being, an essence of the ~~primeval~~ forest animal, and ~~the sun, moon, fire~~ of the animals of day and night, animals of the ~~earth~~ prairie ~~and animals~~ of the mountains as well as of the water, animals of the air ~~of fire, a union of all powers~~–everything, but just human.] TXT_6786/0_N7

182 **Er glaubt sich dann ähnlich jenen natürlichen Kräfte, die ~~ihn schlagen~~ töten, und hofft durch diesen decor** [sic]**, ähnliche Kräfte zu erhalten, oder wenigstens durch dieses Eingeständnis der eigenen ~~der~~ Schwäche, ~~dem~~ Gnade und ein Leben ohne Tod zu führen. Diese ~~Kunst~~ „Künste", entwickelt er endlich zur Kunst. Die Kunst wird ~~dann~~ ein Symbol der eingestandenen Schwäche und ein sich freiwilliges Zurückziehen in das ~~„Zwischenreich"~~ Reich der Abstraktion. In diese[m] „Zwischen~~welt~~reich" von Mann und Gott Erde u. Himmel ~~versucht~~ lebt er ein Leben von Demut. ~~Zu leben und Ergebenheit, in das~~ in ~~das~~ die ~~unvermeidliche die Erkenntnis der Unvermeidlichkeit seines Todes.~~** ["He then believes himself to be similar to the natural forces that kill ~~strike him~~ and hopes to obtain similar forces through this décor, or at least through this personal admission of his weakness, [hopes to obtain] mercy and a life without death. These ~~art~~ 'arts,' he finally develops into art. Art then becomes a symbol of the self-admitted weakness and a voluntary retreat into the ~~"interim"~~ realm of abstraction. In this 'interim ~~world~~ realm' of man and God, earth and heaven, he ~~tries to~~ lives a life of humbleness. ~~To live in acquiescence, in ... the realization of the inevitability of his death.~~"] TXT_6786/0_N6-N7

183 **"civilization** [no closing quotation marks] TXT_6786/0_N7

184 **imaginiäre** TXT_6786/0_N8

185 **~~which he used for the kill~~** TXT_6786/0_N8

186 **He could now kill from a distance and unseen too.** TXT_6786/0_N8

(8) – (10)

(8)-(10). Page 62

(10)

Orangutan constructing his nest.
Similar construction used by primitive man.

9

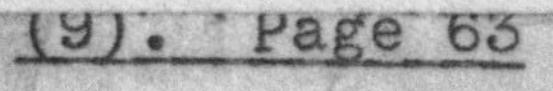

(9). Page 63

(Left): Elevated sleeping nests of orangutans.
(Below and right): Elevated shelters of aboriginals. men

(11)

(11). Page 68

In his fear of death and lack of selfconfidence, man imitates symbols of more powerful forces.

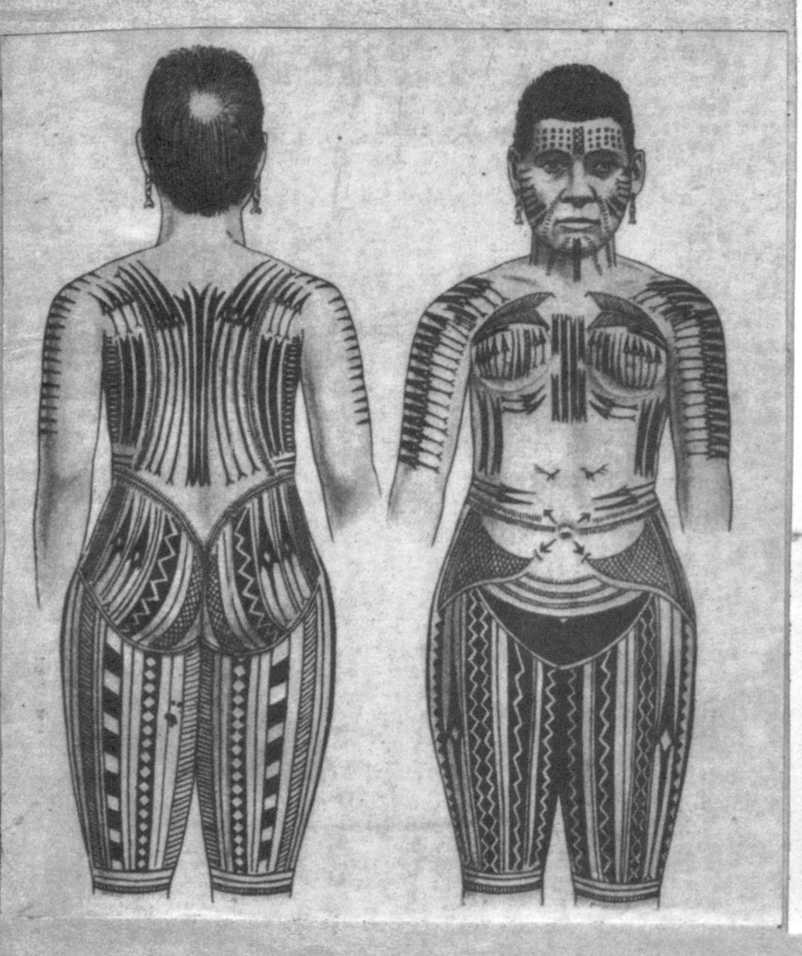

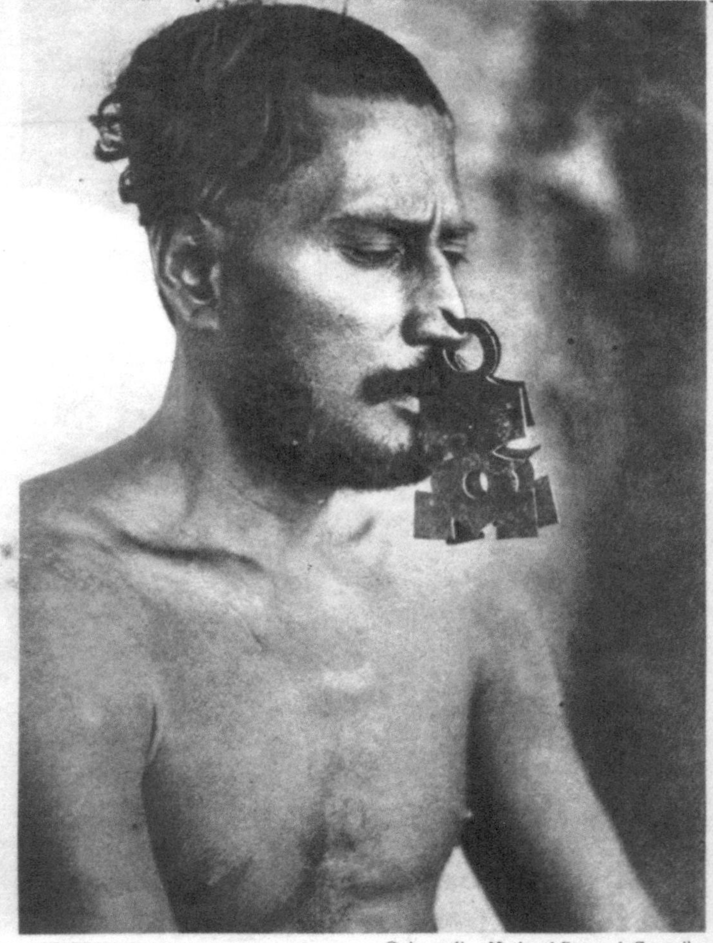

12

(12). By imitating the image of dangerous creatures, he hopes to gain their sympathy.

stick against wood, was indeed a feat! Fire,[187] which, with smoke and flames, devours everything alive, was the same fire—exactly the same as his—that was sent by a far-away hand[188] through clouds and squalls in the form of lightning. To equal such force[189] "from beyond" with his own invention could not have failed to impress man. It probably had a double effect: it made him believe in his power of[190] transformation at will; and it planted in him the belief in a heavenly descent.[191] Both, as he saw, were powers, which no other animal possessed; he could dominate the weaker or the less talented. Later, there loomed in him the vision of a man, who could unite all the powers of forceful nature. Once these qualities accumulated, he could not only subjugate his fellow man and his enemies—not to speak of animals—but he could turn against nature herself and challenge those powers of the "beyond." As a matter of fact, man could never conceive of a God who did not have his image. Only to lesser gods will he allot the symbols of powerful animals and even then they are almost always half man, half animal.[192]

Once primitive man had tested these possibilities, all his aims were devoted to developing and exploiting them.[193] Artificial power[194] was Magic. It was the best defense and the best attack. Artificial power could be used both ways. Therefore, in all his activities he strengthened the liaison with all aspects of nature. He was, and he wanted to be like her. He wanted to be so close to her that he could literally "feel"[195] her secrets. For hunting he often used the skins and make-up of the very animals he hunted, in order to trick them into thinking he was one of them so that he could kill them with ease.[196] The technical superiority he gained through his primitive tools and weapons must have made him feel like a participant in the secret powers of nature. On the other hand, seeing with closed eyes, an experience he had in dreams, was miraculous.[197] This mystery could be explained only as an action from "beyond." As forewarning, as hint, as secret order, the dream was the visible link with invisible forces. And it spelt reality because it dealt with his own environment and the problems of his own life.[198] What a terrifying revelation it must have been to man that someone, unseen by him, not spoken to by him, knew his hopes and fears, plans, and details he had only dimly noted in his most wakeful state of mind.[199] Indeed, how natural for the primitive to put all his belief into this imagery. Without the biological account of birth and death, and only pre-logical experience to live by,[200] primitive man cannot link cause and effect in time and space as we have learned to apprehend it.[201] The birth of a baby is simply the rebirth of a dead person, probably one of his own family or tribe, or of an animal; and not the result of the fertilization of an egg by spermatozoa[202] through the physical relation of a man and a woman.[203] Death is conversion into another state of being, and not the cessation[204] of the heartbeat. Life consists of nothing other than a continuity of cycles. It is continuity. Everything is ever-present. Nothing, therefore, is completely dead.[205] As a matter of fact, death as we understand it does not exist. Death is rather a punishment, a damnation. It is an act of being ordered into EXILE; from there you watch your family; from there you participate in their lives. You become part of their Totem, or you impose Tabus. You either take revenge or help them. Particularly through dreams you take an active hand in their everyday affairs. The day does not consist of twenty-four hours, or 1,440 minutes;[206] the day is not divorced from the night and not isolated from the year; and the year has nothing to do with past and future.[207] Reality is the ever-presence of past and future.[208] This ever-presence is not always seen, or heard, or smelled, or eaten; but it is felt. Time is feeling space, and space the objectivation of emotion.[209] There is only one Reality; and it is the result of a constant interchange of the visible and invisible, the dead and the alive. They interpenetrate. They depend upon each other. All objects, all configurations, are felt transparently. Man is like a house, like a dwelling place. Family members, ancestral and present, and strangers go in and out, as do animals as well as trees and rocks.[210] They stay or disappear,[211] but the Totems never move away. At night, as in dreams,

187 ~~flames~~ TXT_6786/0_N8

188 ~~powers~~ TXT_6786/0_N8

189 ~~effect~~ TXT_6786/0_N8

190 ~~art of~~ TXT_6786/0_N8

191 ~~To equal this effect with his invention and power of transformation (which no animal before him had achieved), that alone could have entitled him to his conceit of being of heavenly descent.~~ TXT_6786/0_N8

192 half man—half tier [animal] TXT_6786/0_N9

193 Another TS draft of this passage shows it preceded by the following: ~~From a cowardly defense, he could progress to offence attack.~~ TXT_6786/0_N9

194 artificial ~~super-~~power TXT_6786/0_N9

195 ~~hear and see~~ TXT_6786/0_N9

196 ~~He used intoxicating drink juices to excel himself to act brutal. He took direct orders from his dreams.~~ TXT_6786/0_N9

197 ~~and unexplainable except with blind faith~~ TXT_6786/0_N10

198 And so true because they dealt with his own environment, the problems of his own life. The dream knew. TXT_6786/0_N10

199 What ~~enormous~~ terrifying revelation that someone unseen by ~~you~~ not spoken to by ~~you~~, knows ~~your secret~~ hopes and fears and details and scopes which ~~you~~ have overlooked ~~your~~self even in ~~your~~ most awakened state of mind. TXT_6786/0_N10

200 Having ~~had~~ not the biological account of birth and death, but rather a pre-logical experience only to live by TXT_6786/0_N10

201 imagerie. [sic] TXT_6786/0_N10 In this manuscript, there are a few deleted words written between the lines of the text with apparent references to Lévy-Bruhl: ~~Pre-logic, instinct, intuition.~~ TXT_6786/0_N10 See also the excerpts on "Dreams" by Lévy-Bruhl quoted later in this section. On the back of the preceding page, there are a number of handwritten notes in pencil: all possessions, all objects, are "possessed" by life power. / magnetic life / interpenetration of the visible and the invisible / poly-dimensional, not one-two-three dimensional language. See fig. B.05. TXT_6786/0_N9verso

202 spermatozoid TXT_6786/0_N11

203 Again here, Kiesler's formulation reflects ideas about the non-biological conception of life in Montagu, *Coming into Being Among the Australian Aborigines.*

204 causation [sic] TXT_6786/0_N11

205 ~~Animals, Pflanzen~~ [plants]~~, Felsen~~ [rocks]~~, Gestirne~~ [stars]~~, Waffen~~ [weapons]~~, Geräte~~ [utensils] ~~are animated in a human way. Even tools have their anima.~~ TXT_6786/0_N11

206 or 1444 [sic] minutes TXT_6686/0_N39 and one thousand four hundred and forty minutes / ~~24x60=1440~~ [handwritten calculation] TXT_6786/0_N11

207 ~~Every object is polydimensional, not only one-, two-, three-, or four-dimensional. It has many lives. It is interpenetrated. Ever-presence of~~ TXT_6786/0_N11

208 ~~Reality is the sum-total of the visible and the invisible.~~ TXT_6786/0_N11 Cf. manuscript notes mentioned in note 201.

209 and space is ~~personified~~ the ~~personification~~ objectification of emotion. TXT_6786/0_N11

210 Family members, past and now, strangers go in and out, and stay whence they like; animals, too; and trees. TXT_6786/0_N11–N12

211 They grow through the house; or change places; or disappear altogether. TXT_6786/0_N12

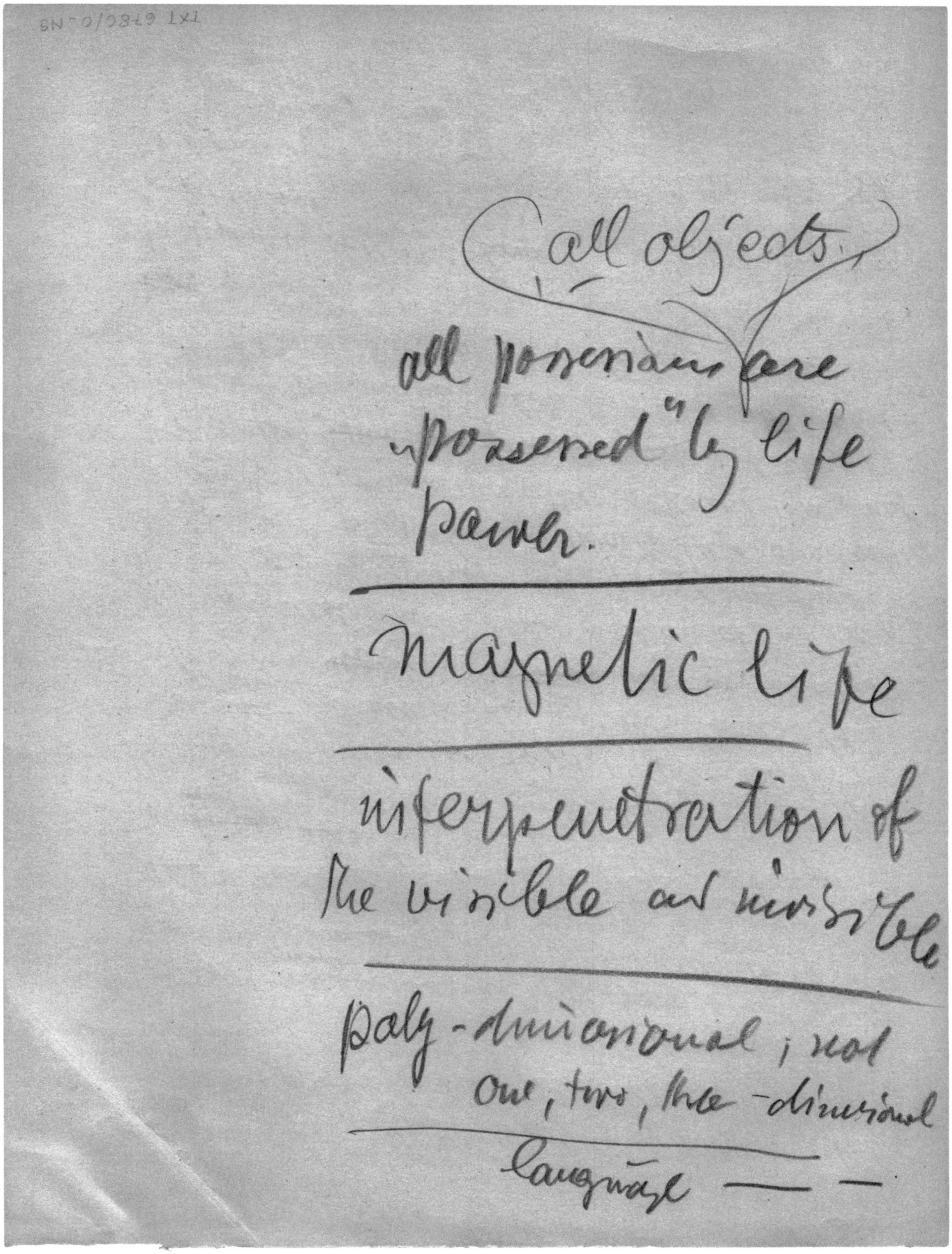

fig. B.05

all objects

all possessions are "possessed" by life power.

magnetic life

interpenetration of the visible and invisible

poly-dimensional; not one, two, three-dimensional language — —

Frederick Kiesler, Part 1, Chapters 6 to 8, opposite side of preliminary draft page with handwritten notes
"... all objects are 'possessed' by life power..." (MS, pencil) ÖFLKS, TXT_6786/0_N9verso

you can see it all better: the house is then illuminated from within. All beings glow luminously while the house itself is skeleton-silent, and dark. Yet, when the morning sun rises, the inside light dies away[212] and the outside begins to glow radiantly. You know the guests have remained: you and they possess one other, and none can be let loose, lest you lose yourself in death, and become part of someone else.[213] And that is damnation.

* * *

The world of experience,[214] as a whole, does not present itself to the primitive mind as it does to us.[215] The world we see provides primitives, as it does us, with a collection of realities perceptible to sense, but in their minds others are added, or rather intermingled, with these data arising out of the mystic forces always and everywhere present.[216] In his closed world, whose space, causation, time, are all somewhat different from our own, communities feel a solidarity with the other beings,[217] or groups of beings—whether seen or unseen—which inhabit it with them. In this sense their world is more complex than our universe, but on the other hand it is complete, and it is closed.

According to the ideas of most primitives, the vault of heaven rests like a dome upon the flat surface of the earth or the ocean. Thus the world ends at the circle of the horizon. In it, space is felt rather than thought of; its directions are weighted with qualities, and each of its regions participates in all that is usually found there.

* * *

The cave is only a small detail of the world as a whole.[218] It is its pl. 13
innermost cell. One by one the other layers of natural environment grow:[219] trees, rocks, mountains, rivers, the ocean, and the sky. They are all part of man's "shelter." They are the architectonics of the great structure of the seen and felt universe.[220] They envelop one's
body continuously. The intertwining growth of branches, lianas and pl. 12a
leaves of the jungle[221] shield him with endless caves of latticework;[222] they form floors, walls, and roofs; they are soft and elastic and yield to pressure.

The clearings in the woods,[223] surrounded by tall trees, provide a shelter supported by a mighty[224] Order of columns; the roof is open; fire in the middle of the floor rises freely; the stars participate through the flying clouds of smoke.

The river protects him from surprise-attack; it is a flowing wall. If someone tries to cross it the water sounds a warning as soon as it is touched.

Below the earth caverns wait with cool covering against the beat of the tropical sun; above, the caves are dry. Lightning does not strike here; squalls and floods cannot enter. The walls are thick. They resound from faraway if strangers come too close. The cave is extensive; it is mountain-deep and mountain-high. It is far beyond the actual need of a shelter.[225] It extends its stony "range" almost to the horizon, where sky and ocean meet; and above it reaches to the sun.[226]

All visible and invisible forces have prepared this home for weak man and powerful animals alike. Nature <u>is</u> Architecture.

212 ~~becomes black~~ TXT_6736/0_N6

213 ~~Man is like a house on feet; they all glow with their own light.~~ They all glow. The house itself is silent-dark. Awake, the House will glow and inside it will be silent-dark. But the guests are there. You know it. You feel them. They are part of you. You possess each other, and none can let loose—least you lose yourself and become part of someone else. [text follows a hand-drawn miniature sketch of a cosmic-like ornament] TXT_6786/0_N12

214 Kiesler labeled these two paragraphs Quote A or B TXT_6786/0_N12 The texts were transcribed with the headings: In: L. Lévy Bruhl: Primitive Mentality / Chapter III Dreams / p. 443-446 TXT_6815/0_N1 Lucien Lévy-Bruhl, *Primitive Mentality*, trans. Lillian A. Clare (London: George Allen & Unwin; New York: Macmillan, 1923), 97, 443-446. English edition of *La Mentalité Primitive* (Paris: Librairie Félix Alcan, 1922). The excerpt from Lévy-Bruhl transcribed in Kiesler's text begins with an opening quotation mark, but no closing quotation mark appears. Excerpts from chapter 3 of Lévy Bruhl's book are mentioned in the outline of Stefi Kiesler's anthology of "Dreams in Literature," as are excerpts from Edward Clodd, *Myth and Dreams* transcribed for but not quoted in any of the drafts of *Magic Architecture*, included in Addenda: Transcriptions and Translations, p. 362.

215 It is not only that its framework differs somewhat, since time, space, and causation are imagined, and above all felt, in a different way; its data are also more complex, and in a certain sense more copious. These sentences are transcribed in TXT_6815/0_N1 but omitted in the MS TXT_6786/0_N12 and later drafts of *Magic Architecture*.

216 data arising out of the mystic forces always and everywhere present, and these are by far the most important TXT_6815/0_N1 Kiesler skips this last phrase and then moves to two different passages from the conclusion of *Primitive Mentality* (Lévy-Bruhl, 445-446), quoted in reverse with the instruction: for quote at the end of page 12 TXT_6815/0_N1 Kiesler also skips the following passage from *Primitive Mentality* (443), included in his transcriptions: Rather it is that their hand acquires its skill by a sort of intuition which is itself directed by acute observation of objects possessing peculiar interest for them... TXT_6815/0_N1

217 communities feel themselves solidary with the other beings TXT_6815/0_N1 (quoted from *Primitive Mentality*, 446). The same phrase is later changed into communities feel a solidarity with other beings. TXT_6736/0_N7

218 For Kiesler's pencil drawings related to plate 13 with the descriptive title The mirror of the caveman, see figs. B.06a-b SFP_6662_N1_N2 A similar ink drawing has the following descriptions of cosmological layers over and under the earth: Light and Shadow of the mirror of A.[rchitecture] / of primitive man. / The Light Unknown / The Light Known / shelter / grave / The Known dark mirror / the unknown dark mirror (fig. B06c) SFP_6666_N1

219 Then are coming all the other layers. TXT_6736/0_N7

220 They are the ~~Archi~~architectonics of the great structure of the ~~cosmos~~, seen and felt. TXT_6736/0_N7

221 of the Urwald; TXT_6782/0_N1 ~~of old and young trees~~ TXT_6736/0_N7

222 endless layers of netting TXT_6782/0_N1

223 The opening in the woods TXT_6782/0_N1

224 With a mächtigen [mighty] column-order TXT_6782/0_N1

225 ~~family~~ shelter TXT_6736/0_N8

226 ~~it is close~~ to the sun. TXT_6736/0_N8

CHAPTER 9

THE SPLIT IN THE UNITY OF VISION AND FACT[227]

Just as the metaphor of poetry is real to the poet so visions represent absolute concretions to primitive man.[228] He has no ability for abstraction.[229] For him everything is incarnate. Logarithms, Semantics, and Art are unknown to him.[230] Instinct, intuition, imagery, and thought are still unified within the nucleus of experience;[231] they cannot be split and isolated.[232] The energy of a common origin binds them and man together.[233] The play of that flow creates magnetic fields of great exuberance. The life of the primitive is chained to the orbits of his ancestry,[234] and similarly his birthplace, his habitat, his hideout are embedded in the cavern of the total sphere of the natural environment.[235]

pl. 13

The hut represents the innermost shell of the world of environments. Rocks and bushes and mountains, brooks and rivers[236] are other shells and spheres which surround him and his groups. The sky is the final dome and roof of his dwelling;[237] the earth is its foundation, and the horizon marks the extent of his home. The total environment of nature is his house and Architecture. Dreams and visions are all here at home with him.[238]

Later, after thousands of years of growth and development, when the persona of the primitive became gradually but steadily more individualized, he detached himself more and more from his family and his group. His personal ties, which formed part of the social structure of the collective group, loosened up the immediate relationships which were then broken one by one.

The cave, too, detaches itself from its natural adherence. It leaves the mountainside. It begins to stand alone, and is built artificially.[239]

Further development of this individuation causes[240] his cave to evolve into the character of a shelter: a newly erected structure.[241]

The vault of the cave is raised on walls and becomes an elevated roof.[242]

Fire, which earlier had burned outside the cave, is[243] now surrounded by protective walls. It is fully enclosed, and so is man.

The open fire now flames against a stone plate placed above it. It is man's first hearth.[244]

pls. 13a–e

He[245] has finally arrived at a new type of habitat, a shelter created by his own hands. It is true that the material is not his own invention; it belongs to the nature of his immediate environment; it is nature. But was man aware of the fact, and is he aware of it now, in house-building? Or does he always blind himself into believing that he can rival nature with his technical ability to imitate the material and form of a natural habitat and be more enduring in his structures than nature herself?[246]

Whatever the truth may be, with the erection of the first hut,[247] man started to build the world of artificial environments we now live in.

Yet, this world, created anew, is not a world of the imagination of the poet, but an extension of the crude mechanics of the first shelter of the caveman, which became the prototype. It is nothing more than the physical protection by roofs, walls, and hearth. Contact with nature is finally re-established by providing holes which serve as windows to look out and doors for entrance and exit.[248] It suffices against hostile climates, men, and beasts. But it has lost its magnetic field. Life, outside and inside of it, is bare of imagination, of poetic exuberance, of joy of living.

Man and house have gained their independence; but interdependence is what creativeness and satisfaction in life calls for, and he had lost the feeling and the technique for it.[249] He dwells in artificial shells which imitate nature.[250] Architecture must wait.[251]

227 Alternative chapter number: **Chapter eight.** ~~**The unity split**~~. TXT_6738/0_N1

228 Here, Kiesler appears to draw from Lévy Bruhl's premise that "primitive mentality is inclined to the concrete" as opposed to the "conceptual" thought processes of Western societies. *Primitive Mentality* (1926), 321. "Concretion" as a dialectical pendant of "abstraction" is also a term employed by Hans Arp, a close acquaintance of Kiesler's. See Jean Arp, "Art concret," first published in the Kunsthalle Basel exhibition catalogue *Konkrete Kunst* (Basel: Benno Schwabe Verlag, 1944), 11–12. For an English translation: "Concrete Art," in *Arp on Arp: Poems, Essays, Memories*, ed. Marcel Jean (New York: Viking Press, 1972), 139–140.

229 **the primitive has no ability** ~~**for abstract thought. He cannot conceive**~~ **of abstraction,** ~~**like we have developed it.**~~ TXT 6783/0_N1 Cf. Lévy Bruhl, *Primitive Mentality* (1926), 402: "[Primitive mentality] feels very strongly, but it hardly ever analyses, nor does it think in abstract terms."

230 **For him everything is** ~~**facts or even his visions are equally concretions**~~ **concrete. Like the metaphors of poetry are real to the poet, so are the visions of the primitive for him absolute concretions.** ~~**Mathematics**~~ **The logarithms or Art per se are unknown to him.** TXT 6783/0_N1

231 **Instinct, intuition, and imagery are still closed within the nucleus of** ~~**event**~~ **and experience.** TXT 6783/0_N1recto

232 **They cannot be split apart and isolated.** ~~**The primitive is participation.**~~ TXT 6783/0_N1recto-verso

233 ~~**There is exuberance created.**~~ TXT 6783/0_N1verso

234 **The life of the primitive** ~~**rests within is magnetically bound**~~ **is** ~~**faithfully**~~ **chained to the orbit of the atom of his family** ~~**group**~~ **and their ancestry.** TXT 6783/0_N1verso

235 **Equally rests his domicile, the habitat, his cave, his shelter** ~~**milieu the framework**~~ **embedded in the total sphere of the natural environment.** TXT 6783/0_N1verso

236 ~~**the ocean**~~ TXT 6783/0_N1verso

237 **roof of his** ~~**shelter**~~ **cave.** TXT 6783/0_N1verso

238 **Dreams, visions,** ~~**daily experience**~~ **and the sensual experiences of the active wake, they all live together and are here at home with him.** TXT 6783/0_N1verso

239 **The cave,** ~~**his home**~~ **where he lives, detaches itself from its** ~~**actual**~~ **adherence. It leaves the** ~~**rock**~~**. It begins to stand alone and is built by him artificially.** TXT 6783/0_N2

240 **evolutes** [sic] TXT 6783/0_N2

241 In the manuscript draft, the paragraph starting with this sentence includes the following annotation in the margin: **Potentials** TXT 6783/0_N2

242 **and becomes** ~~**a frame made to raise the roof and support and build walls underneath, and an opening as chimney for the escape of the smoke.**~~ TXT 6783/0_N2

243 **fire is** ~~**moved inside**~~ TXT 6783/0_N2verso

244 **He closes himself up; and encloses at the same time the fire, because he has now invented the herd,** [hearth] **which burnt until now only outside his cave. He moved it in, and established thus the herd** [hearth]. **The walls became more and more accumulated, as a means of separation. The roof, in the beginning the most important part of his refuge is** ~~**a mere**~~ **over as a** ~~**traditional**~~ **necessity of technical protection. He has** ~~**a door**~~ **an opening in his house through which he enters and exits, his means of contact, from outside to inside and vice versa. This opening filled in with stones against beasts, will in future times become the door, which will shut him off completely at will. His physical isolation is achieved.** This paragraph was eventually crossed out by Kiesler. TXT_6783/0_N2verso

245 **at the same time** TXT 6783/0_N3

246 **or did he blind himself then as now with his pride of his ability to inventing a method to put the materials together in the form of natural habitat?** TXT 6783/0_N3

247 **the first architectural shelters** TXT 6783/0_N3

248 **Contact with nature is provided by lookouts through windows and doors for entrance and exit.** TXT_6783/0_N3verso

249 **he has lost it, the feeling and the technique of it.** TXT_6783/0_N3verso

250 **He dwells in artificial caves.** TXT_6783/0_N3verso

251 In one of the typescripts, under this final paragraph, Kiesler adds a sketch in black ink of a hemispherical structure with a semi-spherical ideogram bearing the following inscriptions: **exit to individuation** / **now** / **return to UNION** / **SPHERE OF THE UNIFIED FIELD OF LIFE**. TXT_6738/0_N3 See fig. B.07a. The same drawing appears in SFP_6665/0_N1 which is included in the preliminary material for Part II, but with a different set of inscriptions around the drawing: **Ascent to Individuality** / **now** / **RETURN TO UNION** / **UNIFIED WITH NATURE** [and below] **The home civilization has build** [sic] ~~**individuality has build**~~. An additional drawing of the same enclosure is in SFP_6665/0_N2. It includes a male and female figure reclining opposite each other on the floor of the hemisphere. See figs. B.07b–c.

(13).

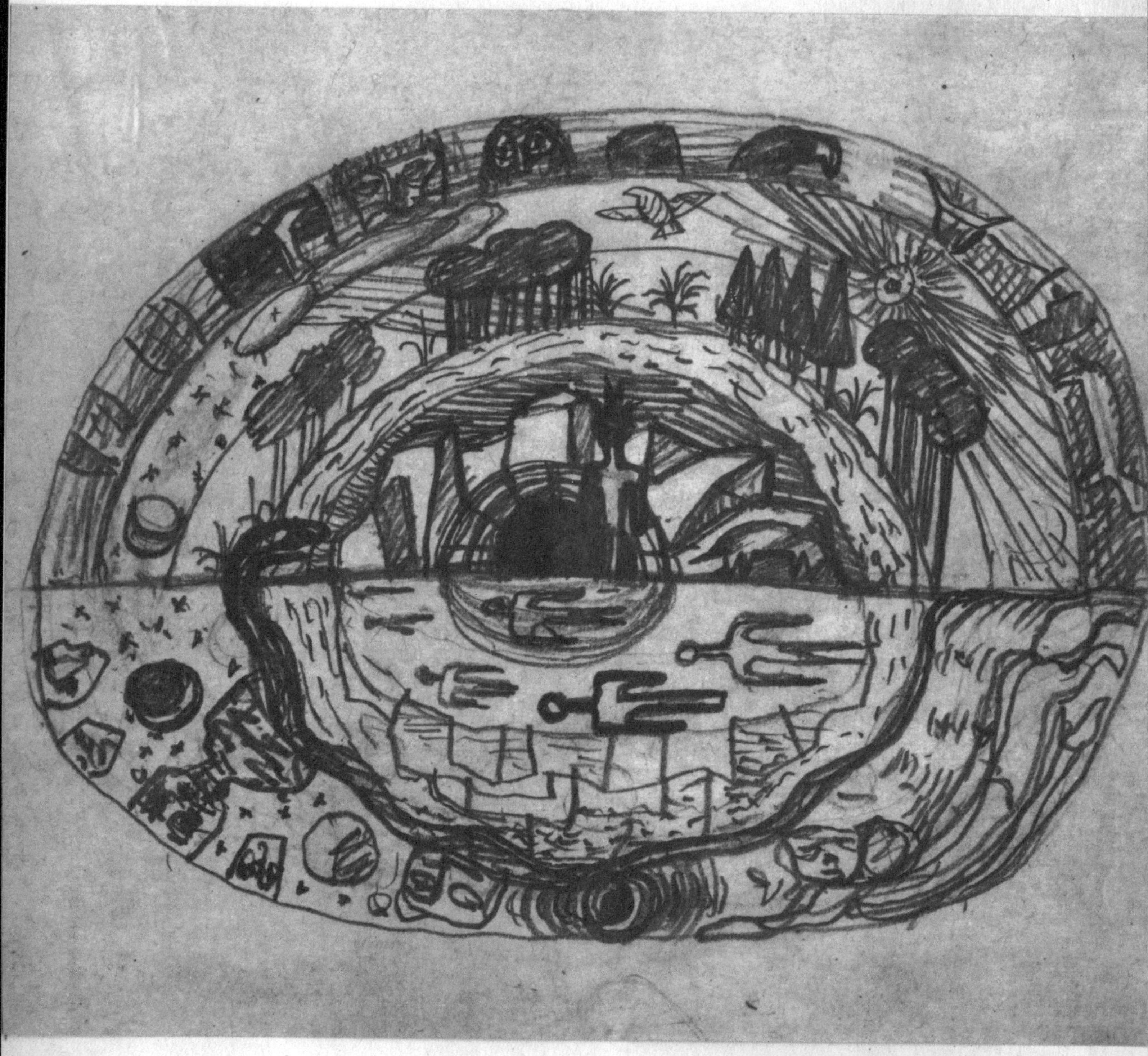

Design of the world of primitive man. His cave is part of the universe. It is not separated. His shelter is the innermost cell of the surrounding layers of rocks, rivers, trees and skies. It is also part of the world below (the dead), and the world beyond (of ghosts and spirits).

(12a).

A perfect photograph illustrating the sheltering nature of a primeval forest. (Men can be seen in center).
(Below): Group of men imitating forms and emotions of animals.
(Monkey-dance, Bali)

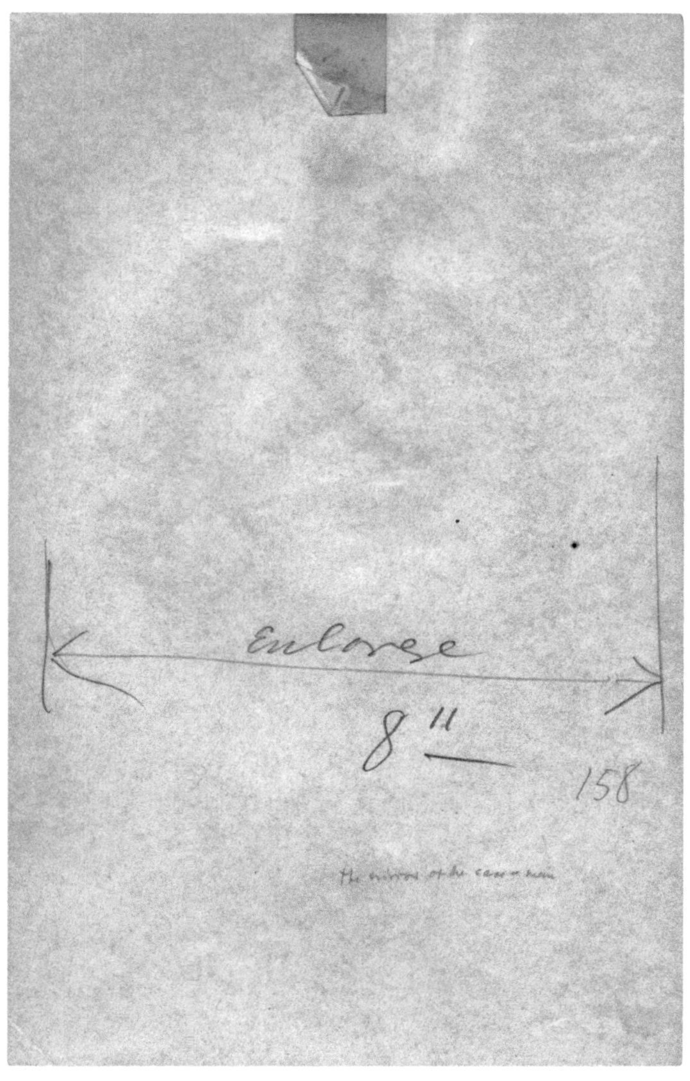

Frederick Kiesler, (Part 1, Chapter 8: The Universe as Architecture) Maquette for plate 13 with hand-written sizing instructions and description: **"The mirror of the cave man"** (MS, pencil) ÖFLKS, SFP_6662/0 N1. Frederick Kiesler, Part 1, Chapter 8, "The Universe as Architecture," hand drawing used in plate 13 and sketch of vertical mirror (pencil) ÖFLKS, SFP_6662/0_N2

Frederick Kiesler, Part 1, Chapter 8, "The Universe as Architecture," preliminary drawing related to plate 13 and sketch of horizontal mirror with descriptions: "Light and Shadow of the mirror of A. / of primitive man. / The Light Unknown / The Light Known / shelter / grave / The Known dark mirror / the unknown dark mirror" (ink) ÖFLKS, SFP_6666/0_N1

(13a)

— The Trees —

Photograph by Gabriel Moulin for Redwood Empire Association

(13). ~~[illegible]~~ (The Forests)

(a,b): Architecture of man, small and great alike, receives and depends on natures insipration, her designs, construction principles, forms and materials.

(Left): Redwoods, California, U.S.A.

(Right): Arcade of St. Peters, Rome, Italy.

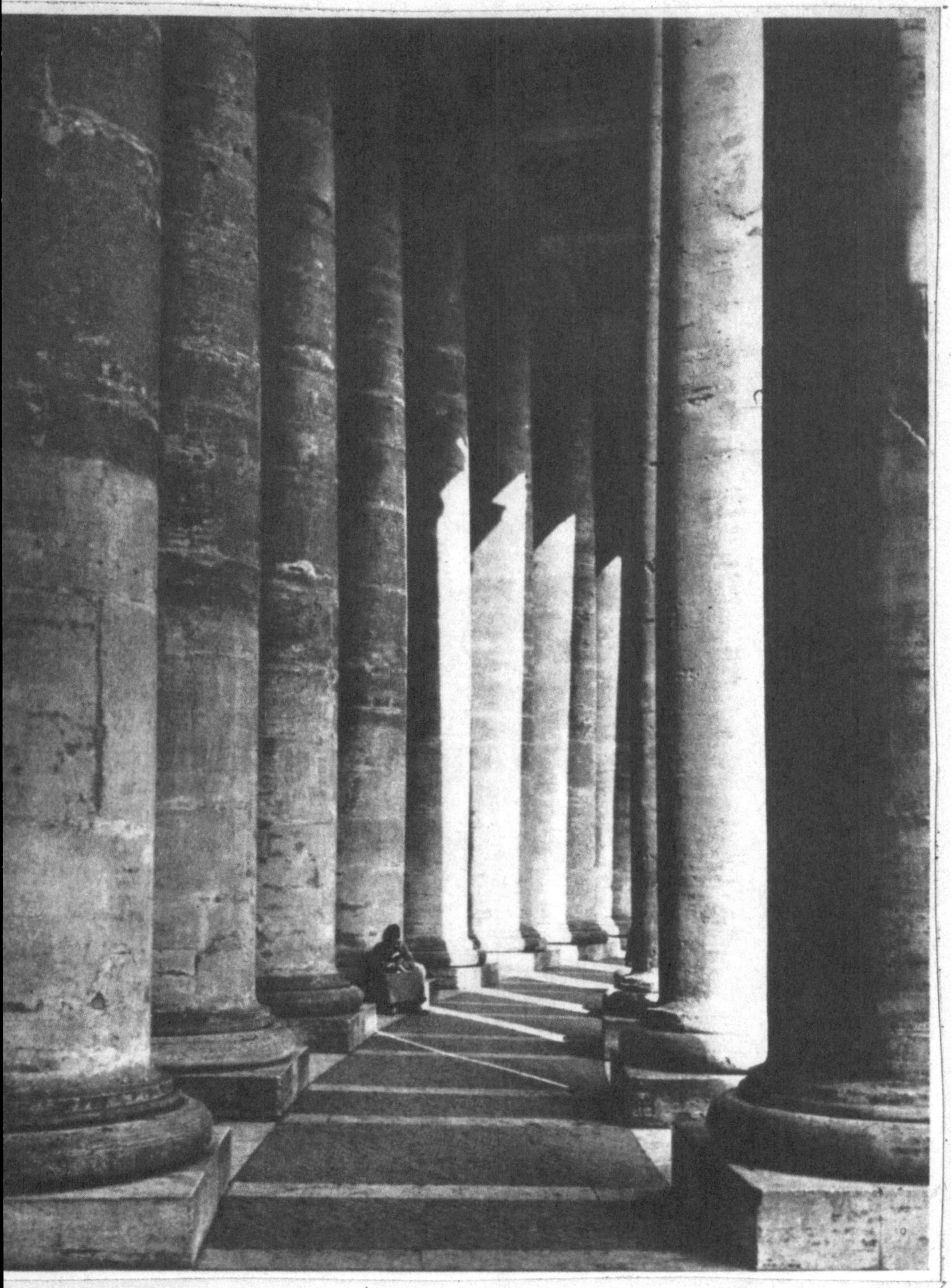

Court of St. Peters, Rome, Italy.

13c

The Mountains

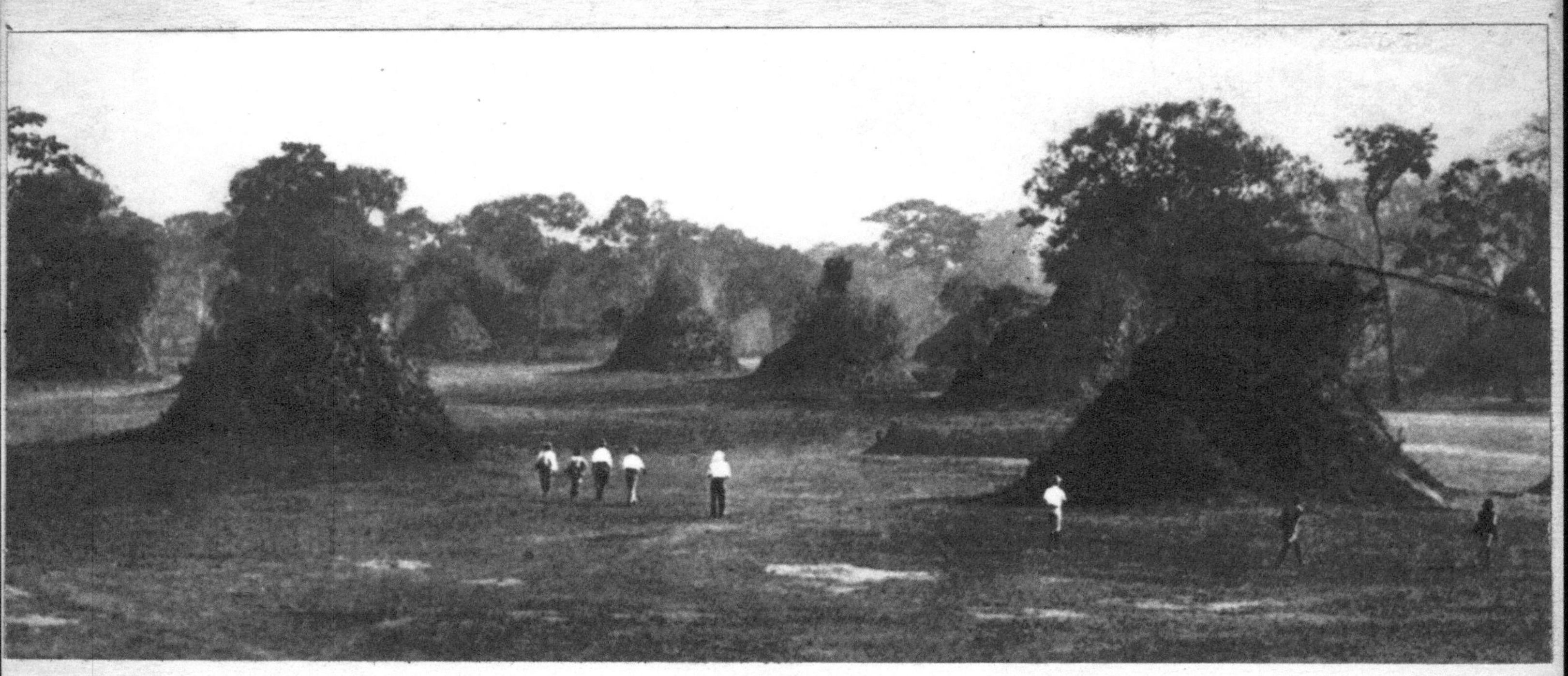

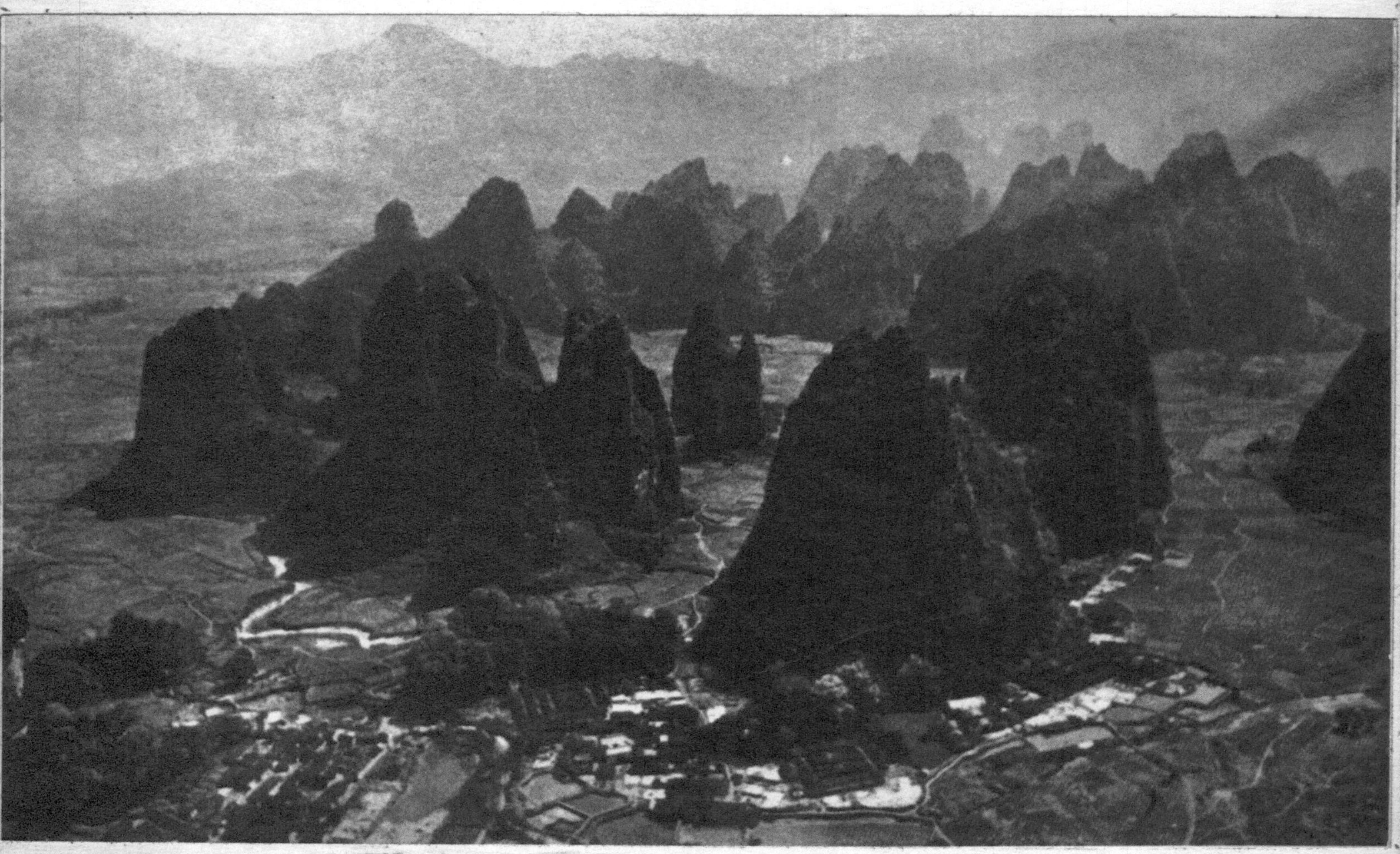

(c): (The Mountains)

Baisc building methods and forms of nature are also used by animals. Above are seen the Termitories of the Termites on a golf course in Johanisberg, Africa. Below: Mountains in Kwangsi Province, China.

(d): (The Rocks)

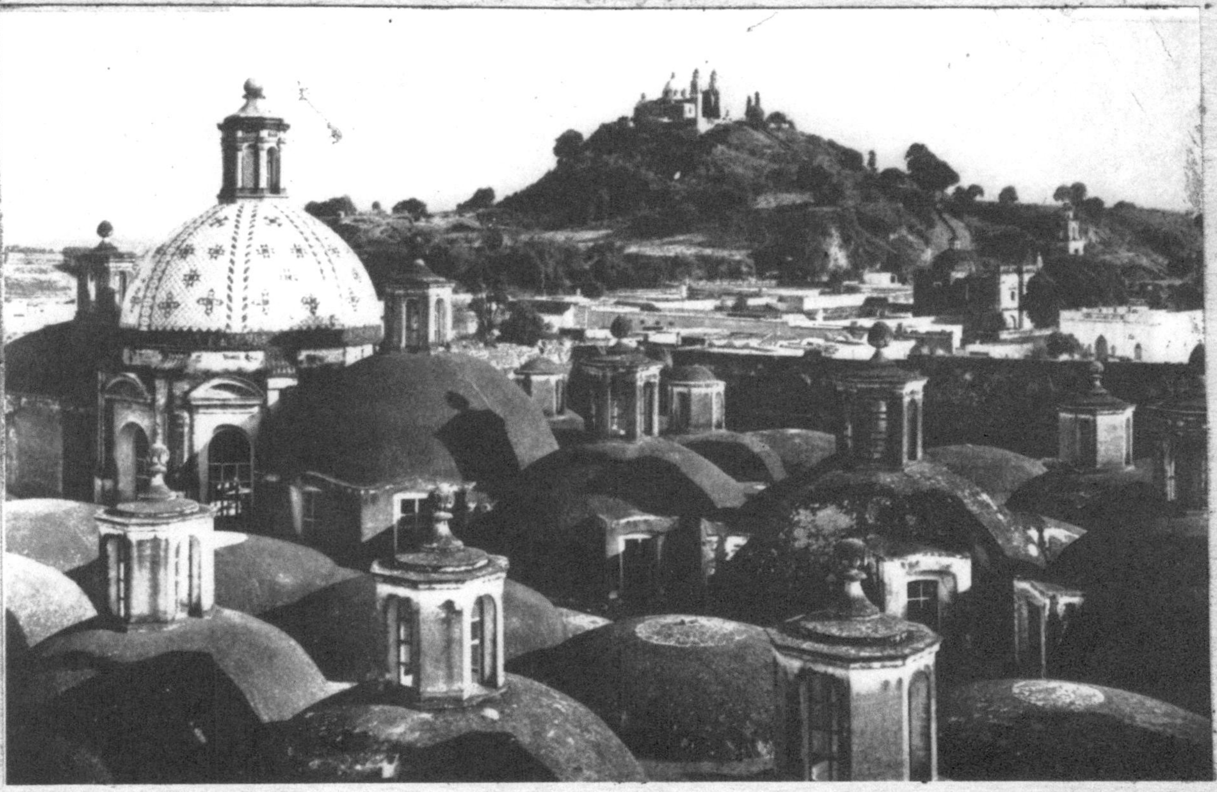

(Below): Boulder landscape, Australia.
(Middle): Shelters, North Africa.
(Above): Domes of the City of a Thousand Churches, Mexico.

(13 e)

– The Animal –

1 SUNDAY	2	3	4	5	SEPTEMBER	6	7	8	9	10
11 SUNDAY	12	13	14	15		16	17	18	19	20
21 SUNDAY	22	23	24	25		26	27	28	29	30

DECEMBER · NOVEMBER · OCTOBER · AUGUST · JULY · JUNE

JANUARY · FEBRUARY · MARCH · APRIL · MAY

Figure 5. Plan of the Tihuanacu calendar with its twelve months and the six weeks of the month of September (the month of Spring and the beginning of the year in the worship and culture of the man of the Andes).

Esquema del calendario Tihuanacu con sus doce meses y las seis semanas del mes de Septiembre (mes de primavera y principio del año en el culto y cultura del hombre en los Andes).

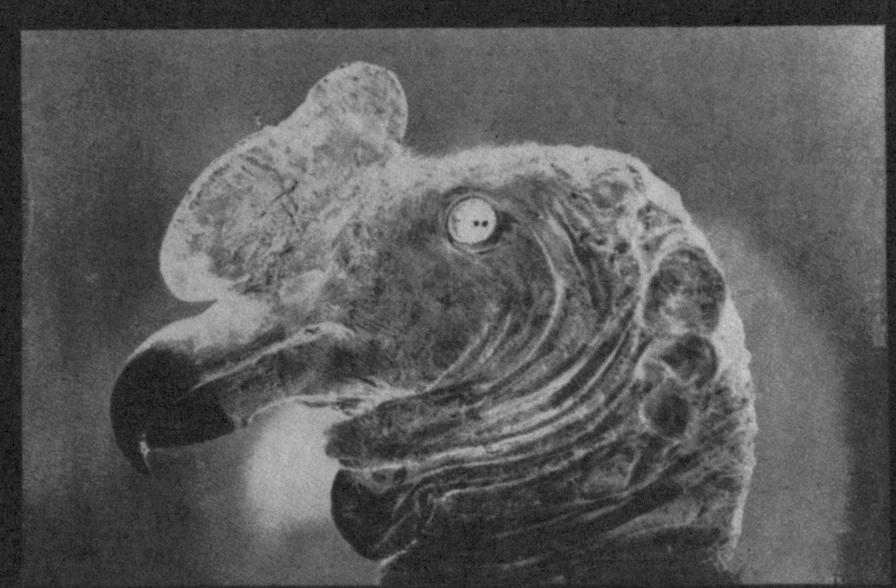

(e): (The Animals)

Head of a Condor of the Andes, South America, and its design as part of an architectural frieze in Tihuanacu.

13e

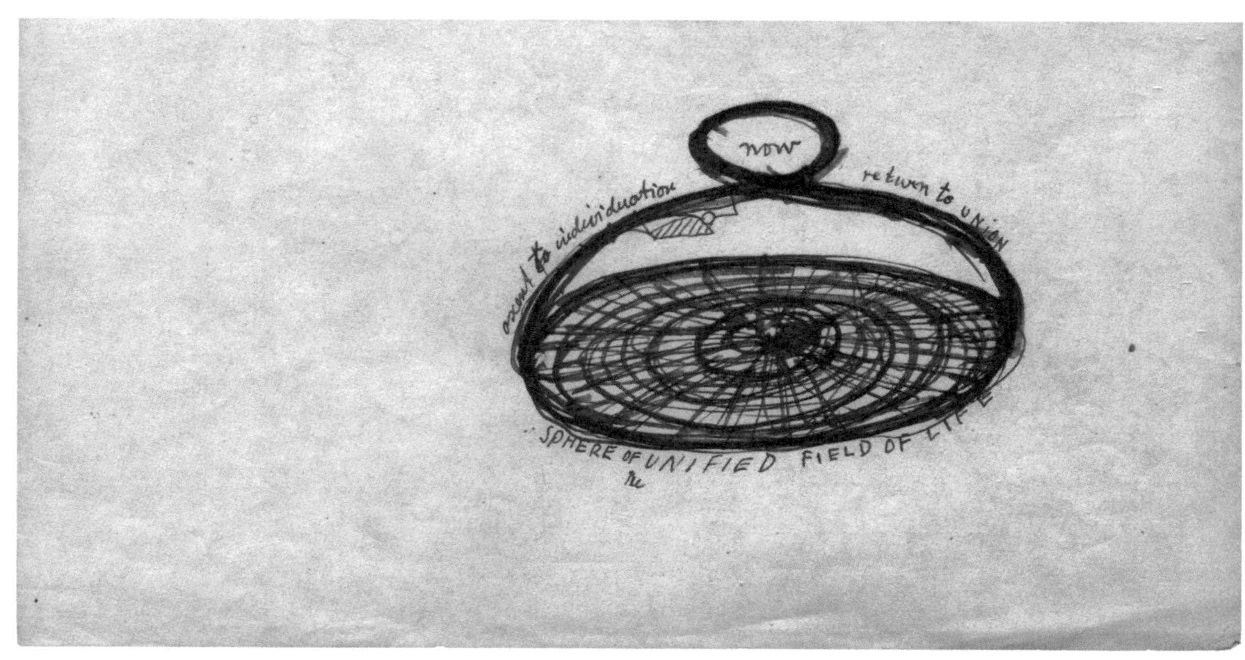

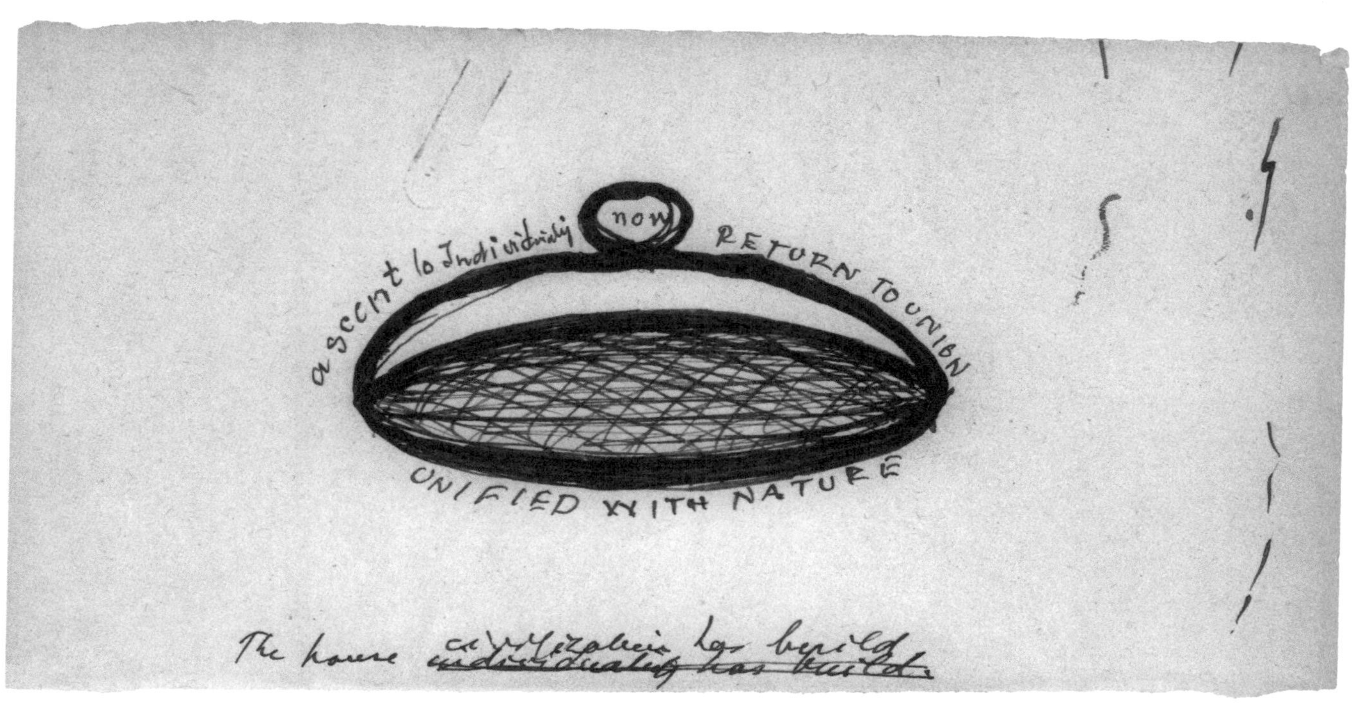

Frederick Kiesler, Part 1, Chapter 9, "The Split in the Unity of Vision and Fact," final page of preliminary draft with drawing and annotations (TS, pencil [colored], ink) ÖFLKS, TXT_6738/0_N3

fig. B.07c

Frederick Kiesler, Conceptual drawing (untitled) (ink) ÖFLKS, SFP_6665/0_N2

1

Above: Leo Frobenius, *Kulturgeschichte Afrikas: Prolegomena zu einer historischen Gestaltlehre* (Zürich: Phaidon Verlag, 1933), 226, fig. 175. ÖFLKS, SCL_6/0

Below: Maynard Owen Williams, "Bali and Points East: Crowded, Happy Isles of the Flores Sea Blend Rice Terraces, Dance Festivals, and Amazing Music in Their Pattern of Living," *National Geographic Magazine* LXXV, no. 3, March 1939, 313–352, photo Williams.

2

Buckminster Fuller, Model for a "Dymaxion House" (1927) from *Art in Our Time: An exhibition to celebrate the tenth anniversary of the Museum of Modern Art and the opening of its new building, held at the time of the New York World's Fair* (New York: Museum of Modern Art, 1939), 307.

2a

Chart by Frederick Kiesler with underlying image from Leo Frobenius and Douglas C. Fox, *Prehistoric Rock Pictures in Europe and Africa From Material in the Archives of the Research Institute for the Morphology of Civilization, Frankfort-on-Main* (New York: Museum of Modern Art, 1937), 47. ÖFLKS, TXT_6740/0_N4

3

Above, from left: Grave of the Longkiput, North Borneo; Rajah Dinda's family sepulchre, Borneo; grave of a Zulu chief, South Africa. *Meyers Großes Konversations-Lexikon*, 6th ed., vol. 19, "Totenbestattungen bei den Naturvölkern" (Leipzig and Vienna: Bibliographisches Institut, 1908), fig. 1; fig. 10; fig. 5. ÖFLKS, SCL_8/0

Below: Western Xia mausoleums, Ningxia, China. Hans Koester, "Four Thousand Hours Over China," *National Geographic Magazine* LXXIII, no. 5, May 1938, 571–614, 591.

4

Kanioka village street (above) and burial hut (below), Kasai-Occidental, Congo. Frobenius, *Kulturgeschichte Afrikas*, 607, 624, pl. 143. 160. ÖFLKS, SCL_9/0

5

Gol Gumbaz, mausoleum of Mohammad Adil Shah, Bijapur. Otto Höver, *Indische Kunst* (Breslau: Ferdinand Hirt, 1923), 87. ÖFLKS, SCL_10/0

6

Pantheon, Rome. Ferdinand Noack, *Die Baukunst des Altertums* (Berlin: Fischer & Franke, 1910), pl. 168. ÖFLKS, SCL_11/0

7

Left: Joseph Ferdinand Cheval, Palais Idéal Facteur Cheval, Hauterives. André Breton, "Le Message Automatique," *Minotaure*, no. 3-4 (1933): 54–65. ÖFLKS, SCL_12/0

Right: Detail of Cheval's palace. "Hatter's Castle," *The Architects' Journal* 95, no. 2457 (Feb 26, 1942): 153–156.

8

Above, left: Orangutan nest. *Meyers Großes Konversations-Lexikon*, 6th ed., vol. 19, "Tierwohnungen," 547–548 (Leipzig and Vienna: Bibliographisches Institut, 1908), fig. 2. ÖFLKS, SCL_13/0

10

Above, right: Construction of round hut, North Queensland. Hermann Klaatsch, *Der Werdegang der Menschheit und die Entstehung der Kultur* (Berlin: Deutsches Verlagshaus Bong & Co), 195, fig. 166. ÖFLKS, SCL_13/0

Below, left and right: H. Ian Hogbin, "Coconuts and Coral Islands," *National Geographic Magazine* LXV, no. 3, March 1934, 265–298.

9

Left: (above) Klaatsch, *Der Werdegang der Menschheit*, p. 71, pl. 10; (below) E. W. Brandes, "Into Primeval Papua by Seaplane: Seeking Disease-Resisting Sugar Cane, Scientists Find Neolithic Man in Unmapped Nooks of Sorcery and Cannibalism," *National Geographic Magazine* LVI, no. 3, September 1929, 253–332. ÖFLKS, SCL_14/0

Right: Brandes, "Into Primeval Papua by Seaplane," 253–332.

11

Clockwise from above left: Royal Bengal tiger. *Wir Tiere...: Erlebnisse und Begebenheiten aus der Welt der Tiere*, ed. Lola Kreutzberg (Berlin: Neufeld & Henius Verlag, 1930), 236, photo Cami Stone; "Medicine Man made by the Oruncha, with the Oruncha Marilla, or Design of the Oruncha," in Walter Baldwin Spencer and Francis James Gillen, *The Arunta: A Study of a Stone Age People*, Vol. 2 (New York: Humanities Press, 1927), fig. 118; "A nose pendant gratifies parental pride," in Hogbin, "Coconuts and Coral Islands," 265–298; Richard Parkinson, *Dreissig Jahre in der Südsee: Land und Leute, Sitten und Gebräuche im Bismarckarchipel und auf den deutschen Salomoinseln* (Stuttgart: Strecker & Schröder, 1907), 533. ÖFLKS, SCL_15/0

13

Frederick Kiesler, *The Universe as Architecture*, drawing (pencil). ÖFLKS, SCL_17/0

12a

Brandes, "Into Primeval Papua by Seaplane," *National Geographic Magazine*, LVI: 3. 264 (Photography by J. Jeswiet) ÖFLKS, CLP_6519/0

Below: "Succumbing to hypnotic ecstasy, men are 'transformed' into monkeys." From Maynard Owen Williams, "Bali and Points East: Crowded, Happy Isles of the Flores Sea Blend Rice Terraces, Dance Festivals, and Amazing Music in Their Pattern of Living," *National Geographic Magazine* LXXV, no. 3 (March 1939): 313-352. (Photography by author) ÖFLKS, SCL_17/0

13a, b

Left: "Redwood families—parents, older children, and infants—grow happily here." From J. R. Hildebrand, "California's Coastal Redwood Realm," *National Geographic Magazine* LXXV, no. 2 (February 1939): 133-184. (Photography by Gabriel Moulin.) ÖFLKS, SCL_17/0

Right: "Huge semicircular colonnades of marble enclose St. Peter's piazza." From W. Coleman Nevils, "The Smallest State in the World," *National Geographic Magazine* LXXV, no. 3 (March 1939): 377-412. (Photography by Philip D. Gendreau.)

13c

Above: "A Golfer's nightmare is the 'ant hill' course in Central Africa." From W. M. Mann, "Stalking Ants, Savage and Civilized," *National Geographic Magazine* LXVI, no. 2 (August 1934): 171-192. (Photography from Tropical Press.) ÖFLKS, SCL_19/0

Below: "Students of Chinese art will recognize these jagged peaks, so common in oriental landscape paintings." From Hans Koester, "Four Thousand Hours Over China," *National Geographic Magazine* LXXIII, no. 5 (May 1938): 571-614. (Photography by author.)

13d

Below: "Natives call this curious rock formation 'many heads'; the tallest would tower above the Empire State Building." From Charles P. Mountford, "Earth's Most Primitive People: A Journey with the Aborigines of Central Australia," *National Geographic Magazine* LXXXIX, no. 1 (January 1946): 89-112. (Photography by author.) ÖFLKS, SCL_20/0

Middle: "Beehive villages are common in the Alep (Aleppo) Plain." From F. A. Schaeffer, "A New Alphabet of the Ancients Is Unearthed," *National Geographic Magazine* LVIII, no. 4 (October 1930): 477-516. (Photography by Maynard Owen Williams.)

Above: "Above the Many-domed City of Cholula rises a huge pyramid that looks like a natural hill." From Luis Marden, "On the Cortés Trail," *National Geographic Magazine* LXXVIII, no. 3 (September 1940): 355-375. (Photography by author.) ÖFLKS, CLP_6517/0

13e

"Plan of the Tihuanacu calendar" and "A condor head". From Arthur Posnansky, *Tihuanacu: The Cradle of American Man*, trans. James F. Shearer (New York: J. J. Augustin, 1945), I-II:76, fig. 5-6. ÖFLKS, SCL_21/0

Animal Architecture and the origin of
man's ability to
~~construct.~~
build.

PART II
ANIMAL ARCHITECTURE AND MAN'S ABILITY TO BUILD[1]

INTRODUCTION
INSTINCT, MEMORY, AND THE DRIVE FOR INVENTION

The world of pre-logical man was free of the stigma of Art and Architecture.[2] Both, as we understand them today, came very much later. The truly primitive lived in unity with nature. His needs derived from her and as she supplied everything, there was no need for inventions.

Although the evolution toward Art and Architecture is difficult to trace, it is very alluring, because it most likely holds the clue to the enigma of: what is our aim in relationship to nature and man?[3] In which directions are we to pursue our efforts in technology and in the art? In sum where do we of the twentieth century go from here?

According to facts formulated by ethnographers and anthropologists, man's ability to construct is closely related to his upright stance and especially to the development of the thumb of his hand.[4]* The ability to grip and hold gave him the manual dexterity necessary for "manufacturing" tools, and once in possession of tools, to create with them more powerful instruments and finally machines.[5]

* we shall find later that this is a false assumption of "facts."[6]

Of course, there are deeper reasons for his "technical attempts"; they are of a psychological nature, but we must always, when considering early man, avoid "splitting" these feelings in our accustomed manner[7] when we try to look into "the inner sanctum" of reasons.

Nevertheless, it is fair to assume that his primary impulse was to protect himself against attack and, with the help of stones and branches, "more easily" to beat off his enemies.[8]

Wundt arrived at a good formulation of the process which led prehistoric man to his ability to build. He says:[9]

Although those instinctual actions cannot be explained either as deliberation or as individual association the hypothesis, to see in them mere reflex-motions, is equally untenable. That the silkmoth secretes silk, the spider its spinning material, the bee wax, this indeed is physically as necessary as the emission[10] of any other secretion. But that these matters are worked up, after their secretion, to such artful creations, how can that be explained by physical organization alone?

That the hexagonal cell of the bee,[11] the intricate cobweb of the spider, the nest of the bird and the cocoon of the caterpillar were in their consciousness from the beginning and that now each of the animals follows a necessary compulsion when it realizes its phantasy into reality, is an assumption in total opposition to what we learn when analyzing human apperception. Conceptions not originated in personal life experiences cannot be proven in man (man is not born with ideas; he must develop and acquire them by experience). The one born deaf does not know of sounds, the blind-born knows no colors.

It is now clear that the instinctive ability of the pianist to play automatically[12] or of man in general to build and to wear clothing has a dual root; a physiological as well as a psychological one.[13] Physiologically: arbitrary reflex motions of the body are, in time, mechanized and standardized through our nervous system. Psychologically: all animals, and especially man, living collectively, invariably learns by imitating.[14]

1 Alternative title (see frontispiece): **PART II: Animal Architecture and the origins of man's ability to ~~construct.~~ build.** TXT_6705/0_N1

2 **The world of pre-logic man was without the ornamentation of Art and Architecture** TXT_6792/0_N1

3 **nature, society, and man?** TXT_6792/0_N1

4 **man's ability to construct ~~to build~~ is closely related to the upright position of his body and particularly to the ~~distinct~~ development of the thumb of his hand** TXT_6792/0_N1

5 **The ability to grip and hold gave him the dexterity of the hand necessary for "manufacturing" tools, and once in possession of tools to create further with tools.** TXT_6792/0_N1

6 **a false assumption based on "facts."** [handwritten annotation] TXT 6705/0_N2 There is no later elaboration on these "facts" in the text of *Magic Architecture*. However, Klaatsch's study on the development of humankind contains an extensive discussion of the development of the thumb and the loss of the "prehensile" or "opposable toe" during the evolution of primates and early humans. See Klaatsch, *Der Werdegang der Menschheit* (1922), 40-49, 84-88. Klaatsch, *The Evolution and Progress of Mankind* (1923), 63-71, 100-102. For Kiesler's drawings of the hands of primates and humans as "building tools," see Addenda: Charts (fig. c.06b). SFP_6664/0_N2

7 **in the manner we are accustomed ~~to think by our own mentality~~.** TXT_6792/0_N2

8 **~~attackers~~** TXT_6792/0_N2

9 **Können derartige Instinkthandlungen** [Those instinctual actions can] **Wundt page 481 (low)** / **bis** [to] **482 (in der Mitte)** [in the middle] / **and 482 (unter)** [below] **bis 483 (oben)** [above]... **Gewohnheiten sein!** [are habits!] / **and** / **page 487 (oben) Es ist nach** [It is after] ... / **bis** / **487 (oben) Nachahmungstriebes** [of the drive for imitation]. TXT_6792/0_N2 These instructions for transcription refer to passages from Wilhelm Wundt, *Vorlesungen über die Menschen- und Thierseele*, 5th rev. ed. (Hamburg; Leipzig: Leopold Voss, 1911). TXT_6730/0 Several passages in these transcriptions are crossed out and only a few sections are translated in the text of *Magic Architecture*. Certain German words are omitted in the Kieslers' translation. While there was a published English translation of Wundt's lectures, it is not used or mentioned among Kiesler's drafts. Wundt, *Lectures in Human and Animal Psychology*, translated from the second German edition by J. E. Creighton and E. B. Titschener (New York: Macmillan, 1912). The first edition of this English translation was published in 1896 and based on the second edition of Wundt's *Vorlesungen* (Hamburg: Voss, 1892). Since the text of Wundt's lectures was considerably expanded and revised before the fifth German edition of 1911 (used by Kiesler), some sentences in the published English translation are entirely different or missing from the Kieslers' translation above. Cf. Wundt, *Lectures* (1912), 392-393, 397-398.

10 **elimination** TXT_5570/0_N55 **elimination** [typed over] **~~secretion~~** TXT_6853/0_N4 to avoid repetition. This is obviously an erroneous word choice for the German *Absonderung* in Wundt's original text, meaning emission or discharge.

11 **~~The assumption~~ That the hexagonal cell of the bee** TXT_6853/0_N4

12 The term "automatically" does not exist in any edition of Wundt's lectures. For Kiesler's gratuitous use of the term, see Sources, Disciplines, and Objects, pp. 27-28 (fig. A.23).

13 **~~The functional necessity develops in the nervous system a will to objectivate that instinctual drive.~~** TXT_6853/0_N5

14 **invariably acquire capacities by learning through imitation.** TXT_6853/0_N5

CHAPTER 1
MAN'S HOUSE IS ANIMAL-ARCHITECTURE.

What is valid for the nest-building of animals is also valid for man.[15] The talent for building is not the exclusive privilege of man; it seems to be nothing else but the extended gesture of defense of the animal-psyche: protection against attack,[16] preservation of food, shielding the weakened sick.[17]

This death-consciousness of animals affects the mechanism of the entire body,[18] not only the hands; the nervous system is constantly on the alert.[19] The individual improvises emergency solutions and robs nature[20] of foliage, twigs, bark, stones, etc. to work them into defense-masks (nests, houses). It is irrelevant if, for this purpose, he has gripping hands or an upright position of the body–he will use the next best part of it[21] to achieve his building if it is of paramount necessity for his survival. He is especially concerned to protect the brood that is still blind, inexperienced, and physically weaker than the parents.[22]

Whether the young are born from eggs or born directly as miniature-animals, like man, there is no major difference:[23] house-building is nothing else but nest-building. Its function is physical protection.[24] For children it is a compulsion, for parents a convenience, and for old people and the sick a necessity.[25] Man's house-building is nothing else but Animal-Architecture.[26]

Building is not an invention of man, but Architecture[27] is. As a matter of fact, animals build,[28] and in many cases what they build is more durable, more economical, more perfect, and genuine in construction-methods, more practical; in short more functional.[29]

* * *

Tools are extensions of the body;[30] as extension of the hand, they further its reach, dexterity, and power to provide physical protection. Nothing really apart from man, tools are his outer self.[31]

* * *

The ability to construct and build for physical protection is a primary function of man and of all animals.

* * *

The creation of any type of physical protection is "animal" function.

* * *

The building of shelter is animal-function in man.[32]

* * *

Architecture starts at a point beyond this animal function, and that is why animals never have Architecture, but they do build perfect shelters.

* * *

The most extraordinary animal shelter is the Termitary of the termites. The most extraordinary animal engineering is the beaver's dam.

CHAPTER 2[33]
THE BUILDING INSTINCT OF ANIMALS: THE TERMITARY OF THE TERMITES

No better illustration of the house as a shield for physical protection can be found than in the homes of the termites.[34] These insect homes, called Termitaries, are relatively so gigantic in dimensions and weight that human beings have nothing to compare with them.[35]

There is probably no insect in our land which has so many natural enemies. One finds the true ant, not the termite, walking round boldly in the daylight, for only reptiles, such as frogs and lizards, which have no sense of taste, try to eat them. Their defense consists of an acid which is secreted for the purpose, and

15 Preliminary MS draft written by Kiesler originally in German (translation in main text): **Was für den Nest-bau der Tiere gilt, gilt auch für den Menschen** TXT_6705/0_N4recto

16 **protection against pain, hunger, and death** TXT_5877/0_N57 **against attack ~~and death~~** TXT_6739/0_N1

17 **Dieses Talent zu bauen ist nicht ein einzigartiges Vorrecht des Menschen; es scheint nicht anders zu sein als ~~eine automatisch gewordene~~ eine erweiterte ~~Schu~~ Abwehrbewegung ~~des Körpers~~ der Tierpsyche - ~~die Angst für~~ zu sein, Schutz vor Schmerz, ~~Lahmlegung~~ Hunger und Tod ~~erfindet~~ den Lebensbedingungen abzuzwingen.** TXT_6705/0_N4recto [This talent for building is not an exclusive prerogative of humans; it seems to be nothing else but ~~an automatically acquired~~ the extended ~~protection~~ movement of defense ~~of the body~~ of the animal-psyche: ~~the anxiety~~ for protection against pain, ~~paralysis~~, hunger, and death, ~~contrives~~ forced by living conditions.] On the automatism of animal building, see Sources, Documents, and Objects, pp. 27, 87.

18 **one's own body** TXT_6739/0_N1

19 **Dieses Todesbewußtsein der Tiere berührt ~~sich~~ die Mechanik des eigenen Körpers (nicht nur die Hände!): totes Material der Natur zu stehlen (wie Äste trockenes Laub, Äste, Sandkörner u.s.f.) und sie zu Schutz-masken (Nester, Häuser) zu verarbeiten;** [This death consciousness of animals affects the mechanics of one's own body (not only the hands!); to steal dead material from nature (like dry foliage, branches, sand grains, etc.) and process them into protective masks (nests, houses);] TXT_6705/0_N4recto; TXT_6730/0_Bverso

20 **Impelling ~~driving~~ the individual being to rob nature of her dead materials** TXT_6739/0_N1

21 **of his physique;** TXT_6739/0_N3

22 **ganz besonders zum Schutze der Brut, die noch blind, unerfahren und physisch schwächer ist, als die Eltern und deshalb den Feinden buchstäblich ausgeliefert ~~sind~~ ist.** [particularly for the protection of the brood, which is still blind, inexperienced, and physically weaker, than the parents and therefore are literally at the mercy of enemies.] TXT_6705/0_N4recto; TXT_6730/0_Bverso **~~hence~~ if this were not done they would literally be handed over to ~~the~~ death at the hands of the enemy. ~~if not protected~~.** TXT_6739/0_N1

23 **~~principal~~ difference** TXT_6739/0_N1

24 **ob nun die Kücken** [sic] **aus Eiern zu Tieren werden, oder direct** [sic] **als Miniaturtiere auf die Welt kommen wie die Menschen–das macht keinen prinzipiellen Unterschied: der Hausbau ist nichts als ein Nestbau. Seine Function** [sic] **ist ~~nichts anderes als~~ physischer Schutz ~~für jung oder alt~~.** [Whether now the chicks transform from eggs to animals, or come to the world directly as miniature animals, this makes no difference in principle: house-building is nothing but nest-building. Its function is ~~nothing else than~~ physical protection ~~for young or old~~.] TXT_6705/0_N4verso; TXT_6730/0_Bverso

25 **Für Kinder zwangsweise, für die Eltern bequemer Weise und für Greise wie kranke notwendigerweise. Der Hausbau des Menschen ist nichts anderes als Tierarchitektur.** [For children, in terms of compulsion; for parents, in terms of comfort; and for the elderly as well as the sick, in terms of necessity. House-building by humans is nothing else than animal architecture.] TXT_6705/0_N4verso; TXT_6730/0_Bverso

26 **animal architecture.** TXT_6739/0_N1

27 **architecture** TXT_6739/0_N2

28 **animals built better** TXT_6739/0_N2

29 **at each L sign–space down and one row of asterisks to give list of aphorisms Relief.** [handwritten instruction for typing to Stefi Kiesler, signaling paragraph sectioning from this point onwards] TXT_6739/0_N2

30 For an alternative understanding of the tool as bodily extension and instrument of attack (instead of protection), see Kiesler's comparison of the "boomerang" and "the tongue of the chameleon" following his reading of a passage from Alexander A. Goldenweiser, *Early Civilization: An Introduction to Anthropology* (New York: Knopf, 1922), included in Addenda: Charts, fig. C.08. TXT_6819/0

31 **~~skin~~** TXT_6739/0_N2

32 **~~and animals~~** TXT_6739/0_N2

33 Alternative chapter numbering and titles: **BUILDING INSTINCT AND TECHNIQUE The Termitary of the Termites** TXT_6740_N2 **Part II. CHAPTER ~~ONE~~TWO. The building instinct ~~and technique~~ of animals. The Termitary of the Termites** TXT_6704/0_N1

34 **The house as a shield for physical protection is no better illustrated than by the home ~~tower which~~ an insect, the ant "Termite," builds and which is called the Termitary. It is ~~more than a house and more than~~ so gigantic in dimensions** TXT_6794/0_N1

35 In his handwritten draft of this chapter, Kiesler includes the following instruction for quotation: **Quote from page 81 "the entomologist who made the acquaintance of the termite for the first time, would be justified in thinking it to be an immigrant from a different planet. To mention but one thing only–the wings ... continue till page 88 ... in great numbers."** TXT_6794/0_N2 verso This is Kiesler's instruction for the first in a long series of extensive quotations from Eugène N. Marais, *The Soul of the White Ant*, with a biographical note by his son, trans. Winifred De Kok (New York: Dodd, Mead, & Co., 1937). These excerpts are transcribed. TXT_6812/0 Only two paragraphs from these pages marked by Kiesler are included in the assembled text, which shows no quotation marks at the beginning of the excerpt, yet does so at its end. TXT_5877/0_N060

also an indigestible outer covering. So effective are apparently these methods of defense that we find certain beetles taking on the form of large black ants so successfully that most animals are deceived by them. The unfortunate termite, on the other hand, is eaten greedily by all other animals. It is a remarkable lesson in nature study to watch the flight of the termite in uninhabited parts of Central Africa. Within a few minutes the surface of the earth is seething with living creatures coming to the feast. Out of the earth crawl frogs, toads, snakes, lizards, and other reptiles. From where they receive the news I cannot tell. Even the tortoise appears. Other insects, crickets, beetles, centipedes, spiders, scorpions swarm in the grass. In the water, just below the surface, one sees hundreds of fish and turtles. Out of the bushes slink jackals, cats, meerkats,[36] apes, and monkeys. There is a temporary truce, except as regards the unfortunate flying termites. They appear to be going to fly merely to die. One begins to understand why nature produces them in such millions, notwithstanding the fact that each pair may be the origin of millions more. Every pair is necessary, because the slaughter is immense. One realizes now why the royal pair are in such a tremendous hurry after they have flown and discarded their wings. The only method of defense the flying termites make use of is flight after dusk. In this way they escape at least the birds which fly by day. But even this may not always happen. Sometimes the flight begins too early and in the twilight hundreds of hawks gather. The night hawks, owls and other night birds continue the feast into the darkest hours of the night.

One realizes that in this case there has been a displacement of the natural means of defense. What the individual queen and king have lost as regards natural means of defense is compensated for by the defenses of the composite animal, the termitary. As soon as the community is formed, the termites never again appear in the daylight, except when injury necessitates this, and even then not in great numbers.

The building material and methods employed are of such functional security that by comparison our modern manufacturing products are mere gambler's dreams. Yet this work is achieved without the builders possessing the benefits of an upright position of the body, nor hands with free, developed thumbs, nor for that matter any hands at all.[37]

One may imagine Nature addressing the queen thus, after her short flight:

"Beloved, you are going to suffer a great loss. Instead of living in this glowing sunlight, you are to spend your days in absolute darkness. Instead of the citizenship of the wide veld, instead of the freedom of the air, of mountains, trees, and plains, you are to spend your days as a prisoner in a narrow vault, in whose confines you will be unable to make the least movement. The annual return of the love season, the search for your beloved and the happy finding, the building of your home and all the happiness bound up in this periodical stirring of the soul, of all this you are to be deprived. But in place of all this, you yourself will become a far more important and wonderful being. Although you will apparently be an immobile shapeless mass buried in a living grave, you will actually be a sensitive mainspring. You will become the feeling, the thinking, the seeing of a life a thousand times greater and more important than you could ever have become. Above all, I will give you protection. The million dangers, the million enemies which threatened your life on every hand, will in your new life fling themselves in vain against your armour."

It was this need for protection which caused the development of the termitary. As individuals the queen and her subjects are the most threatened of all insects. As individuals, in an unprotected

36 **meercats** TXT_6740/0_N2 Marais, *The Soul of the White Ant*, 88: "meercats"

37 [Animals] **"build without hands" in no upright position and thumb.** [handwritten annotation in the margin of the TS for chapter 1 of Part 1] TXT_6739/0_N2 Cf. John George Wood, *Homes without Hands: Being a Description of the Habitation of Animals Classed According to the Principles of Construction* (New York: Harper, 1866). For transcribed excerpts: TXT_6811/0 See also Addenda: Transcriptions and Translations, pp. 363. Kiesler then indicates: **Continue quote: page 91: "One may imagine nature addressing the queen thus, after her short flight: "Beloved, you … till page: 93 … the race is safe, rejoicing inexterminable."** [instructions for the transcription and quotation from Marais, *The Soul of the White Ant*, 91–93] TXT_6794/0_N2verso

environment, the race would never have survived. As a composite animal, the termitary is very nearly perfectly protected. External wounds, destructive attacks which destroy the whole visible form of the termitary, do not touch its real life which goes on as usual as though nothing untoward has happened. The wounds are merely repaired. The queen herself, as brain of the organism, is as well protected as the human brain in its skull. There are very few enemies which ever prove a real danger to the queen. One of the largest is the anteater; some of the most insidious are groups of beetles, which at times completely devastate a weakened termitary. This latter instance is analogous in every respect to the attack on the human body by pathological organisms. The termitary becomes diseased and dies.

The termites achieve a structure of such compact material that we can compare it only to the hard resistance of our massive concrete.[38] No animal, no weather can destroy it. It offers complete protection.[39] The termites incarcerate themselves in the termitary and abandon the light and warmth of the sun so indispensable for the life of any other animal for the sake of a complete enclosure.[40]

All of the termites of a termitary are born in it[41] and most of them die in it without ever having seen the light of day.

Only those females and males[42] who have wings leave the building on a short nuptial flight. They are the potential queen-mothers and future kings, and later the designers of a new termitary. Their flight may take them only a few yards or even less.

There is only a brief time left after the flight for the bridal pair to disappear from the surface of the earth. They must, it is the only moment when their enemies have a chance to see them unprotected (outside the bastion of the termitary)[43] and their enemies numbered by the thousands, are waiting ferociously for the kill.

As soon as the female settles down, it at once discards its wings, waits for the male, and, united with him, immediately starts to dig[44] into the ground. Thus is laid the foundation for a new termitary. As nest, home, and town it will take care of their millions of children.[45]

Let us listen to an ardent observer of the life of the termites, and we shall find the reason for their extraordinary building activities, methods, and results:[46]

In the termite we find three apparently different insects—the queens, the workers, and the soldiers, being produced from one father and mother who are completely different from two of their offspring. If one did not actually know the contrary one would believe the inmates of the termitary to be completely different insects.[47]

With the physical differences go special hereditary memories of instinct. The soldier is armed with the first hypodermic syringe made by nature, which she eventually perfected in the poison fangs of the adder. In his polished head the termite soldier carries a little flask of poison and on his forehead a needle-like tube through which the sticky fluid is squirted. He uses his weapon only against threatening enemies or strangers. The worker has strong, well-made jaws and a glue-producing gland which he uses to construct most complicated building operations. As soon as he has reached adult stature he begins to make gardens, care for and feed the king and queen, tend the hatching eggs, carry food and partially digest it for the benefit of the whole republic. Both these insects are totally blind, neither of them possesses eyes or other organs of sense; nevertheless they are aware of the presence or absence of light through twenty-four inches of compact earth.[48] pl. 14

Let us look at the worker through a magnifying glass. We see them appear one by one from the dark depths, each carrying a tiny grain of earth. Without the least thought, each worker rolls the pebble round and round in its jaws. It covers it with a sticky mucilage, sets it in position in the breach, and vanishes again

38 a structure ~~building~~ of such ~~dense~~ compact material that we can only compare it to the hard resistance of our massive concrete. TXT_6794/0_N1 On the comparison between the building material of the termites and concrete, cf. references on "Beton-form" and "cement" in Wilhelm Bölsche, *Der Termitenstaat: Schilderung eines geheimnisvollen Volkes* [The Termite Colony: Description of a Mysterious People] (Stuttgart: Kosmos, Gesellschaft der Naturfreunde: Franckh'sche Verlagshandlung, 1931), 65. Included among Kiesler's transcriptions from Bölsche's book TXT_6811/0_N3 On Bölsche and Marais, see Sources, Disciplines, and Objects, pp. 25, 87.

39 ~~But that is not all.~~ For greater security ~~they omit a priori all windows and doors.~~ TXT_6794/0_N1

40 for the sake of complete ~~physical~~ enclosure ~~and uninterrupted material protection.~~ TXT_6794/0_N1

41 born ~~in the building and live~~ TXT_6794/0_N1

42 (and ~~some~~ males) TXT_6794/0_N2

43 ~~and kill them~~ TXT_6794/0_N2

44 dig ~~themselves~~ into the ground ~~and thus start immediately the building~~ of a new termitary. TXT_6794/0_N2

45 ~~many hundred thousand children~~ as a nest, home, and town. TXT_6794/0_N2-

46 An earlier TS draft of this section includes a handwritten annotation from Stefi to Kiesler asking him to clarify the length of the quotation from Marais and his marking of previously transcribed excerpts for inclusion in the final text: it starts with C and continues to end? (why numbered C and D?) [deleted] TXT_6740/0_N5 Kiesler himself indicates: Continue quote from page: 124 "In the termite we find three .... Till page: 125 ... four inches of compact earth." TXT_6794/0_N2 verso Before this section, Kiesler also asks for a different passage to be transcribed: continue quote from page 117 "With the feeding and preparation ... till page: 118 ... twelve inches of opaque earth." This last passage is transcribed but ultimately struck out. TXT_6740/0_N6.

47 The margin of an earlier MS contains a struck-through note in Kiesler's hand: ~~How do they see in the dark, having no eyes particularly filled for such purpose at all? How do they feed and drink without ever coming outside?~~ TXT_6794/0_N2 verso

48 Continue quote: page 131: "Let us look at the worker ... till page: 133 (with cuts ... more acute than our own senses." TXT_6794/0_N3

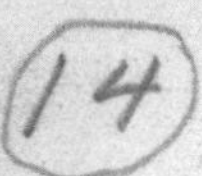

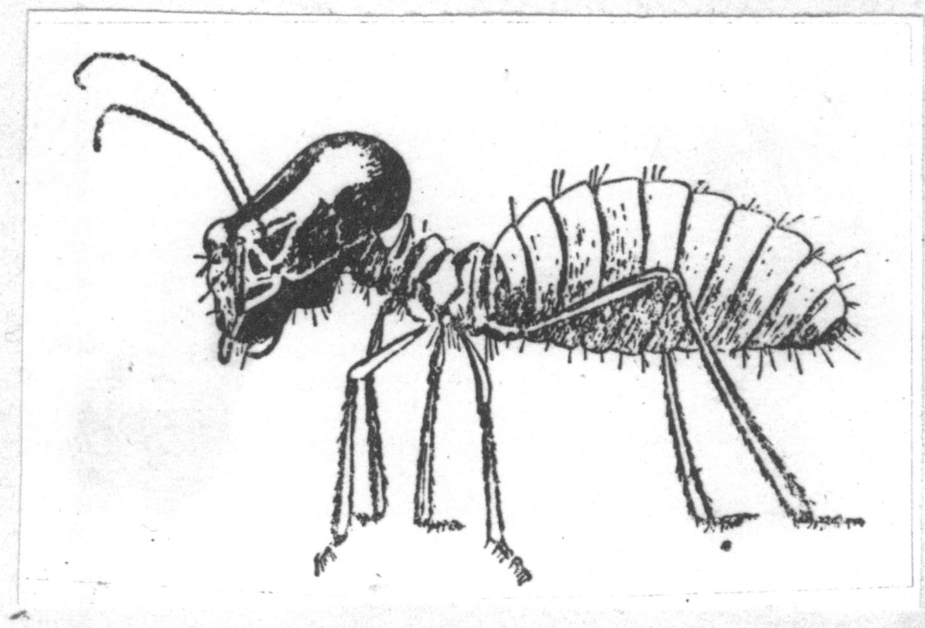

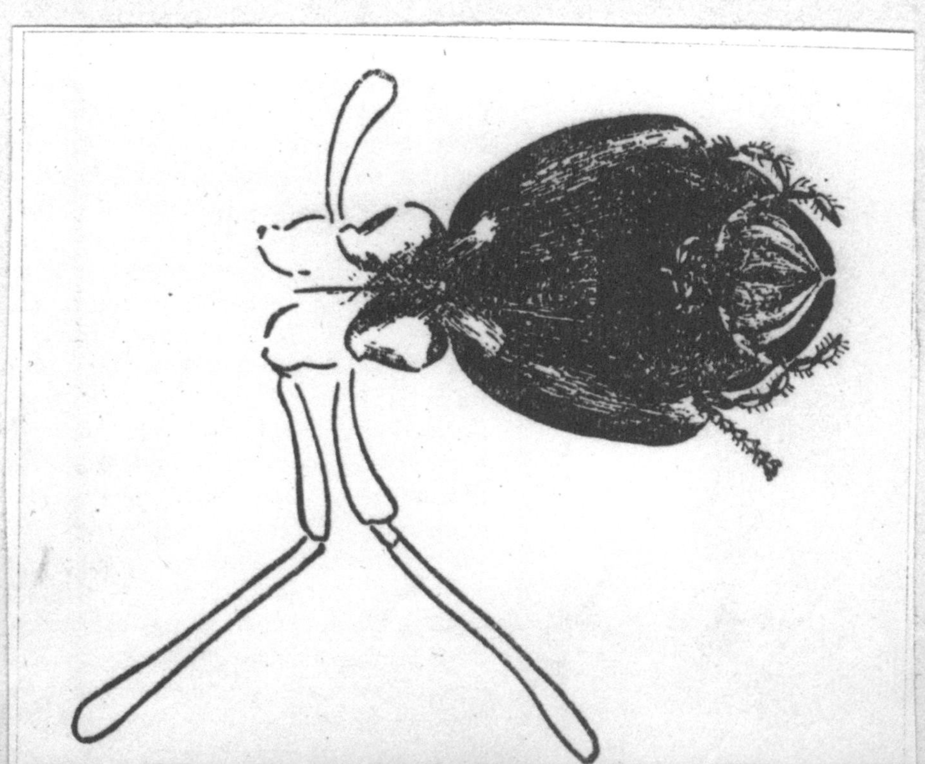

(14).

The Termite-parents give birth to three different types of children. Each has specific functions in creating and maintaining the life and the building of the community.
This is the builder. He is water-carrier, mason, gardener, nurse and feeder. He is blind, has no organs of hearing, sexless.
(Below): Head seen from below, showing mouth-part. These are the tools for building the greatest concrete-like structures in the animal world.

into the depths. No reasonable person can imagine for one moment that every small worker is conscious of the purpose of its work, that it carries in its mind the plan, or even part of the plan of the building operations. The tower breach may be a million times larger than the termite itself. The workers attack the repairs from every side, and are totally blind. We can convince ourselves that the termites at one side of the breach never come in contact with those on the other side. They may fetch their materials from different parts of the nest. If we have any doubt of this we can easily dispel it. Take a steel plate a few feet wider and higher than the termitary. Drive it right through the centre of the breach you have made, in such a way that you divide both the wound and the termitary into two separate parts. One section of the community can never be in touch with the other, and one of the sections will be separated from the queen's cell. The builders on one side of the breach know nothing of those on the other side. In spite of this the termites build a similar arch or tower on each side of the plate, the two halves match perfectly after the dividing cut has been repaired. We cannot escape the ultimate conclusion that somewhere there exists a preconceived plan which the termites merely execute. Where is the soul, the psyche, in which this preconception exists? That is the problem which must be solved.

Where does each worker obtain his part of the general design? We can drive in the steel plate and then make a breach on either side and still the termites build identical structures on each side. It cannot be an inherited tendency, for the termites do not always build the same kind of arch or other structure. We can find a dozen different widths of arch near the surface of a large termitary. These arches are one of the amazing features of the termites' building powers. It cannot be due to the instinctive knowledge of the individual termite. If the termite always built one kind of arch, we might perhaps come to the conclusion that it worked according to instinctive or inherited knowledge. Even then a doubt would exist. We are inclined to imagine the termites thinking and reasoning in our own way. Yet we know that they possess perceptive powers a million times more acute than our own senses.[49]

How can one compare this soul with that of a human being? When one sees a tiny worker hastily placing a single grain of sand on the wall of a building which eventually will become a massive tower twelve or fifteen feet high, millions upon millions of times larger than itself, can one assume for one moment that the worker knows, in the human sense, what the final result of its work is going to be? If this were so its intelligence would be that of a god, compared with our own. His work is naturally due to instinct, as Dr. Bugnion says, but it is not the instinct of the worker. It is the instinct and design of a separate soul situated outside the individual termite.

If we carry our recent experiment a little further, new light begins to trickle through on our problem.

While the termites are carrying on their work of restoration on either side of the steel plate, dig a furrow enabling you to reach the queen's cell, disturbing the nest as little as possible. Expose the queen and destroy her. Immediately the whole community ceases work on either side of the plate. We can separate the termites from the queen for months by means of this plate, yet in spite of that they continue working systematically while she is alive in her cell; destroy or remove her, however, and the activity is at an end.[50]

It was during this journey that I came to a real appreciation of the astounding genius for building which the termites possess. Everyone who is interested in the termite will have read and probably seen photographs of the enormous termitaries which are found in tropical parts of Africa. In the Lowveld of Zoutpansberg I found some giants, nor were these the

49 Continue quote page 134: "How can one compare this soul ... till page 135 (top) ... and their activity is their end." Kiesler's instructions to Stefi for quotation from Marais TXT_6794/0_N3

50 continue quote page 160 (middle) "It was during his journey ... till page: 161 ... to which civilized man is prone." Kiesler's instructions to Stefi for quotation from Marais. TXT_6794/0_N3

exceptions by any means. In some parts of the Limpopo valley these gigantic Termitaries are a very usual feature of the landscape. An engineer friend of mine, Norman Hugel, carefully measured and calculated the weight of earth making up one colossus, and found that it consisted of eleven thousand seven hundred and fifty tons of earth. This termitary belonged to a small Eutermes. Just think of it, eleven thousand seven hundred tons which had been piled up grain by grain, for Eutermes never uses mud for building purposes. They use only microscopic grains of sand; every one is rubbed clean and polished before being coated in a sticky cement; then every tiny stone is carefully placed in the right place. So grain by grain, the termites heaped up a structure weighing eleven thousand seven hundred tons. One would imagine it to take thousands of years to accomplish, but it was hopeless to try to estimate the period of time. There is no doubt that it was a matter of centuries. There is yet another mystery connected with this particular activity of the termites, which I cannot recollect ever to have seen mentioned by other observers. The riddle is simply this: From where does the enormous mass of earth come? One would expect to find a hollow cavity below such a vast excrescence; a hollow in the earth corresponding in size to the superficial mass, because there is no doubt that all the building material is carried from below. No signs of any cavity have ever been found, however, notwithstanding the fact that many of the giants have been intersected in many parts of Africa and have even been totally demolished for purposes of road-making, railway lines, house building, dams, aerodromes and all the many activities to which civilized man is prone.[51]

pl. 15 Now all the architecture of Eutermes is based on the arch. Probably they were the first architects to discover the secret of arch building. It took years of civilization before man discovered how to use the arch in architecture. Those mighty builders, the Egyptians, knew nothing of the arch and limited themselves to two vertical pillars with a colossal stone as crossbeam. The Greeks and Romans did not understand the properties of the arch. It was only in the Middle Ages that architects came to understand fully the value of the arch in building.

It is very interesting to note that we find in the architecture of the termite two stages of development of the arch, analogous to
pl. 15 that in human architecture.

Let us return to Eutermes and examine some new building operations after rain has fallen. One portion of the termitary has a dark stain. If we examine this with a magnifying glass we find that it is a wet patch where the outer crust has disappeared. It is possible to cut away a small piece of this without causing
pl. 16 enough disturbance to make the workers disappear. Now we can examine the building of the first architects of this earth. We see that all the building of Eutermes is based on the arch.[52] This arch is formed in two ways; the first and most primitive is made by inclining two vertical pillars towards each other until they meet. This is the way man, too, made his first arch. But about every eighth worker carries in his mouth a grass-stalk instead of a pebble. He ascends one of the pillars, quickly fastens one end of the stalk with sticky fluid to the top of the pillar, and then rushes away without waiting to see what happens. This is what does happen: The grass-stalk sinks slowly towards the other pillar until its end comes to rest on the summit. There we see another worker waiting in readiness. As soon as the end of the stalk comes within his reach, he stretches up, grips it, and pulls it down to the summit of the pillar where he in turn attaches it with fluid. On this crossbeam the termites plaster tiny pebbles until a perfect arch results. Success is by no means always inevitable. Occasionally the stalk remains vertical instead of sinking down. In these cases the termites simply finish the arch by inclining the tops of the vertical pillars towards each

51 continue page: 167 "Now all the architecture of Eutermes ... till 170 (end) ... the grass–stalks of food." TXT_6794/0_N3

52 Repetition of the same phrase in the original text. See Marais, *The Soul of the White Ant*, 167, 169–170.

page 105

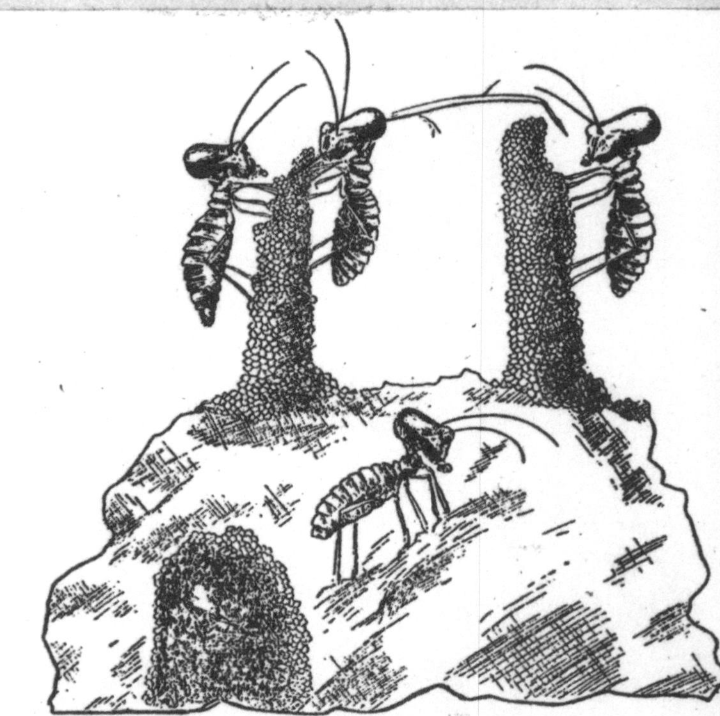

(15). Page 105

Termites building an Arch. (Arch considered to be invention of man.
(left): Erecting two columns out of sand grains.
(right): Laying a grass-stalk across the two columns as a reinforcement of the arch.

rze 105

(16). Similar arch-form made by man. (Thermes of Caracalla, Rome, Italy.)

16 (a): Schematic section through a Termitory, showing tower of superimposed arches. Cell of the queen at base, center.
16 (b): The Colosseum in Rome, also a circular structure of superimposed arches.

16(c): The predecessor of the arch: two columns and a cross-piece of stone. (Doric Order, Greece)

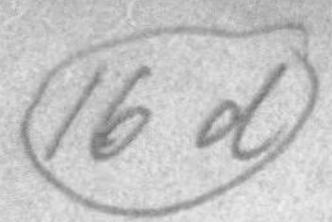

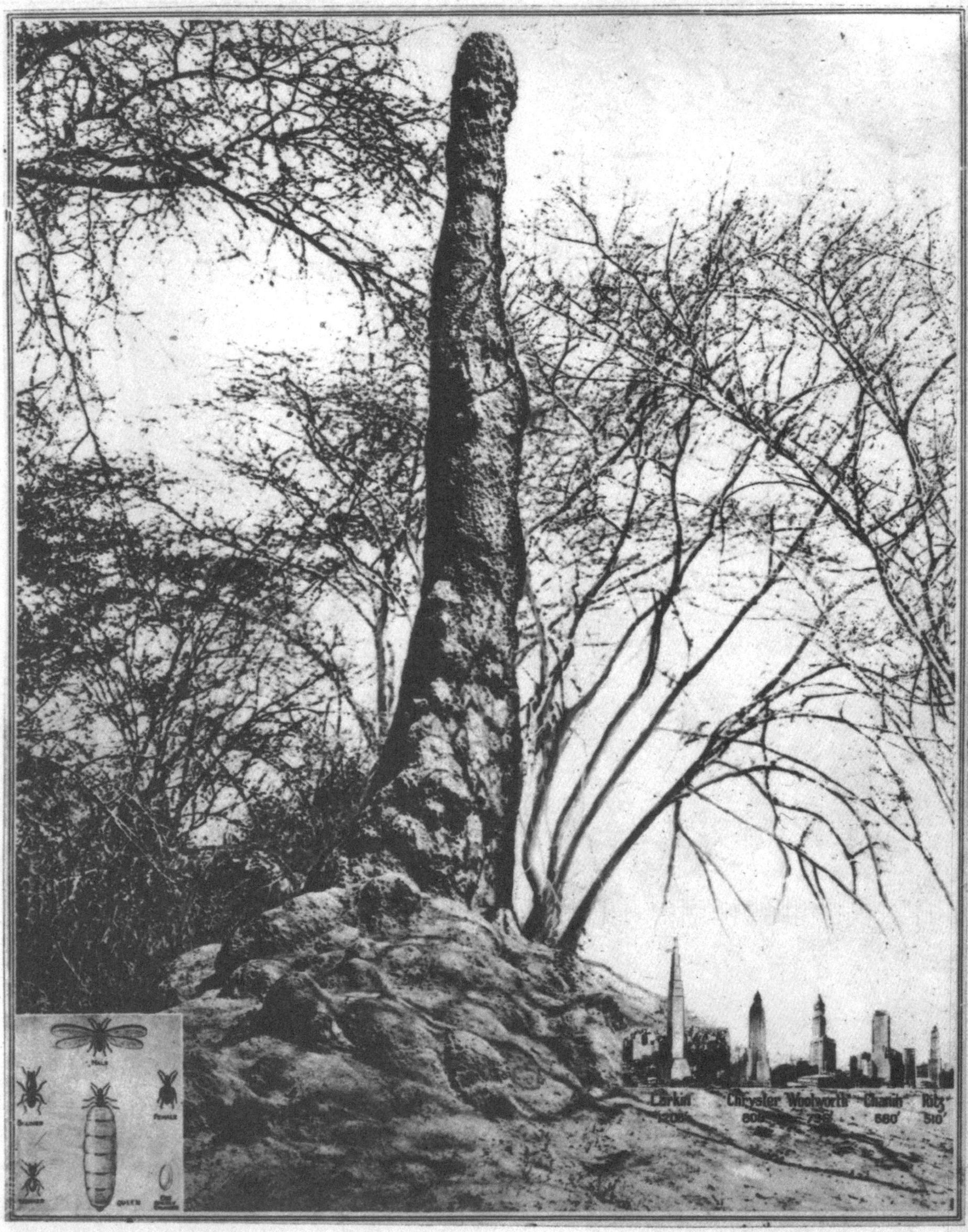

16 (d): A skyscraper for a hundr
four times as high as the Empi
high as:

16 (e): the R. C. A. Building in
height of a white ant - 3/16 o

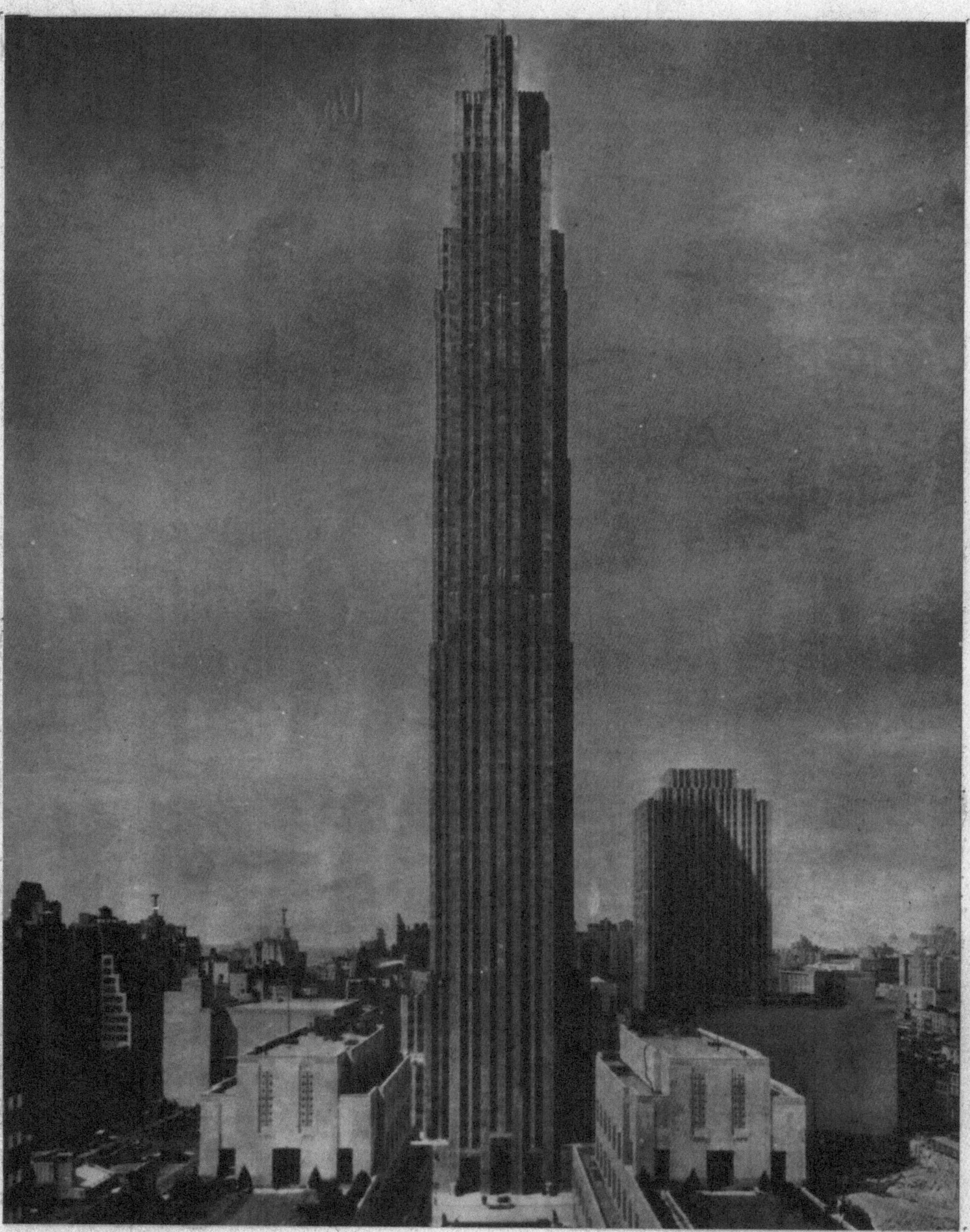

housand inhabitants, relatively
tate Building, and six times as

York City. (As compared to the
inch.)

other until they meet, while the stalk is eventually covered with masonry. Why the stalk is used at all when the termites are able to finish the arch with pebbles only, I cannot tell. Perhaps it is only a rudimentary remainder of a principle which has disappeared. Whatever may be the explanation, I am positive Eutermes never uses the grass-stalks as food.[53]

I believe that the termite was originally a single flying insect exposed to all kinds of dangers. To keep her eggs and offspring safe she took refuge in an underground shelter. Here, just as happens with the bee, Halictus, she came into touch with her young after they were hatched. This was the beginning of community life.

Finally, to cause the community to function well, there was a division of labour. Some of the insects had to build and look for food, others had to protect the nest. Compare the story of Siphonophora mentioned already. The queen who tended to produce offspring more suitable for the various kinds of labour would have a greater chance of survival than one who did not have this tendency. Natural selection began to operate. The present-day soldiers and workers were the fittest types for protection and building operations and the sexual types for reproduction. The queen who had the tendency to produce these three types had more chance of survival and transmitted this tendency to the females born from her. Natural selection thus operated in two directions. The nearer the workers and soldiers came physically to the present-day types, the more chance had the community of surviving. A queen was selected naturally, therefore, who gave birth to all three types. Finally a queen and king were selected who not only produced these three types, but who possessed the psychological power to influence the community and to take the place of the individual instincts of the workers and soldiers.

It is easy to understand why it was an advantage to the community for the sexual sense to be destroyed in all types. Even the sexual types (potential kings and queens) possess no sexuality while they remain in the termitary. Sex in such a community would have been a disturbing influence which would have suspended all protective and other work over long periods. In order to do the best and ceaseless labour, the workers and soldiers had to become mere automata governed by the psychological power of the queen. For the same reason, they lost their sight and the other senses which are the accompaniment of an individual psyche. The soldiers and workers therefore inherit no special instincts from their parents. It is the queen who inherits the power of transmitting the semblance of such instincts to the automatons who work for her.[54]

53 **continue page: 145 (middle): "I believe that the termite ... till end of chapter, page 147.** TXT_6794/0_N3

54 At the end of his instructions for this long series of typed transcriptions from Marais, Kiesler adds a rare **Thank you!!** to Stefi. TXT_6794/0_N3 For further transcriptions from Marais, *The Soul of the White Ant*, not included in this chapter, see TXT_6812/0_N1-N5. These include extracts from pages 1, 3, 11, 12, 15, 16, 17, and 22 of the 1937 edition. For transcriptions from other texts related to the structures of termites, with excerpts from John George Wood, *Homes Without Hands:* (1866), including sections on burrows for humans and animals, as well as "The Brown Ant" and "Termite" (the latter is not transcribed). TXT_6811/0_N1-N3 The same document contains selections from Bölsche, *Der Termitenstaat* (1931). On other termitological studies from that era, see Sources, Disciplines, and Objects, pp. 25, 87. For Kiesler's selections from Wood and Bölsche see Addenda: Transcriptions and Translations, pp. 362–63.

CHAPTER 3[55]

ANIMAL ENGINEERING: THE DAM OF THE BEAVER

The beaver is an animal of the border territory between land and water.[56] He lives on both, he cannot exist without either. On land he does not run the risk of losing security.[57] Land is plentiful, and, in danger, he can change locality or levels. In water, however, a seasonal drought may diminish the water level, and that, according to the destiny of his species, is mortal danger. pl. 17

His first consideration, therefore, is maintenance[58] of a fair water level. Nature will not provide that for him—nor will anyone else;[59] he must do it himself whether or not he can hold an upright position, whether or not his hands are fit for such work, the work must still be done[60] if he and his breed are to survive.[61]

If any modern engineer were asked how to attain such an object, he would probably point to the nearest water-mill, and say that the problem had there been satisfactorily solved, a dam having been built across the stream so as to raise the water to the requisite height and to allow the superfluous water to flow away. Now water is as needful for the beaver as for the miller, and it is a very curious fact, that long before millers ever invented dams, or before man ever learned to grind corn, the beaver knew how to make a dam and insure itself a constant supply of water.

That it does make a dam is a fact that has long been familiar, but how it sets to work is not so well known. In engravings it is generally untrustworthy having mostly been drawn from the imagination of the artist. In most cases the dam is represented as if made after the fashion of our time and country, a number of stakes having been driven into the bed of the river, and smaller branches entwining among them. The projecting ends of the stakes are neatly squared off, and altogether the work looks exactly as if it had been executed by human hands.

Now, in reality the dam is made in a very different manner, and in order to comprehend the mode of its structure, we must watch the beaver at work. When the animal has fixed upon a tree which it believes to be suitable for the purpose, it begins by sitting upright, and with its chisel-like teeth cutting a bold groove completely round the trunk. It then widens the groove, and always makes it wide in exact proportion to its depth, so that when the tree is nearly cut through, it looks something like the contracted portion of an hour-glass. When this stage has been reached, the beaver looks anxiously at the tree, and views it on every side, as if desirous of measuring the direction in which it is to fall. Having settled this question, it goes to the opposite side of the tree, and with two or three powerful bites cuts away the wood, so that the tree becomes overbalanced and falls to the ground. pl. 18

This point reached, the animal proceeds to cut up the fallen trunk into lengths, usually a yard or so in length, employing a similar method of severing the wood. In consequence of this mode of gnawing the timber, both ends of the logs are rounded and rather pointed.[62]

The next part of the task is to make these logs into a dam, ... Some of the dams are of very great size, measuring two to three hundred[63] yards in length and ten or twelve feet in thickness and their form exactly corresponds with the force of the stream, being straight in some parts and more or less convex in others. The dam is formed, not by forcing the ends of the logs into the bed of the river, but by laying them horizontally, and covering them with stones and earth until they can resist the force of the water. Vast numbers of logs are thus laid, and as fast as the water rises, fresh materials are added, being obtained mostly from the trunks and branches of trees which have been stripped of their bark by the beavers. ...[64] Mud and earth are also continually added by the beavers, so that in process of time the dam

55 Alternative chapter numbering and titles: **Chapter Two** TXT_6690/0_N1 **PART II Chapter Two: Animal Engineering and Technique. The Dam of the Beaver** TXT_6698/0_N2

56 **of the borderline between water and land.** TXT_6698/0_N2 **borderland.** TXT_6713/0_N1

57 **Once on land, he is not in danger to lose ground.** TXT_6698/0_N2

58 **the sustaining** TXT_6698/0_N2

59 **~~No one else~~ will ~~do~~ that for him. ~~No one else has advantage of it.~~** TXT_6698/0_N2

60 **His hands fit for much ~~engi~~ work—or not, upright position or not, it must be done** TXT_6698/0_N2

61 Instruction for quotation of transcribed excerpts: **~~And here is how:~~ (quote: If any till ... the end.)** TXT_6698/0_N2 **"Wood, J. G. Rev.: Homes without Hands (Harper 1...?)"** [appended to the transcription of Wood, *Homes Without Hands*] TXT_6698/0_N3 Kiesler selects paragraphs from "Chapter XXI: Social Habitations. Social Mammalia," dedicated to the beaver (431-438; see 432-437 for Kiesler's selections). The first two paragraphs and several other passages from Wood's original text are omitted from the Kieslers' transcription, and there are also small variations from the printed text. TXT_6698/0_N3-N4

62 **~~as seen in the illustration.~~** TXT_6698/0_N4 See illustration of "The beaver and its home," an engraving depicting beavers at work while building a dam, in Wood, *Homes Without Hands*, 434. On page 435, Wood refers to the illustration as follows: "the logs and cut stumps which are given in the illustration were sketched from those objects." See Sources, Disciplines, and Objects, fig. A.24.

63 **2-300** TXT_6698/0_N4

64 Text omitted from the transcription. Wood, *Homes Without Hands*, 436.

(18) page 112

(18). Page 112

A beaver cutting standard size logs for building his shelter.

(17) page 111

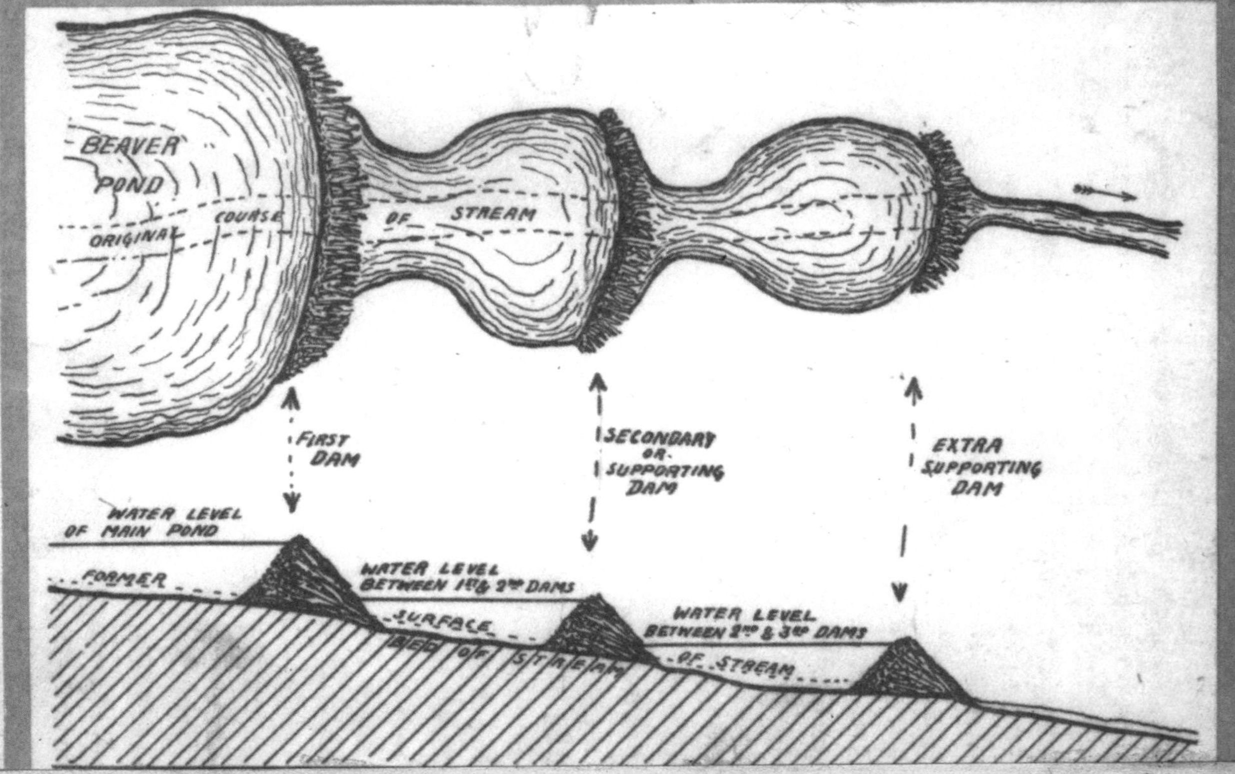

(17). Page 111

Main and subsidiary dam of the beaver, an ingenious engineering feat indispensable for his survival as a land-water animal.

becomes as firm as the land through which the river passes, and is covered with fertile alluvium. Seeds soon make their way to the congenial soil, and in a dam of long standing forest trees have been known to grow, their roots adding to the general stability by binding together the materials.

We have now seen how the beaver keeps the water to the required level and we must next see how he makes use of it. Essentially an aquatic mammal, never walking when it can swim, it therefore makes its houses close to the water and communicating with it by means of subterranean passages, one entrance of which passes into the house, and the other into the water, so far below the surface that it cannot be closed by ice. It is therefore always possible for the beaver to gain access to the provision stores and to return to its house without being seen from the land.

The lodges are nearly circular in form and must resemble the snow-houses of the Inuit in their dome-like quality, and about half as high as they are wide …

*

The same proportions, similar materials, similar assembly and construction methods are employed by many primitive tribes or individuals, today, or at any previous era. pl. 19

The slum-shelter of an East-Indian illustrates this inherently animalistic[65] building method even to the point of the entrance (compare illustration).[66]

CHAPTER 4
THE BUILDING TOOLS OF ANIMALS[67]

Houses are defense mechanisms.[68] The question arises: when is this defense mechanism protective enough to become a standard? And how do the necessary techniques become part of the knowledge of a species?

Through experience parents learn of the inefficiency of the defense powers and mechanisms of their own bodies, and eventually add to them automatically.[69]

This experience is taught to the offspring. And although "cultural development" cannot be inherited physically, it is passed on through parental teaching by animals as well as man.[70]

* * *

Any animal that must build nests, homes, or storage places, will drive toward its objective no matter how badly (from our point of view) nature has equipped its body to procure building-material, carry it, hold, and grip, and mold, and lodge it firmly into position.[71] Animals have no other tools but the parts of their own body. Man has invented others. Man seems to be the only creature of this world that has created tools additional to the mechanisms of his body.[72]

Experience of the weakness and inefficiency of his own animal body as a defense mechanism has forced him to add artificial means of extending its capacity.[73] The discrepancy between his power to think and[74] his power of physical action is so great that he must invent "extensions" of his body's senses, stature, and muscles to bridge the gap between his imagination and the world's reality.[75]

In addition, it seems, man's physical capacities shrink as his mental powers increase. These two poles of his psycho-equilibrium[76] seem to move further and further away from the link of their natural[77] attraction and force man continuously to invent more and more[78] extensive and powerful tools to prevent this ever-widening space from developing into complete cleavage.[79]

Animals like the termites, the beaver, and most others, have finally found the optimum law and form for their homes.[80] They do not

65 inherently ~~primitive~~ TXT_6698/0_N4

66 Kiesler refers to the second illustration of plate 19. See caption and source credit.

67 Alternative chapter numbering and titles: Part II Chapter Three ~~Natural Tools and Tools of Man for Building. Animal Tools for Building (Natural) and Man's Tools (Artificial)~~ TXT_6699/0_N1 Part II Chapter ~~Three~~ Four ~~Either 1. The Building Tools of Animals or 2. Animal Building Tools.~~ TXT_6733/0_N1

68 One can readily see: TXT_6699/0_N1 Houses are defense mechanisms SFP_6665/0_N3r

69 add to them automatically. TXT_5877_N86; TXT_6854/0_N1 add to ~~it~~ them automatically. TXT_6733/0_N1 add eventually to it. / automatically TXT_6699/0_N1 The document TXT_6699/0_N1 is a handwritten manuscript with many corrections (see Sources, Disciplines, and Objects, fig. A.23). On the multiple readings of this passage and the role of automatism in Kiesler's ideas on animal building instinct see Sources, Disciplines, and Objects, p. 27.

70 It is passed ~~on~~ by parental teaching ~~in animal societies as well as~~ by animals as well as man. TXT_6699/0 ~~In this manner the necessity to invent apply "artificial" help is constantly established and standards finally standardized. Animals start to build.~~ TXT_6699/0_N1 Cf. similar references to social and cultural development and inheritance of design skills in humans in Kiesler's article "'On Correalism and Biotechnique': A Study on the Genetics of Building Design," *Architectural Record* 86, no. 3 (1939): 60–75.

71 Any animal ~~will use~~ that must build nests, home, or storage, will drive to achieve it no matter how badly (from our point of view) nature has equipped its body to run for building material, to carry it, to hold and grip it ~~and to manufacture it~~ to mold it, and lodge it firmly into position. TXT_6699/0_N1

72 ~~functions~~ of his body TXT_6733/0_N2 ~~to extend the building capacity of his own animal body.~~ TXT_6699/0_N1-N2

73 to ~~develop~~ artificial means of extending ~~his arms his eyes his building~~ capacities. TXT_6699/0_N2

74 to think and ~~analyze~~ TXT_6699/0_N2

75 he must invent "extensions" of his body ~~capacities~~ (sense, stature, and muscles) to bridge this gap between plan and fact. TXT_6699/0_N2

76 psychic equilibrium TXT_6699/0_N2

77 natural ~~balan~~ [balance?] TXT_6699/0_N2

78 and more TXT_6699/0_N2

79 to prevent the break ~~of the artificial bridge which man erects between these two / over the life-stream~~ [handwritten in the margin and later crossed out] TXT_6699/0_N2 A subheading precedes the following paragraph (it is not transcribed in the TS): Selling Standards for Houses TXT_6699/0_N3

80 and houses. ~~Not so man.~~ TXT_6699/0_N3

pu 115

(19). Page 115

(Top): The finished house of a beaver family (beaver visible repairing roof). Remarkable construction to keep entrance free.
(Below): Compare the similar materials of a primitive shelter (note entrance!) Erected by a Hindu (India, today).

Hindu Shelter in India

pg. 126

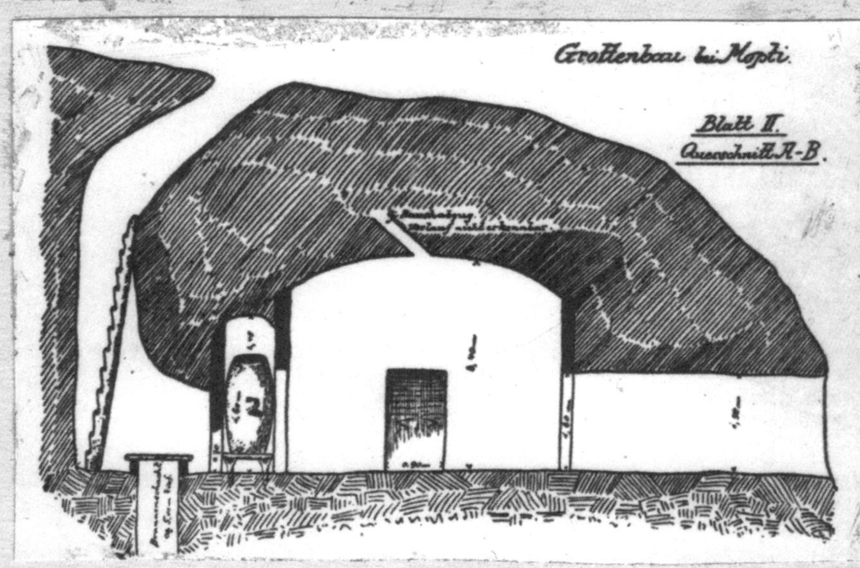

(20). Page 126

(Above): Animal shelters below the ground.
(Middle): Man shelter below the ground (Mopti, West Sudan, Africa).
(Below): Floor plan of same shelter, showing arrangement of living and sleeping quarters.

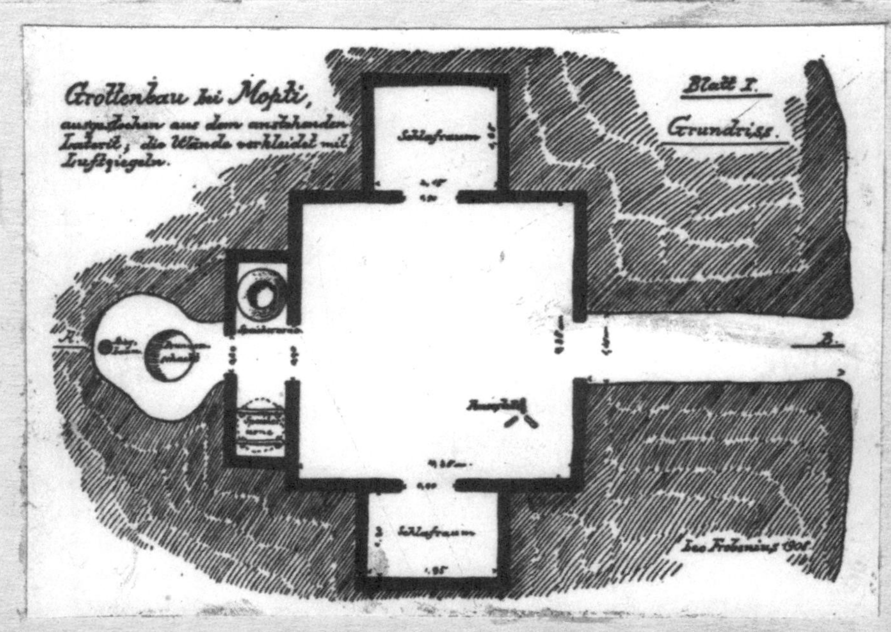

"progress" anymore; they only repeat. It is not so with man. He still progresses. He is still infantile. He[81] is growing. He is now teething strongly –industrially speaking–and has not yet found his peace nor his place and form of shelter.

* * *[82]

The forefoot, later the hand, takes over the duties of the jaw, and the artificial tool takes over the duties of the hand.

This, roughly, is the development from the tools incorporated in the animal-body to the tools added to it by man; man alone makes this addition, and the tools are aptly called: arti-facts.[83]

First:

– All animals use only their body mechanisms (usually the mouth and feet) as tools to construct artificial shelter.
– For building materials they employ the raw parts of nature[84] (such as twigs, branches, sand, stone, feathers, mouth-secretion, and others)–which they find ready-made.

Second:

– The orang utan (forest-man)[85] and the chimpanzee also confine themselves to their body mechanisms as tools to construct artificial shelter, but as soon as their bodies become erect they no longer use the mechanism of the jaw, relying instead on their forefeet or hands to serve as tools.[86]
  Like all their animal predecessors for building material they still use only the raw parts of nature which they find in their immediate environment.

Third:

– In addition to these body mechanisms man invents new tools for the construction of his shelter.
– He uses stones to crack objects and to split them. He finds stone to be more resistant than his fist or finger, harder, and less easily tired.[87] Injuries of the stone do not bleed, as does his hand.
– All the winged, walking, crawling, or floating animals, and man, from primeval to contemporary times, use for building materials only the raw material of their natural environment.[88] Their shelter still consists of sticks and stones, wood, and mud, and sometimes skin.[89]

* * *

Man has become a sculptor; his ancestors were only builders.[90] Suddenly he becomes a transformer of materials[91] after his own will. He adds to nature his own version of form and use. He, formerly only an employee of nature, becomes independent; and opens his own business.[92] He intends to compete. He dreams that he, a slave, will by the sheer invention of tools, enslave nature, and survive more easily, more securely, and more lastingly. An amazing animal indeed! Under any circumstances an amusing adventurer.

* * *

All this still leads him to animal architecture—to better animal architecture, but nevertheless animal architecture. When and how will he give physical expression to the sheltering of his psyche?[93]

CHAPTER 5
MAN, A COMPOSITE ANIMAL OF BUILDING TECHNIQUES[94]

Building a destruction-proof tower for a hundred thousand inhabitants is a task which requires expert organization.[95] A single type of

81 He ~~searches~~ TXT_6699/0_N3
82 Title [Kiesler's placeholder for a chart heading ultimately not added] TXT_6699/0_N4 Cf. charts in reference to "the building tools of animals." SFP_6664/0_N1-N2 included in Addenda: Charts, figs. c.06a–b.
83 Roughly this is the development from ~~the~~ tools ~~of building from the~~ incorporated in the animal body ~~to artificial ones: artifacts~~ to tools added to it by man, and only by man, and which rightly so, one called: arti-facts. ~~One of the reasons, why we are so astound of the houses of animals is, that we~~ [text crossed out and moved two paragraphs later] TXT_6699/0_N4
84 they ~~use ready-made~~ parts of nature TXT_6699/0_N4
85 ~~and the first ape-man~~ TXT_6699/0_N4
86 but they replace the mechanisms of the jaw ~~and mouth~~ with their forefeet or hand as soon as their body becomes erect. TXT_6699/0_N4
87 and untiring. TXT_6699/0_N5
88 As Building-material first man (up to the later type) still uses, like ~~feather and~~ the winged, ~~or~~ walking, ~~or~~ crawling or floating animals before and with him only raw parts of his (immediate) natural environment. TXT_6699/0_N5 For building material primeval man + contemporary man both use like all the winded, walking, crawling or floating animals before their time or of their time, only the raw parts of their (immediate) natural environment. TXT_6733/0_N4
89 sticks and stones, ~~and skins~~ wood and moud [sic] and sometimes skins. TXT_6699/0_N5 [...]tics [illegible] and plastics [handwritten in margin of TS] TXT_6733/0_N4
90 Animal-Man has become a sculptor. His ~~predecessing~~ [sic] ~~animals~~ predecessors have only been builders. TXT_6699/0_N5recto
91 he becomes a ~~fashioner~~ transformer of ~~natural~~ materials TXT_6699/0_N5recto
92 His own business ventures. TXT_6699/0_N5recto
93 When will he give expression to sheltering ~~the spirit of his~~ his spiritual life? TXT_6699/0_N5verso
94 Alternative titles: COMPOSITE ANIMALS [typed with handwritten amendments] Man ~~is~~ a COMPOSITE ANIMAL~~S~~ of building techniques TXT_6732/0_N1
95 ~~The task of~~ building a f[illegible]-proof tower for hundred thousand inhabitants is a ~~job~~ which requires expert organization. TXT_6797/0_N1

termite could not do all the expert work necessary[96] for the erection of so giant a structure. And the miracle happens that from one and the same father and mother three different varieties[97] of children are born: some with eyes–some without; some who fly–and some that cannot; some with shovels and spears–others helpless, without defense weapons or building tools,[98] do nothing but nourish the young.[99] It looks indeed, as Marais[100] puts it, as if through thousands of years of experience and constant need, these variations had to be recreated again and again until they finally reached a differentiation which they could procreate at will.[101]

The children act like different parts of one body.[102] Compared to a unicellular creature, a primordial protozoon for instance, our own body consists of nothing but individual specialized parts (liver, eyes, lungs, etc.),[103] each of which has its own functions and cannot undertake any other. By analogy, Marais calls the Termitary a composite animal,[104] because the life of the parts inside the skin of the building is as specialized for the maintenance of the whole body corporate as it is in our animal bodies of flesh and blood.[105]

Each type of termite is physically and apparently psychologically (if one may say so) born for one and only one task, but all types live and work together for one purpose; and that is, to keep the One building, the Termitary, alive. All members of the enormous family work automatically through the will of the queen,[106] whose role is compared by Marais to that of our brain.[107] Her body-substance, swollen from constant breeding (and therefore very vulnerable), is protected by the building of a special cell,[108] whose vault of massive concrete is the strongest[109] of all the parts of the Termitary. Once the queen dies, all members of the tribe are doomed; the building dries up and crumbles.[110]

I shall go into many details of this building-miracle or monster, but at this juncture I should like to digress[111] and speak of another composite animal. This composite animal apparently has also acquired over a period of hundreds of thousands of years the ability to give forth his own breed with capacities that originally have not been his own. Yet these varied, indeed very varied capacities were not absolute necessities–like those of the termites. Theirs is a matter of life or death, but is not so with our new animal. This animal has acquired its various new needs by a strange liking for the fashions of other species, and has preempted[112] those fashions by simply imitating them continuously over such a long period of time that they ultimately have become his own. I speak of Man.[113]

Look at his building-material and building methods: and look at his buildings!

He is the only animal alive that does not have its own particular building method and type, but combines the building types of most other animals.[114] Architecturally speaking, he is a composite animal of building techniques.[115]

* * *

Every animal has its own–its unique–method of building its nest or home or storage. Only man has different methods; he has as many as there are other types of animals.

Just as man eats everything (meat, vegetables, fruits), he uses all the methods of housebuilding used by other creatures.[116]

For example, he uses:
- the Thatched roof and walls of birds
- the Concrete of termites
- the Earthmounds of the mole
- pl. 19–20 the Timber of the beaver
- the Nettping of the spider
- the standardized Cell-manufacture of the bee[117]

96 **One type of ~~animal~~ body ~~cannot~~ could not do all the ~~specialized~~ expert work necessary**
97 **variations** TXT_6797/0_N1
98 **~~work~~ tools** TXT_6797/0_N1
99 **they do nothing but nursing. ~~u.s. fort~~** TXT_6797/0_N1
100 The name Eugène Marais, the author of *The White Ant*, is persistently misspelled in Kiesler's handwritten draft of this chapter–either as **Maurées** or **Marées.** TXT_6797/0_N1 This is corrected in later typescripts.
101 **these variations had to create, so to say themselves by constant need, and that they finally reached a specialization that they could procreate!** TXT_6797/0_N1
102 **They act like the different parts of one and the same ~~human~~ body. ~~The liver~~** TXT_6797/0_N1
103 **(liver, stomach, etc., etc.)** TXT_6797/0_N1
104 **By analogy Marées** [see note 100] **calls therefore the ~~building~~ Termitary a composite animal** TXT_6797/0_N1
105 **in that of our animal of flesh and blood.** TXT_6797/0_N2 In his study, Marais refers several times to the termitary, as well as higher mammals and human beings, as composite animals whose bodies constitute a "community" of individual organs. See Marais, *The Soul of the White Ant*, 53-65, and Sources, Disciplines, and Objects, pp. 31, 87.
106 **All workers also work automatically through the ~~distant order~~ of the queen** TXT_6797/0_N2
107 **to that of the dominant position of our brain**. TXT_6732/0_N2 Cf. Marais, *The Soul of the White Ant*, 137: "The queen is the psychological centre of the community; she is the brain of the organism which we call a termitary." See also excerpts from Marais transcribed in Part II, chapter 2 of *Magic Architecture*.
108 **like our brain most firmly protected by the skull ~~of any part of the total body by the skull~~ by the building of** [a] **~~strong vault;~~** TXT_6797/0_N2 **like our brain firmly sheltered by the skull** TXT_6732/0_N2 On the structure of the human braincase as a form of architecture, see an article by Ashley Montagu, "The skillful skull," *Technology Review* 45, no. 9 (1943): 3-7, an offprint of which is included in Kiesler's research material; also mentioned in Sources, Disciplines, and Objects, pp. 9-10, 84.
109 **the firmest** TXT_6797/0_N2
110 **the building ~~dies.~~** TXT_6732/0_N2 Cf. Marais, *The Soul of the White Ant*, 135: "If you destroy the queen in one of the two nests adjoining each other, then the termites of that nest cease work and move to the adjoining nest where they apparently swear allegiance to the new queen. If, how-ever, you destroy the queen of a nest which is some distance from another the termites make no attempt to transfer to another nest but die in their old home."
111 **but at this junction I like to side-step** TXT_6797/0_N2
112 **has acquired** TXT_6797/0_N3
113 **man** TXT_6797/0_N3 **~~m~~Man** [handwritten emendation] TXT_6732/0_N3
114 **He is the only animal alive, that does not have its own particular building method and type, like every other animal, but combines for himself by himself all the building types of all the other animals** TXT_6797/0_N3
115 **Constructively speaking ~~he is a composite~~ he is an animal as composite, as they are other species who build ~~ants, beavers, or~~** TXT_6797/0_N3 Cf. Marais, *The Soul of the White Ant*, 76: "the termitary is a separate and composite animal in exactly the same way that a man is a separate composite animal." Marais compares human and termite building in the chapter "The First Architects," in *The Soul of the White Ant*, 159-170.
116 **he uses ~~builds all method like~~ all-methods of housebuilding of ~~every animal~~ other animals.** TXT_6797/0_N4
117 **Thatched roof from birds; earth mounds from ants; stone Concrete from termite; timber from the beaver;** / **method** / **individual netting from the spider; standardized cell manufacture from the bee; ~~mixing of stones~~ holding parts together by mixed fluids–from termites u.s.f** [etc.]**:** ["method" written vertically in left margin along with brackets, suggests the distinction between building materials like concrete and timber, and structural building techniques such as "netting" and "cell-manufacture." TXT_6797/0_N4recto-verso Cf. MS and TS draft versions in figs. B.08 and B.09. TXT_6732/0_N3

Every animal has his own — the only
method of building its nest or home;
only man has different methods — as many as
there are other animals.
Just as man
eats
every-thing
he uses ~~builts all-method~~
~~like~~ of house-building
all-methods of other animals,
~~every-animal~~.
for example:
The thached roof from
birds;
stone Concrete from Termite;
earthmounds from ants;
timber from the Beaver;
~~method~~ methods
weaving netting from the spider;
standardized cell-manufacture from the bee;

Frederick Kiesler, Part II, Chapter 5, "Man a Composite Animal of Building-Techniques," preliminary draft on the building "method(s)" of humans and animals (MS, pencil) ÖFLKS,TXT_6797/0_N4recto

-3 67

ultimately become his own. I speak of man.

Look at his building-material and building methods;
and look at his buildings !

He is the only animal alive, that has not its own,
and particular building-method and type, like every
other animal; but he combines for himself by himself
all the building-types of all the other animals.
Constructively speaking, he is an animals as composite
as the other species who build.

Every animal has its own - the only method of building
its nest or home. Only man has different methods,
as many as there are other animals.

Just as man
eats
every thing
he uses
all methods of house-building of other animals.
For example

The thached roof from birds
Concrete from termites
Earthmounds from ants
Timber from the beaver
Netting from the spider
Cell-manufacture from the bee
Holding parts together by mixed fluids from the
termite, and so forth.

Man is a composite animal of building-techniques.

Frederick Kiesler, Part II, Chapter 5 "Man a Composite Animal of Building-Techniques," preliminary draft with annotations on the "building material and building methods" of humans and animals (TS, pencil [color], ink) ÖFLKS, TXT_6732/0_N3

And the know-how of holding parts together by weaving or the use of fluids which become adhesive through drying, practices common to an infinity of creatures.[118]

* * *

Man is a composite animal in building materials and building techniques.[119]

CHAPTER 6
MAN'S FIRST INVENTION: THE (FIRST) TRANSFORMATION OF DEAD MATERIAL INTO USEFUL TOOLS[120] pl. 19a

(illustrated by annotated drawings)[121]

Splintered stones were small pieces of mountains;[122] they could be weighed by a human hand or even by a clumsy ape without much effort. Most of them were large pieces, some had sharp edges, and pointed like fishbones or like teeth of animal skeletons or shells.

Skeletons were found on the beach, in caves, bush-growths[123] all over the earth surfaces where[124] also birds had fallen dead and decayed.

These[125] bones were as hard as stones sometimes; but most of the time not. They would break when hard hit or often used. But their form fitted well the hand. Their scale was manageable without much effort. If their scale and some of their form could be imitated in stone, which is so much harder, that would help in battles with stronger, bigger animals and could also be used efficiently as a tool in everyday life. Dead material, such bone dead,[126] like inorganic matter, for instance stones, or life material that has become dead, could be transformed into practical tools. This transformation of useless materials would become useful tools. By dying they[127] have lost their original function; but now, without harm to nature, they would become again functional, but in a new way.

This transformation of natural material into artificial objects incorporates a transfunctioning of service. While before it was serving nature, it will now serve man.[128]

CHAPTER 7
THE (SECOND) TRANSFORMATION OF DEAD MATERIAL INTO MAGIC TOOLS OF PHYSICAL ATTRACTION.[129]

After the ape-man had undertaken the transformation of trees (branches) and rocks (stones) into useful implements he started to "fashion" his own body.–[130] pl. 19b

———————————

By instinct all animals have natural likes and dislikes;[131] particularly in regard to smell and taste. A safeguard of survival.–

———————————

All senses are extremely sensitive–the eye.–[132]

———————————

With time (experience) definite preferences are developed.[133] They are taught to the offspring.[134] Mother-love through pain in birth. Later they will develop into the customs and rituals without which man cannot exist happily. –Games. The play of young animals. The erotic element in games. Games involving physical contact.

———————————

118 an infinity of animals TXT_6732/0_N2-N3

119 Man is a composite animal in building materials and building techniques. TXT_6732/0_N3

120 Alternative chapter numbering and titles: PART II / Chapter ~~IV~~ 6 / Man's First Invention / Man's Transformation of ~~Useless~~ Dead Materials ~~of nature~~ into uUseful Tools / ~~His First Invention Creative Discovery and Invention~~ TXT_6742/0_N1

121 See text and sketches in chart by Kiesler (fig. B.10). SFP_6662/N5

122 Splinted rocks, fallen, broken, were small pieces of mountains. Surely they ~~were~~ are part of giants, and therefore part of cosmic power → continue from next page Instruction for transcription of MS with sketches and text. TXT_6742/0_N1

123 bushgrowths [cf. Buschgewächse] SFP_6662/N5

124 were SFP_6662/N5

125 this SFP_6662/N5

126 such [as] bone [from the] dead, like inorganic matter SFP_6662/N5

127 would become useful tools. By deying [illegible] they lost their original function SFP_6662/N5 Here the handwriting is ambiguous. The illegible word could be "dying" or "decaying."

128 See also a different set of sketches of an assortment of prehistoric and Indigenous tools for a chapter originally numbered Part II, chapter two and titled The Transformation / Transfunctioning of USELESS MATERIALS OF NATURE INTO TOOLS in fig. B.11: Dolch aus Kamion Knoch[en] (German for "dagger," derived from the Kamion bone, named for a region in Poland with prehistoric findings) / knöcherne Harpune (German for "bone harpoon") / Tomahawk / Tomahawk SFP 6663/0_N2 Kiesler is copying these artifacts of disparate eras and world areas from a series of illustrations in the first pages of the section "Die vorgeschichtliche Menschheit und ihre Kultur [Prehistoric Humanity and ist Culture]," in Klaatsch, *Der Werdegang der Menschheit* (1922), 253–386; specifically, figs. 192 and 193 (260), and figs. 210 and 211 on (274–275). In the book, the first object (from the bottom left) is described as an engraved bone dagger from Papua, New Guinea, the second as a bone harpoon from the Magdalenian era, the third as a wood and stone ax also from Papua, New Guinea (described by Kiesler as a tomahawk), and the fourth an Indigenous tomahawk made of similar materials from Mesa Verde, Colorado.

129 Alternative chapter numbering and titles: ~~Part III~~ PART II. Chapter ~~V / VI.~~/VII. ~~Towards Artificial Transformation of the Human Figure Body.~~ Chapter 6: The Transformation of Dead Material into Magic Tools of Physical Attraction. TXT_6700/0_N1 The Transformation of Dead Material into Physical Tools of Magical Attraction. TXT_6838/0_N1

130 he gradually starts to fashion his own body. TXT_6700/0_N1 In the handwritten draft of this chapter, Kiesler separates every paragraph from the next one by a long line. In a later typescript, he deletes some of these lines and adds a dash at the end of some paragraphs, all of which connote markings for the typographic layout of the published text. TXT_6700/0_N1; TXT_6743/0_N1

131 By ~~natural~~ instinct, all animals have natural likes and dislikes, a very innate automatism. TXT_6700/0_N1

132 ~~Equal likes and dislikes~~ Plus all senses are ~~equally~~ extremely sensitive–they [sic] eye (sight and vision) too. ~~(That leads to equally selective pleasure.)~~ TXT_6700/0_N1

133 With time (experience) ~~it has developed in man~~ (and animals) definite preferences. TXT_6700/0_N1

134 ~~Man slowly teaches its children the standards of preference and selection.~~ TXT_6700/0_N1

fig. B.10

II, 6 68

C

Man's Transformation of useless Materials of nature into usefull tools.

splintert Stones, were small pieces of mountains; they could be weighed by a human hand or even by a clumsy ape without much effort! Most of them

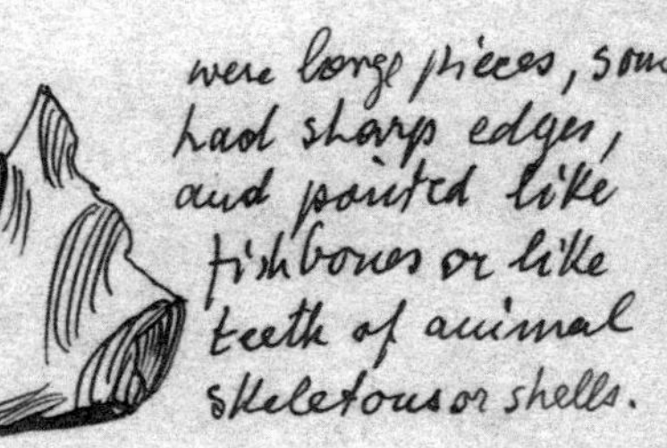

were large pieces, some had sharp edges, and pointed like fishbones or like teeth of animal skeletons or shells.

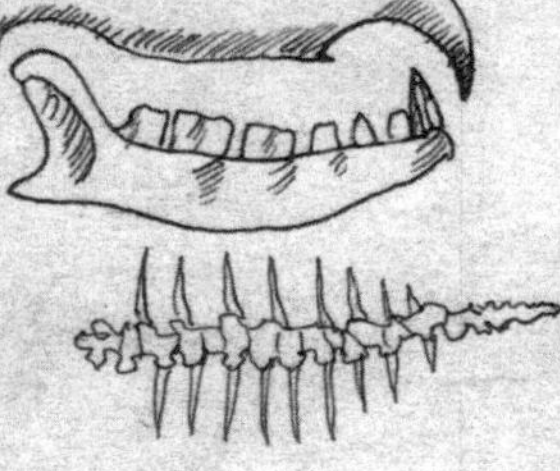

skeletons were found on the beach, in caves, [illegible] all over the earth surfaces, were also birds had fallen dead and decayed.

This bones were as hard as stones sometimes; but most of the time not. They would break when hard hit or often used. But their form fitted well the hand. Their scale was manageable without much

effort. If their scale and some of their form could be imitated in stone, with is so much harder, that would help in battles with stronger, bigger animals and could also be used efficiently

as a tool in everyday life. Dead material, such born dead, like inorganic matter, for instance stones, or life material that has become dead, could be trans-

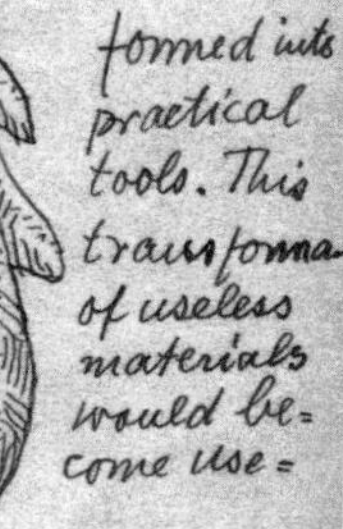

formed into practical tools. This transforma of useless materials would become use-

full tools. By dying their have lost their original function, but now, without harm to nature, they would become again functional, but in a new way.

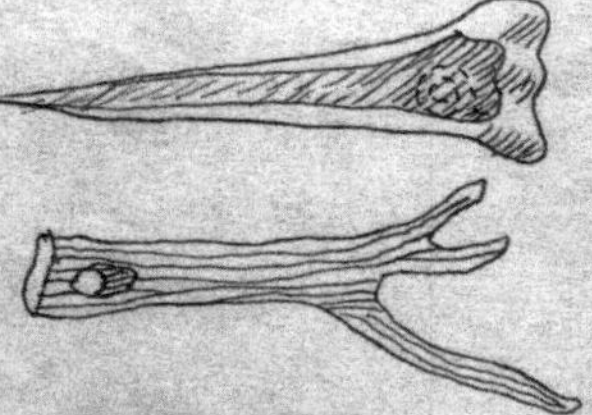

This transformation of natural material into artificial objects incorporate a transfunctioning of service. While before it was serving nature, it will now serve man.

Frederick Kiesler, Part II, Chapter 6: "Man's Transformation of useless materials of nature into usefull [sic] tools," chart with drawings and descriptions (MS, ink) ÖFLKS, SFP_6662/0_N5

fig. B.11

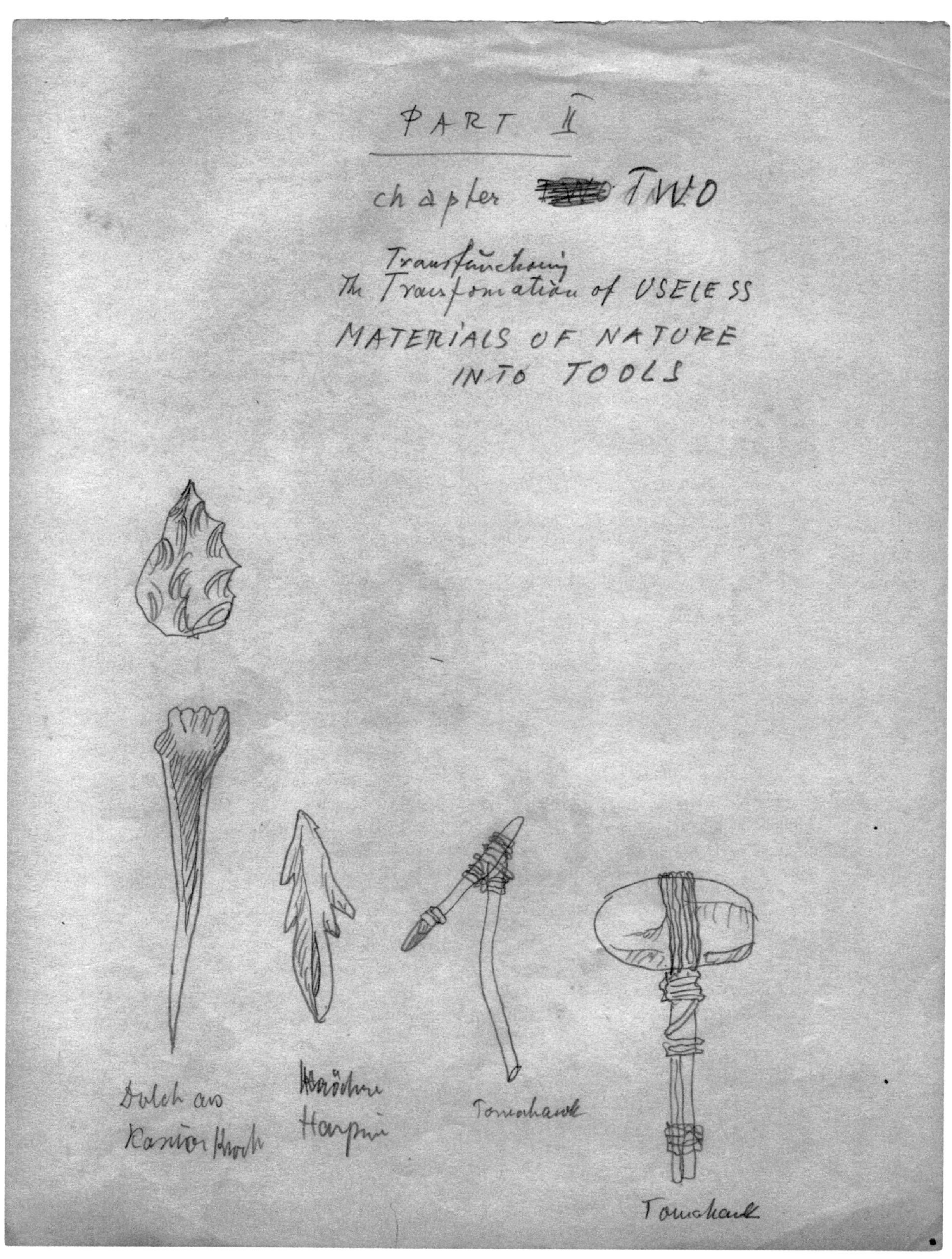

Frederick Kiesler, Preliminary diagram with drawings and descriptions related to the content of Part II, Chapter 6 ("chapter TWO" reflects earlier book manuscript organization): "The Transformation / Transfunctioning of USELESS MATERIALS OF NATURE INTO TOOLS: Dolch aus Kamion Knoch [en] [dagger from Kamion bone] / knöcherne Harpune [bone harpoon] / Tomahawk [sic] / Tomahawk" (MS, pencil) ÖFLKS, SFP_6663/0_N2

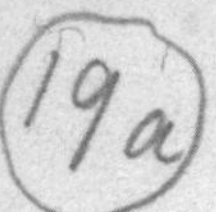

page 128

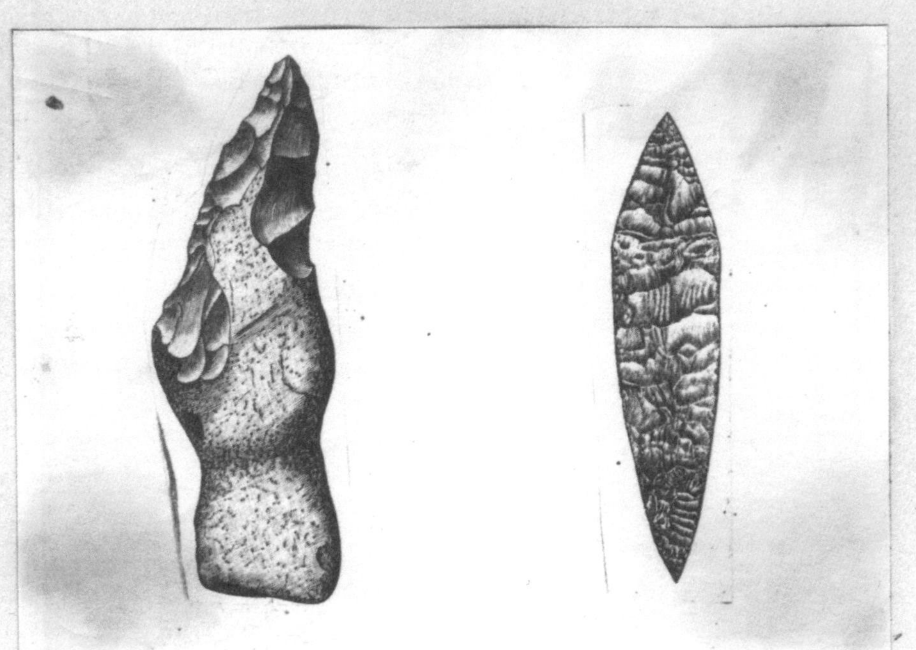

(19a). Page 128

Sculpted stone flint of the paleolithic age (left).
Sculpted stone flint of the neolithic age - and
(below): Sculpted Rock-temple, South India.

Standards of preference[135] are fundamental in sexual selection. This judgment is automatic. Male and female become aware of the reasons for being chosen. Both try to come near "the ideal" and in this way to find security in success.[136]

——————————

Deficiencies of the body (which demonstrate themselves by comparison) urge corrections and alignment with preferred standards.

——————————

One of the first changes in the male body occurred after hunting. He wears the dangerous animal skin, which he killed.–Trophies: teeth-necklaces–given to the females.–Ornaments of shells.

——————————

Hair.–Head-dress.–Beard: in apes very distinctive design[137] in contrast to the naked part of the face. Darwin cleverly pointed to the sexual stimulus of it.[138] Extreme sensitivity of the skin of the face due to beard growth.[139]–Head-shave a sign of mourning.–

——————————

Symbols of strength: Scars. Natural scars imitated as: artificial cicatrization (deformation of nose, ears, skin.)

——————————

Later, tattooing developed of mystic origin into decoration; in connection with taboos.[140] Closely related with self-torture in one form or another.

——————————

Skin: Ointments in primitive tribes very developed, to heighten pleasure of touch and looks. Design and form and color-rhythm emerge and become "beauty."

——————————

MARRIAGE CEREMONIES.[141]

The women have been preparing various substances. Each boy, before the washing, has taken off the most precious ornaments, such as shell-belt, arm-shells, valuable necklaces, and left them with his tabula; so, now the toilet can begin. First comes the anointing with charmed coco-nut oil, always the next stage after washing. When this has been well rubbed all over the skin, by the man himself and not by the women, the latter proceeds to stroke the skin with a mother-of-pearl-shell. Slowly and gently each tabula presses the smooth shell up and down over his cheeks, his arms, and his chest, and laterally across his forehead; reciting a formula, as she does so, in a clear audible voice. The words always spoken towards the boy's face which she is stroking.

Who makes beauty magic?–
To heighten the beauty, to make it come out.
Who makes it on the slopes of Obukula?
I, Tabula, and my mate Kwaywaya.
We make the beauty magic.
I smooth out, I improve, I whiten!
Thy head I smooth out, I improve, I whiten![142]

135 ~~and selection~~ TXT_6700/0_N1

136 **Both try to come near "the ideal ~~of success, That is: the~~ security ~~through~~ in success.** TXT_6700/0_N2

137 **Beard in apes very distinctive ~~decorative~~ design** TXT_6700/0_N2

138 **Darwin cleverly pointed to the ~~erotic~~ sexual ~~influence~~ stimulus of it.** TXT_6700/0_N2 Kiesler's references to the sexual significance of the beard in humans and primates draw from Klaatsch, who devotes several paragraphs on the subject and mentions Darwin. Cf. Klaatsch, *Der Werdegang der Menschheit* (1922), 186; *The Evolution and Progress* (1923), 172: "The connection [of the sexual instinct] with the beard is unmistakable in the case of many of the monkeys, as they have the hairless parts of the face framed with hair. Darwin has very thoroughly described the sexual significance of beards in apes."

139 **Extreme sensitivity of ~~beard – hair~~ of the skin ~~through the~~ of the face through ~~the~~ hair of the face.** TXT_6700/0_N2 Cf. Klaatsch, *Der Werdegang der Menschheit* (1922), 186; *The Evolution and Progress* (1923), 172: "The hairs of the beard are really special organs of a more or less perceptive nature–tactile hairs with a considerable supply of nerves. It is therefore, not surprising that they have been enlisted in the service of sex-life."

140 **Tabus** [German] TXT_5877/0_N99 **Later, ~~much later,~~ Tattooing ~~and Tab~~ developed partly of ~~purely~~ decorative origins ~~and of~~ are in connection with ~~tabus~~ taboos.** TXT_6700/0_N3

141 **marriage ceremonies of the… I.** TXT_6743/0_N3 The following is an excerpt from chapter 3, "The Magic of Love and Beauty," section 4, "Beauty Magic: The Ritual of Adornment," in Bronislaw Malinowski, *The Sexual Lives of Savages* (New York: Liveright; London: Routledge, 1929), II:354–55. The second volume is in Kiesler's personal library. Unlike other transcriptions from texts by other authors typed by Stefi Kiesler, the transcription of this excerpt by Malinowski is done by Kiesler himself in his handwritten draft of this chapter. It contains several errors as well as some deletions and paraphrasing, most of which were not corrected (or were even amplified by further errors) in later typescripts. The edited assembled manuscript in this volume contains corrections according to Malinowski's printed text.

142 Malinowski uses the archaic "Thy" for each of these body parts, which Kiesler originally transcribed as "the" or "they." TXT_6700/0_N4 Cf. Malinowski, *The Sexual Lives of Savages* (1929), II: 355.

(19b)

page 131

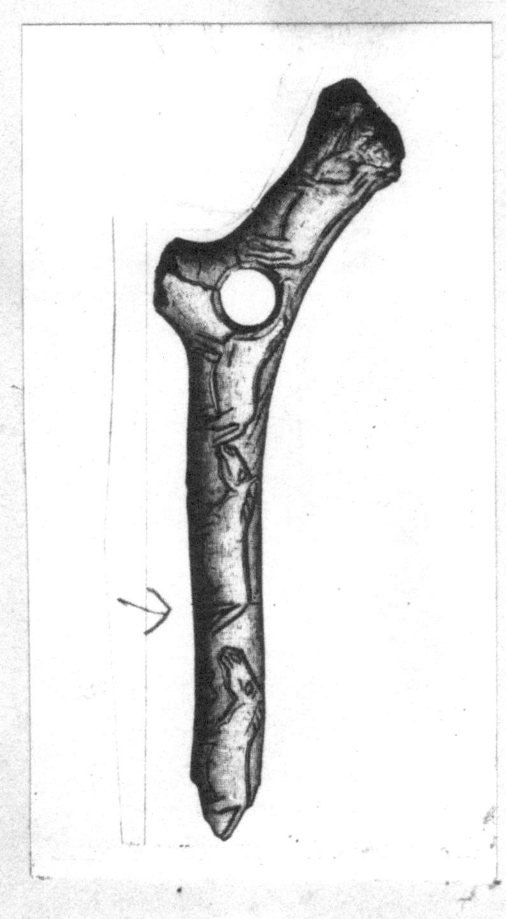

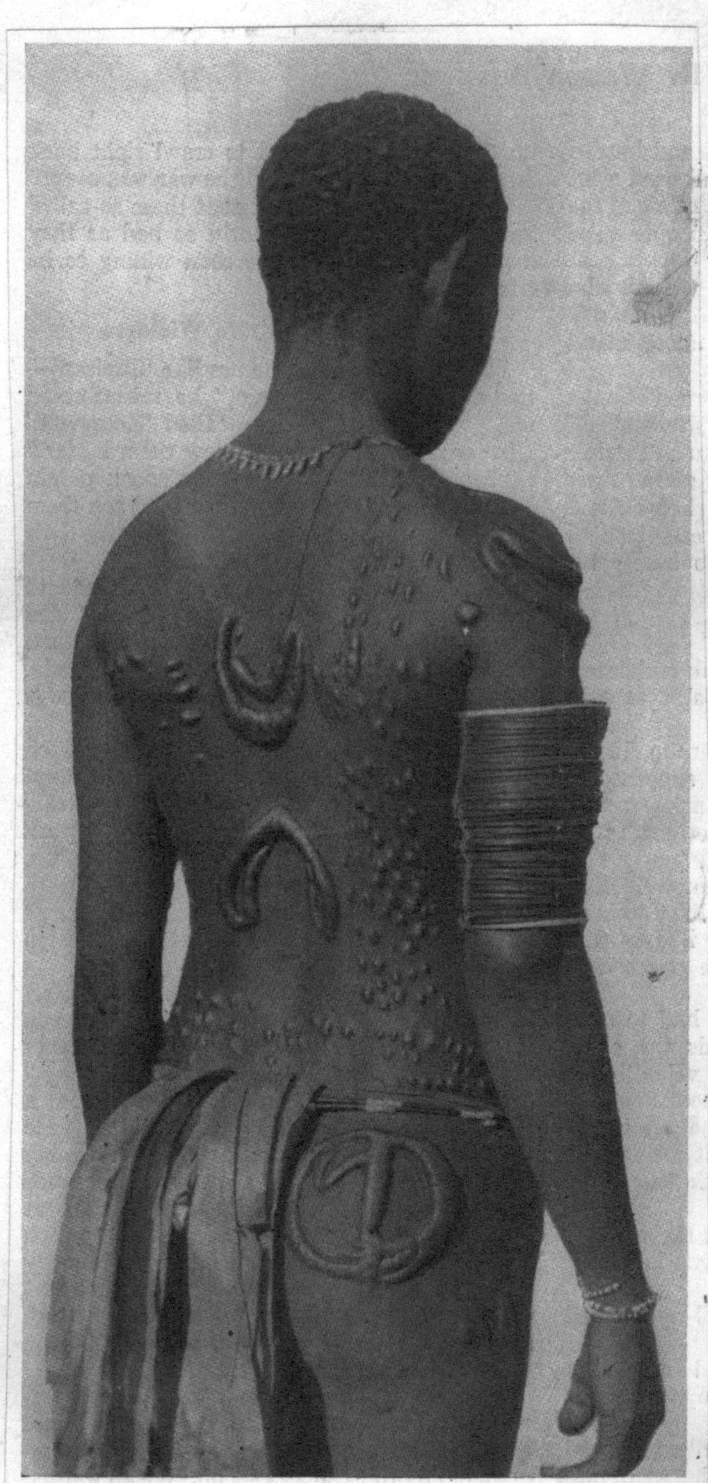

(19b): Engraving to improve the aesthetic aspect of a natural object (bone of the neolithic era).
(right) Cicatrization to improve the aesthetic aspect (women of the Solomon Islands, Pacific).

Thy cheek " "
Thy nose " "
Thy throat " "
Thy neck " "
Thy shoulders " "
Thy breast " "
Bright skin, bright; glowing skin, glowing.
————————————

Of course, like in most creations of man, one can find direct sources of inspiration for them in nature. To change, for instance, the physical "appeal" birds, reptiles, fish, change often their colors or even forms. And often the change is so obvious and comparatively splendid that one speaks of "wedding gowns" animals put on in times of courtship.[143]

With the exception of blushing, man has lost, if he ever had it, the capacity to transform his skin and body, automatically.[144] He had to invent tools and methods to do it. But the drive for it, the instinct, to produce it he shares with the animal kingdom.

* * *

Sex–attraction[145]

To the average normal person, in whatever type of society we find it, attraction by the other sex and the passionate and sentimental episodes which follow are the most significant events in his existence, those most deeply associated with his intimate happiness and with the zest and meaning of life. To the sociologist, therefore, who studies a particular type of society, those of its customs, ideas, and institutions which center round the erotic life of the individual should be of primary importance. For if he wants to be in tune with his subject and to place it in a natural, correct perspective, the sociologist must, in his research, follow the trend of personal values and interests. That which means supreme happiness to the individual must be made a fundamental factor in the scientific treatment of human society.

But the erotic phase, although the most important, is only one among many in which the sexes meet and enter into relations with each other. It cannot be studied outside its proper context, without, that is, being linked up with the legal status of man and woman; with their domestic relations; and with the distribution of their economic functions. Courtships, love, and mating in a given society are influences in every detail by the way in which the sexes face one another in public and in private, by their position in tribal law and custom, by the manner in which they participate in games and amusements, by the share each takes in ordinary daily toil.[146]

CHAPTER 8

THE (THIRD) TRANSFORMATION OF DEAD MATERIAL INTO MAGIC TOOLS OF SPIRITUAL POWER[147]

The same "practical" functional tools undergo a third transformation: the transformation of super-functional expression of Spiritualization. Of Humanization.[148] Of Beautification. Adornment.

The following is the jawbone of a man who died. It has been removed after the ritual first exhumation and is worn as a relic, decorated.

"The skull is made into a lime pot. Other bones are converted to various purposes. The radius, ulna, tibia, and some other bones are carved into lime spatulae to be used with betel and areca nut."[149]

(illustrations)[150]

143 **birds, reptiles, fish, change often their color or even ~~certain~~ forms. And often the change is so obvious and ~~splendid~~ comparatively splendid that one speaks of "weddings gowns" animals put on in times of courtship.** [handwritten addition crossed out in TS] TXT_6743/0_N5 Immediately after there is a transcription of an excerpt from the entry on *Hochzeitskleid*, or wedding dress, in the animal world from *Meyers Großes Konversations-Lexikon*, ultimately not included in later drafts of *Magic Architecture*: **Bei den Tragopanen wird der herrlich lasurblau und zinnoberrot gefleckte Kehlsack zugleich mit zwei blauen Kopfhörnern aufgeblasen, wenn das Männchen vor dem Weibchen seinen Gefiederschmuck entfaltet... Bezüglich der Entstehung des Hochzeitkleides wurde einfach eine Neubildung des Gefieders bei der Mauserung angenommen, doch Schlegel und Gädtke zeigten, dass neben der Erneuerung eine auf verschiedene Weise zustande kommende Verfärbung des bleibenden Gefieders eine grosse Rolle spielt, so dass in manchen Fällen (wie z.B. bei der Zwergmöve** [sic]**, Trauerbachstelze, Lumme, dem Alpenstrandläufer etc.) zur Paarungszeit schneeweisse** [sic] **Federn in das tief glänzendste Schwarz und Schwarzbraun umgefärbt werden können. Ebenso treten Strukturveränderungen ein, die den nachher wieder nachlassenden Metallschimmer der Kolibris und Paradiesvögel hervorbringen, wie dies auch beim Hochzeitskleider der Fische und Kriechtiere zutrifft. Auch das Haarkleid der Säugetiere lasst ähnliche Veränderungen in Färbung, Glanz und Fülle erkennen, ganz besonders stark treten die Neubildung bei der Geweihbildung einzelner Paarhufer hervor.** [In the case of tragopans, if the male unfolds its ornate plumage in front of the female, the wonderfully glaze-blue and vermilion spotted gulan pouch is at the same time inflated with two blue head horns ... With regard to the development of the wedding dress, it was simply assumed that the plumage was newly formed during moulting, but Schlegel and Gädtke showed that in addition to the renewal, a change in color of the permanent plumage, which occurs in different ways, plays an important role, so that in some cases (e.g. the little gull, pied wagtail, guillemot, the dunlin, etc.) snow-white feathers can be re-colored into the deepest shiny black and black-brown during the mating season. Similarly, structural changes occur, which produce the metallic shimmer of the hummingbirds and birds-of-paradise, as is the case with the wedding dress of fish and reptiles, which is reduced afterwards. The mammalian coat also shows similar changes in coloring, shine and fullness. This is particularly pronounced in the new formation of antlers of individual even-toed ungulates.] For the original entry, see "Hochzeitskleid" in *Meyers Großes Konversations-Lexikon*, 6th rev. ed. (Leipzig and Vienna: Bibliographisches Institut, 1905) 9:406–407 (407 for the excerpt transcribed by the Kieslers). See Sources, Disciplines, and Objects, pp. 42 88, and fig. A.35.

144 **With the exception of blushing, ~~a rather negative~~ man has lost, if he ever had it the capacity to transform ~~the colour~~ his skin and body, automatically.** TXT_6743/0_N5 This entire paragraph was handwritten and omitted in later drafts.

145 **Malinowsky** [sic]**, Vol I. page 1. Sex** TXT_6743/0_N6 The following paragraphs come from Malinowski, *The Sexual Lives of Savages* (1929) 1:1–2.

146 **"Klaatch** [sic]**, Evolution p. 178"** TXT_6743/0_N7-N11 Here follows a long (five-page) typewritten transcription of several excerpts from Klaatsch, *The Evolution and Progress*. The same excerpts are transcribed under the heading **Social–family** among the drafts for Part I. TXT_6844/0_N1-N5 In the first copy (TXT_6743), Kiesler crosses out **Social–family** and adds the heading **Sex–marriage**. In the margin, the first and second paragraphs (again transcribed from Klaatsch's 1923 English edition, 178–179) bear the description **home**; the third and fourth (from the same edition, 191–192), **sex**. These last paragraphs of the transcription are not included in other drafts of *Magic Architecture*. In a separate draft handwritten in German, Kiesler adds his speculations on the role of the "sex drive [*Sexualtrieb*]" on the creation of family and human society: **Die zwei Formen der Gesellschaft[:] 1. Sexualtrieb (Homo) - Zusammenleben verschiedenen Geschlechts = Mann + Weib / 2. Geselligkeitstrieb (Sakral)– gleichgeschlechtliche Individuen / 1) (Sexualtrieb entwickelt: Blutsgemeinschaft in: Familie, Sippe, Horde, Stamm. / teils soziale, teils wirtschaftliche Einrichtung der Ehe. 2) Geistige oder Spieltrieb entwickelt: Vereinigungen von Altersklassen, etc.** [The two forms of society (:) / 1. sexual drive (Homo)–cohabitation of the different sexes = husband + wife (Weib) / 2. sociability drive (sacral)–same-sex individuals / 1) (sexual drive leads to consanguinity in: family, kinship, horde, tribe. / partly social, partly economic establishment of marriage. / 2) spiritual drive or play instinct leads to: unification of age classes, etc.] See fig. B.13. TXT_6804/0

147 Beneath the chapter title, the accompanying chart by Kiesler mentions: **"Third"** / **The "SECOND TRANSFORMATION"** (fig. B.12) SFP_6662/0_N6

148 **The same "practical" functional tools undergo a SECOND transformation. The Transformation of super functional expression. Of Spiritualization. Of HUMANIZATION.** SFP_6662/0_N6

149 This passage comes from Malinowski, *The Sexual Lives of Savages* (1:133). The handwritten transcription by Kiesler in his diagram bears quotation marks at the beginning of the paragraph but does not mention Malinowski. It contains several errors, which are reproduced in later typescripts: **line-pat** instead of "lime pot," **concerted** instead of "converted," **relua** instead of "radius, ulna" and **arica** instead of "areca." TXT_5877/0_103; SFP_6662/0_N6 For the original model for Kiesler's sketch of the decorated human jaw, see photograph in Malinowski, *The Sexual Lives of Savages*, plates 34–36 and Sources, Disciplines, and Objects, p. 40.

150 Referring to accompanying chart with text and sketches by Kiesler (fig. B.12). SFP_6662/0_N6

fig. B.12

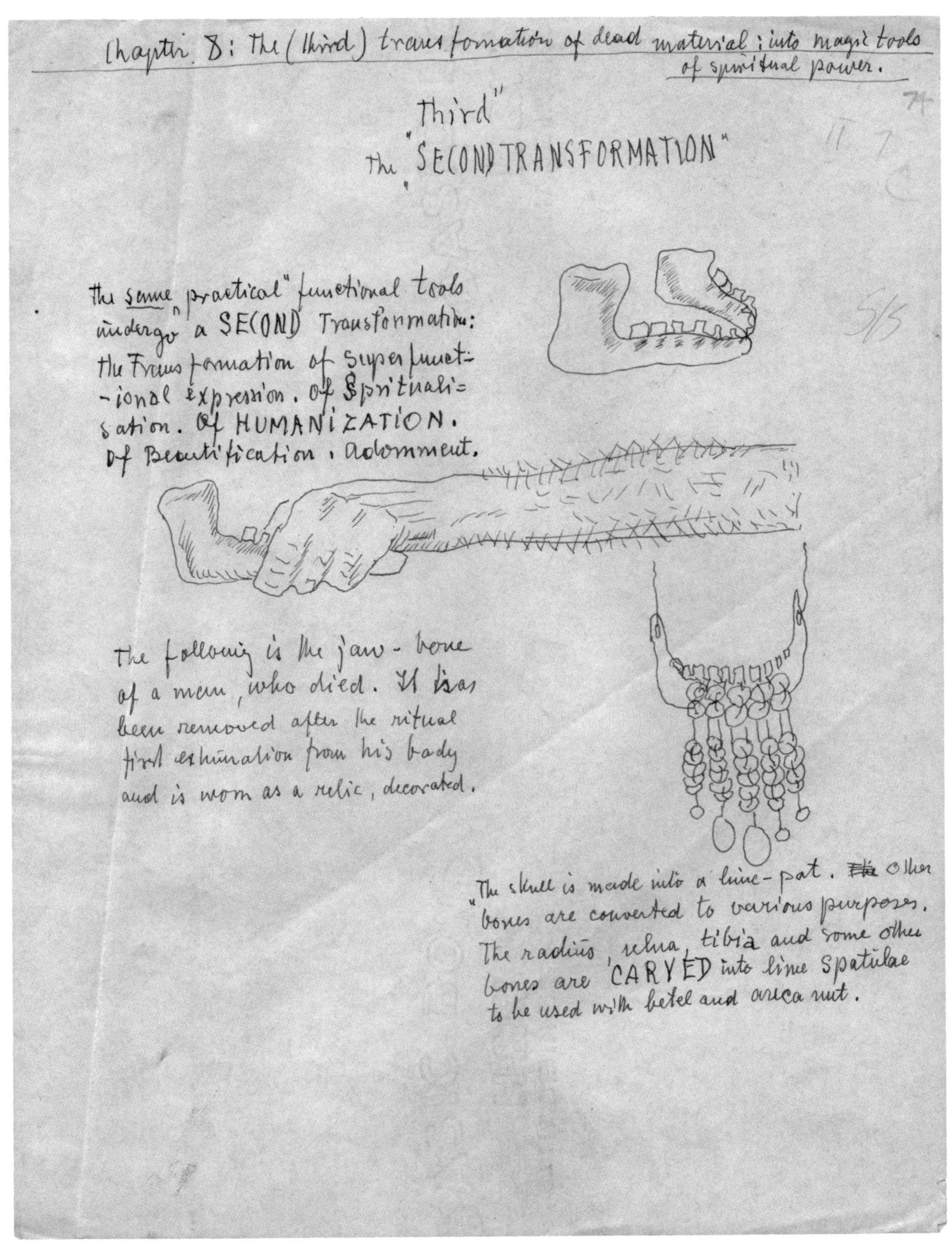

Frederick Kiesler, Part II, Chapter 8, "The (third) transformation of dead material: into magic tools of spiritual power," Chart with ink drawings and handwritten descriptions (MS, ink) ÖFLKS, SFP_6662/0_N6

fig. B.13

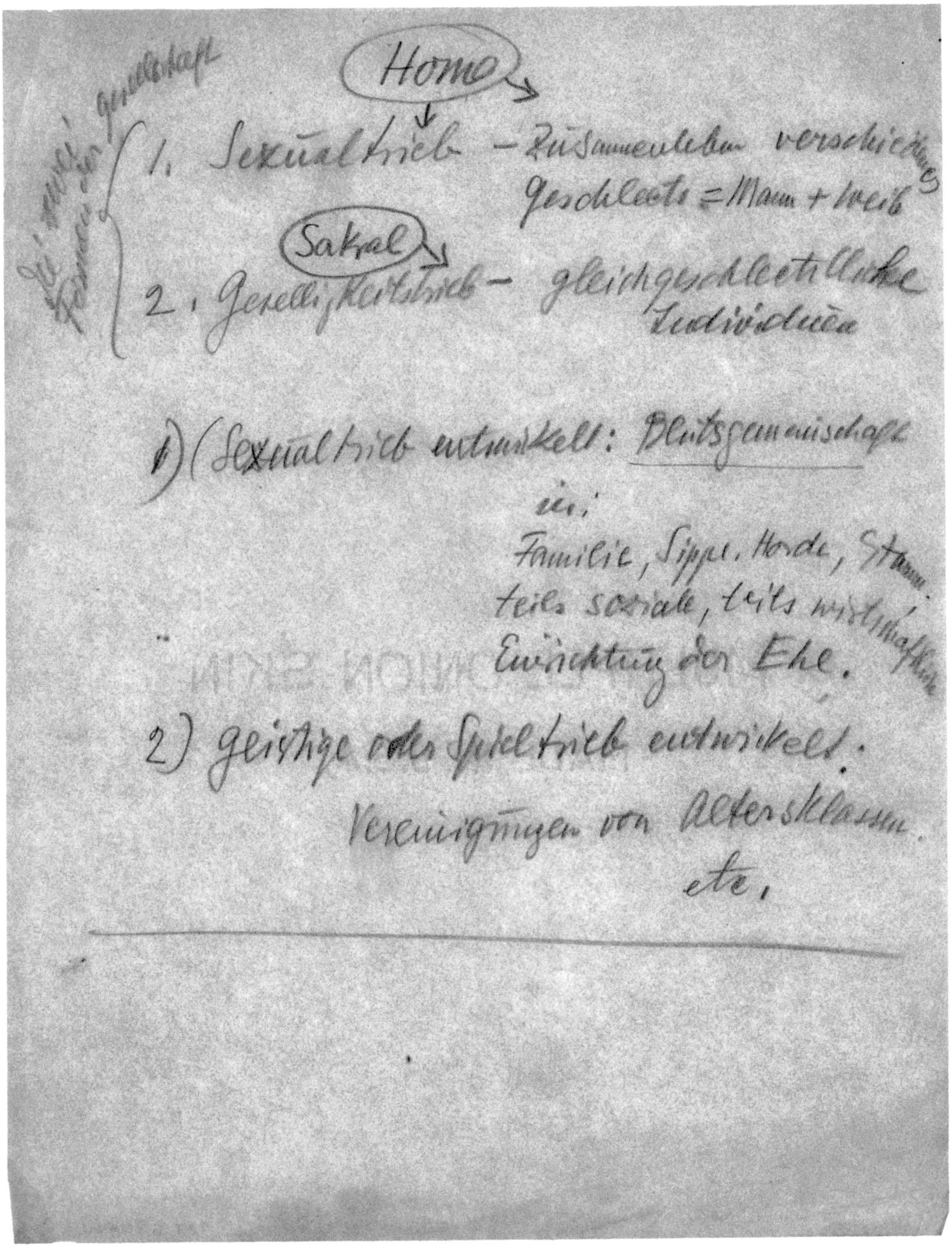

Home

1. Sexualtrieb – Zusammenleben verschiedenes Geschlechts = Mann + Weib

Sakral

2. Geselligkeitstrieb – gleichgeschlechtlicher Individuen

Zweierlei Formen der Gesellschaft

1) (Sexualtrieb entwickelt: Blutsgemeinschaft

in:

Familie, Sippe, Horde, Stamm;
teils soziale, teils wirtschaftliche
Einrichtung der Ehe.

2) geistige oder Spieltrieb entwickelt.

Vereinigungen von Altersklassen.

etc.

Frederick Kiesler, Draft with hand-written notes on "**Sexualtrieb** [sex drive]" related to the content of Part II, Chapter 7, "The (second) Transformation of dead material into Magic Tools of physical attraction" (MS, pencil) ÖFLKS, TXT_6804/0

14
Eugene N. Marais, *The Soul of the White Ant* (New York: Dodd, Mead & Co., 1937), 124–126. ÖFLKS, SCL_22/0

15
Marais, *The Soul of the White Ant*, 168–169. ÖFLKS, SCL_23/0

16
Noack, *Die Baukunst des Altertums*, pl. 172.

16a
"Sky-Scrapers of the Termite World," in *Compton's Pictured Encyclopedia*, vol. 1 (Chicago: F. E. Compton & Co., 1922), 143. ÖFLKS, SCL_24/0

16b
Noack, *Die Baukunst des Altertums*, pl. 137.

16c
Temple of Apollo, Corinth. Noack, *Die Baukunst des Altertums*, pl. 22. ÖFLKS, SCL_25/0

16d
"A Miracle of Building! Ant-Made 'Sky-Scrapers,'" *Illustrated London News* 174, no. 4961, March 16, 1929, 455. ÖFLKS, SCL_26/0

16e
Rockefeller Center under construction, 1934. Source unknown, photo Wurts Bros. ÖFLKS, SCL_26/0

17
Arthur Radclyffe Dugmore, *The Romance of the Beaver: Being in the History of the Beaver in the Western Hemisphere* (Philadelphia: J. B. Lippincott Co., 1914), 41. ÖFLKS, SCL_27/0

18
George Shiras III, "The Wild Life of Lake Superior, Past and Present," *National Geographic Magazine* XL, no. 2, August 1921, 113–204. ÖFLKS, SCL_27/0

19
Above: "A Canadian 'St. Francis': The Beaver's Friend—'Grey Owl' and His 'Little Brothers' of the Wild," *Illustrated London News* 179, no. 4818, August 22, 1931, 278–279. ÖFLKS, SCL_28/0

Below: Member of the Kadu Kuruba, near Mysore. Martin Hürlimann, *Indien: Baukunst, Landschaft und Volksleben* (Berlin: Ernst Wasmuth Verlag A.G., 1928). English edition (also in NYPL): *India: The Landscape, the Monuments and the People* (New York: B. Westermann, 1928), pl. 67.

20
Above: nest of a dormouse, and burrows of a mole, badger, and rabbit. *Meyers Großes Konversations-Lexikon*, "Tierwohnungen," 547–548, figs. 5–8. ÖFLKS, SCL_29/0

Middle and *below*: Frobenius, *Kulturgeschichte Afrikas*, 219, fig. 169.

19a
Above: *Meyers Großes Konversations-Lexikon*, 6th ed., vol. 18, "Kultur der Steinzeit" (Leipzig and Vienna: Bibliographisches Institut, 1907), figs. 10 (left), 3 (right). ÖFLKS, SCL_30/0

Below: Ellora Caves, Mumbai. Hürlimann, *Indien: Baukunst, Landschaft und Volksleben*, pl. 99.

19b
Left: Command staff. *Meyers Großes Konversations-Lexikon*, "Kultur der Steinzeit" (Leipzig and Vienna: Bibliographisches Institut, 1907), fig. 2. ÖFLKS, SCL_31/0

Right: Nakanai woman with scarification marks, New Britain. *Die Große Völkerkunde: Sitten, Gebräuche und Wesen fremder Völker*, Vol. 2 (*Asien*), ed. Hugo A. Bernatzik (Leipzig: Bibliographisches Institut, 1939), 325, fig. 234, photo Henry Ludlow Downing.

AWARENES of the Miraculous

fig. B.14

Frederick Kiesler, Preliminary diagram with “Illustrations” related to bodily transformation into “dream images” via painting and sculpting: “1. Painted Bodies 2. Modeled Hair 3. Clothed 4. Engraved Bodies” related to the content of Part III, Chapter 1, “The Birth of Magic Design” (MS, pencil)
ÖFLKS, SFP_6663/0_N1

PART III
AWARENESS OF THE MIRACULOUS[1]

INTRODUCTION
FROM ANIMAL HOUSING TO MAGIC ARCHITECTURE[2]

That mystic and stirring expectancy of miraculous intervention and of benevolent and unexpected happenings which come to all men at certain psychological moments, forms the foundation of the human belief in magic. There is a desire in every one of us to escape from routine and uncertainty,[3] and it can be said, without exaggeration, that to most men nothing is more cheerless and oppressive than the rigidity and determination with which the world runs; and nothing more repugnant than the cold truths of science, which express and emphasize the determination of reality. Even the most skeptical at times rebels against the inevitable causal chain, which excludes a priori the supernatural and, with it, all the gifts of chance, good fortune and above all the gifts of the imagination of man's creativeness.

Being able to change natural bodies and even his own at times, how much more desirable would it be to lift his own technological manmade[4] ornaments, tools, and houses out of functional limitations into the realm of exuberant affirmation of his self! This awareness has finally struck man,[5] but he is not yet entirely conscious of it.

CHAPTER 1
THE BIRTH OF MAGIC DESIGN[6]

Man discovers his capacity to
convert his own body into a
dream-image[7] through make-up[8]

Man discovers his miraculous capacity to convert his own body into a dream image through make-up. In our time make-up of the face is a matter of surface-beautification.[9] It is—for us—hard to believe that "make-up" once had a deep psychological significance. More than that: it was the "mene tekel" of another, mysterious world.[10] It was a stigma.[11]

The majority of lower societies known to us, has some individuals who undergo even a further initiation. These are the sorcerers, medicine men, shamans, doctors, whatever one chooses to call them. At the time of maturity they have to undergo the tests of all the other young people. But to achieve the ability of fulfilling the important functions that will be entrusted to them, they have to endure still another novitiate (probate), which may last months, even years. During this time they are under the supervision of their teachers, i.e., the practicing sorcerer or shaman.[12]

In regard to the details of the probation period and the effects derived from (seeming death and new birth) one can find that sometimes the analogy turns into identity.

During the initiation no rest is permitted the candidates ... one commands them constant walking or standing until they are totally exhausted and actually no longer know what happens to them. They are forbidden to drink even a drop of water, or to eat. They are made insensible and rigid. "When this condition reaches paroxysm, one can say that they are dead.[13] In other words, the spirits who execute this initiation, kill and then awaken them again to new life. At dawn one of the exorcisers come to the entrance of the cave and there he finds the man (candidate) sleeping; he hits him now with an invisible spear. It pierces through the nape, penetrates the tongue, affecting a big hole and leaves through the mouth. Another spear pierces the head from one

1 Title page (frontispiece): PART III AWARENESS OF THE MIRACULOUS TXT_6825/0_N1

2 Alternative titles: From Animal ~~Architecture~~ Housing to Magic Architecture TXT 6734/0_N1 From Animal Architecture to man's Housing to Magic Architecture TXT_6734/0_N2

3 In the MS Kiesler initially writes certainty before adding ~~un~~UNcertainty TXT_6734/0_N2

4 ~~tools and~~ ornaments TXT_6734/0_N2

5 This awareness has struck ~~him~~ MAN, but ~~it is only the beginning.~~ TXT_6734/0_N2

6 Alternative chapter number and title: ~~Introduction to~~ PART II Chapter ~~III~~ II [preliminary MS] TXT_6788/0 Birth of Design TXT_6734/0_N1 The Birth of Design. ~~by man.~~ TXT_6747/0_N1 Cf. handwritten notes and annotated table-chart on the origins of design. TXT_6806/0_N1-N2 (figs. C.09a-b).

7 ~~The~~ miraculous capacity to convert bodies into dream images through ~~painting and sculpting~~ TXT_6747/0_N1 ~~The conversion of corporeality~~ The miraculous capacity to convert bodies into dream images through painting and sculpting TXT_6788/0_N1 The conversion of corporeality into dream images through painting and sculpting [Erased chapter title over a set of drawn illustrations depicting the bodily transformation into "dream images" via painting and sculpting:] 1. Painted Bodies 2. Modeled Hair 3. Clothed 4. Engraved Bodies (fig. B.14). SFP: 6663/0_N1

8 make up. (painting) TXT_6734/0_N1

9 a matter of decorative beautification. TXT_6788/0_N1

10 it was the "mene tekel" of another, mysterious world, which originated the ~~sign of~~ "making" of the painted face. TXT_6788/0_N1 "Mene tekel": the writing on the wall, Aramaic; Daniel, Book V.

11 "I quote in Levy Brühl; Denken der Naturvölker / from page .... 318 (unter 11 lines) / and from page ... 319 (oben: aber was ... till ... worden ist." TXT_6788/0_N1 ~~I quote L. Lévy-Bruhl:~~ TXT_6747/0_N1 A quotation follows from Lévy Bruhl's text in German with the note übersetzt! [translated]. The transcription omits part of the main text as well as all footnotes of the original text. TXT_6747/0_N1-2 Cf. Lévy-Bruhl, *Das Denken der Naturvölker* (1926), 318–319. For the Kieslers' English translation of these excerpts from the German edition of Lévy-Bruhl transcribed above, see TXT_6747/0_N4-N5 Their translation differs from the English edition of Levy-Bruhl's text published in the 1920s: *How Natives Think* (1926), 354–355. For the same passages in the original French edition, Lévy-Bruhl, *Les fonctions mentales dans les sociétés inférieures* (1910), 417–418.

12 Cf. Kiesler's handwritten notes on shamanism and magic: Hingabe → Mystik, Shamanismus → Magie / Ultima ratio der Mechanik (Devotion-Mystic, Shamanism-Magic/ last resort of mechanics) The phrase "ultima ratio der Mechanik" is also used by Frobenius in a section on "architecture" of his *Kulturgeschichte Afrikas*, 213. See reproduction of the handwritten text (fig. B.15) under the notes of this page. TXT_6828/0_N6

13 In this and the following paragraph, Lévy-Bruhl quotes from Baldwin Spencer and Francis James Gillen, *The Native Tribes of Central Australia* (London: Macmillan and Co., 1899), 523–525 (all editions of Lévy-Bruhl's book mention 524–525). In connection to the same passage, Lévy-Bruhl also cites a series of similar ethnographic descriptions on the "graduation" practices of the "medicine man" by Spencer and Gillen in *The Northern Tribes of Central Australia* (London: Macmillan and Co., 1904), 480–484. Cited in Lévy-Bruhl, *Das Denken der Naturvölker*, 319. One of Kiesler's plate illustrations (plate 11) is a detail from a photograph of a "medicine man" with a painted pattern on his face and body included in the same chapter of *The Native Tribes of Central Australia* excerpted by Lévy-Bruhl (Spencer and Gillen [1899], 527, fig. 105). No edition of Lévy-Bruhl's studies includes any illustrations, which suggests that the Kieslers might have referred to the original publications he was citing in search of image material. This particular photograph of the "medicine man" also appears in Spencer and Gillen, *The Arunta; A Study of a Stone Age People*, vol. 2 (New York: Humanities Press, 1927), n.p., fig. 118. Ashley Montagu uses *The Arunta* as a source for most of the plates of his *Coming into Being Among the Australian Aborigines*, but his book is sparsely illustrated and does not include this particular photograph.

Hingabe ; Schamanismus
↓ ↓
Mystik Magie
ultima ratio der Mechanik

ear to the other. The victim falls down dead and is carried immediately into the depth of the cave (the abode of the spirits). There, the iruntarinia (spirit) removes from the body of the victim all the inner organs and replaces them with entirely new ones. (This operation is identical with the one the initiated of the tribe have to endure during their seeming death) ...[14] He then returns to life, but in a state of madness (likewise the initiated)... For several days the candidate shows more or less a strange behavior, until one observes one morning that he painted a wide stripe across the upper part of his nose with fat and coaldust. All signs of madness disappear and one knows that a new medicine man is admitted."

This black streak of charcoal and oil which shows now across the face of a human, appears a sign from another world.[15] It is the imprint of dream. No doubt, it was initiated in the medicine-man-life as a dead. He has come back. He has the knowledge of the secret powers. He has been stigmatized.[16]

The making of designs will mean now: contact with the unknown. Calling the forces from within and from beyond. The design was born a symbol of magic power.[17]

CHAPTER 2

Man discovers that the fingers
of his hand are magic wands for
the transformation of surfaces into
images through the application of paint[18] pl. 21

These forerunners of ours in the dim past seem to have practiced in the depth of long caves a peculiar kind of "sympathetic magic" involving naturalistic representations of animals required for food.[19] pl. 22

The colours, in both paleolithic and neolithic times, were generally made with natural ochres powdered of pounded and mixed with some fatty substance. This has disappeared and one can only guess at its nature. It may have been liquid like oil, but this is doubtful; on the other hand marrow-fats were easily obtainable. There is, however, the difficulty that fat is not liquid, as it has penetrated into the microscopic interstices of the rock. The organic matter has disappeared, but the mineral pigment has become, as it were, part of the rock itself, except when the rock is bituminous. Though different pigments, derived from the various natural ochres, etc. were used, the present tints are also due to the fact that there has been a gradual change of colour brought about by atmospheric action.[20]

CHAPTER 3

Man discovers that by making grooves
(engraving) in hard stone objects held in
his hand he can transform soft stone
surfaces into images[21] pl. 23

[22] But whatever primitive man at that period did—was transformation of the surface. He did not go into the form as a whole and changed it to represent his vision. That happened much later. (If he changed the form of a stone or bone it was only for practical, utilitarian purposes, like tools for defense and food.)

With a hard piece of stone, a so-called "stone flint," man engraves designs into another (somewhat softer) stone. He plays now with a tool (flint) which normally serves him only for utilitarian purposes.[23] (Rock carvings in Spain & Africa).[24]

14 Ellipses in the original French text by Lévy-Bruhl while quoting from Spencer and Gillen, *The Native Tribes*. The number of ellipses differs in the German edition and also varies in the Kieslers' transcription of the same passage in German and their translation into English. Cf. TXT_6747/0_N2; TXT_6689/0_N03

15 **appears a sign~~, or a stigma~~ from another world.** TXT_6788/0_N2

16 **He has come back. ~~stigmatized.~~** TXT_6788/0_N2

17 **Design was born a magic symbol.** TXT_6788/0_N2

18 Alternative chapter numbers and titles: **Discovering the Finger of His Hand a Magic Wand for the Frame Formation of Rock Surfaces Through Application of Make-up (Painting)** TXT_6734/0_N1 **PART III Chapter ~~IV–V~~ two ~~The Discovery~~ of ~~the Paint-Shik~~** [sic] **~~as~~ a Magic Wand~~.~~** / **Transformation of Rocks ~~(through painting).~~** / **~~wall painting.~~** TXT_6825/0_N2 The manuscript draft includes drawings of rocks with human, animal, and vegetal symbols (fig. B.16).

19 The following passages are quoted from Henri Breuil and Miles Crawford Burkitt, *Rock Paintings of Southern Andalusia: A Description of a Neolithic and Copper Age Art Group* (Oxford: Clarendon Press, 1929), 1, 4. The first paragraph was preceded by a (partially erased) handwritten note by Stefi Kiesler indicating the book's title and page numbers: **Rock Paintings of Southern Andalusia** / **p. 1 → / p. 4** TXT_6746/0 The second paragraph was preceded by struck-through text transcribed from Breuil **~~(Some notes must now be made on the pigments used by the old prehistoric folk and how they were prepared.)~~** TXT_6746/0

20 Kiesler intended to use a number of additional excerpts from Breuil's study of rock paintings. For Kiesler's notes and further transcriptions from Breuil's study, as well as Frobenius's *Kulturgeschichte der Afrika*, see TXT_6813/0/N1-N3verso; TXT_6814/0 and Addenda: Transcriptions and Translations, pp. 360–62.

21 Alternative chapter numbers and titles: **PART III Chapter ~~III IV V~~ III. The discovery of the chisel as a magic wand for the TRANSFORMATION of ~~Rock~~ stones through grooves (engraving) ~~(from sculpting).~~** TXT_6825/0_N3recto (fig. B.17) **Discovery of the chisel as a magic wand for the transformation of stone surfaces through grooves (engraving)** TXT 6734/0_N1

22 This paragraph and the following were handwritten and accompanied by a sheet of drawings that were annotated on the reverse. The passage was not transcribed in later drafts. See fig. B.17. TXT_6825/0_N3recto-verso

23 **~~The tool had first to be direct, like the stone flint, before it could become indirect, namely a tool for producing another tool, which will have greater bearing. With that status~~ re-production ~~began.~~** TXT_6825/0_N3recto (fig. B.17) Cf. the following formulations: **First and second state of tools. Natural ~~The~~ tools had first to be discovered, like the stone flint, before it could become a tool for another more powerful tool It first had to be a direct tool (I. state); later it developed into an indirect tool (II. state).** TXT 6806/0_N3

24 **Insert A (from Antiquity)** [instruction to insert a transcription] TXT_6825/0_N3 recto **from: Antiquity, vol XI. No 41 March 1937, p. 58.** TXT_6825/0_N4 For copies of the same transcribed excerpt cited as **"Scandinavian Rock paintings," Antiquity, March 1937 (Part 3 Chap. 3)**, see TXT_6745/0; TXT_6745/1. For the published article: Grahame Clark, "Scandinavian Rock-engravings," *Antiquity* 11 (March 1937): 56–69, here 58. Kiesler also reproduces a number of illustrations from this article in plates 22 and 23.

fig. B.16

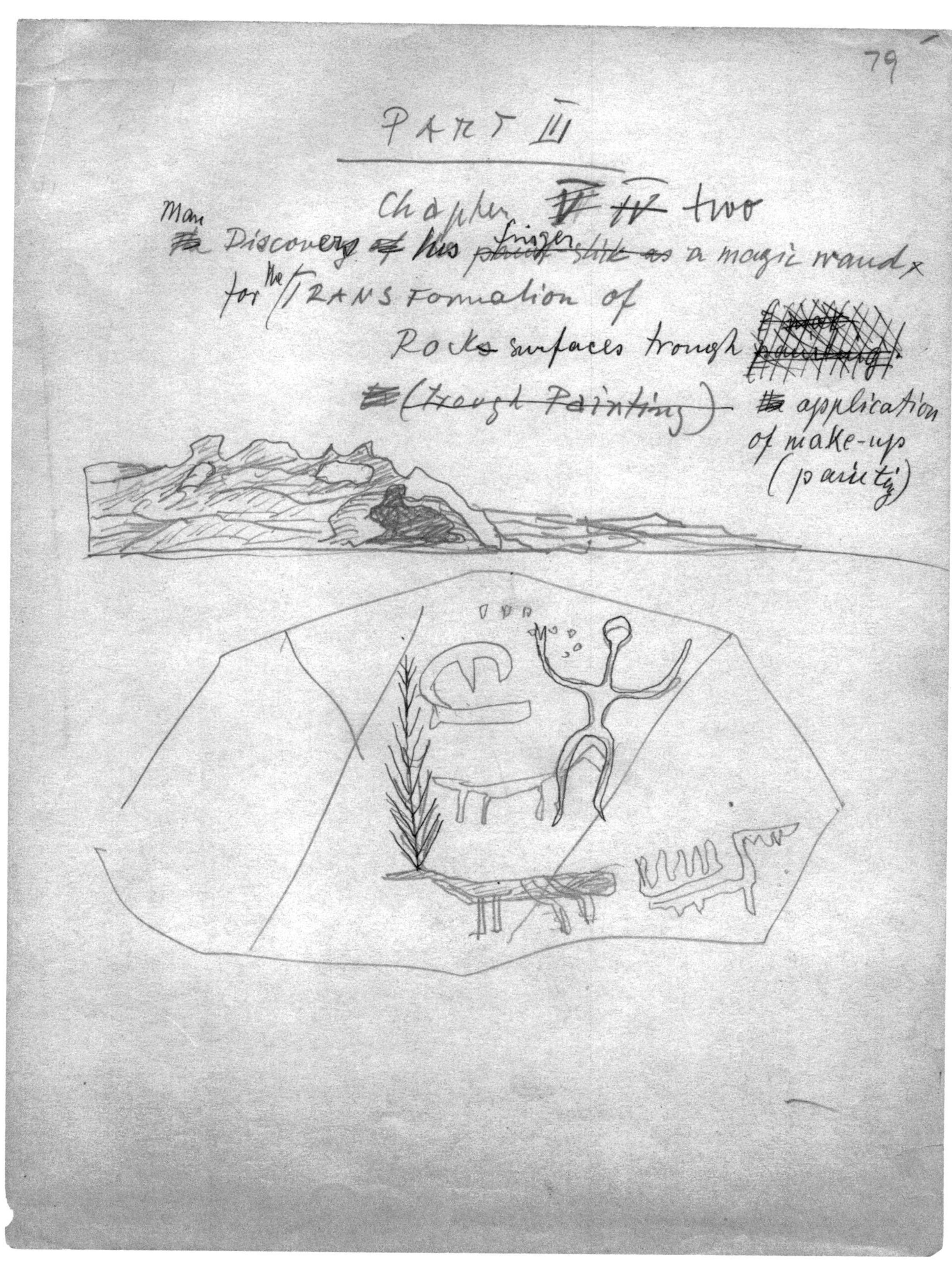

Frederick Kiesler, Part III, Chapter 2 "Man discovers his fingers are magic wands…," preliminary diagram with notes: "Man discovers his finger …. a magic wand for the TRANSFORMATION of Rock surfaces through application of make-up (painting) (MS, pencil) ÖFLKS, TXT_6825/0_N2

(21)

(21). Page 149

Present-day photograph of an Australian Aborigine making cave-painting, (apparently) in the same manner as those of the pre-historic cave-paintings of the European stone-age.
Below: The cave of Ayers Rock, Central Australia, (Same man seen in Entrance.)

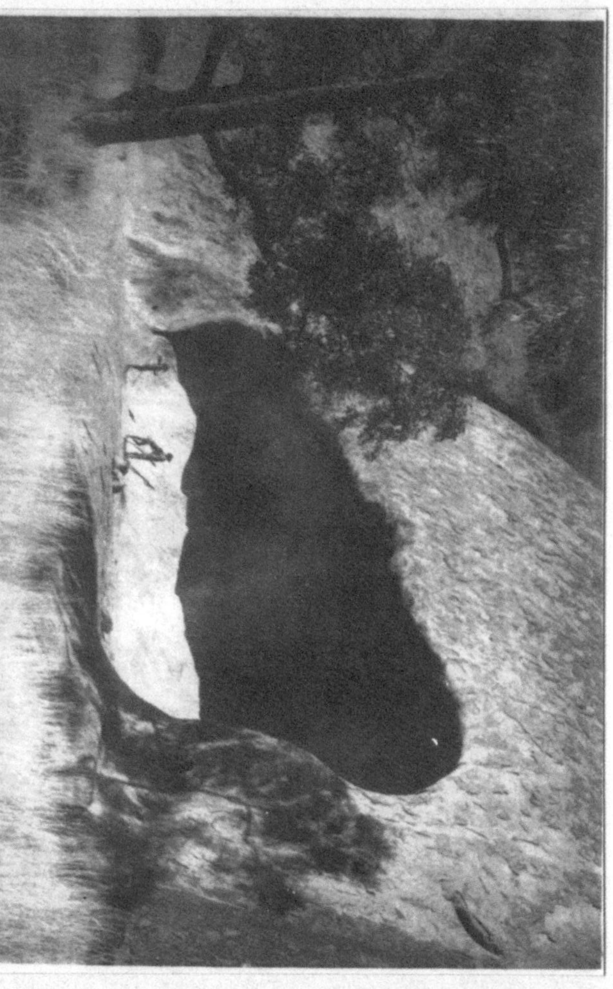

pre 149

(22)

page 149

(22). Three styles (a,b,c) of engravings of the stone-age.
Below: Similar design filled in with chalk for clearer reading.

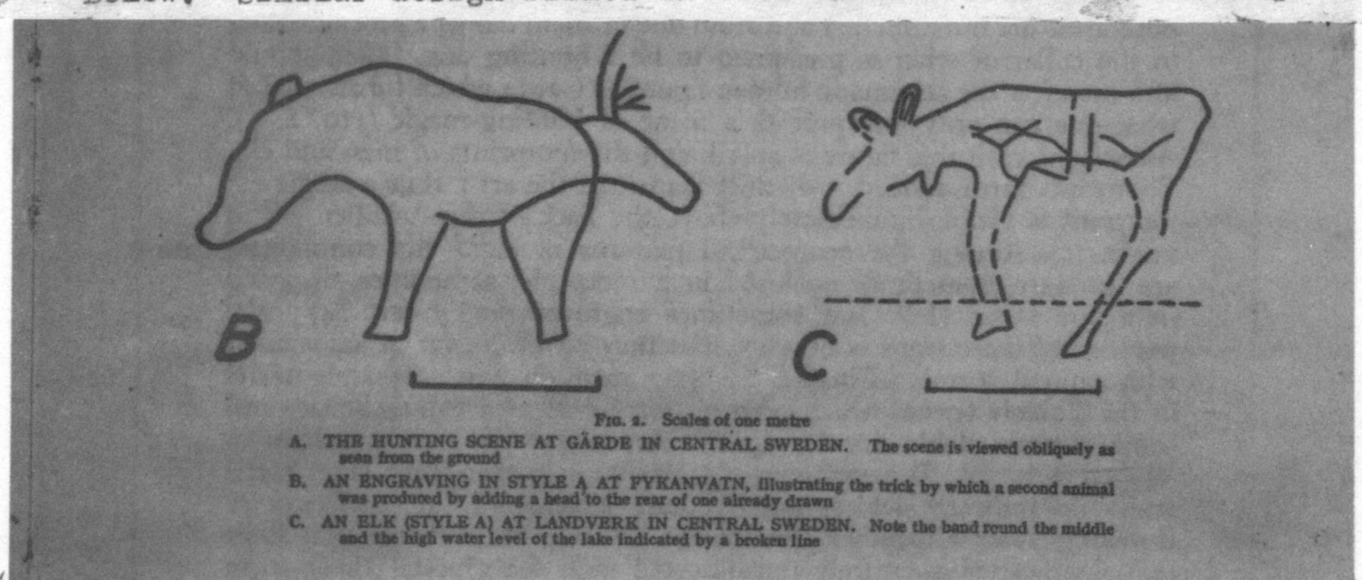

FIG. 2. Scales of one metre

A. THE HUNTING SCENE AT GÄRDE IN CENTRAL SWEDEN. The scene is viewed obliquely as seen from the ground

B. AN ENGRAVING IN STYLE A AT FYKANVATN, illustrating the trick by which a second animal was produced by adding a head to the rear of one already drawn

C. AN ELK (STYLE A) AT LANDVERK IN CENTRAL SWEDEN. Note the band round the middle and the high water level of the lake indicated by a broken line

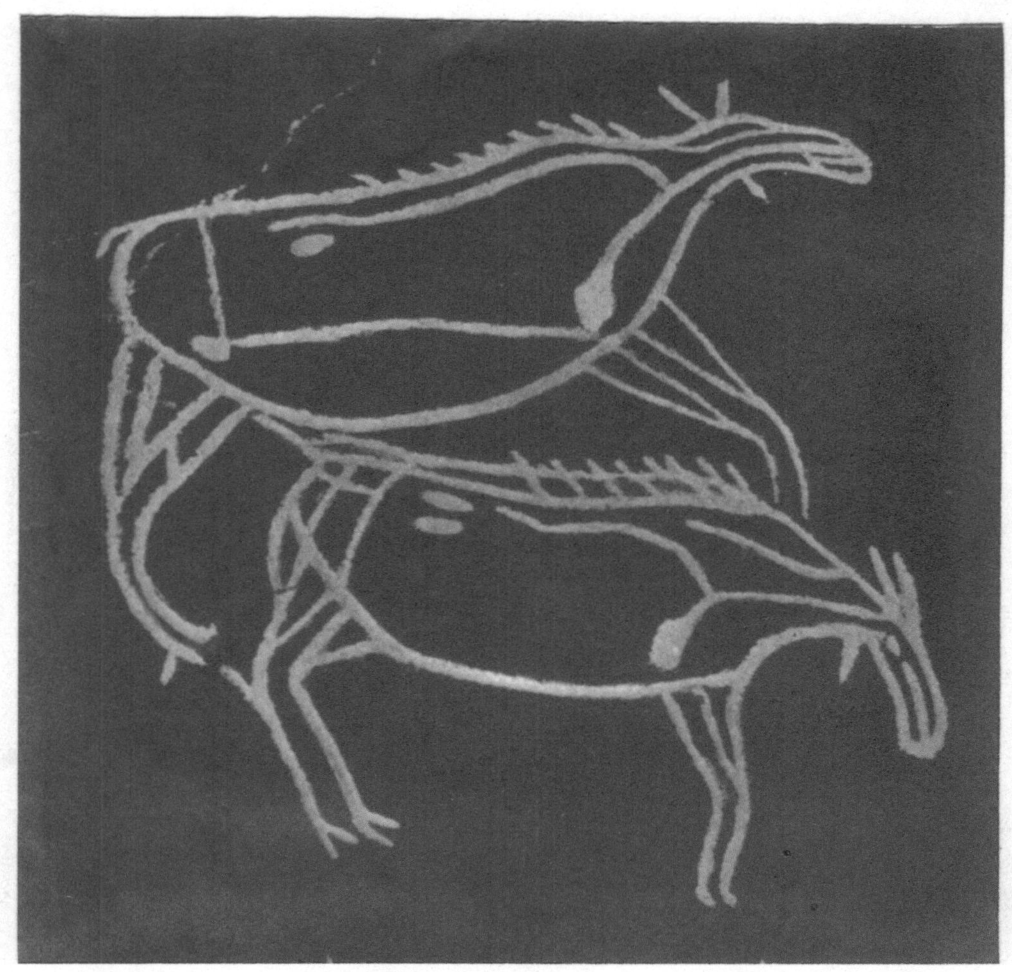

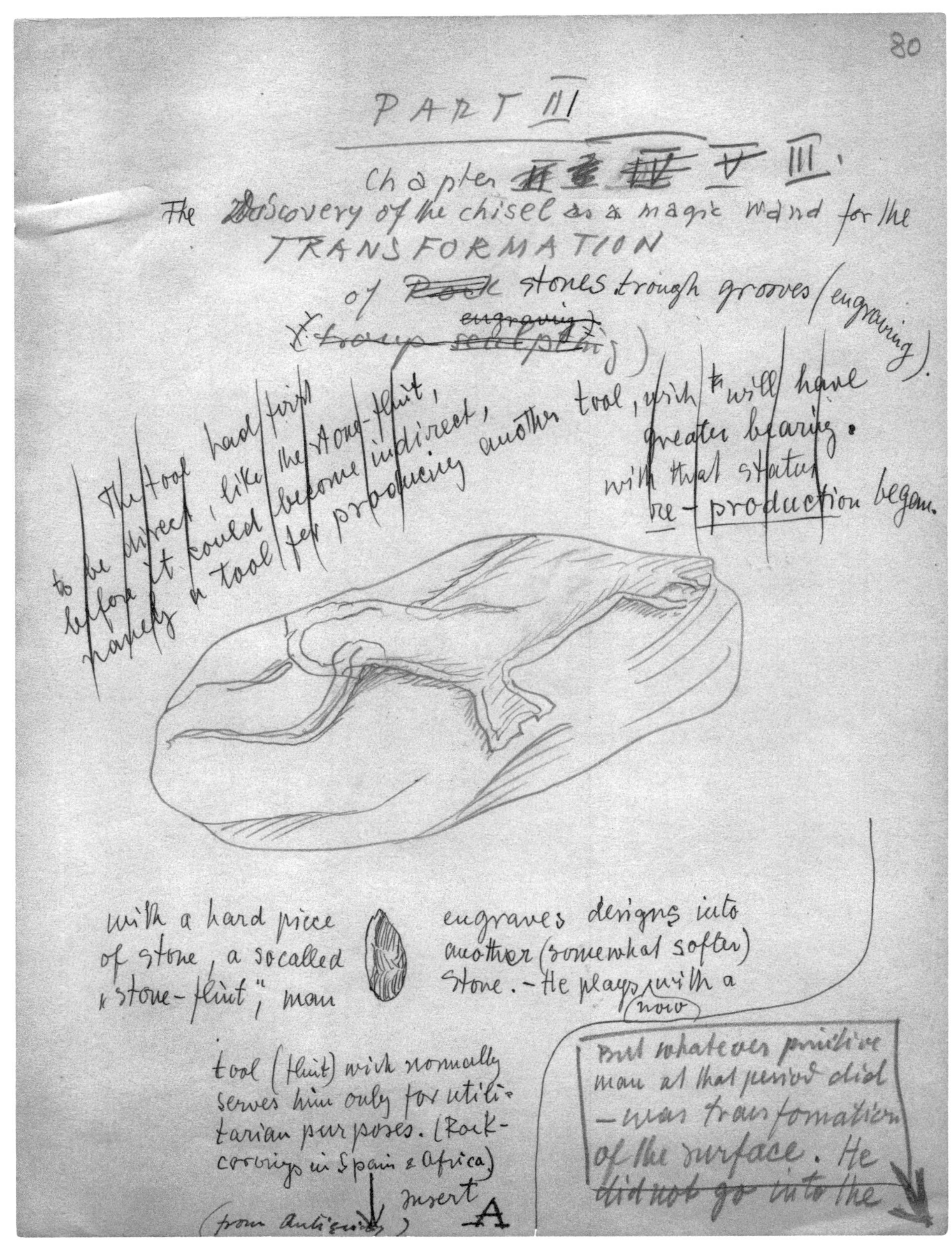

Frederick Kiesler, Part III, Chapter 3, "Man discovers that by making grooves..." preliminary diagram with notes: "The discovery of the chisel as a magic wand for the TRANSFORMATION of stones through grooves (engraving) ..." (MS, pencil, ink) ÖFLKS, TXT_6825/0 N3recto

In producing the engravings direct incision was possible only where the rock was sufficiently soft and at present it has been recorded only at Hell, a place much frequented by tourists from Trondheim,[25] for reasons quite unconnected with prehistoric archeology. A second technique, that of grinding into the rock-surface (Schleiftechnik), is of particular interest because it is only found employed on engravings of style A, thus serving to support the reality of the sub-division made on purely stylistic grounds. The third and commonest technique, that of pecking, by which a line was produced by the junction of a great number of shallow pits, was occasionally employed on engravings of style A, but exclusively on those of style B, as well as on the later Bronze Age group. Such pecked outlines are often difficult to see, but the technique is well demonstrated by Plate V, the original of which was taken while the rock surface was still glistening after heavy rain.

CHAPTER 4
DISCOVERY AND AFFIRMATION OF THE SUPERFLUOUS[26]

His eyes are no longer bent to the ground but are fixed towards the horizon.[27] Man not only stands erect, he walks erect; he has risen to the state of human being.

The visions of his inner sight[28] have now grown to maturity and are seeking a way by which they might come to life.

The new skill of his hands is spreading this imagery[29] over the surfaces of his cave. He tries to grasp the mysteries of the world he lives in by halting them and then projecting outward their reflections in the mirrors of his inner eye.[30]

The conflict between logic and dream has shattered his peace of mind. He becomes restless with idle inquiries.

* * *

pl. 24 The first artistic impulses appear at the end of the Mousterian[31] period.[32] They grow and perfect themselves in the Aurignacian period and reach their height in the Magdalenian period.[33]

After the Magdalenian period (approximately 10,000 B.C.) prehistoric archives yield no more animal drawings and only a very few traces of ornamental art. The reason may be, that man, at that time, devoted himself entirely to his first try of domesticating animals and tilling the ground, and had neither the leisure nor the same totemistic-magical representational beliefs of the Magdalenian man, who was a hunter essentially.

This highly developed prehistoric art suddenly vanishes and this increases additionally its fascination.[34]

25 **Trondjem** TXT_5877_0_N110. For images of engravings style A and style B described by Grahame Clark in this paragraph, see plates 22 and 23.

26 Alternative parts, chapters, and titles: **PART II** / **CHAPTER VI** / **Illustration: The Discovery of the Superfluous** [see original drawing by Kiesler not included in the assembled text, fig. B.18] TXT_6825/0_N5 **Part ~~II~~ III. Chapter ~~VI~~ IV. Discovery and affirmation of the Superfluous (Art)** TXT_6795/0

27 **By now man has developed his own body. His eyes are not more ~~fixed to the~~ bent ~~towards~~ to the ground but fixed towards the horizons** TXT_6795/0

28 **He has developed his own thoughts and feelings. In addition to his eyes ~~He has the capacity to …~~ has developed an inner sight.** TXT_6795/0

29 **spreading his imagery ~~of his inner life~~** TXT_6795/0

30 **by halting and then projecting ~~and halting~~ outward their reflections in ~~the image of~~ the mirrors of his self ~~outwards~~. He becomes restless with idle inquiries.** TXT_6795/0

31 **Moustérien** TXT_5877/0_N11

32 This quotation comes from the popular speleological memoir *Ten Years under the Earth*, by Norbert Casteret. It is the Kieslers' own English translation of the 1936 German edition: Norbert Casteret, *Zehn Jahre unter der Erde: Höhlenforschungen eines Einzelgängers*, trans. (from the French) Friedrich von Oppeln-Bronikoswki (Leipzig: F. A. Brockhaus, 1936). TXT_6857/0_N3 For the Kieslers' transcriptions from this edition, see TXT_6821/0 Original French edition: *Dix ans sous terre: Campagnes d'un explorateur solitaire* (Paris, Perrin, 1933); English edition (not used in *Magic Architecture*): *Ten Years under the Earth*, ed. and trans. June Barrows Mussey (New York: Greystone Press, 1938).

33 Cf. Casteret, *Zehn Jahre unter der Erde* (1936), 65; *Ten Years Under the Earth* (1938), 53: "The very first prehistoric art appears at the end of the Mousterian epoch; it multiplies and improves during the Aurignacian and reaches its height with the Magdalenians." The Kieslers' transcription and translation includes the following paragraph, which they crossed out and which was not used in *Magic Architecture*. **Though it is quite an unthankful task to express the chronology of prehistoric ages in figures (because its duration dumbfounds the layman or seems unbelievable to him), we rely on the most serious scientific estimations for these three periods. The calculations of the most cautious and best-known scholars places back the Mousterian period 50,000 years, the Aurignacian 25,000 and the Magdalenian between 20,000 and 15,000 years B.C.** TXT_6857/0_N3 For the rest of the Kieslers' translated transcriptions from Casteret's book not used in the main draft of *Magic Architecture*, see TXT_6839/0

34 **its ~~secret~~ fascination. ~~for us.~~** TXT_6857/0_N3 Cf. Casteret, *Zehn Jahre unter der Erde* (1936), 67; 56: "After the Magdalenian epoch, there are among prehistoric remains hardly any traces of animal art, and very few of decorative art. This may have something to do with the fact that man thereafter, absorbed in his first efforts to domesticate animals and practices cultivation, had neither the leisure nor the magical beliefs of the Magdalenian hunters. Prehistoric art, thus highly developed, yet without successors, still fascinates us across the ages. Many of its secrets still remain to tantalize us."

(23)

(23)b

page 152

page 179

(23b). Page 179

(below)
Extraordinary discovery(only recently) of an animal clay sculpture in the caves of Montespan, France.
The animal sculpture is headless; so are all similar animal sculptures found in the same cave. On the floor near them skulls of real bears were found. These were apparently attached by means of a dowl to the headless figures. preceding ceremonial rites before a bear [illegible]t. This bear hunt was re-enacted inside the cave as an expression of sympathetic magic. All animal sculptures are pierced by arrows and stone weapons.

Illustration →

(23)

page 152

(23). Page 152

Showing technique of achieving designs in stone by making holes and cuts.

(23b)

page 179

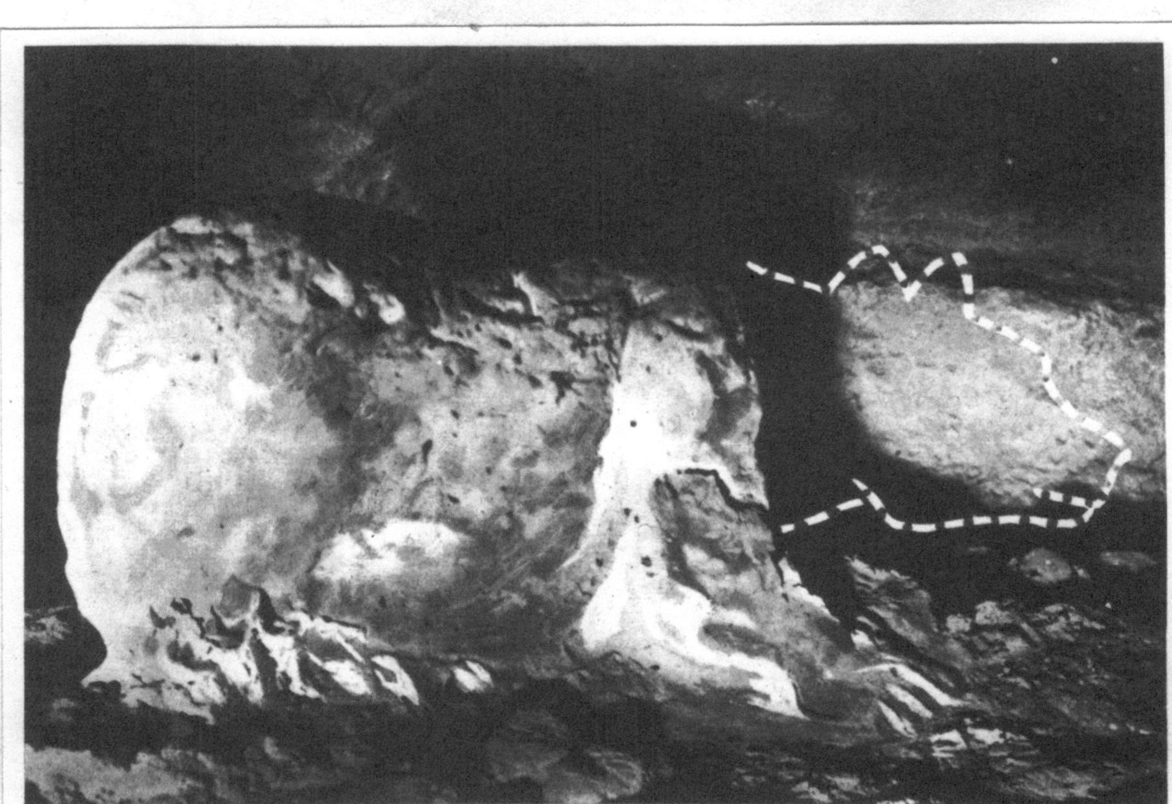

← caption in back

Frederick Kiesler, Preliminary drawing with description "Illustration: The Discovery of the Superfluous" related to the content of Part III, Chapter 4 "The Discovery and Affirmation of the Superfluous" (part and chapter numbers on this sheet reflect earlier book manuscript organization) (pencil) ÖFLKS, TXT_6825/0_N5

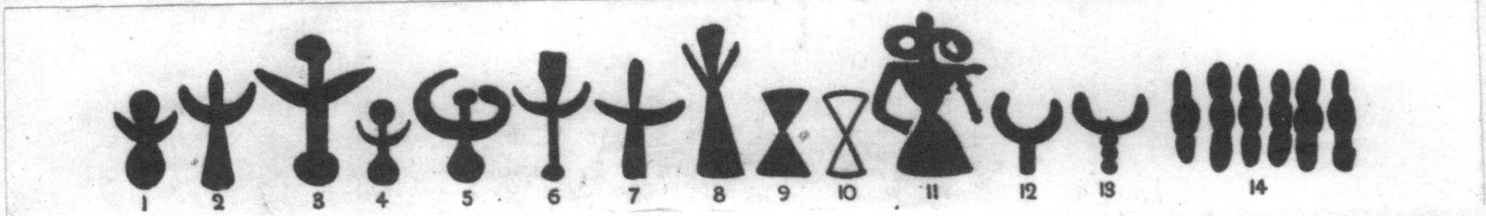

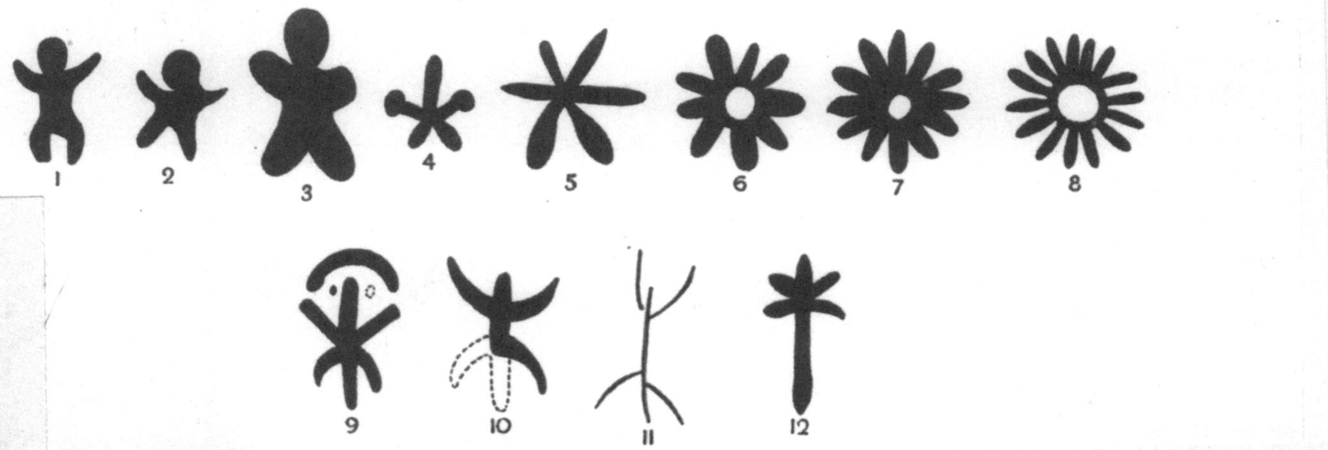

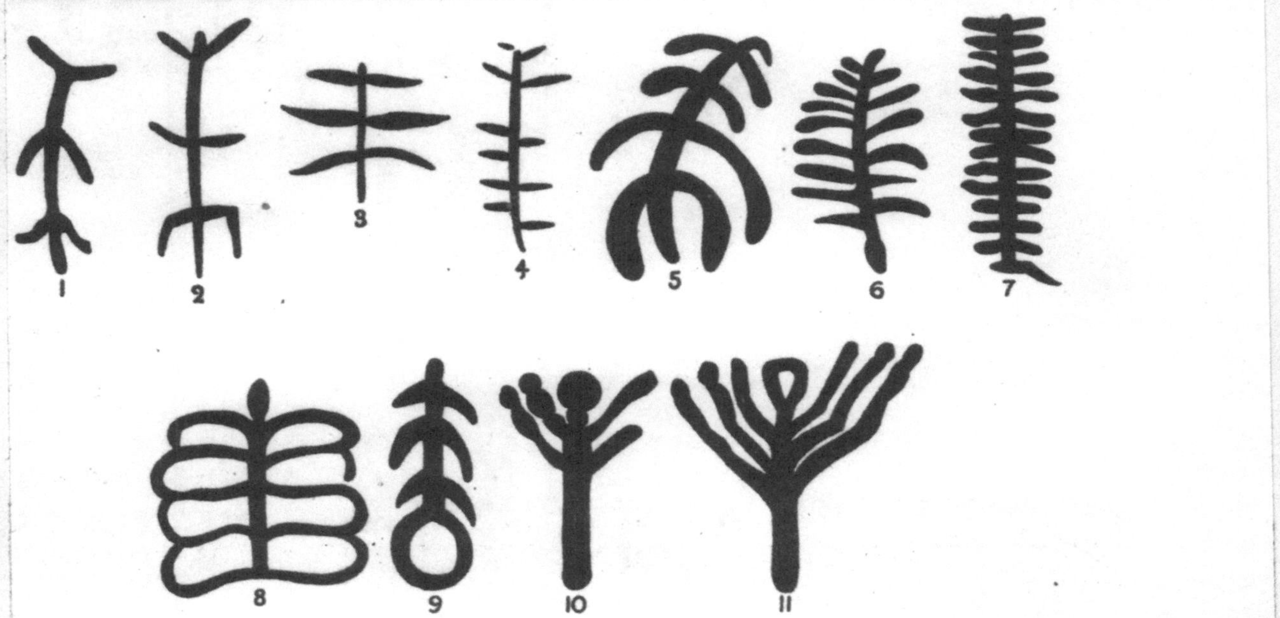

(24). Page 154

5 rows of (stylized) rock paintings showing various abstractions of the human figure (except for the star-design which denotes a hut on stilts).

(below):

The cave of Las Figuras where paintings were found (Southern Andalusia, Spain. Neolithic and copper-age group).

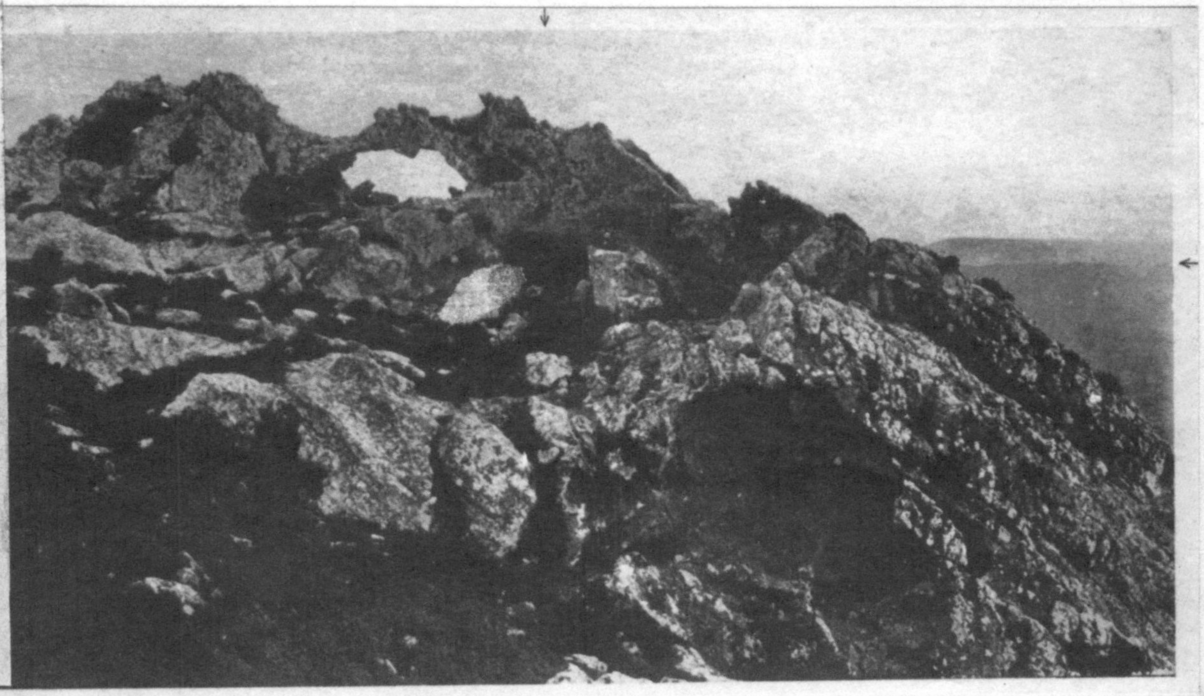

21
"Customs of 20,000 Years ago still exist among the Aborigines of Central Australia" and "According to legend, the marsupial mole, Itjaritjari, created this sacred cave." Charles P. Mountford, "Earth's Most Primitive People," 89–112, photos Mountford. ÖFLKS, SCL_32/0

22
"Scales of one metre, A. The hunting scene at Gärde in central Sweden. The scene is viewed obliquely as seen from the ground; B. An engraving in style A at Fykanvatn, illustrating the trick by which a second animal was produced by adding a head to the rear of one already drawn; C. An elk (style A) at Landverk in central Sweden." Grahame Clark, "Scandinavian Rock-engravings," *Antiquity* 11 (January 1, 1937): 56–69, photos J. G. D. Clark. ÖFLKS, SCL_33/0

23
"Rock-engraving (Arctic, Stlye B) in pecked technique at Ekeberg, near Oslo." Clark, "Scandinavian Rock-engravings," 69, pl. V, photo J. G. D. Clark. ÖFLKS, SCL_34/0

23b
"Tonbär [Clay bear]." Norbert Casteret, *Zehn Jahre unter der Erde, Höhlenforschung eines Einzelgängers* (Leipzig: F. A. Brockhaus, 1936). ÖFLKS, SCL_34/0

24
"Typical human symbols" and "View of the Tajo de las Figuras from the North." Henri Breuil and Miles Crawford Burkitt, *Rock Paintings of Southern Andalusia: A Description of a Neolithic and Copper Age Art Group* (Oxford: The Clarendon Press, 1929), (row 1) 8, fig. 9, series I; (rows 2–3) 6, fig. 4, series D (rows 4–5) 8, fig. 8, series H; and (photo) pl. II. ÖFLKS, SCL_35/0

THE SUPERFLUOUS BECOMES A NECESSITY

PART IV
ART AND THE UNKNOWN[1]

INTRODUCTION
THE SUPERFLUOUS BECOMES A NECESSITY

With the growth of his logical powers man became conscious of his earthly insecurity.[2]

The physical shelter was not sufficient for survival because he had begun to live a twofold existence;[3] there was his own, the visible life, and the other the invisible, ancestral life.

* * *

It was in Art that primitive man found the link between the Known and the Unknown.

* * *

He had already acquired fire, which was warming his cave;[4] and which was part[5] of the other world. It was the same fire that split the skies and the trees, but which he had captured and tamed to serve his immediate necessities. But this acquired power was not enough. His peace of mind was not complete. He remained disquieted[6] during the night when the imagery of dreams obsessed him, because he was unable to capture and tame them.

Dreams were like the light of the moon. Coming on brighter and wider, and disappearing again; and the memories of them haunting him during the day; there was no escape from them either "outdoors" or "indoors." Neither his rock shelter, nor his hut could protect him from them; nor were his stone tools and bone weapons able to conquer the apparitions. These enemies were in him; yet he could not capture them. They infested[7] his body, using it for their shelter and flying in and out of it, after their like, with the erratic energy of bats flapping their way through skeleton houses. There was nothing he could do but make friends with them, or at least try to make friends.

Above all man displayed the greatest reverence to the next of kin of these ghostly visions–the dead. He started to share food with them, placing it at haunted spots;[8] he shared his wealth, his clothing, his ornaments and tools[9] with the dead. He bestowed precious gifts on them, and built them homes of elaborate design.

Graves were always of greater importance to primitive man than his own habitat.

They were indeed the trespass from the known world to worlds unknown.

The door from the known to the unknown could be opened or locked with the Key of Art.

Primitive man discovered the key, and he clung desperately to it.

Art, the Superfluous, becomes a necessity. It expresses itself first in rituals and group ceremonials, individually. Sorcerers, elders, and chiefs use it as a power over the members of their clan.[10] Art is not abstract. It is useful. It is magical. pl. 25

* * *

The Imagery of Art becomes the bridge over the gap between Life and Dream, which had developed since man's primordial days.[11]

It heals the breach in the UNITY of man and nature, between his weakness and the strength of supernatural forces.

Art becomes the visual bond between nature and supernature;[12] without it man cannot live anymore; he either falls into the stupor of the animal (in him) or into the complete detachment of the imagination.[13]

1 Alternative title later used to title the introduction to Part IV (frontispiece): **PART IV. THE SUPERFLUOUS BECOMES A NECESSITY** TXT_6737/0_N1

2 Pleistocene man / With ~~the~~ his logic growing, ~~his~~ man's earthly insecurity ~~grew~~ became dangerously conscious. TXT_6796/0_N1 With ~~his~~ the growth of his logical powers ~~growing~~, the dangers of man's earthly insecurity became ~~dangerously~~ conscious to him. TXT 6737/0_N1

3 because there was apparently a double life he was living TXT_6796/0_N1

4 warming ~~his food and~~ his cave TXT_6796/0_N1

5 was ~~a visible sign~~ of the other world TXT_6796/0_N1

6 He remained unruhig [disquieted, anxious] TXT_6796/0_N1

7 They used TXT_6796/0_N2

8 placing it at ~~places in forests in~~ TXT_6796/0_N2

9 by sharing his wealth and clothing and ornaments and tools for meals. TXT_6796/0_N2

10 The superfluous becomes a necessity for the expression of extra-ordinary qualities of rituals and ceremonials of individual man, such as sorcerers, elders, chiefs. TXT 6701/0_N1

11 Art becomes the link over the gap which developed since his primordial days between Life and Dream. TXT_6701/0_N1

12 In addition to **supernature**, Kiesler uses the term **overnature** probably as a translation of the German Übernatur in a table-chart illustrating the "birth of design," included in Addenda: Charts, fig. C.09b. TXT_6806/0_N2

13 or into ~~madness the~~ complete detachment of madness TXT_6701/0_N1 It leads to a life of isolation and madness. TXT _6737/0_N4 Editor's query referring to "It": ~~The absence of Art?~~ TXT_6858/0_N5

(25)

page 159

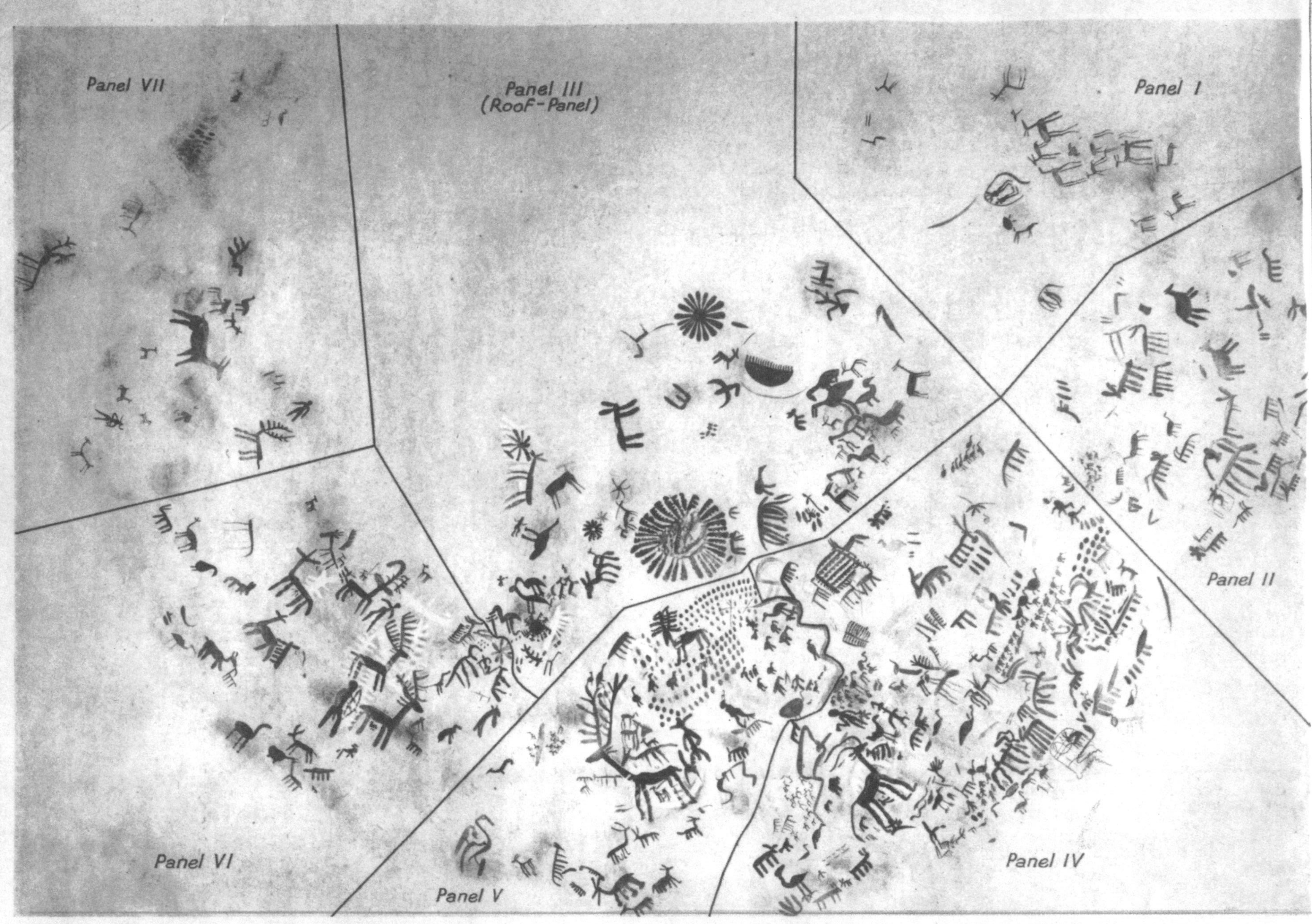

(25). Page 159

Complete decoration of the main cave of Las Figuras, (Southern Andalusia, Spain) showing ceiling and side-panels. (Designs of men, animals, birds and huts).

CHAPTER 1
THE MEANING OF MAGIC[14]

Today the term "Magic" evokes both: repute and disrepute.[15]

Disrepute because it is associated usually with the trickeries of conjurers and, from the times of the Middle Ages, with sorcery. But those and their like[16] are pseudo-performers only like the advantage-takers of any type of art and vocation.

The truth is: at the root of every invention of man, be it mechanical or teleological or both, and alike in Art, is the belief in the possibility of superhuman power.

Without the belief in the magic power of creation, both civilization and culture are unthinkable.[17] Magic is the mother of invention. And every invention is a tool for increased power of the human being, down and up the scale of his make-up.

The chroniclers (like the historians) of social events[18] who write about what other people have created, are often rather confusers than clarifiers, as they claim to be. If the public would be in direct contact with creations and creators, the original thought and meaning would have a greater chance of contact. As it is, the interpreters (teachers) have intertwined themselves with the work and its creator and have taken their place.

With regard to "Magic," they have split it for convenience's sake into black and white (evil and good). Magical practices are of three types: sympathetic (mimicry), divination (clairvoyance), thaumaturgy (wonder-working, alchemy).[19]

The history of magic is bound up with the history of science as well as with folk-lore, primitive culture, and the history of religion.[20] Sometimes our authors have spoken of natural magic, but I rather wonder whether there could well be any other kind, since man must always reckon with his natural environment.[21] It is not without reason that the Magi stand out in Pliny's pages[22] not as mere sorcerers of enchanters but as those who have gone farthest and in most detail—too curiously, in his opinion—into the study of nature. It is not without reason that we have found experimentation and magic so constantly associated throughout our period. After all it was not surprising that magic, which was both curious and tried to accomplish things, should investigate nature and should experiment. It is even possible that magicians were the first to experiment, or shared that province with the first inventors and the useful arts, and that natural science, originally philosophical and speculative, took over experimental methods in a crude form, as well as the conception of occult virtue, from magic. As Sir James Frazer has said, "Here is a body of men relieved, at least in the higher stages of savagery, from the need of earning their livelihood by hard manual toil, and allowed, nay, expected and encouraged, to prosecute researches into the secret ways of nature."[23]

It is therefore perhaps not surprising that men like Galen, Apuleius, Apollonius, and Dunstan were accused of magic by their contemporaries; that men like Gebert, Michael Scot, and Albertus Magnus were represented as magicians in later, if not contemporary legend; that Lithica and Roger Bacon tell us of the danger of sages being accused of magic; that in the Book of Enoch, Cyprian, Firmicus, and Picatrix confuse magic with other arts and sciences; and that no one of our authors, try as he may, succeeds in keeping magic entirely out of science or science entirely out of magic.

Be that as it may, if the anthropologists are correct in asserting that magic forms a greater part of the life and thought of early man and of all primitive peoples, it is evident that only gradually would the science and thought of civilized peoples free themselves from the old habits and instincts. Modern science cannot exempt itself from its own theory of evolution as Julius Firmicus exempted the Roman emperor from the rule of the

14 **~~Magic is the negation of death.~~** handwritten introductory statement crossed out with red pencil TXT_6840/0_N1

15 **–The term magic is both in disrepute and in repute of glamour.** TXT_6697/0_N1

16 **and their ~~pseudo-professionals~~** TXT_6697/0_N1

17 **~~Invention and Magic~~** TXT_6697/0_N2

18 **(like the historians of social events)** TXT_6697/0_N2

19 All of these categories of magic are analyzed in Lynn Thorndike's *History of Magic*, which Kiesler quotes below. **Now: quote Thorndike: …** TXT_6697/0_N3 **~~Thorndike~~** [erased in the margin] TXT_6840/1_N2 See Lynn Thorndike, *A History of Magic and Experimental Science during the First Thirteen Centuries of Our Era* (New York: Columbia University Press, 1923).

20 Cf. Thorndike: "Yet our material has conclusively shown that the history of magic is bound up with the history of science as well as with folk-lore, primitive culture, and the history of religion." The rest of Kiesler's text comprises a quotation from Thorndike, *History of Magic*, 2:977-978.

21 Thorndike often refers to notions of "natural magic" because of the association of "magicians" with the study of natural objects. In the case of Pliny's *Natural History*, examined in detail in the first volume of his *History*, Thorndike comments: "The most striking fact is that the magicians are cited again and again concerning the supposed properties, virtues, and effects of things in nature—herbs, animals, and stones. These virtues are, it is true, often employed in an effort to produce wonderful results, and often too they are combined with some fantastic rite or superstitious ceremonial performed by a human agent. But in many cases either no rite at all is suggested or merely some simple medicinal application; and in a few cases there is no mention of any particular operation or result, the magicians are cited simply as authorities concerning the great but unspecified virtues of natural objects." Thorndike, *History of Magic*, 1:64-65.

22 **It is not without reason that the Magi stands** [sic] **out in Pliny's pages**. TXT_5877/0_N119; TXT_6840/0_N2 Cf. Thorndike, *History of Magic*, 2:977: "It is not without reason that the Magi stand out in Pliny's pages." Thorndike refers to magicians as "Magi" in Pliny's *Natural History*. See, Thorndike, "The Science of the Magi," in *History of Magic*, 1:64-72, especially 65 for where he first makes the same statement: "Indeed, they [the magi] stand out in Pliny's pages not as mere sorcerers or enchanters or wonder workers, but as those who have gone the farthest and in most detail—too far and too curiously in Pliny's opinion—into the study of medicine and nature."

23 Thorndike quotes from J. G. Frazer, *The Golden Bough: Magic Art and the Evolution of Kings* (London: Macmillan, 1911), 1:246-247. A copy of the 1929 edition exists in the Kiesler estate library.

stars. Science did not come down from above nor invade from without. It grew up in the very midst of superstition and mental anarchy, just as the states of modern Europe had their beginnings in feudal society. As the kings in the Middle Ages had to govern under feudal limitations and even by feudal means, so science for a long time not merely was opposed by the unscientific attitude, but was itself tinged by fantastic theories and false data. It is scarcely a paradox to say that during our Roman and medieval period the laws of magic were better defined and understood than those of science. Yet the scientific attitude, like the spirit of nationality, was at work in this seeming chaos; gradually it shook itself free from error, and, by the increasing application of truly scientific methods, won a similar triumph to that which the sovereign political power gained by its gradual development of governmental institutions.[24]

CHAPTER 2
MAN PART OF THE COSMOS AND MAN APART FROM THE COSMOS[25]

Note: (Pertaining to the transformation from the mystic image-less belief to visual objectivations: Idols, shrines.)[26]

CHAPTER 3
ARTIFACTS, SYMBOLS, AND ART[27]

Man has fabricated certain tools;[28] he has invented instruments of practical use. They had their origin in his ability to create objects for use-necessity.

Earlier, man had developed his instinct for physical adornment.[29] For many occasions women and men alike wore necklaces, decorated their hair and their bodies.

They combined[30] their decorative attributes with meaning. They took parts of nature (which is to them true power) and applied them to their own bodies.[31] Animal feathers, leaves and branches, stones, bones,[32] and others became symbols of strength, success, and security.

With time they felt so much in unity with the animal kingdom that they identified themselves with many aspects of it. And in a further development man let a magician play for him the animal roles of the super-powers of heaven. He did not as yet have the self-confidence to play God himself.

And so the man-artist makes[33] "animals play the part of cosmic bodies: Antelopes personify stars, the lion and eagle the sun, the steer the moon … and heaven and earth play the role of man and wife in sexual attraction."[34]

24 See also the transcription of another quotation from Thorndike on "nature in Gothic architecture and sculpture" (Thorndike, *History of Magic*, 2:537) not used in the main text of *Magic Architecture* included in Addenda: Transcriptions and Translations, p. 368. TXT_6827/0

25 Alternative chapter numbers and titles: Part IV: Chapter ~~one~~ 2 ~~Introduction~~ Man Part of the Cosmos and Man Apart of the Cosmos. TXT_6744/0_N2 Chapter 1: Man Part of the Cosmos and Man Apart from the Cosmos. (to be translated?) [question in the list of contents regarding translation of excerpts by Lévy-Bruhl] TXT_6702/0_N5

26 (Pertaining to the ~~transference of~~ mystic (image-less) belief ~~into~~ visual objectivation in: idols, shrines~~, temples~~) TXT_6744/0_N1 Following this paragraph are further notes from Kiesler: Levy-Bruhl: IXth Chapter: Uebergang zu höheren Typen der Ge[is]tesbetätigung [Transition to higher mental operations] See excerpt. page 326 / (Do not type / Transl.) [handwritten instruction for translation] TXT_6744/0_N1 Follows transcription in German of excerpts from the ninth chapter of Lucien Lévy-Bruhl, *Das Denken der Naturvölker*, ed. Wilhelm Jerusalem, trans. P. Friedlander, 2nd ed. (Vienna-Leipzig: Braumüller, 1926), 326–329. Ultimately these excerpts were neither translated nor included in later drafts. There is an additional transcription from the same section in the German edition of Lévy-Bruhl with fewer paragraphs transcribed. TXT_6744/0_N2-N6; TXT_6810/0_N1-N2 On the content of these extracts from Lévy Bruhl, see Sources, Disciplines, and Objects, pp. 44–46 and fig. A.37.

27 Alternative parts, chapter numbers, and titles: Chapter ~~TWO~~ 3 TXT_6715/0_N1 PART ~~III~~ IV ~~Introduction~~ chapter 2: Artifacts, Symbols, and Art. The first page of this MS with the text of Part IV, chapter 3 includes the last four paragraphs of Part IV, "Introduction." TXT_6701/0_N1

28 Man has by now fabricated certain tools TXT_6701/0_N1

29 has before ~~with~~ Man ~~his instinct for~~ developed his instinct for physical adornment. TXT_6701/0_N1verso Before, man has developed his instinct for physical adornment. TXT_6835/0_N1

30 They now combine TXT_6701/0_N1verso

31 and ~~marked~~ their own bodies TXT_6701/0_N1verso

32 crafty jaw-bones TXT_6701/0_N1verso

33 ~~lets~~ animals TXT_6715/0_N2

34 die Tiere spielen die Rolle der Gestirne; Antilopen die der Sterne, Löwe und Adler die der Sonne, der Stier die des Mondes; …. Himmel & Erde spielen die Rolle des Menschen in der Paarung TXT_6816/0_N1 Transcribed excerpt from Frobenius, *Kulturgeschichte Afrikas* (1933), 168. Another draft includes an instruction in Kiesler's hand for inserted text: Insert from the beginning → TXT_6701/0_N3 No inserted text exists beyond this point in this MS or later TS drafts of the chapter. Another MS with a similar chapter title contains a different text by Kiesler that is related to the problematics of the Introduction and chapter 3 of Part IV but was never transcribed: ~~Part III.~~ Part IV. Chapter VI ~~Introduction~~ Artifacts, Décor, and ART): The language of design was apparently automatically developed as an outgrowth of a natural desire to give expression to a state of wonder. Every child builds first no matter what materials fall into their hands and plays the part of the magician: pebbles, sand, pieces of wood, or anything that may be found by him. To construct or to design is as natural in the development of man as it is in the individual. One of the most important ~~factor~~ of such early exercises is making one's own feelings visible to others is ~~the fact of~~ their apparent "uselessness." They appear, at least to the bystander, superfluous, to immediate necessity nothing but play~~full~~; yet they ~~appear~~ emerge as prominently in every child's life as the seasons in nature. ~~No matter what land of the earth.~~ And what is equally important, man attaches himself to this exercise with almost desperate "tenacity", ~~like~~ and ~~leans on it~~ leans on it like the blind ~~wanderer~~ on his stick. Once he has ~~taken grip~~ of it, he (and society) never leaves it. ~~The~~ Superfluous Design becomes increasingly a cherished necessity. The more fully developed "designs" of early man have been found chiefly in the caves of Dordogne and in Spain. The psychological foundation of these developed exercises we find well-described in Frobenius, who says: TXT_6808/0_N1-2 The MS does not mention the passages to be quoted from Frobenius, who refers to the caves of Dordogne in his *Kulturgeschichte Afrikas*, 63, in a passage transcribed by the Kieslers. TXT_6814/0_N1. See Addenda: Transcriptions and Translations, p. 360.

(25x) page 170

(25x). Page 170

Configuration of Myth and Magic into Architecture. (Rajarami Temple, India).

CHAPTER 4
MYTH AND MAGIC[35]

pl. 25x The fact is that the simplest meaning of the Greek word "myth" is the right one: <u>a myth is a story, myth is narrative or poetic literature</u>.[36] It need be no more philosophic than any kind of literature. It need be no more philosophic than any kind of literature. Myth is therefore art and must be studied as such. Myth is a mode of cognition, a system of thought, a way of life, only as art is. It can be opposed to science only as art is opposed to science. There is no question of one defeating the other. They are complementary and fulfill different needs. The romantic fear that science may destroy myth betrays an acquiescence in the misinterpretation of myth which science sometimes gives us: namely that it is frivolous or delicate nonsense. There are no eras in recorded history when science has banished myth: though there are[37] eras when human thought in general has become superficial.

* * *

Myth is much more akin to the naive assumptions and techniques of magic than to religion.[38] Magic does not of itself imagine discreet spirits of deities, but only efficacious preternatural forces residing in animals, objects, and men, which can be manipulated by human compulsion. Myth should be thought as a dramatic picturization of magical forces as they clash, interact or harmonize with each other.

The idea of discreet spirits inhabiting and motivating objects is not primary as E. B. Tylor and Herbert Spencer thought; it is secondary and does not take into account the universal practice of magic. To the savage, <u>mana</u>[39] or preternatural power is impersonal; he apprehends it as an immediate quality of things, just as color, sound, size, shape, and motion are immediate qualities. As the savage envelops the world in his own emotions, things assume dramatic qualities: they are, in the words of Dewey, "poignant, tragic, beautiful, humorous, settled, disturbed, comfortable, annoying, barren, harsh, consoling, splendid, fearful; are such immediately and in their own right and behalf."

Magic, and all the benefits it is supposed to bring, depends upon this fusion of power, quality, and object: without it "things fall apart;" the world becomes chaotic and dangerous when it can no longer be enveloped in the tissue of human emotion. When objects and qualities become efficacious by being fused with power, they are subject to the compulsive techniques of magic. Beside being a compulsive technique–a pseudo-science as Frazer says–magic is obviously an esthetic activity. <u>Magic is immediately available to art, and art to magic</u>.[40] Primitive literature is shot through with magic and we may regard it as mythical when it fortifies the magical view of things, when it reaffirms the vibrant dynamism of the world, when it fortifies the magical view of things, when it reaffirms the vibrant dynamism of the world, when it fortifies the ego with the impression that there is magically potent brilliancy in the world. Myth is not vaporous, abstract, or unreal; it is a "blaze of reality."

Like other kinds of literature, myth performs the cathartic function of dramatizing the clashes and harmonies of life in a social and natural environment. But myth can be understood as the esthetic leaven which heals or makes tolerable those deep neurotic disturbances which in primitive culture are occasioned by the clashing attitudes of magic and religion. This collision of forces, as Radin points out in his Primitive Religion,[41] is partly the result of the priest's struggle to achieve a dominant economic position. Coincident with his war upon the people is his war against magic. For magic is the prerogative of mankind in

35 **Richard Chase, Notes on the Study of Myth (Partisan Review, Vol. XIII, No. 3 p. 338)** Bibliographic citation in Stefi Kiesler's hand for the transcription that follows. TXT_5877/0_N124 See Richard Chase, "Notes on the Study of Myth," *Partisan Review* 8, no. 3 (Summer 1946): 338-346. This entire chapter, including the title is taken from Chase's article. For Kiesler's relation to contemporary literature on myth and magic, including the work of Richard (Volney) Chase, see Sources, Disciplines, and Objects, pp. 46, 59, 88-89.

36 Emphasis also in the original article, Chase, "Notes on the Study of Myth," 339.

37 **<u>are</u>** [emphasis Kiesler] TXT 6841/0_N1 Cf. Chase, "Notes on the Study of Myth," 339.

38 **Myth and Magic** TXT 6841/0_N1 appears as the section heading in the original article (Chase, "Notes on the Study of Myth," 341) but is crossed out in the TS and used as chapter title. TXT_5877/0_N124

39 Emphasis Chase, "Notes on the Study of Myth," 344.

40 Emphasis Kiesler TXT 6841/0_N2

41 Chase is referring to Paul Radin, *Primitive Religion: Its Nature and Origin* (New York: Viking Press, 1937).

general; it exalts human power; it places the world and the gods at the disposal of mankind. The priest's task is to transmute magic into religion, to overcome the subjectivism on which magic depends, to present spirits and gods as clearly conceivable objective beings, to transfer magical power to the gods and make man obeisant before them. Mythology is full of the tension created by this universal struggle, and many myths may be said to array the propaganda of men, animals, and magical beings against the propaganda of the gods. But art is constructive where life is destructive. Myth keeps the dilemma operative and resolves the contesting forces into useful experience.

I am aware too that no complete account of myth can be undertaken without wider references to human needs and aspirations than those I have chosen here. The method of pragmatic naturalism seems to me the only fruitful method of studying myth—yet that method leaves us with the feeling that we have made art too functional, too outward looking, too optimistic. Psychoanalysis may be misleading as psychology, but the "pleasure principle" and the desperate "instincts" of sex and death give myth a dramatic richness unknown to contemporary pragmatism, or at least not yet assimilated by it.[42]

CHAPTER 5
THE PSYCHO—PLASTIC—ERA[43]

Once Paleolithic man had accumulated enough associations to be conscious of "experience," he becomes more and more aware of his being as an individual.[44] He is no longer a man of the herd.[45] The rule of the instinct loses power to the will of thought, which becomes preponderant.[46] He will gradually take his and his family's faith into his "own hands." He emerges from the cave and builds his own hut, independent of natural protection. pl. 26

Until now the collective spirit of the group has been his only security, and he still needs it when he detaches himself from the herd.[47] Without it he is lost in the mysterious network of life forces. The instinctive memory of the protective "collective spirit" must therefore be kept alive. Although he is no longer in direct contact with it, his memory recreates it in visual symbols.

These symbols are wholly realistic. They represent animals which he fears or needs and always tried to appease.[48] Since certain animals are the good spirit (Totems) of each family, such an animal is property of all members (and also of their ancestors) and represents therefore a collective symbol.[49] And since birth, initiations of many kinds, and death are common to all members of the clan or tribe, certain creatures and apparitions, painted or sculpted,[50] will serve them all, and replace the collective spirit of the herd instinct. pl. 26

Primitive man has now proceeded to the neolithic age and beyond and has arrived at the capacity for psycho-plastic expression in his growth of detachment from the "collective spirit" which binds him to the natural environment of animals, rocks, and trees.[51] He wears animal-heads, which he has shot and transformed for his use. He deliberately imitates his dreams of ghosts and spirits through masks of his own making. He is still naive and animal enough to believe[52] that they will transmit[53] their power to him.[54] By mimicking like with like, man invents practical or sympathetic magic.

*CAVE-PAINTING[55]

The most vivid representation of a prehistoric sorcerer was discovered by Count Begouen and his three sons, in the Three Brother Grotto at St. Giron (Ariège).[56]

This witchman whose body was painted with the ritual red and black, is represented nude and dancing. Count Begouen writes: "On his hands he wears gloves of lion's paws with sharp claws, has a

42 The original transcription includes an additional sentence from Chase, "Notes on the Study of Myth," 346, which was later crossed out in the TS: **Myth is, in the phrase of Renan, "simultaneous humanity."** Cf. TXT_6841/0_N4; TXT_5877/0_N127

43 Alternative chapter numbers and titles: **PART [II] III IV. Chapter ~~III II 3~~ 5 Psycho–plastic–Era** TXT_6716/0_N1 **Part II: Chapter III. Psycho-plastic Era** TXT_6789/0_N1

44 **aware of his ~~own personality~~** TXT_6789/0_N1

45 **He is not more der Herdemensch** TXT_6789/0_N1

46 Cf. Kiesler's diagram on **The Law of Preponderance** included in Addenda: Charts, fig. C.10. TXT_6817/0_N1

47 **The collective spirit, ~~the belief~~ of the group was the security till now and he still needs it, ~~but slowly he forms his own~~ when he detaches himself from the herd.** TXT_6789/0_N1

48 **They represent ~~the~~ animals, trees and ~~death corpses~~ death, which he fears and tried ~~to~~ always to appease.** TXT_6789/0_N2

49 **a collective ~~spirit~~** TXT_6789/0_N3

50 **certain ~~idols, symbols~~ painted, sculpted, or build** [sic] TXT_6789/0_N3

51 **the detachment from the "collective spirit" of the animal and nature ~~into his own realm~~ at the capacity of psychoplastic expression.** TXT_6789/0_N4

52 **to belief** [sic] **in it himself to the fullest extent.** TXT_6789/0_N5

53 **~~trandescent~~** [sic] TXT_6716/0_N2

54 **Not only does he himself believe in it, but he makes some animals believe in his masks and costuming. In Africa, Spain, France, and in the Malayan Islands, Rock paintings and Cave-engravings have been found, which show how the hunter approached herds of animals disguised in their own skins and skeleton, and making them believe of being one of theirs, kills with ease.** TXT_6716/0_N2 Omitted in later drafts.

55 Handwritten note on preliminary TS: **Casteret Psycho-plastic-era I (painting) (Part IV, Chapter 5)** TXT_6752/0_N3 The text that follows is a series of excerpts on cave "painting" and "sculpture" from Casteret's memoir in the Kieslers' English translation of the German edition: Casteret, *Zehn Jahre unter der Erde* (1936), 68–69. For the Kieslers' transcriptions from the German edition (including hand corrections by Stefi Kiesler), see TXT_6821/0; TXT_6821/1; TXT_6752/0_N5 For the omission of certain passages with Casteret's racial remarks contained in the passages transcribed and translated by the Kieslers yet not included in the final text, see Sources, Disciplines, and Objects, p. 86.

56 Cave of the Trois-Frères.

(26)

page 106

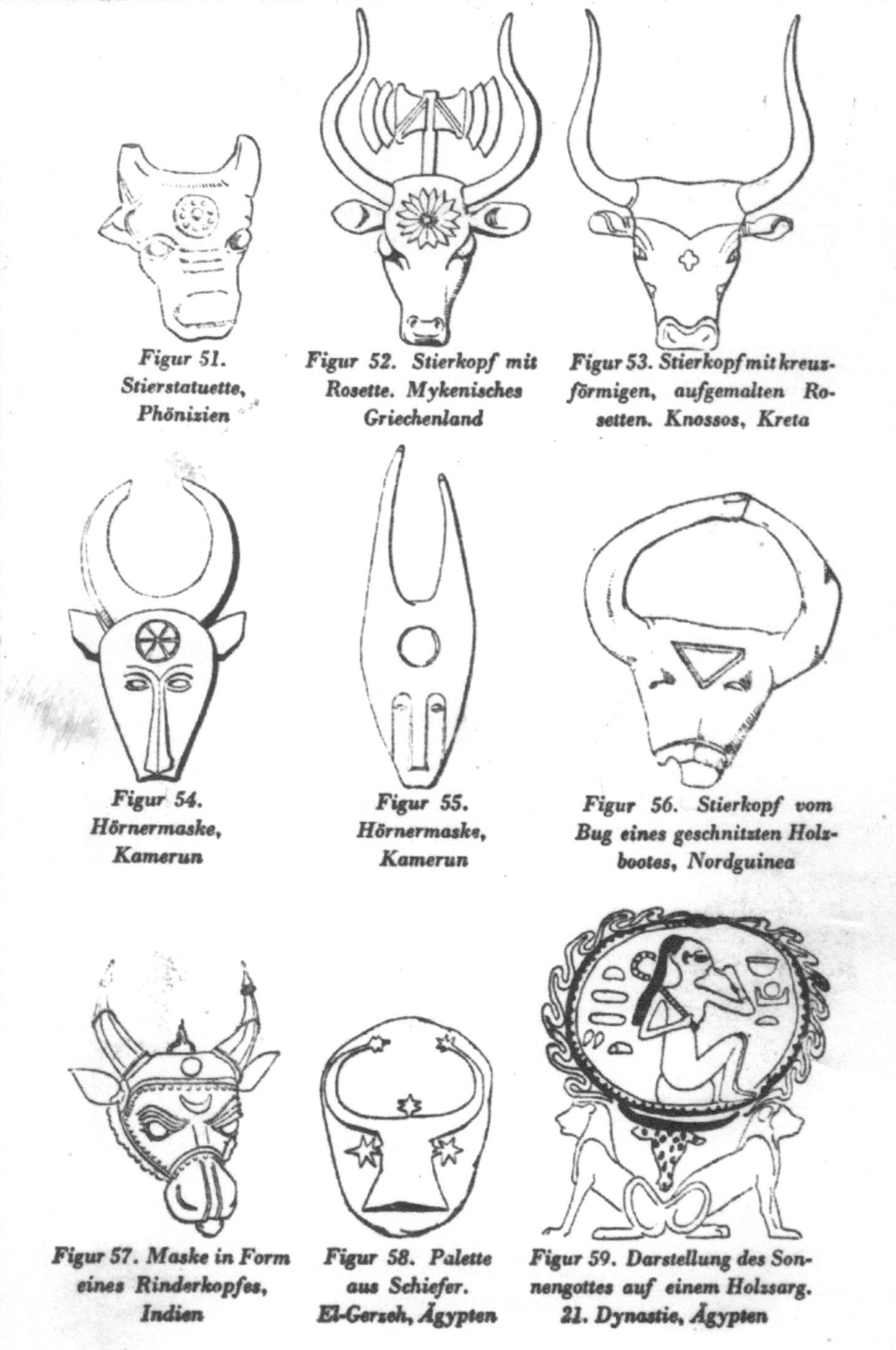

Figur 51. Stierstatuette, Phönizien

Figur 52. Stierkopf mit Rosette. Mykenisches Griechenland

Figur 53. Stierkopf mit kreuzförmigen, aufgemalten Rosetten. Knossos, Kreta

Figur 54. Hörnermaske, Kamerun

Figur 55. Hörnermaske, Kamerun

Figur 56. Stierkopf vom Bug eines geschnitzten Holzbootes, Nordguinea

Figur 57. Maske in Form eines Rinderkopfes, Indien

Figur 58. Palette aus Schiefer. El-Gerzeh, Ägypten

Figur 59. Darstellung des Sonnengottes auf einem Holzsarg. 21. Dynastie, Ägypten

(26). Page 106

In order to simulate power, early man adopts the image of powerful animals for himself, even for the portrayal of his gods. And, as a psycho-plastic expression, he does that invariably, no matter in what land he is born. (Steer-headed designs found in Phoenicia, Greece, Crete, Africa, Northern Guinea, India etc.)

mask with a bison-beard, an eagle's beak, wolf ears and antlers, eyes of an owl, and to his back is fastened a horse tail. With these insignia he believed to have acquired the full magic power and all the physical characteristics of those animals: the courage of the lion, the sharp vision of the eagle during day and the owl's at night time, the sharp ear of the wolf, the perseverance of the bison and the swiftness of the horse and stag."

This sorcerer is painted on a wall three meters[57] above the ground and in the depth of a cave five hundred meters away from the entrance. He has the place of honor in a natural amphitheater. Painted on the wall, at his feet, one sees a long row of animals. Lions, tigers, bisons, reindeers, bears, and wild asses with wounds, arrows and clubs drawn into their bodies, in short, all the attributes of the hunt. On the clay-floor, preserved with piety, one can still see the foot marks of the men, who held their ceremonials in that room.

In the light of these many-thousands-of-years-old records, one can imagine in all probability the appearance of the prehistoric sorcerer in this gigantic cave. All alone, he walks through the subterranean labyrinths, getting some light from a stone-lamp, consisting of a moss wick swimming in animal fat. In his awe-inspiring disguise he enters his sanctuary to execute the secret ceremonies of his belief. Drawing his magic actions on the wall he strives for the blessings of his tribe by the invisible powers.

He prays in his fashion for the protection of his kin against lions, tigers, bears; prays, that they never should be short of bison, horse, and reindeer meat; that the warriors in their fights, and the hunters in their pursuit be blessed with success.[58]

*

The primitives represented those animals whom they intended to kill. With magic rituals they applied wounds to these pictures and thus killed the animal symbolically, in order to be sure to kill it in reality in their hunts.

This explains the marks, holes, arrows, axes, and clubs on numerous animal drawings. Sometimes the intention of the hunter is even clearer: he shows the animal entering the trap or net or being killed by a shower of stones.

*

Until recently red Indians performed the famous bison dance. The hunters were clad in bison skins and danced in ritual motions or presented sham-fights. It purposed nothing else but a magic action to either secure success of the future hunt or to charm the herd to its own hunting grounds.[59]

Similar ceremonies and pantomimes are performed by the Inuit[60] on the eve of the seal hunt and the great fish haul. Before an emu chase takes place, the Australians draw a picture of that bird on the floor and pour over it arrows and pronounce terrible threats.

One could quote an endless succession of such usages from all countries and in all time. All folklore is full of it even that of civilized peoples.[61]

CAVE-SCULPTURE[62]

Following along the passage in the cave it suddenly widens and forms a cavern—called hall of the bears—which is the most interesting part of the entire cave structure. pl. 23b

In a radius of ten meters there lie around on the floor a lot of clay forms, a regular prehistoric museum, whose main piece is the headless stature of a bear.

57 **3 metres** TXT_6752/0_N4

58 Cf. Casteret, *Zehn Jahre* (1936), 71-72 and Norbert Casteret, *Ten Years under the Earth*, ed. and trans. June Barrows Mussey (New York: Greystone Press, 1938), 60-61. The painted and plastic representations inside the Trois Frères cave are also discussed in Frobenius's *Kulturgeschichte Afrikas*, 65-70. Following this is a section of three paragraphs from the Casteret transcription in German with the note **Casteret p. 37** which is crossed out and not translated into English TXT_6752/0_N5; TXT_6821/1_N6 Cf. Casteret, *Zehn Jahre* (1936), 37; *Ten Years* (1938), 21. See Sources, Disciplines, and Objects, p. 22.

59 Cf. Casteret, *Zehn Jahre* (1936), 60; *Ten Years* (1938), 48.

60 Original text uses the dated term "Eskimos."

61 Cf. Casteret, *Zehn Jahre* (1936), 62f; *Ten Years* (1938), 50.

62 Handwritten note on preliminary TS: **Psycho-plastic-era II. (Part IV, Chapter 5) / Cave-sculpture / Casteret p. 35** TXT_6752/0_N7

This bear lies in the same position as the great sphinx of Gizeh; he is 1.10 meters long and 0.60 high. Like the lion, he looks toward the exit, but does not lean against the wall. He is about a meter away and set on a small pedestal.

The statue is massive as it is fit for such animal. It has no head[63] and apparently never had one, because the cut at the throat is just as weathered as the rest of the body and shows no traces of being severed, as it is evident in the statue of Gizeh.

Also this bear shows numerous mutilations. He is pierced with round holes, seemingly originating from violent spear-stabs in the vital parts of the body. Yet, on account of its massiveness and wide base it withstood time.[64] Even the water that flowed down from the ceiling over his back and flanks did not harm it; partly, only, it is armored with a very hard crust of a lime-mixture which guaranteed its long age.

Between his front paws one sees the skull of a young bear and in correct scale, which led the scholars to very peculiar conclusions. For, this skull fell down from the statue on which it was fastened with a wooden dowel whose marks are still visible but the dowel itself rotted away on account of the humidity. So, originally the Bear of Montespan was a clay sculpture with a genuine bleeding head. What to think of this extraordinary and really exciting combination of a headless statue with a genuine head, is only possible if we imagine the terrifying rituals that once took place in this mountain castle.

One meter behind the bear, a horse is engraved deep into the clay floor; the neck, covered with enigmatic signs, seemed to have had a long fluttering mane. The entire floor of the hall is covered with about thirty reliefs, thirty to fifty centimeters long and ten to fifteen centimeters deep. It seems that they form an entire herd of horses whose bodies are marked with yet undecipherable signs just as many others of the Montespan animals.[65]

* * *

CHAPTER 6
THE IDEO—PLASTIC—ERA[66]

pls. 27, 25a–b

[67]Man arrived at his next phase, which, to agree with Max Verworn, could be designated as the ideo-plastic.[68]

As earlier he had expressed his faith and feelings through the imagery of the animal kingdom, he now proceeds to personify himself as the heaven, the earth, and the animals of both those spheres.

Architecturally, emphasis is put on monuments expressing the power of their invisible protectors[69] which are now made "real" in sculptures and buildings of gigantic dimensions.[70]

At this period families of the clan still live alongside each other in groups. They form a sort of alignment and huddle together in streets or in circles of one sort of another.[71] But each family shelters in an individual hut. Of course, the ancient "spots" where the elders of the clan would meet for the discussions of their hunts or tribal fights, or ceremonial rites, have now emerged from the haphazards of open nature, and have become "meeting houses" within the "village." Here the collective spirit is particularly preserved and with it the aura of mysticism based on the tradition of ancestral totemism and its dream world. The power associated with this cult finds on the "tribal-houses" decorative expression through special designs applied, by carving of posts and furnishings, and naturally, by a greater emphasis of height and mass of construction.[72]

The individual hut of the "average family" remains nothing but a profane shelter.[73]

63 **The animal has no head** TXT_6752/0_N7

64 **it withstood, and so the body remained unharmed.** TXT_6752/0_N7

65 There seems to be no transcription of the German text on which this translation of the excerpt on "cave sculpture" from Casteret is based. Cf. Casteret, *Zehn Jahre* (1936), 34–35; *Ten Years* (1938), 17–19.

66 Alternative part and chapter numbers: **Part II Chapter IV Ideo-plastic era** TXT_6790/0_N1 **PART ~~III~~ IV Chapter ~~IV III IV 4~~ 6 Ideo–Plastic–Era** TXT_6714/0_N1 **ideo-plastic & psycho-plastic** page with handwritten notes inside frame by Kiesler, see fig. B.19 TXT_6580/0

67 In addition to plate 27, marked in the TS, a second pair of plates numbered 25a and 25b present two contrasting examples of "ideo-plastic" versus "physio-plastic expression" in building structures represented by architectural models in Peruvian pottery and a project by Le Corbusier. See plates 25a and 25b, and Sources, Disciplines, and Objects, p. 13.

68 **Man's progress having been merciless pursuit** [sic] **by nature, he arrives at his next phase, which with M. Verworn can be appropriately designated as the ideoplastic.** TXT_6790/0_N1 **Having been mercilessly pursued by nature in his progress, man arrived at his next phase, which, agreeing with Max Verworn, we can designate as the ideo-plastic.** TXT_6714/0_N1 See Kiesler's transcription of excerpts from Max Verworn's "Zur Psychologie der primitive Kunst [On the psychology of primitive art]" addressing the distinction between physio-plastic, ideo-plastic, and psycho-plastic art. Included in Addenda: Transcriptions and Translations in English translation pp. 363–64. TXT_6823/0; TXT_6823/1

69 **Architecturalle** [sic] **ideoplastic man lives still in huts and in groupings together, but they have put emphasis on monuments expressing the ~~protector of spirits~~ power of their invisible protectors** TXT_6790/0_N3

70 **By sacrificing all their devotion to the Gods in power, the people take upon themselves gladly the neglect of their own quarters because no matter in what manner their own life might be clad, its good fortune does solely depend on the good will of the Gods. All their care is concentrated on creating "altars" for their sacrifices "of many colors" and of incorporating with all possible technical perfection all the insignia of powerful nature, which, in their belief expresses the guarantee for successful survival.** Entire paragraph crossed out in the TS, with a side note by Stefi Kiesler: **this paragraph omitted? (no blue bracket)** [crossed out]. TXT_6751/0_N2

71 **At this period, the families of the clans live ~~separately in huts but~~ still alongside each other in groups of a street or in circles of one sort or another, but they house themselves in individual huts. They have certain community houses as part of their "village."** TXT_6789/0_N6

72 **and mass of ~~building~~ construction.** TXT 6714/0_N3

73 **~~more or less.~~** TXT 6714/0_N3

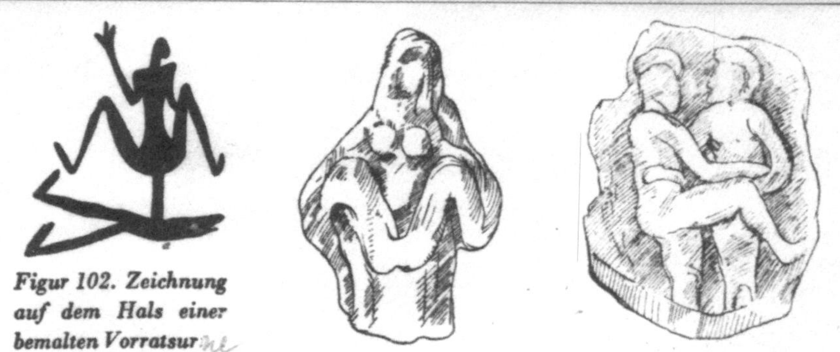

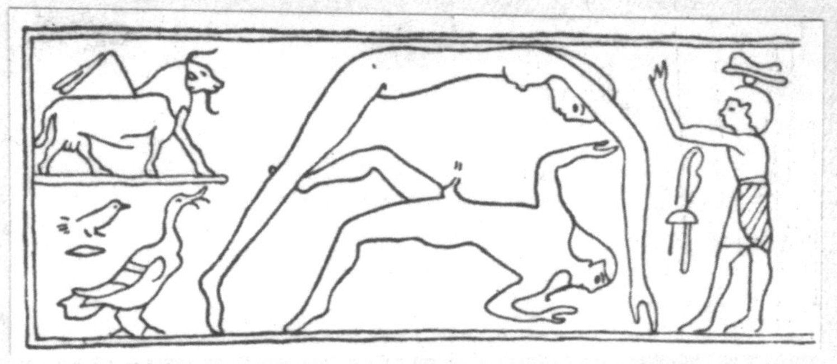

(27). Page 183

The psychic relation of man to the Cosmos changes perpetually. In these designs and sculptures, man is shown identifying himself with heaven (woman) and earth (man). (Ideo-plastic expression).

(28). Page 189

Below: Earth and heaven, rain, ocean, bird of the Sun. (Inside of a painted bowl, Africa.) (Expression of Abstract Design).

Ref.: to (25a) and (25b) page 183

(25a). Page 183

Peruvian Pottery in the form of houses and temples. An ideo-plastic imaginative expression of an every-day tool.

(25b). Below: Barren houses of our machine-age. A physio-plastic expression, which cares mainly for the physically organic. (Project by Le Corbusier. One family houses, 20th century, France.)

CHAPTER 7
THE ERA OF METAMORPHOSIS[74]

The organization of families, whether powerful or weak,[75] has grown more complex. Kings rule them in their earthly fights for existence, and priests rule them in their heavenly[76] martyrdom.[77]

The division into dwellings, ritual-building, and state palaces has become very marked.

The "average" man sacrifices now not only to "Spirits" and Gods, but pays also tribute to the supermen of his tribe and to the dignitaries of his society.

In this many thousands of years, associations of experience have produced memories, handed down in symbolic engravings and writings; history became conscious, time and space.

Gradually man has used all the paraphernalia of his natural surrounding stones, and bones, trees raw[78] or carved, animal heads, claws and feathers, fat of the eye, and the liver of a brother-man as special amulets of occult security.[79] There was really nothing more left to draw from for illusory power. He had exhausted the visual wealth of nature.

His personality is stuffed with riches; he feels equal with nature's populace and through the development of his technical skill in many respects superior to her.

Man begins to project himself into the skies, and plays a superior role previously occupied by the sun, the moon, the stars, the dawn and dusk, night and light. Zeus, king of the man-gods and a power over the earth-man, has a strong human stature; the shake of his (still) leonine coronet of hair is sufficient to set off disastrous thunder and lightning.[80] Man forces his personality on nature. His gods are many; they live and die like him. They ferry between heaven and earth and the planets. They masquerade and transform themselves into humans or animals of the earth. They participate in and even form (like the spirits of the cavemen) the large and petty affairs of earthly man.[81]

This is the era of metamorphosis. Its orgy of inter-change of creature, man, and cosmos is the culminating soporific in the ancestral stupor of man.[82]

CHAPTER 8
THE ERA OF ABSTRACTION[83]

Just as death announces itself through illness toward the end of a life, so in Greece there emerged slowly but determinedly, a spirit, which, summarizing the long deistic and earthly concepts, built its structure of meditation in terms of philosophy, that is to say in between the spatial conglomeration of the forces of godly and earthly motives and emotions.[84] pl. 28

These philosophers, who promenaded rather than ran, and some of the poets, artists and architects, erected a superstructure of abstraction. The mere honesty of thought and calcule culminated in a plastic creation, the Parthenon, which surpassed any powerful expression hitherto achieved by others.[85] Man had reached the height of plastic creativeness.[86] He demonstrated his ability to rely upon himself as creator of artistic concepts, but as a member of society[87] he still lived in slums.

CHAPTER 9
PHYSIO—PLASTIC—ERA

Note: (Man concentrates upon his physical well-being and develops his strife for materialistic security.)

(large sheet)[88] pls. 25a*–25b*

74 Alternative part and chapter numbers: Part III Chapter Three The Era of Metamorphosis. TXT_6793/0_N1 PART ~~III~~ IV Chapter ~~Three FOUR 5~~ 7 TXT_6722/0_N1

75 powerful and less powerful TXT_6793/0_N1

76 ~~spiritual~~ TXT_6722/0_N1

77 The subsequent paragraphs are part of a handwritten draft TXT_6722/0_N1-N2. They are not transcribed in any of the typewritten drafts of this chapter and are not included in any of the assembled versions of Kiesler's book manuscript. Cf. TXT_6750/0; TXT_5877_N137-138.

78 ~~as found~~ TXT_6793/0_N2

79 ~~power and security~~ TXT_6793/0_N2

80 Zeus ~~with powerfull~~ King of the man-gods and over the earth man, has a powerful human stature. The shake of his (still) lionesk [sic] ~~head back~~ hair-corona is sufficient to set off a disastrous thunder and lightning. TXT_6793/0_N3 On the royal powers of the "lion head" in African and early Greek cultures, see the sixth section "Lion (Löwe)" in Frobenius, *Kulturgeschichte Afrikas*, 63-102 (the first pages of which are included in the Kieslers' translated transcriptions TXT_6814/0_N5-N7).

81 the large and petty affairs of earthly creatures such as man, animals, and plants. TXT_6793/0_N4

82 the culminating feast of ancestral stupor in man. TXT_6793/0_N4

83 Alternate chapter numbers: Part III Chapter Four The era of abstraction TXT_6791/0_N1 PART ~~III~~ IV Chapter ~~Four FIVE 6~~ 8 The Era of Abstraction TXT_6859/0_N2

84 Stefi Kiesler queries the following paragraph: long paragraph in manuscr. indicated to omit? Kiesler then replies: please add second paragraph → fig. B.23 TXT_6859/0_N1 On the exchanges between Frederick and Stefi Kiesler as recorded on the book manuscript of *Magic Architecture*, see Annotated Chronology and Note by the Editors.

85 which surpassed any borrowed Form or Color ~~of man~~ either from the earth or from the heavens ~~which other nations have adopted~~ TXT_6859/0_N2

86 spiritual creativeness TXT_6859/0_N2

87 but as ~~he plays with the imagery of gods~~ TXT_6859/0_N2

88 Kiesler notes only 25b* in the TS but the plates intended for this chapter show part of a diptych (25a* and 25b*).

fig. B.19

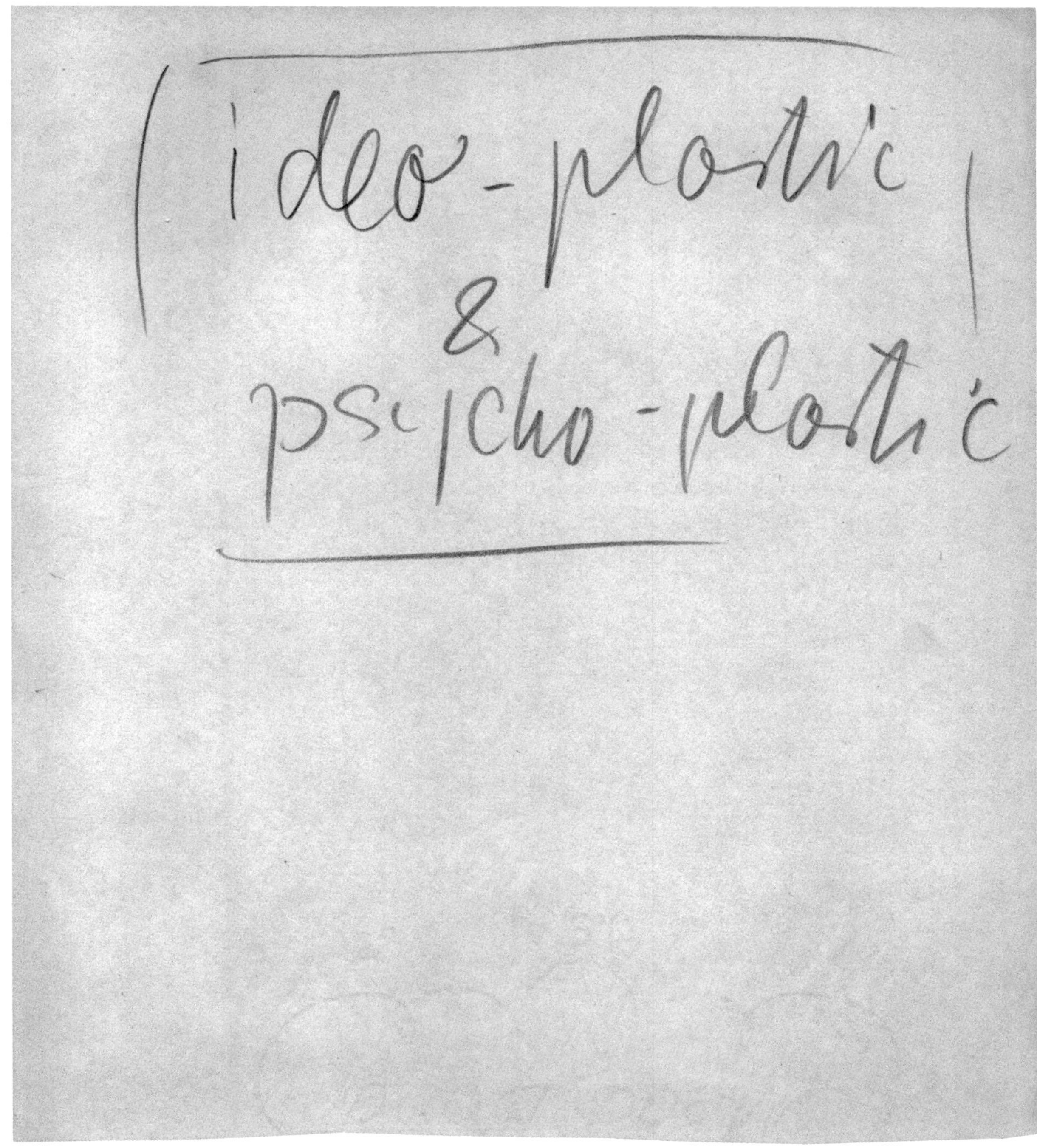

Frederick Kiesler, Handwritten notes: "ideo-plastic & psycho-plastic" related to the content of Part IV, Chapters 5 "The Psycho-plastic era" and 6 "The Ideo-plastic era" (MS, pencil) ÖFLKS, TXT_6580/0

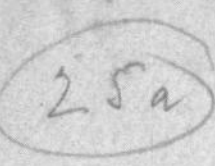

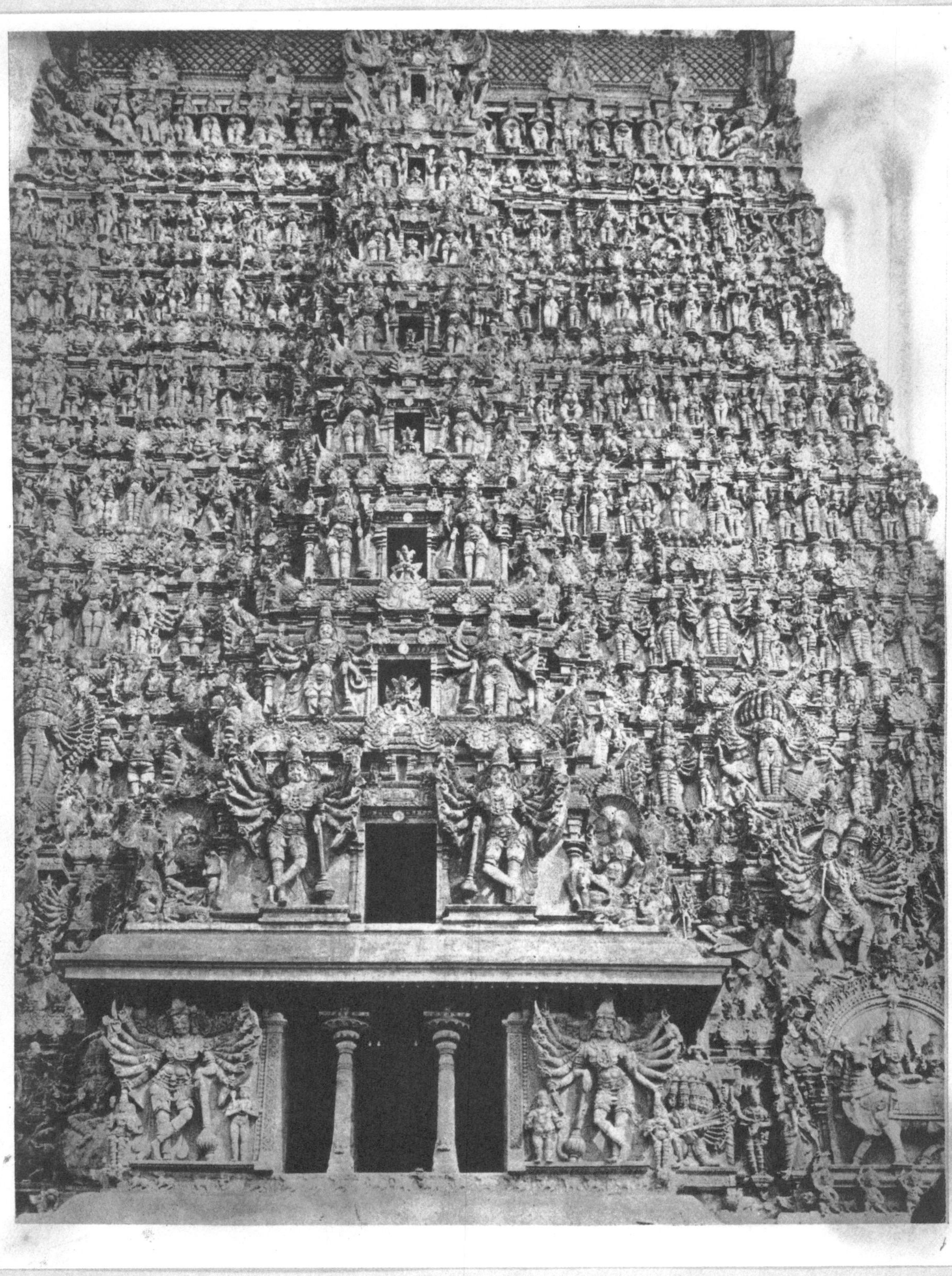

Psycho-plastic expression.
(wall of temple in Madura, India.)

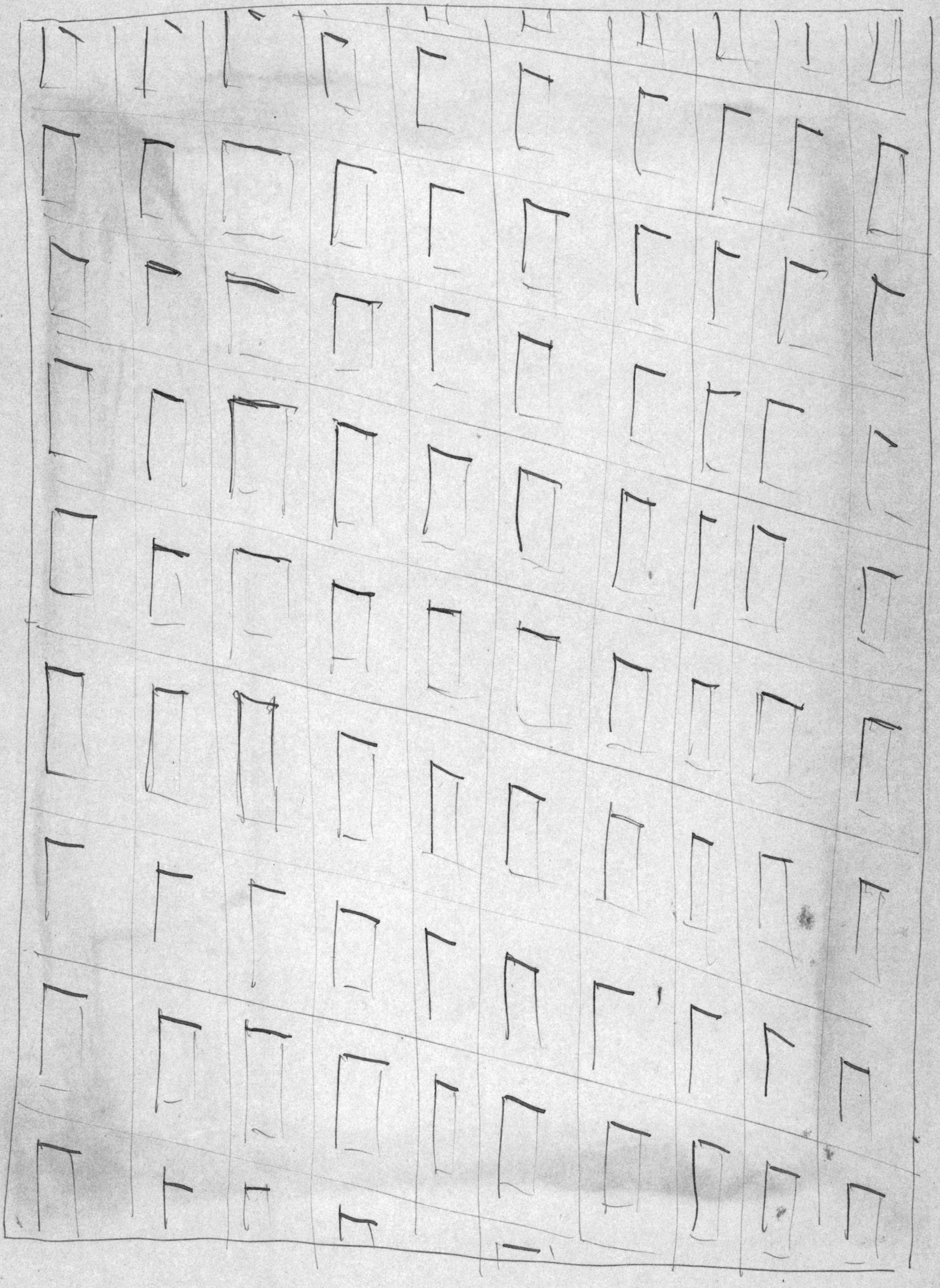

Physio-plastic expression.
(wall of R.C.A. building, Rockefeller Center, New York, U.S.A.)

25
"Las Figuras. Key-plate, showing division into seven panels." Breuil, *Rock Paintings of Southern Andalusia*, pl. I. ÖFLKS, SCL_36/0

25x
Rajarani Temple, Bhubaneswar. Hürlimann, *Indien: Baukunst, Landschaft und Volksleben*, pl. 123. ÖFLKS, SCL_37/0

26
Animal masks, heads, and symbols. Frobenius, *Kulturgeschichte Afrikas*, 137, figs. 51–59. ÖFLKS, SCL_39/0

27
Early terracotta reliefs and painting on an Egyptian wooden coffin with female and male symbolic figures. Frobenius, *Kulturgeschichte Afrikas*, 155, figs. 101–104. ÖFLKS, SCL_40/0

28
"Painted bowls, Elam. Susa." Frobenius, *Kulturgeschichte Afrikas*, 169, figs. 114–115. ÖFLKS, SCL_40/0

25a
Early Chimu vases. Philip Ainsworth Means, *Ancient Civilizations of the Andes* (New York: Charles Scribner's Sons, 1931), 82, figs. 17–19. ÖFLKS, SCL_38/2

25b
Le Corbusier, *Kommende Baukunst*, trans. Hans Hildebrandt (Stuttgart: Deutsche Verlags-Anstalt, 1926), 222. ÖFLKS, SCL_38/2

25a*
Ramanathaswamy Temple, Rameswaram. Hürlimann, *Indien: Baukunst, Landschaft und Volksleben*, pl. 9. ÖFLKS, SCL_38/0

25b*
Frederick Kiesler, Sketch of the facade of the R.C.A. building, Rockefeller Center. ÖFLKS, SCL_38/0

Part V
slums for the Body,
Dream Architecture for Rituals

fig. B.20

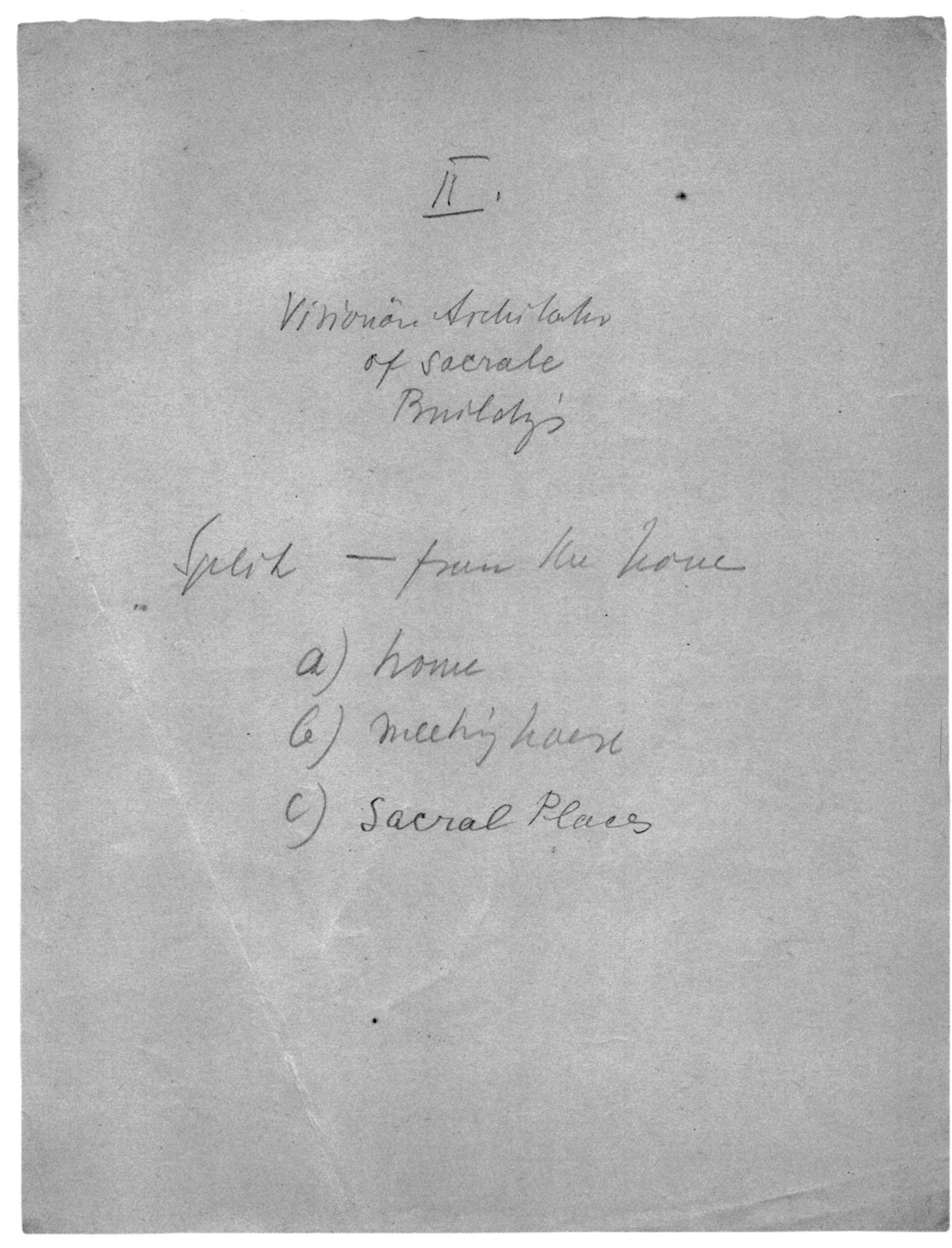

II.

Visionäre Architektur
of sacrale
Buildings

Split — from the home

a) home
b) meeting house
c) Sacral Places

Frederick Kiesler, Handwritten notes: "Visionaire Architektur of sakrale Buildings / Split - from the home / a) home b) meeting house c) sacral places" related to the content of Part v, Chapter 1 "The Split in Vision and Fact standardized" (MS, pencil) ÖFLKS, TXT_6805/0

PART V
SLUMS FOR THE BODY
DREAM ARCHITECTURE FOR RITUALS[1]

INTRODUCTION
IMAGE—WORSHIP[2]

As, century after century, the ages roll on, polytheism comes back under the disguise of Mariolatry and the adoration of saints; image-worship becomes as rampant as in old Egypt; adoration of relics takes the place of the old fetish-worship; the virtues of the ephod pale before those of holy coats and handkerchiefs; shrines and calvaries make up for the loss of the ark and of the high places; and even the lustral fluid of paganism is replaced by holy water at the porches of the temples. A touching ceremony—the common meal originally eaten in pious memory of a loved teacher— becomes metamorphosed into a flesh-and-blood sacrifice, supposed to possess exactly that redeeming virtue which the prophets denied to the flesh-and-blood sacrifices of their day; while the minute observance of ritual is raised to a degree of punctilious refinement which Levitical legislators might envy. And with the growth of this theology, grew its inevitable concomitant, the belief in evil spirits, in possession, in sorcery, in charms and omens, until the Christians of the twelfth century after our era were sunk in more debased and brutal superstitions than are recorded of the Israelites in the twelfth century before it.[3]

A candid Mexican of the time of Cortez, could he have seen this Christian burial-place, would have taken it for an appropriately adorned Teocalli. The professed disciple of the God of justice and of mercy might there gloat over the sufferings of his fellowmen depicted as undergoing every extremity of atrocious and sanguinary torture to all eternity, for theological errors no less than for moral delinquencies; while, in the central figure of Satan, occupied in champing up souls in his capacious and well-toothed jaws, to void them again for the purpose of undergoing fresh suffering, we have the counterpart of the strange Polynesian and Egyptian dogma that there were certain gods, who employed themselves in devouring the ghostly flesh of the spirits of the dead. But in justice to the Polynesian, it must be recollected that, after three such operations, they thought the soul was purified and happy. In the view of the Christian theologian the operation was only a preparation for the tortures continued forever and aye.

CHAPTER 1
THE SPLIT IN VISION AND FACT STANDARDIZED[4]

pl. 29 In all parts of the civilized western as well as eastern worlds we find abundant architectural samples of the standardized splitting of life's experience into vision and fact. People everywhere built shelters for homes, homes for their "dream"—visions of temples, and for their homes of the imagination—suitable for social rituals, the palaces of kings, and the castles of the rich.[5]

Even measured by the health standards of their own period the people themselves actually lived in slums, particularly in those countries where—at the same times—some of the best samples of sacred architecture were built.[6] This split is vividly illustrated by the embedding of great monuments in the slum living quarters of the people who built them.[7]

1 Alternative titles (frontispiece): **<u>Part v</u> ~~The Unity of Vision and Fact Reality~~** / **~~led in~~** [illegible] / **~~Nothing but Dreams~~** / **Slums for the Body,** / **Dream Architecture for Rituals.** TXT_6726/0_N1recto **Introduction:** / **Slums for the body** / **...** TXT_6726/0_N1verso

2 **Huxley (<u>Encore</u>–Jan. 1943).** TXT_6753/0_N1 **T. H. Huxley Evolution of Theology <u>Encore</u>, June 1943.** TXT_6836/0_N1 The Introduction to Part v is an excerpt of an essay by Thomas H. Huxley, "The Evolution of Theology," as published in *Encore*. See Thomas Henry Huxley, "The Stocks and the Stones: From the Evolution of Theology," *The Magazine Encore, A Continuing Anthology* 3, no. 17 (June 1943): 704–708. For the original source of the essay, see Sources, Disciplines, and Objects, p. 89.

3 Several lines of Huxley's *Encore* essay are omitted in the Kieslers' transcription. See Sources, Disciplines, and Objects, pp. 61–62.

4 **~~Slums for the Body—Dream Architecture for Rituals.~~** The chapter subtitle eventually became the title of Part v. TXT_6753/0_N3

5 Cf. Kiesler's handwritten notes on the development and progressive split of sacred architecture from house building (fig. B.20): **II. Visionaire Architektur of sakrale Buildings** / **Split—from the home** / **a) home b) meeting house c) sacral places** TXT_6805/0

6 **particularly in those countries where the best samples of ~~magie~~ architecture were built. This split is illustrated in Greece of the time of the Parthenon 434 B.C.; by the Hagia Sophia of Anthemios and Milet (537 A.C.); by the terrace temple of Deir-el-Bahar (1580–1447) in India; and by the Pyramids of Egypt.** [Handwritten addition] In his draft, Kiesler crosses out this list of monuments and includes another handwritten note: **for dates only →** TXT_6726/0_N2verso

7 Following this passage Kiesler added a handwritten instruction indicating chapter 1 as the introduction to Part v, including an outline of its contents: **STEFI—repeat but from outline—Part 5—chapt's 2–8.** TXT_6726/0_N2 The TS by Stefi includes a partial list of chapters in Part v: **Egyptian Pyramid and Street** / **Aztec Pyramid and Houses** / **Parthenon and Street** / **Indian Temple and Street** / **Gothic Cathedral and Street** / **Hagia Sophia and Street** / **Skyscrapers and Houses** [handwritten addition] TXT_6753/0_N4 See also handwritten list of contents for Part v. TXT_6702/0_N6-N7 noted in "Content."

(29) pge 197

(29). Page 197

The split of Architecture into buildings for the spirit and in shelters for the body.
Above: Churches in Pisa, Italy - and -
Below: Shelter-huts for the people to live in.

CHAPTER 2[8]
EGYPTIAN PYRAMID AND TOWN

pl. 30 Picture
Pyramid of Gizeh

Historians and architects have worked their quills to sweat to find a functional reason for the form of the Egyptian pyramid and gave up. Because it is too evident that the "functional" shelter for a mummy tomb does not need a giant pyramid. Nor have any monumental buildings of the Egyptian style of architecture that shape. Where does it come from then? Egyptian temples with their gigantic colonnades or plutocratic dwellings of any of the Egyptian periods are not "pyramidic." Could it be that some builder saw magic in man's make-up? The earthboundness of his body, the gravitation of his weight unerringly towards the earth, while at the same time his dreams point continually upward.[9] The pyramid is an accomplished expression[10] of these two forces: earth and heaven–bound.

Magic Architecture for the Death[11]

1. The Pyramid
2. The House of <u>Everyman</u> in Egypt[12]

Matter and Form
Nature
Art
Vegetative
Platonic Idea
Organic Mass
Anorganic
Metaphysical

<u>Magic Architecture for the Death in Egypt</u>
<u>The Pyramid</u>
<u>Tomb above</u> ground
No underground Tomb
A Tent?
The roof?
Therefore eternal symbol of the House
(<u>Not</u> in Egypt)

a Tent ?

Nothing but rest, no uplift ... for going in and out

CHAPTER 3
AZTEC PYRAMID AND DWELLINGS[13]

Behind the unheard-of luxury of the court was concealed the misery that naturally accompanies all despotic governments. The king, the nobles, the priests, the officers, and the privileged classes, lived in abundance; the people, bound to the soil, oppressed, badly fed, with no hope of seeing their condition improve, toiled to supply, not their own needs, but those of the great. Between the king and his vassals there was an impassable chasm; and the latter, the soldiers especially, considered death as blessing, for it opened to them the gates of a world where their sufferings would cease forever.[14]

* * *

Built in the middle of the city, this vast temple, which had the form of a truncated pyramid, covered, with the temples annexed, all the place now occupied by the cathedral of Mexico–the great square and the adjoining streets. The wall, sculptured with intertwined serpents, which surrounded it, formed a square, according to Cortez, large enough to contain a village of five hundred houses.

8 **~~belongs to Part Two~~** / **Part v, Ch. 2** TXT_6832/0 The following TS text was not transcribed in later drafts and is not part of the assembled book manuscript; it has been added by the editors.

9 **~~the entity of~~ his ~~vision~~ points ~~incessantly and~~ continually upward** TXT_6832/0

10 **Thi~~s~~ pyramid is ~~the most perfect~~ expression** TXT_6832/0

11 The charts with sketches and text on the Egyptian pyramid included in this chapter make up part of an earlier assembled manuscript (see Kiesler's page numbers on top of each page). These pages were not transcribed in later drafts and are not included in any of the existing assembled drafts of *Magic Architecture* (figs. B.21, B.22). TXT_6829/0_N11-N12 Kiesler's preliminary drafts for this chapter also indicate a footnote with a quotation from Schopenhauer in German on inorganic nature. **<u>Footnote to "Pyramid"</u>** / **Schopenhauer: Zur Metaphysik und Aesthetik (<u>Parerga</u> II)** / **213.**/ **"Die unorganische Natur, soweit sie nicht etwa aus Wasser besteht, macht, wenn sie alles Organische sich darstellt, einen sehr traurigen, ja, beklemmenden Eindruck auf uns. Beispiele davon sind die bloss nackte Felsen darbietetemdem** [sic] **Gegenden, namentlich das lange Felsenthal, ohne alle Vegetation, nahe vor Toulon, durch welches der Weg nach Marseille führt: im Grossen aber und viel eindringlicher wird es die Afrikanische Wüste leisten. Die Traurigkeit dieses Eindrucks des Unorganischen auf uns entspringt zunächst daraus, dass die unorganische Masse ausschliesslich <u>dem Gesetz der Schwere</u> gehorcht, nach deren Richtung daher hier Alles gelagert ist.–Dagegen nun erfreut uns der Anblick der Vegetation unmittelbar und im hohen Grade; natürlich aber umso mehr, je reicher, mannigfaltiger, ausgebreiteter und dabei sich selbst überlassen sie ist. Der nächste Grund hierfür liegt darin, dass in der Vegetation <u>das Gesetz der Schwere als überwunden erscheint</u>, indem die Pflanzenwelt sich <u>in der seiner Richtung gerade engegengesetzten</u>** [sic] **<u>erhebt</u>: hiedurch kündigt <u>sich unmittelbar das Phänomen</u> des Lebens an, als eine neue und höhere Ordnung der Dinge. Wir selbst gehören dieser an: sie ist uns das Verwandte, das Element unseres Daseins.** [emphasis Kiesler] TXT_6829/0_N10 Quoted from Arthur Schopenhauer, "Zur Metaphysik des Schönen und Aesthetik," in *Parerga und Paralipomena: Kleine Philosophische Schriften, Schopenhauer's Sämmtliche Werke*, Grossherzog Wilhelm Ernst edition (Leipzig: Insel-Verlag, 1920), V: 464-466 (section 213). The copy in Kiesler's personal library includes pencil marks at the beginning and end of the passage, indicating a potential footnote. There is no translation of this extract by the Kieslers. For a published English translation of the same passage: Arthur Schopenhauer, *Parerga and Paralipomena: Short Philosophical Essays*, trans. E. F. J. Payne (Oxford: Clarendon Press, 1974), 2:425. Other excerpts from Schopenhauer's aesthetics figure among the set of readings Kiesler compiled for the students of his Laboratory for Design Correlation at Columbia University: "Chapter XIX. Zur Metaphysik des Schönen und Aesthetik," sections 205, 206, 209, 211 in *Parerga und Paralipomena: Sämmtliche Werke* (1920), V: 453, 456, 460, 462. TXT_3572/0_N29-32

12 Deleted German text inside the chart: **~~An ägyptian House of everym~~ 2. The House of <u>Every-Man</u> in Aegypt** / **Materie ←Natur und Form ←Kunst** / **vegetabilisch / platonische Idee** / **organische Masse** / **unorganische** / **metaphysisch** TXT_6829/0_N11 A preliminary compilation of materials for this chapter also included a transcription of excerpts on the Egyptian pyramid from Egon Friedell, *Kulturgeschichte des Altertums. Leben und Legende der vorchristlichen Seele Erster Teil: Ägypten und Vorderasien* [Cultural History of Antiquity. Part I: Life and Legend of the Prechristian Soul] (Zurich: Helikon Verlag, 1936), 153-158, 446-448: **p. 153 Friedell** [handwritten note by Stefi Kiesler] TXT_6829/0_N1 **Egon Friedell: Kulturgeschichte des Altertums. 1.Teil: Ägypten und Vorderasien Helikon Vlg. 1936 First Chap**[te]**r, page 155.** / **Page 157.** / **Chapter Four. Page 446.** TXT_6829/0_N3, N5-6 These excerpts were not translated and therefore not used in later drafts. Included in English translation, in Addenda: Transcriptions and Translations, pp. 366-67. There, another set of unused transcriptions by the Kieslers (centered on the legend of Atlantis) copies earlier sections of Friedell's book. On the Kieslers' use of Friedell, see Sources, Disciplines, and Objects, pp. 50, 68-69. TXT_6822/0

13 **Pt 5 / Ch. 3–**/ **pge -195 (top)** / **p. 142-143** / **p. 329-330** / **p. 161-163** / **~~p. 195 top only →~~ From "The Aztecs" by Lucien Biart** / **Chicago 1887**. TXT_6753/0_N5 Instructions for quotation from Lucien Biart, *The Aztecs: Their History, Manners and Customs*, trans. J. L. Garner (Chicago: A. C. McClurg & Co., 1887). For the original publication (not used by the Kieslers), see Lucien Biart, *Les Aztèques: Histoire, moeurs, coutumes* (Paris: A. Hennuyer, 1885). Lucien Biart, a French author and Americanist specializing in Mexican archeology and ethnography, originally trained as a physician and lived in Mexico in the 1860s where he conducted zoological research during the French and Austrian colonization. See also Sources, Disciplines, and Objects, pp. 61, 89.

14 Biart's original text (the final paragraph of chapter 9 of his book) concludes with: "Oppressor and oppressed: do not these two words, unfortunately, sum up the history of man in all ages and in all countries?" This was omitted from the Kieslers' transcription and the manuscript of *Magic Architecture*. Biart, *The Aztecs*, 195. See Sources, Disciplines, and Objects, p. 61.

fig. B.21

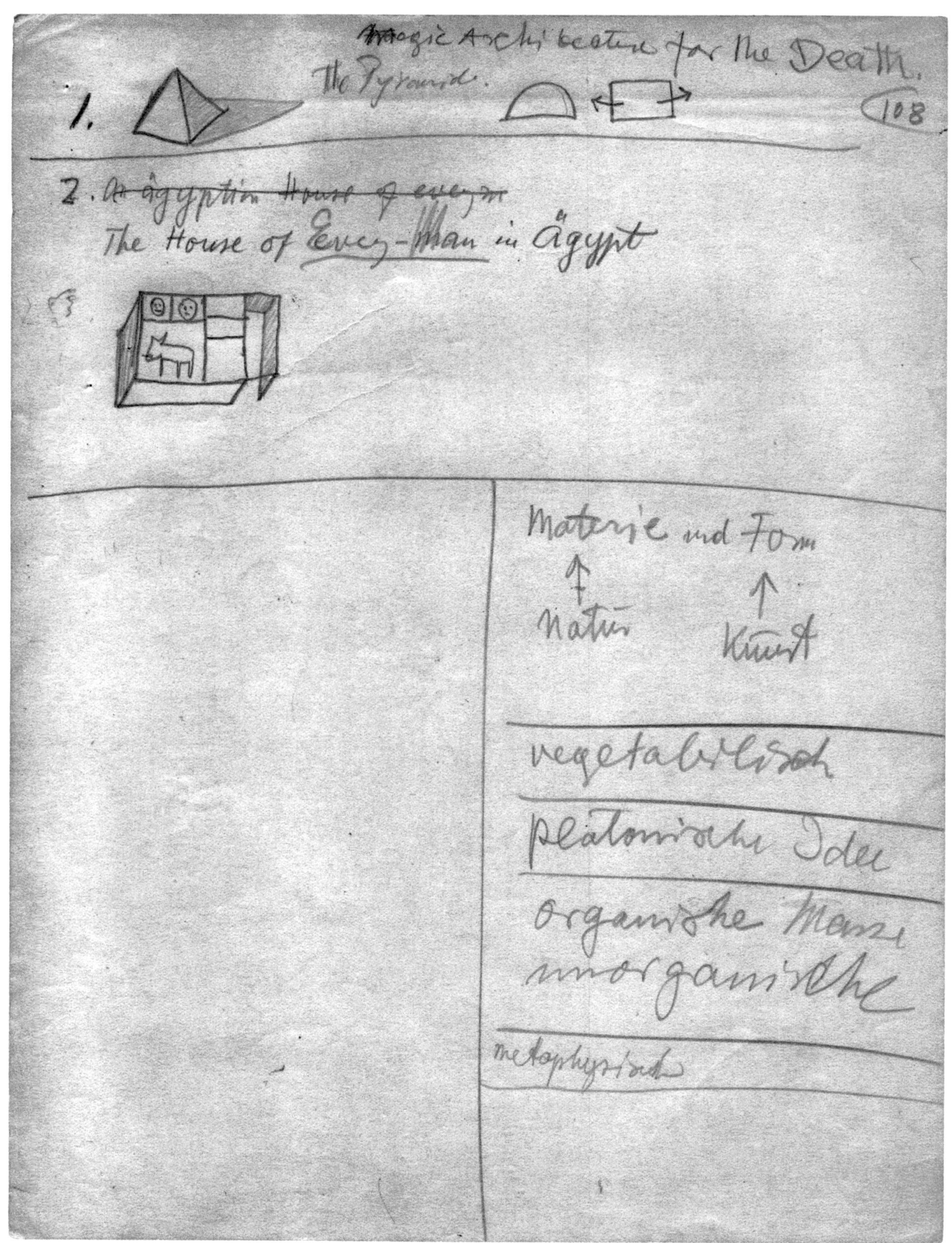

Frederick Kiesler, Preliminary chart related to Part v, Chapter 2, "Egyptian pyramid and town": "Architecture for the Death./ 1.The Pyramid / 2.The House of Every-Man in Ägypt [Egypt] / Materie ←Natur und Form ←Kunst [Materials ←Nature and Form ←Art] vegetabilisch [vegetal] / platonische Idee [platonic idea] / organische Masse [organic mass] / unorganische [inorganic] / metaphysisch [metaphysical] (MS, pencil) ÖFLKS, TXT_6829/0_N11

fig. B.22

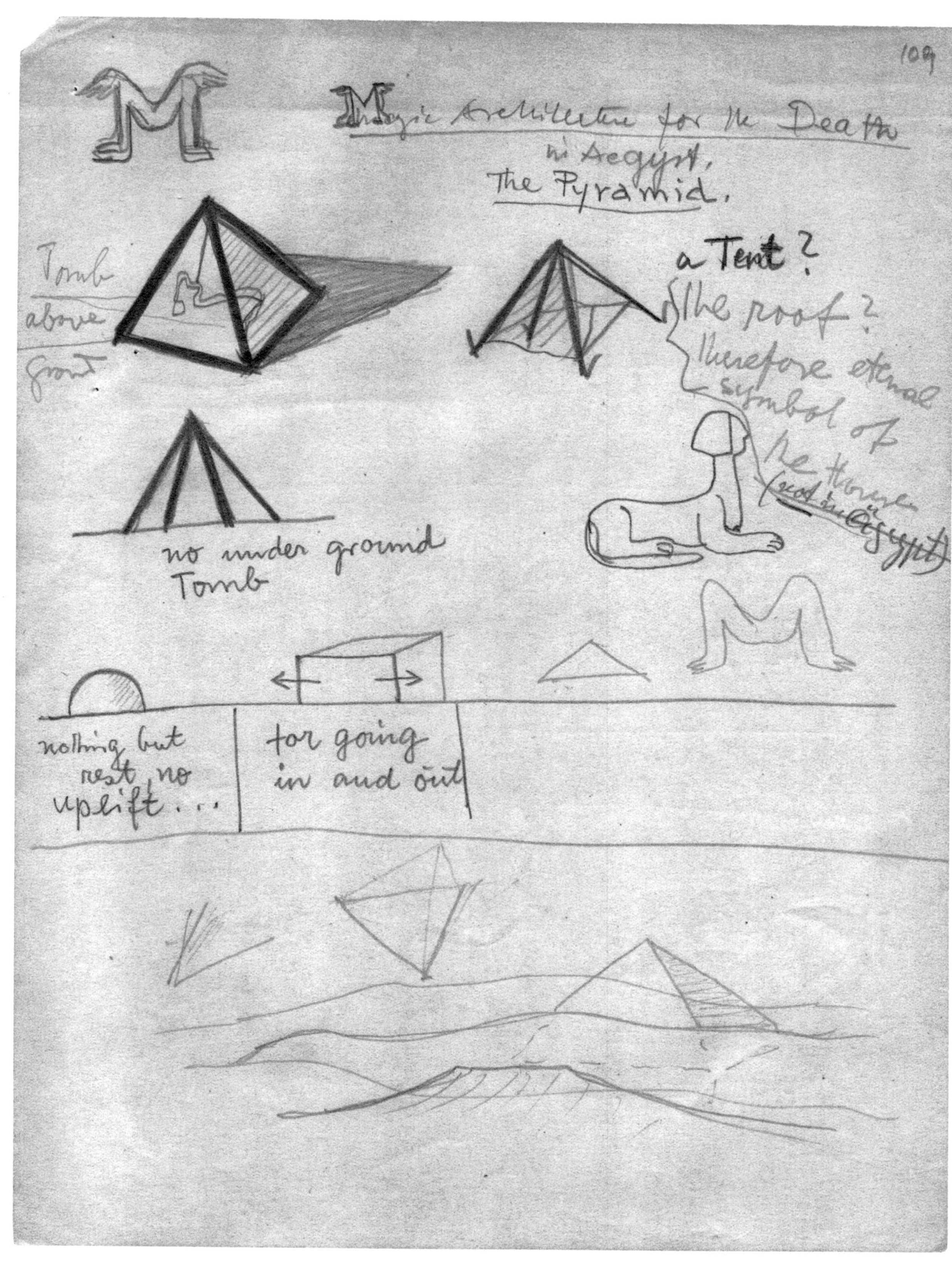

Frederick Kiesler, Preliminary chart related to Part v, Chapter 2, "Egyptian pyramid and town": "Magic Architecture for the Death in Aegypt [Egypt] / The Pyramid. / Tomb above ground / no underground Tomb / a Tent? / The roof? / Therefore eternal symbol of the House / (not in Ägypt) [Egypt] / nothing but rest, no uplift ... / for going in and out" ÖFLKS, TXT_6829/0_N12

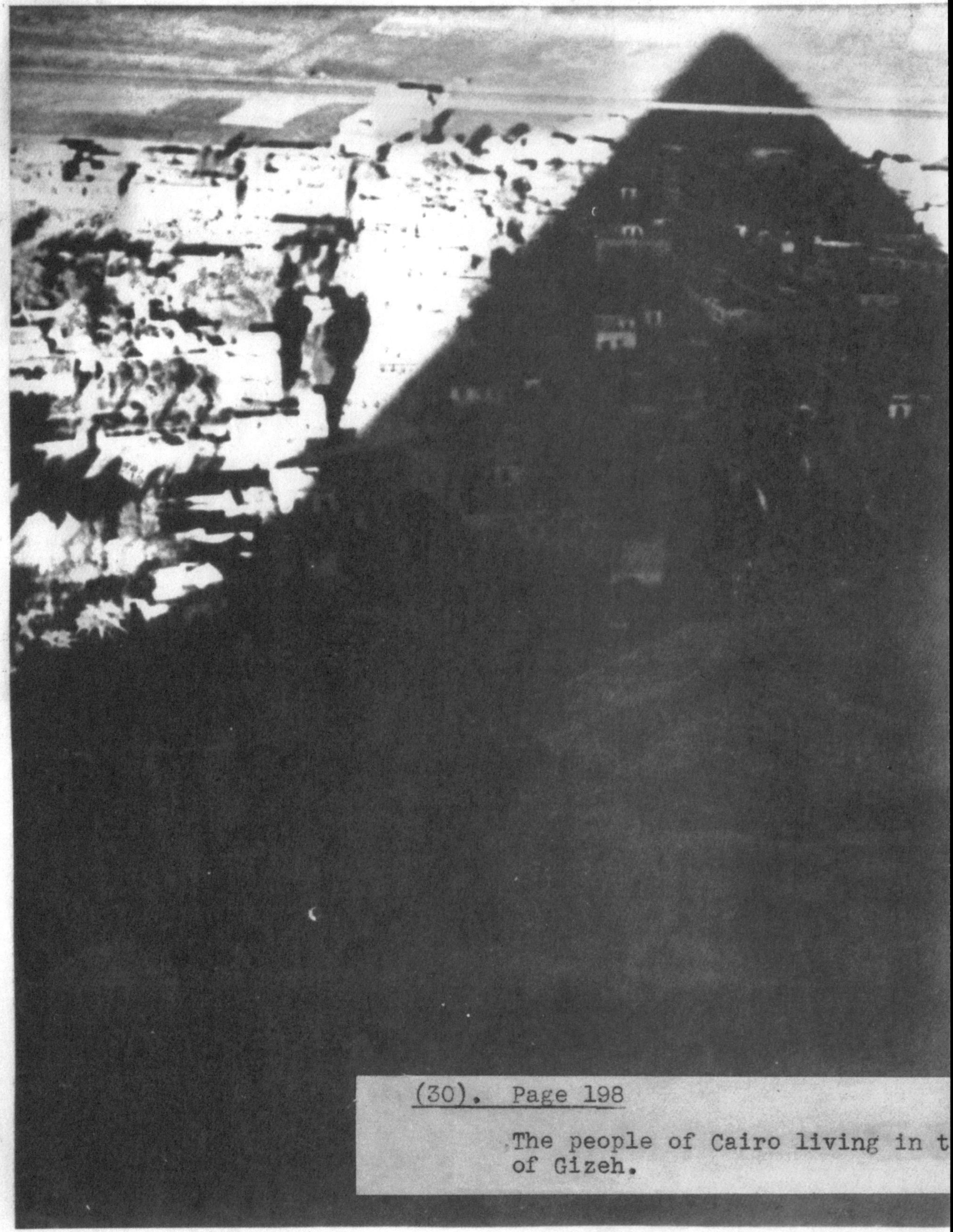

(30). Page 198

The people of Cairo living in t
of Gizeh.

page 198

hadow of the great Tomb-pyramid

Made of stone and mortar, this wall, which was very broad, was surmounted with battlements, and furnished with four gates facing the four cardinal points. A broad road extended from the eastern gate to Lake Tezcoco.[15] The other three gates opened upon the three principal streets of the city, which were long and broad, and which extended over the lake, as far as the villages of Iztapalapan, Tacuba, and Tepejacac.[16] Each of these gates was ornamented with stands of offensive and defensive arms. In case of necessity the soldiers manned them.[17]

The interior court enclosed by this wall was paved with stones so highly polished that the horses of the Spaniards could not venture into it without running the risk of falling. In the middle of this court arose the vast truncated pyramid, having according to some the form of a parallelogram, according to others that of a square.[18]

* * *

The walls of the dwellings of the poor were made of bamboo and bricks dried in the sun, and sometimes of stones held together with clay. To cover their roofs the Aztecs used long weeds of agave-leaves placed one upon the other, like our tiles. One of the principle supports of these houses was often a tree of medium height, which, in addition to the shade it afforded, lessened the cost of construction. These houses had but one room, in which was the fireplace, the furniture, the utensils, and in which the family and domestic animals lived together. If the proprietor was in comfortable circumstances, two or three rooms, an oratory, a "temascalli," and a granary were added to the house.[19]

The dwellings of the nobles and of the wealthy people were built of stone. They had two stories, with the rooms well arranged; and the roof, made of timber-work, was flat and served for a terrace. The walls, whitened and carefully polished, shone in such a manner that the first Spaniards who arrived before Mexico believed they were of silver. The foundation of these houses was of masonry; sometimes they were crowned with battlements or towers. Generally they had a garden, and a pond supplied with running water.[20]

* * *

[21]It is not known what sort of sacrifices the Toltecs offered to their gods; as to the Chichimecs,[22] they remained a long time without temples, and presented nothing to the objects they worshipped—the sun and the moon—but flowers, fruits, and incense. None of the peoples of Anáhuac, moreover, had any idea of human sacrifices until the Aztecs furnished them with the example. pl. 31

Among the latter the sacrifices varied, according to the god that was being honored, in the number of victims as well as in the manner they were killed. In most cases the breast of the unhappy being doomed to die was opened; but others were burned, drowned, flayed, or condemned to die of hunger in the grottos where the dead were buried. Others, small in number, fell in the duels the Spaniards called gladiatorial combats. Generally, these atrocious acts were committed in temples, for they all had an altar set aside for these religious murders. That of the temple of Mexico called "techcatl" was a block of green jade, its upper surface convex, three feet high and five feet long.

The ordinary ministers of sacrifice were six in number; they inherited their office. The chief among them was called Topiltzin;[23] but at the moment he was performing his terrible functions he took the name of the god to whom he was sacrificing. He wore a red vestment, suggestive of the scapular, ornamented with cotton fringe. On his head he had a crown of green and yellow feathers; from his ears emeralds were suspended, and from his lower lip a feather of "tentetl," of a blue color. The others were clothed in white robes bordered with black. Their hair was dishevelled, and their foreheads were bound with ribbons ornamented with round

15 Modern spelling is Texcoco.
16 Modern spellings are Iztapalapa and Tepeyacac.
17 The last sentence in the transcription is altered from the published English translation: "In case of necessity soldiers repaired there, to arm themselves." Biart, *The Aztecs*, 142–143.
18 Biart, *The Aztecs*, 143.
19 Modern spelling is temazcalli.
20 Biart, *The Aztecs*, 329–330.
21 All images included in plate 31 are reproduced from an article by the German ethnologist and Americanist Walter Krickeberg from the popular German illustrated journal *Koralle*, included in Kiesler's research clippings. "Menschenopfer für den Sonnengott: Wie die Azteken den Fortbestand der Welt sichern wollten [Human sacrifices for the Sun God: How the Aztecs wanted to secure the continuing existence of the world]," *Koralle* 24 (June 19, 1938), 852–853 (853 for the illustrations). See also Bibliographies: Research Clippings.
22 Modern spelling is Chichimecas.
23 Also called Quetzalcóatl.

page 200

(31). Below: Aztec Pyramid erected for human sacrifices.
Center: Illustration of sacrifice.
Right: The sculpted stone block upon which the human-being is laid, and the Urn into which his blood will flow.
Above: Sculpted Stone-Knife (for the extirpation of the human heart).

Stätte der Menschenopfer. Eine Rekonstruktion der Tempelpyramide von Tenayuca, auf der den Göttern Gefangene geopfert wurden.

bits of various colored papyrus. Their entire body was painted black, except around the mouth, which they daubed with white. Once in possession of a victim, these executioners carried him naked to a grand altar, on which they extended him, having first indicated to the assistants the idol to which they were about to offer the sacrifice, so that they might adore it. Four of the priests then held the unhappy being still by the legs and arms, while another kept him from moving his head, with the aid of an instrument of wood or stone, made in the form of a horse-shoe, and sometimes representing a curved serpent. The stone of the altar being convex, the body was bent in an arch, with the breast and stomach prominent, and the victim could make no resistance. The Topiltzin then approached and, with a knife of jasper or chalcedony, in accordance with the rite, opened the breast of the prisoner, tore out his heart, offered the palpitating trophy to the sun, and then threw it to the feet of the idol to burn it and to contemplate its ashes with veneration. If the idol was large and hollow, they placed the bleeding heart in its mouth with the aid of a golden spoon, and daubed its lips with the blood. When the victim was a prisoner-of-war, they cut off his head to preserve it for the Tzompatli,[24] and the body was then thrown on the lower step of the temple. There, the officer or soldier who had captured him seized the prey, carried it away, had it cooked, and served it to his friends at a banquet. They ate only the thighs, the arms, and the breast. As to the trunk, it was reduced to ashes or given as food to the animals of the royal menagerie. The Otomites quartered the victim and sold the remains in the market.[25]

CHAPTER 4
INDIAN TEMPLE AND STREET[26]

pl. 32

CHAPTER 5
PARTHENON AND HOUSE[27]

pl. 33

CHAPTER 6
GOTHIC CATHEDRAL AND TOWN

pl. 34

CHAPTER 7
HAGIA SOPHIA AND HOUSES

CHAPTER 8
SKYSCRAPER AND STREET

CHAPTER 9[28]
CATHEDRAL OF THE HOLY GRAIL

pl. 35

This project is particularly interesting because it has been designed after the description of an architectural fantasy within the framework of an epic poem (Titurel), written in the thirteenth and fourteenth centuries by Wolfram von Eschenbach and Albrecht von Scharfenberg.

It is the effort to overtop in design any Gothic cathedral planned. Quote:[29] "The Grail takes the skies to the far East[30] because Christianity of the West is unworthy of his blessings. There he hovers[31] over a mountain top in India. Titurel, son of an ancient line of kings of France, follows him. The king orders the mountain top cut and highly polished. One morning, he finds the floor plan of a cathedral miraculously engraved into it."

The full description of its plan, its building material, is contained in the epos "Titurel," and it was closely followed by Sulpiz

24 Modern spelling is tzompantli.
25 Biart, *The Aztecs*, 161-163.
26 Chapters 4-8 contain no text other than their titles and plate captions. Chapters 7-8 lack plates as well. Kiesler's journal clippings include the article by Maynard Owens Williams, "New Delhi Goes Full Time," *National Geographic* 82, no. 4, October 1942, 465-494. Also mentioned in Bibliographies: Research Clippings.
27 Kiesler's research clippings include two additional printed images of the Parthenon related to plate 33. Like the image montaged on Kiesler's plate, they, too, are extracted from Ferdinand Noack, *Die Baukunst des Altertums* (Berlin: Fischer & Franke, 1910), plates 17-18. CLP 6474/0_N1-N2
28 **Part v Chapter 9 The Cathedral of the Holy Grail** TXT_6754/0_N1
29 Text appears with and without quotation marks. TXT_6754/0_N1; TXT_5877_N157 Cf. the German text transcribed from Josef Ponten (with Heinz Rosemann and Hedwig Schmelz), *Architektur die nicht gebaut wurde* [Architecture that was not built] (Stuttgart: Deutsche Verlags-Anstalt, 1925), 1:17. TXT_6754/0_N2 The "Temple of the Holy Grail" is only the second architectural object described by Ponten in his account, following the description of Deinokrates' project for Mount Athos (included in Part vi of *Magic Architecture*). See also Sources, Disciplines, and Objects, pp. 62-65.
30 **to ~~India~~ …** TXT_6754/0_N1
31 **There he ~~draws in circles~~ over** TXT_6754/0_N1

(32)

page 206

(32). Page 206

So called Gapura of Madura, India. The people who built this magic monument live in slum-shelter. (See houses left and right).

(33)

p. 207

(33). Page 207

Great Architecture for the Gods, Slums for the people who built it. (Parthenon, Greece, and a dwelling of a family.

Dwelling to be replaced by a contemporary reconstruction.

(34)

pg. 208

(34). Page 208

To appease the Gods, a populace easily sacrifices its wealth and health. It builds cathedrals for Gods they never saw; but mere shelter for themsleves. (~~Tourney, France~~). Tournai (Belgique)

?

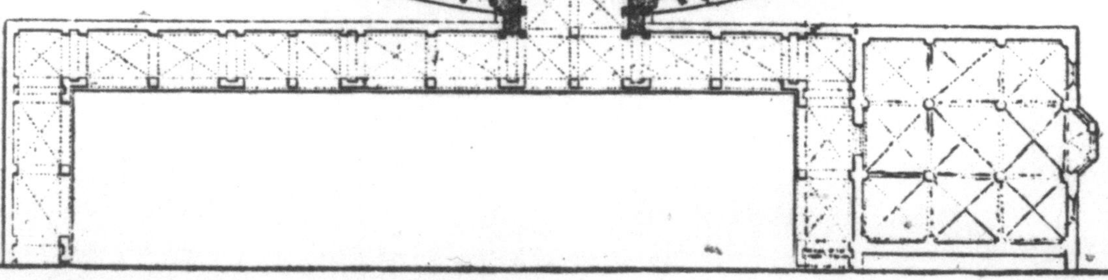

page 212

(35). Page 212

Floor plan and elevation drawing of a Cathedral for the Holy Grail. A project never built. (By Boisseré, after the description of a vision by Tituerel.)

Boisserée, the architect of the eighteenth century.[32] "The top[33] of the central spire carries a garnet of such luminosity that it illuminates all paths of the forest for those who seek refuge, and lost their way in the darkness of the night."[34]

(Text available in German)[35]

CHAPTER 10
THE GOTHIC ARCH[36]

I was much less impressed by what I could find in books[37] than by pl. 36
references in pure fiction to the awfulness of Gothic art—particularly by one writer's confession that the interior of a Gothic church, seen at night, gave him the idea of being inside the skeleton of some monstrous animal; and by a far-famed comparison of the windows of a cathedral to eyes, and of its door to a great mouth, "devouring the people." These imaginations explained little; they could not be developed beyond the phase of vague intimation: yet they stirred such emotional response that I felt sure they had touched some truth. Certainly the architecture of a Gothic cathedral offers strange resemblances to the architecture of bone;[38] and the general impression it makes upon the mind is an impression of life. But this impression or sense of life I found to be undefinable—not a sense of any life organic, but of a life latent and daemonic. And the manifestation of that life I felt to be in the <u>pointing</u>[39] of the structure.

Attempts to interpret the emotion by effects of attitude and gloom and vastness appeared to me of no worth; for buildings loftier and larger and darker than any Gothic cathedral, but of a different order of architecture—Egyptian, for instance—could not produce a like impression. I felt certain that the horror was made by something altogether peculiar to Gothic construction, and that this something haunted the tops of the arches.

To any experienced eye, the curves of Gothic arching offer a striking resemblance to certain curves of vegetal growth—the curves of the palm-branch being, perhaps, especially suggested. But observe that the architectural form suggests more than any vegetal comparison could illustrate. The meeting of two palm-crests would indeed form a kind of Gothic arch; yet the effect of so short an arch would be insignificant. For nature to repeat the strange impression of the real Gothic arch, it were necessary that the branches of the touching crests should vastly exceed, both in length of curve and strength of spring, anything of their kind existing in the vegetable world. The effect of the Gothic arch depends altogether upon the intimation of energy. An arch formed by the intersection of two short sprouting lines could suggest only a feeble power of growth; but the lines of the tall mediaeval arch seem to express a crescent force immensely surpassing that of nature. And the horror of Gothic architecture is not in the mere suggestion of a growing life, but in the suggestion of an energy supernatural and tremendous.

Of course the child, oppressed by the strangeness of Gothic forms, is yet incapable of analyzing the impression received: he is frightened without comprehending. He cannot divine that the points and the curves are terrible to him because they represent the prodigious exaggeration of a real law of vegetal growth. He dreads the shapes because they seem alive; yet he does not know how to express this dread. Without suspecting why, he feels that his silent manifestation of power, everywhere pointing and piercing upward, is not natural. To his startled imagination, the building stretches itself like a phantasm of sleep—makes itself tall and taller with intent to frighten. Even though built by hands of men, it has ceased to be a mass of dead stone: it is infused with Something that thinks and threatens—it has become a shadowing malevolence, a multiple goblinry, a monstrous fetish![40]

32 For the original description and engravings by Boisserée (reproduced among Kiesler's plates for *Magic Architecture* from Ponten, *Architektur* II:2), see Sulpiz Boisserée, *Ueber die Beschreibung des Tempels des heiligen Grales in dem Heldengedicht: Titurel Kap. III* (Munich: Königliche Bayerische Akademie der Wissenschaften, 1835).

33 **The pic** [sic] **of the central ~~steeple~~** TXT_6754/0_N1

34 This sentence appears with and without quotation marks. TXT_6754/0_N1; TXT_5877/0_N157 Cf. Ponten, *Architektur die nicht*, 1:18; transcribed by the Kieslers. TXT_6754/0_N3

35 Cf. Ponten, *Architektur*, 1:16–19. See TXT_6754/0_N2-N4 for the full set of excerpts transcribed from Ponten's chapter on the Cathedral of the Holy Grail.

36 **To type.** / **<u>Gothic.</u>** / **Page 214** / **215, 216, page 221, 222 Part v, Chapter ~~8~~ 10** / **retype** CLP_6464/0_N1verso Typing instructions by Kiesler written on the front page of a short essay titled "Gothic Horror" by the Greek-American-Japanese writer Lafcadio Hearn. The essay was clipped from a collection of essays by Hearn titled *Shadowings* (Boston: Little, Brown and Company, 1900), 213–222; 214–216, 221–222 for the two transcribed excerpts from the essay. See figs. B.23a-b.

37 **~~them~~ books**. CLP_6464/0_N3recto The Kieslers' transcription omits the first sentence of this paragraph: "Books about architecture were disappointing." Hearn, *Shadowings*, 214–215.

38 Drawing on Hearn's "resemblance" between Gothic architecture and "bone architecture" (Hearn, *Shadowings*, 215), Kiesler sketched a pair of Gothic arches with the statements—**(emotional) Bones only exist to carry flesh** / **(abstract) Bones without flesh**—on the back of the first torn page from Hearn's book (fig. B.23a). CLP_6464/0_N1recto Also a quotation from Hearn on the Gothic arch appears on the reverse of the folio that includes the photograph of Gothic arches from the Chartres Cathedral reproduced in plate 36 from Elie Faure's *La Vie des Formes* (1921): "but the lines of the tall medieval arch seem to express a crescent force immensely surpassing that of nature." Lafcadio Hearn, *Shadowings*, 221. See clip, SCL_48/0 and sources for plate 36.

39 Emphasis Hearn, *Shadowings*, 215.

40 On Gothic architecture, see also the following excerpt from Lynn Thorndike, *A History of Magic and Experimental Science during the First Thirteen Centuries of Our Era* (New York: Columbia University Press, 1923), II:536–537. This accompanies the Kieslers' transcriptions with the handwritten note: **<u>Nature in Gothic Architecture and Sculpture</u>** / **<u>Thorndike, History of Magic</u> Vol. 2, p. 537** but is not included in any of the assembled drafts of *Magic Architecture*. TXT_6827/0_N1-N2; _6829_N12-N13 It is included in Addenda: Transcriptions and Translations, p. 368.

(36). Page 214

Below: Gothic arches and their awe*inspiring effect described by Lafcadio Hearn. (Cathedral of Chartres, France).
Above: The inspiration: the ribs of a palm tree.

Photograph by Loran Kahle

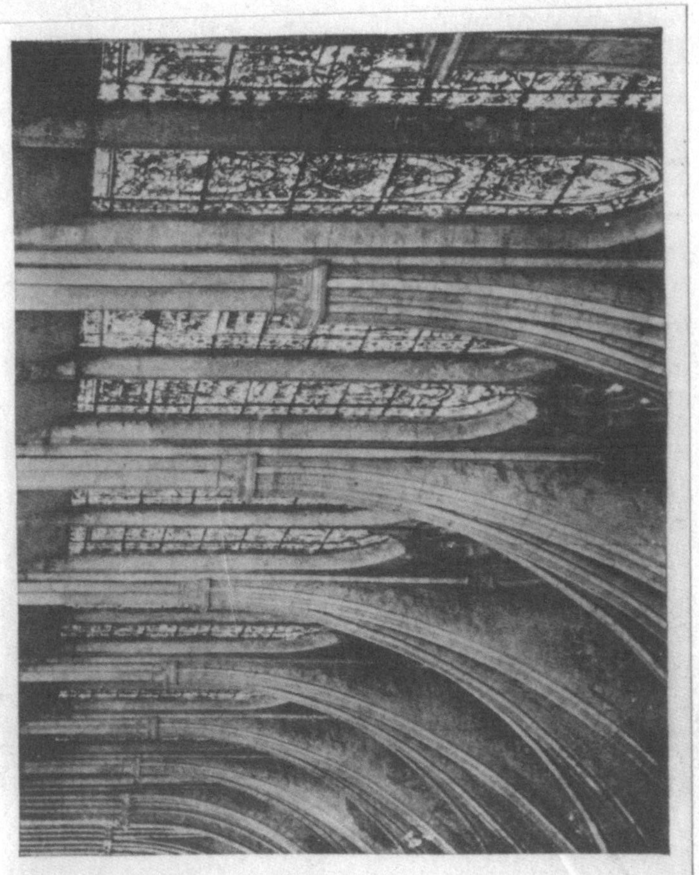

page 214

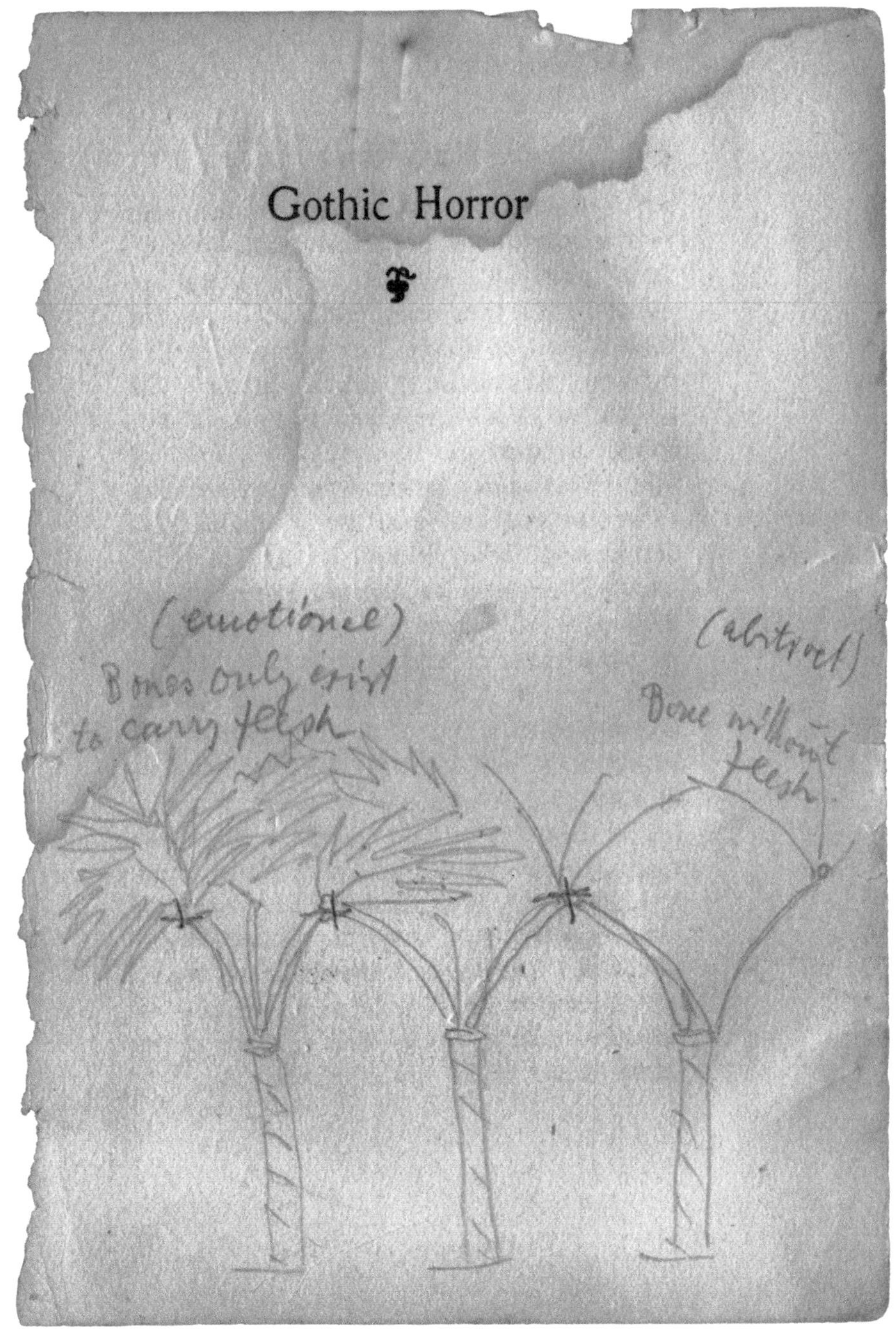

"Gothic Horror," Title page torn from Lafcadio Hearn, *Shadowings* (Boston: Little, Brown, and Company, 1919) with drawing and notes by Frederick Kiesler: "(emotional) Bones only exist to carry flesh / (abstract) Bone without flesh" related to Part v, Chapter 10 "The Gothic Arch" (pencil)
ÖFLKS, CLP_6464/0_N1recto

*fig.*B.23b

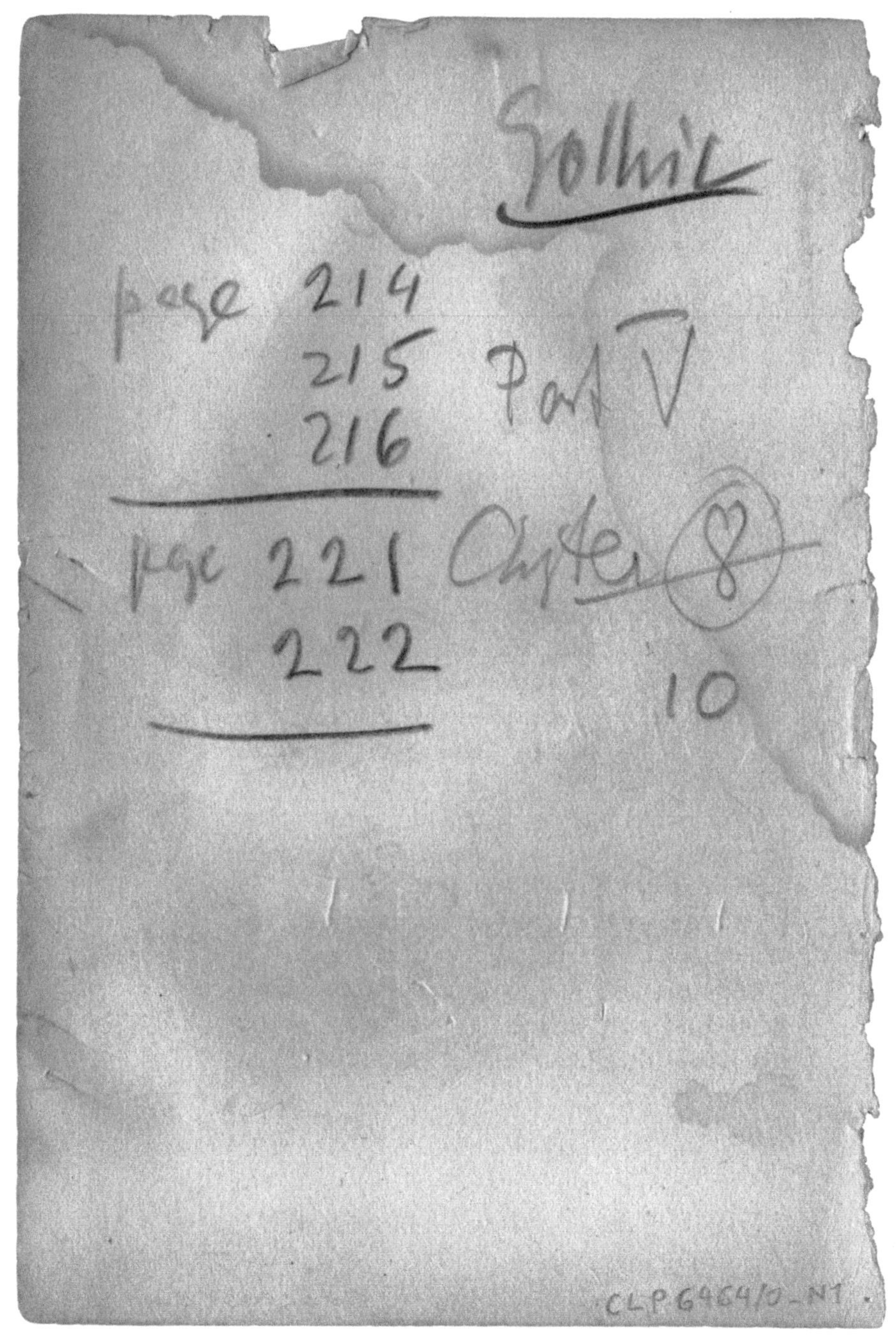

Verso of title page of "Gothic Horror" torn from Lafcadio Hearn, *Shadowings* (Boston: Little, Brown, and Company, 1919) with notes by Frederick Kiesler on pages to be transcribed ([color] pencil) ÖFLKS, CLP_6464/0_N1verso

29
Above: "Baptistry and Cathedral with Clocktower, southwest view." Max Hauttmann, *Die Kunst des frühen Mittelalters* (Berlin: Propyläen-Verlag, 1929), 414. ÖFLKS, SCL_41/0

Below: Huts of the Albu Muhammed Ma'dan (marshland) tribe. John van Ess, "Forty Years Among the Arabs," *National Geographic Magazine* LXXXII, no. 3, September 1942, 385–420, photo Field Museum of Natural History.

30
George Hoyningen-Huene and George Steindorff, *Egypt* (New York, J. J. Augustin, 1943), 38–39, photo Hoyningen-Huene. ÖFLKS, SCL_42/0

31
Walter Krickeberg, "Menschenopfer für den Sonnengott: Wie die Azteken den Fortbestand der Welt sichern wollten," *Koralle* 6, no. 24 (June 19, 1938): 852–853. ÖFLKS, SCL_43/0

32
Ramanathaswamy Temple, Rameswaram. Hürlimann, *Indien: Baukunst, Landschaft und Volksleben*, pl. 2. ÖFLKS, SCL_44/0

33
Montage by Frederick Kiesler with view of the Acropolis from Noack, *Die Baukunst des Altertums*, pl. 99. ÖFLKS, SCL_45/0

34
"Tournai Cathedral [Belgium], southwest view," from Max Hauttmann, *Die Kunst des frühen Mittelalters* (Berlin: Propyläen-Verlag, 1929), Plate XVII. . ÖFLKS, SCL_46/0

35
Left: "Grundriß [plan]," *Right*: "Der Tempel des Grals (nach Boisserée) [The Temple of the Grail (after Boisserée)]." Josef Ponten, *Architektur die nicht gebaut wurde* (Stuttgart: Deutsche Verlags-Anstalt, 1925), (left) II:3, pl. 4; (right) II:2, pl. 2. ÖFLKS, SCL_47/0

36
Above: Anne Rainey Langley, "I Kept House in a Jungle," *National Geographic Magazine* LXXV, no. 1, January 1939, 97–132, photo Loran Kahle.

Below: Elie Faure, *History of Art*, Vol. 5, *The Spirit of the Forms*, trans. Walter Pach (New York: Harper & Brothers, 1921), 187, fig. 88. ÖFLKS, SCL_48/0

Part VI
Painters
as
Dream-Architects

fig. B.24

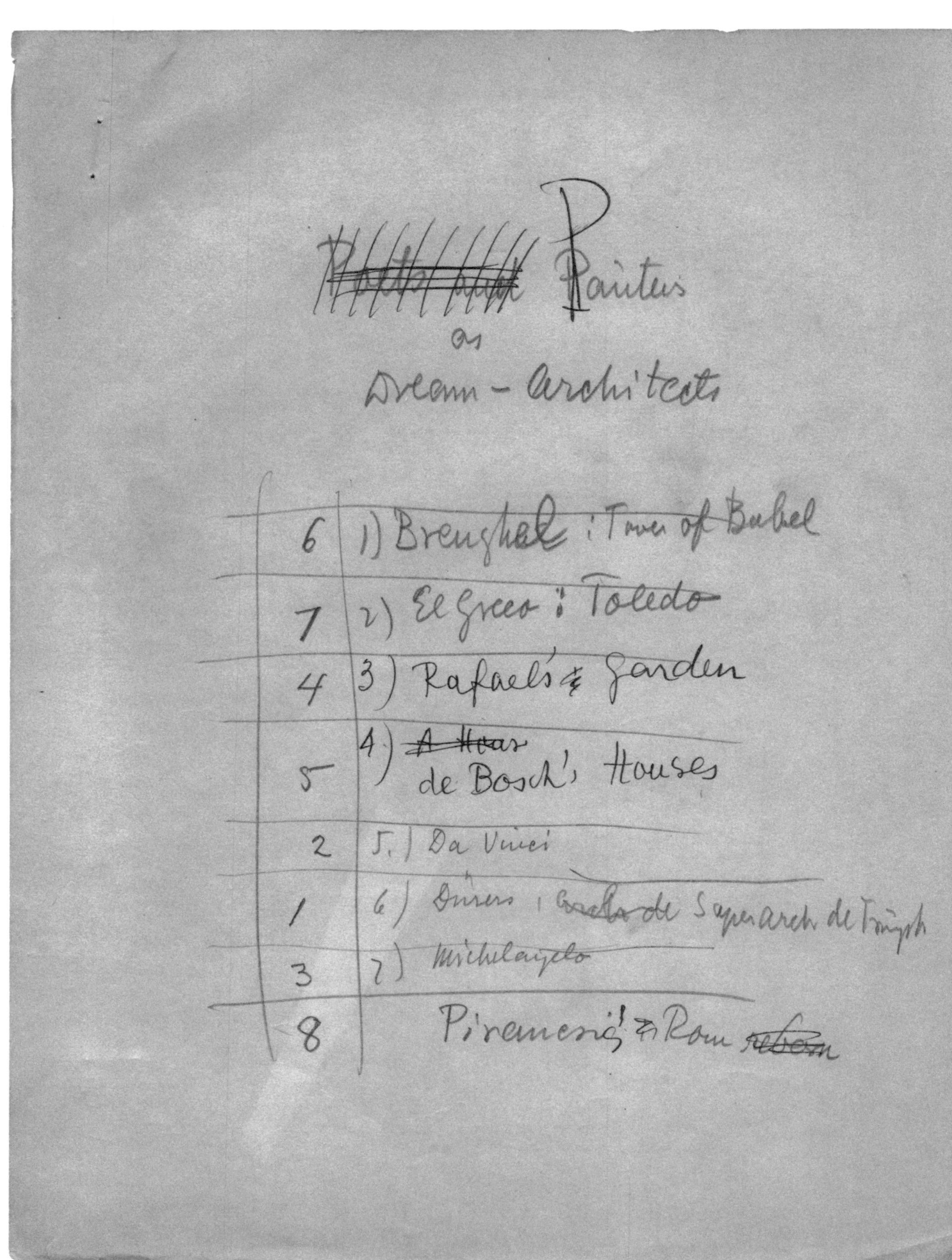

~~[illegible]~~ Painters
as
Dream-Architects

6	1) ~~Breughel~~ : Tower of Babel
7	2) El Greco : Toledo
4	3) Rafael's garden
5	4) ~~A Hous~~ de Bosch's Houses
2	5.) Da Vinci
1	6) Dürers : [illegible] Superarch de Triumph
3	7) Michelangelo
8	Piranesi's Rom ~~[illegible]~~

Frederick Kiesler, Part VI, "Painters as Dream-Architects," preliminary draft with alternate lists of chapters (MS, pencil, ink) ÖFLKS, TXT_6729/0_N2

PART VI
PAINTERS AS DREAM-ARCHITECTS[1]

INTRODUCTION

Both poets and painters have excelled in creating architecture in the magic sense because they are free of all technical considerations[2] and are set–a priori–to portray the essential. To them however, the essential is the expression, the form; it is not, as it is for the architect, a question of the rebuilding and ordering of organic material. Material is used solely for the expression of the emotional and spiritual, be it the portrayal of the house of Everyman, the small town, churches, bridges, walls, doors, floors, or ceilings.

Although it might seem that poetry and the plastic arts would by their very nature permit the creator the free flow of his inner sight,[3] we find only in the very best of these "designers" a realization worthy of their privileges. *)[4]

*The others superimposed their sentimentality upon the buildings of their imagination or upon the buildings which confront them and in this way wash whatever facts present themselves with the tints of timidity,[5] the very stigma of the petty bourgeois. Their presentations are weak, idealized vistas, one could really say the world seen by man in retirement.

CHAPTER 1
DÜRER'S SUPER-ARCH OF TRIUMPH

pl. 37 Dürer's project for a "Super-Arch of Triumph"[6] for Maximilian. (Original engraving at Public Library, New York.)[7]

CHAPTER 2
DA VINCI: CONCEPT OF CATHEDRAL[8]

pl. 38 Sketches for a new type of Cathedral designed by Leonardo da Vinci.[9]

pl. 39 and Francesco Cossa
Detail from: The Legend of St. Hyacinth[10]

CHAPTER 3
MICHELANGELO: CONCEPT OF ST. PETER'S CATHEDRAL

A comparison of Michelangelo's model for St. Peter's Dome and the deviation in actual execution by those who followed him.[11]

(Two photographs and two small plans)[12]

CHAPTER 4
BRUEGEL'S TOWER OF BABEL[13]

pl. 40 Tower of Babel by Pieter Bruegel the Elder (1563).[14]

A project of great structural soundness, logic, and realism. A circular pyramid in setbacks. It is the earth raising its head out of the sea of her endless plains, hills and mountain ranges until that upward lift is halted by a cloud lowered from the skies.[15]

CHAPTER 5
pl. 40x
HIERONYMUS BOSCH'S HOUSES (A) AND TOOLS (B)[16]

1 Title sheet (frontispiece): **PART VI: Painters as Dream Architects** TXT_6729/0_N1 Following the title sheet for Part VI is a handwritten chapter list with a different order than what appears in later typewritten versions: **~~Poets and~~ Painters as Dream Architects 1) Breugel: Tower of Babel 2) El Greco: Toledo 3) Rafael's Garden 4) ~~A Hous~~ de Bosch's Houses 5) Da Vinci 6) Dürer's ~~arch de~~ Superarch de Triumph 7) Michelangelo.** Kiesler renumbered all chapters on his table and added **Piranesi's Rom ~~reborn~~** as the eighth and final chapter of Part V (fig. B.24). TXT_6729/0_N2

2 **Poets and painters ~~too~~ excelled in creating architecture ~~and so much more~~ in the magic sense because they ~~were~~ freed of all technical considerations** TXT_6729/0_N4

3 **the free flow of his ~~imagination~~** TXT_6729/0_N4

4 Footnote by the author in MS not included in later drafts. TXT_6729/0_N4 * / **Footnote omitted?** [handwritten footnote symbol and query by Stefi Kiesler added in TS] TXT_6761/0_N1 The assembled TS draft shows a footnote symbol but no text. TXT_5877/0_N162

5 **in this way ~~sugar coat~~ whatever facts present themselves with the tints of timidity** TXT_6729/0_N4

6 **~~Arch de~~ Super-arch de Triumph** TXT_6729/0_N1; TXT_6729/0_N3

7 In his handwritten draft, Kiesler asks Stefi for a reproduction: **photo?** TXT_6729/0_N3 The photograph, reproduced in plate 39 is from an installation view of the set of engravings by the school of Dürer. These were on permanent display in Astor Hall of the New York Public Library. The NYPL does not own the "original engraving" or set of engravings for this project as Kiesler writes. Most of the original drawings and woodblocks are in Vienna's Albertina Museum. See also sources for plates at the end of Part VI.

8 **Concept of Cathedrals** TXT_5877/0_164

9 On Leonardo's architectural drawings, see Josef Ponten (with Heinz Rosemann and Hedwig Schmelz), *Architektur die nicht gebaut wurde* (1925), 1:46; 2:42 (fig. 84). Kiesler's library contains three books on Leonardo da Vinci: Richard Muther, *Leonardo da Vinci* (Berlin: Bard, Marquardt & Co, 1907); an English edition of Sigmund Freud, *Leonardo da Vinci: A Study in Psychosexuality*, trans. A. A. Brill (New York: Random House, 1947); and the catalogue for a traveling exhibition of models based on Leonardo's drawings organized by IBM: Ludwig Heinrich Heydenreich, *Leonardo da Vinci: The Scientist* (New York: International Business Machines Corporation, 1951).

10 Handwritten addition TXT_5877/0_164 No mention of Cossa in any of the preliminary drafts. TXT_6761/0_N3

11 Cf. Kiesler's reference (text and cartoon) to the dome of Saint Peter's by Michelangelo in his book *Contemporary Art Applied to the Store and its Display* (New York: Brentano's, 1930), 75. It is a cartoon with the attribution "Design by ELISE" depicting Michelangelo in sixteenth-century garb demonstrating his drawing to a modern-day business manager who rejects it, while a clerk in the background shows the artist the door. Cf. the chapters on St. Peter's and Michelangelo as an architect, in Ponten, *Architektur*, 1:47-58.

12 These photographs and plans do not exist among the plates for *Magic Architecture*. Nevertheless, Kiesler's copy of the German edition of Le Corbusier's *Towards an Architecture* contains page markers with photostat requests (in Kiesler's handwriting) for the photographs and drawings of the dome of St. Peter's, including Michelangelo's design. See Le Corbusier and Hans Hildebrandt, *Kommende Baukunst* (Stuttgart: Deutsche Verlags-Anstalt, 1926), 140-143. Ponten's publication also includes a series of drawings of St. Peter's facade according to Michelangelo and others, as well as a photograph of its dome later reproduced in the German edition of Le Corbusier. See Ponten, *Architektur*, 2:50-52 (figs. 98-100). Cf. Ponten, *Architektur*, 2:51; and Le Corbusier and Hildebrandt, *Kommende Baukunst*, 140.

13 **sep. sh.** [annotation indicating a separate sheet] TXT_6729/0_N4 In this TS draft, the text for the Tower of Babel immediately follows the introduction. As noted earlier, the initial list of projects and artist-designers for Part VI presents the Tower of Babel as chapter 1. Both clues suggest that Kiesler initially planned to start Part VI on the architecture of painters with Breugel's *Tower of Babel* but then opted for a more chronological sequence.

14 **Peter Breughel the Older** TXT_5877/0_N166 Kiesler's research material includes a page from an article with an illustration of Bruegel's *Tower of Babel* (at the Kunsthistorisches Museum in Vienna), titled "Der Turmbau zu Babel (Wien)." The page is clipped from an article on the philosophy of language by the linguist Ernst Lewy, "Das Wesen der Sprache" published in the journal *Faust: eine Monatsschrift* für Kunst, *Literatur und Musik* 4, no. 6 (1926), 3-12; 9 for the illustration. CLP_6541/0 On the role of the Tower of Babel in Kiesler's text, see Sources, Disciplines, and Objects, pp. 52-53, 89.

15 The second chapter of Egon Friedell, *Kulturgeschichte des Altertums* (1936), 215-336, in which the author describes the Babylonian and Egyptian civilizations, is named after the Tower of Babel.

16 Alternative chapter titles: **~~A Hous~~ de Bosch's Houses.** TXT_6729_N2 **A HOUSE by Hieronymus de Bosch** TXT_6729_N6 **and tools (b)** [handwritten annotation on the TS] TXT_5877/0_N167 Throughout drafts, Kiesler refers to Hieronymus Bosch (1460-1516) as Hieronymus de Bosch (his name is corrected in the edited manuscript). See earlier note in "Content" for the same chapter in the annotated text. Only one plate (a detail) from Bosch's triptych *The Garden of Earthly Delights* (1503-1515) is included in the plates for *Magic Architecture*. It depicts musical instruments, described by Kiesler as "Magic music-instruments." In terms of contemporary interest in Bosch among the surrealists, one has to mention the extensive yet unpublished study by Kiesler's close acquaintance, Nicolas Calas on Bosch's triptych. For a summary of his research, see the article in *Life* magazine: "Hieronymus Bosch's

(37)

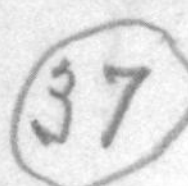

page 220

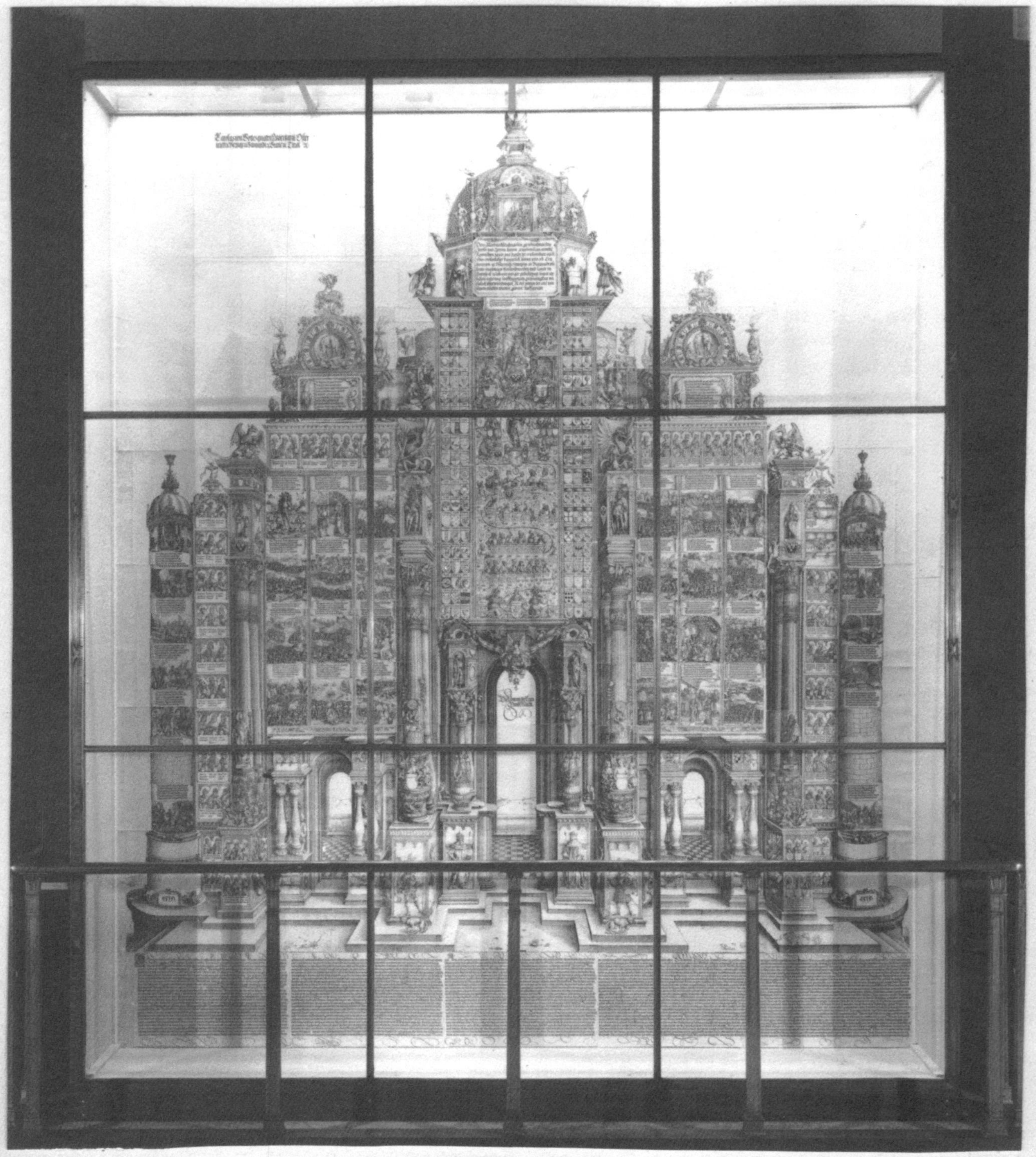

(37). Pages 219, 220

A Dream of Magic Architecture by Albrecht Durer.

page 221

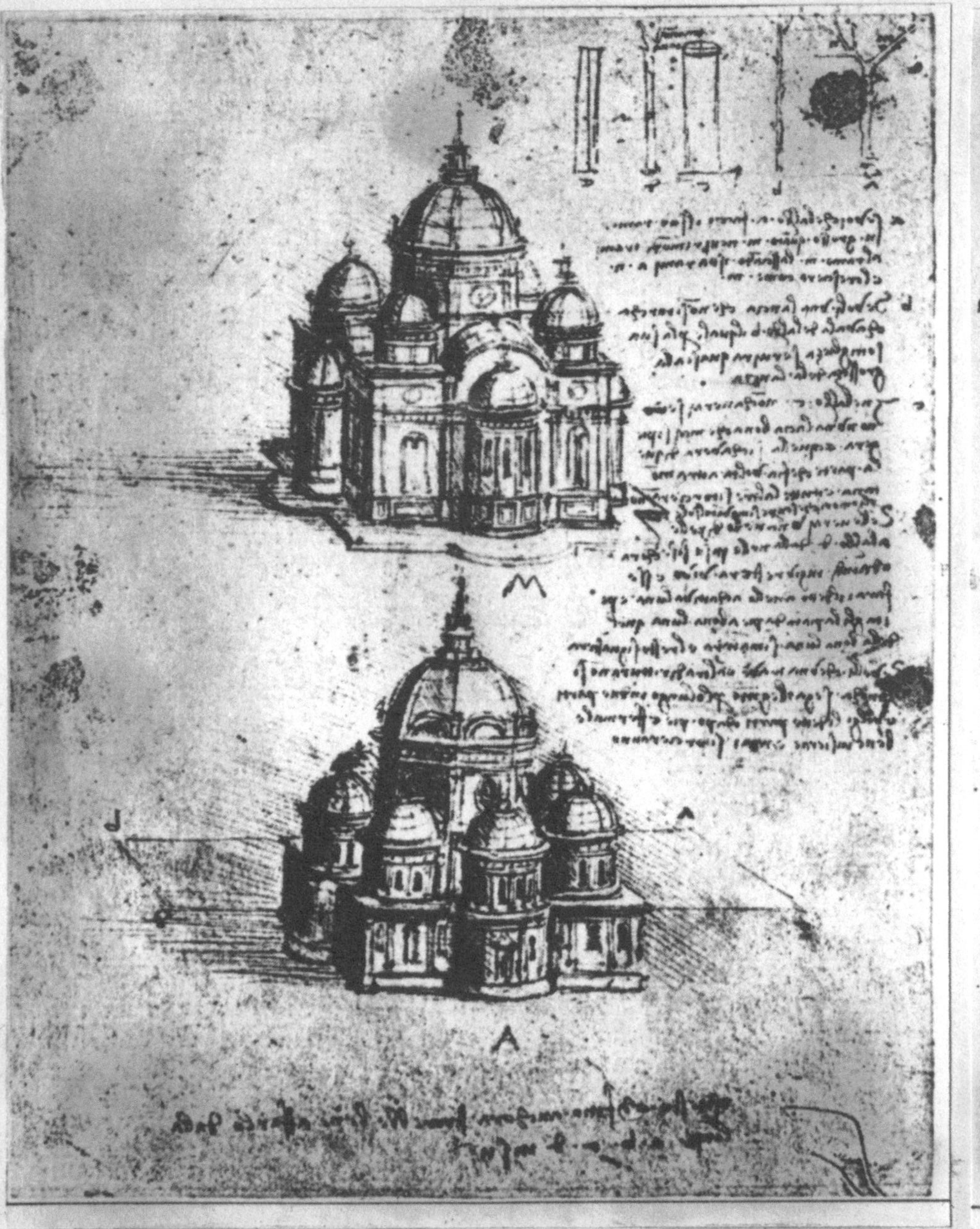

(38). Page 221

Leonardo da Vinci does not investigate the possibilities of new functional designs for cathedrals; he plays with the plastic arrangements of traditional forms.

page 221

(39). Fantastic Architecture by a painter. An exciting interplay of natural and architectural forms. (Detail of a Fresco by Cossa, Italy

page 223

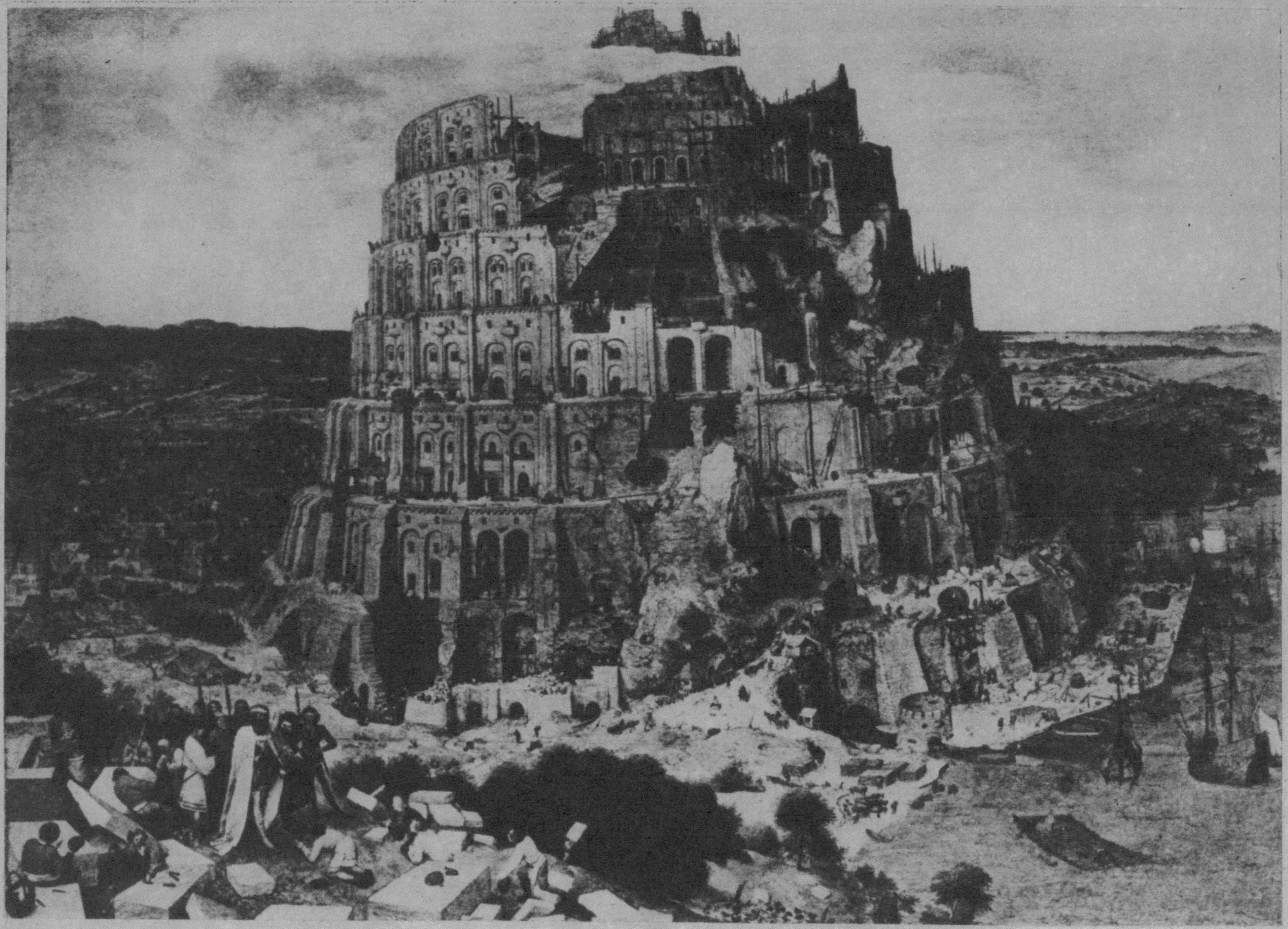

(40). Page 223

Vision of a [illegible] work of Architecture. (The Tower of Babel by Peter Breughel, the older).

(40x). Page 220

Magic music-instruments. (Detail of a painting by ~~de~~ Bosch).

pl. 41

CHAPTER 6
EL GRECO'S TOLEDO

[17]View of Toledo by El Greco (1541-1614).

The View of Toledo is the only landscape strictly speaking, which El Greco is known to have painted. To be sure, we catch mysterious glimpses of cities looming far off behind the struggling figures of Laocoön and his sons, or swimming phantom-like in the valley beyond the still figure of Christ crucified, or remote and small behind the uplifted foreleg of Saint Martin's white horse. And those who have visited Toledo will not fail to remember the curious vista panoramica[18] by Greco which hangs in his house there. It too represents Toledo, yet it is less a landscape than a topographical chart. Viewed from the North, Toledo is shown spread out across the top of its hill almost in profile. At the right of the picture, prominently displayed, is a young man didactically exhibiting a map of the city, and at the left sits a river god pouring from his jar the Rio Tajo.

If the vista panoramica in the Casa del Greco possesses topographic statements which constitute it more a chart than a landscape, the artist's landscape in the Metropolitan Museum is so highly charged with imagination that it could perhaps better be entitled a Vision of Toledo than a View. In that barren part of Castile the grass is green for only a few brief weeks in spring, but even in spring one would fail to find such virulent greens as Greco except under the baleful illumination of an impending storm such as we see in the dream of Toledo. Against the dark clouds, the buildings appear spectral, almost phosphorescent, yet several may be identified. On the hillock to the left he shows the medieval castle of San Servando. The artist painted the city from a point across Tajo to the northeast. The old Moorish bridge called Alcantara spans the river and the long spire of the cathedral rises at the crest of the hill–that being where Greco chose to place it for reasons triumphantly justified by the results, although in fact it stands far to the right in the center of the town.[19]

Greco's genius[20] has not only transformed Toledo's real buildings into something[21] designed by nature herself, but earth and sky themselves have become architecture in the truest sense of the word. This whole chunk of nature–vegetable and inorganic[22] as well as artifacts–appears hypnotized into the immobile structure of architecture, but remains ready at the same time to release exuberant magic[23] at the slightest contact with the human eye.

This is not an idealized landscape; it is not make-believe. This is a new reality, in which facts and figures are only a small part of the whole truth. and El Greco's: Mount Sinai[24]

pl. 41a

CHAPTER 7
RAPHAEL'S GARDENS[25]

This is also a good occasion to speak about rocks and trees which have been transformed into architectural expression: I refer to landscape gardens. All types of vegetation and even rock formations are subjugated to a ground plan of geometric design or as in the case of the formal French gardens of the eighteenth century and particularly of the English of the nineteenth century into three-dimensional plasticity. Hedges are cut into square blocks and walls, niches are carved out of bushes,[26] and domestic animals are sheared out of the mass of wildly grown foliage. They indeed represent a perverse image of man's ability to dream.[27] (Comparison with Raphael's gardens).

CHAPTER 8
THE RELIGIOUS DEVELOPMENT OF THE ROMAN EMPIRE[28]

Garden of Delights: Scholar offers a solution to painting which has baffled the world since 1500," *Life* 27, no. 20, November 14, 1949, 75-82.

17 ***) From the Bulletin of the Metropolitan Museum of Art, June 1945** TXT_6729/0_N6 An earlier draft shows the description of the painting in quotation marks. TXT_6729/0_N5-N6 The text that follows is a transcription of a brief article by Harry B. Wehle, "Notes on the Cover," *The Metropolitan Museum of Art Bulletin* 3, no. 10, June 1945, see cover and illustration opposite 233.

18 "Vista panoramica" is italicized in Wehle's text. Wehle is referring to *View and Plan of Toledo* (*Vista y plano de Toledo*; ca. 1608).

19 Here the quotation from Wehle ends. The original article contains an additional sentence omitted from the transcription, which references the events of the Spanish Civil War in Toledo concerning the siege of Alcázar: "Foursquare beyond the cathedral stands the massive Alcazar, the stronghold which succumbed a few years ago only after months of continuous shelling." Wehle, "Notes on the Cover." On this and other omissions of references to contemporary political events in Kiesler's transcriptions, see Sources, Disciplines, and Objects, p. 61.

20 **Greco's ~~magic power~~** TXT_6729/0_N5 The last two paragraphs of the chapter on El Greco are Kiesler's own text.

21 **Toledo's real buildings ~~as if they were~~ designed by nature herself** TXT_6729/0_N5

22 **~~vegetative~~ and ~~u~~inorganic ~~and the~~ as well as the artifacts** TXT_6729/0_N5

23 **to release its exuberant magic ~~powers~~** TXT_6729/0_N6

24 Handwritten addition TXT_5877/0_N170 Kiesler is referring to El Greco's *View of Mount Sinai and the Monastery of St. Catherine* (1570-1572), which is not mentioned in any preliminary drafts but just added in the TS of the assembled version.

25 Alternative chapter numbers and titles: **Rafael's Garden** TXT_6729/0_N2 **P. VI–8 Raffael** TXT_6761/0_N3 **P.VI–7 (Raffael.** TXT_6759/0_N1 Illustrations for this chapter are missing. Ponten's book on "architecture not built" refers to Raphael's garden designs for the Villa Madama (completed by Antonio da Sangalo the Younger), including a number of original drawings. Ponten *Architektur*, 1:45-47 (45 on the garden designs); 2:38-41 (figs. 76-83).
Ponten and his co-authors draw from the classic study of Raphael as an architect by Heinrich Geymüller, *Raffaello Sanzio studiato come architetto con l'aiuto di nuovi documenti* (Milan: Hoepli, 1884). Kiesler was also interested in Raphael's depiction of landscape in paintings, as in the artist's *Madonna del Prato* (*Madonna of the Meadow*, 1505-1506), now at the Kunsthistorisches Musuem in Vienna, and also known as *Madonna Belvedere* since the painting was part of the imperial collection at the Austrian Palace. Kiesler's collection of reference images for his *Vision Machine* (1937-1941) contains a reproduction of Raphael's *Madonna of the Meadow* (1506) from Adolf Paul Oppé, *Raphael* (London: Methuen, 1909), plate 32. PHO 1107/0.

26 **Niches are carved ~~into leaves and branches~~ out of bushes** TXT_6729/0_N6

27 This paragraph is not included in the assembled manuscripts of *Magic Architecture*. It was originally part of the text included in chapter 6 following Kiesler's description of El Greco's landscape as a form of "architecture" that is "designed by nature." TXT_6729/0_N6 However a typed transcription of the same passage is cut and clipped on a page with the note **P.VI–7 Raffael,** which indicates that Kiesler considered using it as an introduction and narrative transition to a chapter on Raphael's gardens he never completed. TXT_6759/0_N2

28 Alternative chapter title: **Part Six Chapt. 8** / **PIRANESI's Rom** [German] / **~~Rome Reborn–By engraving~~** / **Projects: The Via Appia, The Arena, The ~~Coreiere~~ Carceriere** [sic]. Kiesler consistently misspells *carceri* throughout. It has been corrected in the edited text. TXT_6756_N1 Early versions of this chapter include only Kiesler's text on Piranesi (see also following note). However the previous TS draft includes a four-page appendix prefaced by a bibliographic note and a new chapter title: **Wells: Short History of the World** / **continues after the Piranesi** / **Part six : Chapter 8** / **"The religious Developments under the Roman Empire and Piranesi's Rome"** TXT_6756/0_N3 Apparently Kiesler was originally planning to include a longer excerpt from H. G. Wells, "Religious Developments under the Roman Empire," in *A Short History of the World* (New York: Macmillan, 1922), 208-213. (No particular edition is mentioned in Kiesler's drafts.) As he notes above, the quotation would come "after" his commentary on Piranesi's Rome. Ultimately Kiesler selected only the first paragraph of the transcription and placed it before the description of Piranesi's projects. Cf. TXT_6834/0; TXT_6756/0_N3-N6; TXT_5877/0_N172

page 226

(41). Page 226

A painter's transformation of an existing city into a dream-vision. (Toledo, Spain, by El Greco).

41a

page 228

(41a). Page 228

Magic mountains built like Architecture. (~~Very remindful~~ Reminiscent of the towers built by Termites.) (Mount Sinai, painted by El Greco.)

The soul of man under that Latin and Greek empire of the first two centuries of the Christian era was a worried and frustrated soul. Compulsion and cruelty reigned; there were pride and display but little honour; little serenity or steadfast happiness. The unfortunate were despised and wretched; the fortunate were insecure and feverishly eager for gratifications. In a great number of cities life centered on the red excitement of the arena, where men and beasts fought and were tormented and slain. Amphitheatres are the most characteristic of Roman ruins. Life went on in that key. The uneasiness of men's hearts manifested itself in profound religious unrest.

ROME REBORN—BY ENGRAVING

Projects: The Via Appia, The Arena, The Carceri[29] (large) pl. 43

Just as the human body, long ill, rallies before the very end and displays, to the surprise of the watchful laymen,[30] a sudden vitality—even a lust for life, so it appears, that the eighteenth century brought decaying Europe[31] once more in its cultural rhythm to Life and Death, to an exuberant expression of the will to Architecture.[32]

The Baroque of Italy and Germany[33] is testimony of it; after that Europe's architecture is ridden by death agonies.[34]

The types of projects like those of Juvara, of Scamozzi, of Bernardo Buontalenti of the sixteenth century, are taken up in their untimely expression and developed to[35] a state of formal frenzy by most of the eighteenth-century designers, painters, architects, and sculptors.[36] This is no wonder–the unification of the plastic arts was the[37] ambition of the day. Even the theater showed sets whose milieus were literally embedded in a visual orgy of imaginary architecture.

(work of the Bibienas and their School)

Among all of the builders and painters of the eighteenth century there was one who seemed to summarize everything out of the centuries before him, that was plastically expressive and who tried desperately to form a new world out of the ruins of the old. His name was Giambattista Piranesi, Designer and Engraver.[38] He was born in 1707 [sic] in Venice. If ever there was an antique dealer in Architecture, it was he. He is probably the only interior decorator who has dealt wholesale in cities. His love was Rome.

If Piranesi had not left us his perspectives for the "carceri," one could easily call him the greatest faker[39] of monumental Architecture of all periods; but with those etchings before us we must recognize his outstanding ability to project visions with automatic immediacy;[40] they strike us like thunderous flashes from the mysterious world of man's imagination. A talent such as that is too rare in any land, at any time; and so, the apparent faker becomes the truest fakir of design in architecture.[41] To many his projects for Rome will appear prodigious; in all honor to him, they are only prestidigious.[42] Their magic is not inherent, but exhilarating nevertheless.

* * *

With the end of the eighteenth century, man's beliefs have very much come down to earth; he no longer worships the sun, the stars or giant mountains; the only thing he now fears is disease.

Weakened ethics and morals have created an ever more decaying society. Dream and fact lost even the surface unity they had in the Renaissance and became dual.[43] The citizen's vision lost humility, and facts were blind. The make-believe of knowledge was simulated by a wig whose white color was borrowed from wisdom's old age and whose curlicues were lent by the frivolity of youth.[44]

In architecture the dissolution of form progressed to the ultimate;[45] nothing remained of the firm body but the cringing ornament of its surface.[46]

29 Rom reborn in Dream by engraving -not built. Project: The Via Appia; The Arena; The Carceriere TXT_6781/0_N1 Piranesi / Rome Reborn–by Engraving / Project / Plural? [handwritten query by Stefi Kiesler] / The Via Appia, The Arena, The ~~Coreiere~~ Carceriere TXT_6727/0_N1

30 to the surprise of the ~~laymen's logic~~ TXT_6781/0_N1

31 decaying Europe ~~of the Renaissance~~ TXT_6781/0_N1

32 will tof Architecture [handwritten correction] TXT_5877/0_N173 will to Architecture TXT_6781/0_N1

33 The Barock [German] of Italy~~,~~ ~~France~~ and Germany TXT_6781/0_N1

34 after that, Europe's ~~cities are~~ ridden by death. TXT_6781/0_N1

35 developed to ~~great power~~ TXT_6781/0_N2

36 Painters, Architects, and Sculptors alike. TXT_6781/0_N2

37 was the ~~program~~ TXT_6781/0_N2

38 Throughout his drafts, Kiesler refers to Piranesi as Gianbattista Piranesi, designer and engraver TXT_6781/0_N2 Gianbattista Piranesi, dDesigner and eEngraver [handwritten capitalizations] Erroneously in the following sentence (as well as in other drafts), he cites his birth year as 1707 instead of 1720. TXT_6727/0_N2; TXT_5877/0_N173

39 Faker TXT_6781/0_N2verso

40 we recognize a temperament with the highest ability to project visions with automatic immediacy TXT_6781/0_N2verso

41 the apparent Faker becomes the truest Fakir of Design in Architecture. TXT_6781/0_N2verso

42 Kiesler's adjective refers to the art of the prestidigitator, whom he also references in Part VII while referring to magic techniques. TXT_6781/0_N2verso

43 The dualism of ~~decaying society created the Architecture~~ dream and fact was not even anymore on the surface ... unified as in the Renaissance. ~~The Rokoko~~ ... TXT_6781/0_N3 ~~The dualism of~~ dream and fact ~~was not unified anymore, not even on the surface, as in~~ the Renaissance. TXT_6727/0_N3

44 whose white color was borrowed from ~~the~~ old age ~~of~~ wisdom and its curlicues ~~from~~ the frivolitiesousness [sic] of youth. TXT_6727/0_N3

45 to the Ultimat. TXT_6727/0_N3

46 ~~(which led to the Rococo.)~~ TXT_6727/0_N3 Kiesler's notepad, which contains initial drafts for several chapters included in Parts VI–X, indicates that a fragment titled A Project for the Rococo is to immediately follow the last paragraph of this chapter. TXT_6781/0_N3 The section on the Rococo was ultimately moved to Part VIII. See notes on Part VIII, chapter 2.

(42)

page 231

(42). Page 231

Amphitheatres are the most characteristic expressions of the Roman Empire. "The unfortunate were despised, wretched and sacrificed; the fortunate were insecure and feverishly eager for gratification."
(Above: Ruin of the Colosseum, Rome)
(Below: Life inside it.)

<u>(43). Large sheet</u>

Magic Architecture - faked. Project for rebuilding the Via Appia in Rome, with an accumalation of replicas of famous antique buildings. (Engraving by Piranesi)

37
Albrecht Dürer, *Arch of Honor (for Maximilian I)*, 1515, installation view, Astor Hall, New York Public Library, New York, on display 1911–1970s, photo undated. ÖFLKS, SCL_49/0

38
Leonardo da Vinci, "centralized building studies." Ponten, *Architektur die nicht gebaut wurde*, 2:42, pl. 84. ÖFLKS, SCL_50/0

39
Picture gallery of the Vatican with detail of fresco by Francesco del Cossa. Richard Hamann, *Die Frührenaissance der italienischen Malerei* (Jena: E. Diederichs, 1909), fig. 156, photo D. Anderson. ÖFLKS, SCL_51/0

40
Pieter Bruegel the Elder, The Tower of Babel (1563). Ernst Lewy, "Das Wesen der Sprache," *Faust—Monatsschrift für Kunst, Literatur und Musik* 4, no. 6 (1925–1926): 3–12. ÖFLKS, SCL_52/0

40x
Hieronymus Bosch, *The Garden of Earthly Delights*, detail (1503–1515). Source unknown. ÖFLKS, SCL_53/0

41
El Greco, *View of Toledo* (ca. 1599–1600). Harry B. Wehle, "Notes," *The Metropolitan Museum of Art Bulletin* 3, no. 10 (June 1945). ÖFLKS, SCL_54/0

41a
El Greco, *Mount Sinai* (ca. 1570–1572). Source unknown. ÖFLKS, SCL_55/0

42
Above: "Kolosseum, Rom" (Colosseum, Rome). Noack, *Die Baukunst des Altertums*, pl. 137.

Below: "Scene in Roman Coliseum [sic!] and Roman Coins" (detail). J. G. Heck, *Iconographic Encyclopaedia of Science, Literature, and Art*, vol. 1, division IV, History and Ethnology, trans. and ed. Spencer F. Baird (New York: Rudolph Garrigue, 1851), pl. 15. ÖFLKS, SCL_56/0

43
"Piranesi: vision for the Via Appia." Ponten, *Architektur die nicht gebaut wurde*, 2:108, pl. 107. ÖFLKS, SCL_57/0

Part VI
Magic Architecture

fig. B.25

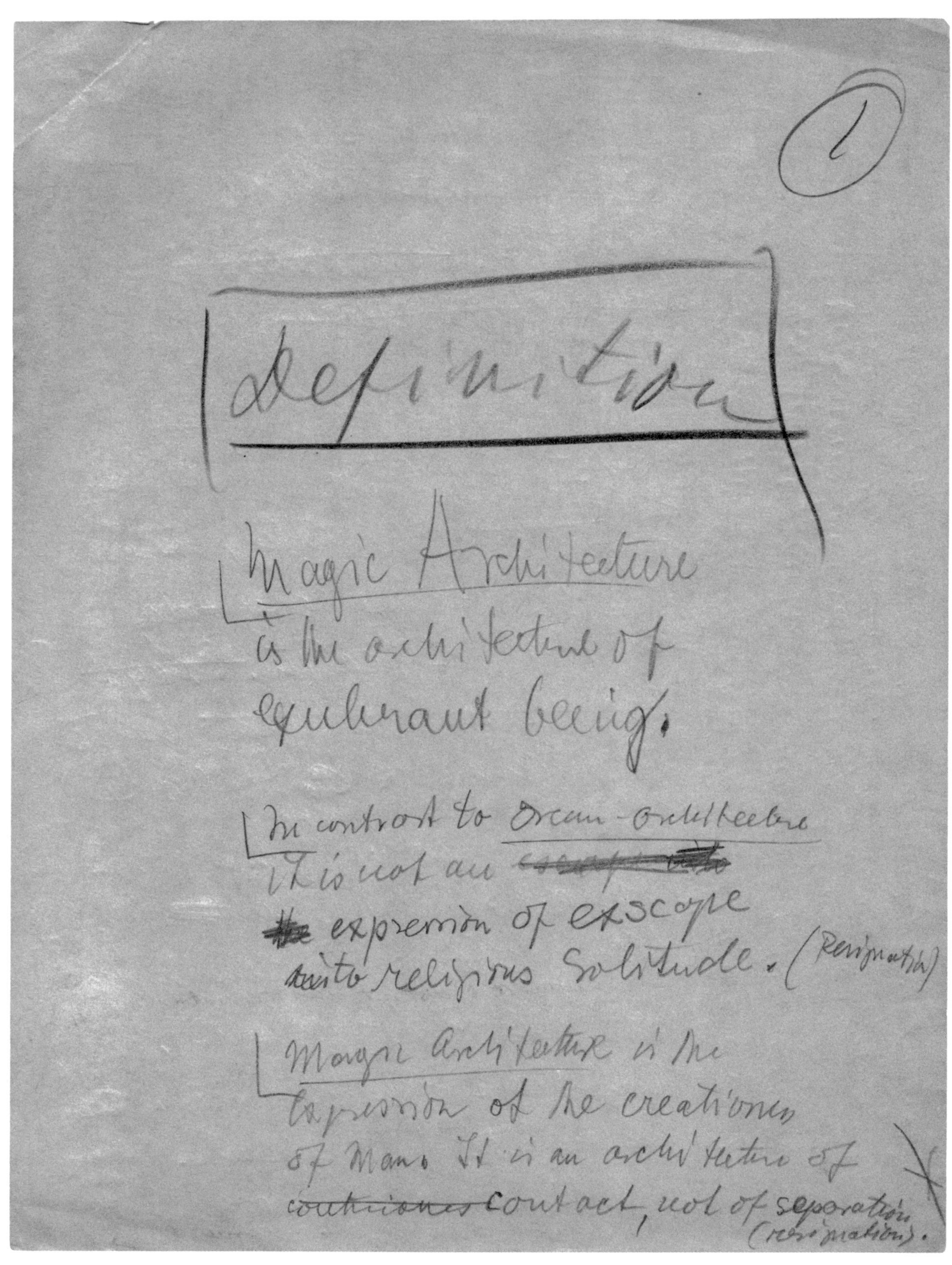

Definition

Magic Architecture
is the architecture of
exuberant being.

In contrast to Dream-architecture
it is not an
expression of exscape
into religious solitude. (Resignation)

Magic Architecture is the
expression of the creativeness
of Man. It is an architecture of
contact, not of separation
(resignation).

Frederick Kiesler, Part VII, Introduction, preliminary draft: "Definition / Magic Architecture is the architecture of exuberant being. …" (MS, [color] pencil) ÖFLKS, TXT_6695/0_N1recto

PART VII
MAGIC ARCHITECTURE[1]

INTRODUCTION
DEFINITION[2]
TOWARDS MAGIC ARCHITECTURE[3]

Magic Architecture is the architecture of exuberant being.[4]

In contrast to Dream Architecture it is not an expression of escape into religious solitude.[5]

Magic Architecture is the expression of the creativeness of man. It is an architecture of contact,[6] not of separation (resignation). Its emphasis is on participation, not on isolation.[7]

Being a constant environmental companion, it performs wonders in the development of mankind, just as sunlight performs wonders in the development of plants.

Magic Architecture is a generator. It can operate in any scale. Any cell of habitation is a nucleus for a powerhouse of joyful living. Neither wealth nor cash, nor building material, nor social power are needed to accomplish it. It follows the old rule of accomplishing the most with the least. It relies on self-confidence, and self-confidence in the discovery of natural capacities. It holds the balance between the two extremes of man: a. desire for the machine, and b. the denial of science.[8] Its magic consists solely in the discovery of capacities[9] in the natural ore of a being–and by refining it brings forth the latent qualities.[10]

Magic Architecture is, of course, unthinkable without its sociological roots in a society[11] of free will and sacrifice. Its magic cannot be performed[12] like the tricks of a prestidigitator.[13] Its power to stimulate the evolution of unheard-of capacities in man can be part only of the structure of a society devoted to such ideals.[14]

Magic Architecture is not dream architecture, like temples or castles; it is the architecture of everyday, every-moment reality,[15] an implement of contact. Contrary to popular belief it is not an expression of mysticism, but a tool of realism,[16] the expression of man's desire for imaginative living as opposed to standardized routine.[17]

Magic Architecture is the incarnation[18] of love for life.
Magic Architecture is ~~the~~ reality of Dreams.
Magic Architecture is Dream-Reality.
Magic Architecture is the embodiment of Dream-Reality.
Magic Architecture is the Shelter of Dream-Reality.
Magic Architecture is the Reality of Dreams.
Magic Architecture is the incarnation of Dream in Reality.

CHAPTERS 1–3
VISIONS OF CITIES[19]

1 Mount Athos
2 Sforzinda
3 The City of the Sun

CHAPTER 1
MOUNT ATHOS BY DINOCRATES

pl. 44 We find[20] that from time to time the desire of man for unity breaks through the frustration of usurpating powers, be they exploiting religion, patriotism, nationalism, or wealth and creates projects of extraordinary human significance, such as Dinocrates' for the peninsula Chalchidiké in Greece.

1 Title sheet (frontispiece): **Part VII Magic Architecture** TXT_6718/0_N1

2 ~~DEFINITION~~ **Part VII. Introduction: Magic Architecture** [handwritten addition] TXT_6718/0_N2 **DEFINITION** TXT_6688/0_N1-N2 In this alternate version of the assembled book manuscript, a longer text titled "Definition" appears first among the manuscript's front matter, preceding the "Note to the Publisher" and "Content" to serve as an opening statement on what "is magic architecture." Kiesler gradually condensed the text of the "Definition" to only two paragraphs by deleting some of his opening statements and moved it to the "Introduction" to Part VII (fig. B.26a). Here, the excised paragraphs are restored. The first pages of both MS and TS versions show the initial sentences marked with a paragraph symbol indicating that the text should be structured as a manifesto of a sequence of short aphoristic statements (figs. B.25, B.26b). TXT_6695/0_N1; TXT_6755/0_N1

3 **Introduction: Towards** [handwritten insertion by Kiesler on the TS] **Magic Architecture (fig. B.26b)** TXT_6755/0_N1

4 Cf. Kiesler's contemporary unpublished text "Economy and Exuberanz" described in Sources, Disciplines, and Objects, pp. 56, 89.

5 **(Resignation)** TXT_6695/0_N1

6 ~~continuous~~ **contact** TXT_6695/0_N1

7 ~~Architecture is here technological~~ [crossed-out, unfinished sentence] **Magic Architecture is not dream-Architecture, like that of ~~Churches~~ Temples or Castles, it is the Architecture of every-day every-night Reality ~~Except that it does not take~~ Magic Architecture is a tool of realistic life.** These sentences of the "Definition" were ultimately moved to the final paragraph of Kiesler's introduction to Part VII with a few revisions. TXT_6695/0_N1verso; TXT_6688/0_N1

8 **It holds the balance between reliance on ~~technological gadgets~~ and the denial of science.** TXT_6695/0_N2

9 ~~natural~~ **capacities** TXT_6695/0_N2

10 **and ~~develops it, by providing a "suitable climate."~~ / ~~develops its inherent higher standards.~~** TXT_6695/0_N2

11 ~~free~~ **society** TXT_6695/0_N2

12 ~~looked upon~~ TXT_6695/0_N2

13 **prestidigiateur** [sic] TXT_6695/0_N2 **prestidigitator** TXT_6718/0_N **prestigitator** [sic] TXT_6755/0_N2; TXT_5877/0_N177 Instead of "magician," Kiesler uses the old-fashioned English-Latin term prestidigitator or the French *prestidigitateur* (from *presto* plus *digitus*–quick with one's fingers–and similar in meaning to the Greek *tachydaktylourgos*) to emphasize the difference between his understanding of magic versus trickery based on manual dexterity. See also his use of the term "prestidigious" in reference to Piranesi's projects in Part VI, chapter 8.

14 **Its power to evolute unheard of capacities in man can be part only of a ~~total~~ structure of a society devoted to such ideals. That is nothing new. Every religious community has produced extraordinary architectural developments and styles.** TXT_6695/0_N2

15 **every-day every-night Reality** TXT_6695/0_N1verso; TXT_6688/0_N1

16 Cf. sentence in earlier paragraph excised from the handwritten text of "Definition:" **Magic Architecture is a tool of realistic life.** TXT_6695/0_N1verso; TXT_6688/0_N1

17 Multiple definitions of magic architecture appear in a handwritten draft by Kiesler not transcribed or included in any versions of the assembled manuscript (fig. B.27). Here it has been added by the editors to the main text of this introductory chapter. TXT_6803/0 Yet another "definition" scribbled in a preliminary draft states: **Magic Architecture is the omnipotence of desire and thought (made ~~real) build~~ concrete. (build.)** (See Sources, Disciplines, and Objects, fig. A.46.) TXT_6749/0_N1 On the multiple definitions of "magic architecture," see Sources, Disciplines, and Objects, pp. 56–57

18 the ~~shelter~~ TXT_6803/0

19 Alternative and additional chapters, later moved to Parts VI, IX, X (see fig. B.28):

~~Dream Towns~~
1. Mount Athos
2. Sforzinda
3. Scheerbart: Dream City of glass
4. Cities of a New Globe (Bruno Taut)
~~3. Rome reborn by Piranesi~~
~~4. Cities of a new Globe by Bruno Taut~~
3. The City of the Sun TXT_6718/0_N4

20 **We find however** TXT_6755/0_N5

fig. B.26a

Part VII.

Introduction: Magic Architecture

DEFINITION

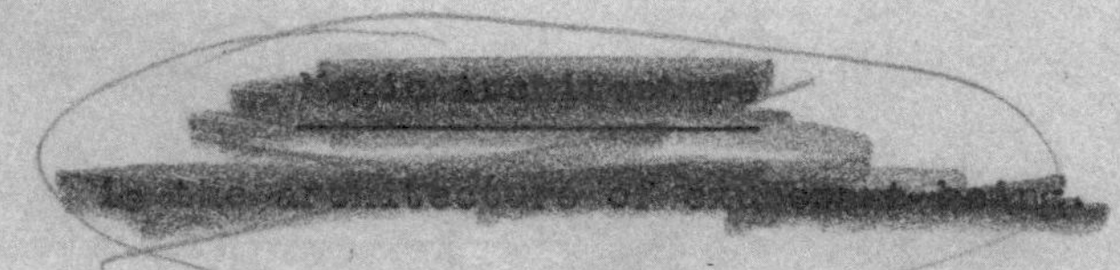

In contrast to Dream Architecture, it is not an expression of escape into religious solitude (Resignation).

Magic Architecture is the expression of the creativeness of man. It is an architecture of contact, not of seperation (resignation). ITS emphasis IS on participation, not ON isolation.

Magic architecture is not dream-architecture, like that of temples or castles; it is the architecture of every-day, every-night reality. Magic architecture is a tool of realistic Life. It performs wonders in the development of mankind, just as sunlight performs wonders in the development of plants. Being a constant environmental companion. Magic architecture is a generator. It can operate on any scale. Any cell of

Frederick Kiesler, Part VII, Introduction, preliminary draft with deleted sections: "Magic Architecture is the expression of the creativeness of man." (TS, pencil) ÖFLKS, TXT_6718/0_N2

fig. B.26b

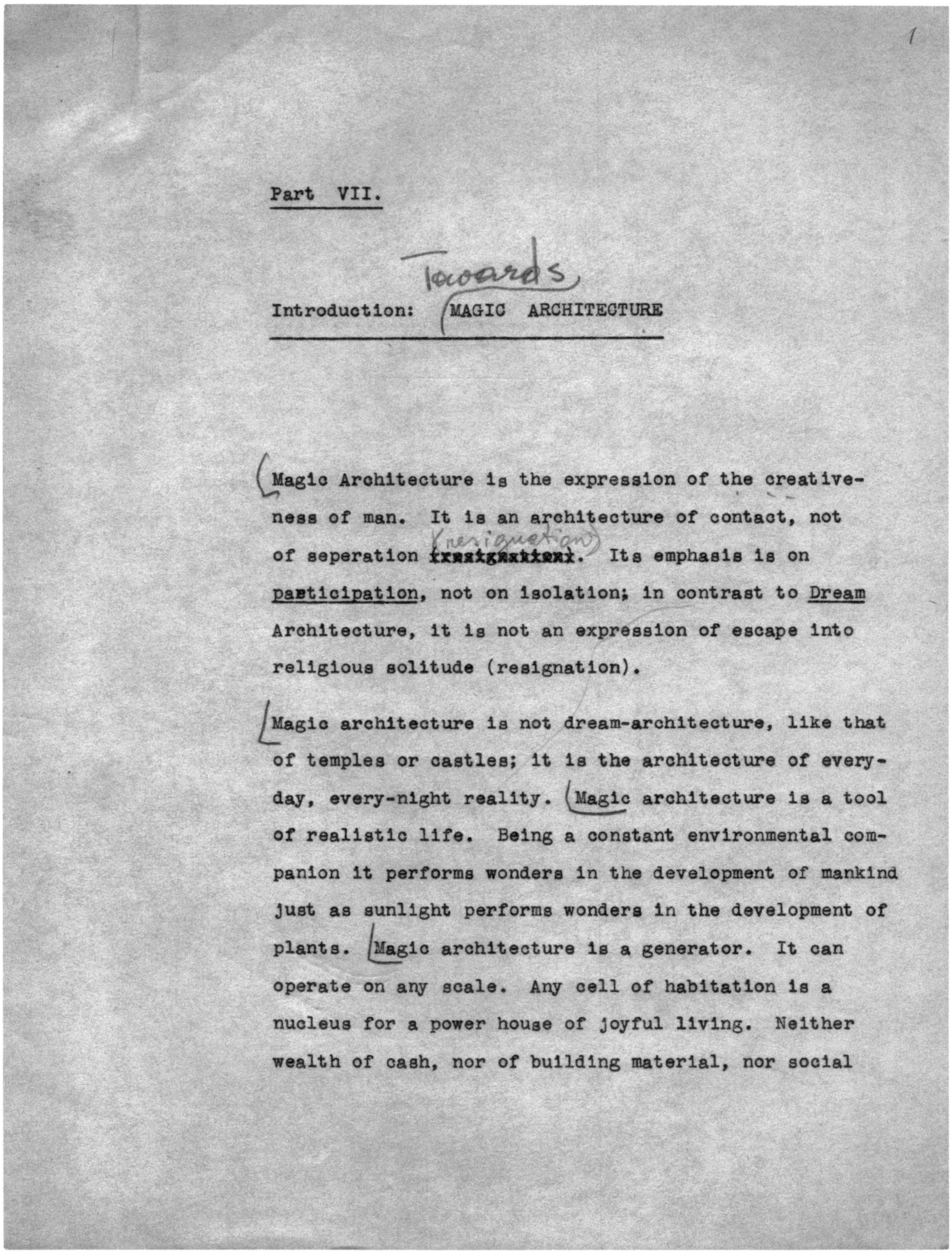

1

Part VII.

Towards

Introduction: MAGIC ARCHITECTURE

Magic Architecture is the expression of the creativeness of man. It is an architecture of contact, not of seperation (resignation) ~~xxxxxxxxxxx~~. Its emphasis is on participation, not on isolation; in contrast to Dream Architecture, it is not an expression of escape into religious solitude (resignation).

Magic architecture is not dream-architecture, like that of temples or castles; it is the architecture of every-day, every-night reality. Magic architecture is a tool of realistic life. Being a constant environmental companion it performs wonders in the development of mankind just as sunlight performs wonders in the development of plants. Magic architecture is a generator. It can operate on any scale. Any cell of habitation is a nucleus for a power house of joyful living. Neither wealth of cash, nor of building material, nor social

Frederick Kiesler, Part VII, Introduction, preliminary draft with hand written additions: "Towards MAGIC ARCHITECTURE" (TS, pencil) ÖFLKS, TXT_6755/0_N1

Magic Architecture is the ~~shelter~~ incarnation of love for life.

Magic Architecture is ~~the~~ reality of Dreams.

Magic Architecture is Dream-Reality.

Magic Architecture is the embodiment of Dream-Reality.

Magic Architecture is the Shelter of Dream ~~Reality~~ -Reality.

Magic Architecture is the Reality of Dreams.

(Dreams in Reality).

Magic Architecture is the the incarnation of

Frederick Kiesler, Preliminary draft with notes towards a definition of Magic Architecture: "Magic Architecture is the incarnation of love for life. …" related to the content of Part VII, Introduction (MS, pencil) ÖFLKS, TXT_6803/0

fig. B.28

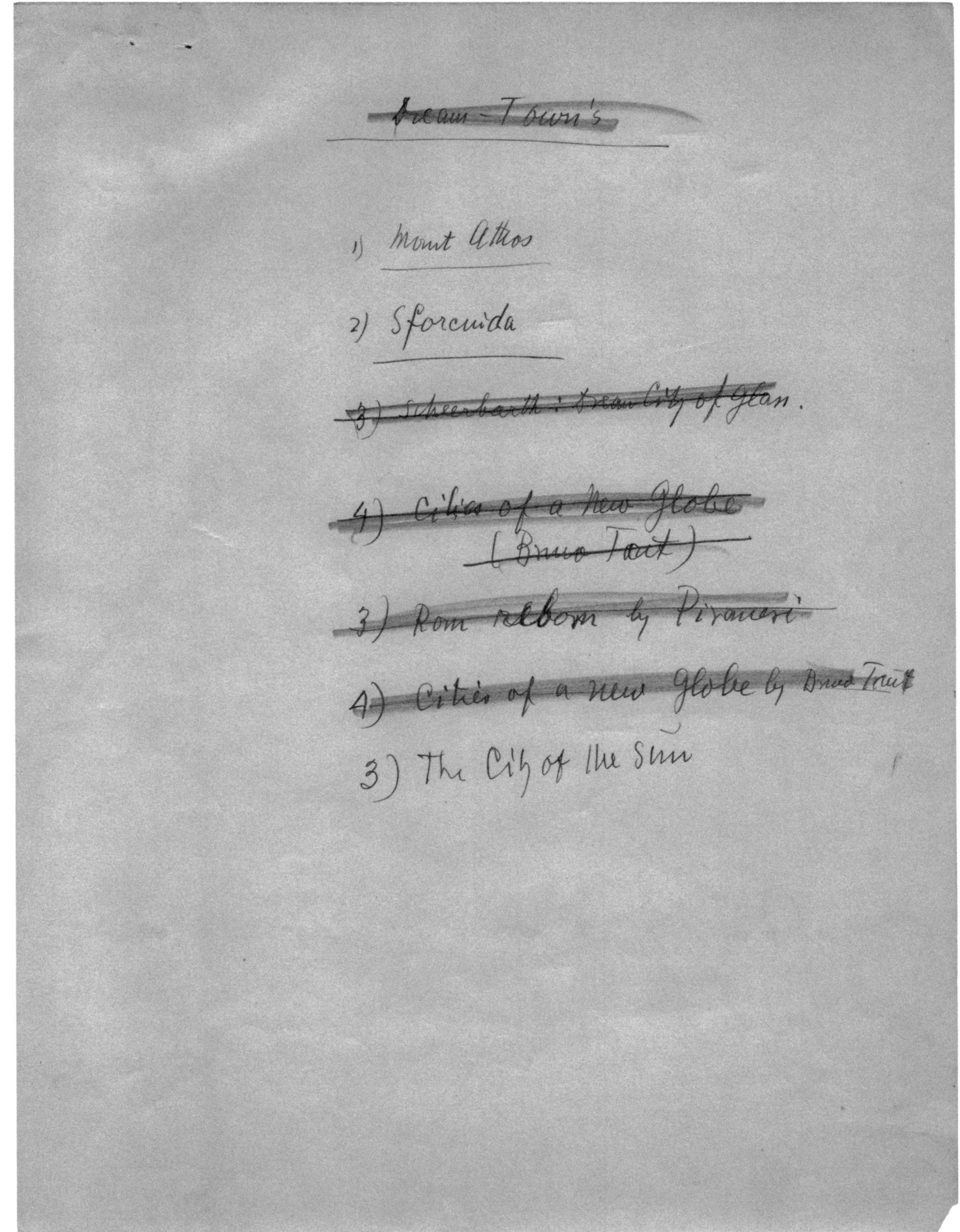
~~Dream-Town's~~

1) Mont Athos

2) Sforcinda

~~3) Scheerbarth: Dream City of Glass.~~

~~4) Cities of a New Globe (Bruno Taut)~~

~~3) Rom reborn by Piranesi~~

~~4) Cities of a new Globe by Bruno Taut~~

3) The City of the Sun

Frederick Kiesler, Preliminary list of chapters (including deletions) for Part VII, "Magic Architecture (MS, ink) ÖFLKS, TXT_6718/0_N4

Der Macedonische Berg Athos in Gestalt eines Riesen, wie der Dinocrates, des Großen Alexanders Architect, solchen Bau angegeben. Vitruv: Praefat: L. 2. Strabo: Li. 13

I. B. F. v. E. del.

page 240

(44). Page 240

Magic Architecture - never built. Project for the transformation of Mount Athos, in Greece, into an ideal town dominated by a symbolic figure of Alexander the Great. The left hand holds the town, the right hand distributes the rivers. (Project by Dinocrates, Architect of Alexander the Great, drawn by Fischer von Erlach.)

He was the architect of Alexander the Great and proposed to transform the Mount Athos into "a giant figure whose left hand holds a city of 10,000 inhabitants, and whose right hand unites in a bowl the dispersed rivulets and rivers of the country in one focal point before they precipitate into the Aegean Sea. It is said that Alexander considered this idea worthy of his greatness and dignity but forsook[21] the commemoration of his reign for the reason that such a large city, placed as it was, could not rely on enough fields and farms to feed its population."[22]

(Excellent reproduction after illustration by Fischer von Erlach.)[23]

CHAPTER 2
FILARETE'S CITY SFORZINDA

The Project of Sforzinda[24]

Filarete, named also Antonio Francesco Averlino, born 1410 in Florence,[25] has provided us with a city plan and designs of their main buildings of extraordinary significance for that period as well as for the problems of architecture. His is a typical dream city never built. There is an excellent account (not translated into English) by himself.[26] He calls the city Sforzinda because he was proposing this plan to his master the Prince Sforza. It is a most exact account of the materials to be used, how the workers are to be organized, and he calculated that he would need 103,000 workers. He also uses astrologers for the proper moment to start important buildings; it is found that the best date for the inner city is: the 15th of April 1460, 10.21 a.m. "In the foundation will be laid most valuable symbolical objects to be found by future archeologists when our time has become the antiquity." Not one important detail of such an enterprise is forgotten in the description contained in a tractate and in excellent drawings.

His description of the city of Sforzinda sounds like an oriental fairytale, yet it is a keen study in city planning, extremely imaginative in the use of building materials and an extraordinary criticism of the morals of living and warring. The concept of his Tower of Vice and Virtue cannot be topped by any surrealist or postwar streamlining.

This Architecture-never-built[27] should be elaborately accounted for from his own descriptions and profusely illustrated.

FILARETE'S CITY SFORZINDA[28]

An architecture not built, and, on the whole, not meant to be built, is found in Filarete's little-known book.[29]

To evoke in Prince Sforza the desire to build on a great scale, Filarete wrote this peculiar book, in which the architect plans in all its details an entire city, to be called after his master: Sforzinda. pl. 45–46

For us this work is interesting because, aside from its artistic and human content, it tells us a good deal about the ideals of city planning in the closing Middle Ages and the beginning of the Renaissance.[30] It is also rich in its views on cultural history and society in general. This story of Onitoan (Antonio in reverse)[31] is written in the first person: "I convince the prince to build a city. My plan is accepted, and the building starts immediately. In the environment there is lime, sand, mud for bricks marble, porphyry, precious stones, and tuff. The necessary amount of bricks, lime for the city wall, number of workers, contracts, and wages are calculated. On the first workday the fundaments are laid for the wall and towers. The building of the wall proceeds rapidly; on the tenth day the wall is finished with the exception of the round towers.

I need 12,000 master-workmen, for each master-workmen seven skilled workmen,[32] 84,000 in all, 6,000 unskilled laborers,[33] in toto 102,000 men. The master workmen, each day, supervise the

21 **forsake** TXT_5877/0_N179

22 **Part VII Chapter 1 Mount Athos** TXT_6755/0_N4 This paragraph is based on an excerpt translated from a larger section titled "Athos" in Ponten, *Architektur die nicht gebaut wurde* (1925), 1:15, initially transcribed in German from the original. TXT_6755/0_N4

23 Kiesler refers to the well-known illustration by Fischer von Erlach from his *Entwurf einer historischen Architektur* (Vienna, 1721), reproduced in Ponten, *Architektur*, 2:1, fig. 1.

24 TS with Kiesler's summation in English of Filarete's textual "project" based on an account of "The city of Sforzinda by Filarete" [Die Stadt Sforzinda des Filarete], in Ponten, *Architektur*, 1:32–38. This brief introductory text is not included in the assembled manuscript. TXT_6831/0_N1

25 Filarete's real name was Antonio di Pietro Averulino. The name mentioned here (Antonio Francesco Averlino) and year of birth are cited in *Meyers Grosses Konversations-Lexikon*, 6th ed. (Leipzig and Vienna: Bibliographisches Institut, 1904), 6:562.

26 Ponten's account is based on a bilingual (German-Italian) edition of Filarete's *Libro architettonico*: Wolfgang von Oettingen, *Tractat über die Baukunst nebst seinen Büchern von der Zeichenkunst und den Bauten der Medici* (Vienna: Carl Graeser, 1896), in Ponten, *Architektur*, 1:164.

27 **A/architecture-never built** [handwritten capitalization] Kiesler's phrase echoes in English the original title of Ponten's *Architektur* (Architecture that was not built), even if neither the title of the book nor the name of its author are cited among Kiesler's drafts. TXT_6831/0_N1

28 **The City Sforzinda by Filarete** TXT_6863/0 Title heading for a set of transcriptions in German based on Ponten's account of Filarete's textual project. Ponten, *Architektur*, 1:32–38 The Kieslers' transcription is idiosyncratic. Sometimes, the original text is paraphrased, while clauses or single words are omitted. Translations of certain words in the following passages, such as "proletariat" for *Kleinleute*, or "sports arena" for *Kampfplatz*, are worth noting.

29 **is found in the hardly known book by Filarete.** TXT_6862/0_N1

30 **Beginning Renaissance** TXT_6755/0_N6 **Beginning the Renaissance** TXT_5877/0_N180

31 **(Antonio verkehrt)** TXT_6863/0_N1 Onitoan Nolivera is not "reversed" but an anagram of Filarete's name: Antonio Averlino.

32 **Gesellen** TXT_6755/0_N6

33 **under-workers** TXT_6755/0_N6

(45) text on (46)

page 242

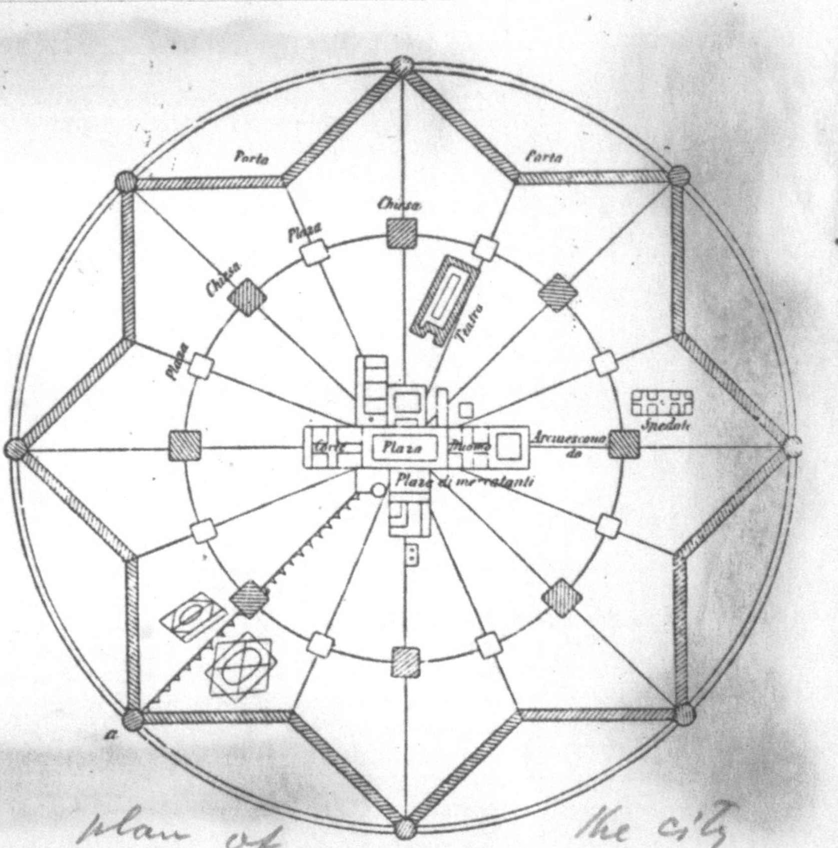

plan of the city

(46)

(45 and 46). Page 242

Magic Skyscrapers of the middle ages - planned but not built. They are units of the plan of the ideal city "Sforzinda", planned for Count Sforza of Italy by his architect, Filarete. According to the description of how and with what material it was to have been built: "103,000 workmen are to lay thirty million bricks a day." (Geometric plan of city, location and buildings. (45)

Buildings of

page 242

"Sforzinda"

laying of thirty million bricks. One thousand architectural foremen are needed. The total number of workers thus is 103,000.

The presence of His Highness, the Prince, is urgently asked for about eight to ten days, so that the working men keep up respect. Each working unit is kept separately from the other, each guarded by ten men of the cavalry and fifty of the infantry, during work and leisure. Disobedience is punished with death. Workers have to feed themselves.[34]

The wall is erected. The cautious prince asks a reliable astrologer for the favorable time when to begin the building of the inner city. He calculates as the best date: April 15, 1460, at ten o'clock and twenty-one minutes.

Into the foundations are deposited a lot of precious and symbolic items, so that future archeologists, when digging up our city, then a world of antiquity, should have great pleasure. Among others: millet–symbolizing the city's need for food; water–useful and clear, an ideal for future citizens; milk–innocent and unbloody, shall keep away the citizens from quarrelsomeness; wine–used with measure is curative, using one's forces rightly; oil–means peace and also victory; honey–reminds of the diligent and strictly monarchic bees.

Then comes a holiday when the prince determines the sight and plan of the citadel. The castle is reachable only by a long detour of a geometrical labyrinth that would tire an invading army. The cross section of the city is an octagon star; at the end of each of the eight radiating points are erected towers. At the eight inside courts of the star the eight gates are located. Closely, in front of them, just as many piazzas, smaller marketplaces: the straw-market, the wood-market, the wine, oil, wheat-market, etc. Around them will be the quarters for the artisans and proletariat.[35] Between the supply-market squares, formed in a circle, are located the eight parish churches. The sixteen star-streets unite in a Splendor-piazza in the city center, a forum with the municipal buildings, the seat of the prince, the dome, and the stock exchange. This main piazza is situated on a hill; all streets fall out from here to the exterior, providing for a simple solution of canalization.

The prince approved the plan, and we started to build immediately.

With the perfectly organized work system all groundwork is done in four, all fundament work in eight days. And now the specific task of building begins. The prince leaves for two to three weeks."

*

And the story continues: The Dome is built. There is a building for the prince, the bishop, for the aristocracy, the merchants, and the house of the architect Onitoan which, at the same time, is the Hall of Fame for artists. The building of the city continues; the town hall, prison, custom house, convents, hospitals, the mint plant. Now follow the private houses, the theater, buildings for the proletariat, the bridges; canalization over a bridge; the aqueduct.

The harbor is next. The book speaks of an enormous harbor-fort, sixteen stories high, crowned with a colossal picture of the prince on a horse. It speaks of hanging gardens, forges, and enormous forge-hammers; the descriptions go over to a sort of "pedagogical province"; educational institutions for boys and girls; houses in which the administration, clothing, employees, alimentation, sleeping quarters, accident insurance, a sports arena for boys are taken care of. Everything is laid out and fully described.[36]

Also the detailed administration of the entire city of Sforzinda is laid down after an antique ideal; the distribution of land of the environment, the work house, treatment of criminals, the work of the slaves and the free, the consular magistrate, the

34 Here Ponten offers (in parenthesis) an ambivalent and ironic comparison with modern working conditions in the building operations of Weimar Germany, not included in the Kieslers' transcription: "Die geplagten Baumeister von heute sehen, auf wie einfache Weise man die Fragen der Sozialfürsorge, des Streik- und Koalitionsrechtes lösen kann." [The plagued master-builders of today see how easy it is to solve the issues of social welfare, the right to strike and the right to organize]. Ponten, *Architektur*, 1:53. See Sources, Disciplines, and Objects, p. 64.

35 **Quarters for ... the proletariat** This is the Kieslers' translation of Ponten's more politically neutral term "Kleinleutequartiere."

36 **houses in which** [deleted words] **are taken care of: administration, employees, alimentation, clothing, sleeping, accident insurance; a sport arena for boys.** TXT_5877/0_N184 **houses in which the administration, clothing, employees, alimentation, sleeping quarters, accident insurance are taken care of, a sport arena for boys, everything is laid down and described** TXT_6755/0_N9

high Council and the smaller commissions, laws for luxury and taxes, and finally the Civil-list of the prince.

*

The crowning of the fantastic is Antonio's House of Virtue and Vice.

Filarete contrived the following allegory: "On a steep mountain stands, on the tip of a diamond, Virtue, a garnished figure with a sunlike face. She holds a laurel and a palm in her hands. At her feet springs a honey source at which bees nip. At the Mount of Virtue lies a grotto which houses Vice.

A satyr, holding in his hands dishes with food and drinks, and dice. He sits on a wheel whose spikes are seven animals. They spit ordure and in the puddle formed by it, a pig wallows."

For his ideal house he thought of the form of a mountain,[37] but of civil form since it must be habitable. In the square understructure lies a court; from it rises a round building of ten stories, consisting of two joining concentric cylinders, separated by a ring gangway or corridor ring, that passes through the building. In the inner cylinder is a tubular shaft. These cylinders are connected with seven diagonal arch systems on which one walks like on bridges from one cylinder to the other, in three different heights. In the tubular shaft is a spiral staircase that leads through the entire giant structure to the platform. In the axis of the staircase is the water pipe. It is beautiful to walk on the platform of the outer cylinder between nude genii who carry the roof. From one of the bridges one reaches the platform of the inner cylinder. There rises, above the shaft, a cupola, carried by the nine Muses, and on top of the cupola stands, crowning the whole, the colossal statue of Virtue.

The three lowest stories of the inner cylindric building serve for the practice of vice. And opposite, in the outer ring are the taverns and gambling rooms. On the second floor live the ladies of pleasure, directly over them, on the third floor, the police, because vice requires bridling, the writer teaches us. The seven following stories are given to the seven sciences; the first story (the fourth in the structure) for logic, pictured as a woman with double-dress in multi-colors (very unfriendly to philosophers), the next for rhetoric, etc., and the last for astrology. These rooms in the cylinders are in reality only stately halls; the real study rooms, the seminaries are located somewhere in the very roomy block, so that professors don't have to climb too high, the friendly architect informs us.

The one who studies himself up through all these rooms reaches the platform—but to set foot on it is permitted only to those who distinguish themselves in all the sciences, and also those militarists with decorations, and strangers who want to visit the building—for Filarete is Italian...

(rough draft of translation)

(Profusely illustrated with original drawings, unpubl. in English).[38]

CHAPTER 3
THE CITY OF THE SUN BY CAMPANELLA[39]

Campanella, born in Southern Calabria in 1568, became at a very early age a Dominican monk and was interested rather in physics than in theology. By attacking the prevailing Aristotelian philosophy, he soon roused enemies against him, and was imprisoned[40] on the charge of conspiring to overthrow the Kingdom of Naples and to found a republic. He was tortured seven times during twenty-seven years of confinement in fifty

37 **he thought of the form** TXT_6862/0_N4 **he thought out the form** TXT_5877/0_N185 **he thought / out / of the form** TXT_6755/0_N9 These translations render Kiesler's transcription of the German phrase in Ponten: **hat er sich eigentlich die Gestalt eines Berges gedacht** [He actually thought of the shape of a mountain]. Cf. Ponten (1925), 1:36. TXT_6863/0_N4

38 **(Profusely illustr. ~~b~~ with orig. drawings (unpubl. in English)** [handwritten note by Stefi Kiesler referring to Filarete's treatise and/or Ponten's book. See TXT_6755/0_N11 for her research notes on a copy of Ponten at the NYPL TXT_6878_N1-N3 and Sources, Disciplines, and Objects, pp. 52, 54]. Filarete's treatise would be fully translated and published in English along with a manuscript facsimile in 1965, the year of Kiesler's death: *Filarete's Treatise on Architecture: Being the Treatise by Antonio di Piero Averlino, Known as Filarete*, trans. John R. Spencer (New Haven: Yale University Press, 1965). For the 1896 German-Italian edition of Filarete's treatise, see note 26 in this chapter.

39 **Part VII Ch. 3 ~~Introduction~~ (by Charles M. Andrews for Ideal Empires and Republics, Dunne Publ. 1901)** [bibliographic note later crossed out] TXT_6843/0_N1; TXT_6755/0_N12 The introductory text of this chapter is an excerpt from the introduction by the American historian Charles McLean Andrews to *Ideal Empires and Republics: Rousseau's Social Contract, More's Utopia, Bacon's New Atlantis, Campanella's City of the Sun* (New York: Walter Dunne, 1901), vii–xvii (xiii–xiv for the quoted passages).

40 **imprisoned** [underlined by hand] TXT_6843/0_N1; TXT_6755/0_N12

41 **customs and manners** TXT_6693/0_N1 **manners and customs** [as per Andrews, *Ideal Empires*, xiv] TXT_6843/0_N1; TXT_6755/0_N12

42 **retype p. 1** [handwritten note by Stefi Kiesler regarding excerpts from Andrews' introduction] TXT_6755/0_N12

43 **from same book** [note for a transcription from Andrews] TXT_6755/0_N13; TXT_6843/0_N2 Cf. Andrews, *Ideal Empires*, 275, 278–279.

different prisons, and was often deprived of the means of study and writing.

After his release in 1626, he withdrew to France; and in 1639 died in a convent of his order. The Civitas Solis seu idea republicae philosophicae, written in prison, is believed to have been the beginning of a large work, of which the first part was to deal with the laws of nature, the second with the manners and customs of man,[41] the third with the organization of the state, the fourth with the economic bases of society. It was, as Campanella himself says, the counterpart of Plato's Republic, and on the scientific side was based on Telesius. It formulated for the first time a complete socialistic system on a scientific foundation, and, in France, especially furnished a model for later ideal communities.

The city with its seven walls, its compact organization, its carefully divided labors, and rigorous discipline, reflects the monastic experiences of the writer; but the principles, the accordance with which the state is governed, the social relation determined, and industry controlled, are such as to interest all men in all ages.

Collectively, the inhabitants labor for the common good; individually, each seeks the perfecting of his body and soul, the care of the young children, and the worship of God. Government is entrusted to the wisest and ablest, and laws are made and administered only so far as they promote the object for which all are laboring.

The essences of life are equality, sacrifice of self for the community, the banishment of egotism; and peculiar features are the community of wives and goods, common meals, state control of produce, and of children after a certain age, dislike of commercial exchange, depreciation of money, love of all for manual labor, and the high regard which all show for intellectual and artistic pursuits.

It is a remarkable fact that in spite of Campanella's sufferings his work should maintain consistently the loftiest ideals.[42]

* * *

Excerpt from Campanella's book "The City of the Sun," "(a poetical dialogue between a Grandmaster of the Knights Hospitalers and a Genoese Sea Captain, his guest.)"[43]

Grand Master

– Tell on, I pray you! Tell on! I am dying to hear more.

Captain

– The temple is built in the form of a circle; it is not girt with walls, but stands upon thick columns, beautifully grouped. A very large dome, built with great care in the center or pole, contains another small vault as it were rising out of it, and in this a spiracle, which is right over the altar. There is but one altar in the middle of the temple, and this is hedged round by columns. The temple itself is on a space of more than three hundred and fifty paces. The temple itself is on a space of more than three hundred and fifty spaces. Without it, arches measuring about eight paces extend from the heads of the columns outwards, whence other columns rise about three paces from the thick, strong and erect wall. Between these and the former columns there are galleries for walking, with beautiful pavements, and in the recess of the wall, which is adorned with numerous large doors, there are immovable seats, places as it were between the inside columns, supporting the temple. Portable chairs are not wanting, many and well adorned. Nothing is seen over the altar but a large globe, upon which the heavenly bodies are painted, and another globe upon which there is a representation of the earth.

Furthermore, in the vault of the dome there can be discerned representations of all the stars of heaven from the first to the sixth magnitude, with their proper names and power to influence terrestrial things mark[ed] in three little verses for each.

There are the poles and greater and lesser circles according to the right latitude of the place, but these are not perfect because there is no wall below. They seem too, to be made in their relation to the globes on the altar. The pavement of the temple is bright with precious stones. Its seven golden lamps hang always burning, and these bear the names of the seven planets.

At the top of the building several small and beautiful cells surround the small dome, and behind the level space above the bands of arches of the exterior and interior columns there are many cells, both small and large, where the priest and religious officers dwell to the number of forty-nine.

A revolving flag projects from the smallest dome, and this shows in what quarter the wind is. The flag is marked with figures up to thirty-six, and the priests know what sort of year the different kinds of wind bring and what will be the changes of weather on land and sea. Furthermore, under the flag a book is always kept written with letters of gold.

Grand Master

– I pray you, worthy hero, explain to me their whole system of government; for I am anxious to hear it.

Captain

– The great ruler among them is a priest whom they call by the name Hoh, though we should call him Metaphysics…[44]

CHAPTER 4
MAGIC ARCHITECTURE, HOLY AND PROFANE

pl. 47 a) Michelangelo's Sistine Chapel[45]

A comparison study of a Renaissance project planned and built, adequately treated.

(Of course, there are many in that period where fact and vision were attempted in unification to produce magic architecture–and many that failed. The selection must be careful and discard those projects, perhaps well known, that are nothing more but a conglomeration, however *raffiné* contrived, of over-rich architecture in design and material and embellished with frescoes, sculptures, and artisan's craftwork.)

Such a study alone could fill a book, and a very necessary one: because these "faked," grandiose pieces of architecture and décor had, through their easy effect, an enormous influence on public and designers and have produced a "false capitalism" in building styles up to our time.

pl. 48 b) Houses of Pompeii[46]

The sheltering functionalism of walls negated. Frescoes employed to pen vistas of land, buildings, etc.,[47] non-existent in reality, but with utmost details realized as visions. Excellent examples of architecture which goes beyond "functionalism" and "décor" in home design.

There are superb examples existing especially of the so-called second style period of Boscoreale near Pompeii. These are true examples of the ability of the architect to induce transfiguration of building materials into spiritual functions.

44 **Metaphysics** TXT_6755/0_N14; TXT_6843/0_N3 In these two typescript copies of the transcription, the final "s" of "Metaphysics" is crossed out with a typed slash, echoing the German *Metaphysik*. The text of the assembled version mentions **Metaphysics** TXT_6693/0_N5 as does the printed text of Andrews, *Ideal Empires*, 279.

45 **Magic Architecture Holy & Profane / a) Michelangelo Sistine Chapel / b) Houses of Pompeji** [sic; handwritten final chapter list by Stefi Kiesler; see fig. B.29b] TXT_6755/0_N15 **Part VII Chapter. 4, b) Michelangelo's Sistine Chapel / Part VII Chapt. 4, a) ~~The Dream Architecture of Pompeï~~ Houses of Pompeji / Pompeji comes first →** TXT_6831/0_N2 In this TS, Kiesler uses an arrow to reverse the order of sections a and b and Stefi marks the alternative sequence in her chapter numbers (fig. B.29a). The same TS includes text which is not transcribed in any of the later drafts but has been restored in the Main Text. Assembled versions of *Magic Architecture* include only the two section titles in the original order, also observed in the plate illustrations. TXT_5877/0_N187-N188

46 **~~The Dream Architecture of Pompeï~~** TXT_6831/0_N2

47 **u.s.f.** [etc.; handwritten addition] TXT_6831/0_N2

~~Part VII Chap. 4, (6)~~ C 30

Michelangelo's ~~The~~ Sistine Chapel

a ~~One~~ comparison study of a Renaissance project planned and built, adequately treated.

(Of course, there are many in that period where fact and vision were attempted in unification to produce magic architecture -- and many that failed. The selection must be careful and discard those projects, perhaps well known, that are nothing more but a conglomeration, however raffiné contrived, of over-rich architecture in design and material and embellished with frescoes, sculptures and artisan's craft work.)

Such a study alone could fill a book, and a very necessary one: because these faked, grandiose pieces of architecture and décor had, through their easy effect, an enormous influence on public and designers and have produced a "false capitalism" in building styles up to our time.

Pompeji comes first

~~The Dream Architecture of Pompei~~ Houses of Pompeji { Part VII Chapt. 4, (5) C

The sheltering funtionalism of walls negated. Frescos employed to open vistas of land, buildings, non- existent in reality, but with utmost details realized as visions.

Excellent examples of architecture which goes beyond "functionalism" and "decor" in home design.

There are superb examples existing especially of the so called second style period of Boscoreale near Pompei. These are true examples of the ability of the architect to induce transfiguration of building materials into spiritual functions.

Frederick and Stefi Kiesler, Part VII, Chapter 4, preliminary draft with text omitted from later versions and proposed alteration of chapter structure ("Pompeji comes first") by Frederick Kiesler (in ink) and marked by Stefi (in pencil) (TS, pencil, ink) ÖFLKS, TXT_6831/0_N2

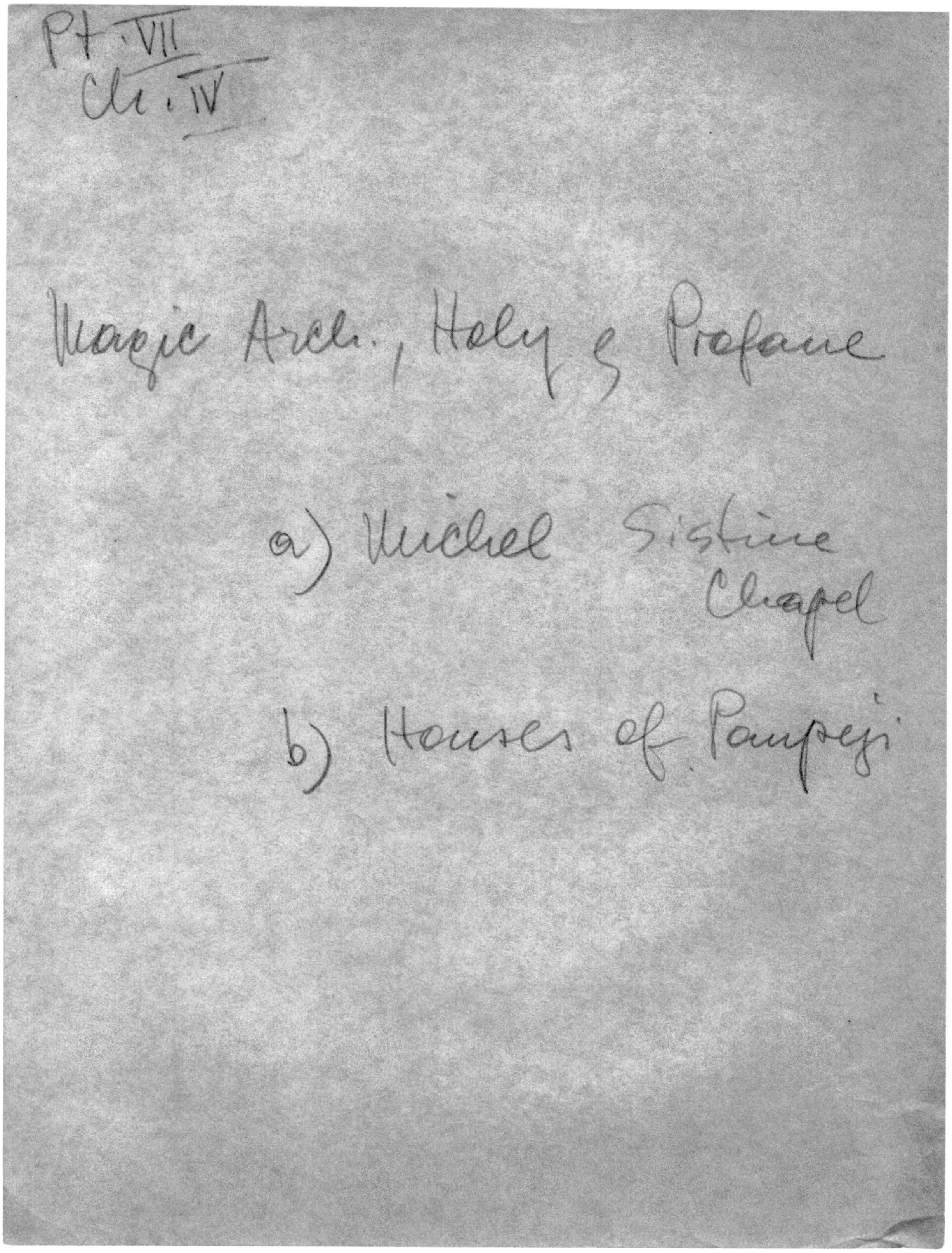

fig. B.29b

Pt. VII
Ch. IV

Magic Arch., Holy & Profane

a) Michel Sistine Chapel

b) Houses of Pompeji

Frederick and Stefi Kiesler, Part VII, Chapter 4: "Magic Arch[itecture], Holy & Profane," preliminary draft in Stefi Kiesler's hand noting final chapter structure (MS, pencil) ÖFLKS, TXT_6755/0_N15

Page 255

(47 and 48). Pages 255, 256

These are two samples of how interior-walls of buildings can be transformed to stimulate the imagination.

Left: Interior of St. Peters in Rome during a mass. (The Pope center, low.)

Right: Pompeian fresco.

44
"Fischer von Erlach, The Macedonian Mount Athos in the shape of a giant, as Dinocrates, architect of the great Alexander, specified such construction (1721)." Ponten, *Architektur die nicht gebaut wurde*, 2:1, pl. 1. ÖFLKS, SCL_58/0

45–46
"Filarete, the fifteenth-century ideal city of Sforzinda, including the labyrinth and fort (below, left) and city plan (below, right), and (overleaf) tower, harbor fort, Zogalias tower, and temple." Ponten, *Architektur die nicht gebaut wurde*, 2:24–25, 28, pl. 38, 42, 44–45, 54–55, 65. ÖFLKS, SCL_59/0; ÖFLKS, SCL_60/0

47–48
Left: "American Saint: Mother Cabrini is First Citizen of US to be canonized in Rome," *Life*, July 22, 1946, 30–31. ÖFLKS, SCL_61/0

Right: Roman villa, Pompeii. Noack, *Die Baukunst des Altertums*, pl. 127.

Part VII½

Dance of Death

fig. B.30

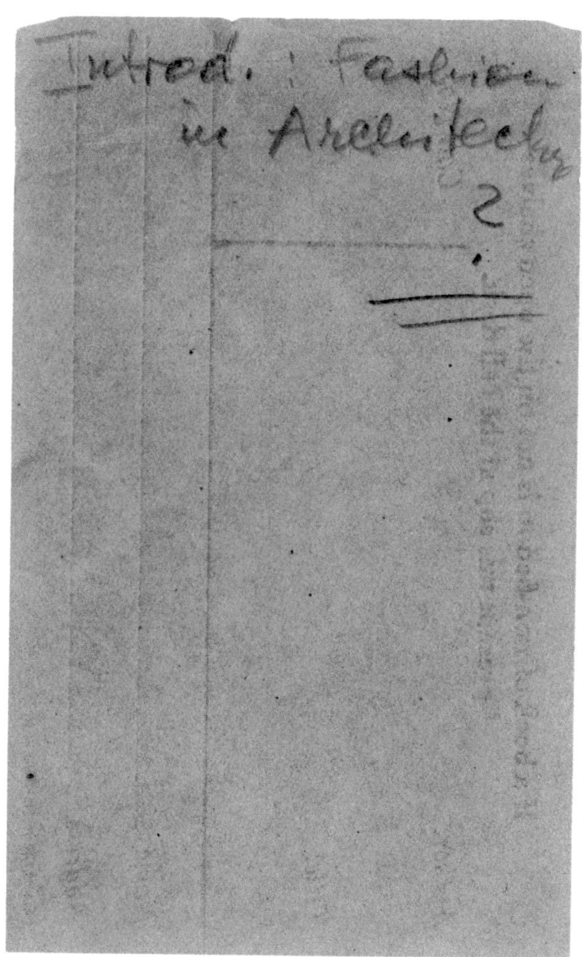

Frederick Kiesler, Part VIII, Introduction, preliminary draft on the back of library slip: "Intro[duction]: Fashion in Architecture?"
(MS, pencil) ÖFLKS, TXT_6826/0_N2

PART VIII
REALISM OF WEALTH[1]

INTRODUCTION
FASHION IN ARCHITECTURE[2]

CHAPTER 1
LUST IN STONE (FOUNTAIN BY PAULUS DECKER)

pl. 49

Description of a fountain by Paulus Decker who was court architect at Bayreuth, 1731.[3]

Paulus Decker was architect of the duchy Pfalz-Sulzbach, court architect of Bayreuth. "The Royal Master Builder" was the title of his powerful corpus of engravings capturing the high impetus of his imagination. The year 1731.[4]

The first of the pleasure-fountains is the Muses' fountain. The muses are scattered throughout this liquid world. One has to note the pressing power of this water; thick columns rise from mussel-shaped shells, the tuba sound of the winged Fama strikes the curling water surface of the column as a straight solid jet of water, as does the cry of the eagle on the other side. The second is the Fountain of the Gods–glass balls dance on the curling water surface without ever falling down. The third fountain is based on the battle of the Lapiths and the Centaurs: the hydraulic pressure of the waterworks for these liquid artifices is so strong, that not only the tuba sound becomes massive but furthermore allows Zeus to hurl three flashes of thick waterjets out of each hand like lances...[5]

CHAPTER 2
TOTENTANZ OF ARCHITECTURE[6]

A PROJECT OF THE ROCOCO[7]

(Every emotion ends in motion, and dies as a skeleton of mechanization.)[8]

THE ROCOCO IN FRANCE (TRIANON)

Description of the Trianon.[9]

1 Alternative part numbers and titles (frontispiece): **Part VII½ Dance of Death** TXT_6826/0_N1 **Part VIII Totentanz der Architecture** [Dance of Death of Architecture] TXT_6830/0_N1 See also handwritten list of contents. TXT_6702/0_N10 mentioned in editors' notes in "Content."

2 **Introd.: Fashion / in Architecture / ?** [handwritten note on the back of a library book request slip (fig. B.30)] TXT_6826/0_N2recto-verso. Despite Kiesler's professional involvement with shop window design (including his designs for Saks Fifth Avenue in 1928) and his publication *Contemporary Art Applied to the Store and its Display*, none of his writings on fashion have survived. In 1944, he designed the exhibition *Fashion of the Times*, 3rd edition, organized by the *New York Times*. See exhibition brochure: MED 5984/0. On Kiesler and fashion, see Sources, Disciplines, and Objects, p. 67.

3 The following is the editors' translation of the Kieslers' German transcription of an excerpt from a chapter titled "Der Fürstliche Baumeister [Royal Master Builder]" in Ponten, *Architektur die nicht gebaut wurde* (1925), 1:73–77 (74 for the Kieslers' selection). It contains a brief introductory text and description of Decker's "pleasure fountains." Kiesler's transcriptions remained untranslated in later drafts and were not included in any of the assembled versions of *Magic Architecture*. Here they are included in a translation by the editors. TXT_6826/0_N2; TXT_6830/0_N2.

4 **Anno 1731.** Cf. Ponten, *Architektur*, 1:74. The date follows Ponten; his main text mentions 1731 (a mistake), while his bibliography correctly lists the three original publication dates of Decker's work: Part 1 (1711), Appendix (1713), and Part 2 (1716); Ponten, 1:165. Ponten's text also includes the complete title of the publication: "Fürstlicher Baumeister oder *Architectura Civilis*, wie Großer Fürsten und Herren Palläste / mit ihren Höfen / Lusthäusern/ Gärten / Grotten / Orangerien / und anderen darzu gehörigen Gebäuden füglich anzulegen / und nach heutiger Art auszuzieren; zusamt den Grund-Rissen und Durchschnitten / auch vornehmsten Gemächern und Sälen eines ordentlichen Fürstlichen Pallastes. [Royal master builder or *Architectura Civilis*, such as Great Princes' and Lords' Palaces / with their courts / pleasure-houses / gardens / grottoes / orangeries / and other buildings belonging to it / and to decorate them in the manner of today; together with the floor plans and sections / of even the most distinguished chambers and halls of a proper royal palace.]" Ponten, *Architektur*, 1:74.

5 Ponten's ornamented description of the three "free-standing pleasure-fountains" follows his survey of Decker's other landscape structures for his projected royal environs, including monumental entrance gates, gardens, grottoes, and labyrinths. Cf. Ponten, *Architektur*, 1:75–76.

6 Alternative chapter title: **Pt VIII: Totentanz der Architecture** [Dance of Death of Architecture] TXT_6830/0_N1 This title corresponds to that of Part VII ½ (Dance of Death) in the hand-drawn title sheet for this section.

7 Kiesler's library includes the book by the Viennese essayist and playwright (as well as collaborator of Franz Kafka) Franz Blei, *Das Rokoko: Variationen über ein Thema* (Munich: Georg Müller, 1911). For Kiesler's criticism of Rococo architecture and the architectural display of wealth, see his 1956 *Art News* article on Mozart cited in editors' notes for Part IX, chapter 1. On Kiesler's views of Rococo architecture and his contemporary culture of "wealth" in Europe and the United States, see Sources, Disciplines, and Objects, pp. 66–67, 90.

8 **A Project of the Rococo / Every emotion ends in motion, and dies as a skeleton of mechanization** [handwritten on manuscript draft; transcribed to a typescript but not included in any versions of the assembled manuscript] TXT_6830/0_N1 In the MS draft, the statement on the Rococo follows a handwritten draft on Piranesi, which suggests that Kiesler was thinking of a chapter on the Rococo immediately following the last chapter of Part VI on Piranesi. TXT_6781/0_N3

9 No description of the Grand (or Petit) Trianon in Versailles exists among Kiesler's drafts.

(49)

(49). Page 259

A fountain in exhuberant design. (By the court architect, Paulus Dekker, 18th century.)

page 259

Joh. Balthasar Probst Sculps.
27.
Bronnen .
Ieremias Wolff excud. Aug. Vind.

49
"Lustbronnen [pleasure fountain]."
Ponten, *Architektur die nicht gebaut wurde*, 2:96, pl. 178.
ÖFLKS, SCL_62/0

the Poets Architecture

fig. B.31

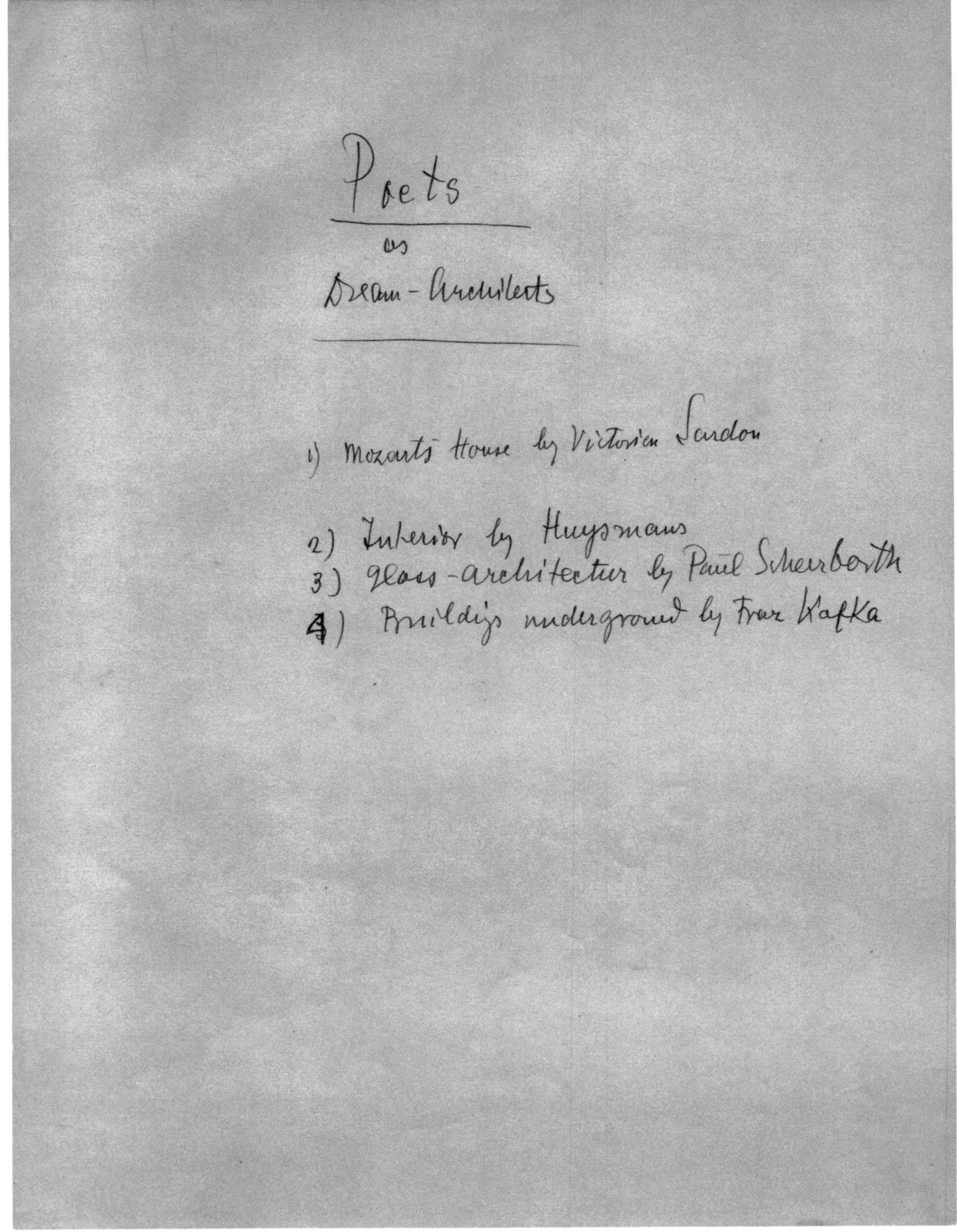

Poets

as

Dream-Architects

1) Mozarts House by Victorien Sardou

2) Interior by Huysmans

3) glass-architectur by Paul Scheerbarth

4) Buildings underground by Franz Kafka

Frederick Kiesler, Part IX, preliminary draft titled "Poets as Dream-Architects" with alternative list of contents (MS, ink) ÖFLKS, TXT_6721/0 N2

PART IX
THE POET'S ARCHITECTURE[1]

INTRODUCTION
CASTLES IN THE AIR[2]

CHAPTER 1
MOZART'S HOUSE BY VICTORIEN SARDOU

pl. 50 A poet retreats from everyman's gold rush into a dream habitat.[3]

(Excellent descriptions of unusual construction and material used.)[4]

CHAPTER 2
AN INTERIOR BY HUYSMANS[5]

A description of the magic effect of extraordinary building materials, their emotional and psychological power.

A poet's guide to the meaning of Architecture.[6]
(Quote parts of text)[7]

CHAPTER 3
GLASS ARCHITECTURE BY PAUL SCHEERBART[8]

A writer[9] describes the future habitation of mankind.

CHAPTER 4
THE BUILDING BY FRANZ KAFKA[10]

Description of an imaginary town underground.[11]

1 Alternative part number and titles (frontispiece): **~~PART VIII~~ 9 The Poets Architecture** TXT_6721/0_N1 See also handwritten list of alternative titles (fig. B.31):
Poets
as
Dream Architects
1 **Mozart's House by Victorien Sardou**
2 **Interior by Huysmans**
3 **Glass-Architectur by Paul Scheerbart** [In his spelling of Architecture, Kiesler sometimes misses the final "e" as in the German Architektur.]
4 **Buildings underground by Franz Kafka** TXT_6721/0_N2

2 No introduction exists. The title could be a reference to skyscrapers and/or glass architecture (see chapters in Parts IX and X).

3 **"An Exterior MOZART'S HOUSE by Victorien Sardou / A poet retreats from the everyman's gold rush into the dream world of a habitat he considers worthy of a man of genius (quote part of description.), who died in poverty."** TXT_6833/0_N2 and TXT_6763/0_N1 **~~Flight~~ from the violence of everyman's goldrush, a poets retreat retreats into the dream-world to build what he considers the magic habitat.** TXT_6781/0_N12

4 Sardou's etching, *La Maison de Mozart (Ville basse)*, first appeared in *Revue spirite* in 1858 along with an account of the French dramatist's description of the habitations of spirits on planet Jupiter, including the "house of Mozart." Sardou's description was allegedly dictated by the spirit of the seventeenth-century sculptor and scientist Bernard Palissy, who also guided his design. See, Victorien Sardou, "Des habitations de la planète Jupiter," *Revue spirite: Journal d'études psychologiques* (August 1858): 222–232. The original etching was owned by André Breton and is still part of his collection. It is described in Breton's well-known article "Le message automatique" (*Minotaure*, nos. 3–4 [1933], 55–65), which is preceded by a reproduction of Sardou's aquatint with the caption "La Maison de Mozart en Jupiter, eau-forte automatique exécutée en neuf heures par Victorien Sardou (*La revue Spirite*, 1858)" alongside an excerpt from Sardou's text. Kiesler created a photostat of Sardou's engraving from his personal copy of *Minotaure*, which was reproduced in plate 50 of *Magic Architecture*. PHO_7213/0 See Sources, Disciplines, and Objects, fig. A.51. An excerpt from Breton's article features among Kiesler's transcriptions of readings for his students in the Laboratory for Design Correlation at Columbia University. TXT_3572/0_N7-N8. Other drafts include the following: **a man of genius** [Mozart], **who died in poverty** TXT_6833/0_N2; TXT_6763/0_N1 Kiesler's research material includes a magazine clipping with the transcription of a letter containing an account of Mozart's death by one of his contemporaries: "Über Mozarts Tod: Ein Brief von Sophie Haibl an Nikolaus Nissen," in *Insel-Almanach: auf das Jahr 1926* (Leipzig: Insel-Verlag, 1926), 50–53; reprinted from Albert Leitzmann, *Wolfgang Amadeus Mozart: Berichte der Zeitgenossen und Briefe* (Leipzig: Insel-Verlag, 1926), 178–181. CLP_6562/0_N1-N3 The Kieslers owned several books on Mozart, including: Hugo Leichtentritt (ed.), *Mozarts Briefe* (Berlin: Deutsche Bibliothek, 1912); W. J. Turner, *Mozart. The Man and his Work* (New York, NY: Doubleday, 1938). In his work as a scenographer, Kiesler did the stage designs for several Mozart operas at the Juilliard Opera Theater in New York: *The Abduction from the Seraglio* (1938), *Cosi fan Tutte* (1940), *The Magic Flute* (1940, 1949), and *The Marriage of Figaro* (1942). On the occasion of Mozart's bicentennial, he contributed an essay for *Art News*, which includes a rebuttal of eighteenth-century Rococo architecture (particularly in Austria): "Mozart's music is neither frivolous nor lecherous, it is Form through and through without décor. Rococo *is* décor: décor *par excellence*. But in 1789 all the curvilinear Rococo frames were condensed into a single barren, raw wooden rectangle: the guillotine." Frederick Kiesler, "Mozart: 1956–1756; A modern artist appraises Mozart the artist as his bicentennial opens with a huge Rococo show at the Nelson Gallery, Kansas City," *Art News* 54, no. 9, January 1956, 22–25 and 58 (here, 25). For the original draft, see TXT_904/0; TXT_905/0 This later (dis)association between Mozart and the Rococo may retroactively explain the inclusion of Sardou's "House of Mozart" following Kiesler's unwritten chapter on the Rococo.

5 **~~The~~ Interior ~~of Plush glass~~ / by / Huysmans.** TXT_6781/0_N13 There are no extracts from any of Joris-Karl Huysmans' novels among Kiesler's drafts, and no books by Huysmans have survived in the Kiesler estate library. The reference to "interior of plush-glass" in the crossed-out text points to the extraordinary interior concocted by Des Esseintes, the reclusive protagonist of Huysmans' *À rebours* (translated in English as *Against Nature*), first published in 1884. A German edition was later published: Joris-Karl Huysmans, *Gegen den Strich* (*À rebours*), trans. M. Cupsius (Berlin: Schuster und Loffler, 1897).

6 **~~The~~ poet's guide to the meaning of Architecture. / A description of the magic effect of extraordinary building materials, their emotional and psychological power. →** [a hand-drawn arrow reverses the order of the two sentences, fig. B.32] TXT_6781/0_N13

7 No quotations from Huysmans exist in any of the drafts of *Magic Architecture*, but *À rebours* is mentioned in an "Outline" for Stefi Kiesler's planned "anthology" or "collection of Dreams in Literature" (uncatalogued drafts). See also Annotated Chronology, p. 378.

8 **The Glass–Architecture–Novel / by / Paul Scheerbart.** TXT_6833/0_N1; TXT_6781_N10 See Paul Scheerbart, *Glasarchitektur* (Berlin: Verlag der Sturm, 1914). For the English edition, see "Glass Architecture," translated by James Palmes, in Paul Scheerbart and Bruno Taut, *Glass Architecture and Alpine Architecture*, ed. Dennis Sharp (New York: Praeger, 1972), 39–74. No transcriptions of excerpts from Scheerbart's text exist, and no book by Scheerbart survives in the Kiesler estate library. Kiesler did not meet Scheerbart during the years he lived in Berlin, but he was familiar with the ideas of Bruno Taut and other members of the Gläserne Kette (Glass Chain) group, who were inspired by Scheerbart's architectonic visions, through encounters with members of art and architectural collectives such as the Novembergruppe and the Arbeitsrat für Kunst.

9 **a ~~german~~ writer** TXT_6781_N10

10 **Frank** [sic] **Kafka** TXT_5877/0_N198 **Franz Kafka** TXT_6763/0_N1; TXT_6763/0_N2

11 **~~The Buildings underground~~ / ~~by~~ ~~Franz Kafka~~.** TXT_6763/0_N1 **Part IX Ch. 4 The Building by Franz Kafka (discovery of an imaginary town underground.)** [handwritten additions to TS] TXT_6763/0_N2 Kafka does not appear in Kiesler's writing pad draft, which includes the rest of the literary figures mentioned in Part IX. TXT_6781/0 No excerpts from Kafka's stories are transcribed, and no works by Kafka have survived in the Kieslers' library. However, excerpts from Kafka's diaries and letters (and the published collection *Tagebücher und Briefe* (Prague: Heinrich Mercy Sohn, 1936) are included in Stefi Kiesler's unpublished collection of dream narratives (see also Annotated Chronology, p. 378). The reference to "an imaginary town underground" points to the burrow building structure described by the animal narrator of Kafka's short story "Der Bau," translated in English as "The Burrow." Kafka's short story was first published in a journal in 1928 and was later republished in a collection of short stories: Franz Kafka, "Der Bau," in *Beim Bau der Chinesischen Mauer: ungedruckte Erzählungen und Prosa aus dem Nachlass*, ed. Max Brod (Berlin: Kiepenheuer, 1931), 77–130. For the first English edition: Franz Kafka, "The Burrow," in *The Great Wall of China, and other pieces*, trans. Willa and Edwin Muir (London: Martin Secker, 1933), 48–81.

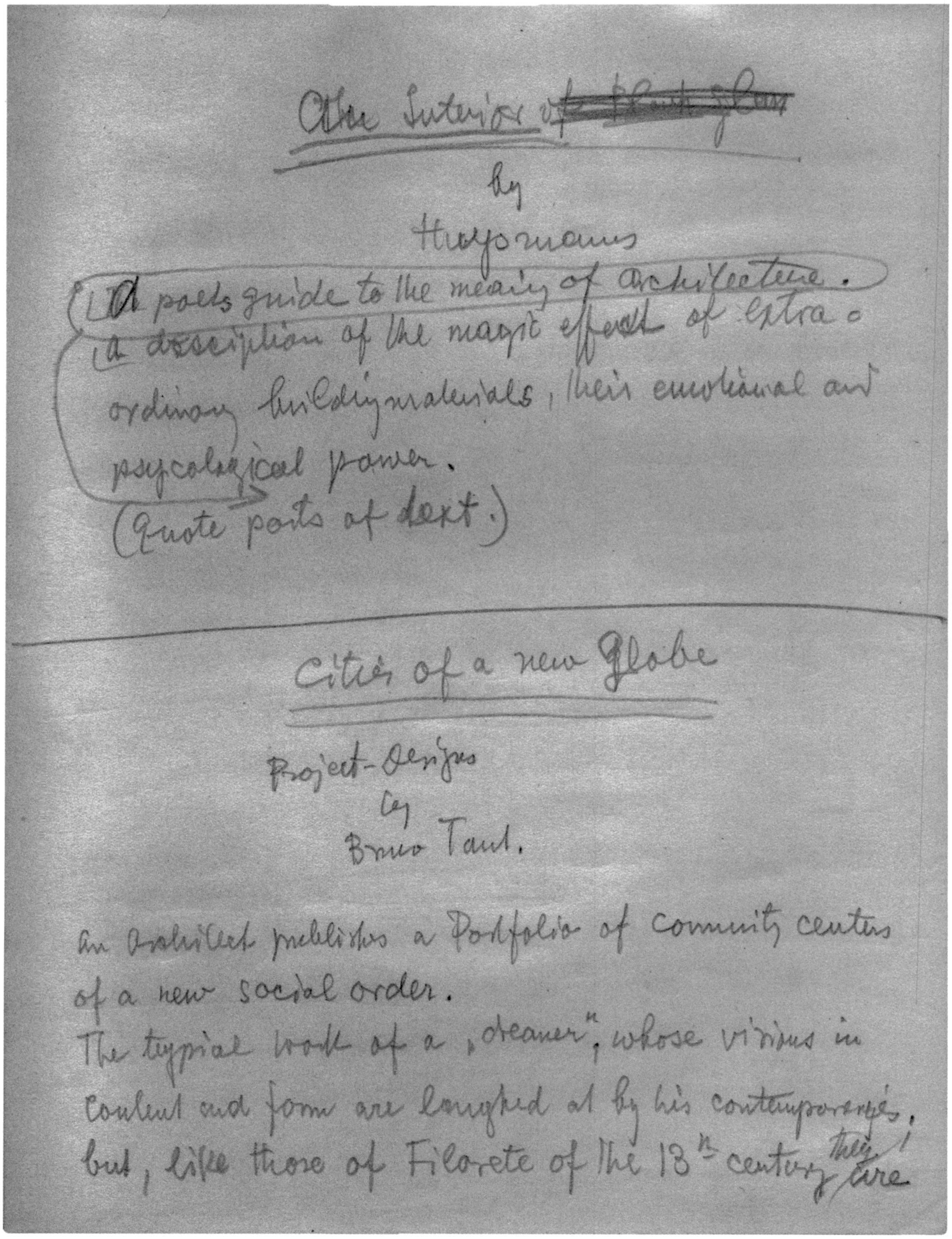

fig. B.32

The Interior of

by

Huysmans

A poets guide to the meaning of architecture.
A description of the magic effect of extra-ordinary buildingmaterials, their emotional and psycological power.
(Quote parts of text.)

Cities of a new Globe

Project-Designs
by
Bruno Taut.

An Architect publishes a Portfolio of community centers of a new social order.
The typical work of a „dreamer", whose visions in content and form are laughed at by his contemporaries, but, like those of Filarete of the 13th century they are

Frederick Kiesler, Page from the architect's note-pad with consecutive descriptions of "An Interior by Huysmans" and "Cities of a new Globe by Bruno Taut" used in Part IX, Chapter 2 and Part X, Chapter 2, respectively, in later versions of the book manuscript (MS, pencil) ÖFLKS, TXT_6781/0_N13

page 263

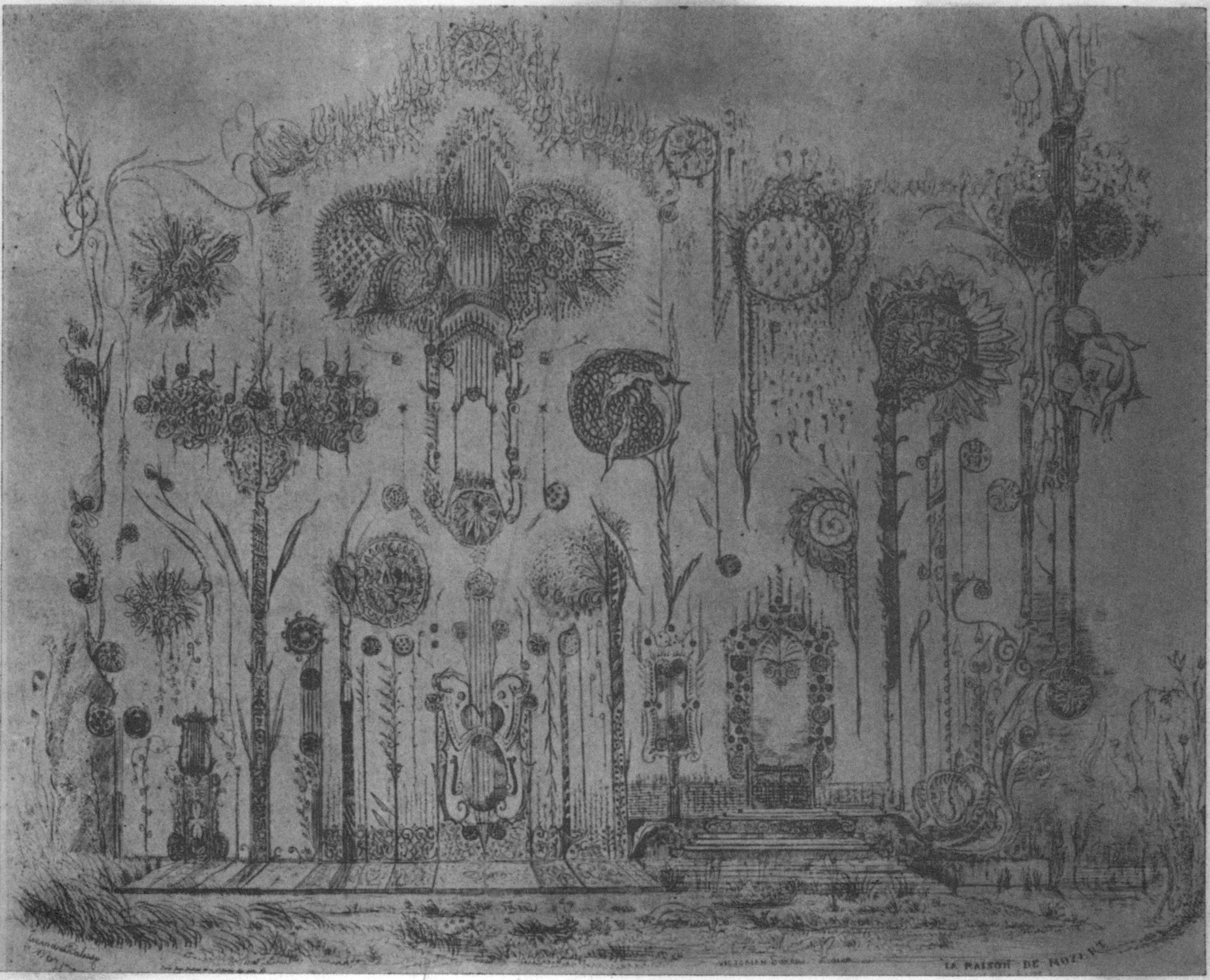

(50). Page 263

A French poet's (Victorien Sardou) dream-design of a house for Mozart.

50
Victorien Sardou, "La Maison de Mozart (Ville basse)" (c. 1858), *Minotaure* 3–4 (1933): 54, preceding the article by André Breton, "Le message automatique," ibid., 55–65. ÖFLKS, SCL_63/051a

Part VII
Flares of a new
Unity of Vision and Fact

fig. B.33

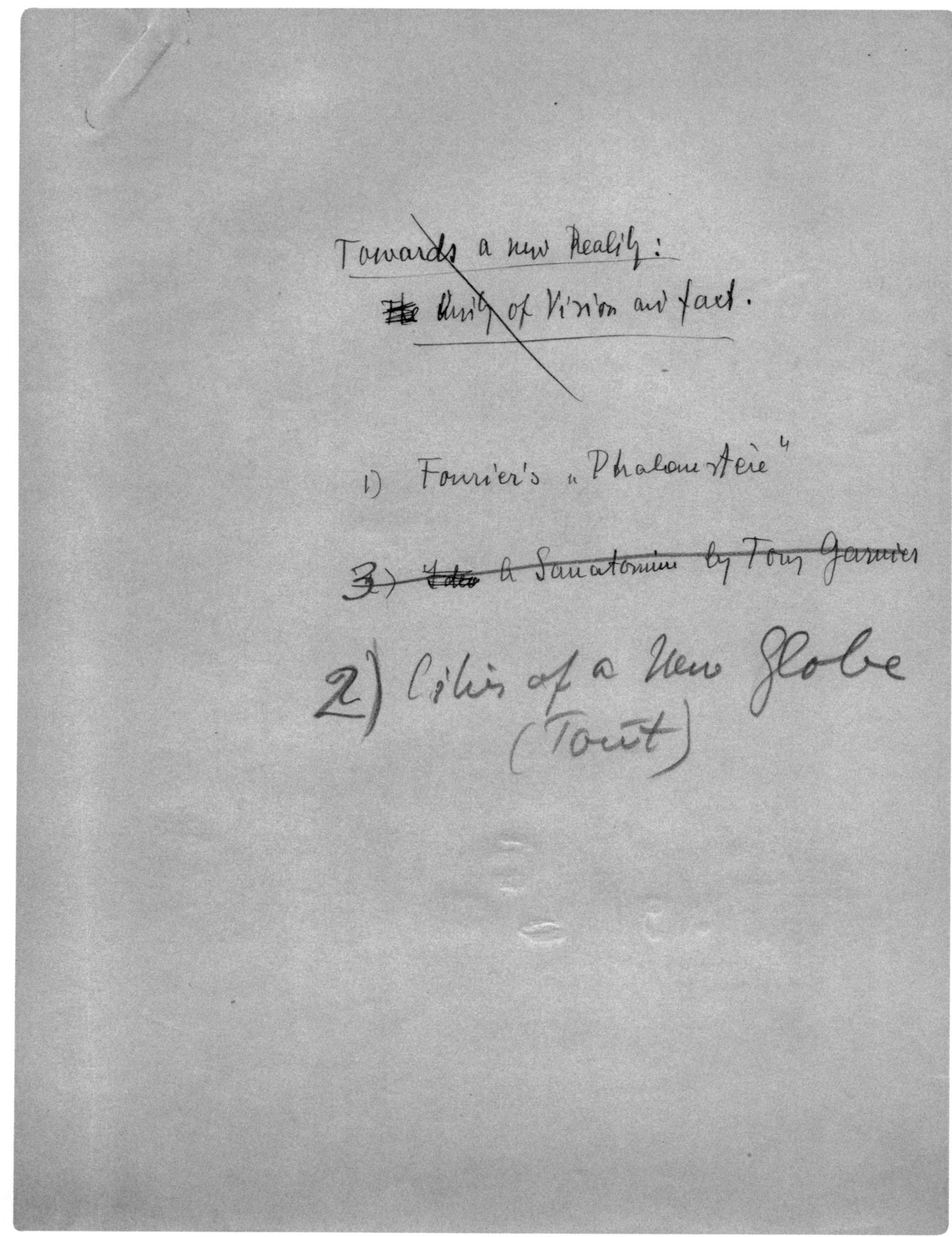

~~Towards a new Reality:~~
~~Unity of Vision and fact.~~

1) Fourier's „Phalanstère"

~~3) Idea A Sanatorium by Tony Garnier~~

2) Cities of a New Globe
(Taut)

Frederick Kiesler, Draft for Part x (formerly Part viii), "Towards a new Reality: Unity of Vision and Fact" with alternative list of contents, including deleted chapter title: "A Sanatorium by Tony Garnier" (ms, pencil, ink) ÖFLKS, TXT_6824/0_N2

PART X
FLARES OF A NEW UNITY OF VISION AND FACT[1]

INTRODUCTION
SOCIO-ARCHITECTURAL UTOPIA AND THE REALITY OF INDUSTRY

Shelter cannot be accounted for only in stones or bricks (or plastics, if you like); it covers all fields of human behavior.[2]

Philosophy is shelter[3] just as poetry is: a system invented and one evolved[4] to explain or guard man in his struggle for existence,[5] and his delight of its intervals. Structures of the intellect are methods of protection, just as well as buildings of brick.[6] These buildings, of course, cannot be touched by hands or with our eyes,[7] but they are real, nevertheless, and structures and shelters they are!

The social structures, such as the family, the clan, tribe, a monarchy, or a socialist community—they all are meant as: sheltering means; and in that respect they are more direct, more realistic, more "touchable" than philosophy or poetry although not as much as houses; they are social edifices, an outer layer[8] or the nucleus of philosophy or poetry, and that is why we are at greater ease when we come in contact with them[9]—naturally. Our senses (of immediacy) are limited in number and capacity, and we therefore like to believe in things which we can not only behold, but also hold; which we can not only grasp, but also grip.[10]

With regard to architecture,[11] this state of being was catastrophic: whatever was satisfactory to the direct touch of man's senses (such as felt by hands and eyes), was unsatisfactory to his inner senses; and whatever physical being was satisfactory to his inner senses belonged to nature: fauna, flora[12]—the other man or woman. What man built was ugly and inefficient. He was a poor imitator. Nature's flesh, skin, and plumage was beyond his reach. He abandoned the hope of building Architecture,[13] he resigned himself to shelter. More immediate problems, such as hunger and sex had to be dealt with; there was no refuge from that—no natural cave would satisfy this urge.[14] Social structures had to be built first. They meant food for everyone and protection for the family and its offspring.[15]

CHAPTER 1
FOURIER'S "IDEAL PHALANX"

(An architectural plan for the unification of Work, Residence, and Play.)[16]

CHAPTER 2
"CITIES OF A NEW GLOBE" BY BRUNO TAUT

pls. 51, 51a–b

The Surface of the Earth transformed: Project Designs by Bruno Taut.

An architect published a portfolio of community centers for a new social order.[17]

The typical work of a "dreamer," whose visions in content and form are laughed at by his contemporaries, but, like those of Filarete of the fifteenth century,[18] they are nothing else than the continuity of man's desire for an order[19] which will produce the greatest possibility of individual productivity and freedom.

1 Alternative part number and title (frontispiece): Part VIII / FLARES of a new ~~REALITY~~ Unity of Vision and Fact / ~~Fusion Reality & Fact:~~ TXT_6824/0_N1 The numbering of the title sheet reflects an earlier structure of the book's final section, which remained in flux. The title for Part X references the title of the general introduction to *Magic Architecture*: The Unity of Vision and Fact. Earlier drafts show an alternative list of contents below the title (figs. B.33, B.34). TXT_6824/0_N2-N3

2 ~~The Term / The meaning of~~ shelter cannot be accounted for ~~in~~ only stones or bricks (or plastics, if you like); it covers all fields of human behavior ~~materialistic as well as spiritual~~. TXT_6723/0_N1

3 a ~~method of~~ shelter TXT_6723/0_N1

4 evoluted [sic] ~~by man~~ TXT_6723/0_N1

5 ~~his existence and in his~~ his struggle for existence TXT_6723/0_N1 This follows the Darwinian expression *Kampf ums Dasein*, also used frequently by Klaatsch.

6 Structures of the intellect are ~~more indirect~~ methods of protection, ~~they are not akin to buildings~~ TXT_6723/0_N1

7 ~~It is true,~~ these buildings cannot be touched by hands ~~(like houses or tools)~~ or ~~by our~~ eyes TXT_6723/0_N1

8 they, the social edifices, are a ~~more~~ outer layer of them, TXT_6723/0_N1

9 in ~~direct~~ contact with them TXT_6723/0_N1

10 not only grasp, but also grip. TXT_6723/0_N1 The terms "grasp" and "grip" correspond to the German verbs *begreifen* (mentally grasp or conceive) and *greifen* (physically grip or snatch).

11 that is one of the reasons why architecture ~~leaves~~ always / tended / more to the materialistic function than to the spiritual. The human body is ~~the~~ shelter of the will. [handwritten passage entirely excised] TXT_6723/0_N2

12 birds, trees TXT_6723/0_N2 ~~birds, tree's~~ fauna, flora TXT_6762/0_N2

13 building houses TXT_6723/0_N2 building architecture TXT_6762/0_N2

14 like a missing home. TXT_6723/0_N2

15 Follows: / Das Reich der Träumer / (H. Sassmann) / page 13 (unter) til page 14 (middle: Völker chemie [chemistry of peoples]) / then page 7 (Bei den zahlreichen [in the numerous] ...) till page 9 (oben) TXT_6723/0_N3 Kiesler includes these handwritten instructions for excerpts from the preface of Hanns Sassmann, *Das Reich der Träumer. Eine Kulturgeschichte Österreichs vom Urzustand bis zur Republik* [The Empire of Dreamers. A Cultural History of Austria from the Primal State to the Republic] (Berlin: Verlag für Kulturpolitik, 1932). Sassmann: Das Reich der Träumer p. 13–14 / p. 7–9 TXT_6710/0_N1-N3 In his preface, Sassmann addresses historiographic methodology and includes references to Egon Friedell's "ideological" conception of history in his *Kulturgeschichte der Neuzeit* [Cultural History of the Modern Era]. These paragraphs were neither translated nor mentioned in later drafts. See translation of the Kieslers' transcriptions included in the Addenda: Transcriptions and Translations, p. 368.

16 An earlier draft includes an alternative title and chapter list where Kiesler reverses the chapters on Garnier and Fourier. TXT_6781_N15 The same reversal of order occurs in a TS draft before the chapter on Garnier's sanatorium is ultimately crossed out. See TS with chapter number by Stefi and corrections by Frederick in fig. B.35). TXT_6767/0; TXT_6833/0_N5 Kiesler produced a series of illustrations for André Breton's book on Fourier, *Ode à Charles Fourier* (Paris: Éditions de la Revue Fontaine, 1947). On Garnier's unrealized projects for sanatoria, see Sanatorium Franco-Americain (1916–1917) for Lyon, and Sanatorium de Saint-Hilaire du Touvet (1923), as well as drawings of hospitals (1904/1917): Tony Garnier, *Une Cité Industrielle: ètude pour la construction des villes* (Lyon: Baise et Goutagny, 1919).

17 Plate 51 for *Magic Architecture* includes a reproduction of Taut's drawing titled "Eine Arbeitsgemeinschaft" [A working community], in *Die Auflössung der Städte oder Die Erde–eine gute Wohnung: oder auch: der Weg zur alpinen Architektur* (Hagen: Volkwang Verlag, 1920), plate 2.

18 Filarete of the thirteenth-century TXT_6781/0_N13; TXT_6728/0

19 they are ~~clearly~~ nothing else but the ~~lively expression~~ of man's desire for ~~a system or~~ order TXT_6781/0_N13-N14

fig. B.34

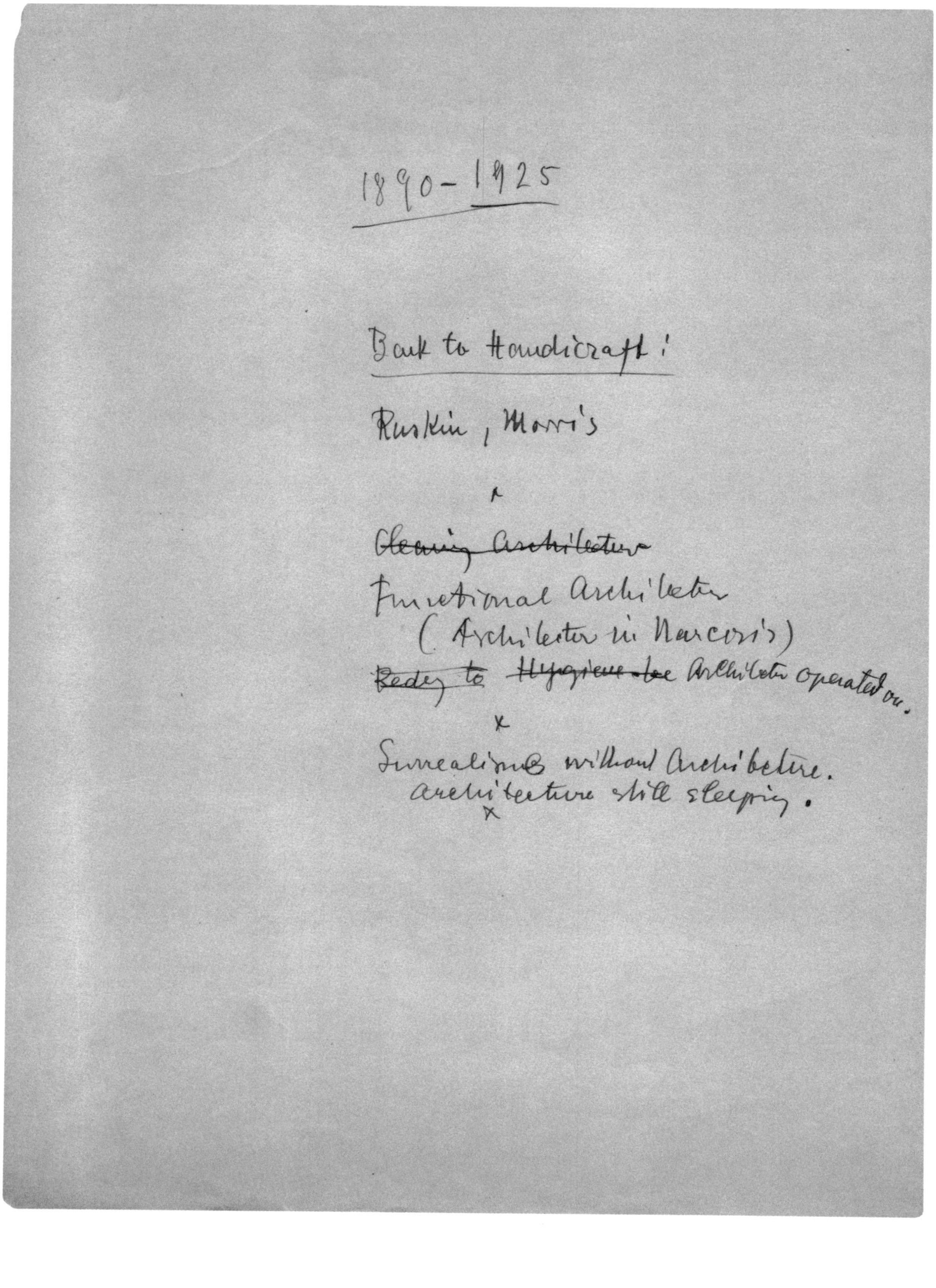

1890–1925

Back to Handicraft!

Ruskin, Morris

x

~~Sleeping Architecture~~

Functional Architecture
(Architecture in Narcosis)
~~Ready to Hygiene~~ Architecture operated on.

x

Surrealism without Architecture.
architecture still sleeping.
x

Frederick Kiesler, Part x (and former "Part VIII"), Preliminary draft on architectural developments in the period "1890–1925" (and beyond) with projected list of contents and associative notes: "Back to Handicraft: Ruskin, Morris … Functional Architecture (Architecture in Narcosis) … Surrealism without Architecture. Architecture still sleeping." partly related to contents of Part x (and "Part VIII" in earlier versions of the book manuscript) (MS, ink) ÖFLKS, TXT_6824/0_N3

fig. B.35

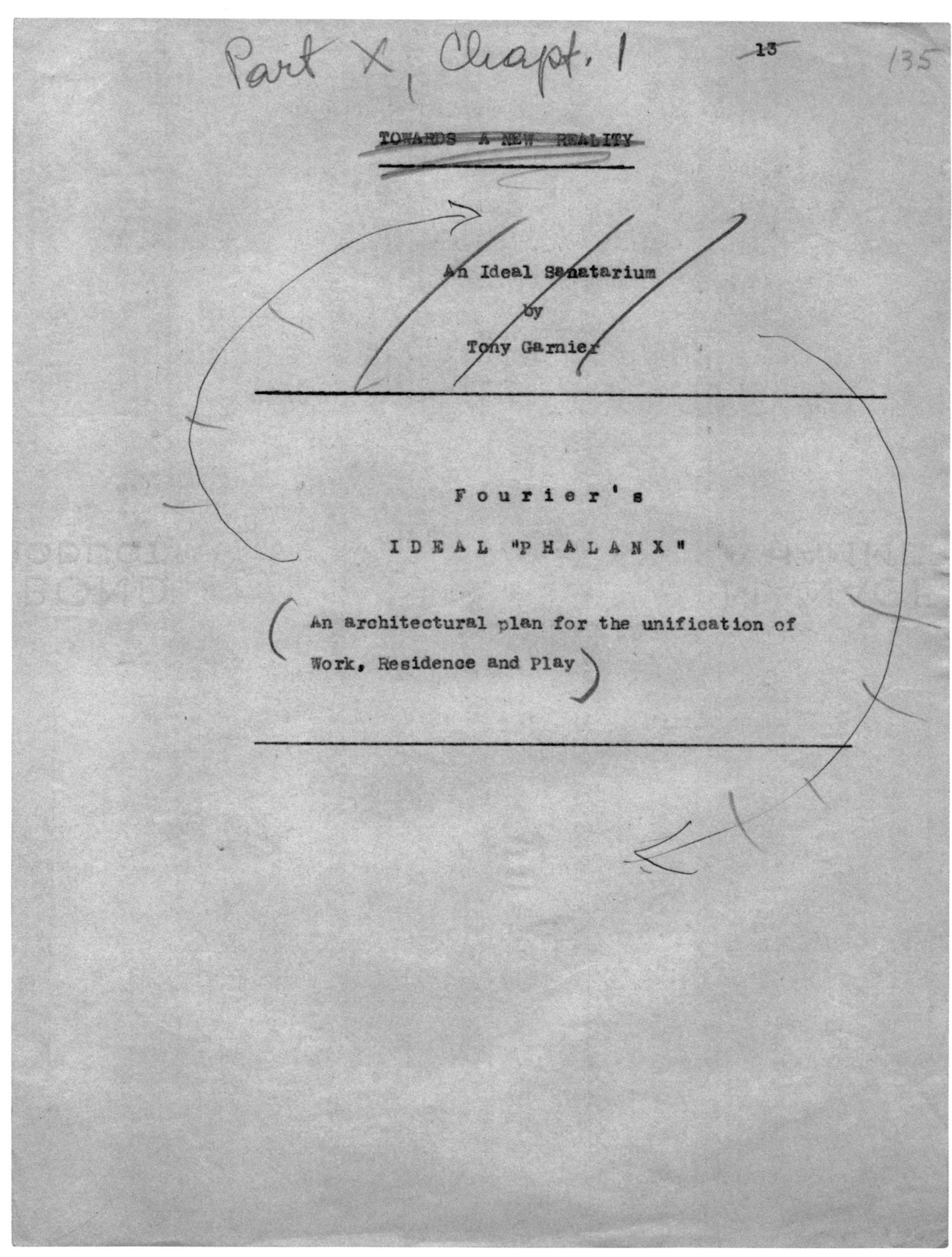

Part X, Chapt. 1 ~~13~~ 135

~~TOWARDS A NEW REALITY~~

~~An Ideal Sanatarium~~

~~by~~

~~Tony Garnier~~

Fourier's

IDEAL "PHALANX"

(An architectural plan for the unification of
Work, Residence and Play)

Frederick and Stefi Kiesler, Part x, Chapter 1, "Fourier's Ideal Phalanx," preliminary draft from an earlier version of the book manuscript with deleted title "TOWARDS A NEW REALITY," deleted chapter on "An Ideal Sanatorium by Tony Garnier" and reversal of chapter order by Kiesler (final chapter number noted by Stefi Kiesler) (TS, pencil, ink) ÖFLKS, TXT_6767/0

(51) page 272

vision

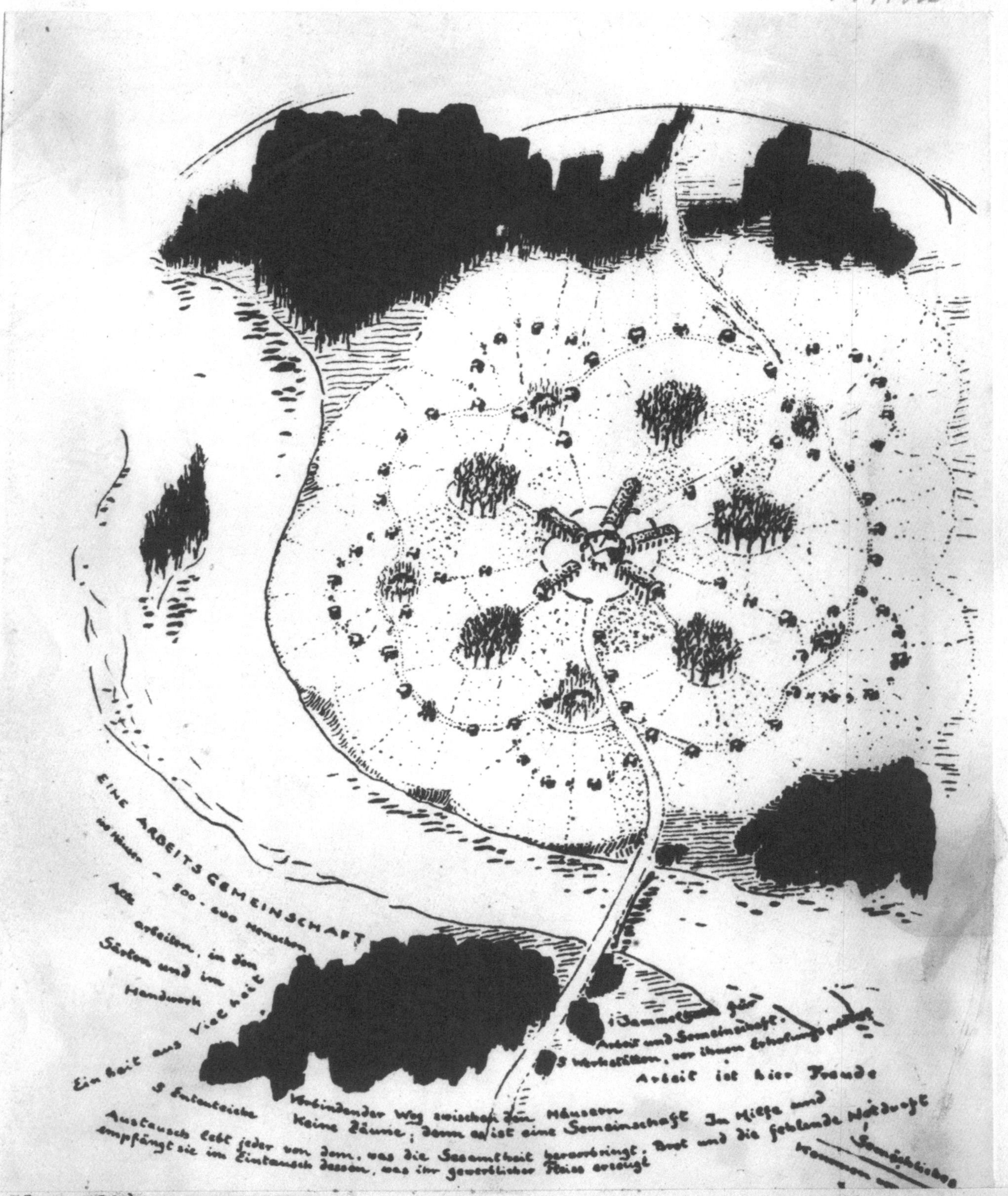

<u>(51, 51a, 51b). Page 272</u>

Left: Vision of a community where "work is joy" (early 1920's by Taut.)
Right; above: A large community, (New York) and existing fact, where work is physical and nervous strain.
Right, below: A plan of the 1930's, where a practical application of the experiences of vision and fact in building is demonstrated. More breathing space, more elbow-room, more greens; more privacy.

Fact

New Reality

(Quotations and Reproductions such as:

"Alpine Architecture"
"Dissolution of Cities":
new architectural forms out of new
"aims of life"[20]...)

CHAPTER 3
REACTION: BACK TO CLASSICISM[21]

(large sheet) pl. 52
Schinkel's project (1781)[22] for a Palace
of King Otto of Greece on the Acropolis.

Before the end of their earthly journey, very great men, even cynics like Voltaire, turned backward in a last, desperate attempt to get hold of some vision,[23] accredited by history;[24] they wanted to associate themselves with some light, if only an imaginary one, for the sake of ensuring their survival.[25]

In the South of Europe, Piranesi tried every possible stylistic cure to revive Italy's Architecture. In the North the more cold-blooded Schinkel clad his broken teutonic body in the one and only Chiton-toga that, for him, seemed to hold the guarantee for the continuity of glory: the Classic Greek.

Fortunately his project was never executed. His neo-classicism might have been a calming solution[26] for the frivolous North, but no one from anywhere outside of Greece may bring Greek Architecture to the Acropolis.

And that which was true in the past is true now and will always continue to be true.[27] The smallest chunk of marble from Greek earth is worth more to the revival of Architecture anywhere, than whole carloads of Phidian sculptures on pedestals in museums.[28]

Furthermore, no matter how studious, no matter how skillful and talented it may be, the Architecture of a previous period, revived for a contemporary expression, is not healthy and powerful enough to prevent the natural flow of the contemporary; in the best of cases it only serves as a short procrastination of the end.[29]

CHAPTER 4
MAGIC IN STEEL: THE EIFFEL TOWER[30]

[31]The religions derived from the "Supernature" of the skies, of the monuments of the earth and from giants and Holy men, have finally consumed the energy of their fire.[32] pl. 53

Artists, poets, architects escaped into the formalities of the Esthetics.[33] The public still wore rosaries, but in moments of danger science became more reliable than prayers.

Architecture became nothing but shell and skeleton dressed in period costumes. It was neither fact nor vision.

Neither Asia, nor Asia Minor, lusty suppliers of Prophets for many a century, nor the fruitful valleys of the Nile, nor the Greece of Athens or the Italy of Rome, nor any other peninsula of Europe, or the Mainland could create a new belief; it was dead on vision. Without a content Architecture was impossible.[34]

* * *

As some rivers[35] disappear underground and appear in far off regions to continue their flow, so the old will toward belief appeared unexpectedly in another continent, and burst into a geyser of dreams.[36] It was the Revolution of 1776 and the land–America.

Sixteen years later, in 1792, the French Revolution followed. The last Gods on pedestals fell. Man was alone, and was ready to take all responsibilities upon himself.

20 **(Quotations and Reproductions such as: / "Alpine Architecture" / "Dissolution of Cities" / "New Architectural Forms out of new Aims of Life" ... / ...)** TXT_5877/0_N203 The TS of the assembled version erroneously capitalizes all the words of the final phrase as if they were a different book title, similar to *Alpine Architecture* or *The Dissolution of Cities*. Kiesler's original MS includes a double colon after "Dissolution of Cities" which indicates that what follows is a quotation from or a reference to Taut's book and not a different publication: **Quotations and Reproductions such as: / "Alpine Architecture." / "Dissolution of Cities.": / new Architectural Forms / out of new "aims of life" ... / ...** TXT_6781_N14 See the statement in one of the handwritten texts accompanying Taut's drawing of *Wohnhäuser* [dwelling houses]: "Andere Lebensinhalte erzeugen andere Lebensformen" [Other life purposes generate other life forms], in *Die Auflösung der Städte*, plate 7. See also Taut, *Alpine Architektur* (Hagen: Volkwang Verlag, 1919). Neither of these early German volumes survive in Kiesler's library, which includes other publications by Taut, such as *Bauen–Der neue Wohnbau* (Leipzig/Berlin: Klinkhardt & Biermann, 1927) and *Fundamentals of Japanese Architecture* (Tokyo: Kokusai Bunka Shinkokai, 1936).

21 Alternative titles: **P. x. Ch. 3 / Reaction: Back to Classicism / NIGHTMARE BEFORE DEATH / Dawn.** TXT_6765/0_N1 **Actions and Reactions / a nightmare before Dawn / Schinkel's Project for a rebuilding of the Acropolis / ~~The~~ Abstract Magic of Steel / The Eiffel Tower** TXT_6708/0_N1-N2 These titles precede a typescript of this chapter, alternatively titled **Part III: Towards a New Magic Architecture.** The naming reflects an earlier organization of the book manuscript into three parts. Kiesler was apparently thinking of starting this third and final section on a "New Magic Architecture" with a chapter on the "return" to Schinkel's "classicism" followed by one on the Eiffel Tower. Ultimately, both chapters were incorporated in Part x.

22 **Nightmare before Death / Schinkel's Project (1781) for a Palace of King Otto of Greece on the Acropolis** TXT_6781/0_N6 The year in this MS is an error made during transcription; 1781 is the year of Schinkel's birth, and his project for the palace was developed in 1834. Ponten's survey includes a long section on Schinkel's "unbuilt" projects: "Ungebautes von Schinkel," in Ponten, *Architektur die nicht gebaut wurde* (1925), 1:82–89; 2:116-125 (figs. 202–216), including his project for the Palace of King Otto on the Acropolis, 1:83; 2:118 (figs. 210–211).

23 **Very great men ~~and~~ sarcasts ~~as~~ like Voltaire turned before the end of their earthly ~~life existence~~ backward in a last, desperate attempt to get ~~even~~** [illegible] **~~in self deceit,~~ hold of ~~something~~** TXT_6781/0_N6

24 **however short** TXT_6781/0_N6

25 **to associate himself with ~~for~~ an imaginäre survival.** TXT_6781/0_N6

26 **Fortunately ~~it was never built. He was a good architect. Perhaps~~ his neo-classism might have been a ~~temporary~~ calming solution** TXT_6781/0_N6

27 **And that held for then, holds for now, and ever.** TXT_6708/0_N3 **And that ~~what held for then held for now, and ever~~** TXT_6781/0_N7

28 **The smallest chunk of touched marble in Greece is more worth to the revival of Architecture anywhere, than whole carloads of Phidean sculptures on pedestals in Museums.** TXT_6781/0_N7

29 **And equally: no matter how ~~clever skillful~~ studious, no matter how skillful and talented, ~~no~~ Architecture of a previous period, ~~applied~~ is revived for a contemporary experience, it is not healthy and powerful enough to prevent the natural flow of the contemporary. It is deceit. And in the best cases only a short procrastination of the End.** TXT_6781/0_N7

30 Alternative chapter titles: **~~The~~ Magic in steel: The Tower by Eiffel** TXT_6708/0_N1: **~~The~~ Abstract Magic of Steel / The Eiffel-Tower** TXT_6781/0_N8 **MAGIC IN STEEL The Tower by Eiffel** TXT_6708/0_N5 **P. x, 4/1 MAGIC IN STEEL The Tower of Eiffel** TXT_6764/0_N1

31 The image of an illuminated Eiffel Tower at night (plate 53) is reproduced from Kiesler's newspaper clipping of the August 17, 1945, edition of the *New York Herald Tribune*. It bears the heading: "As Paris Celebrated the Surrender of Japan" and caption: "The Eiffel Tower illuminated by searchlights following the official announcement of Japan's surrender to the allies." See also Sources, Disciplines, and Objects, p. 62.

32 The first four paragraphs are numbered (1–4) in earlier drafts of this section. TXT_6781/0_N8; TXT_6708/0_N5 Numbers are eliminated in the final TS. TXT_5877/0_N206

33 **flüchteten sich in die Aesthetik** [sought refuge in Aesthetics] TXT_6781/0_N8

34 **~~From a far away land where pagan men / tribes / still murdered their fellow brother / kin / in pagan rituals, a new type of belief was born: the love ... for Everyman.~~** TXT_6781/0_N9

35 **Like some of the rivers ~~of the past~~** TXT_6781/0_N9

36 **so appeared the old will to ~~Vision~~ belief unexpectedly in another continent. ~~It was~~ and burst into a geyser of ~~visions~~ dreams.** TXT_6781/0_N9

(52). Large sheet

After the American and French Revolutions, ideas for better living conditions were inspiring the architects. Something new had to be done, but some designers turned back to classicism for inspiration and produced false ideals like this attempt to reconstruct the Acropolis, for the purpose of housing a German king.
(Project by Schinkel, 1781).

(53)

page 277

(53). Page 277

Magic in Steel

A new building material gave new possibilities in construction.
(The Eiffel Tower, Paris, France.

* * *

In the meantime a new material was processed into readiness for him–steel. The Eiffel Tower rose; the first building without hermetic enclosures–open.[37] It was a superfluous monument from the physio-functional point of view, but <u>the</u> very necessity for a link with the superfluous:[38] Art and Imagination.[39]

* * *

Soon another material developed into a state where it could stimulate more than shelter–glass. The building of the Crystal Palace followed. The transparency of walls freed the in and out for unrestrained contact. Architects became inspired engineers; engineers became architects. The spark of magic caught the imagination; new materials, new methods of construction, new social structures were devised.[40]

CHAPTER 5
THE CITY IN SPACE

("De Stijl" magazine, April 1925, by Kiesler)[41]

The new city will bring with it the solution of the problems of traffic and hygiene; make possible the diversity of private life and the freedom of the masses. It is not built to suffice in itself, but, by the strictest economy of means, to create the greatest possible abundance.

There will exist no longer houses dooming man, which shout at him: "Sleep well, eat well, and take a gasp of air now and then." And with the disappearance of houses conceived in this spirit, the streets of huddled cubes will be resolved into free living and working areas.

* * *

Compulsion directs the new form of the city:

> The Country-City:
> the division of city from country will be abolished.
>
> The Time-City:
> time is the measure of the organization of its space.
>
> The Space-City:
> it floats freely in space in a decentralized federation dictated by the ground formation.
>
> The Automatic-City:
> the processes of daily life are mechanized.

What are houses but coffins towering up from the earth into the air? One story, two stories–a thousand stories. Walled up on two sides, on ten sides. Stone entombed–or wood, clay, concrete. Coffins with airholes.

* * *

What interests everyone is: how does one LIVE among these curved or straight walls? From what sort of life, of NEW life, do these four or X faces arise?

Instead of ornament, plain walls; instead of art, facts[42]–these are your demands. But we must have organic building; the city in space; functional architecture: <u>Elasticity of Building adequate to the Elasticity of Living.</u>

37 See handwritten draft with sketch of the Eiffel Tower (fig. B.36): **all open ~~and a self-supporting network~~** TXT_6781/0_N10 **~~all~~ open throughout.** TXT_6708/0_N6

38 **A superfluous monument from a physio-functional point of view; but <u>the very necessity for hungry hope</u> for those who build.** TXT_6781/0_N10

39 **Art and Imagination** is a handwritten addition in the final TS and does not exist in any other draft. TXT_5877/0_N207

40 **social structures ~~for living together.~~** TXT_6781/0_N10

41 English translation of excerpts from Kiesler's early "Manifesto: Vital Construction, Space-city, Functional Architecture," first published as Frederick Kiesler, "Manifest. Vitalbau-Raumstadt-Funktionelle Architektur," *De Stijl* 10/11 (1924–1925): 141–146. Sections of Kiesler's spatial manifesto had previously appeared in English in his first book, *Contemporary Art Applied to the Store and its Display* (New York: Brentano's, 1930), 48. The translation of the original essay for both *Magic Architecture* and *Contemporary Art* is the same, with the addition of the final sentence on the "elasticity of building." See also Annotated Chronology, pp. 375, 397.

42 **Instead of art; ~~architecture~~ facts** [handwritten addition] TXT_5877/0_N209 Cf. the original text published in 1925: "Statt Kunst Architektur" [Instead of art, architecture] and Kiesler, "Manifesto," *De Stijl*, 146.

*

In the meantime a new material was processed into readiness for him: steel. The Eiffel-tower rose, a superfluous monument from a physio-functional point of view; but the very necessity for hungry hope for those who build.

Soon another material developed into a state were it could stimulate more than shelter: glass. The building of the Christalpalace followed. ⊗ Architects became inspired engineers; engineers became architects. The spark of magic has caught the imagination. New materials, new methods of construction, new social structures.

The first building without aesthetic enclosures, all open

⊕ The transparency of walls freed the ~~eye~~ in and out for unrestrained contact.

The Glass-Architecture-Novel
by
Paul Scheerbart
a writer describes the future habitation of mankind.

Frederick Kiesler, Page from the architect's notepad including preliminary drafts for Part x, Chapter 4, "Magic in Steel: The Eiffel Tower" and Part ix, Chapter 3, "Glass-Architecture by Paul Scheerbart" (ms, pencil) ÖFLKS, TXT_6781/0_N10

CHAPTER 6
THE DOUBLE-PERSONALITY OF THE SKYSCRAPER:[43] BUSINESS AND ART (SPECIAL ILLUSTR.)

The impetus of the new Idea was too primordial, too powerful. Over-enthusiasts,[44] misunderstanding, and reaction followed. The split in the dualism continued except that the Cathedral became the sky-scraper,[45] the home a sales-object.[46]

Architecture could not hold pace with business development. The results were veritable building-monsters. Without waiting for a contemporary concept to emerge, steel, stone, clay, wood, and glass were combined in haste[47] and heaped upon each other until they reached the sky.

The Woolworth Building, New York

The church wisely had planted the Cross[48] on top of its structures to put a reverent stop to its spires and keep them from reaching too high; it was not so with the skyscraper.[49] It borrowed the Church's ornateness but ended in a flat top; it was as if the skyscraper had become physically exhausted,[50] but then it always seemed to revive and with its last efforts convulsively clinched centuries of ritual buildings into one single miniature crown, and set it upon its own broad shoulders.[51]

Pseudo-Magic Crowns
of skyscrapers.

Illustrations[52]

Pyramid of Egypt or Aztec? Standard Oil Bldg., New York.	Gothic Church or Woolworth Bldg. New York?	Renaissance Colonnade with Persian spires or Grand Central Office Bldg.?	Campanile of Venice or Life Insurance Bldg., NY ?

* * *

The ancient Religion of Gods was finally replaced by the religion of goods. The question was not: to be or not to be; the question was: to have or not to have.

* * *

Once, leaders in design were the masters of their guild, when leadership was called for; now, the gods were replaced by half-gods, who, in ancient times were helper's helper.

* * *

Many designs of old master buildings were pirated to make them fit twentieth-century firms of architects;[53] many imperial graves of past periods were broken into and robbed of their relics. But these raiding parties were, and still are for the flow of the innermost trends, what the microbes are for the bloodstream. They are dangerous when they multiply too fast; they are death carriers.[54]

* * *

Through the first world war[55] Europe's revolutionary spirit became widespread. Freed from imperialism, tzarism, and monarchism, the populace began to plan on a large scale for the realization of better social systems,[56] and, logically, their every-day architects (in the past immune to progress)[57] designed better architectural orders.[58]

43 (Border–Monument of two worlds: / Business and Art / Mass and Individual.) [subtitle appears in handwritten manuscript] TXT_6709/0_N1

44 Overenthusiasm TXT_6781/0_N11; TXT_6709/0_N2

45 The cathedral ~~of Religion changed into~~ the skyscraper. TXT_6781/0_N11

46 The slumbering Dancers of the golden calf started to get up. [sentence excised in later typescripts] TXT_6781/0_N11; TXT_6833/0_N1

47 were combined to skip time TXT_6781/0_N11

48 The church had wisely put the cross ~~on~~ atop ~~of its spire~~ with reverence TXT_6781/0_N11

49 not so the skyscraper, and set it ~~himself~~ upon ~~his~~ broad shoulders. TXT_6708/0_N2

50 He borrowed the church ornat [sic], but ended in a flat (top) the result of exhaustion. TXT_6781/0_N11

51 Awakened, he clinched centuries of ritual building in a last effort into one single miniature crown and set it himself upon the ~~roof~~ shoulders TXT_6781/0_N11

52 Original drawing was reduced by fifty percent and pasted on the TS used for the assembled typescript. (fig. B.37) SFP_6662/0_N4; TXT_5877/0_N211. [The Magic crowns of skyscrapers] / The Tops of Skyscrapers / ~~The~~ Pyramid of Egypt or Aztec ? (The Standard Oil Blg. in New York.) / St. Peters or? (The life insurance Blg in New York) MS with original sketches of two historicist skyscraper crowns (fig. B.38) different from those of the four similar skyscraper crowns used in the assembled typescript. TXT_6781/0_N11-12 ~~Tops of Skyscrapers~~ Different set of small pencil sketches of historical building types and historicist skyscraper tops (fig. B.39). TXT_6768/0-N3 Mysteries of Sky Handwritten table with four building descriptions and alternate general title (fig. B.40). TXT_6768/0_N6

53 Many old master buildings were lynched to make them fit the prejudices of twentieth century ~~designer firms~~ TXT_6781/0_N16

54 They ~~bring death to the body~~. TXT_6781/0_N16

55 ~~After~~ the first world war TXT_6781/0_N14

56 Freed from ~~the~~ Imperialism, Tsarism, and Monarchism the populace ~~of most Europe~~ began on a large scale ~~to dream of~~ TXT_6781/0_N14

57 their everyday architects (always immune to progress) and engineers TXT_6781/0_N14

58 Freed from Imperialism, Czarism and Monarchism, the populace dreamed of new social–and logically of new architectural orders. TXT_6800/0_N1-N2 This is part of a preliminary MS outline on "twentieth-century developments" with an overview of some of the projects mentioned in Part X. For Kiesler's outline, see Addenda: Drafts.

fig. B.37

Frederick Kiesler, Part x, Chapter 6, "The Double-Personality of the Skyscraper: Business and Art," line drawing for "special illustration" titled "Pseudo-Magic Crowns of Skyscrapers," with sizing instructions for reproduction (pencil) ÖFLKS, SFP_6662/0_N3

fig. B.38

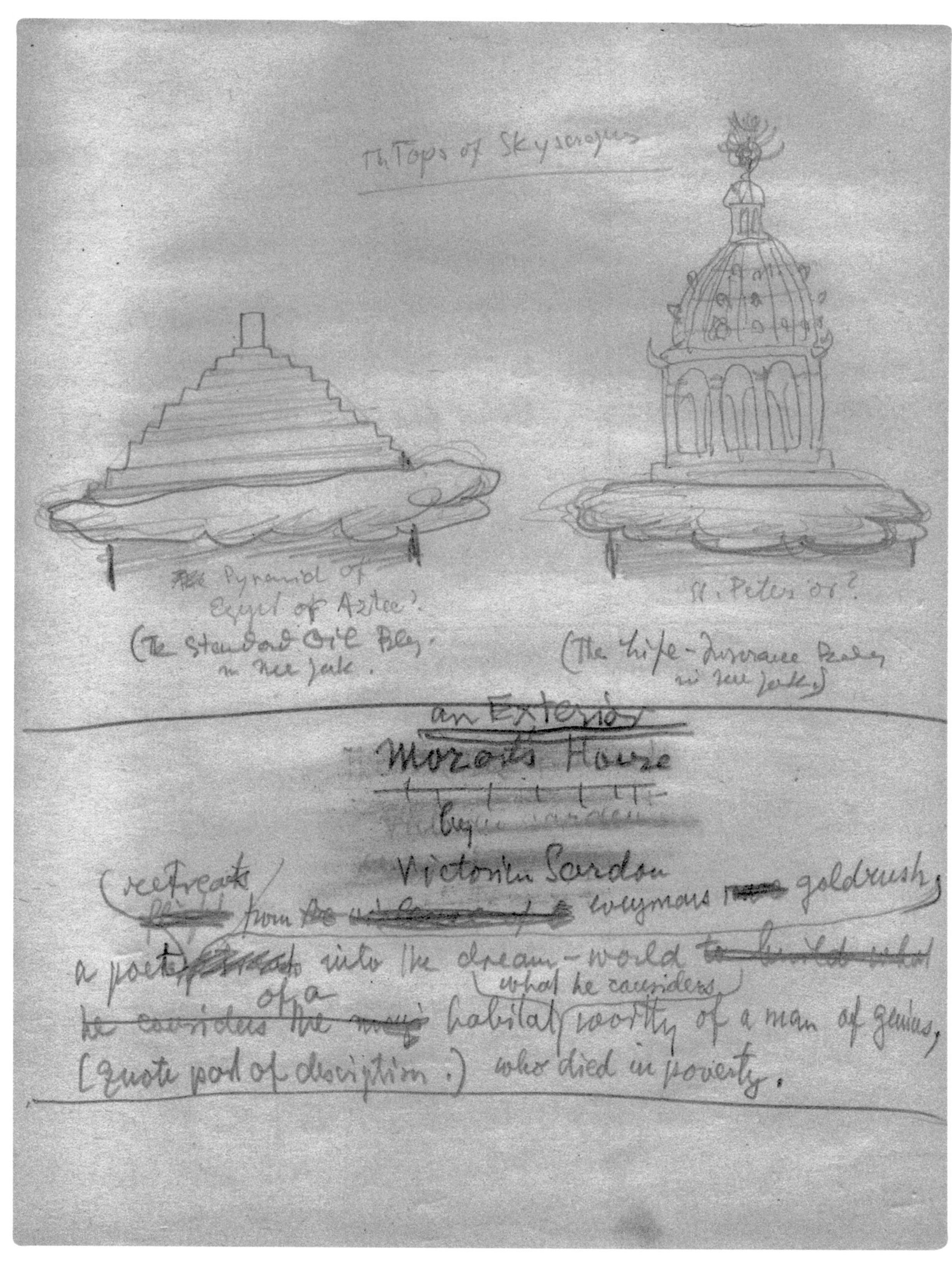

Frederick Kiesler, Page from the architect's notepad including preliminary sketches of "The Tops of Skyscrapers," related to Part x, Chapter 6, "Illustration" drawing (MS, pencil) ÖFLKS, TXT_6781/0_N12

10

into one single miniature crown, and set it upon its own broad shoulders.

(The Magic Crowns of Skyscrapers)

Tops of Skyscrapers

Illustr.

Illustr.

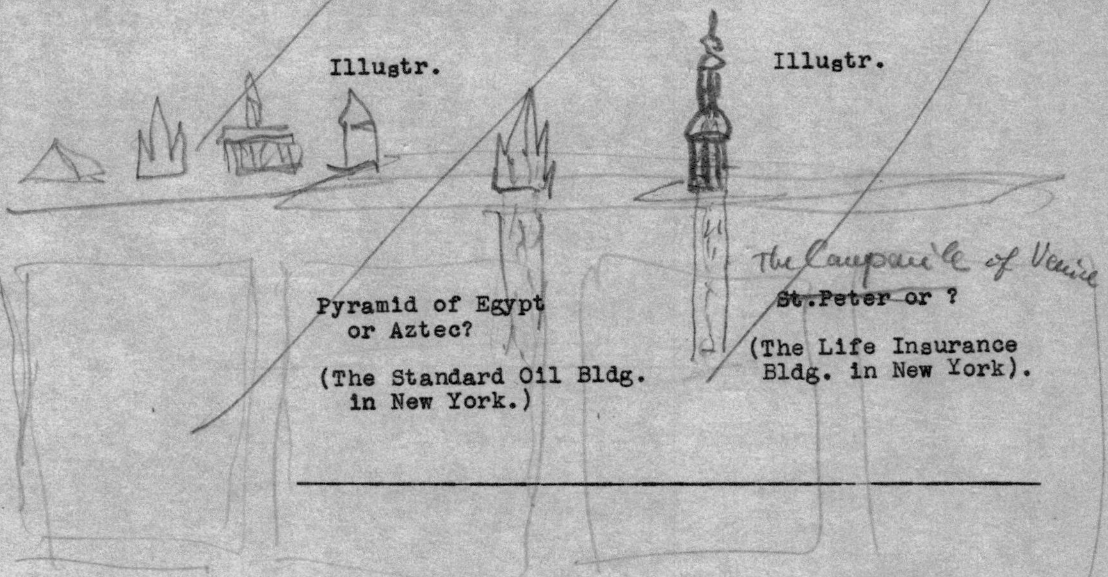

Pyramid of Egypt or Aztec?

(The Standard Oil Bldg. in New York.)

The Campanile of Venice

St. Peter or ?

(The Life Insurance Bldg. in New York).

Corrected?

Through the first world war Europe's revolutionary spirit became wide-spread. Freed from imperialism, tzarism and monarchism, the populace began to plan on a large scale for the realization of better social systems, and, logically, their every-day architects (always immune to progress) and engineers for better

Frederick Kiesler, Sketches for Part x, Chapter 6, "The Magic Crowns of Skyscrapers," ÖFLKS, TXT_6768/0_N3

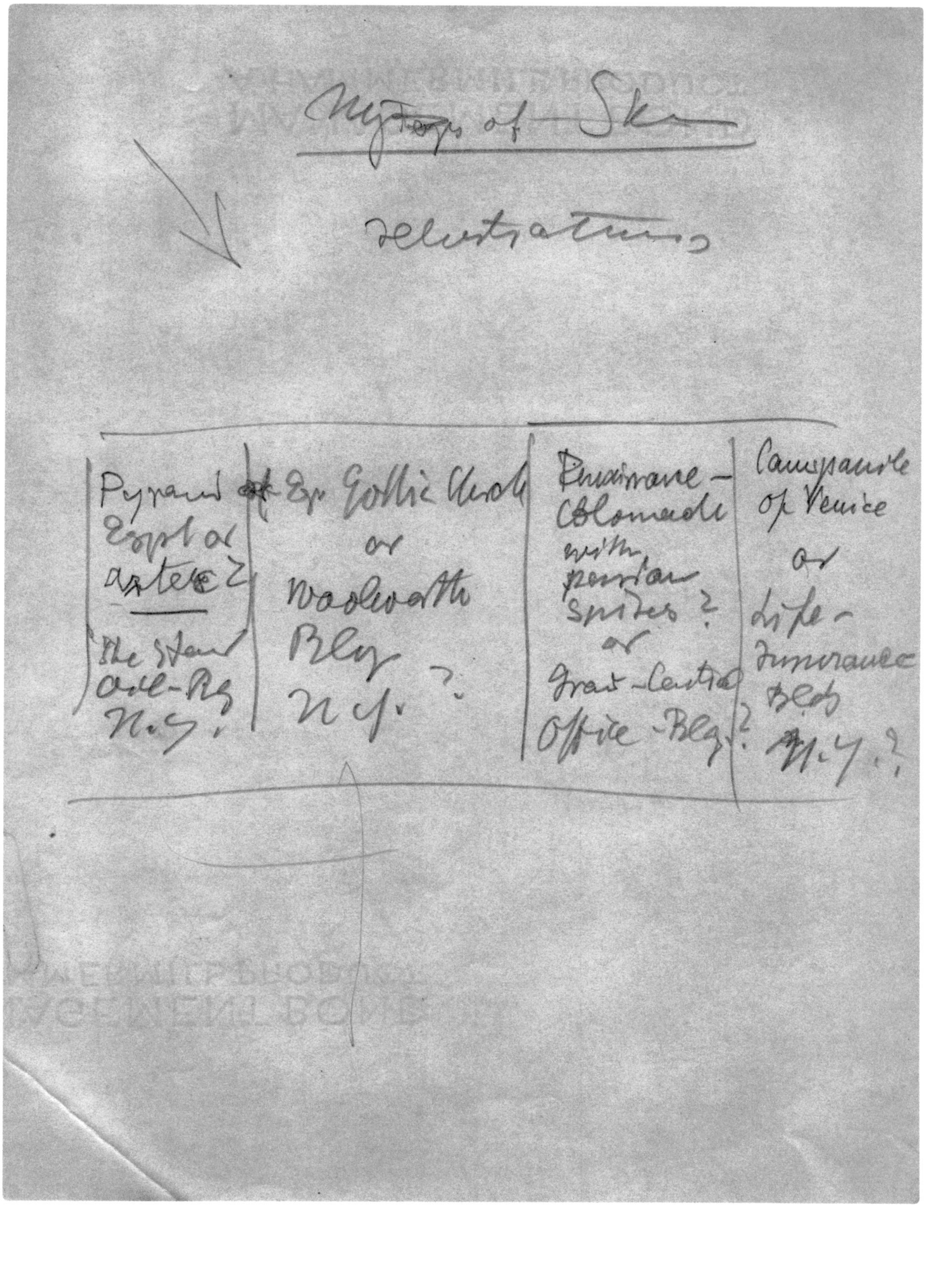

fig. B.40

Frederick Kiesler, Draft for Part x, Chapter 6, "NY Tops of Sky[scrapers] Illustrations," ÖFLKS, TXT_6768/0_N6

Business did not yet start to take full advantage of these awakening desires for wealth of "Everyman." Designs were still too related to dreaming to be profitable enough in comparison with the prevailing standards. They let individuals and small industries pioneer, demonstrate, and fail. They watched the delirious crowd. The opportunity to take over[59] came after the second world war.[60]

CHAPTER 7
REACTION: BACK TO HANDICRAFT: THE VICTORIAN ERA

To guard progress, men in England recommended a direct return to nature.[61] To live primitively and to build accordingly. They preached handicraft. (Ruskin, Morris). They established schools and theories of imitating the woodcarver, the silver smith, etc.;[62] they opposed the growing power of machinal production, the machine that seemed to them the very Anti-Christ of beauty. The confusion created by the new religion of "Men for Men"[63] was growing more and more complex. At the same time the miners of Wales got their first decent shelter to live in, by claims of the machine age. Here in the deepest dark of the mine-pit men were indeed working for men, and the belief in a better future had developed firmness.[64]

In the meantime the losing majority[65] above the ground redecorated their homes. They had hands and machines[66] turn out softest velvets, satins, plushes,[67] and laces to dress their homes. A queen, symbolized by her bloated figure,[68] the overstuffiness and superficial richness of this Victorian era[69]

* * *

The holy mask laid upon the cancerous growth of the tissues to assure healing, science finally [was] replaced by a knife, which went beyond the surface[70] and cut the parasite out of hiding.

In the dualism of Vision and Fact, science was resurrecting facts.[71] Vision was only retained as a stimulus to facts.

CHAPTER 8
HYGIENE OF FUNCTIONAL ARCHITECTURE[72]

In architecture, architects[73] cleaned buildings inside and outside of ornamental growths, intarsias of multiple materials, and construction. Simplicity was the aesthetics of the new beauty. Ornament was considered a crime (Loos) against economy and esthetics.[74] Functionalism was the goal. The human house was considered nothing else but a machine (Corbusier).[75]

CHAPTER 9
FLIGHT INTO THE DREAM WORLD OF SURREALISM (ART WITHOUT ARCHITECTURE)

It was after the First World War;[76] before the second was in progress, another European group developed a counter-action.[77] Starting in literature, it flooded into painting and sculpture, and into architecture by way of fantastic furnishings.[78] They did not design houses. In the dualism of Vision and Fact, surrealism[79] resurrected Vision. Fact was only retained as an ingredient[80] of man's subconscious. In truth, Vision should[81] create out of itself, automatically. The new esthetics were anti-machine. Man's house does not matter as long as his mind is sheltered by subconscious living.[82]

59 **The opening for taking over** TXT_6781/0_N15

60 Excerpts in the TS are copied from two different sections of Kiesler's MS notepad, which includes the initial chapter drafts of Part X. Between these two narrative parts is a list of contents for a section titled **Towards a New Reality** with three chapters: **Garnier**, **(Garden-Cities)**, and **Fourier** (see previous notes). TXT_6768/0_N3; TXT_6781/0_N14-N17

61 **To protect the body of progress, men in England tried even to recommend a direct return to nature** TXT_6799/0_N1 **guard of ~~the body against~~ progress** TXT_6860/0_N1

62 **u.s.f.** [etc.] TXT_6799/0_N1

63 **Maen for Man** TXT_6799/0_N1

64 **Here in the deepest dark of the mine-shacht** [shaft] **men were indeed working for man, and the belief in a better future had caught depth and firmness.** TXT_6799/0_N2

65 **the losing ~~bureaucrats~~** TXT_6799/0_N2

66 **they had ~~tools~~ and machines** TXT_6799/0_N2

67 **peluches** appears in the final assembled manuscript TXT_6694/0_N2 **plushes** in the original MS by Kiesler TXT_6799/0_N2

68 **her <u>aufgedunsene</u>** [bloated] **figure** TXT_6799/0_N2

69 **superficial richness of ~~her century~~. / */3 small countries carried against this sensual trend, the burden of truth. Holland through Berlage, Austria through ~~Wagner, Loos~~** [paragraph excised in the MS] TXT_6799/0_N2 On the omission of this paragraph, see Sources, Disciplines, and Objects, p. 72.

70 **The holy mask laid upon the cancerous growth ~~of the tissues~~ to assure healing was replaced by a knife which went beyond the ~~skin~~** TXT_6799/0_N3

71 In the **~~world~~ dualism of Vision and Fact science ~~relied on instruments~~** TXT_6694/0_N3

72 In manuscript TXT_6799/0_N3 and its corresponding typescript TXT_6860/0_N2, the text on hygiene immediately follows the last paragraph of chapter 7 without a break. A handwritten note was later inserted into the typescript: **Part x, chapter 8 The hygiene ...**

73 **Architecture did the same as science, that is retaining vision as a "stimulus to facts"** [see last sentence of previous chapter] TXT_6799/0_N3

74 On Kiesler and Loos, see Annotated Chronology, p. 376.

75 Cf. also handwritten chapter outline for Part X with the following headings: **~~Cleaning Architecture~~** / **Functional Architecture** / **(Architecture in Narcosis)** / **~~Hygiene~~** / **Architecture ~~Ready to be~~ operated on ... Surrealism without Architecture. Architecture still sleeping."** TXT_6824/0_N3 (fig. B.34)

76 **This was after the First World War** TXT_6799/0_N4; TXT_6860/0_N2 Here, Kiesler references the advent of hygiene, functionalism, and machinism in architecture covered in chapter 8. Earlier drafts show this paragraph as a continuation of chapter 7 (which also incorporated the text that would later appear as chapter 8 in the assembled manuscript; see previous note). A break was later introduced with the note: **Part x, chapter 9 Flight ...** TXT_6860/0_N2

77 **another European group ~~planted a new~~ counteraction** TXT_6799/0_N4

78 **by way of ~~new forms for furnishing~~ fantastic ~~interiors chiefly~~ furnishings.** TXT_6799/0_N4

79 **surrealism (this was the name of the movement)** TXT_6799/0_N4

80 **as a ~~stimulant~~** TXT_6799/0_N4

81 **~~act auto~~** TXT_6799/0_N4

82 **Man's House is anyone as long as his mind is sheltered by subconscious living.** TXT_6799/0_N4

CHAPTER 10
THE TWENTIETH CENTURY'S SECOND QUARTER: TOWARDS A NEW REALITY

pl. 54

(Claude-Nicolas Ledoux)[83]

The spiritual deflation of the Architecture of the nineteenth century in Europe and elsewhere was a rapid decline from the low level of eighteenth-century Rococo, which, at least, had retained the sensuousness of ornament.[84] By the nineteenth century, stone and wood had been carved out of their last possibilities—only the fringe remained.

Stone and wood, used by primitive man as found in nature, were later on subjected to crafty treatments to make them more pliable to man's will;[85] like certain animals, the two materials, were, so to say, more and more domesticated until they were slaves and learned to behave as obediently as live material ever can.[86]

To suppress the urge toward freedom of material—live or dead—man finally crushed it completely, destroyed its form and function, literally pulverized it.[87] With other natural products domesticated (such as milk, oil, and spirits), he hoped to form new plastics, materials that would be easier to control and would stand up and shelter him with less reluctance to obey his orders.[88]

The architect, the builder, and not least of all the inhabitants, will be confronted with materials, processes, and forms, which never existed[89] before in man's building history. Man has taken the last step in the artificiality of building-construction. How is he equipped to take the responsibility for such a new constellation?[90]

* * *

Claude-Nicolas Ledoux[91]

With the middle of the twentieth century, we, the inheritors of chaos, have, strangely enough, the very best of possibilities in our power to eliminate the barriers separating Vision and Fact,[92] to unify and intertwine them inseparably. Architecture will then have the magic life of exuberance.[93] Worship then will no longer be confined to religious structures, nor will industrial, agricultural, or administrative work places be dominated by the doom of economic necessity, but no matter where man exercises his will to life, natural and technological environment will be adequate, more than that, it will be stimulating in developing his maximum of creative productivity.

Man often has been close to the realization of such an "utopia";
pl. 55 this was last so in France at the end of the eighteenth century.[94] But "Investments" have always planted money deep into the roots of kingdoms and republics.[95] Every new law, meant for the equal distribution of the fruits of the revolution was transformed to permit profiteering.[96] Wars with their need for armament, clothing, and food, the prohibitive law importing merchandise from England, in short, every and all measures executed in the interest of the country, first by the Constituent, then the Convention, then the Committee of Public Safety, then the Directorium, could be used by Commerce[97] for its advantage; it was always possible to cut up the carcass for sale. In the midst of the bloody scenes of the Revolution "Commerce" sat at the harvest and cold bloodedly calculated the profits, earned by this or that new law passed by the head of power.[98] It had its agents everywhere, in the clubs, in the Convent, in the committees of safety and charity, among the delegates in the provinces, in the leading groups of army administration, in the leading groups of civilian administrations for the newly conquered provinces and cities—everywhere investment's profit[99] was enormous. Commerce celebrated orgies as never before, and hardly ever after. Great fortunes grew up faster than mushrooms; the spirit of speculation and commerce radiated

83 Alternative part number and titles: **PART III TOWARDS A NEW MAGIC ARCHITECTURE** TXT_6708/0_N2 **PART III TOWARDS A NEW MAGIC ARCHITECTURE** TXT_6781/0_N4 The following paragraphs (up to the section with the subheading Ledoux) initially formed an introduction to **Part III Towards a new Magic Architecture**. This would have been followed by the chapters on **Schinkel's Project for a Palace of King Otto on the Acropolis** and **Magic in Steel: The Tower by Eiffel**. This "final" chapter (Part x, chapter 10) in the assembled versions of the later manuscript is essentially a montage of a number of different fragments whose themes veer from the nineteenth and twentieth centuries back to the late eighteenth. On the reverse structure of this final chapter, see Sources, Disciplines, and Objects, p. 71.

84 **The spiritual deflation of the Architecture of the nineteenth century in Europe and elsewhere had naturally its inert expression in its plastic form with the Rococo—only the rim remained. ~~The firmness was gone~~.** TXT_6781/0_N4

85 **to make it more pliable for man's wishes** TXT_6781/0_N4

86 **as folgsam** [obediently] **as live material ~~can~~ ever ~~do~~ can.** TXT_6781/0_N4

87 **Man sensing that der Drang nach Freiheit selbst im toten Material noch zu lebendig ist um jede Art Revolte unmöglich zu machen** [the urge for freedom even in dead material is still too alive to make any kind of revolt impossible], **masked it finally completely, destroyed its form and function, ~~and~~ literally pulverized it.** TXT_6781/0_N4 Similar notes on the pulverization of material in the Rococo illustrated by Kiesler's own sketches can be found in the four-part "narrative outline" for the book manuscript, included in Addenda: Drafts.

88 **materials which will easier and with less reluctance obey his orders to stand up and shelter him.** TXT_6781/0_N5

89 **materials, processes, and forms, that is evident, which never existed** TXT_6781/0_N5

90 **a new ~~order?~~** TXT_6781/0_N5 **Primitive man found the material ready made for him (tools, hands, so the new man today finds it ready made.** This paragraph was enclosed in a rectangular frame deleted in later drafts TXT_6781/0_N5 The manuscript draft continues with the section **Nightmare before Death**, and the chapters on Schinkel and the Eiffel Tower.

91 **Claude-Nicolas Ledoux** [handwritten subheading added to the TS] TXT_5877/0_N216 While describing the events at the end of the eighteenth century including the aftermath of the French revolution, the rest of the text does not contain any specific references to Ledoux. However plate 55 includes two of Ledoux's projects (as well as a project by Lequeu) reproduced from Kiesler's copy of Emil Kaufmann, *Von Ledoux bis Le Corbusier: Ursprung und Entwicklung der autonomen Architektur* (Vienna: Rolf Passer, 1933). See Sources, Disciplines, and Objects, p. 72. In earlier manuscript and typewritten drafts, the following paragraphs until the end of chapter 10 appear *after* the various sections marked as "Epilogue" in the assembled manuscript. TXT_6798/0_N4-N6; TXT_6720/0_N4-N7 This is an additional clue that the final sections of the book manuscript were reorganized while others were omitted.

92 **the best possibilities in our power ~~to create out of the dualisms of wish and reality~~ to eliminate the barriers separating Vision and Fact ~~in Life~~** TXT_6798/0_N5

93 **Architecture will then have the Magic of a ~~century, which~~ life of exuberance. / ~~(Temple–Home)–Work–administration–communication–Recreation.)~~** / **~~Aristophanes and Voltaire~~** [headlines inserted in the middle of the page; see references to these two authors at the end of this chapter] **/ ~~The unification of the generic parts which constitute a society of today~~ Places of worship** TXT_6798/0_N5

94 **Last in France ~~after the~~ at the end of the eighteenth century~~; he missed it again~~** TXT_6798/0_N5verso

95 Kiesler writes "investment" in place of "capital." See Sources, Disciplines, and Objects, p. 62.

96 **~~Here too~~ Every new law meant ~~for liberation was transformed~~ for the equal distribution of the fruits of the Revolution was transformed into profiteering: ~~for~~ die Güter Konfiskationen, die Assignatenwirtschaft, das Maximum** [the confiscation of goods, the Assignat economy, the maximum] TXT_6798/0_N5 verso **confiscation of property, the workings of assignats, the maximums, the rationing** TXT_6720/0_N5 This text was omitted in the assembled typescript. TXT_5877/0_N216 Following the German words in his manuscript draft, Kiesler calls for a quotation without mentioning the title of the book: **quote: from Book page 15 and 16** (which might suggest a possible source for the text above). TXT_6798/0_N5verso Kiesler's library includes the memoirs of the French Revolution by Nicolas-Edme Rétif, or Restif de la Bretonne in a German edition: Rétif de la Bretonne, *Revolutionsnächte* (Munich: Hyperionverlag, 1920).

97 **~~capital understood to use it~~** TXT_6720/0_N5 Kiesler often uses expressions such as "commerce" or "investment" to avoid references to "capital." See Sources, Disciplines, and Objects, p. 62.

98 **this or that new law of the ~~power~~ heads.** TXT_6720/0_N5

99 **everywhere ~~capital's interests~~** TXT_6720/0_N5

(54)

(54). Page 293

Utopias of the Machine age - not built.
(Left top) The so-called "Horizontal Skyscraper", a terraced building, which provides every family of a community of 500 families, with indoor and outdoor living quarters, recreation facilities for grown-ups and for children, cooperative stores, restaurants etc. A small town in one building, where costs of building and maintaining it are reduced to a minimum.
(By Kiesler, New York, 1931)

The horizontal Skyscraper. (Kiesler)

(Below, left) The heart of Paris razed and rebuilt as an ideal business center. Skyscrapers take the place of many streets of small slum-houses, and create in wide spacing from each other a city of much air, sunshine, gardens and speedways.
(Le Corbusier, Plan Voisin, Paris, 1925.)

the ideal Business-City (Le Corbusier)

Utopias

page 293

he Machine-Age.

Skyscraper in Glass, Steel and Copper.
(F.L. Wright)

(55)

(55). Page 296

Two dream houses of an architect in search for Magic Architecture, but not yet found.
(Left) Villa with observation tower.
(Right) House for a Forester. (Below the section through the house showing arrangements of floors and rooms inside.)
(Ledoux, France, 1755).

Dream-House II.
by Ledoux

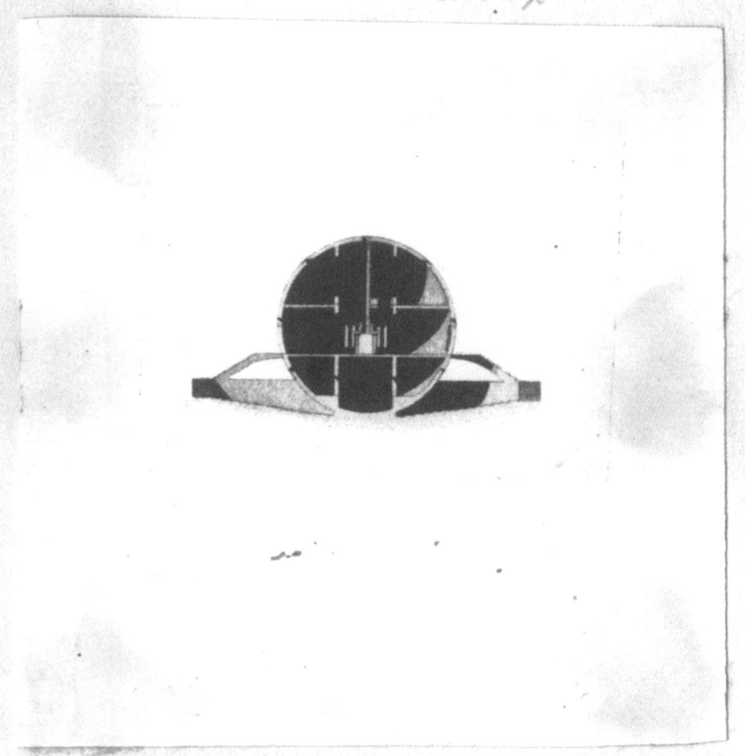

(Section of plan)

further and wider, and controlled and ruled the entire public and private life of men.[100]

And as one was forced, during the Revolution, to live externally in very simple, economic, and virtuous ways, just as the virtuous principles of a Rousseau demanded it, so now the long artificially frustrated thirst for pleasure burst out and was addicted to love with such eccentricity as the "ancient régime" under Louis xv, and the Court of Versailles never practiced.

Then came Napoleon,[101] and the Sons and Daughters of the Revolution again became soldiers for an Emperor-Dictator. And the stampede of their military exercising buried deeper and deeper into the ground their own heroes who tried to liberate them from the obsession of [possession at] the knife's edge of the Guillotine.[102]

It might well be, that up in the skies of history Aristophanes, who watched with satire the rise of Greece's democracies,[103] is now inviting Voltaire, who watched his time with skepticism, to[104] take a slow flying walk-around the Earth,[105] to observe peoples, who again have started a march on Peace through an even greater Arc de Triomphe of hardened Blood, the size of which, they, good students of social might well be disturbed by a strange noise pulsating from an enormous Architecture,[106] never heard of before. Somewhere along their route, their whisper might well be disturbed by a strange noise pulsating from an enormous silvery bird.[107]

Our wise men think they dream.

The men inside the bird, do not; they are flying.[108]

Their ancestors had dreamed about it for thousands of years,[109] talked, wrote, experimented, and always failed. This generation did it.[110]

And equally will they, not because of, but in spite of our civilization, and with it, transform the habitats of man, of this cosmic island into magic Architecture.[111]

~~Finis~~[112]

100 ~~all bearings~~ of men. TXT_6720/0_N5

101 Then came Napoleon. TXT_6798/0_N5verso

102 And the stampede of their military exercising buried deeper and deeper into the ground, the heroes, their own, who tried to liberate them from the obsessions of possession. / the edge of the guillotine [last phrase added on the margin] TXT_6798/0_N6 who tried to liberate them from the obsession of possessions ~~to~~ at the knife's edge of the Guillotine. TXT_6720/0_N6 who tried to liberate them from the obsession of the knife's edge of the Guillotine. TXT_5877/0_N219

103 The following paragraphs are not transcribed in any of the assembled versions of the book manuscript. They first appear in the MS TXT_6798/0_N6recto-verso and are then transcribed in two TS drafts: TXT_6720_N5-N6; TXT_6769/0_N3 This last document is an "incomplete" typescript draft of chapter 10 of Part x in which the paragraphs beginning with Aristophanes and Voltaire follow the paragraph on Napoleon. They are ultimately crossed out and do not appear again in later transcriptions of the same chapter (fig. B.41). For the original MS drafts, see figs. B.42a–b.

104 ~~to talk things over back down~~ TXT_6798/0_N6

105 ~~Globe~~ TXT_6798/0_N6

106 good students ~~of the past~~ TXT_6798/0_N6

107 ~~Their murmurs~~ Somewhere along their ~~walk~~ route, ~~of walk~~ their whisper might well be disturbed by a strange noise pulsating from an enormous ~~silver~~ silverous Bird. TXT_6798/0_N6recto-verso

108 The men inside the bird ~~did~~ not ~~dream~~; they ~~were~~ flying. TXT_6798/0_N6verso

109 millions of years TXT_6798/0_N6verso

110 The ~~youngest~~ generation ~~won.~~ TXT_6798/0_N6verso

111 in spite of ~~and~~ our ~~technological inventions~~, and with ~~them~~ transform ~~our~~ habitats of this cosmic island into ~~the~~ magic Architecture [followed by excised and illegible words] (fig. B.42b) TXT_6798/0_N6verso

112 The word **Finis** hovers at the bottom of the penultimate page of this handwritten draft (see fig. B.42a) and is not transcribed in any of the typescripts. Yet it could serve as a clue that Kiesler was considering, at some point, to end this final chapter and perhaps his book manuscript with this cross-temporal dream narrative. TXT_6798/0_N6recto

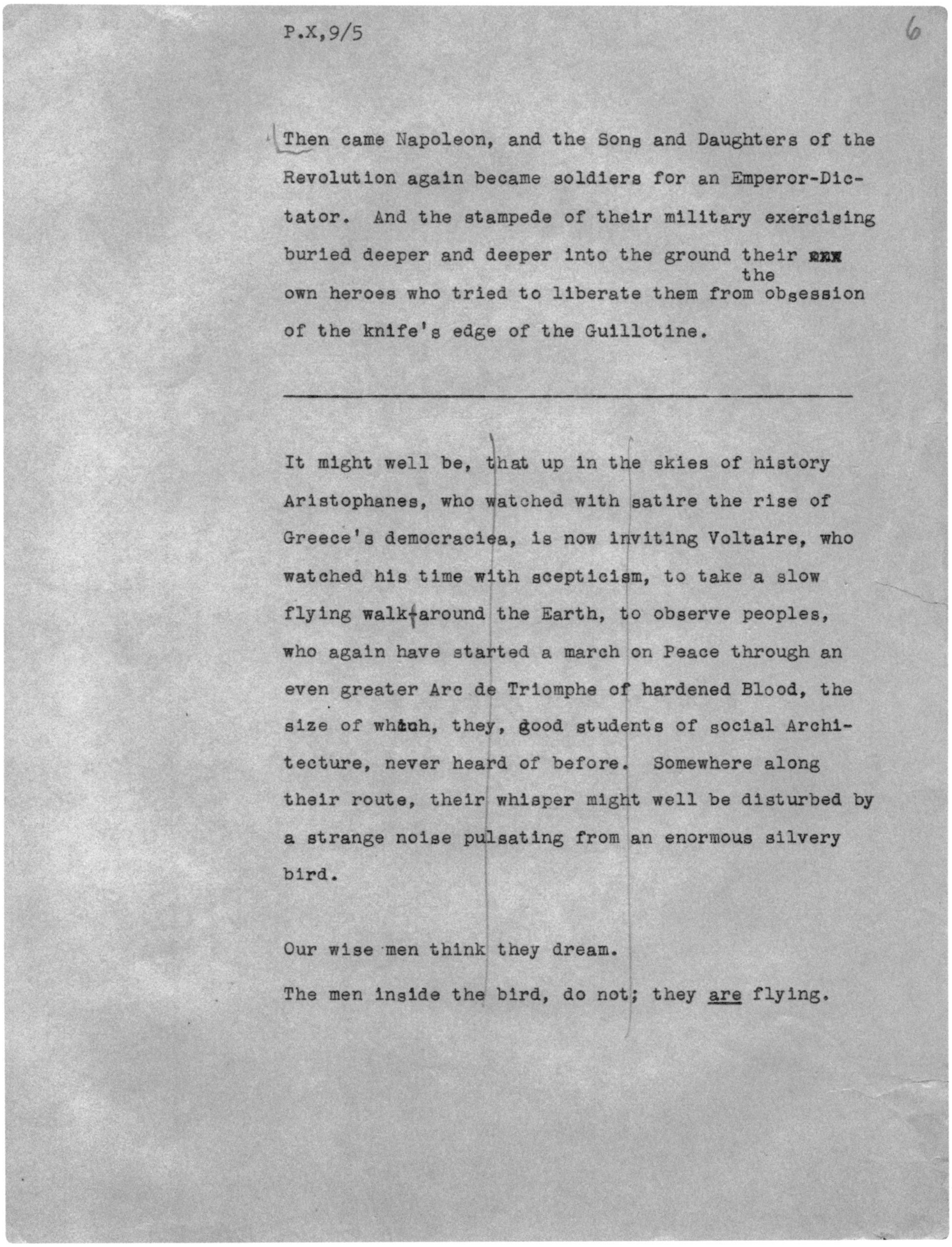

P.X,9/5 6

Then came Napoleon, and the Sons and Daughters of the Revolution again became soldiers for an Emperor-Dictator. And the stampede of their military exercising buried deeper and deeper into the ground their xxx own heroes who tried to liberate them from the obsession of the knife's edge of the Guillotine.

It might well be, that up in the skies of history Aristophanes, who watched with satire the rise of Greece's democracies, is now inviting Voltaire, who watched his time with scepticism, to take a slow flying walk around the Earth, to observe peoples, who again have started a march on Peace through an even greater Arc de Triomphe of hardened Blood, the size of which, they, good students of social Architecture, never heard of before. Somewhere along their route, their whisper might well be disturbed by a strange noise pulsating from an enormous silvery bird.

Our wise men think they dream.

The men inside the bird, do not; they are flying.

Fredrick Kiesler, Draft for Part x, Chapter 10 [former Chapter 9], starting with the phrase: "Then came Napoleon", including deleted final paragraphs (ts, pencil) ÖFLKS, TXT_6769/0_N2

9

of the Revolution became again Soldiers for an Emperor-Dictator. And the stampede of their military exercising boried deeper and deeper into the ground, the heroes, their own, who tried to liberate them from the obsessions of possession.

the cage to guillotine & of the

It might well be, that up in the skies of history Aristophanes, who watched with satire the rise of Greece's democracy, is now inviting Voltaire, who watched his time with skepticisme, to take a slow flying walk around the Earth, to observe peoples, who again have started a march to Peace through an even greater Arc de Triumph of Hardened Blood, the size of which they, some good students of some Architecture never heard of before. Somewhere along their route, their wisper, might

Frederick Kiesler, Preliminary draft for the concluding section of Magic Architecture (eventually Part x, Chapter 10) with paragraphs deleted from later versions ÖFLKS, TXT_6798/0_N6recto

fig. B.42b

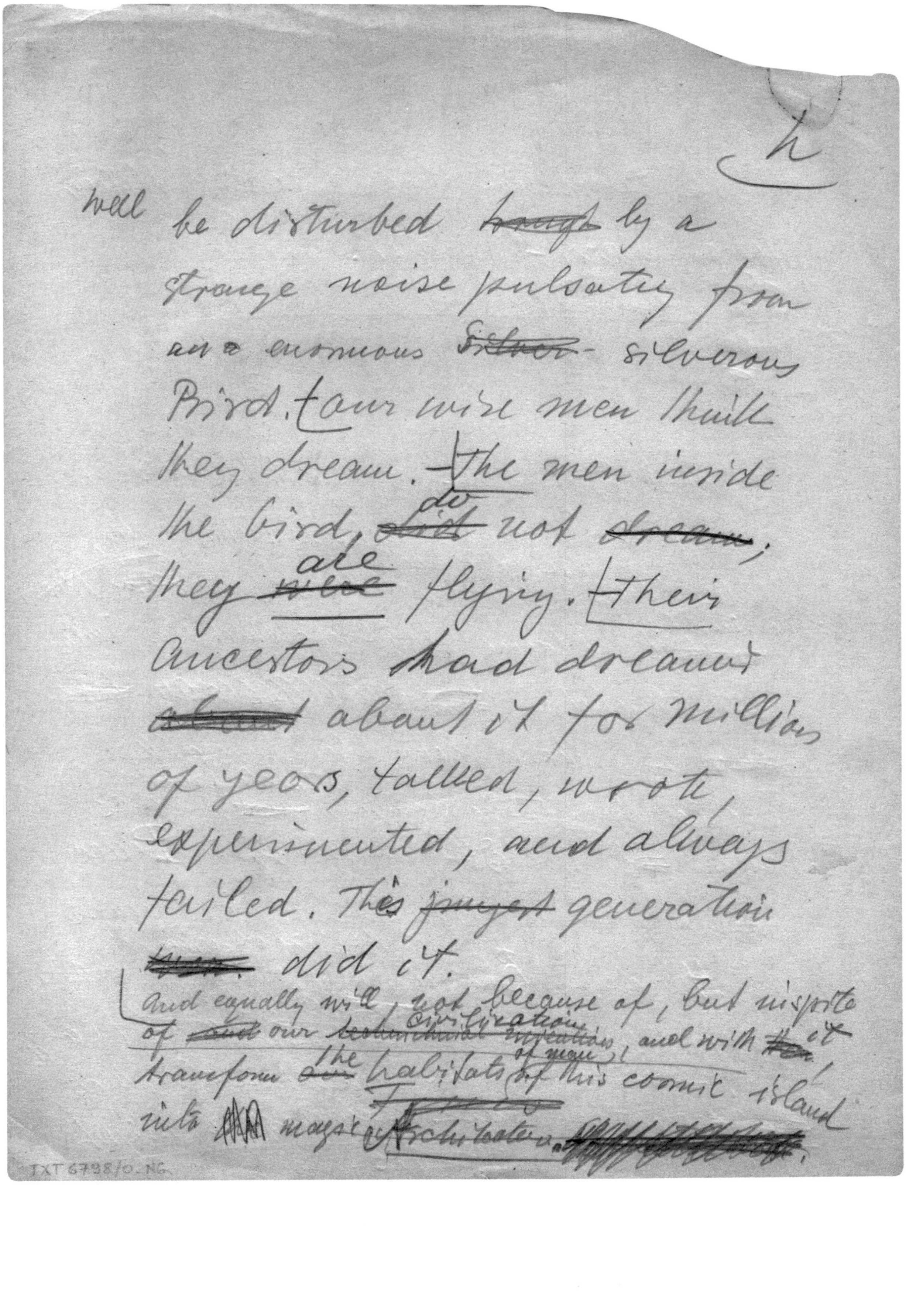

4

will be disturbed by a strange noise pulsating from an enormous silverous Bird. Our wise men think they dream. The men inside the bird, do not; they are flying. Their ancestors had dreamed about it for millions of years, talked, wrote, experimented, and always failed. This generation did it.

And equally will, not because of, but inspite of our civilization, and with it transform the habitats of man of this cosmic island into magic Architecture.

TXT 6798/0_N6

Frederick Kiesler, Frederick Kiesler, Preliminary draft for the concluding section of Magic Architecture (eventually Part x, Chapter 10) with paragraphs deleted from later versions ÖFLKS, TXT_6798/0_N6verso

EPILOGUE AND PROLOGUE[113]

MAN'S SHELTER BECOMES MAGIC ARCHITECTURE pl. 55x

Between the two world wars, Russia as well as the United States defined their interpretation of freedom. With regard to housing Russia put the preponderance of desirability on the collective, the United States upon the individual house.[114] America, having won the first war, could go forward into realization; Russia, defeated, could only trail her ideals. After the second war, both were victorious, and both are expected to pursue Architecture into a state of utmost satisfaction of their ideals.[115]

All important to a new Architecture is the fact that no matter what the tactics and techniques of present-day planning are, the basis for a new social belief has been expanded from the confines of little Greece of 500 B.C. to the wide extent of all the nations of the globe.[116] The effects of the social revolution in America and Europe, and the two world wars have steadily increased the radius of contact among different nations and races of this earth.[117] Just as social barriers[118] between different economic groups begin to disappear, so it may be hoped that psychological barriers to understanding between different peoples of the world may be reduced to insignificance.[119]

Not last among the considerations is the evolution of technology which helped to bring about such contacts. From the communication by word of mouth of tribal-time through phonetic and visual symbols to printing,[120] from morse-code to wireless, communication and information has become immediate. Resistance to verbal contact over wide Space and Time has been overcome, and resistance to visual contact over wide areas will soon be overcome by television.

We all must realize that "buildings" cannot become "Architecture," which is a fusion of Vision and Fact, unless Vision[121] first has been established, firmly rooted and kept alive.[122]

SECTION ONE[123]
AS TO FACTS

Building-methods from handicraft to industrial manufacturing have progressed to a degree where the barrier to ownership and price is being gradually brought down (prefabricated houses.)[124]

SECTION TWO
AS TO MATERIALS AND MECHANICS[125]

The solidity of the monolithic homes[126] of pre-history finally has developed into the transparency of plastics and nettings, making the transformation of densities (walls) a matter of easy control for contact of individuals or their isolation.[127] (The Space-House).[128] pl. 56

SECTION THREE
AS TO DESIGN

The interchange of the indoor and the outdoor in homes has been pioneered since the turn of the century in many a plan and building. pl. 57
The aim is to overcome a priori a separation of nature and house (Le Corbusier: Pavilion, Paris; F. L. Wright, USA, Adolf Loos.)[129]

SECTION FOUR
AS TO EQUIPMENT pl. 58

The American dogma of mass production[130] has always called for a service-design to reduce physical labor in Home and Factory to an ever growing minimum. American industry has, in the large,

113 Part TEN ~~Chapter 9:~~ EPILOGUE and Prologue [handwritten addition] / ~~Shelter becomes Architecture~~ / Man's shelter becomes Magic Architecture. TXT_6861/0_N1 Part X / Chapter 9 / ~~Introduction~~ / ~~Modern times~~ / ~~(Future)~~ / / Epilogue? / Fuller / Kiesler TXT_6720/0_N1 This manuscript title sheet, with its various titles of "introduction" and "epilogue," speaks for the reversible logic of organization in Kiesler's textual montage, in which the end can also function as beginning, and the same text serves as both "epilogue" *and* "prologue," resulting in an "endless" structure. (fig. B.43)

114 Russia put the preponderance on the collective, the United States on the individual Home. TXT_6798/0_N1 Cf. Kiesler's design for an exhibition on American architecture sent to the USSR by the National Council of American-Soviet Friendship, 1944-45. See Annotated Chronology, p. 378 and Sources, Disciplines, and Objects, pp. 35, 74.

115 After the second war both were victorious ~~re-organized~~ and both are expected to pursue architecture from year to year into a state of utmost satisfaction of her ideals [that is, architecture's ideals; not those of Russia and the United States as it appears in the text of the assembled manuscript] TXT_6798/0_N1

116 ~~The growth of discords of this growth in contact is by now, from the small beginnings of Greece of 500 b.c. world wide.~~ TXT_6798/0_N2

117 first the social Revolution in England and Russia, and second: the two world wars have steadily increased the contact among different nations and Races of this earth ~~globe.~~ TXT_6798/0_N1-N2

118 ~~the economic~~ barriers TXT_6798/0_N2

119 might disappear finally TXT_6798/0_N2

120 to ~~mobil~~ printing TXT_6798/0_N2

121 a Vision TXT_6798/0_N3

122 ~~Throughout all ages Individuals have carried "Ideas"~~ ~~(The Endless.~~ Kiesler: The Endless) [paragraph with reference to Kiesler's projects excised] TXT_6798/0_N3

123 In Kiesler's handwritten manuscript, the paragraphs describing technical "facts," "materials," "design," and "equipment" are part of a continuous text following the previous section of his epilogue with no individual headings. TXT_6798/0_N3 In a later TS, Kiesler writes section on the margin of each paragraph, indicating that each one should become a different programmatic section. TXT_6798/0_N3

124 where the barrier of price to ownership is being gradually ~~reduced~~ brought down. (Prefabricated House.) TXT_6798/0_N3

125 As to materials / and mechanics [handwritten insertion] TXT_6798/0_N3

126 ~~walls~~ houses TXT_6798/0_N3

127 making ~~transformation rooms~~ the transformation of walls into vistas a matter of easy control of contact or isolation. TXT_6798/0_N3

128 (The Space Haus–Kiesler) TXT_6798/0_N3 Cf. Kiesler's "Space-House" exhibition model for Modernage Furniture Company, New York, 1933 and related published essays: "One Living Space Convertible into Many Rooms," *Home Beautiful* 44, no. 1 (January 1934), 32–33, and "Notes on Architecture. The Space House. Annotations at Random." *Hound & Horn* 37 (January-March 1934): 292–297.

129 The aim: to overcome a priori separation of nature and house. (Le Corbusier: Pavilion, Paris.) TXT_6798/0_N4 Wright and Loos are missing from the initial MS draft and its transcription in the TS TXT_6720/0_N3 Their names are handwritten in later typescripts: F. L. Wright, USA TXT_6861/0_N3; Adolf Loos TXT_5877/0_N223

130 The American dogma of mechanization [handwritten addition] TXT_6720/0_N4

progressed in this respect rapidly,[131] and has the lead over all other nations.

(Service tower in Fuller's Dymaxion)[132]

SECTION FIVE
SCIENCE AND ARCHITECTURE[133]

A Laboratory Test of Biotechnical Design

The new method of approach to design problems, called Biotechnique, was developed in the last ten years at the architectural "Laboratory for Design-Correlation" of Columbia University.

Biotechnique is based on investigations of the interrelationships of natural and man-made organisms, with particular reference to human housing.[134]

Perhaps the simplest way to explain its meaning is to say that it deals with the incapacity of society to provide and sustain a healthful and healthy Shelter for each of its members and to deal adequately with these demands for all income levels.

As an outgrow of the laboratory studies, a Mobile Home-Library has been built to test the validity of the new design approach. It has proven very satisfactory.[135]

Although the study deals with the problem of book-storing in the home,[136] the methods of investigation employed are valid for all
pl. 59 building-cells in architecture.[137]

* * *

The result proved organic fusion[138] between the physiological and psychological demands.

The mechanical solutions form an integral part of highly developed functions. The effect is, with its elements of surprise and transformation, truly magic.

* * *

(illustrated with drawings of types of houses of the future)[139]

APPENDED:

pl. 60 1 A Metabolism-Chart of the Mobile Home-Library.[140] It analyzes the effects of technological environment upon man, particularly as a stimulant to higher productivity and as a factor in reducing fatigue moments.

2 Plan, elevation, and construction-details of the Mobile Home-Library.

3 Chart of the four standard types in manufacturing products.

131 ~~It is leading all in that respect, with the aim to free human energy~~ for American Industry mostly progressed in this respect TXT_6720/0_N4

132 Fuller's: Dymaxion TXT_6720/0_N4 Service timer in Fuller's Dymaxion [handwritten addition] TXT_6861/0_N3

133 Alternative title: Part x. follows Epilogue / <u>Section five: Science and Architecture</u> [handwritten addition] TXT_6842/1_N1 This fifth section of the epilogue does not exist in the MS draft containing the first four sections. TXT_6798/0_N3-N4

134 with particular reference to human housing. [handwritten addition] TXT_6842/0_N1; TXT_6842/1_N1

135 ~~It has proven very satisfactory.~~ [crossed out by hand in the TS] TXT_6842/0_N1

136 the problem of books in the home TXT_6842/0_N1; TXT_6842/1_N1

137 See also an annotated drawing of the "Mobile Home-Library" by Kiesler included among the preliminary material for *Magic Architecture* with note by Kiesler Include <u>Biotechnique</u> and descriptions of some of its mobile features: Dream-curtain / Reading-Light / reading - lounge with Book - table. SFP_6658/0

138 the result is a perfect fusion TXT_6842/0_N1; TXT_6842/1_N1

139 In other typescripts the phrase in brackets is missing. TXT_6842/0_N2; TXT_6842/1_N2 Kiesler's plates (54, 56, 59) contain images of several of his own projects including the "Mobile Home-Library" designed and built by his Laboratory for Design Correlation at Columbia University (plate 59).

140 ~~is attached.~~ TXT_6842/0_N2; TXT_6842/1_N2

fig. B.43

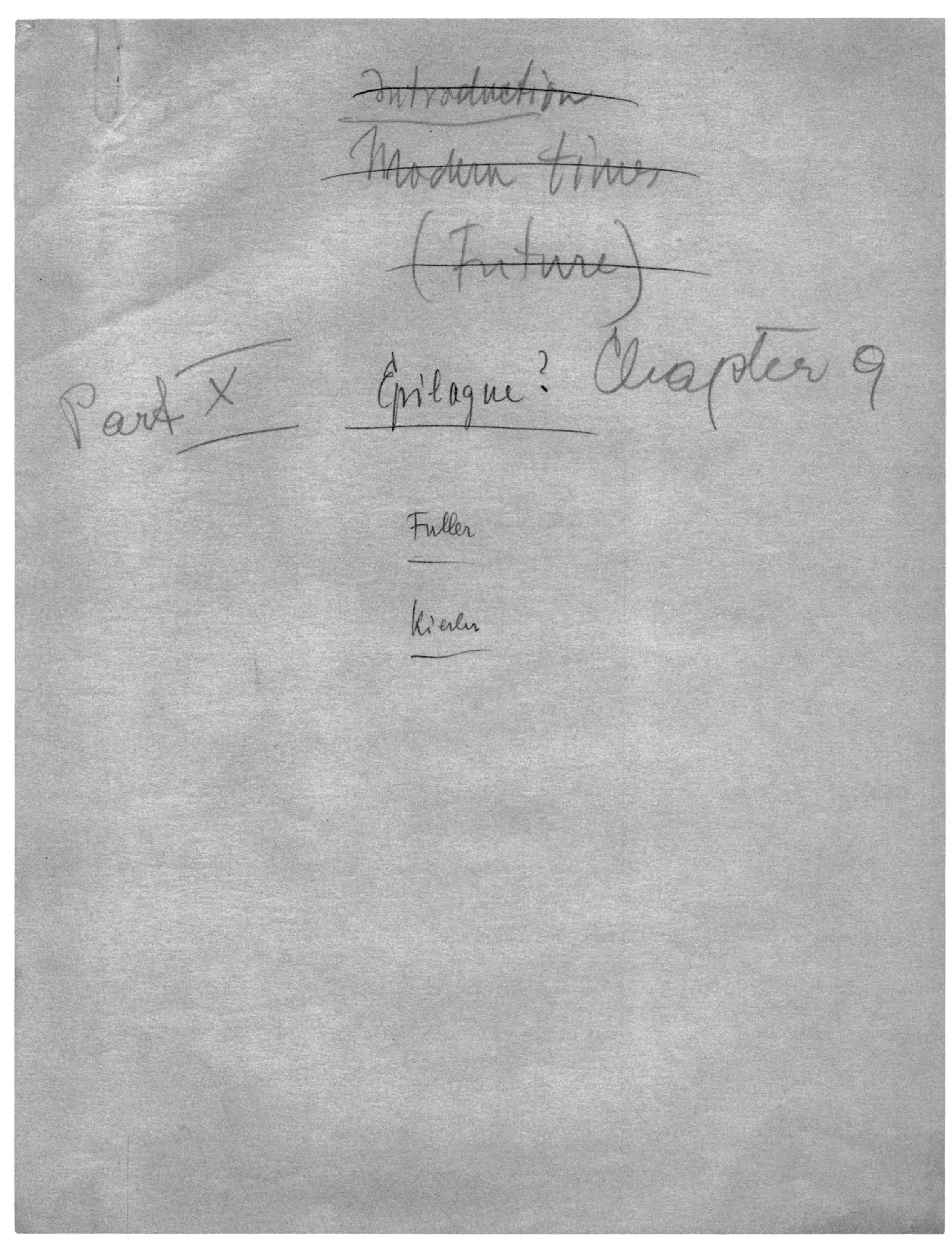

Frederick Kiesler, draft previously titled "Introduction: Modern Times (Future)" or "Epilogue?" marked for Part x, chapter 9. ÖFLKS, TXT_6720/0_N1

(55x)

page 300

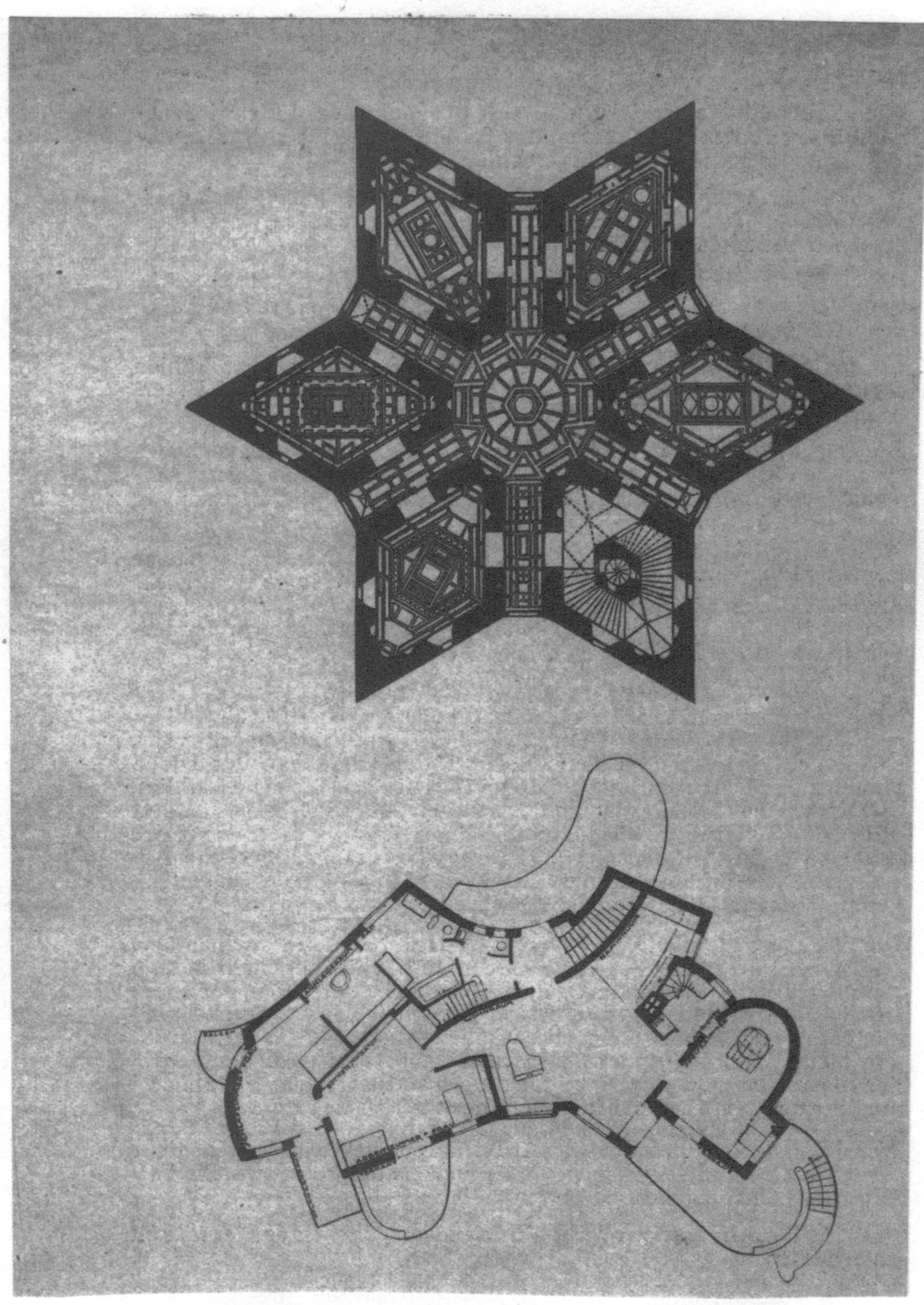

(55x). Page 300

In search of a floor plan for a house that would eliminate the rigidity and formality of 19th century villas. (above) (Below) Plan for a house of rooms in a free-flow-plan.
(By Haering, 1925).

55x

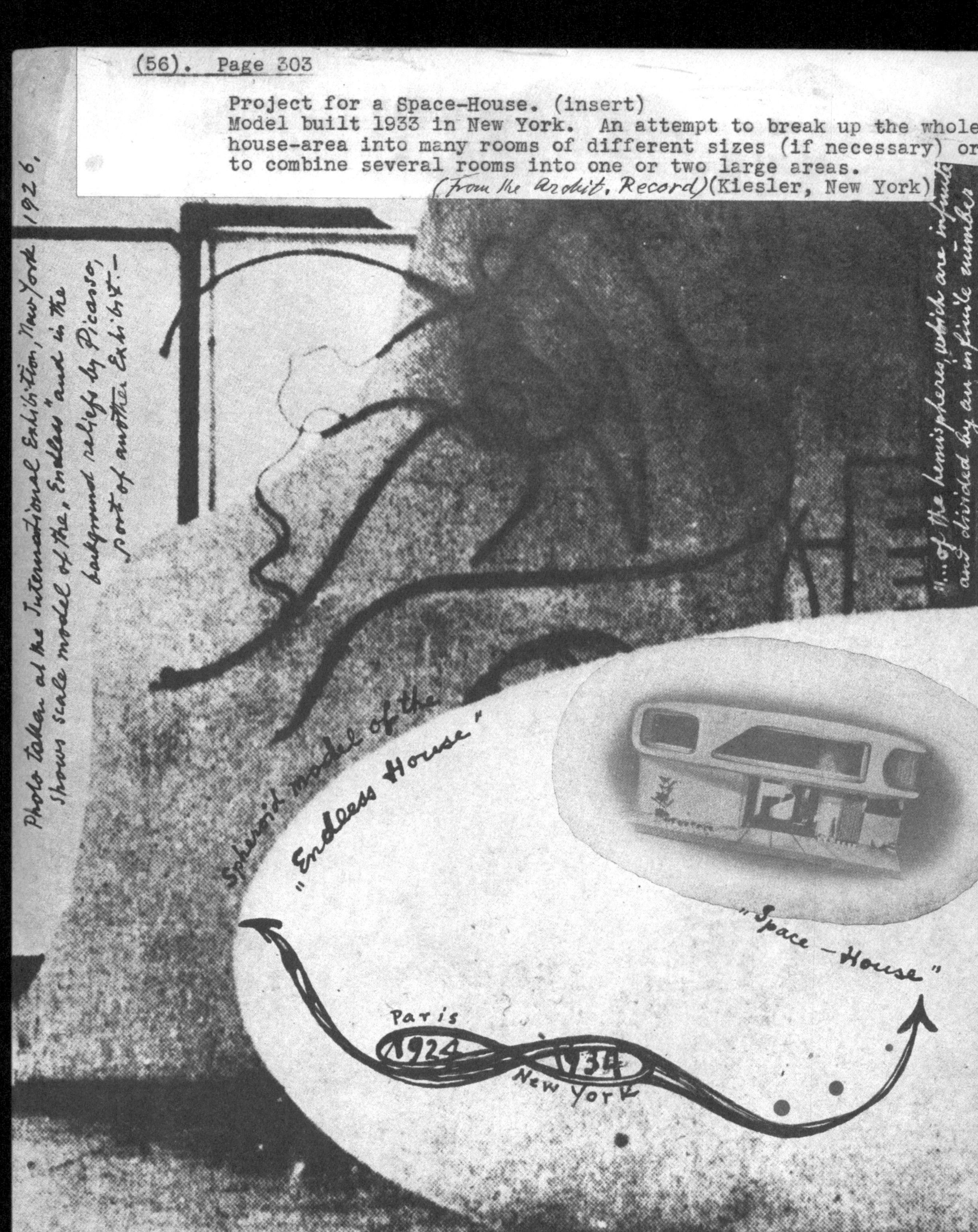
(56). Page 303

Project for a Space-House. (insert)
Model built 1933 in New York. An attempt to break up the whole house-area into many rooms of different sizes (if necessary) or to combine several rooms into one or two large areas.
(From the Archit. Record)(Kiesler, New York)

of lines in such a way that every
man has always one of these lines
between his feet.
men shall speak and touch and
embrace each other while
standing in different hemispheres
and shall understand
each other's language."

da Vinci

both of these projects were designed by Kiesler,
„structures in continuous tension" to facilitate
pre-and-fabrication in moulds for plastics, as well
as to shelter those „continuous mutations" of the
life-force, which seem to be part of the „practical"
as well as of the magical.

page 304

Ad. Loos: Pilsen, 1907

(57). Page 304

An attempt to create a magic living quarter. Combination of various materials, exotic and profane; of three-in-one areas; a study in comfort for nerves and physical relaxation.

(by Loos, Pilsen, Europe, 1907)

page 305

(58). Page 305

Prefabricated physical comfort. Efficiency in service-designs of a contemporary one-family house. All service-equipment (such as heating, cooling, kitchen, baths etc.) are concentrated in the cneter of a circular house-plan.

(Dymaxion House by Fuller, Wichita, Kansas, 1945).

(59)

(59). Page 308

Attempt at a scientific approach to design in Architecture. This is a library for every man's home, (left). Its advantages, adaptable to the various demands of apartments, amount of books (right), and price levels. Knock-down, prefabricated units (extreme right). Product of the Laboratory School of Architecture, Columbia University. The result (here illustrated) proved an organic fusion between the physiological and the psychological demands.

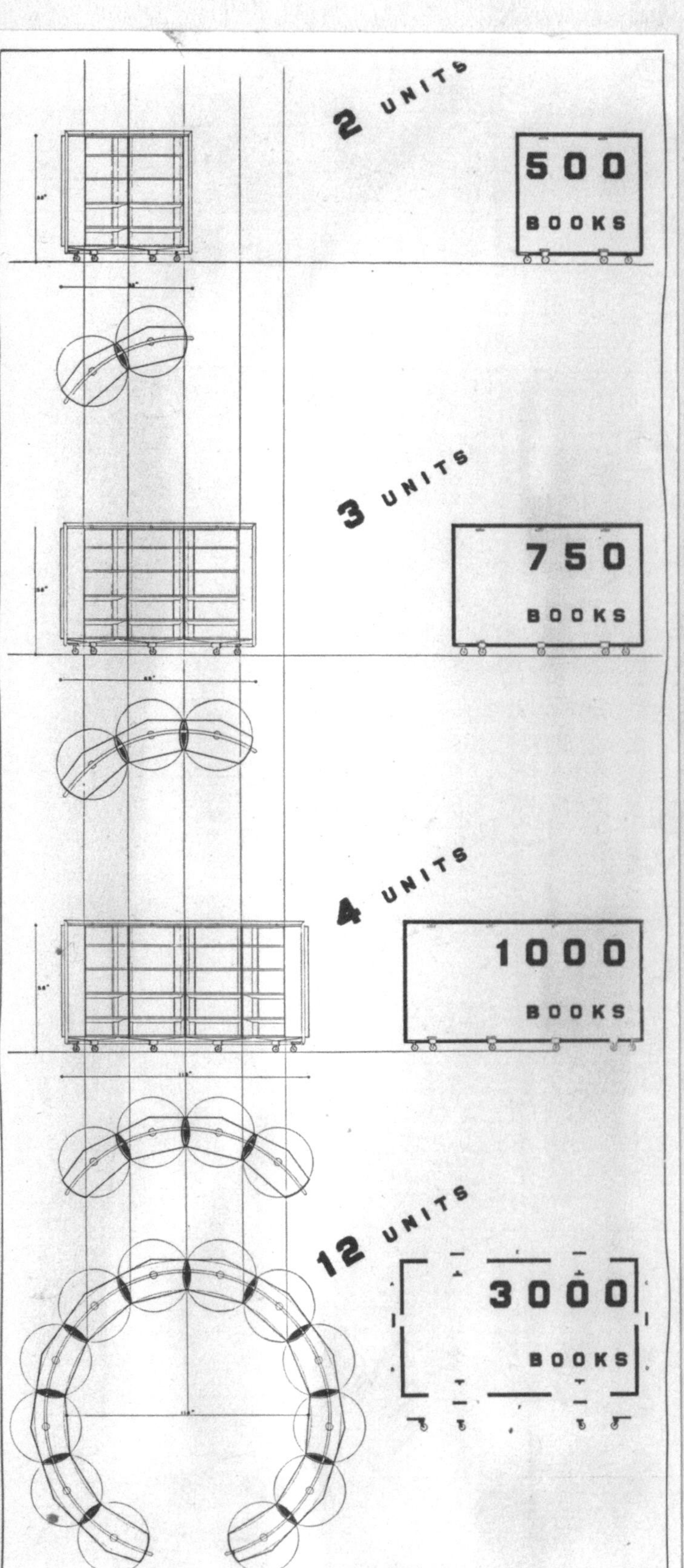
2 UNITS
500
BOOKS
3 UNITS
750
BOOKS
4 UNITS
1000
BOOKS
12 UNITS
3000
BOOKS
Patent Pending

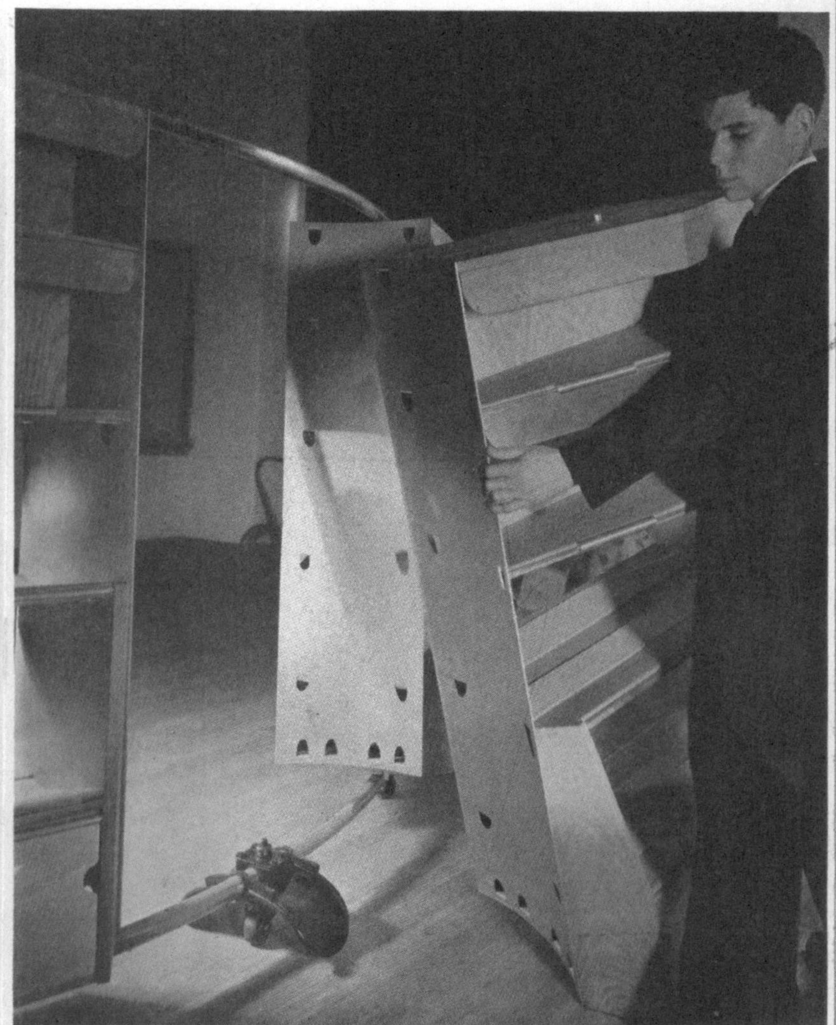

(60). Page 309

(Chart, appended)

We all live most of our life-time inside houses, either in living quarters or work-rooms or recreation buildings. Would it not have been desirable, therefore, to investigate and to find out by proper measuring, what influence these 'artificial' environments have upon our health, physical and mental? Yet it seems such scientific investigations have not yet been done, at any period.

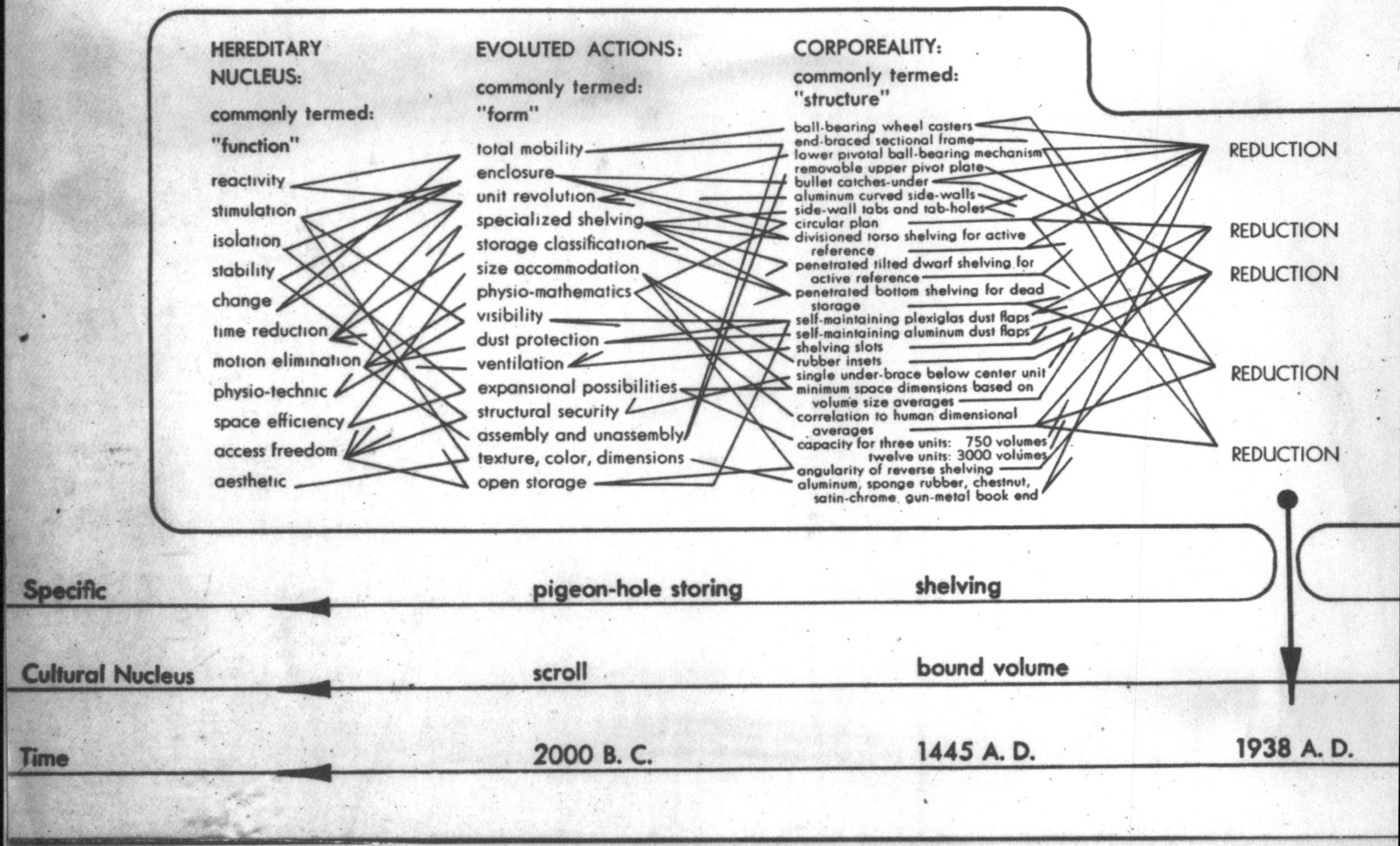

HEREDITARY NUCLEUS:
commonly termed:
"function"

reactivity
stimulation
isolation
stability
change
time reduction
motion elimination
physio-technic
space efficiency
access freedom
aesthetic

EVOLUTED ACTIONS:
commonly termed:
"form"

total mobility
enclosure
unit revolution
specialized shelving
storage classification
size accommodation
physio-mathematics
visibility
dust protection
ventilation
expansional possibilities
structural security
assembly and unassembly
texture, color, dimensions
open storage

CORPOREALITY:
commonly termed:
"structure"

ball-bearing wheel casters
end-braced sectional frame
lower pivotal ball-bearing mechanism
removable upper pivot plate
bullet catches-under
aluminum curved side-walls
side-wall tabs and tab-holes
circular plan
divisioned torso shelving for active reference
penetrated tilted dwarf shelving for active reference
penetrated bottom shelving for dead storage
self-maintaining plexiglas dust flaps
self-maintaining aluminum dust flaps
shelving slots
rubber insets
single under-brace below center unit
minimum space dimensions based on volume size averages
correlation to human dimensional averages
capacity for three units: 750 volumes
twelve units: 3000 volumes
angularity of reverse shelving
aluminum, sponge rubber, chestnut, satin-chrome, gun-metal book end

REDUCTION
REDUCTION
REDUCTION
REDUCTION
REDUCTION

Specific	pigeon-hole storing	shelving	
Cultural Nucleus	scroll	bound volume	
Time	2000 B. C.	1445 A. D.	1938 A. D.

Reproduced here, therefore, is a first investigation of that aim: a metabolism chart of the effects of the new mobile home library upon those who use it. It analyzes the effects of technological environment upon the human being, particularly as a stimulant to higher productivity and as a factor in reducing fatigue moments.

(From the Architectural Record, Report of Laboratory, Columbia University, New York, 1937.)

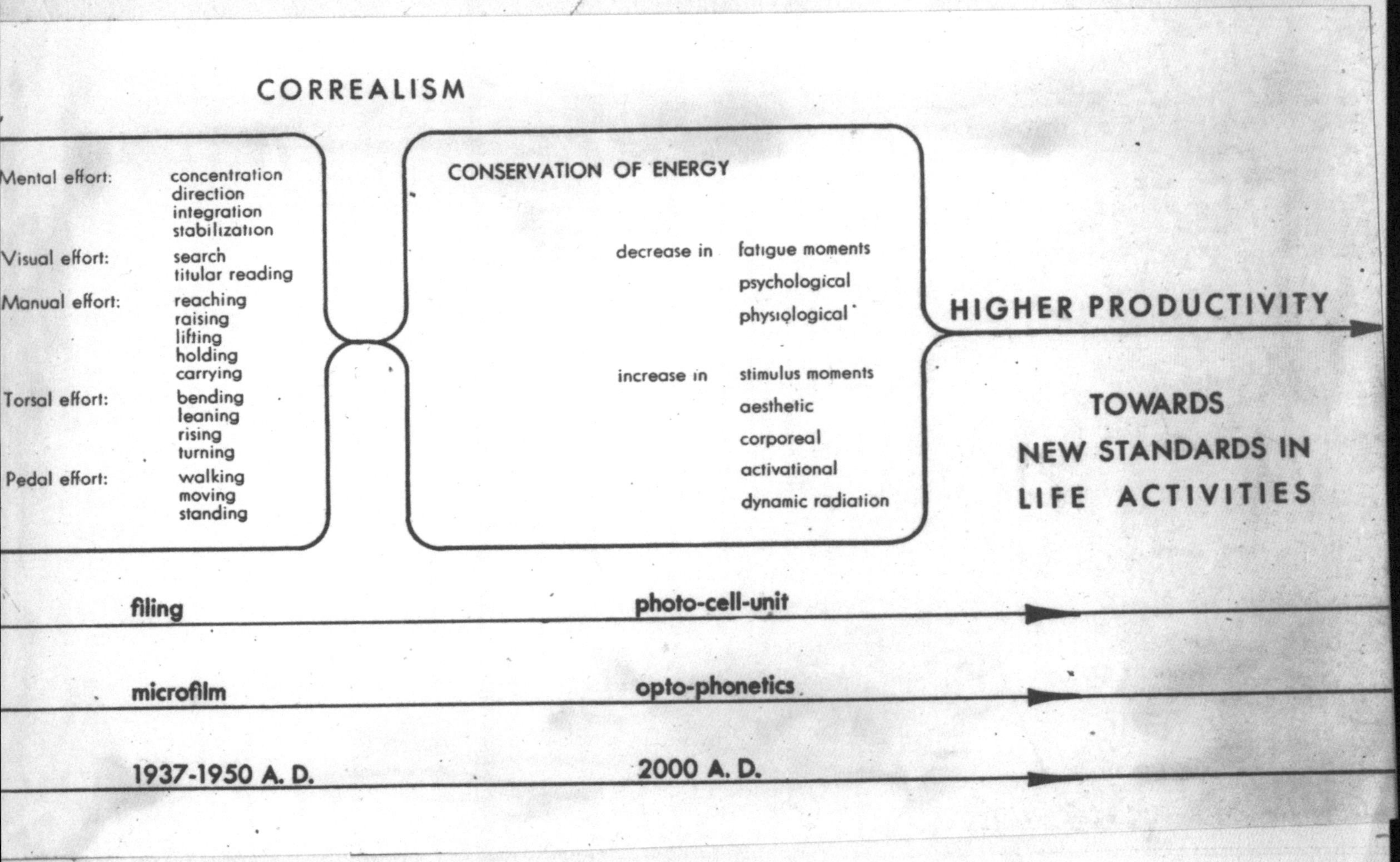

CORREALISM

Mental effort: concentration, direction, integration, stabilization

Visual effort: search, titular reading

Manual effort: reaching, raising, lifting, holding, carrying

Torsal effort: bending, leaning, rising, turning

Pedal effort: walking, moving, standing

CONSERVATION OF ENERGY

decrease in fatigue moments: psychological, physiological

increase in stimulus moments: aesthetic, corporeal, activational, dynamic radiation

HIGHER PRODUCTIVITY

TOWARDS NEW STANDARDS IN LIFE ACTIVITIES

filing → photo-cell-unit

microfilm → opto-phonetics

1937-1950 A. D. → 2000 A. D.

51
Left: Bruno Taut, *Die Auflösung der Städte, oder: Die Erde eine gute Wohnung, oder auch: Der Weg zur Alpinen Architektur* (Hagen: Folkwange, 1920), pl. 2. ÖFLKS, SCL_64/0

51a
"Downtown New York." *Photography, 1839–1937* (New York: The Museum of Mocern Art, 1937), pl. 85, photo McLaughlin Aerial Surveys. ÖFLKS, SCL_64/0

51b
"Blick auf die neue Stadt" (view of the new city). M. R. M., "Die alte und die neue Stadt: Gesunder Lebensraum für kommende Geschlechter," *Koralle* 7, no. 15 (April 16, 1939): 532–533. ÖFLKS, SCL_64/0

52
Karl Friedrich Schinkel, Royal Palace on the Acropolis, 1834. [Note that in his caption Kiesler mistakes the birth year of the architect for the date of the unrealized project.] Ponten, *Architektur die nicht gebaut wurde*, 2:118, pl. 210/211. ÖFLKS, SCL_65/0

53
"As Paris Celebrated the Surrender of Japan," *New York Herald Tribune*, August 17, 1945, 17. ÖFLKS, SCL_66/0

54
Above: Frederick Kiesler, terrace houses, perspective, ca. 1931. (Design related to Kiesler's project for a "Horizontal Skyscraper" [1925]). ÖFLKS, SCL_67/0

Below: "Eine Stadt der Gegenwart. Diorama der City [A city of the present. City diorama]." Le Corbusier, *Städtebau*, trans. Hans Hildebrandt (Stuttgart: Deutsche Verlags-Anstalt, 1929), foldout n.p.

Right: Frank Lloyd Wright, St. Mark's Church-in-the-Bouwerie, New York, 1929. Source unknown.

55
Left: Jean-Jacques Lequeu, country house with observatory. Emil Kaufmann, *Von Ledoux bis Le Corbusier: Ursprung und Entwicklung der Autonomen Architektur* (Vienna: Rolf Passer, 1933), 27. ÖFLKS, SCL_68/0

Right: Claude-Nicolas Ledoux, spherical house for a forester, 1789. Kaufmann, *Von Ledoux bis Le Corbusier*, 31.

55x
Montage of the plan of Sommer Palace Star by Giovanni Maria Aostalli, Giovanni Lucchese, and Bonifaz Wohlmut (Hvězda, near Prague, ca. 1555-1558), and Hugo Häring, plan of a House (1922) as published in Adolf Behne, *Eine Stunde Architektur* (Stuttgart: Wedekind & Co, 1928), 10. ÖFLKS, SCL_69/0

56
Frederick Kiesler, "Endless House" [photomontage], *VVV*, No. 4 (1944): 60–61. Photo taken at the International Exhibition, New York 1926. Shows scale model of the "Endless House" and in the background reliefs by Picasso, part of another exhibit. Inscriptions handwritten by Kiesler on the magazine illustration. ÖFLKS, SCL_70/0

57
Adolf Loos, living room of the apartment of Wilhelm Hirsch, Pilsen (1907). Franz Glück, *Adolf Loos, Illustré de 32 reproductions en héliogravure* (Paris: Éditions G. Crès et Cie, 1931). ÖFLKS, SCL_71/0

58
"The 8,000 LB. House: Fuller's $6,500 four-room industrialized unit is round," *Architectural Forum* 84, no. 4 (April 1946): 129–137. ÖFLKS, SCL_72/0

59
Frederick Kiesler, "Mobile-Home-Library" model and drawings as reproduced in his article "'On Correalism and Biotechnique': A Study on the Genetics of Building Design," *Architecture Record* 86, no. 3 (September 1939): 60–75. ÖFLKS, SCL_73/0

60
Frederick Kiesler, "'On Correalism and Biotechnique,'" 60–75. ÖFLKS, SCL_74/0

ADDENDA

fig. C.01

Note to the Publisher.

The book is divided into three sections:

1) Prehistory (30 illustr.) .... 150 pages text

2) From the Egyptian Era to the French Revolution (30 illustr.) .. 150 pages text

3) From the French Revolution to Present Times (40 illustr. incl. designs for future housing types) .... 200 pages text

Total ....100 illustrations ...... 500 pages text

The fact that I have almost completed the writing of the first nine chapters gives the outline an over-weight on the first section.

But the book should be viewed from the content-outline and not from these nine chapters. They are included merely to clarify important issues involved.
In other words: The book deals only with <u>contemporary problems</u> throughout, but it traces them through history in order to justify and clarify our own problems at stake.

Sample chapters as to writing:

The Introduction to Part I

The Universe as Architecture, Part I, Chapter 8

With my present plan, this book will have approximately five hundred pages of text and one hundred and fifty illustrations, in varied sizes, of which at least thirty can be line-cuts.

Frederick Kiesler, First page of preliminary "Note to the Publisher" with added handwritten text (TS, pencil) ÖFLKS, TXT_5877/0_N14

The alternate drafts in this section comprise preliminary book proposals, outlines, and lists that were ultimately not part of the assembled manuscript of *Magic Architecture*. Included here are preliminary notes to the publisher and editor, a partial three-part outline, another outline in four parts, early synopses of Parts I and X, and a list of unbuilt architectural projects. Most of the typescripts and manuscripts are untitled and were not copied, transcribed, or edited. They appear here in their original unedited form, including most of Kiesler's handwritten deletions, corrections, and misspellings.

The following preliminary "Note to the Publisher" contains an early schematic book outline in three "sections." The typed draft was part of a book proposal submission that included the list of contents and a selection of chapters. (fig. C.01)[1]

Note to the Publisher

The book is divided into three sections:

1) Prehistory (30 illustr.) 150 pages text
2) From the Egyptian Era to the French Revolution (30 illustr.) 150 pages text
3) From the French Revolution to Present Times (40 illustr. incl. designs for future housing types) 200 pages text
   Total 100 illustrations 500 pages text

The fact that I have almost completed the writing of the first nine chapters gives the outline an over-weight on the first section.[2]

But the book should be viewed from the content-outline and not from these nine chapters. They are included merely to clarify important issues involved.

In other words: The book deals only with contemporary problems throughout, but it traces them through history in order to justify and clarify our own problems at stake.

Sample chapters as to writing:
The Introduction to Part I
The Universe as Architecture,
Part I, Chapter 8

With my present plan, this book will have approximately five hundred pages of text and one hundred and fifty illustrations, in varied sizes, of which at least thirty can be line-cuts.

Another draft with additional guidelines for the editor accompanying Kiesler's proposal and (partial) manuscript submission.

Note to the Editor

This outline is in many parts more elaborate than is customary. The elaboration was necessary in order to clarify the very complex material that had to be evaluated to make a proper presentation of the origin of Shelter and Architecture.[3] These parts, however, should not be considered as finished or completed. They are not more than extended research data.

Only the introduction, Preamble to Architecture
Part ..., Chapter ....
and, The Universe as Architecture,
Part..., Chapter...
are presented as finished samples of writing.[4]

*

The book will consist of approximately 800 pages.[5] Of these: 600 pages[6] to be continuous text
200 pages illustrations
the 200 pages of illustrations divide themselves in:
100 pages of half tones (30 full pages) and 70 half and quarter page sizes and
100 pages of large and small line cut drawings within the main illustrations.[7]
Two charts at the end of the book.

The script will close with the usual index of names and a section[8] of Annotations and Data with reference to the main text. This appendix will be concerned chiefly with important factual details, which could not be included in the body of the book without disturbing the flow of the text.[9]

The following untitled outline for Parts II and III summarizes the main theoretical and historical argument of the book. It reflects an earlier organization of Kiesler's book project as a tripartite history, in contrast to the ten parts that appear in the later version. This partial synopsis draws heavily on Lévy-Bruhl's idea of "participation."

PART II
Introduction

Caveman –
in perfect symbiosis with nature, the members of his clan; no God–no symbols

Primitive Aborigine-man –
starts individualization of the members of the clan, and loses the direct sense of participation; the unity is split: he replaces the collective spirit by images of it–he creates myths and symbolizes their powerful individuals in plastic and pictorial images. Forces of Nature are objectivized as Gods; and objects made by man are personalized.–

The symbiosis of the caveman with nature and family is re-established via Gods and their images. The direct contact is lost.–

In building shelter the split manifests itself in three ways:

1. the hut[10] (home–family)
2. the community–place (adminitration groups)
3. The sacral–locality (temple communities)

It is very interesting to recognize in these early categories the same basic order of building– types which we still pursue today.

Since thousands of years the greatest architectural emphasis was laid in reverse order, namely: first on the sacral–buildings, second on community–administration-buildings; and last–or none–on the home structure. The home remained physio-functional.

*

It is only in the late eighteenth century that old and oldest social ideas, tending to foster again the unity of man, society, natural, and technological environment–were strong enough to shake the belief in separation and in the false prophecies of happiness incorporated therein. It appeared that this happiness was based on sacrifice and fear, an aspect which linked this mentality very closely with the life of persecution, fear, and guilt of the caveman.

Of course, all hopes of the majority of the populace, went, architecturally speaking, into religious structures.

In democratic lands these hopes concentrated in a super-architecture of administration buildings and not in religious structures. The emphasis is laid upon economic wealth as security from fear.

PART III
Towards a New Unity of Men and Environment

But with the reawakening of the Spirit of primordial participation, the strive for acceptance of factual life, grew. Without being fatalistic it tends towards a symbiosis of science and faith, which unerringly moves to the establishment of the House and its corollaries as the nucleus of architectural expression. It thus abandons the buildings of the psychic periphery, namely the Temple and the Administration-center, as the primary factor of attention, importance, and adoration and does not delegate the responsibility to outer-spheres. For the first time in Man's history the architectural emphasis[11] is on the house and the home. Man again strives to be part of the structure of the total environment,[12] but this time, without the sacrifice of his innermost individuality.

The following incomplete draft presents a more extensive preliminary book outline in four parts with a narrative description of each section. This outline is closer to the later structure of the book in ten parts. The TS has many handwritten additions by Kiesler. No "clean" copy exists, suggesting the outline was not sent to publishers. The same draft includes an "excursus" with Kiesler's sketches and notes drawn freely from the previous outline (figs. C.02a–b), as well as an illustrated chart on the relation between the evolution of religious systems throughout human history and the emergence of "everyman's architecture."

The manuscript to be divided into four parts, of which the first and the last are the smallest.

First Part
Samples of architecture of primitive cultures. Vision and reality form perfect integration; the people live in unity with their environment, which is both: an expression of physical function and of spiritual necessity. (Africa, The Pacific, American Indians.)[13]

Second Part
The unity of Dream and Reality lost. Split in Home and Worship center. The poor homes of the people of Egypt and Greece b.c. Imagination is confined to temples, Royal Palaces, and buildings of war (fortification), for social or religious rituals, particularly for the dead. Some perfect samples of Dream-Architecture. Their fame rests on enormous dimensions, weight, or the overemphasis of the superfluous: Parthenon or Poseidon Temple of Paestum (middle of 7th cent. b.c.). The Hagia Sophia by Anthemios and Milet (537);[14] the Terrace-Temple of Deir-el-Bahar (1580–1447).[15] (India, China.)[16]

Pompeii:[17] Transformation of walls into fairy lands of Architecture and Nature. Desire for an integrated life of Vision and Reality. Excellent examples of[18] Architecture which goes beyond "functionalism" in home-design.

[Kiesler's side notes on the second part]
China
Japan
India
Discrepancy
Peru

~~Third Part~~
The gigantic projects of the Renaissance and particularly of the Barock–not executed. The Bibienas and their school. (18th cent.) Juvara; Scamozzi (16th cent.); Bernando Buontalenti (16th); Piranesi (1707–1778) [sic][19] (18th).[20] Projects of the French, German and Italian Rokoko;[21] Schinkel's project for the Acropolis (19th).

Dream structures of engineers. (Eiffel tower)

The beginning of the twentieth century with its new plans for cities, communities; Inventions for unprecedented comforts in home and communication.

The twentieth century again directs its attention towards a more practical Architecture. Particular interest is focused upon the interrelation of outdoor and indoor-living.[22]

But the imagination cannot s'enfuir[23] into religious buildings or into temples of Wealth–it is now directed toward the Home of Everyman; toward the conquest through Technology[24] and its serviceability for developing a more creative life. Toward healing the breach between wish and reality.[25] (Tony Garnier; Le Corbusier; Tatlin[26] (Russia); Fuller (America) and others.[27]

[Kiesler's side notes on this part]
Bosch
Projects of "Ideal Gardens"
formal and intimate
(England)
Projects of film-architecture
(The Ghost goes West by
René Clair)
Mellies' early films
H. G. Wells: Things to Come
Disney Films.

The Fourth Part
Should account in a short chapter [about] ideas in buildings that are purely imaginary, ~~to the point of sheer insanity~~. They are curiosa[28] with regard to architecture.
The flight from reality into a fictitious world in which the pathologically neurasthenic lives, has produced some extraordinary designs for castles-in-the-air. Children too, usually up to the age of twelve–retain and express im ....[29] of visionary buildings.
The spontaneity of their drawings and buildings in sand and of their building blocks are fascinating as expressions of ideas of fairy lands of architecture.

And not last are the inventors and hobbyists. The US Patent Office alone has some of the most astounding dreams of "practicability" in store. While we all "normal" people look at first somewhat pitiable at them, yet, these "cranks," it will be well to remember for most of our technical conveniences were first looked upon as tricks, even such inventions as electricity, humorously called at the time elec-trick. Yet they all tend toward one goal only: to improve the lot of mankind; to improve its physical and mental well-being; to make the dream an everyday reality.

[Kiesler's side notes for the fourth part]

This section will prove an excellent antidote for those readers wh[o], still in the throes of their everyday "appointments," may feel the main chapters and projects of this book are taking them for a ride. In fact, it does. But it leads them through a detour of the imagination to their inner-self. The last chapter will therefore easily prove to them where the lines are to be drawn between phantoms of the insane and the masterpieces of imaginary architecture.

The book to have 250–300 pages with approximately 32 pages of illustrations and some pages of line-cuts. It should sell for about $3.50 and be ready in manuscript in one and a half years from signing of the agreement.

Footnote:

Of particular interest is the now famous structure of the French postman Cheval, built of fish shells collected during his thirty years of walking in distributing letters along the coast of his district. He might be called the Henri Rousseau of architecture.[30]

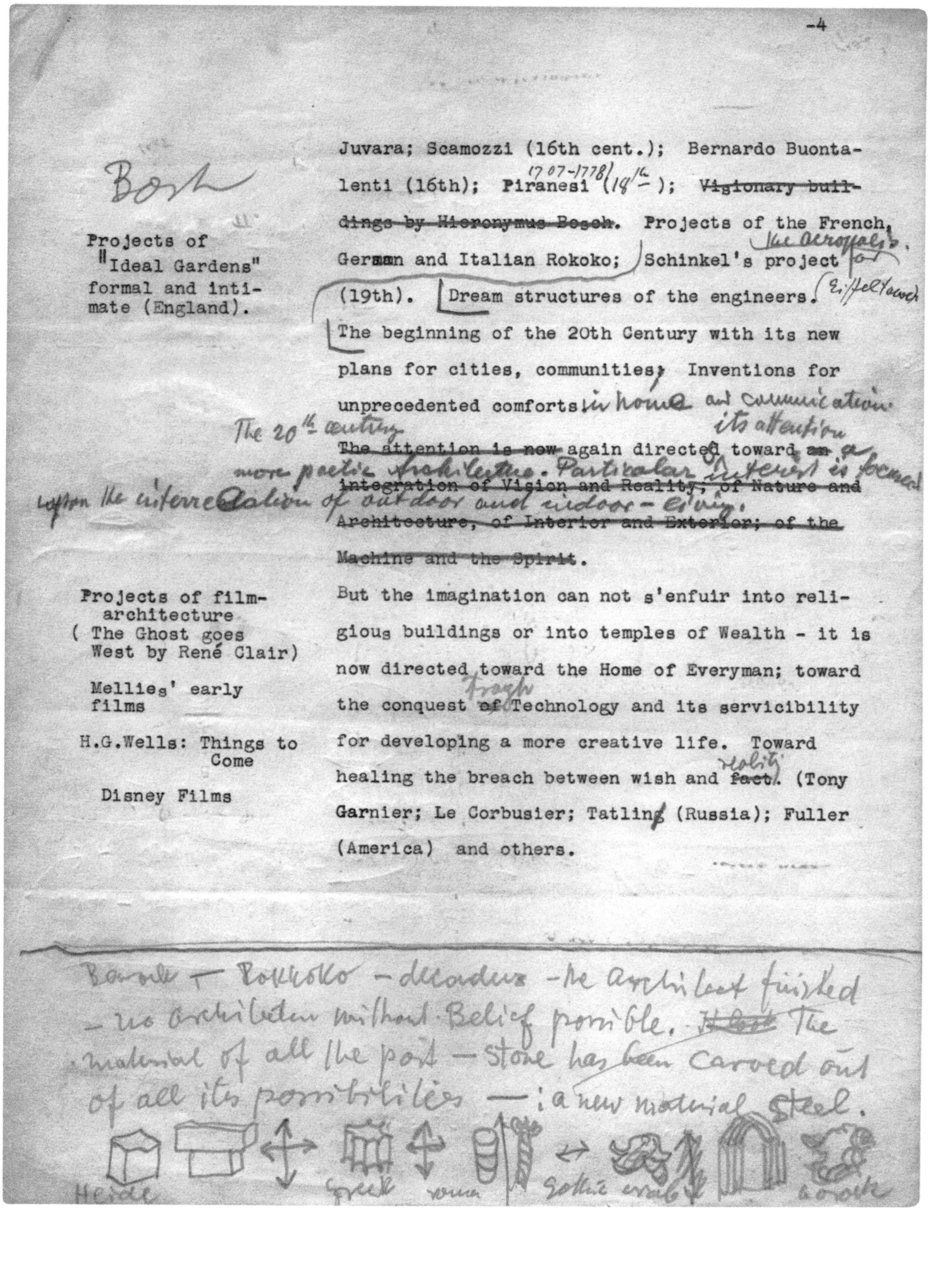

-4

Bosch

Projects of "Ideal Gardens" formal and intimate (England).

Juvara; Scamozzi (16th cent.); Bernardo Buontalenti (16th); Piranesi (1707–1778) (18th); ~~Visionary buildings by Hieronymus Bosch.~~ Projects of the French, German and Italian Rokoko; Schinkel's project for the Acropolis (19th). Dream structures of the engineers. (Eiffel tower)

The beginning of the 20th Century with its new plans for cities, communities; Inventions for unprecedented comforts in home and communication.

The 20th century its attention ~~The attention is now~~ again directed toward ~~an~~ a more poetic Architecture. Particular Interest is focused upon the interrelation of outdoor and indoor-living. ~~integration of Vision and Reality, of Nature and Architecture, of Interior and Exterior; of the Machine and the Spirit.~~

Projects of film-architecture (The Ghost goes West by René Clair)

Mellies' early films

H.G.Wells: Things to Come

Disney Films

But the imagination can not s'enfuir into religious buildings or into temples of Wealth - it is now directed toward the Home of Everyman; toward the conquest through ~~of~~ Technology and its servicibility for developing a more creative life. Toward healing the breach between wish and reality ~~fact~~. (Tony Garnier; Le Corbusier; Tatling (Russia); Fuller (America) and others.

Baroque + Rokkoko – decadence – the architect finished – no architecture without Belief possible. The material of all the past – stone has been carved out of all its possibilities — ; a new material steel.

Heide Greek roman gothic arab Baroque

Preliminary book outline of *Magic Architecture* in four parts. Page with handwritten annotations and an addendum with sketches on Baroque and the Rococo, decadence, and the pulverization of materials. TS, pencil. ÖFLKS TXT_6800/0_N5recto

fig. C.02b

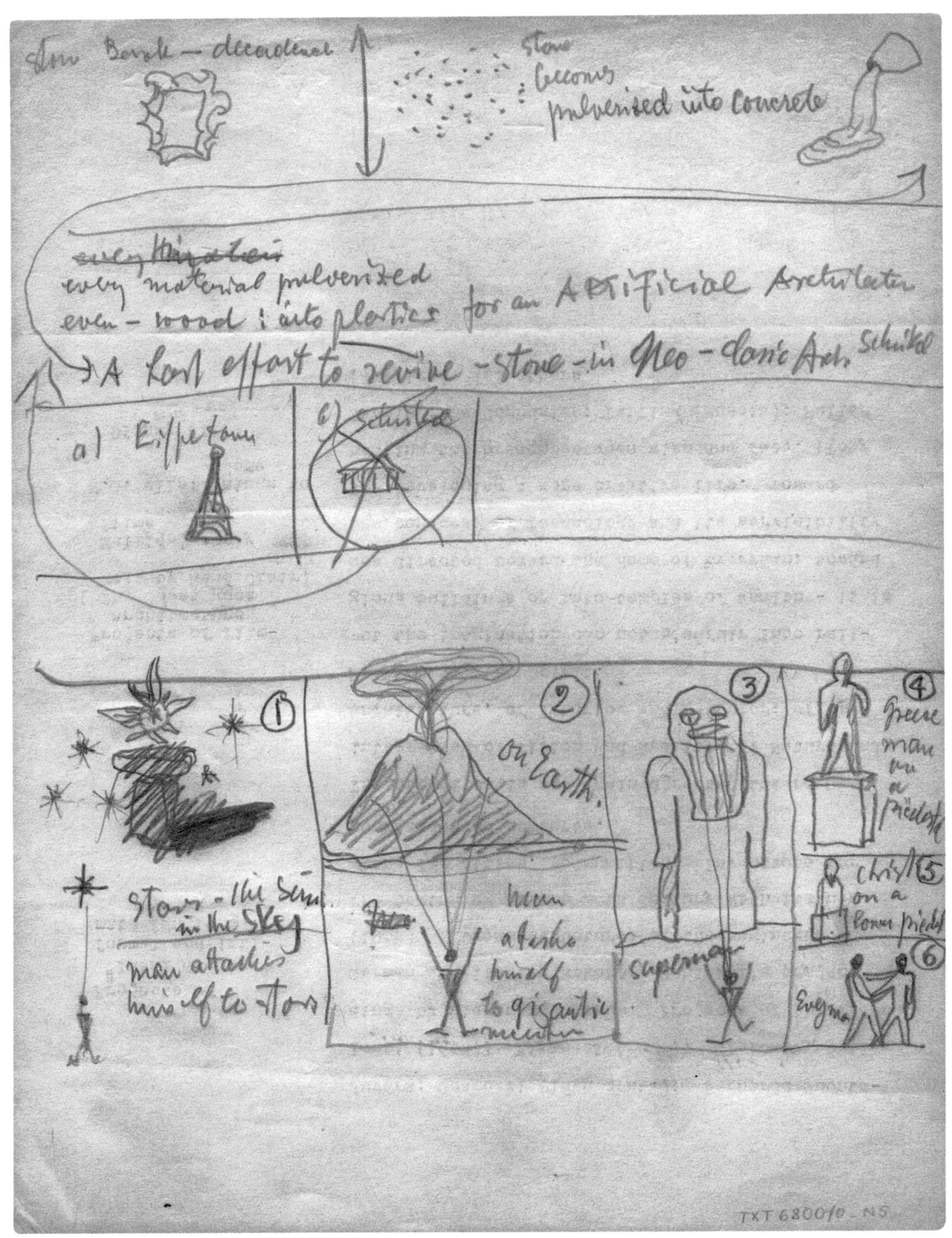

Preliminary book outline of *Magic Architecture* in four parts. Verso of previous page (C.01A) with sketches of the Eiffel Tower, Schinkel, and a preliminary chart on "The Orbit of Ecstasy" in six stages—all material for the third part (later Parts VIII and X). TS, pencil. ÖFLKS, TXT_6800/0_N5verso

This draft was initially part of a general outline with an overview of what in the previous outline was described as the book's "first part." It was then partially converted into a sample "chapter 3" to be accompanied by illustrations but was not used in later versions of the manuscript.

PART ONE

Chapter Three: Man creates society and organizes t[h]oughts.[31]

In this chapter

Samples of Architecture of primitive cultures are discussed where vision and reality form a perfect integration.

The people live in harmonious unity with their environment. It is difficult to draw a line to separate vision from fact. Their houses as well as their artifacts are an undivided expression of physical[32] as well as of spiritual necessities.

They live mostly an outdoor life, therefore are their houses in Form and Function "primitif"; and no attempt at "Architecture" is formed. The house is no more than the nucleus of a wider shell, which is nature itself, her earth, rocks, bushes, forests, and the skies above. The building material which is taken directly from the environment makes the house so much part of nature.[33]

Picture No 1.

Utilitarian household objects of Trujillo in form of houses, and temple pyramids (Inca, Peru). (Illustration)[34] (see figs. c.03a-b)

What we call decorative patterns, be they birds, flowers, lakes, mountains, streams, or so-called abstract designs, have no further meaning but the falsified beautification, a superficial estheticism and therefore a wasteful selling attribute. In contrast to this state of mind[35], I quote, to underline the deep significance of any formation or de-formation, pictorial, plastic, or architectural, in primitive cultures:[36]

It is impossible to detach from any useful objects of these periods, what we call the decorative pattern. Vision and fact are so inter-related in material, form, and technique of the configuration, and it is only in this way capable to fulfill its function of practicability. In the culture of today[37] we readily ca wash off or scrape off decorative patterns without destroying the utility of the object. It is purely mechanical in its intention;[38] but as to mechanics, it is not developed enough. It serves habits of routine.

2 Picture
(Inca city in Ucayali Valley, discov. 1911)[39]
Built into and around the rock, not only acting as a shelter in a physical sense, but also in a spiritual one, the form of the "high mountain" is stimulating in a visionary manner and evokes the dream image of a divine power. Resting, there is the fortress city, tenderly nestled, cast-on. The embrace is physical and spiritual. Weapons and physical strength are not enough in battle. Mechanics alone are not enough for action, faith must permeate the body deeper and in a more general way than blood and oxygen.

3 Picture
Totem (Alaska)
Haida–Indian house showing the incorporation of the Totem pole.[40]

4 Picture
Face mask made of black leather with sewn on yellow leather stripes, which are reproducing the tattoo of the woman's face. Worn by the Angekok when healing illnesses. Cumberland Golf, Baffinland.[41]

5 Picture
Alaskan mask
According to (Inuit) religion, every being and every object has a shadow or a look-alike image among the spirits; the grotesque wooden masks of the Alaskan (Inuit), for example, are supposed to represent these shadowy doppelgangers.[42]

6 Picture
Sioux chief Black Rock in full ornament with the buffalo coat and the horned hood decorated with ermine furs and eagle feathers (The insignia of the war chief).[43] (fig. c.04a)

7 Opposing picture
A modern commander in chief (Eisenhower) in field uniform. (fig. c.04b)

The equalization to natural powers is visualized in primitive tribes through many attributes on their body. Painting it, carving it, and forcing parts of the body like ears, into distorted growths, or even the skull into distorted shape, "unnatural" procedures in our sense. They are, however, nothing else but the desire to heighten the power of the individual not only facing his opponent–fellowman, but also for himself, as a self-assertion. Associating his body with symbols that do not come from human beings but from animals or terrestrial or heavenly bodies, the sight of which alone heightens his power, his energies and his hopes, for miraculous achievements, gives him psychological security.

Modern man relies on machines for supernatural power. He has discarded visual magic.[44] He rather uses the chemical extract of nature, may they be stones,[45] animals, plants, or cosmic rays. For the self-assertion of his psyche he tries to use his bankbook, or in a case of failure the medicine-man-analyst. And through him, it seems, modern man carved himself unknowingly an underpassage back to the dwellings of the subconscious,[46] where the different types of the species[47] however separated through space and times, still dwell together in perfect harmony. The self-betrayal of modern man, in denying himself the magic power of belief (faith), has led him to endless incantations of mechanical activities to deaden the whisper of his inner voice. But just as the super power of the electron hides itself in micro-minuteness, so is the whisper of his inner voice bound to drown out one day the t[h]underous clutter of his mechanical thoughts.

Thus the desire of both civilizations, aboriginal and modern, to prepare themselves for the conquest of more territory than their stomachs and minds can digest, has led to the preponderance of thaumaturgy in primitive and of the mechanical hocus pocus in modern man.

For Part ONE:

(1

?) TAMBerma[illegible], Togo-land of earth, imitation of castles

Süd-Amerika

1) Prähistoric Town of Pucará (Puna de Jujuy)

2.) Tongefäße ~~in Form~~ aus Trujilo in Gestalt von Häusern und Tempelpyramiden
page 398

3.) Ruinen der INCA-Festung MACHU-Picchu
page 381

4) menschengestaltige Tonurne der Aruak des Amazonendeltas (page 235)

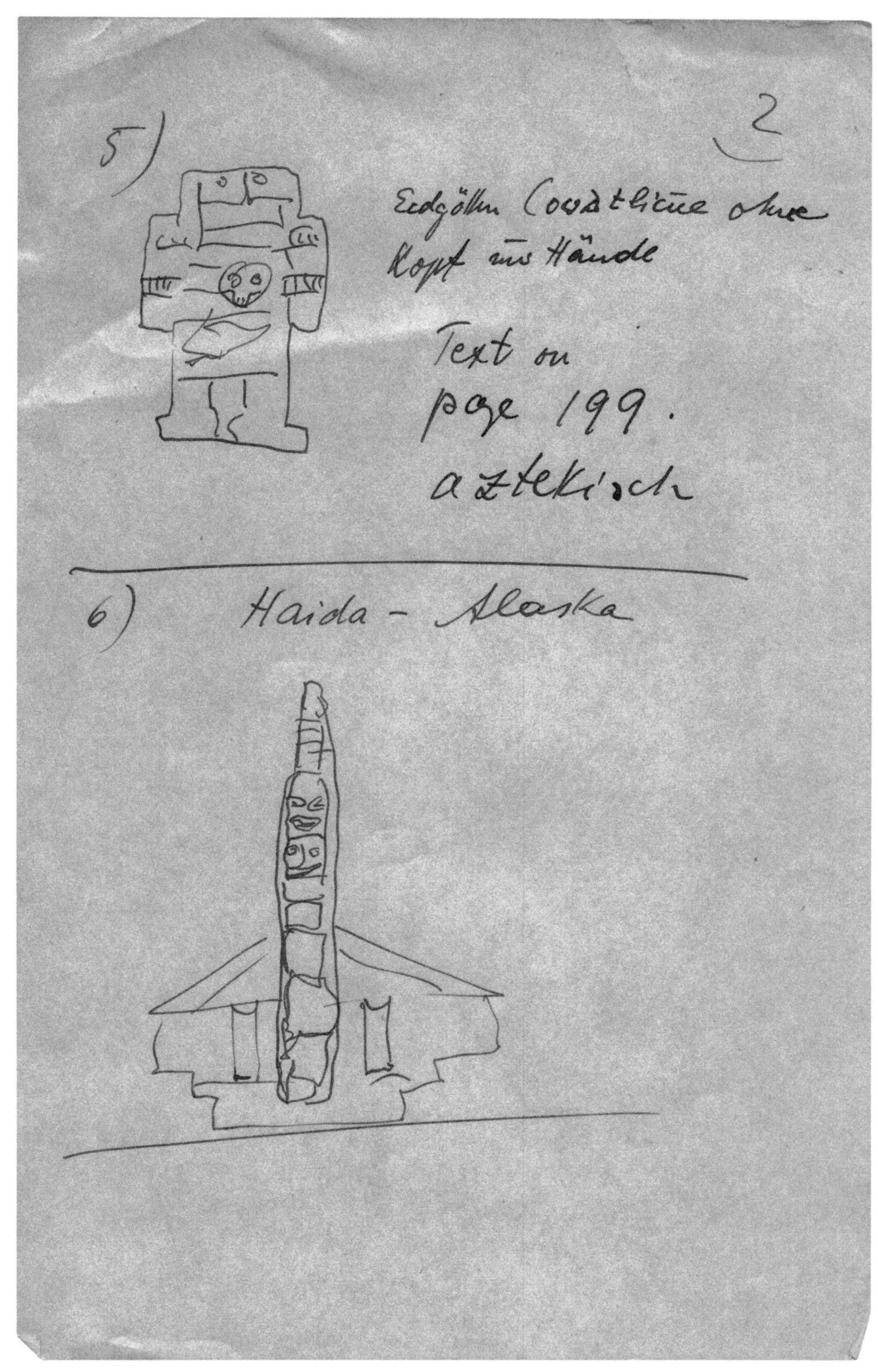

Preliminary outline of "First Part." Notepad with handwritten notes and sketches on illustrations for "Part One" copied from Georg Buschan ed., *Illustrierte Völkerkunde.* Volume I: *Vergleichende Völkerkunde: Amerika – Afrika*, 2nd ed. (Stuttgart: Strecker und Schröder, 1922) (ink)
ÖFLKS, TXT_6876/0_N1–N2

fig. C.04a

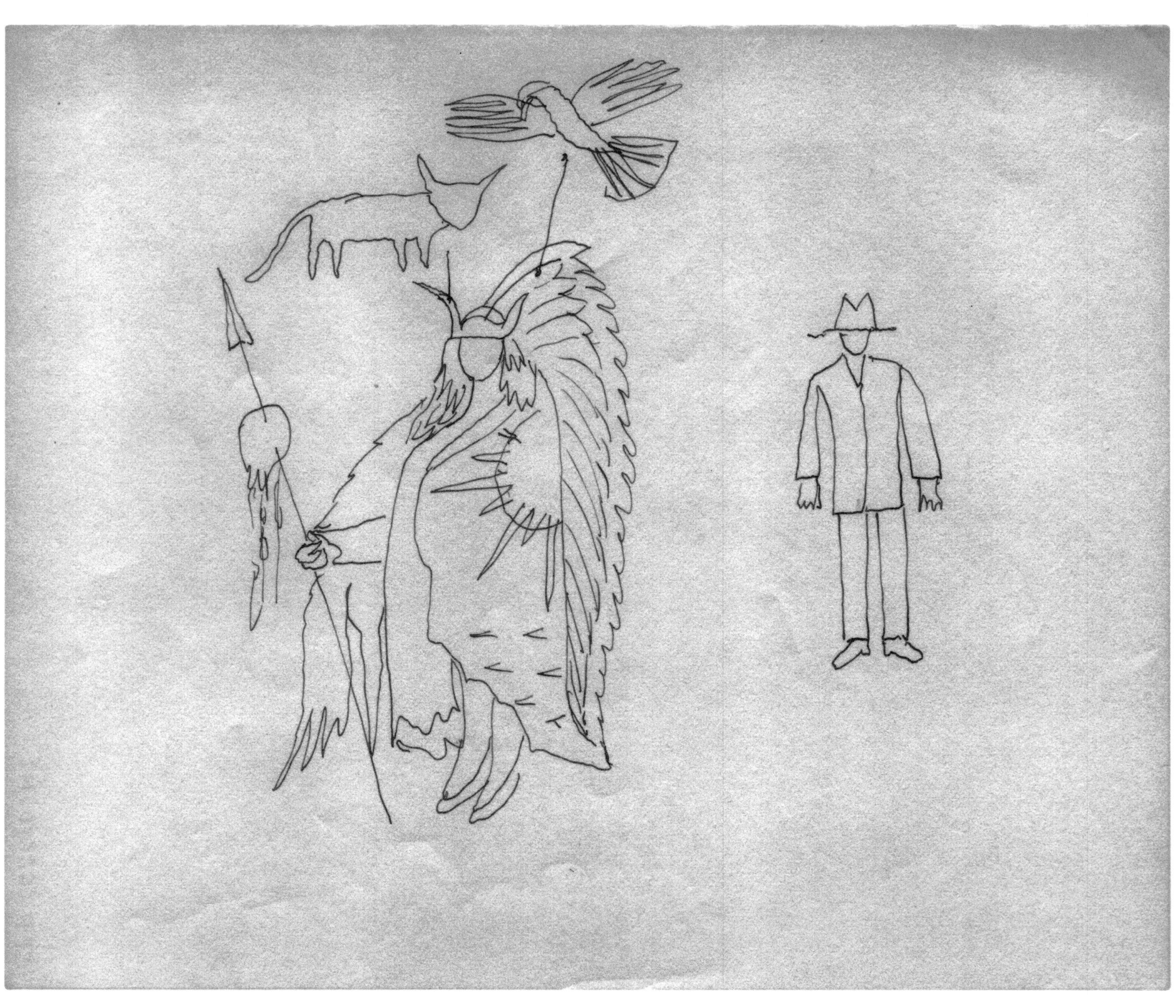

Preliminary outline of "First Part." Sketches of "Sioux chief Black Rock" (after a painting by George Catlin) and a "modern commander in chief (Eisenhower)." (ink) ÖFLKS, SFP_6666/0_N2a

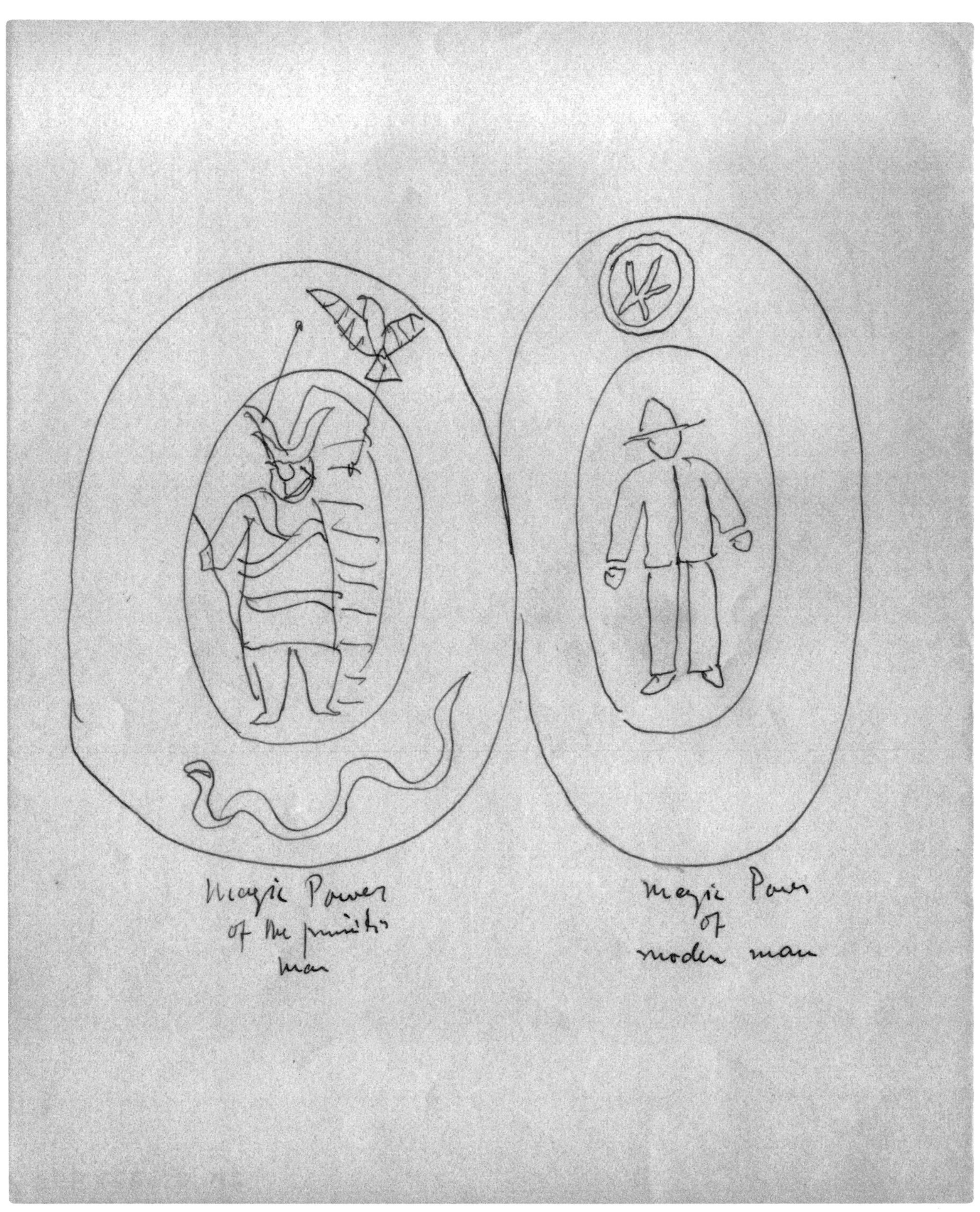

"Magic Power of the primitive man" and "Magic Power of modern man," drawing for a preliminary outline of the "First Part" of *Magic Architecture*.
(ink) ÖFLKS, SFP_6666/0_N2b

This synoptic description could be a fragment, an excerpt from an alternative draft to what later became Part x of *Magic Architecture*, or the final part of an outline accompanying a book proposal. The text itself offers developments in the architecture of the twentieth century. Similar statements made here can be found throughout Part x in later versions of the manuscript.

The beginning of the [twentieth century] **with its new ideas**[48] **for city planning, garden cities and communities, which flourished due** [to] **the revolutionary spirit in Europe after the first world war. Freed from Imperialism, Czarism and Monarchism, the populace dreamed of new social - and logically of new architectural orders.**[49] **(Bruno Taut's**[50] **"Alpine Architecture", "Dissolution of Cities", "New Architectural Forms out of new aims in life.") Most interesting projects by the architect of Max Reinhardt Play house-Arena in Berlin Herr Hans Poelzig**[51] **for Salzburg in Austria: ein Festspielhaus**[52] **called Mozarteum. It's an attempt to create a contemporary Barock to parallel Mozart's Barock-city Salzburg.**

New impetus to special designs came from the advances made in steel-construction and the achievements of engineering starting with the Crystal Palace in London. Steel and glass and new plastics. The growing industrial age stimulated by international competition promises unprecedented control in homes. Utopian invention in furnishings, air-conditioning, Bathing, gadgets. (Eiffel tower project for London; the bathtubs of Benjamin Franklin. The American Congress forbids bathtubs by decree as immoral. Paul Sheerbart's "Glass-Architecture").[53] **Reaction to the**[54] **overgrowing influence of the machine expresses itself clearly in the architectural project for "better living." A "return to nature" or at least a better coordination to land, sea and vegetation is expressed in the plan of breaking down walls between indoor and outdoor, exterior and interior. (Frank Lloyd Wright. Le Corbusier. "The horizontal Skyscraper."**[55] **Fuller's "Dymaxion House.") Mass-production fosters mass-education, and the planners and architects scheme now not for Emperors, Land- or -industrial Magnates but for: everyman. They promise the "paradise" not in Heaven and not somewhere in the country - but in every Home.**[56] **Are these projects <u>utopia</u> like those of the past?**[57] **Saint'Elia** [sic] **–/ Skyscraper-City/ ... –sky streets** (fig. c.05b)

The following untitled document (fig. c.05a) contains a list of unrealized projects from antiquity to the modern era. The majority of these projects are described in chapters of Parts vi–x of *Magic Architecture*. There are, however, notable exceptions, such as the projects by Poelzig and Tatlin, not included in later drafts of the Main Text. Several of the projects in this list are described in Josef Ponten, *Architektur die nicht gebaut wurde* (Architecture that was not built) (1925), from which Kiesler draws several of his references to projects by artists and architects, most of which remained unrealized or were built not according to their intentions.

Concerning the entry on Rabelais, Kiesler is referring to the Abbey of Thélème, an unconventional monastic complex described in François Rabelais's *Gargantua and Pantagruel* as rendered in the nineteenth century by the architect Charles-Auguste Questel in two lithographs first published in Charles Lenormant, *Rabelais et l'architecture de la renaissance. Restitution de l'abbaye de Thélème* (Paris: Crozet, 1840), plates 1–2. Questel's "reconstruction" is described and reproduced in Ponten, *Architektur die nicht gebaut wurde* (vol. 1, 38–39; vol. 2, fig. 65) but is not mentioned in other drafts of *Magic Architecture*. The years listed in the entries for Schinkel and Cheval are those of the architects' birth. The entry for "Ren" is Christopher Wren's St. Paul's Cathedral. On top of this page, Kiesler notes: **modern Man is absolete** [sic] On the back of the same folio, there is the following aphorism handwritten by Kiesler:

The desirable state of a country: Productivity of man–not in manufacturing, but in fully realizing himself.[58]

modern man is obsolete,

Dinokrates:
Project for the peninsula Kalkidike in Greece for Alexander the Great

Filarete:
Project for the town of Sforcinda. Filarete born 1410 in Florence.

Rabelais:
Description of an extraordinary piece of architecture designed by architect Questel.

Leonardo Da Vinci:
Sketches for new types of cathedrals

Sulpiz Boisserée:
Gothic cathedral of the Gral. Executed after the medieaval text of the Titurel.

Giambattista Piranesi:
born 1720. His projects for the Via Appia and for the race arena as well as his drawings for prisons.

Paulus Decker:
Projects for a fountain of "Lust"

Friedrich Schinkel:
1781. Project for a palace of King Otto of Greece on the Acropolis.

Hans Poelzig:
Project for the Mozarteum in Salzburg.

Ferd. Postman Cheval:
1836. His dream castle built at Hauterives. France

Bruno Taut:
Ideas for the dissolution of the City. New community designs.

Bruegel: Tower

El Greco: Toledo

Corbusier:
Plan Voison, skyscraper city

Kiesler:
The horizontal skyscraper. The Endless House.

Renn – St. Paulus-Cathedral

Buckminster Fuller:
The Dymaxion House.

Scheerbart

Huysmans

Tatlin:
Project for a building for the Third Internationale, 1919.

Garnier!

List of unbuilt architectural projects and their authors with handwritten additions. See Parts VI to X of *Magic Architecture*.
TS, pencil. ÖFLKS, TXT_6800/0_N3recto

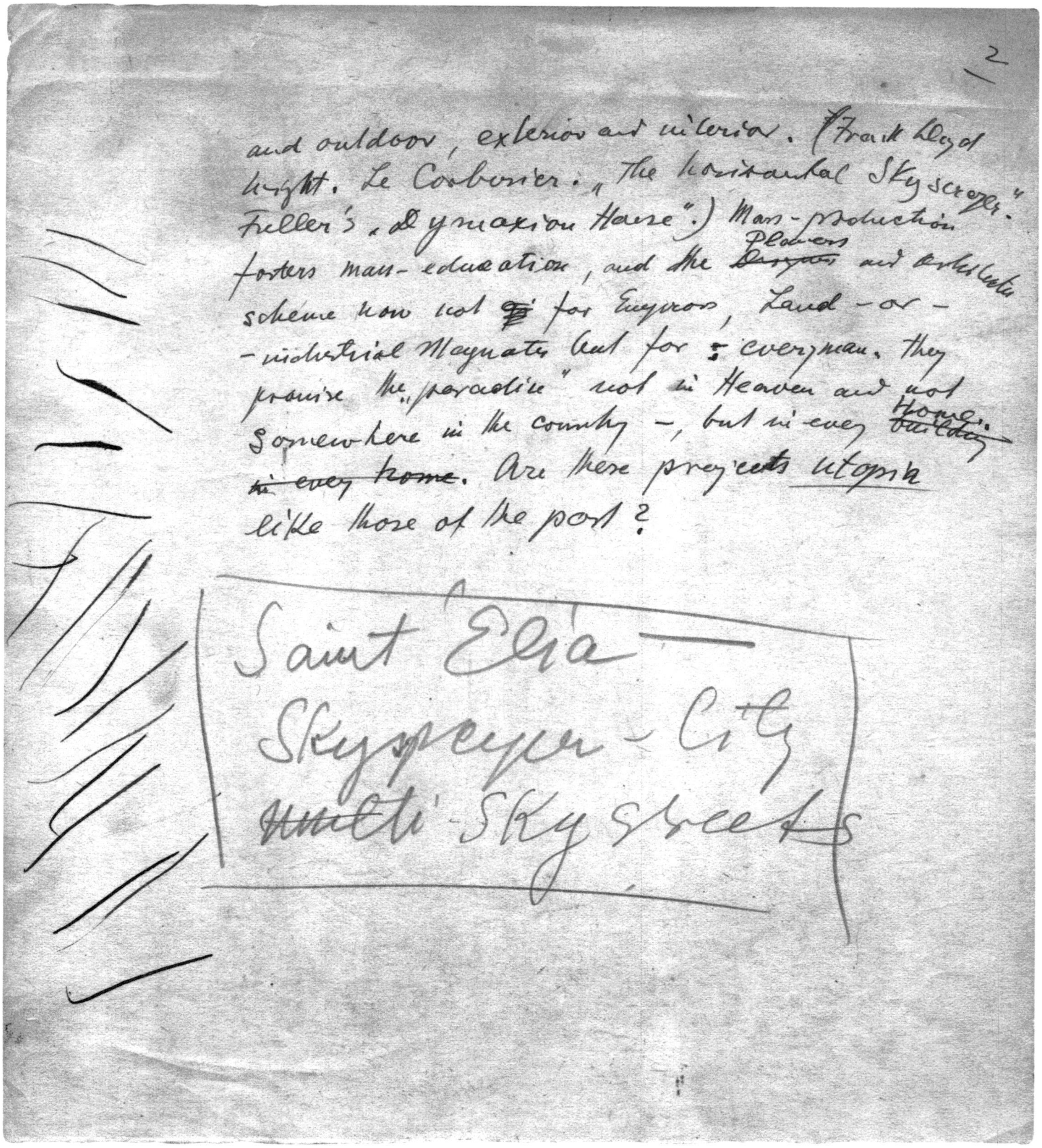

2

and outdoor, exterior and interior. (Frank Lloyd Wright. Le Corbusier: „The horizontal Skyscraper." Fuller's „Dymaxion House".) Mass-production fosters mass-education, and the ~~Designers~~ Planners and architects scheme now not for Emperors, Land-or-industrial Magnates but for everyman. They promise the „paradise" not in Heaven and not somewhere in the country –, but in every ~~building~~ Home. ~~in every home.~~ Are these projects utopia like those of the past?

Saint Elia
Skyscraper-City
~~multi~~ Sky streets

Preliminary manuscript draft on twentieth-century developments (see Part x of *Magic Architecture*). Handwritten draft with addendum on Antonio "Saint'Elia [sic]–Skyscraper-City Sky streets." Ink and pencil. ÖFLKS, TXT_6800/0_N2

1 TXT_5877/0_N14 See also a letter from Kiesler to Hugh Garvey, August 6, 1946, quoted in Annotated Chronology, p. 378. For Kiesler's selection of chapters for reading and sample chapters of writing, see Main Text, fig. B.02.

2 Kiesler probably refers to the nine chapters on "prehistory" included in Part I, whose structure remained essentially the same in later stages of the book manuscript.

3 **That was necessary for a proper evaluation of the general structures of the content; ~~particularly for the part which deals with the origins of shelter in architecture.~~** TXT_6724/0_N1

4 The fact that this proposal does not include part or chapter numbers for what are essentially the writing sampled in the previous Note to the Publisher indicates that by this point Kiesler was considering revising the overall structure of his book manuscript. Changes in the overall number of pages mentioned in the following paragraph point in the same direction.

5 **700 pages** TXT_6724/0_N2

6 **500 pages** TXT_6724/0_N2

7 **within the main text or within the main illustrations.** TXT_6724/0_N2

8 **a rich section** TXT_6724/0_N2

9 **It will chiefly concern itself with elaborate factual details, which could not be included in the text without disturbing the ease of its continuity.** TXT_6724/0_N2 **without disturbing the flow of the text, ~~but which are vital information.~~** TXT_6711/0_N2 Only a few annotations were drafted but never ultimately completed or included in later versions of the book manuscript. See Annotations and Data mentioned in Part I, chapter 1.

10 **the ~~cave~~** TXT_6802/0_N1

11 **~~architecturally and sociologically speaking / expressed,~~** TXT_6802/0_N3

12 **Man is again ~~tending~~ to be part of the ~~total~~ structure of the environment** TXT_6802/0_N3

13 **(Africa, ~~New Caledonia~~, ~~Alaska~~) The Pacific, American Indians** inserted by hand. TXT_6800/0_N4

14 Kiesler refers to Anthemius of Tralles and Isidorus of Miletus whose design for the Hagia Sophia was completed in 537 CE.

15 See, Deir el-Bahari mortuary temple complex in the Theban Necropolis, Luxor, Egypt; first temple constructed in fifteenth-century BCE.

16 **India, China** added by hand TXT_6800/0_N4

17 **~~The Projects of Pompeji, Italy / Projects for imaginative architecture in houses vividly planned in Pompeji, Italy.~~** TXT_6800/0_N4

18 **~~creative~~** TXT_6800/0_N4

19 These incorrect dates are a handwritten addition. See, Giovanni Batista Piranesi (1720–1778).

20 **~~Visionary buildings by Hieronymous Bosch.~~** TXT_6800/0_N5

21 See figs. C.02a–b.

22 These two sentences are handwritten additions substituting the following: **~~The attention is now again directed toward an integration of Vision and Reality, of Nature and Architecture, of Interior and Exterior, of the Machine and the Spirit.~~** TXT_6800/0_N5

23 French for abscond TXT_6800/0_N5

24 **the conquest of Technology** TXT_6800/0_N5

25 **between wish and fact** TXT_6800/0_N5

26 **Tatling** TXT_6800/0_N5

27 Closed parenthesis is missing. TXT_6800/0_N5

28 **~~typical~~ curiosa** TXT_6800/0_N6

29 incomplete word TXT_6800/0_N6

30 **~~just as Rousseay~~** [sic] **~~was called the master of primitive painting in France.~~** TXT_6800/0_N6 For illustrations of Ferdinand Cheval's mausoleum "structure," see plates 6 and 7 in the Main Text.

31 **Part ONE** / **~~Chapter Two~~** / **~~Primitive Architecture~~** / **~~The manuscript to be divided into four parts of which the first and last are the smallest, the second and third the largest.~~** / **~~First Part~~** TXT_6807/0_N2

32 **of physical ~~function and~~** TXT_6807/0_N2

33 **Places of worship??** [handwritten in the margin by Kiesler] TXT_6807/0_N3 Cf. Kiesler's drawings of his vision of such unified world around the nucleus of a cave dwelling included in MA I.1, figs. B.06a–c.

34 **~~(Picture)~~** TXT_6807/0_N3 As noted in Sources, Disciplines, and Objects (p. 13), Kiesler selects the picture of the Trujillo house-vessels and the rest of the illustrations sampled in this "chapter" from a German ethnological compendium comparing America and Africa: Georg Buschan, ed., *Illustrierte Völkerkunde Vol. 1: Vergleichende Völkerkunde: Amerika – Afrika*, 2nd edition (Stuttgart: Strecker und Schröder, 1922), 398, fig. 158. For Kiesler's handwritten notes and sketches from this volume see figs. C.03a–b. TXT_6876_N1–N2

35 **in contrast to our state of mind** TXT_6876/0_N1–N2

36 **"/quote (missing)** handwritten note indicating that a quotation is missing TXT_6876/0_N1–N2

37 **In ~~our~~ culture** TXT_6876/0_N1–N2

38 **~~and the satisfaction of a purpose it is to serve is wholly dependent as to beauty on its price and as such unsatisfactory~~** TXT_6876/0_N1–N2

39 Kiesler provided German descriptions for the following passage, as well as for pictures 4–6. The text that appears in these sections has been translated by the editors. **Eingebaut in und um den Felsen, nicht nur physisch schutzsuchend, sondern auch spirituell, die Form des Hochberges, der visionär anregend ist und das Traumbild einer göttlichen Macht hervorruft. Hingelag**[er]**t ist die Festungsstadt, angeschmiegt, angegossen, zärtlich.** / **Die Umarmung ist physisch und geistig. Waffen und physische Stärke sind nicht genug im Kampf. Die Mechanik allein ist nicht genug zur Aktion, Glaube muss den Körper tiefer und allgemeiner durchsetzen als Blut und Oxygen.** TXT_6807/0_N3; TXT_6876/0_N1–N2 Kiesler refers to a photographic view of the "Machu Pichu Inca stronghold" reproduced in *Illustrierte Völkerkunde*, 381, fig. 150.

40 See, *Illustrierte Völkerkunde*, Plate I ("Hausbau der Nordamerikaner").

41 **Gesichtsmaske aus schwarzem Leder mit aufgenähten gelben Lederstreifen, die die Tataui**[e]**rungdes Frauengesichts wiedergeben. Vom Abgekok bei Krankheitsheilungen getragen. Cumberland Golf, Baffinland.** [handwritten text in German translated by the editors] TXT_6807/0_N4 See, *Illustrierte Völkerkunde*, 89, fig. 10.

42 **Jedes Wesen, jeder Gegenstand besitzt nämlich nach dem Galuben der Eskimo einen Schatten oder ein spirituelles Abbild; die grotesken Holzmasken der Alaska-Eskimo sollen z.B. diese schattenhaften Doppelgänger darstellen.** Handwritten text in German translated by the editors. TXT_6807/0_N4

43 **Siouxhäuptling Black Rock in vollem Schmuck mit dem Büffelmantel un**[d] **der mit Hermelinfellen und Adlerfedern verzierten Hörnerhaube (Dem Abzeichen des Kriegshäuptlings)** Handwritten text in German translated by the editors. TXT_6807/0_N4 See Kiesler's drawings on the theme of "magic power" in "primitive man" and in "modern man" (figs. C.04a–b), in which the former is represented as a Sioux Chief after George Catlin's painting of Black Rock and his family (1854) (reproduced as frontispiece in *Illustrierte Völkerkunde*) and the latter as then "commander in chief" Dwight D. Eisenhower. SFP_6666/0_N2a–N2b

44 **?** [handwritten in the margin] SFP6666_N2a–N2b, TXT_6807/0_N4

45 **~~minerals~~** SFP_6666/0_N2a–N2b

46 **back to ~~the subconscious of his primitive youth, which dwells in harmonious brotherhood with the souls of primitive men at the bottom of~~** SFP_6666/0_N2a–N2b

47 **types of man** TXT_6807/0_N6

48 **The beginning of the 20th Century with its ~~emphasis on~~** TXT_6800/0_N1

49 Cf. Part X, chapter 6: **Freed from imperialism, tzarism, and monarchism, the populace began to plan on a large scale for the realization of better social systems, and, logically, their every-day architects (in the past immune to progress) designed better architectural orders.**

50 **Bruno Taut's ~~designs~~** TXT_6800_N1

51 **~~concerns itself~~ wi[th]** TXT_6800_N1

52 German for festival hall

53 **~~Greater contact among nations~~** TXT_6800_N1

54 **Reaction to the ~~danger of~~ overgrowing influence** TXT_6800_N1

55 See illustration of Kiesler's project among those by Corbusier and Wright, plate 54. See also Kiesler's pencil sketch of a chart on the emergence of "Every Man" earlier in the Addenda fig. C.02b.

56 **~~building, in every home~~** TXT_6800_N2

57 Compare the handwritten description of Sant'Elia's project (fig. C.05b) with the list of unbuilt projects in the following document (fig. C.02a). TXT_6800_ N3

58 TXT_6800/0_N3verso

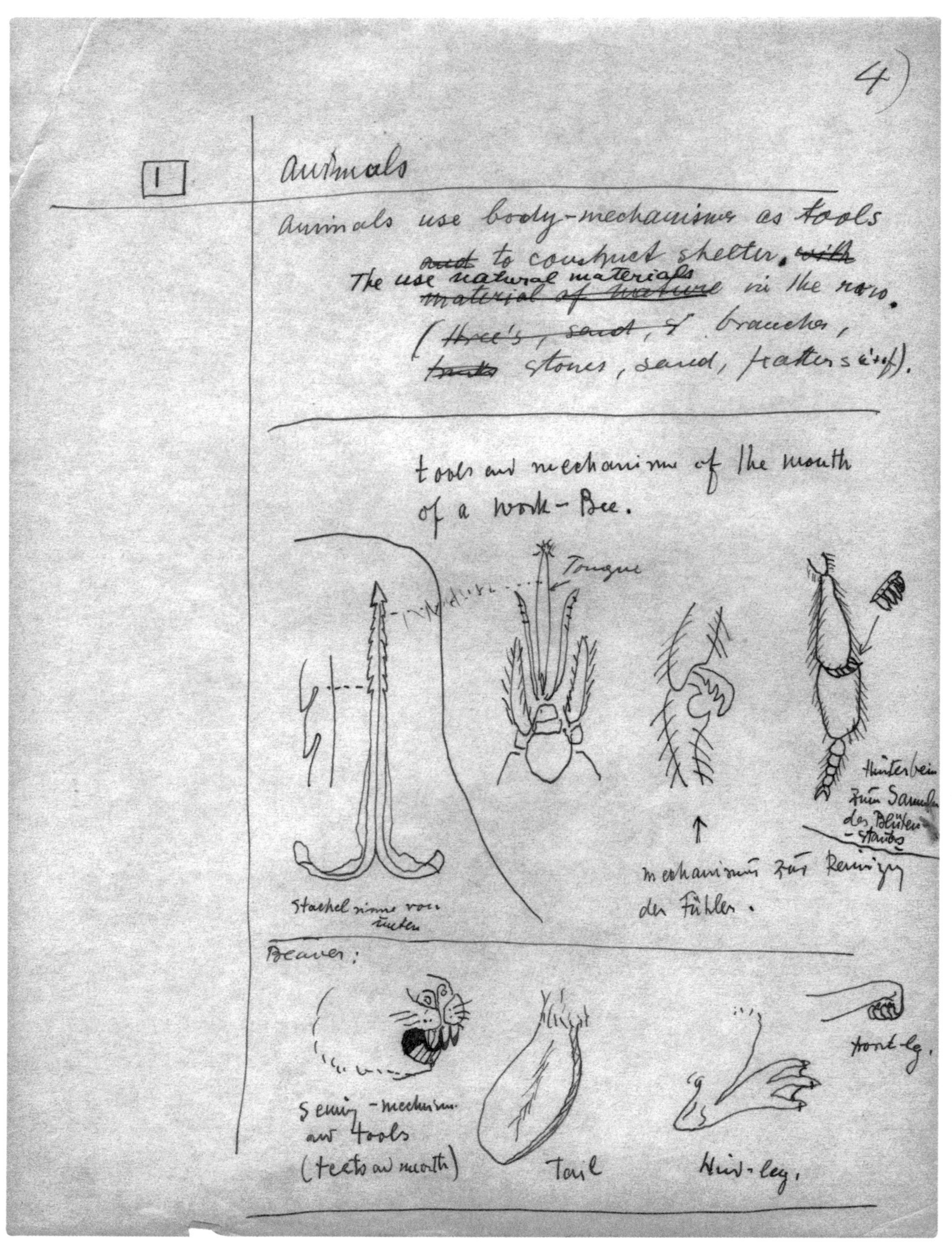
4)
I
Animals
Animals use body-mechanisms as tools to construct shelter.
The use natural materials in the raw.
(branches,
stones, sand, feathers etc).
tools and mechanisms of the mouth
of a work-Bee.
Tongue
Hinterbein zum Sammeln des Blüten-Staubs
mechanismus zur Reinigung der Fühler.
Beaver:
Sawing-mechanism and tools (teeth and mouth)
Tail
Hind-leg.
front-leg.

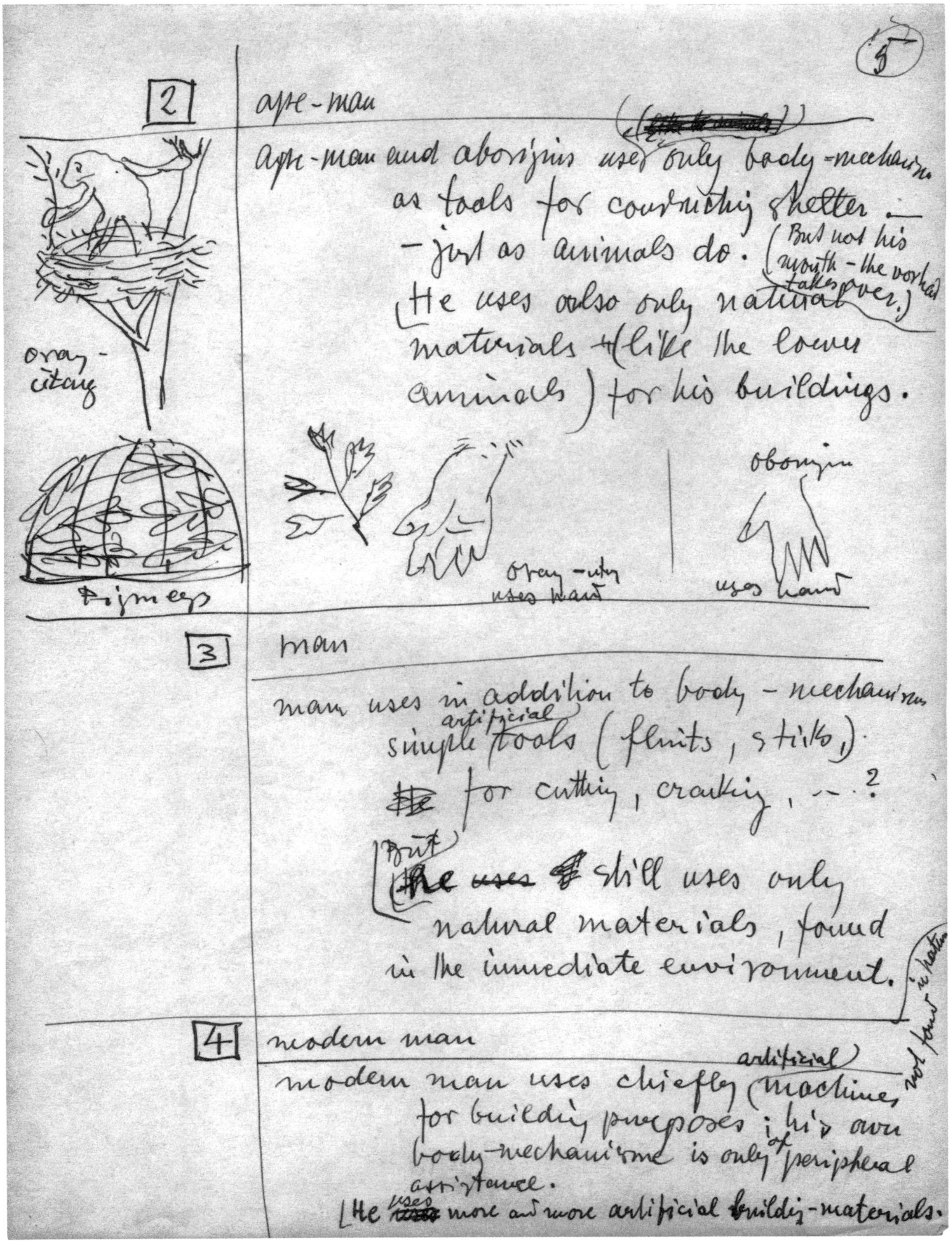

5

[2] ape-man

(~~[illegible]~~)

ape-man and aborigines uses only body-mechanism as tools for constructing shelter. — just as animals do. (But not his mouth – the verbal takes over.)
[He uses also only natural materials (like the lower animals) for his buildings.

orang-utang

Pigmees

orang-utan uses hand

aborigine uses hand

[3] man

man uses in addition to body-mechanism simple artificial tools (flints, sticks,) for cutting, cracking, ...?

[But ~~he uses~~ still uses only natural materials, found in the immediate environment. (not found in nature)

[4] modern man

modern man uses chiefly (artificial) machines for building purposes; his own body-mechanism is only of peripheral assistance.
[He uses more and more artificial building-materials.

Building Tools of Animals and Humans Two-page preliminary chart, with drawings and descriptions on the building tools of animals in comparison with those of humans. Although not used in later drafts, these charts correspond to Part II, chapter 4 of *Magic Architecture*, "The Building Tools of Animals." (ink) ÖFLKS, SFP_6664/0_N1–N2 *figs.* C.07a–b

(A) Tools for ATTACK

and

(B) Tools for defense

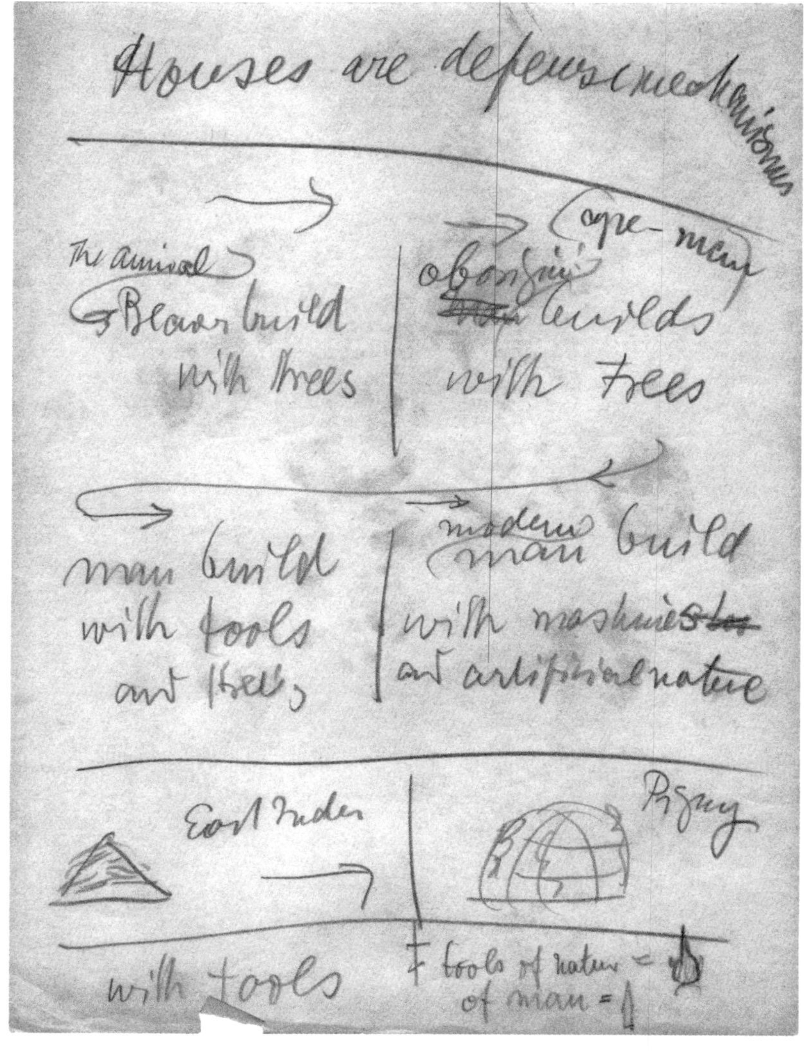

Notes on two types of "tools." Like the previous two-page chart, these statements and the ensuing table-chart, not used in later drafts, correspond to Part II, chapter 4 of *Magic Architecture*: "The Building Tools of Animals." (pencil) ÖFLKS, SFP_6665/0_N3recto-verso

fig. C.08

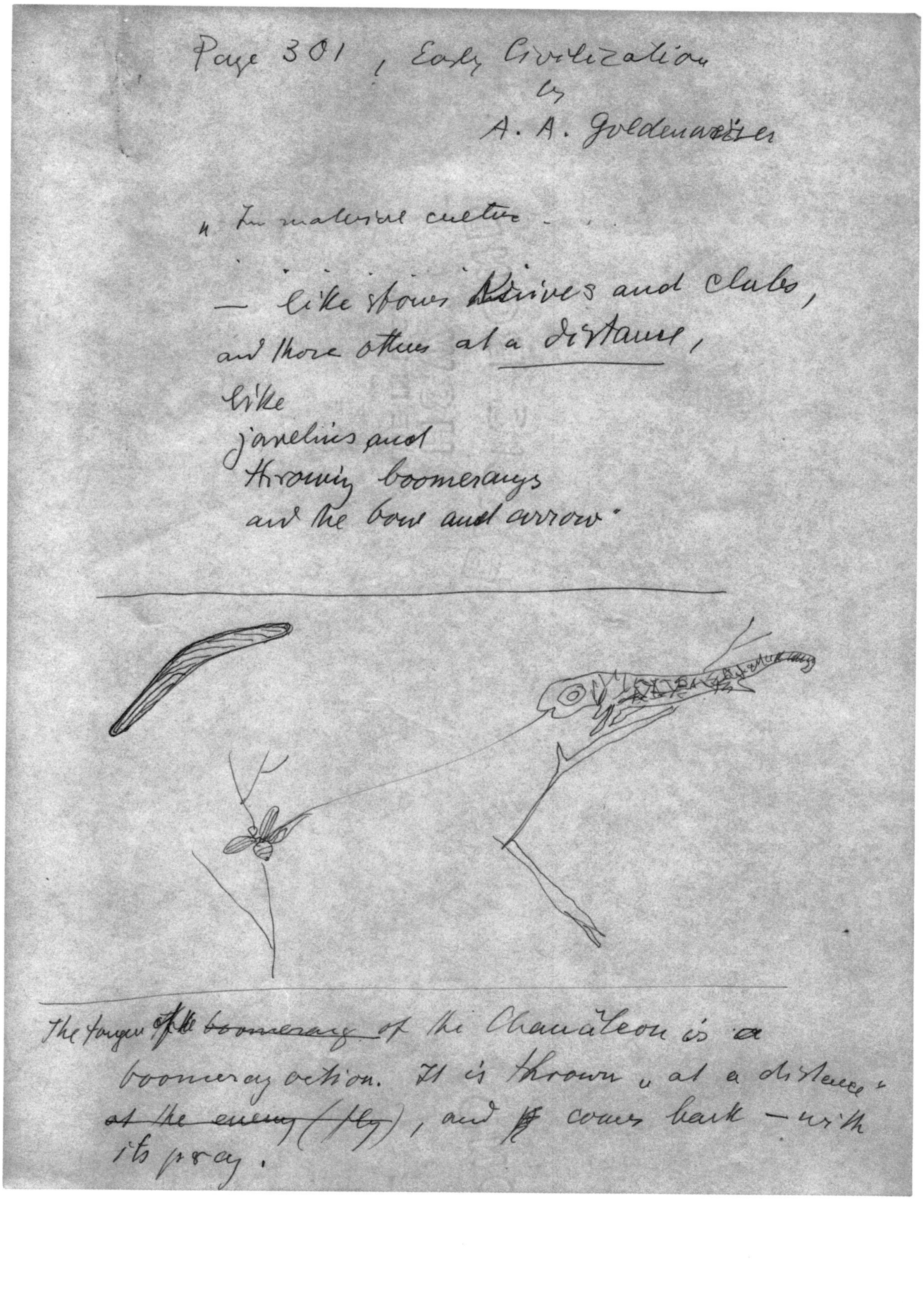

Page 301, Early Civilization
by
A. A. Goldenweiser

"In material culture . . .

— like stones knives and clubs,
and those others at a distance,
like
javelins and
throwing boomerangs
and the bow and arrow."

The tongue ~~of the boomerang~~ of the Chameleon is a
boomerang action. It is thrown, at a distance,
~~at the enemy (fly)~~, and it comes back — with
its prey.

Kiesler copied this brief excerpt from an anthropological textbook by the Kiev-born American anthropologist Alexander Alexandrovich Goldenweiser. It is followed by Kiesler's sketch of an Australian boomerang and a chameleon capturing an insect from a distance. A number of chapters in Part I of *Magic Architecture* refer to a non-objectified mortal threat striking from a distance, while chapters in Parts II and III mention the development of weapons in Indigenous cultures. The entire paragraph from Goldenweiser marked for quotation reads: "In material culture, for example, some things are universal. Everywhere there is some form of habitation; some means of transportation is used, by land, by water, or both; some garments are worn, however scant; some tools, however crude, are employed for cutting and hammering; some weapons appear and among these are those used in close combat, like stones knives and clubs, and those others that strike at a distance, like javelins and throwing boomerangs, and the bow and arrow." Alexander A. Goldenweiser, *Early Civilization: An Introduction to Anthropology* (New York: Knopf, 1922), 301–302. The book exists in the Kieslers' library. See also editors' notes in the Main Text for Part II, chapter 1. (ink) ÖFLKS, TXT_6819/0

fig. C.09a

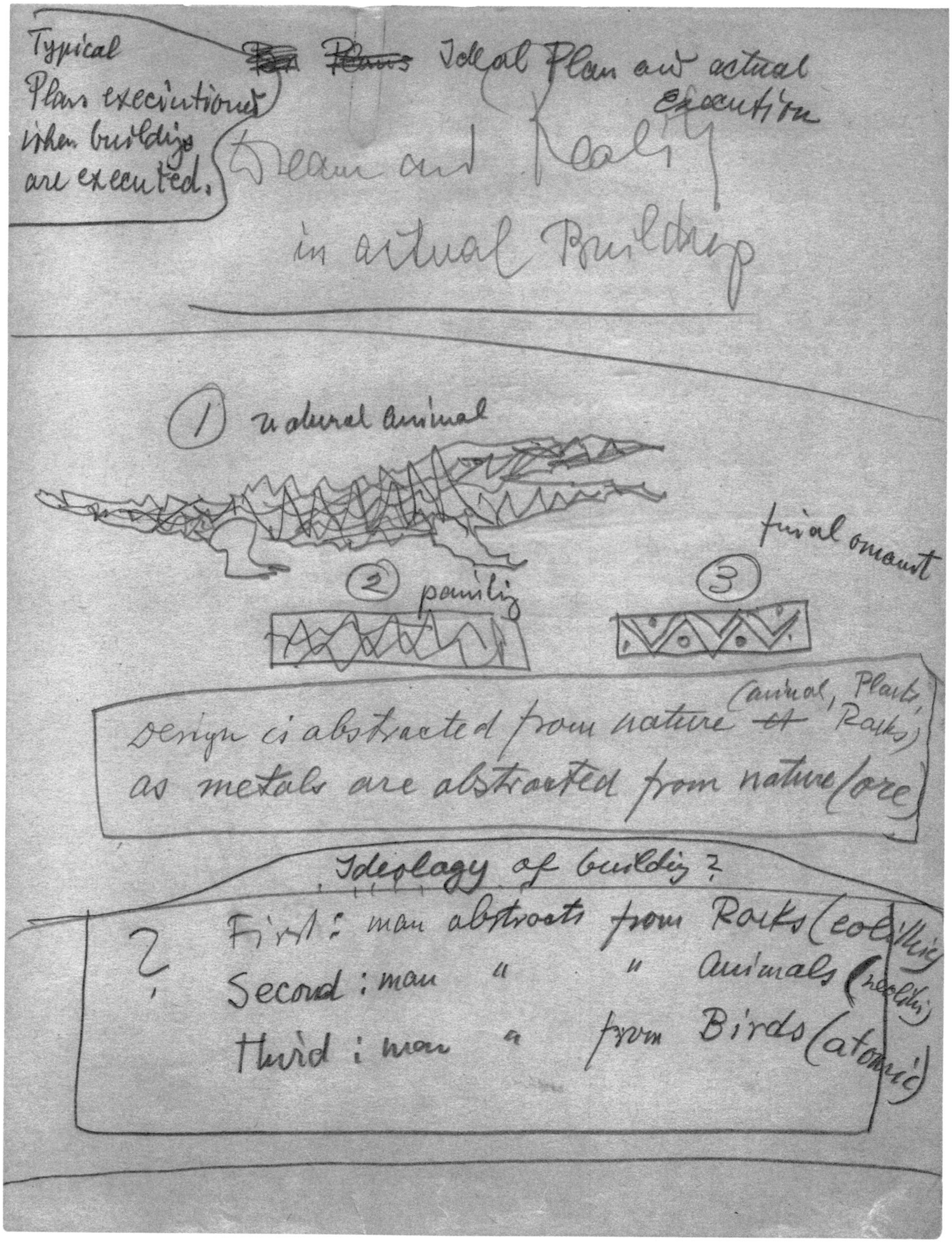

Typical
Plans executions
when buildings
are executed.

~~Plans~~ Ideal Plan and actual
execution

Dream and Reality
in actual Buildings

(1) natural animal

(2) painting

(3) final ornament

design is abstracted from nature ~~at~~ (animal, Plants, Rocks)
as metals are abstracted from nature (ore)

Ideology of building?

?

First: man abstracts from Rocks (eolithic)
Second: man " " animals (neolithic)
Third: man " from Birds (atomic)

fig. C.09b

Notes on the relation between dream, reality, and execution followed by further notes and a chart on the relation between earth extraction in nature and the origin of abstraction in (applied) art and (over)nature. "Over nature" here renders the German *Ubernatur*, or "supernature" used in medieval theological discourses (Scholastic theology in particular). Kiesler is perhaps conflating *Übernatur* with the Nietzschean *Übermensch*, often translated into English as "Overman," or "Superman" (the term is mentioned in Kiesler's "Orbit of Exstacy" chart), which could have a number of repercussions for his diagram on the origin of abstraction and design. While not transcribed in later drafts, the chart and associated notes correspond to the content of chapters in Part IV, particularly chapter 8, "The Era of Abstraction." See Sources, Disciplines, and Objects, pp. 40-41. (pencil) ÖFLKS, TXT_6806/0_N1-N2

fig. C.10

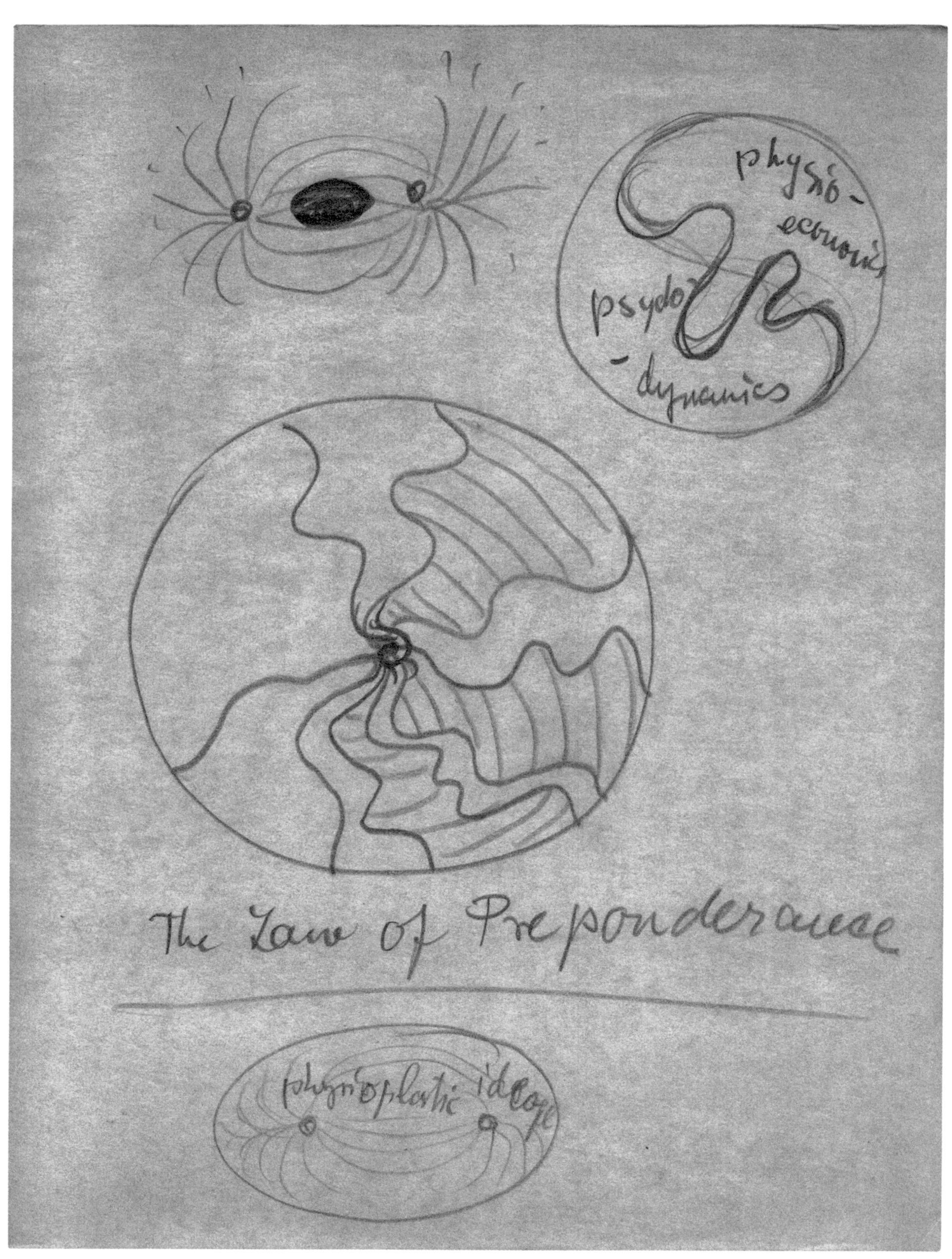

"The Law of Preponderance"
Chart corresponding to the content of Part IV, chapters 5 and 9. On the origin of terms "physio-plastic" and "ideo-plastic" in the writings of Max Verworn, see Part IV, chapters 6 and 9. (pencil) ÖFLKS, TXT_6817/0

fig. C.11

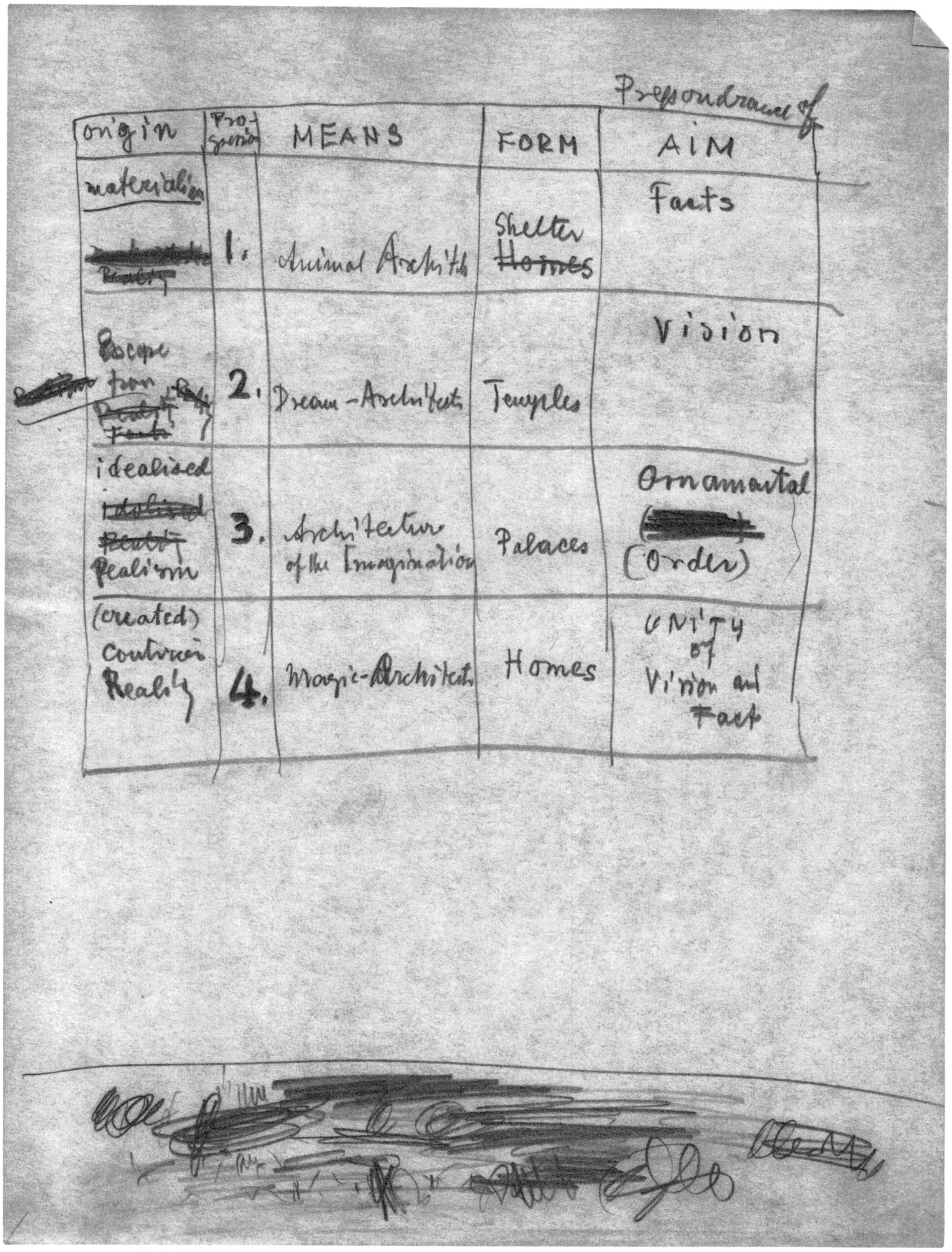

Preponderance of

origin	Progression	MEANS	FORM	AIM
materialism	1.	Animal Architecture	Shelter	Facts
Escape from	2.	Dream-Architecture	Temples	Vision
idealised Realism	3.	Architecture of the Imagination	Palaces	Ornamental (Order)
(created) contrived Reality	4.	Magic-Architecture	Homes	UNITY of Vision and Fact

Table chart illustrating the "progression" from "Animal" to "Magic Architecture" based on the "preponderance" of "origin," "form" and "aim." (pencil) ÖFLKS, TXT_6817/0_N2

the Orbit of Ecstasy

A CHART

fig. C.12a–b

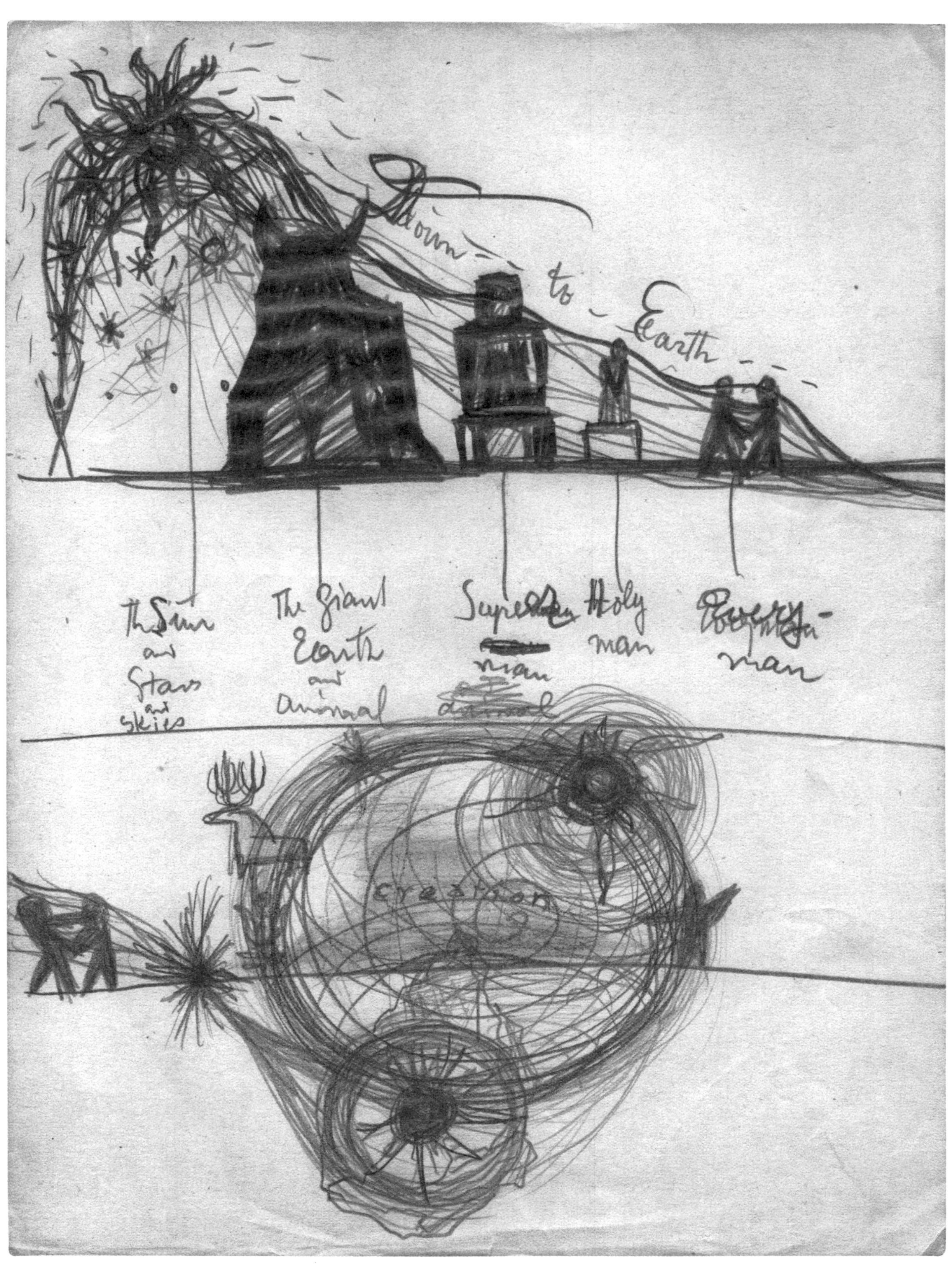

The Orbit of Exstasy

Title sheet and chart illustrating the progression from natural and anthropomorphic religion to the ideology of “everyman.” Compare with Kiesler’s preliminary version of a similar chart concluding with “Every-man” sketched in one of the preliminary book outlines (fig. c.02b). A “chart” with the same title figures in an earlier draft of the book’s “Content,” as an appendix to the “Epilogue” (following Part x of *Magic Architecture*). Subtitled “The home as nucleus of Magic Architecture accomplished,” it suggests that in an earlier version of the book manuscript, “The Orbit of Exstasy” was envisioned as the final chart of *Magic Architecture* (the assembled version of the manuscript finishes with the “metabolism chart” of Kiesler’s “Mobile Home-Library,” see plate 60). (ink) ÖFLKS, SFP_6667/0_N1–N2

A selection of transcriptions from books or other publications made by the Kieslers while working collaboratively on *Magic Architecture*, which were ultimately not incorporated in the final manuscript.

A number of transcriptions from German texts were slated for translation but never materialized. These are included here, translated by the editors whenever an English edition does not exist. Titles of books, chapters, or articles, along with page numbers included in the transcription were normally added by hand on the typewritten text either by Stefi or Frederick Kiesler (indicated in bold). Most of these are included except in instances of redunancies.

Transcriptions from Breuil and Verworn include original text and afterthoughts by Kiesler related to *Magic Architecture* that were not used in later drafts, but are included in this section. This heterogeneous assembly of transcribed leftovers from texts by anthropologists, philosophers, naturalists, cultural historians, and the popular press constitute a supplementary "reader" accompaying the main text of *Magic Architecture*, a large percentage of which consists of lengthy quotations by the same or other authors, not unlike the thick reader(s) with xeroxed typewritten transcriptions of English, French, and German texts (left in the original language) that Kiesler prepared for the students of his Laboratory for Design Correlation at Columbia University in the late 1930s and early 40s.

List of Excerpts

The Associated Press, "Atomic Blue Glow Kills Scientists: Army Reports Accidents Caused no Blast, Debris or Noise," *The Sun* (New York, NY), June 28, 1946, 21.

Selections of the following article have been transcribed. The paragraph structure and quotation marks follow the original newspaper text. The name and place of the newspaper are added on the TS by Stefi Kiesler, who provided the transcription. Kiesler's archived newspaper clipping of the article includes pencil markings noting paragraphs to be transcribed. See Sources, Disciplines, and Objects, fig. A.01.[59]

The army today described an atomic chain reaction set up on May 21 at the Los Alamos atomic laboratory, which burned a scientist fatally, as a blue glow with "no explosion in the sense that there were no mechanical effects, no debris, no noise."

The detailed report of the Army gave this description of the accident:

"An accident occurred when a piece of equipment slipped. This brought the material swiftly together beyond the critical point. This resulted in a tremendous energy release within millionths of a second, which was evidenced to the persons present through a sensation of heat and visual perception of a blue glow around the material.

"In the words of one of the men present, 'It was as if you were standing near an arc welder when he struck the arc.'

No Blast or Noise

"The blue glow resulted from the ionization of air particles by radiation emanating from the fissionable material. There was no explosion in the sense that there were no mechanical effects, no debris, no noise.

"In the millionths of a second in which this occurred, the immediate area and all in it were bombarded by intense high energy gamma rays and neutrons of all energies—fast, intermediate and slow. There were no beta and no alpha radiation.

"Dr. Slotin, at the instant of the mishap, knocked the equipment apart, thus halting the intensifying radiation and averting serious consequences, possibly death to his companions. He was grasping part of the equipment with his left hand at the moment of the accident.

"The medical men began to treat the accident victims as soon as they were admitted to the hospital," the report said. "This treatment, in general, consisted of many transfusions of whole blood and plasma and fluids, principally glucose and saline."

The report said that the burns suffered by Slotin were compared to a "three-dimensional sunburn," explaining: "The skin burns from the radiation are superficial, but as the rays penetrate the body they burn deep, resulting in injury and destruction of tissue and blood cells."

Daglian, whose burns were less severe, died in twenty-six days after the accident.

Leo Frobenius, *Kulturgeschichte Afrikas: Prolegomena zu einer historischen Gestaltlehre.* [Cultural History of Africa: Prolegomena to a historical Theory of Representation] [Zurich: Phaidon Verlag, 1933), 63–65.

English translation by the editors. Word emphasis in the transcription follows the original published text only on some occasions. These transcriptions were not translated or incorporated in the assembled text of *Magic Architecture*, yet they correspond in content with Part IV, chapter 2.

***Frobenius*, p. 63**[60]

The visual art [*Bildkunst*] of the Mesolithic has been preserved only in a single part of the earth as long as such art was attached to a formation of the earth's surface that has been sustained from that period. Even if in those times earthen or wooden buildings have been erected aboveground, such structures cannot exist anymore. However, there is no reason to assume they existed. We now know the subterranean world of ancient times, the vast caves of the Dordogne. Everything was rediscovered in there approximately in the condition in which they used to be after their human use had ceased: the accumulation of the light bowls, the tools, the clay sculptures—except for the footsteps. If there had been a basic building art [*Baukunst*] aboveground at that time, it could be assumed that it would have been documented in some way in this underworld. However, the more we get to know the details of the furnishing of this subterranean, lightless, eternally nocturnal afterlife, we shall be compelled to increasingly take them as former homesteads of a sacred purpose [*Heimstätten sakraler Bestimmung*]. This is at least true for the most important sites.

Now, the clarification of the progressive discovery of culture in general, as well as of the germination of the cultural phenomena, forces us to determine that at the "beginning [*Anfang*]," a division into profane and sacral life cannot at all be thinkable. The curve can only run from a flatly animalistic attitude towards the relationship with nature in the signification of the environment [*im Sinne der Umwelt*] to the formulation of emotional grasping [*Ergriffenheit*], whose first expressions ensued the germs [*Keime*] of the "creative Paideuma." The emotional grasping was always identified with the sense of sacredness [*Heiligkeit*]. The capacity for emotional grasping increased. The human being was taken by one substance after the other, until the total phenomena of the environment as well as life were finally summarized in a strong encompassing feeling of life [*Lebensgefühl*] full of sacred essence. In this first culmination everything was sacred: the furthest as well as the nearest, the smallest as well as the largest, the essential for life, the self-evident, the everyday [*das Alltägliche*]. Also the gathering food, like food itself; clothing [*Tracht*], like dwelling [*Hausung*]. We will see that even the union of the sexes was specifically subject to this attitude, for which Walter F. Otto coined a good saying: the myth was already alive back then and germinated in action. We do not yet know when to date the zenith of the sacral period [*Sakralperiode*]; however, the possibility of finding this point is granted. Namely, by means of ethnographic facts and in the essential core [*Wesen*] of early human arts. Today we anticipate, that it must have been close to the "sacral regicide [*sakraler Königsmord*]," since from this psychological complex [*Komplex*] the separation of the profane takes place at great speed. In this culmination point, human beings still experienced the cosmos in the earthly mirror image [*irdisches Spiegelbild*] and even played themselves the role of the essential core of cosmic unity. Out of this highly sacral condition, monarchy, priesthood, and class hierarchy detached themselves on one side, while laws on the other, profane side. "Religion" became the domain of sacral reserves [*sakrale Reservate*] following the profane other. From now on, this almost historical trajectory races along the path of an increasingly pervasive profanation, until it finally finds its highest triumphs in the principle of causality [*Kausalitätsprinzip*] and the "ignominious dismissal of speculative metaphysics"[61] in Materialism.

***Frobenius*, p. 242**[62]

The transition from emotional gripping [*Ergriffenheit*] to conceptual grasping [*Begreifen*] is and remains (at least for us) the Alpha and the Omega of every formation of culture. It runs as an all-determining factor through the history of individual human beings and peoples, as well as through the history of culture and art. Herein, the being of culture [*Kultursein*] corresponds to the world of appearances [*Gestaltwelt*], especially the appearance of culture that is most obvious to the human eye, that of plants. And if we seem to lack the plant-like steadiness in our cultural being, this only signifies a difference in degree, which emerges from our inherent difficulty in gaining above all a disposition [*Einstellung*] at the right distance. It shall not by all means be denied (especially at first observation) that this difficulty is significant. However, if it is possible to recognize such immense phenomena like the metaphysical curve, namely, to perceive how by being emotionally affected by the core of the environment [*das Wesen der Umwelt*] has led humanity from spontaneous, isolated and sporadic dispositions to complete self-identification (devotion to the point of self-abandonment) with the environment, and following that, via a process of factualization [*Vertatsächligung*], oozing down, drop by drop into profanation until it has led to the glorification of the conceptual grasping of facts; furthermore, if it is possible to peel out processes within the trajectory from the richness of signification [*Sinnerfülltheit*] to the capacity for interpretation [*Deutungsfähigkeit*], then life finally begins to manifest itself in the awareness of culture [*Kulturerschlossenheit*].

This way of observation ostensibly interprets the garden of the culture-world and the art-world as an abundance of wonders, but no longer of magical conjuring [*magische Zauberei*]. The latter would correspond to the assumption of possibilities which interrupt or bend the course of nature by its capacity to stand against nature [*Naturwidrigkeit*]. On the contrary in wonder, the higher potency of natural circumstances may be glimpsed. Therefore, it is obvious that in the spiritual creations of humankind as well as in its poetry, the miraculous appears as a phenomenon of mysticism emerging from devotion. The magical [*Zauberische*] grows out of the primitive need of the "ego" to free itself from the incomprehensible reality and thus to gain instruments of power from magic. Hence it is quite natural that the narratives of magical things [*zauberische Dinge*], powers, events easily found their way into the literature of the Hamites, but hardly into that of the Ethiopians.

***Frobenius*, p. 247**

Each clan led its own life. There are no markets between them and they have only been introduced here and there by the High Sudanese. But if these state-builders do not watch over their maintenance, they soon deteriorate because the small clans have no need for exchange. The traffic in the immediate vicinity is enough. Each clan produces what is necessary for itself. Only instances of death and cultic rituals, as well as very rarely more expansive hunting operations, unite them. All the world, men and women, the elderly and the children, are diligent in farming. The fields and plantations are remarkably well-kept where these weak communities [*Gemeindeschwachen*] are not exposed to the danger of the marauding High Sudanese.

These people are of staggering intensity in work as in piety. Yet this is so natural to them that they are not aware of it, and, as a result of their completely self-evident commitment, they are also unable to talk about it. Considering their inability to execute anything other than consequentially and silently, they experience everything with a fervor that easily leaves the impression of an indifferent composure on strangers.

Their entire life is filled with the rhythm of the great Being [*des grossen Seins*], expressed by the transformation from becoming to perishing and becoming again [*von Werden zum Vergehen und Wiederwerden*]. This transformation of being is the content of their life and determines the course of things and its contemplation. Just as seed sowing, growth, harvest follow on seed sowing, growth, harvest time and again, so too are birth, maturation, old age, death superseded by rebirth, maturation, old age, death. Rhythm sublimates eternity. Fertility of the earth, fructification and human progeny, these are the three pivotal points of the course of time; everything is revolving around them from the coarsest to the finest.

***Frobenius*, p. 247**

The life of the Ethiopian culture of mysticism ascends in three stages. The first is given in the integral development [*Vollentwicklung*] of the clan, whose magnificent primitivity [*grossartige Primitivität*] was sketched in the previous section. The second is achieved with the formation of the people into a community [*Gemeinde*], the third in that of the state [*Staat*]. Now it has already been explained that in their initial unity (to concur with Walter F. Otto), myth and poetry arise in the nature of life unspoken, and only in a later stage are cladded by words.

Henri Breuil, Miles Crawford Burkitt, and M. F. Montagu Pollock, *Rock paintings of Southern Andalusia: A Description of a Neolithic and Copper Age Art Group* (Oxford: Clarendon Press, 1929), 85–86 (emphasis not in the original). With a preface and conclusion by Frederick Kiesler

These excerpts were not included in the text of *Magic Architecture*, yet a different section of the study of Andalusian rock paintings by Breuil and others was quoted in Part III, chapter 2. Similar references to rock paintings based on texts by Frobenius are made in Part I, chapter 1. The following transcriptions are preceded and followed handwritten text by Kiesler, which further suggests that he originally intended to use these excerpts as part of a chapter. Emphasis was added by Kiesler.

The abbé Henri Breuil takes a similar point of view. He too finds that probably most, if not all, of these Rock paintings had a sacral origin; –and even sacred meaning.

From our architectural point of view he verifies the assumption that these designs belong to a type of assembly-caves rather than to home-caves, – a fact which is very important.[63]

The prominent position occupied by a number of the larger sites is significant. Thus, the rock-shelter of Las Figuras opens in a sandstone cliff visible for miles around, and from it there is an extensive view. The same is true of another site, outside our area, in the mountains of Jaen. While many of the smaller and less important sites are tucked away and difficult to find, practically speaking all the important ones are thus prominently situated. Another point to be remembered that in the two cases just mentioned the rock-shelters were certainly never used as homes. Las Figuras, indeed, could not have so served, for the floor of the entrance passage slopes steeply upwards, making a firm foothold difficult, and no traces can be seen of in the rock walls such as would have been required had there been any wooden platform. Many of these larger sites, however, lie close to natural springs of water. Might we argue from this that somebody–priest or guardian–had charge of the paintings, and that they were in sacred spots where seasonal and other important rites were duly performed by the population of the district?

It is unscientific, however, to assume similarity of motive in every case, and two other localities tell us a very different story. The first–the rock-shelter Gabal, in the Vélez Blanco district, a good deal farther to the east than our area–is at the base of a cliff above a long steep scree. It must have been a very suitable spot for a habitation, and, in fact, is still extensively used by the local goatherds both for themselves and their flocks. No trace of painting has been found on its walls, but over the arch of the doorway, in a little shallow niche difficult to get at without the help of a ladder, a number of paintings of human beings in the hour-glass form can be seen. Another site, Fuente de la Asa, in the same district, is reached by a narrow ledge along the side of a cliff, the ground rising perpendicularly on the left hand and falling steeply away on the right. Again no trace of paintings has been found in the shelter itself; but in a shallow ledge, there are a number of figures, including punctuations and a human being. The position of the paintings would surely suggest that at these two places at least they were designed as a sort of talisman to protect the home. In any case, home decoration was not the object the painter had in view.

The last rock-shelter to be considered–San Bartolomé–lies in our district, and has already been described in due place. The paintings occur on the inner side of a projecting curtain of rock behind which the investigator has to squeeze himself. Quite clearly San Bartolomé I was never a home, and home decoration therefore again ruled out. Equally clearly it does not enter into the category of the prominent larger sites. The concealment of the paintings is, however, very noteworthy and suggests the possibility that they may have had some sacred significance.

As regards the paintings at many of the smaller sites which do not seem to enter exactly into any of these three categories, it is impossible to be sure of the motives which prompted their production. That home decoration was intended appears, however, to be exceedingly unlikely.

Man at this early stage lived so much with the "conscience of instinct" that he far from being an artist (in our sense of profession) could paint and carve like dance and speak.

The fact that he lived in constant terror (of nature and spirits) did not prevent him (or rather fostered it) to feel in unison with the universe, an incarnate part of the whole and therefore wholly "being."

Edward Clodd, *Myths and Dreams* (London, Chatto and Windus, 1885), 10–11.

Clodd's study is also mentioned in Stefi Kiesler's outline for a book on dreams in literature.[64]

Man, in his first outlook upon nature, was altogether ignorant of the character of the forces by which he was environed; ignorant of that unvarying relation between effect and cause which it needed the experience of ages and the generalisations therefrom to apprehend, and to express as laws of nature. He had not even the intellectual resource of later times in inventing miracle to explain where the necessary relation between events seemed broken or absent.

His first attitude was that of wonder, mingled with fear–fear as instinctive as the dread of the brute for him. The sole measure of things was himself, consequently everything that moved or that had power of movement did so because it was alive. A personal life and will was attributed to sun, moon, clouds, river, waterfall, ocean, and trees, and the varying phenomena of the sky at dawn or noon, at gray eve or black-clouded night, were the manifestation of the controlling life that dwelt in all. In a thousand different forms this conception was expressed. The thunder was the roar of a mighty beast; the lightning a serpent that darted at its prey, an angry eye flashing, the storm demon's outshot forked tongue; the rainbow a thirsty monster; the water-spout a long-tailed dragon[.] This was not a pretty or powerful conceit, not imagery, but an explanation. The men who thus spoke of these phenomena meant precisely what they said. What does the savage know about heat, light, sound, electricity, and the other modes of motion through which the Proteus-force beyond our keen is manifest? …

Wilhelm Bölsche, *Der Termitenstaat: Schilderung eines geheimnisvollen Volkes* [The Termite Colony: Description of a Mysterious People] (Stuttgart: Kosmos/Franckh'sche Verlagshandlung, 1931) 65, 67–68, 10, 12–13.

Text transcribed by the Kieslers from the original German publication and translated by the editors.[65]

When termitaries are tested for durability, there is something about them, that could not by any means be compared to agglomerations of merely crumbled earth or of raw wood. You only have to think of the iron-solid mantle of such a huge hill. The termite does not simply build with earth or wood which have been fragmented to smaller or larger pieces: it builds with both in the form of concrete [*Betonform*], joining the parts with cement, that in the beginning is moisty, but subsequently rock-hard. However, the termite produces this cement layer [*Zementeinlage*] from its own body, as it were to "digest" the foreign material by itself for a second time for the purpose of building.

… As such a building, measuring twelve meters in height and twenty meters in width at the base, commands all respect, due to the incredible mass of additional production, that is thrown into the pure construction work by the digestion apparatus of the termite beyond the actual task of nutrition–comparable to the Cathedral of Cologne or an Egyptian pyramid pasted together from the salvia or gastric juice of their builders.

… Even from these simple basic observations it became unmistakably clear, that every construction was proceeding according to plan and to "certain methods of construction."

It was not an ant-like amassing, but every little tip formed, when completed, a permanently cemented pillar. At the same time the whole was dominated by a general building design, that was followed adamantly.

... That the termitary is definitely a systematic unified construction [*planmässiger Einheitsbau*] like our cathedral and the pyramids, could be proven by Escherich with species from Ceylon:[66] Each species, in contrast to the others, had its specific height, which it did not exceed. It seemingly required thirteen years for the execution of a dome of 2.5m in height, to which another two years could be added for the initial existence of the respective colony underground.

... Termites gorge in [human] culture [*fressen in der Kultur*] by devouring the curtains, wallpaper, clothes, linoleum, leather, wool, even ivory. Whole houses collapse because of them, the magnificent and sumptuous palace of the English governor of Calcutta had to be demolished because of the termites' gorging in 1814.

Liner ships of the port were infected until sinking. The entire capital of St. Helena, Jamestown, was in extreme danger from termites that were accidentally introduced. Books, too. Humboldt complained, that almost no book in South America is older than fifty years. At Schönbrunn [palace] near Vienna, termites brought in by accident destroyed the beautiful greenhouses, just as they also destroyed the irreplaceable woodwork of the National Museum in America.

John George Wood, *Homes without Hands: Being a Description of the Habitation of Animals Classed According to the Principles of Construction* (New York: Harper, 1866), 19–22, 148.

These selections were not used in *Magic Architecture*, but Kiesler quotes extensively from the book by the British clergyman, naturalist, and historian of race in his description of beaver dams in Part II, chapter 3.[67]

Of all the mammals the mole is entitled to take first place in our list of burrowers. This extraordinary animal does not merely dig tunnels in the ground and sit at the end of them, but forms a complicated subterranean dwelling place, with chambers passages, and other arrangements of wonderful completeness. It has regular roads leading to its feeding grounds; establishes a system of communication as elaborate as that of a modern railway, or to be more correct, as that of the subterranean network of metropolitan sewers. ...

The Brown Ant

It is a noteworthy fact that the ant will always avail itself of any accidential circumstances that may assist it in building. For instances taking advantage of a straw that happened to cross one another, and to convert them into beams with which to support the ceiling. It began the work by depositing the little clay pellets in the angles formed by the straws, and then lay several rows of the pellets along the side of each straw. The ceiling grew rapidly and on account of the extemporized beams, was necessarily of much greater strength.

Max Verworn, *Zur Psychologie der primitiven Kunst* [On the Psychology of Primitive Art] (Jena: Gustav Fischer, 1917), 5–15, 20–28, 34.

The transcription omits phrases indicated in brackets in this English translation by the editors. For a chart with handwritten notes by Kiesler after his reading of Verworn, see fig. C.13.[68]

... Artistic production is a means of human expression of sensations and ideas, of thoughts and feelings.

... Such means of expression [...] are capable of giving us a glimpse into the emotional and imaginative life of peoples of whom no spoken or written word will ever bear witness. ...

[...] It arises on the one hand from the preoccupation with the art of the child, on the other hand from the preoccupation with the primitive art of today, as well as the art of prehistory, which has experienced a resurgence of interest since the discovery of the Spanish and French cave paintings in the last decades.

... Anyone who critically reviews the artistic productions of prehistoric humans from the oldest to the youngest periods, will be struck by the enormous contrast between the artistic achievements of the Paleolithic mammoth and reindeer hunters and those of the peoples from the Neolithic, Bronze Age, and Iron Age. The drawings of reindeer, bison, horses, etc. of the former are in their overwhelming majority of an astonishing true-to-life quality and fidelity to nature both in posture and movement; the idols, the animal and human figures on urns and bronze implements of the latter periods appear without exception in stiff, conventional, thoroughly stylized form, without a trace of fidelity to nature and lively movement. ...

Of course, and I would like to emphasize this right from the beginning, the split that separates the Paleolithic from the Neolithic and later art is in reality not as sharp as one has probably often believed. [...] the stylizing trend of art did not appear either suddenly or immediately. It was already being prepared in the final section of the Paleolithic reindeer period. As Abbe Breuil...

The contrast in the general character of the Paleolithic and the later art is undoubtedly there. It has already been clearly expressed in the relative literature. But how is it founded in psychology? I must confess that this contradiction made a particularly deep impression on me, when, years ago, I first got to know the Paleolithic wall drawings in the caves of the Dordogne in their almost overwhelming abundance. As I was pondering the strange contrast on a lonely train ride, the first perspectives for its psychological understanding came to me. The problem has stuck with me ever since. It has become the reason for me to make detailed studies on the mental life of primitive humans in various directions. These studies partly coincided with other psychological and purely physiological studies, with which I have been occupied for a long time. ... in the following, I will communicate some results from these various types of studies.

Visual art is essentially the reproduction of optical impressions and ideas.

[...]The ideas we have about individual objects are completely dependent on the richness of our associative life [*Assoziationsleben*], because the ideas influence each other by association. All thinking is based on the associative combination of the individual ideas. The richer the life of the imagination [*Vorstellungsleben*] is developed, the greater will be the danger that the imagination, i.e. the memory image [*Erinnerungsbild*] of an object, will be changed by associations from the most different sides, i.e., by innumerable factors which have not sprung from the immediate, sensorial perception of the object. The motor innervation [*motorische Innervation*] is here the resultant of innumerable associative processes in the large imaginative fields. Therefore, it is not the pure memory image of the object that is expressed in the drawing, but more or less what the draftsman thinks and knows about the object. A thoroughly ideoplastic art develops contrary to physioplastic art.

*

Children's drawings provide the most brilliant evidence of this. Children's art is thoroughly ideoplastic from the very beginning. I have conducted my experiments on farmers' children from remote villages, who have more opportunity to observe nature...

[...]When the child draws a horse, or a cow, or a man, it draws everything it has learned about it. In the case of the horse it draws the head, the mane, the torso, the tail, four legs, the hooves, etc., but the whole is not a horse. ... The cases in which the child draws body parts visibly through the clothes are particularly characteristic as it had previously happened in many cases within the very ideoplastic art of ancient Egypt. ...

The child draws his knowledge, his thoughts, his reflections, not the object as it is really seen. [...] This is how drawings of wagons are created in which the wagon's hull and the drawbar are seen from above, and the wheels are seen from the side, spread out next to the hull, as in the ideoplastic wagon drawings on Bronze Age rock paintings in Sweden or in the Early Iron Age urns from Austria. ...

[...] The art of the child is from the start a thoroughly ideoplastic art. The child's art is therefore not to be situated parallel with the purely physioplastic art of the Palaeolithic period, as one could have thought following basic biogenetic laws, but with the strictly ideoplastic art of later times.

... With a few [but important] exemptions [which will demand our special attention], the art of [nearly all] indigenous peoples [*Naturvölker*] of today, is fully ideoplastic. In the artistic representations of gods, demons, animals, celestial objects, etc., they express fantastic, mystical, religious and mythological ideas. These representations are a faithful reflection of the creations of a rampant, bizarre imagination, which is filled with fear of ghosts at every turn, as it is characteristic for the psychic life [*Seelenleben*] of these peoples. The primitive thinking of these peoples is not like the critical and, I would like to say, even experimental thinking of the modern man of culture, which immediately tests every emerging thought against the known facts of reality. It is still a very short-winded thinking, which is not able to form long, logical series of thoughts and does not consider wide-ranging consequences. It rather theorizes in the closest connection to the momentary situation and therefore, continuously creates contradictions that come to pass unnoticed. Thus, it occurs that the naive speculations of these peoples on the surrounding world are far away from any truth of nature. And so it happens that the most adventurous creations of an excited imagination do not raise any critical concerns. And this appears in the most striking way, both in their words and in their images. According to his mythology, the Haida Indian draws a fantastic bird-headed man into the moon carrying a water bucket and a bush, because this myth tells that the moon once drew a man up to itself together with his bucket and the bush he was holding on to, so that it rains as soon as the man tips over his bucket. Thus, the Zuni Indian draws the heart of a deer in red color visible through the chest and communicating with the mouth. This is in accordance with his idea that the red soul, the blood, escapes from the mouth when shot in the chest. Thus, the Giljake [today known as the Niwchen people] and Golde [Nanai] are carving a raw human figure with a toad on the chest as an amulet against chest pain[...]

In contrast to these peoples, including the Negroes of Africa as well as the Indians of America, the inhabitants of the South Sea Islands as well as the Mongol tribes of North Asia, there is a very small group of peoples whose art has a much more, although no longer purely physioplastic character.

*

Primitive art has all the more physioplastic features, the more sensual observation stands in the foreground. It has the more ideoplastic features, the more the life of the imagination [*Vorstellungsleben*] of peoples becomes paramount. The most powerful impulse for the development of the life of the imagination in prehistoric times was given by the conception of the idea of the soul [*Seelenidee*]. The religious conceptions that sprang from this idea provided the most favorable conditions for the emergence of ideoplastic art. **(not entirely correct) K.**[69]

What follows is a transcription of Kiesler's theoretical reflections on Verworn's typological distinctions in art (fig. C.13):

Natur **physio-plastische Kunst endet?? in? realistische? Photography?** [physioplastic art ends? In? realistic photography?] / **ideo-plastische ... memoric? ~~abstract~~ art** [ideoplastic art ends in memoric abstract art?] **~~psycho-plastic~~ ... ~~metamorphic~~** [~~psychoplastic~~ art ends in metamorphic?] **abstract ... ~~geometric~~ logarythmic?** [abstract art ends in ~~geometric~~ logarithmic?

dream **... psychoplastic ... (unrealist? metamorphic)** [dream, psychoplastic art ends in unrealist, metamorphic?]

from nature	**a**	**physioplastic art = realistic**
from memory	**b**	**ideoplastic art = ~~memory stylized~~ illustrative**
from memory & nature	**c**	**abstract art = mathematical, logarythmic, geometric, decorative**
from dream-ing /??	**d**	**psychoplastic art = metamorphic**

Period Antiquae???	**a**	**gesichtlos** [faceless]
	b	**Masken** [masks]
	c	**totale Verkleidung** [total cladding]

Egon Friedell, *Kulturgeschichte des Altertums. Leben und Legende der vorchristlichen Seele Erster Teil: Ägypten und Vorderasien* [Cultural History of Antiquity. Part I: Life and Legend of the Prechristian Soul] (Zurich: Helikon Verlag, 1936), 38–40 and 44–45 (Atlantis), 153–158 (Egypt), 446–448 (Mycenae).

Excerpts originally transcribed in German, here in English translation by the editors. The central and most extensive set of these transcriptions corresponds to Part V, chapter 2 of *Magic Architecture* on the Egyptian pyramid, which contains no text by Kiesler. The preceding excerpts from *Kulturgeschichte des Altertums* on the antediluvian city of Atlantis (whose worship of the dead Friedell compares to that of Egypt) echo descriptions of literary architectural utopias in Part VII, but also include references to "telepathic" phenomena mentioned in Part I of Kiesler's book manuscript. Finally, the transcription of the paragraphs on Mycenean culture from the concluding section of Friedell's volume is again occasioned by references to the pre-Homeric worship of the dead (which for Friedell is "almost Egyptian") and its expression in archaic funereal monuments.

Atlantis

In 1882, Ignatius Donnelly published a book titled *Atlantis, the Antediluvian World* which caused a similar sensation as the discovery of the Martian canals by Schiaparelli around the same time. The book explained that the sunken Atlantis was a large continent in the middle of the ocean. Its highest peaks were Madeira and the Azores, which still rise above the sea level today. In the course of a history spanning many thousands of years, the Atlantians spread not only over their island, but also flooded over to Mexico, South America, West Africa, Southern Europe: at the time when the empire witnessed its greatest territorial expansion, it stretched from the Cordilleras to the Near East. Atlantis was divided into three altitudinal zones: the area of the volcanic mountains, the plateaus [*Tafelländer*] where the kings resided, and the "great plain." The climate was subtropical, very pleasant; and from here all human culture originated. From the Atlantians originated not only the construction of bricks and silk, the cultivation of cereals and refined fruits, the domestication of cattle and horses, but also the compass and gunpowder, steel making and paper manufacturing, astronomy and the alphabet, as well as circumcision to protect against American syphilis. Atlantis, the paradisiacal land of fertility and peace, is the Garden of Eden, the island of the blessed, Olympus, Asgard, a dream image of a

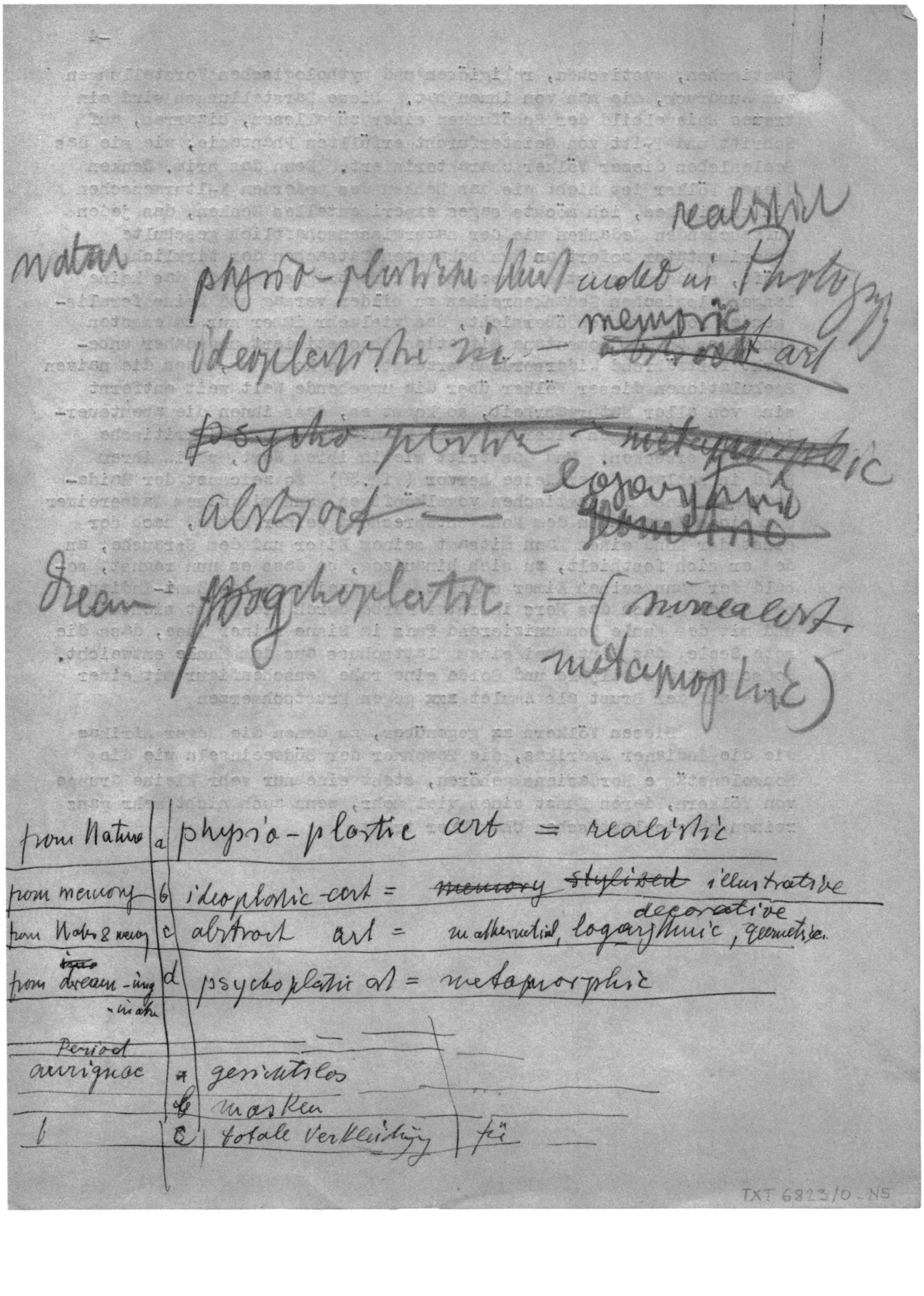

fig. C.13

realistic

natur physio-plastische Kunst nicht in Photography

ideoplastische ... memoric ~~art~~ art

~~psycho plastic — metamorphic~~

abstract art — logarythmic ~~geometric~~

dream psychoplastic (surrealist. metamorphic)

from Nature	a	physio-plastic art = realistic
from memory	b	ideoplastic-art = ~~memory~~ ~~stylised~~ illustrative decorative
from Nature & memory	c	abstract art = mathematical, logarythmic, geometric
from dream-ing / trance / -making	d	psychoplastic art = metamorphic

Period			
aurignac	a	gesichtslos	
	b	masken	
b	c	totale Verkleidung	fü

Frederick Kiesler, theoretical reflections (in German and English) and chart on "physio-plastic" and "psycho-plastic" art following the reading of Max Verworn, which informs Part IV, chapters 5–9 of *Magic Architecture*. (pencil) ÖFLKS, TXT_6823/0_N5verso

more beautiful past that persists among all peoples. In Mexico and Peru, Egypt and Babylonia, the last remnants of Atlantean civilizations have survived. [38–39]

The cultural analogies between Native Americans and the ancient Egyptians are also quite astonishing. Both worshipped the solar disk, embalmed the dead bodies and built pyramids according to the same principles of celestial orientation of the internal architecture. [40]

In fact, even the primitive sees something like magic in our system of mastering nature. In both cases it is a question of insights into the essence of nature, gained by the training and exercise of certain mental skills, i.e. a kind of miracle. A pale reflection of the other insights into nature, as possessed by the Atlantians, can still be seen today in the phenomena of telepathy, whereby we must think of the highest achievements ever observed in this field. However, among the Atlantians telepathy was increased to telekinesis and teleplasticity, to the power of remote movement [*Fernbewegung*], remote radiation [*Fernstrahlung*] and materialization. If these appear as fairy tales to us, it is because we have lost two abilities that they still possessed. As we are able to grasp the exterior of everything with the greatest virtuosity, they were able to penetrate into its interior. Thus, by having truly experienced what was "happening on the inside," and how "social" relations are existing among us, similarities existed across the whole of nature. Therefore, the parts of nature were almost the same to them as the limbs of our body are to us. We grasp reality by intelligence, they grasped it by "sympathy". They breathed with nature like the unborn child through its mother. We are just able to control the inorganic, because the mind is a mere mathematician and engineer, helpless in the face of life. To quote Bergson: "Intelligence is characterized by a natural incomprehension of life."[70] [44–45]

While our mastery of nature is therefore mechanical, the mastery of the Atlantean was vital. [45]

p. 153, Friedell

The pyramid is nothing more than a huge tomb with a coffin chamber beneath. One of its main purposes was protection from tomb raiders. The immensely thick masonry of the firmest rock was impenetrable, and the narrow entrance through which the coffin was brought inside was hidden in the most ingenious way. Nevertheless, even the pyramid tombs were breached, but certainly not without state patronage, and this was then often no less a gigantic accomplishment than the construction itself. Therefore, the pyramid tombs were abandoned in the New Kingdom and started to use rock tombs, which were even more inaccessible. Nevertheless, a way was always found, and no tomb was discovered that was not in a looted or at least plundered condition. The motive was not always greed, but also political or religious opposition, and most recently it is of scientific nature. It is strange, by the way, that very few people have any feeling for the blasphemy that lies in ripping a corpse out of its coffin and putting it in a museum. Despite all these attacks, however, some hiding places are certainly untraceable and Mariette used to say that there are a lot of mummies that will absolutely never see the light of day again.

To each pyramid belonged a whole extensive complex. Its main parts belong to the so-called gate building, followed by a temple in the valley on the bank of the Nile, the covered ramp, which, up to four kilometers long, led to the plateau of the desert and the mortuary temple, which was located at the feet of the pyramid, and was divided into a wide vestibule and a deep peristyle. In addition, there were large magazines. The decorum of the rooms was of imposing simplicity: the floor of snow-white alabaster, the walls of bright red granite, along with mighty square pillars and throughout larger-than-life statues of the king made of green stone, no reliefs, no inscriptions. It becomes clear that the complexes of these ancient temples, which were called "barbaric" by Strabo from his Greek point of view, have originally been of wooden construction. They are wooden construction translated into stone.

Teil: Ägypten und Vorderasien
[Part 1: Egypt and Near East]
First Chapter, p. 155

It has been calculated that the stone material which was required for the Cheops pyramid would fill five truck trains, each as long as the Vienna–Paris route. The quarries from which it came were located fifteen kilometers from the pyramid field, besides having to cross the Nile. The granite for the temple buildings even came from Aswan, which is about one thousand kilometers away from Giza. The tremendously heavy blocks had to be lifted up many stories high. Simple machines such as levers, rollers, cranes and pulleys were certainly used by the Egyptians. There is also a famous tomb painting depicting the transportation of a colossus: 172 men pull on ropes a wood sledge on which the 6.5-meter statue is tied; pieces of leather protect it from being abraded by the ropes. On the pedestal stands someone who pours water to prevent the planks from catching fire from the friction, a guard claps his hands to set the pace, people with tools and water carriers follow. If the pyramids really were built in this primitive way, it would remind us of the fabulous achievements of certain insects. The entomologist [McCook][71] has measured the nests of a Pennsylvanian ant species and compared them to the Cheops pyramid. Calculating from the dimensions of the insect, the nests are 84 times as large as the Cheops pyramid. And the city that the animals had created was made up of 1600 such nests; "next to such settlements," [McCook] added, "London and New York are nothing but villages." As for the astonishingly exact processing of the building blocks, one can recall the honeycomb cell, which is of such absolute regularity that Réaumur proposed it as an international standard measure. "If," says Maeterlinck in his wonderful book on the life of bees, "a spirit from another world descended to earth and desired to see the most perfect creation of the logic of life, we should show him the plain honeycomb." Furthermore, the shell that the Helix pomatia builds is a much more disturbing issue. It is rolled up according to the laws of a curve, which is called "logarithmic spiral" or snail curve and is a so-called transcendental curve. This cannot be expressed by our algebraic equations. Therefore, this common mollusk is obviously a higher mathematician than man. Perhaps the feats, which the horses of Elberfeld accomplished at their time, belonged to this context, too: among other things, they drew square roots and cube roots from multi-digit numbers with a speed in which they outperformed most people. One tends to marvel at all these achievements because they are based on mere instinctual activity. In reverse, one would have to declare: only because these achievements are instinctive, they could come about. The deeper we descend, the more confidently we can see the working of organisms; all the narrower, however, becomes the circle of their activity and the domain of their genius. The spirit goes astray because it is free, because it is creative; instinct hits the center because it is compulsory and non-original.

p. 157

The four sides of the Cheops pyramid are placed exactly according to the four cardinal directions. A section running from north to south through the top of the pyramid coincides with the plane of the so-called "ideal meridian", which traverses the majority of continents and the fewest seas. The entrance tunnel to the subterranean tomb housing the pharaoh had an incline of twenty-seven degrees. It has now been calculated that at the time of Cheops, star *a* in the constellation of the Dragon was the Polaris. The height of its lower culmination was twenty-seven degrees: hence its rays fell directly on the dead Pharaoh, the "earthly Polaris." Our solar year has 365,242 days. If one divides the exact side length of the pyramid by this number, one receives a measure, which is repeated in the dimensions of the corridors and chambers in a striking way. Therefore, it has been called "pyramid meter [*Pyramidenmeter*]." This pyramid meter is exactly the ten millionth part of half of the polar axis of the earth. If one divides the pyramid meter into further twenty-five parts, one arrives at the "pyramid inch." The circumference of the basis of the Cheops pyramid amounts to 36524.2 pyramid inches: it thus reproduces the number of the anniversaries. If you multiply the height of the pyramid by one billion, you get the distance of the earth from the sun, a number which today's astronomy has only reached after long erroneous paths and with the help of the most complicated apparatuses. Only the most trivial philistine could speak of nothing but coincidences, and rightly the Abbé Moreux, the director of the observatory in Bourges, has said that all the conquests of modern science are found in the pyramid. The most famous astronomers of the world: Newton, Herschel, Flammarion and others, have very seriously and thoroughly studied the mystery of the pyramid. …

Chapter Four, p. 446

The climate was much heavier and much more contrasting than in historical times: the winters were harsh, the summers tropically hot. The land was still widely covered with dense forests, with wolves and wild boars, buffalo and bears inhabiting them. Even the lion still roamed the mountains and the ancient Greek heroic legend has preserved his memory with veneration. The "Mycenaeans" certainly possessed the horse already when they immigrated; but they were neither an equestrian people nor a seafaring one. As in ancient Israel and Rome, the father of the house still held full sway over family and servants and acquired a wife by purchasing a bride. He is his own priest and makes daily sacrifices in his yard to the gods of the tribe. On ceremonial occasions, this is done by the tribal duke or the great king. These gods are partly animal-headed. When Homer calls Hera cow-eyed, Athena owl-eyed, he no longer knew that this was once to be taken quite literally. Even the Minotaur, of whom the Greeks still knew to tell stories in later times, was probably nothing else than a Cretan god-king Minos with a bull's head, to whom probably human sacrifices were offered. Much like in the Christian Middle Ages, the popular imagination populated forest and meadow, river and swamp, night and mist with supernatural beings. There were nymphs in trees, rocks, springs, mountain ghosts and will-o'-the-wisps, unicorns, fiery steeds and other wild and gentle animals that were inhabited by gods. The highest and most comprehensive deity, however, is [*Ge*], the earth, the all-mother of mankind, as Demeter the protector of agriculture, to which she bestows the eternal blessing of the harvest, and of female sexual life, which she also provides with the power of fertility. Her husband was the horse-shaped Poseidon, originally a deity of the earth, too. Therefore, he is still regarded as the cause of earthquakes in the later Hellenic faith. At his side, Zeus still takes a second place. Later, as we know, it was the contrary: Zeus becomes the father of men and king of the gods and Poseidon a specialized god who has to be content with the sea: "The whole role of Poseidon in the Odyssey," says Carl Schuchhardt so beautifully, "is that of a departing thunderstorm." Such "rudiments" of earlier beliefs are still found several times in Homer. The classic example is the funeral celebration that Achilles hosts for Patroclus. Abundant amounts of wine, oil and honey, blood, fat and meat are sacrificed. Horses, dogs and even humans are slaughtered, splendid fighting games conclude the feast. All this testifies to a fervent belief in a powerful and lasting survival after death, which Homer no longer possessed. It seems almost Egyptian. All this happens for no one else than for the dead: the sacrificial animals, which are completely burned, shall feed him in the afterlife, the 12 murdered noble Trojan youths, the noble steeds and dogs shall serve him, the competitions shall honor and delight him. The Greeks' belief in the soul around the time of Agamemnon was different and stronger than the Homeric one: for the latter a life without sea and sun was an unimaginable void, for the former the forces of earth and darkness still had the full potential of a second, even higher life. The rationalistic and actually atheistic question, how a shadow without body and light should then originate in the underworld, did not exist for them.

Characteristic for the Mycenaean dwelling was the megaron, a quadrangular main room, covered and heated by a stove, which is not found elsewhere in the South. Its whole structure clearly points to the colder North. In the Cretan palaces, the building purposes are ventilation and cooling. The same contrast is seen in the clothing: The Cretans only used to wear a loincloth, while the Greeks kept the chiton even in the milder climate. In the houses of the nobles, one first entered a propylon decorated with columns, which led into a forecourt: this was also surrounded by columns and contained the altar; and only then could one reach the Megaron, whose floor was beautifully painted and bore the magnificent throne-seat of the feudal lord. The walls, the ceiling and even the round stove in the center were covered with stucco and paintings. The smoke went off through an opening in the ceiling; windows were missing. For this reason, Homer speaks of the "shady megaron," which is again, a significant contrast with Crete, where light flooded from everywhere through rooms, staircases and roofs. A bathroom was never missing: in Tiryns, its floor consisted of a single huge block of stone and the clay tub was colored with ornaments. The graves were usually laid out in such a way that a long narrow passage, the dromos, led through a narrow antechamber, the stomion, which could be closed off, to the spacious tomb chamber. The main room, however, was the adjacent dome-shaped sacrificial hall. This also shows that the cult of the dead must have played a much greater role in Mycenaean times than later. There are even some remains of corpses that indicate embalming. When the Greeks spoke of the "graves of heroes," they meant these primeval cultic sites.

Lynn Thorndike, *A History of Magic and Experimental Science During the First Thirteen Centuries of our Era* (New York: Columbia University Press, 1923), II: 536–537.

Other excerpts from Thorndike's history are quoted in Part IV, chapter 2 on "the meaning of magic." These selections correspond to Part V, chapters 6 and 10, which refer to the Gothic cathedral and the Gothic arch, respectively.[72]

Nature in Gothic Architecture and Sculpture

One has only to examine the sculpture of the great thirteenth-century cathedrals to see that the craftsmen of the towns were close observers of the world of nature and that every artist was a naturalist too. In the foliage that twines about the capitals of the columns in French Gothic cathedrals it is easy to recognize, says M. Mâle, a large number of plants: "The plantain, arum, ranunculus, fern, clover, coladine, hepatica, columbine, cress, parsley, strawberry-plant, ivy, snap-dragon, the flower of the broom and the leaf of the oak, a typically French collection of flowers loved from childhood."[73] *Mutatis mutandis*, the same statement could be made concerning the carved vegetation that runs riot in Lincoln cathedral. "The thirteenth century sculptors sang their *chant de mai*. All the spring delights of the Middle Ages live again in their work—the exhilaration of Palm Sunday, the garlands of flowers, the bouquets fastened on the doors, the strewing of fresh herbs in the chapels, the magical flowers of the feast of Saint John—all the fleeting charm of those old-time springs and summers, the Middle

Ages, so often said to have little love for nature, in point of fact gazed at every blade of grass with reverence." But it is not merely love of nature but scientific interest and accuracy that we see revealed in the sculptures of the cathedrals and in the note-book of the thirteenth century architect, Villard de Honnecourt, with its sketches of insect as well as animal life, of a lobster, two perroquets on a perch, the spirals of a snake's shell, a fly, a dragonfly, and a grass-hopper, as well as a bear and a lion from life, and more familiar animals such as the cat and the swan. The sculptors of gargoyles and chimeras were not content to reproduce existing animals, but showed their command of animal anatomy by creating strange compound and hybrid monsters–one might almost say, evolving new species–which nevertheless have all the verisimilitude of copies from living forms. It was these breeders in stone, these Burbanks of the pencil, these Darwins with the chisel, who knew nature and had studied botany and zoology in a way superior to the scholar who simply pored over the works of Aristotle and Pliny.

Hanns Sassmann, *Das Reich der Träumer. Eine Kulturgeschichte Österreichs vom Urzustand bis zur Republik* [The Empire of Dreamers: A Cultural History of Austria from the Primal State to the Republic] (Berlin: Verlag für Kulturpolitik, 1932), 13–14, 7–9.

Translated by the editors. All underlining was added by hand to the typed transcription and does not correspond to the original. Kiesler asks for the two paragraphs transcribed from Sassmann to be added at the end of the text that served as the "Introduction" to Part x, but these excerpts were not translated and not included in later drafts.[74]

We are aware how doubtful all the exploration of history [*Geschichtsergründung*] could be, if we–in contrast to historical materialism–do not perceive an economic problem in all historical movements, but a metaphysical-biological phenomenon which has not yet been unraveled and its causes lie beyond the laws of nature that are perceptible to us. We start from the assumption that the purpose of all historical events is not the preservation of an existing, but the creation of a new, unprecedented human type [*Menschenart*]. We regard historical process as an enduring creation from which we can observe the great historical movements. Out of the great historical movements, we always see new peoples in new life forms emerging from the substance of the past, as if a chemist was at work with all his systematic handling of mixing and unmixing. All the past eras of the world appear to us like tremendous, accomplished experiments of a certain chemistry that mixes and separates spirits, souls and peoples: a Chemistry of peoples [*Völkerchemie*].

Of all the numerous attempts in modern philosophy of history, there have mainly been two recent methods that provided serviceable historical systems [*Geschichtssysteme*]: the ideological and the materialistic conception of history. The ideological conception of history, which culminates in Treitschke's dictum that "humans," i.e., the heroes of humankind and their ideas make history, has experienced a unique evolution towards romanticism in the past years thanks to Doctor Egon Friedell, the Viennese philosopher of history and his epoch-making "Cultural History of the Modern Age [*Kulturgeschichte der Neuzeit*]." Friedell substitutes the term "genius" for the term "hero," thus seeing all history as the "history of the spirit [*Geistesgeschichte*]." He concludes that epochs are objectivized [*objektivieren*] in "great men." That all dark drives and unredeemed thoughts, slumbering in the subconsciousness of contemporary subjects, clearly appear in "representative men" and constitute their essence. Every epoch-making genius is thus entirely the creature of its time. But at the same moment, time receives all its drives and life-forming thoughts from this genius and thus becomes a creation. Nevertheless, both are confronted with the inexplicable fact that the genius and his time remain estranged in their deepest essence: the genius appears as an "exotic monster and pathological original," its time appears to him without any relation to his will [*Wollen*] and his accomplishment. "The genius," as Friedell formulates in his third thesis, "has nothing to do with his time and the time has nothing to do with him." By ingeniously transforming synthesis into a second antithesis, Friedell only seemingly entangles the reader in a confusing contradiction. In reality, he convinces him of something that no unprejudiced person has dared to express since the beginning of the Enlightenment: that all historical matters are metaphysical in their ultimate origin. Friedell's logical development of the ideological conception of history shifts the synthesis of the opposition of genius and time into the fourth dimension. History is thus rooted in the transcendent–and the three contradictory Friedellian theses of the epoch-making genius convince us of this fact. This is the last conclusion that the ideological method can reach with its historical system.

59 TXT_6820/0_N1-N2; CLP_6463/0

60 **Belongs to Part II, Chapter VI** The chapter number reflects an earlier organization of the manuscript. TXT_6814/0_N1

61 In the published text, Frobenius parenthetically attributes this last phrase to the German cultural historian Victor Hehn, which is excised from the transcription. Frobenius, *Kulturgeschichte Afrikas*, 65.

62 Another selection of transcriptions from a later section of Frobenius's book. See Frobenius, *Kulturgeschichte Afrikas*, 242–249. The title and page numbers were added by hand on the TS by Stefi Kiesler. TXT_6818/0_N1-N3

63 **The prominent position …… → Belongs to Part II, Chapter VI/6** Handwritten instruction for quotation by Kiesler. The chapter number reflects an earlier organization of the text. TXT_6814/0_N4-N5

64 TXT_6809/0_N1-N2

65 TXT_6811/0_N3

66 Bölsche refers to the study of the entomologist Karl Escherich, *Termitenleben auf Ceylon: Neue Studien zur Soziologie der Tiere zugleich ein Kapitel kolonialer Forstentomologie* [Termite Life in Ceylon: New Studies on the Sociology of Animals and a Chapter of colonial Forest Entomology] (Jena: Gustav Fischer, 1911).

67 TXT_6811/0_N1-N2

68 TXT_6823/0_N5verso

69 **(nicht ganz korrekt) K.** Quotation marks, comment, and title added in Kiesler's hand on the typewritten transcription of this paragraph. TXT_6823/0_N1

70 "L'intelligence est caractérisée par une incompréhension naturelle de la vie." Bergson's phrase is quoted in the original French. Friedell, Kulturgeschichte des Altertums, 45.

71 Both the original publication and the Kieslers' transcription erroneously refer to the entomologist Henry Christopher McCook as "MacCook."

72 TXT_6827/0_N1-N2

73 Thorndike inserts a footnote, not included in Kiesler's transcription: Èmile Male, *Religious Art in France in the Thirteenth Century*, translated from the third edition by Dora Nussey (New York: Dutton & Co, 1913), 52.

74 TXT_6710_0/N1-N3; TXT_6723/0_N3

ADDENDA: BIBLIOGRAPHIES

MAIN TEXT

Books and Journal Articles transcribed by the Kieslers and quoted or mentioned in *Magic Architecture* and related drafts. Numbers in brackets indicate Part/Chapter of the main text in which these sources are quoted or mentioned.

Andrews, Charles M., ed. *Ideal Empires and Republics: Rousseau's Social Contract, More's Utopia, Bacon's New Atlantis, Campanella's City of the Sun.* With an introduction by Charles M. Andrews. New York: M. W. Dunne, 1901. [VII/3]

Baring-Gould, Sabine. *Cliff Castles and Cave Dwellings of Europe.* Philadelphia: Lippincott / London: Seeley and Co., 1911. [I/6]

Biart, Lucien. *The Aztecs: Their History, Manners and Customs.* Translated by J. L. Garner. Chicago: McClurg & Co., 1887. [V/3]

Bölsche, Wilhelm. *Der Termitenstaat. Schilderung eines geheimnisvollen Volkes.* Stuttgart: Kosmos / Franckh'sche Verlagshandlung, 1931. [transcribed, not quoted, relates to II/2]

Breuil, Henri, and Miles Crawford Burkitt. *Rock Paintings of Southern Andalusia: A Description of a Neolithic and Copper Age Art Group.* With the collaboration of Sir Montagu Pollock. Oxford: The Clarendon Press, 1929. [III/2]

Burton, Robert. *The Anatomy of Melancholy.* With an introduction by Holbrook Jackson. 2 vols. London: Dent / New York: Dutton, 1932. [I/1]

Casteret, Norbert. *Zehn Jahre unter der Erde, Höhlenforschungen eines Einzelgängers.* Translated by Friedrich von Oppeln-Bronikowski. Leipzig: F. A. Brockhaus, 1936. [III/4; IV/5]

Chase, Richard. "Notes on the Study of Myth." *Partisan Review* XIII, no. 3 (Summer 1946): 338–346. [IV/4]

Clark, Grahame. "Scandinavian Rock-engravings." *Antiquity* 11 (January 1, 1937): 56–69. [III/3]

Clodd, Edward. *Myths and Dreams.* London: Chatto and Windus, 1885. [I/8]

Friedell, Egon. *Kulturgeschichte des Altertums: Leben und Legende der vorchristlichen Seele.* Zurich: Helikon-Verlag, 1936. [V/2; VI/4]

Frobenius Leo. *Kulturgeschichte Afrikas: Prolegomena zu einer historischen Gestaltlehre.* Zürich: Phaidon-Verlag, 1933. [I/1; IV/3]

Frobenius, Leo, and Douglas C. Fox. *Prehistoric Rock Pictures in Europe and Africa: From Material in the Archives of the Research Institute for the Morphology of Civilization, Frankfort-on-Main.* New York: The Museum of Modern Art, 1937. [I/1]

Hearn, Lafcadio. "Gothic Horror." In Lafcadio Hearn, *Shadowings*, 213–222. Boston: Little, Brown, and Co., 1900. [V/10]

Huxley, Thomas Henry. "The Stocks and the Stones. From the Evolution of Theology." *Encore* III, no. 17 (June 1943): 704–708. [V/Introduction]

Kiesler, Frederick. "Vitalbau–Raumstadt–Funktionelle Architektur." *De Stijl*, no. 10/12 (1924–1925): 141–146. [I/5; X/5]

Klaatsch, Hermann. *Der Werdegang der Menschheit und die Entstehung der Kultur.* Edited after the death of the author by Adolf Heilborn. 2nd and extended edition. Berlin; Leipzig; Vienna; Stuttgart: Deutsches Verlagshaus Bong & Co., 1922. [I/1; I/2; I/3; I/4; I/6; I/7; II/Introduction; II/6; II/7]

Klaatsch, Hermann. *The Evolution and Progress of Mankind.* Edited and enlarged by Adolf Heilborn. Translated by Joseph McCabe. New York: Frederick A. Stokes Company, 1923. [transcribed but not quoted, related to parts I and II]

Lévy-Bruhl, Lucien. *Primitive Mentality.* Translated by Lillian Clare. London: Allen / New York: Macmillan, 1922. [I/8]

Lévy-Bruhl, Lucien. *Das Denken der Naturvölker.* Edited and with an introduction by Wilhelm Jerusalem. Translated by Paul Friedländer. 2nd edition. Vienna-Leipzig: Braumüller, 1926. [I/3; I/4; III/1; IV/2]

Malinowski, Bronisław. *The Sexual Lives of Savages in North-Western Melanesia.* 2 vols. New York: Liveright / London: Routledge, 1929. [II/7; II/8]

Marais, Eugene N. *The Soul of the White Ant.* New York: Dodd, Mead & Co., 1937. [II/2; II/5]

Meyers Großes Konversations-Lexikon. Vol. 6. 6th edition. Leipzig and Vienna: Bibliographisches Institut, 1904. [VII/2]

Meyers Großes Konversations-Lexikon. Vol. 9. 6th edition. Leipzig and Vienna: Bibliographisches Institut, 1905. [II/7]

Montagu, M. F. Ashley. *Coming into Being Among the Australian Aborigines: A Study of the Procreative Beliefs of the Native Tribes of Australia.* With a foreword by Bronislaw Malinowski. New York: E. P. Dutton & Company, 1938. [I/4]

Ponten, Josef. *Architektur die nicht gebaut wurde.* With the collaboration of Heinz Rosemann and Hedwig Schmelz. 2 vols. Stuttgart: Deutsche Verlags-Anstalt, 1925. [V/9; VI/2; VI/3; VI/7; VII/1; VII/2; VIII/1; X/3]

Sassmann, Hanns. *Das Reich der Träumer. Eine Kulturgeschichte Österreichs vom Urzustand bis zur Republik.* Berlin: Verlag für Kulturpolitik, 1932. [X/Introduction]

Scheerbart, Paul. *Glasarchitektur.* Berlin: Verlag der Sturm, 1914. [IX/3]

Schopenhauer, Arthur. "Zur Metaphysik des Schönen und Aesthetik." In Arthur Schopenhauer, *Parerga und Paralipomena: Kleine Philosophische Schriften*, Grossherzog Wilhelm Ernst Edition. Leipzig: Insel-Verlag, 1920. [V/2]

Taut, Bruno. *Alpine Architektur.* Hagen: Folkwang, 1919. [X/2]

Taut, Bruno. *Die Auflösung der Städte, oder: Die Erde eine gute Wohnung, oder auch: Der Weg zur Alpinen Architektur.* Hagen: Folkwang, 1920. [X/2]

Thorndike, Lynn. *History of Magic and Experimental Science.* 8 vols. New York: Columbia University Press, 1934–1958. [First two volumes originally published by Macmillan, New York, 1923] [IV/1; V/10]

Verworn, Max. *Zur Psychologie der primitiven Kunst: ein Vortrag.* Jena: Gustav Fischer, 1908. [IV/6]

Wells, H. G. *A Short History of the World.* New York: Macmillan, 1922. [VI/8]

Wood, John George. *Homes without Hands: Being a Description of the Habitation of Animals, Classed According to Their Principle of Construction.* New York: Harper, 1866. [II/2; II/3]

Wundt, Wilhelm. *Vorlesungen über die Menschen- und Thierseele.* 5th revised edition. Hamburg; Leipzig: Leopold Voss, 1911. [II/Introduction]

PLATES

Books, illustrated journals, and newspapers, visual material from which is used by Kiesler in the illustrations of his plates. Numbers in brackets indicate plate illustrations.

"A Canadian 'St. Francis': The Beaver's Friend–'Grey Owl' and His 'Little Brothers' of the Wild." *Illustrated London News* 179, no. 4818, August 22, 1931. [19]

"A Miracle of Building! Ant-Made "Sky-Scrapers." *Illustrated London News* 174, no. 4961, March 16, 1929. [16d]

"American Saint: Mother Cabrini is First Citizen of US to be Canonized in Rome." *Life*, July 22, 1946. [47/48]

Art in Our Time: An exhibition to celebrate the tenth anniversary of the Museum of Modern Art and the opening of its new building, held at the time of the New York World's Fair (New York: Museum of Modern Art, 1939). [2]

"As Paris Celebrated the Surrender of Japan." *New York Herald Tribune*, August 17, 1945. [53]

"Mach Dich Grösser vor dem Feind!" *Koralle* 7, no. 22 (May 31, 1939): 809–811. [12]

Brandes, E. W. "Into Primeval Papua by Seaplane: Seeking Disease-resisting Sugar Cane, Scientists Find Neolithic Man in Unmapped Nooks of Sorcery and Cannibalism." *National Geographic* LVI, no. 3, September 1929. [9; 12a]

Breuil, Henri, and Miles Crawford Burkitt. *Rock Paintings of Southern Andalusia: A Description of a Neolithic and Copper Age Art Group.* With the collaboration of Sir Montagu Pollock. Oxford: The Clarendon Press, 1929. [24; 25]

Burnett, Wanda. "Yank Meets Native." *National Geographic* LXXXVIII, no. 1, July 1945. [12]

Casteret, Norbert. *Zehn Jahre unter der Erde, Höhlenforschung eines Einzelgängers.* Translated by Friedrich von Oppeln-Bronikowski. Leipzig: F. A. Brockhaus, 1936. [23b]

Clark, Grahame. "Scandinavian Rock-engravings." *Antiquity*, vol. 11 (January 1, 1937): 56–69. [22; 23]

Compton's Pictured Encyclopedia, vol. 1. Chicago: F. E. Compton & Co., 1922. [16a]

Dugmore, Arthur Radclyffe. *The Romance of the Beaver: Being in the History of the Beaver in the Western Hemisphere.* Philadelphia: J. B. Lippincott Co. / London: William Heinemann, 1914. [17]

Ess, John van. "Forty Years Among the Arabs." *National Geographic* LXXXII, no. 3, September 1942. [29]

Faure, Élie. *History of Art, Vol. 5 The Spirit of the Forms.* 5 vols. Translated by Walter Pach. New York and London: Harper & Brothers, 1921. [36]

Frobenius Leo. *Kulturgeschichte Afrikas: Prolegomena zu einer historischen Gestaltlehre.* Zürich: Phaidon-Verlag, 1933. [1; 4; 20; 26; 27; 28]

Frobenius, Leo, and Douglas C. Fox. *Prehistoric Rock Pictures in Europe and Africa: From Material in the Archives of the Research Institute for the Morphology of Civilization, Frankfort-on-Main.* New York: The Museum of Modern Art, 1937. [2a]

Hamann, Richard. *Die Frührenaissance der italienischen Malerei.* Jena: E. Diederichs, 1909. [39]

Hauttmann, Max. *Die Kunst des frühen Mittelalters* (Berlin: Propyläen-Verlag, 1929). [34]

Heck, J. G. *Iconographic Encyclopaedia of Science, Literature & Art.* Plates. Vol. 1, Division IV., History and Ethnology. Systematically arranged by J. G. Heck. Translated from the German, with additions, and edited by Spencer F. Baird. New York: Rudolph Garrigue, 1851. [42]

Hildebrand, J. R. "California's Coastal Redwood Realm." *National Geographic* LXXV, no. 2, February 1939. [13]

Hogbin, H. Ian. "Coconuts and Coral Islands." *The National Geographic* LXV, no. 3, March 1934. [10; 11]

Hoyningen-Huene, George, and George Steindorff. *Egypt.* New York, J. J. Augustin, 1943. [30]

Höver, Otto. *Indische Kunst.* Breslau: Ferdinand Hirt, 1923. [5]

Hürlimann, Martin. *Indien: Baukunst, Landschaft und Volksleben.* Berlin: Ernst Wasmuth Verlag A.G., 1928. [*India: The Landscape, the Monuments and the People.* Bombay: D. B. Taraporevala Sons & Co., 1932.] [19; 19a; 25x; 25a; 32]

Kaufmann, Emil. *Von Ledoux bis Le Corbusier: Ursprung und Entwicklung der Autonomen Architektur.* Vienna and Leipzig: Verlag Dr. Rolf Passer, 1933. [55]

Kiesler, Frederick J. "'On Correalism and Biotechnique': A Study on the Genetics of Building Design." *Architecture Record* 86, no. 3 (September 1939): 60–75. [59; 60]

Klaatsch, Hermann. *Der Werdegang der Menschheit und die Entstehung der Kultur.* Edited after the death of the author by Adolf Heilborn. 2nd and extended edition. Berlin; Leipzig; Wien; Stuttgart: Deutsches Verlagshaus Bong & Co., 1922. [9; 10]

Koester, Hans. "Four Thousand Hours Over China." *National Geographic* LXXIII, no. 5, May 1938. [3d; 13c]

Kreutzberg, Lola, ed. *Wir Tiere…: Erlebnisse und Begebenheiten aus der Welt der Tiere.* Berlin: Neufeld & Henius Verlag, 1930. [11]

Krickeberg, Walter. "Menschenopfer für den Sonnengott: Wie die Azteken den Fortbestand der Welt sichern wollten." *Koralle*, vol. 6, no. 24 (June 19, 1938): 852–853. [31]

Kulka, Heinrich. *Adolf Loos. Das Werk des Architekten.* Vienna: Anton Schroll, 1931. [57]

Langley, Anne Rainey. "I Kept House in a Jungle." *National Geographic* LXXV, no. 1, January 1939. [36]

Le Corbusier. *Kommende Baukunst.* Translated by Hans Hildebrandt. Stuttgart: Deutsche Verlags-Anstalt, 1926. [25b]

Le Corbusier. *Städtebau.* Translated by Hans Hildebrandt. Stuttgart: Deutsche Verlags-Anstalt, 1929. [54]

Lewy, Ernst. "Das Wesen der Sprache." *Faust–Monatsschrift für Kunst, Literatur und Musik* 4, no. 6 (1925–1926): 3–12. [40]

M. R. M. "Die alte und die neue Stadt: Gesunder Lebensraum für kommende Geschlechter." *Koralle* 7, no. 15 (April 16, 1939): 532–533. [51b]

Mann, W. M. "Stalking Ants, Savage and Civilized." *National Geographic* LXVI, no. 2, August 1934. [13c]

Marais, Eugene N. *The Soul of the White Ant.* New York: Dodd, Mead & Co., 1937. [11; 14; 15]

Marden, Luis. "On the Cortés Trail." *National Geographic* LXXVIII, no. 3, September 1940.

Means, Philip Ainsworth. *Ancient Civilizations of the Andes.* New York and London: Charles Scribner's Sons, 1931.

Meyers Großes Konversations-Lexikon. 6th edition. Vol. 18. Leipzig and Vienna: Bibliographisches Institut, 1907. [19a; 19b]

Meyers Großes Konversations-Lexikon. 6th edition. Vol. 19. Leipzig and Vienna: Bibliographisches Institut, 1908. [3a; 3b; 3c]

Mountford, Charles P. "Earth's Most Primitive People: A Journey with the Aborigines of Central Australia." *National Geographic* LXXXIX, no. 1, January 1946. [13d; 21]

Nevils, W. Coleman. "The Smallest State in the World: Vatican City on its 108 Acres is a Complete Sovereignty Internationally Recognized." *National Geographic* LXXV, no. 3, March 1939. [13]

Noack, Ferdinand. *Die Baukunst des Altertums.* Berlin: Fischer & Franke: 1910. [6; 16; 16a; 16b; 16c; 33; 42; 48]

Parkinson, Richard. *Dreissig Jahre in der Südsee: Land und Leute, Sitten und Gebräuche im Bismarckarchipel und auf den deutschen Salomoinseln, Vol. 1.* Stuttgart: Strecker & Schröder, 1907. [11]

Photography, 1839–1937. New York: The Museum of Modern Art, 1937. [51a]

Ponten, Josef. *Architektur die nicht gebaut wurde.* With the collaboration of Heinz Rosemann and Hedwig Schmelz. 2 vols. Stuttgart: Deutsche Verlags-Anstalt, 1925. [35; 38; 43; 44; 45; 46; 49; 52]

Posnansky, Arthur. *Tihuanacu: The Cradle of American Man*, vol. 1–2, 4 vols. New York: J.J. Augustin, 1945. [13e]

Sardou, Victorien. "La maison de Mozart dans Jupiter (*La revue spirite*, 1858)." Excerpted in *Minotaure*, no. 3–4 (1933): 54. [50]

Schaeffer, F. A. "A New Alphabet of the Ancients Is Unearthed." *National Geographic* LVIII, no. 4, October 1930. [13d]

Shiras, George, III. "The Wild Life of Lake Superior, Past and Present." *National Geographic* XL, no. 2, August 1921. [18]

Taut, Bruno. *Die Auflösung der Städte, oder: Die Erde eine gute Wohnung, oder auch: Der Weg zur Alpinen Architektur.* Hagen: Folkwang, 1920. [51]

Wehle, Harry B. "Notes." *The Metropolitan Museum of Art Bulletin* 3, no. 10 (June 1945). [41]

Williams, Maynard Owen. "Bali and Points East: Crowded, Happy Isles of the Flores Sea Blend Rice Terraces, Dance Festivals, and Amazing Music in Their Pattern of Living." *National Geographic* LXXV, no. 3, March 1939. [1; 12a]

RESEARCH CLIPPINGS

Journal and newspaper articles in Kiesler's collection of clippings related to his research on *Magic Architecture* but not quoted in the text or reproduced in the plates.

"Ancient Towers in the North of Scotland." *The Illustrated Magazine of Art* 2, no. 11, 1853.

"Building for Defense." *Architectural Forum* 79, no. 6 (June 1941): 423–434.

"Das Robot-Pferd." *Koralle* 7, no. 21 (May 28, 1939): 774.

"Der Traum-Palast: Ein Landbriefträger und sein gigantisches Steckenpfernd." *Koralle* 7, no. 1 (January 8, 1939): 34–35.

"Deutscher Stil: Zur Deutschen Architektur-Ausstellung." *Koralle* 6, no. 6 (February 13, 1938): 17–181.

"Entschleiertes Wunderwerk: Von der Internationalen Automobil- und Motorrad-Ausstellung 1938, Berlin." *Koralle* 6, no. 8 (February 27, 1938): 280.

"Mutation Minks: Successful Breeding of Rare Variations Produces White and Blue Pelts." *Life*, January 28, 1946.
"Peiping: China's Ancient Capital is Rich in Art Treasure." *Life*, April 29, 1946.
"Rock-Pictures." *Chamber's Journal* VI, no. 283 (June 1, 1889).
"Seltsame Hütten der Eingeborenen in Yambuya (Kongostaat)." *Das Buch für Alle* 43, no. 18 (1908): 399, 403.
"So oder So: Vexierbilder mit und ohne tiefere Bedeutung." Koralle 7, no. 45 (November 12, 1939): 1523.
"Space Shapes: They Measure Room People Need to Perform their Everyday Tasks." *Life*, May 7, 1945s.
"The 8,000 LB. House: Fuller's $6,500 Four-Room Industrialized Unit is Round." *Architectural Forum* 84, no. 4, April 1946.
"The Bomb Explodes: Photographs of Actual Detonation Show Blinding Flash and Fireball." *Life*, July 22, 1946.
"The Life of the Bee." *Life*, August 11, 1952.
"The World of the Insects." *Life*, August 8, 1955.
"Wie sehen die Naturvölker das Tier?" *Koralle* 6, no. 31 (August 7, 1938): 1094–1096.
"Wo Steine reden: An Irans uralten Karawanenstraßen." *Koralle* 7, no. 22 (May 31, 1939): 812–813.
Berg, Bengt. *Tiger und Mensch*. Berlin: Reimer, 1934.
Binder, Heinrich. "Das 'Buch der Wilden': Gelehrsamkeit ist das Vergnügen an Dingen, die mitunter trügen." *Koralle* 7, no. 11 (March 19, 1939): 368.
Bonnier, Gaston. "Socialism Among Bees." *The Independent* 65 (1908): 833–839.
Borland, Hal. "Engineers Without College Degrees." *New York* Times, January 24, 1960.
Breton, André. "Le Message Automatique." *Minotaure*, no. 3–4 (1933): 55–65.
Buß (Buss), Georg. "Badeleben in alter Zeit." *Velhagen & Klasings Monatshefte* 19, bd. 2 (1904–1905): 497–514.
Buttler, Werner. "Pits and Pit-dwellings in Southeast Europe." *Antiquity* 10, no. 37 (March 1936): 25–36 [Reprint/translation from *Bonner Jahrbücher* CXXXIX, 134-144, Darmstadt, 1934].
Cavins, Lorimer Victor. *The Wonderland of Knowledge: A New Pictorial Encyclopedia*. Edited by Paul Randall, Bertha Maude White, and Roderick Grant. Chicago: Publishers Productions, Inc., 1937.
Chandler, Douglas. "The Transformation of Turkey: New Hats and New Alphabet are the Surface Symbols of the Swiftest National Changes in Modern Times." *National Geographic* LXXV, no. 1, January 1939.
Corbach, Otto. "Chinas Hintertür: Wird Burma zur Etappe des Ostasien-Krieges?" *Koralle* 7, no. 7 (1939): 215–217.
Dr. K. W. "Der tanzende Gott: TANDAWA–das Gleichnis vom Wandel der Schöpfung." *Koralle* 7, no. 2 (January 15, 1939): 42–43.
Dr. K. W. "Das Rätsel von Angkor: Eine Tempelstadt mitten im Urwald." *Koralle* 7, no. 5 (1939): 139–141.
Dunning, G. C., and R. F. Jussup. "Roman Barrows," *Antiquity* 10, no. 37 (March 1936): 37–53.
E. L. "Wo ist der Sitz der Seele?–Eine Frage, die alle Zeitalter bewegte." *Koralle* 7, no. 38 (September 24, 1939): 1356–1357.
Eberl-Elber, Dr. R. "Geheimbund der Frauen: Afrikanische Busch-Schulen, die kein Mann betreten darf." *Koralle* 6, no. 13 (March 31, 1938): 442–443.
Fritsche, Herbert. "Stammt der Mensch vom Affen ab?–Eine alte Streitfrage, die den Laien wie die Wissenschaft interessiert." *Koralle* 6, no. 28 (July 17, 1938): 994–996.
Frobenius Leo. *Erythräa: Länder und Zeiten des heiligen Königsmordes*. Berlin: Atlantis Verlag, 1931.
Gann, Thomas William Francis. *Ancient Cities and Modern Tribes: Exploration and Adventure in Maya Lands*. New York: Charles Scribner's Sons, 1926.
Gutheim, F. A. "Architecture Yesterday and Today." *Survey Graphic* XXXIII, no. 10 (October 1934): 488–489, centerfold.
H.B. "Der Medizinmann kommt…: 'Sprechstunde' in Hinterindien." *Koralle* 7, no. 15 (April 16, 1939): 534–535.
Haibl, Sophie. "Über Mozarts Tod: Ein Brief von Sophie Haibl an Nikolaus Nissen." In: *Insel-Almanach: auf das Jahr 1926*. 50–53. Leipzig: Insel-Verlag, 1926. [Reprinted from Leitzmann, Albert. *Wolfgang Amadeus Mozart. Berichte der Zeitgenossen und Briefe*. 178–181. Leipzig: Insel-Verlag, 1926.]
Hawaiian Sugar Planters' Association (advertisement), *Collier's*, November 7, 1936.
Hedin, Sven. *Jehol. Die Kaiserstadt*. Leipzig: F. A. Brockhaus, 1932.
Helfritz, Hans. *Chicago der Wüste*. Berlin: Reimar Hobbing, 1932.
Heyck, Eduard. "Aus den Frühtagen der Menschheit." *Velhagen & Klasings Monatshefte* 21, no. 2 (1907): 461–474.
Hutchison, Isobel Wylie. "Riddle of the Aleutians: A Botanist Explores the Origin of Plants on Ever-misty Islands Now Enshrouded in the Fog of War." *National Geographic* LXXXII, no. 6, December 1942.
Janeway, Eliot. "Modern Life and Cloistered Oxford." *Travel* 67 (October 1936): 16–19, 53–55.
Karlson, Paul. "Vorstoss ins Unsichtbare: Eine Meisterleistung deutscher Technik: Das Elektronen-Mikroskop." *Koralle* 6, no. 32 (August 14, 1938): 1119–1121.
Karlson, Paul. "Ein Tier aus hunderttausend Tieren: Das rätselhaft Wesen der Termite." *Koralle* 6, no. 42 (October 23, 1938): 1483–1486.
La Motte, Ellen N. "The Ruins of Angkor." *Harper's Monthly Magazine* CXL, 1920, 365–378.
Lamb, Harold. "Mountain Tribes of Iran and Iraq." *National Geographic* LXXXIX, no. 3 March 1946.
Meyers Großes Konversations-Lexikon. 6th edition. Vol. 8. Leipzig and Vienna: Bibliographisches Institut, 1904.
Meyers Großes Konversations-Lexikon. 6th edition. Vol. 23 (Jahres-Supplement 1910–1911). Leipzig and Vienna: Bibliographisches Institut, 1912.
Moore, W. Robert. "The Cities That Gold and Diamonds Built: Transvaal Treasures Have Created Bustling Johannesburg and Fostered Pretoria, Administrative Capital of the South African Union." *National Geographic* LXXXII, no. 6, December 1942.
Moore, W. Robert. "Nevada, Desert Treasure House." *National Geographic* LXXXIX, no. 1, January 1946.
Moore, W. Robert, and Frederick Simpich. "Change Comes to Bible Lands." *National Geographic* LXXIV, no. 6, December 1938.
Morden, Florence H., and Francis Price Knott. "House-Boat Days in the Vale of Kashmir." *National Geographic* LVI, no. 4, October 1929.
Müller-Wulckow, Walter. *Die deutsche Wohnung der Gegenwart*. Königstein i. Taunus: K. R. Langewiesche Verlag, 1930.
P. K. "Erfinder sind kuriose Leute: Warum einfach, wenn es auch kompliziert geht?" *Koralle* 7, no. 8 (February 26, 1939): 282–283.
Sch., H. "Lebensraum Stadt: Wie Zeiten und Völker das Problem der großen Siedlung zu lösen suchten." *Koralle* 6, no. 20 (May 22, 1938): 698–701.
Soby, James Thrall. "T. Cole: Reviving an ancestor." *Art News* XLVII, no. 9, January 1949.
Simpich, Frederick, and Richard H. Stewart. "New Mexico Melodrama." *National Geographic* LXXIII, no. 5, May 1938.
St. "Die älteste Handschrift der Welt? Eine Sternkarte – in Stein gemeißelt." *Koralle* 7, no. 8 (February 26, 1939): 271.
Step, Edward. "Go to the Ant." *The Illustrated London News*, May 17, 1924.
Stirling, Matthew W., and Richard H. Stewart. "Great Stone Faces of the Mexican Jungle: Five Colossal Heads and Numerous Other Monuments of Vanished Americans are excavated by the Latest National Geographic-Smithsonian Expedition." *National Geographic* LXXVIII, no. 3, September 1940.
Thomas, E. Richmond. "Plants That Defy Drought." *Travel* 67 (October 1936): 13–15, 57.
Williams, Maynard Owen. "New Delhi Goes Full Time." *National Geographic* LXXXII, no. 4, October 1942.

OFFPRINTS

Offprints by the anthropologist M. F. Ashley Montagu in Kiesler's research files

"On The Origin of the Domestication of the Dog." Reprinted from *SCIENCE* 96, no. 2483 (July 31, 1942): 111–112.
"Bronislaw Malinowski (1884–1942)." Reprinted from *ISIS* XXXIV, pt. 2, no. 94 (Autumn 1942): 146–150.
"Four on War." Reprinted from *The Technology Review* XLV, no. 6 (April 1943): 315–316, 334, 336, 338.
"Bloody: The Natural History of a Word." Reprinted from *Psychiatry: Journal of the Biology and Pathology of Interpersonal Relations* 6, no. 2 (May 1943): title page, 175–190.
"Edward Tyson, M.D., F.R.S. 1650–1708 and the Rise of Human and Comparative Anatomy in England: A Study in the History of Science." Philadelphia: The American Philosophical Society: 1943.
"The Skillful Skull." Reprinted from *Technology Review* 45, no. 9 (July 1943): 483–486.

LIBRARY SLIPS

Library slips from Kiesler's research on bees (ca. mid-1950s).

Avebury, John Lubbock. *Ants, Bees, and Wasps: A Record of Observations on the Habits of the Social Hymenoptera*. 1882.
Butler, Colin G. *The World of the Honey Bee*. London: Collins, 1954.
Canning Williams, *The Story of the Hive: A Bee-Lover's Book*. London: A. & C. Black, 1928.
Cowan, T. W. *The Honey-Bee: Its Natural History, Anatomy, and Physiology*. London: Houlston & Sons, 1890.
Curtis, George DeClyver. *Bee's Ways*. Boston: Houghton Mifflin, 1948.
Evrard, Eugene. *The Mystery of the Hive*. London: Methuen, 1923.
Frisch, Karl von. *Bees: Their Vision, Chemical Senses, and Language*. Ithaca: Cornell University Press, 1950.
Herrod-Hempsall, William. *Bee-Keeping: New and Old Described with Pen and Camera*. London: British Bee Journal, 1930.
Hurpin, Jean. *La cité merveilleuse. Histoire des abeilles à travers les* âges. Lausanne: Spes, 1935.
Latham, Allen. *Allen Latham's Bee Book*. London: Hale, 1949.
Nixon, Gilbert. *The World of Bees*. London: Hutchinson, 1954.
Ribbands, Ronald. *The Behaviour and Social Life of Honey Bees*. London: Bee Research Association, 1953.
Stuart, Frank S. *City of the Bees*. London: Allen & Unwin, 1947.

All bibliographies compiled by Clemens Finkelstein

MAGIC ARCHITECTURE
AN ANNOTATED CHRONOLOGY

GERD ZILLNER

fig. C.14

Curriculum Vitae
Frederick Kiesler
architect

1923 Berlin. Active member of "De Stijl", group of the modern architects: J.P.Oud, Theo van Doesburg, Mies van der Rohe, Eesteren, Corbusier, and others.

1924 Working for the City of Vienna. Built ~~the~~ Festival Theatre as Director and Architect of the Festival of the City of Vienna. Lectures at the Museum of Modern Art and Industry. Demonstration of a new exhibition method.

1925 Architect of the architectural and theatre section of the World's Fair "Exposition des Arts Décoratifs et Industrielles Modernes, Paris". ~~Demonstration of new city planning. New correlation of living and working quarters. Built one family residence.~~

Publishing manifesto on new city planning and demonstrations of new construction methods at World's Fair.

1926 Architect of the "International Exposition of Theatre Arts" at Steinway Hall, New York.

1927 Plans for a Museum of Modern Art~~s~~ for the "Society Anonyme", N.Y. (President: Miss Katherine S. Dreier).

1928 Architect for Saks, Fifth Avenue, (Exhibitions) New York. ~~Windows and Interiors.~~

1928 Architect for the Film Guild Cinema, New York.

1929 Published book on Contemporary Art, Architecture and Industry, for Brentano's, New York.

1930 Rebuilt Weyhe (?) Book-Store N.Y.C.

1930 Plans for the residence of Mr. Alfred de Liagre, Byrdcliff, N.Y.

1931 ~~Working on a~~ Commissioned to write book "From Architecture to Life" ~~for Brewer,~~ Warren & Putnam, New York. dealing with all problems of new housing.

1931 Finishing ~~the~~ plans of "Nucleus House". Scheme for ~~the~~ individual and collective ~~housing~~ shelter planning.

~~1931 Winning the competition for a modern Civic Center, Woodstock, N.Y.~~

1931 In charge of the modern rooms exposition of "Audac", Union of American Industrial Designers, at Grand Central Palace, N.Y.

1932 Member Executive Committee, Housing Section of the Welfare Council of New York City.

1932 Collaborating on ... Plans for a National Housing Exhibit.

1932 Consulting architect Public Housing Conference, New York.

1933 Built full size model of a "SPACE-HOUSE" at Exposition, New York City.

1933 Lectures at ... Design Center, New York.

Significant articles on
Mr. Kiesler's contributions
can be found in:

1. DE STIJL 1922–1930
1. Vanity Fair (Hall of Fame), May 1929
2. Architectural Record, August 1930
3. Advertising Arts, January 1931
4. Audac, American Designer's Yearbook, 1931
5. Architectural Forum, December 1932
6. Theatre Arts Monthly, June 1933
7. Theatre Arts Monthly, May 1934

(See Architectural Forum, House & Home, N.Y. Times Magazine)

1933 Lecture on ~~new housing~~ the Nucleus-Concept of Housing Faculty of the Social Science Division University of Chicago.

Frederick Kiesler, Curriculum Vitae with handwritten annotations, mid-1930s. (TS, pencil) ÖFLKS, TXT_6869/0_N1

The story of Frederick Kiesler's *Magic Architecture* is convoluted, stretching over a period that includes several years of research and writing, as well as correspondence with publishers and grant institutions, leading eventually to the failure of its publication. The following chronology is an attempt to trace this incomplete—or in the words of its author, "endless"—history, typical of Kiesler's projects. Its main sources are the correspondence held at the archive of the Kiesler Foundation in Vienna and the Kiesler Papers at the American Archives of Art at the Smithsonian Institution in Washington, DC, centered on Kiesler's interactions with publishers and sponsoring institutions, as well as meetings with editors. Furthermore, the yearly planning calendars of Stefi Kiesler, Frederick's first wife, are an invaluable source of information, documenting the numerous meetings of everyone involved in the making and publishing of *Magic Architecture*.

The following summary is by no means a complete chronology of Frederick Kiesler's life and work.[1] It is a highly selective chronicle recording a list of dates, directly or indirectly related to the making of *Magic Architecture*. Facts and documents that may appear marginal or unrelated to one another become significant when read alongside the architect's manuscripts, as well as the editors' critical annotations.[2]

Two cautionary warnings must be made in advance. The first relates to the nature of temporal frames in this chronology and the limitations of dating. While most of the documents mentioned here are from 1945 to 1949, several other dates in the decades before and after World War II are also represented, since they impact Kiesler's interconnected theoretical projects following or proceeding *Magic Architecture*. Additionally, while letters to editors and diary entries bear a date, neither the preliminary manuscript and typescript drafts nor any of the assembled versions of the final, yet still-unfinished typescript are dated by Kiesler. Therefore, it is not possible to establish via the documents an exact date for either the origin or the completion of the work. Even if Kiesler's newspaper clippings and photostats have a date of printing, they only allow a *terminus post quem*. References in Kiesler's "Note to the Publisher" accompanying his book proposal—such as allusions to the challenges that "lie ahead of us after this Second World War"—suggest that major work on the book had been carried out towards, or soon after the end of World War II, during a moment still vulnerable to wartime destruction and the emergence of the Cold War.[3]

The bulk of the typewritten chapter samples sent to publishers was presumably prepared by Stefi, circa 1946 and early 1947, when Kiesler was corresponding with acquisitions editors, but one cannot be sure when the architect's preliminary manuscripts and sketches were first drafted. The annotated chronology alongside Kiesler's research clippings contain dates and clues indicating that at least some of the architect's encounters with people, publications, and events that inform *Magic Architecture* date from the 1930s, while his failed publication efforts, as well as resuscitations of earlier research, drag into the mid-1950s, factoring among the very last writings he was able to complete before he died in 1965. Therefore, instead of trying to establish exact production dates, the aim of this annotated chronology is to destabilize and ultimately expand the very practice of "dating" a text, particularly when it concerns a book project unhinged by a date of publication.

A second problem arises from the multidirectional nature of Kiesler's research process, which was often channeled into a number of different paths and led to overlapping projects. Inevitably, then, the documents and dates of this chronology do not refer exclusively to *Magic Architecture*, but also to Kiesler's other book and exhibition projects that progress parallel to the development of *Magic Architecture* and eventually outgrow and substitute it.

1925

Architect Josef Hoffmann invites Frederick Kiesler to design and organize the Austrian theater section at the *Exposition Internationale des Arts Décoratifs et Industriels Modernes* in Paris (April 28 to October 1925). Kiesler's contribution is a large display structure, which also serves as a model for his theoretical project *City in Space* (*Raumstadt*), a futuristic vision of an urbanistic superstructure. Following the Paris exposition, Theo van Doesburg publishes Kiesler's manifesto "City in Space—Functional Architecture" in *De Stijl*.[4] Kiesler would refer repeatedly to this text later in his career. Excerpts from the same manifesto translated into English would be included in his first book, *Contemporary Art Applied to the Store and Its Display* (1930), as well as the last sections of *Magic Architecture*.[5] (X.5) A contemporary publisher's announcement for forthcoming Bauhaus books lists a title by Kiesler, *New Forms of Demonstration. The City in Space*, following volumes "about architecture" by Mies van der Rohe and Le Corbusier. However, Kiesler's offering does not materialize.[6]

1926

On January 19, Frederick and Stefi Kiesler leave Paris and set sail for New York to install the *International Theatre Exposition* at the Steinway Building. The show opens on February 27. Although they do not intend to stay and their start in America is anything but smooth, New York City becomes their permanent home. Kiesler's promised curatorial fees are not paid, envisaged projects vanish into thin air, and whenever the Kieslers manage to save enough money for their return trip, a new and even more promising project appears on the horizon that postpones their departure. On the recommendation of Katherine Dreier, Kiesler starts to work with Harvey Wiley Corbett and accepts small occasional commissions, such as designs for shop windows.

1927

Stefi Kiesler starts working at the New York Public Library (NYPL). Her position as Foreign Language Specialist, managing the acquisition of foreign, predominantly French and German books is instrumental in Kiesler's extensive literature research while working on various projects, including *Magic Architecture*.[7] Several of the books, excerpts from which are transcribed for *Magic Architecture*, originate in the collections of the NYPL, and many of the photostats used as illustrations for *Magic Architecture* and other projects bear the NYPL stamp, as well as Stefi's handwritten image credits.

1930

Kiesler publishes his first English-language book with the New York publishing house Brentano's. Disguised as a manual on shop window design and with a page layout meticulously designed by Kiesler, *Contemporary Art Applied to the Store and Its Display* is essentially a theoretical account of the European avant-garde, one of the earliest critical appraisals of modern art to be published in the United States.

The same year, Kiesler redesigns the New York-based Westermann Bookstore, which specialized in "general & scientific books in all languages."[8] Several books used by Kiesler in the text and illustrations for *Magic Architecture*, such as the 1926 German edition of Le Corbusier's *Vers une Architecture*, bear the Westermann sticker. During World War II, the bookstore becomes infamous for serving as a drop-off point for Nazi spies, leading Kiesler to omit this commission from later resumes.[9]

1931

A heavily annotated, typewritten curriculum vitae lists "Working on a book 'From Architecture to Life' for Warren & Putnam, New York. Dealing with all problems of new housing."[10] (fig. C.14)

1932

Kiesler gives a lecture presentation on Adolf Loos's "Ornament and Crime" at the Brooklyn Museum, New York, on January 31. Among the working drafts of the lecture are transcriptions of passages from Loos's writings, translated into English by Stefi.[11] Kiesler knew Loos personally and greatly admired his senior colleague from Vienna. He also repeatedly claimed to have worked on a project for the Vienna Settlers Movement (*Siedlerbewegung*) while in Loos's studio, but no evidence of his involvement exists.

1933

Commissioned to design the showroom for Modernage Furniture Company in New York, Kiesler turns the shop into a full-scale model of his *Space House*. Along with this project, he writes texts that theorize his approach to architecture. These essays anticipate important aspects of his later architectural and design ideas, especially his theory of "correalism." Chart-diagrams for a "Morphology of Architecture" and a "Progression Chart of Architecture" foreshadow *Magic Architecture* in terms of emphasizing the correlation between architecture and socio-economic systems.[12]

1934

Kiesler is hired by the Juilliard School of Music, serving as Director of Scenic Design from 1934 to 1952. The position secures him a modest but regular income that allows more time for theoretical projects.

1937

The Museum of Modern Art stages the exhibition *Prehistoric Rock Pictures in Europe and Africa* (April 28 to May 30, 1937). Stefi Kiesler notes in her calendar, "April 28 lecture Frobenius."[13] (fig. C.15a) In the following week, the name "Montagu" appears in Stefi's calendar for the first time. (fig. C.15b) Eventually a friend of the Kieslers, Ashley Montagu completed his PhD in the Department of Anthropology at Columbia University that year and would later teach anatomy and physical anthropology on the East Coast while publishing on urgent social issues, such as race and feminism.[14]

1937–1941

Kiesler teaches at the School of Architecture at Columbia University, where he founds and leads the Laboratory for Design Correlation. Research material, especially for his *Vision Machine*, overlaps with the research on human nature that informs *Magic Architecture* (for example, the evolution of human perception, especially vision, and the role of dream images).[15]

Between 1937 and 1939, Kiesler publishes a series of articles on "Design Correlation," including articles on Marcel Duchamp's *Large Glass*, architecture for animals, folk spectacle, and the history of photography, culminating in "On Correalism and Biotechnique. Definition and Test of a New Approach to Building Design."[16] This latter essay is illustrated with photographs of the *Mobile Home Library* and diagrams of Kiesler's theory of "correalism." A photomontage of the library and Kiesler's "Metabolism Chart of Correalism" are also included among the final illustration plates of *Magic Architecture*.

March 25, 1939
An entry in Stefi's calendar from March 25, 1939, mentions her participation in a protest march against the German occupation of Czechoslovakia.[17] This is perhaps the only personal document by the Kieslers that comments directly on events related to the Nazi occupation. Nevertheless, the Kieslers were well informed about political events prior to World War II and wartime developments. So far, the fates of their families cannot be fully reconstructed.[18]

One of Kiesler's personal losses during this period is directly linked to the Nazis' perfidious exploitation of former Jewish citizens who had managed to escape or emigrate. His personal belongings were deposited in a warehouse in Vienna before he was contacted by the Viennese shipping company Caro & Jellinek to pay for their transport to Switzerland and storage costs—otherwise Kiesler's effects would be sold by the Viennese auction house Dorotheum. This was common practice of VUGESTA (Verwaltungsstelle für jüdisches Umzugsgut der Gestapo, the Gestapo Office for the Disposal of the Property of Jewish Emigrants). All of Kiesler's possessions, including drawings, etchings and books, were apparently lost during transport.[19]

1940S

The Kieslers become anchor points for exiled artists and writers arriving in New York after the defeat of France by the German Reich. This is especially true for the surrealist artists such as Marcel Duchamp, Roberto Matta, Gordon Onslow Ford, Kurt Seligmann, Max Ernst, and André Breton. Among the frequent guests in the Kieslers' penthouse apartment at 56 7th Avenue was Duchamp, who, at some point, became their subtenant, and Onslow Ford, who rehearsed his famous presentations at the New School for Social Research in the Kiesler home.[20]

JUNE–JULY 1941

Kiesler discusses a possible book project on architecture with Doubleday. In a letter dated June 27, he refers to previous correspondence with Doubleday editor Kenneth McCormick about a publication. Kiesler states that "there is great need for information in the field of architecture and industrial design. It only depends upon which part one sees best fit to attack first." He proposes a meeting and Stefi notes an appointment with the publisher on July 7.[21]

1942

Kiesler publishes the essay "Some Testimonials of Dream Images" in the first issue of the surrealist magazine *VVV*.[22] He also designs the exhibition *Art of This Century*, showcasing Peggy Guggenheim's collection of modern art by converting two tailor shops into a gallery-museum. He uses his research at Columbia University for the display, especially for the "Surrealist Gallery." In a press release for the October 20th opening, he formulates a "Note on Designing the Gallery," which includes phrases that reappear almost verbatim in the manuscript of *Magic Architecture*, for example, "Primitive man knew no separate world of vision and Fact."[23]

1942–1944

Kiesler becomes involved in a project for the redesign of several displays at the American Museum of Natural History in New York, spearheaded by Albert E. Parr, the newly appointed director. Over the course of 1942 and 1943, Parr exchanges ideas with Kiesler, who had gained recognition for his innovative design for *Art of This Century*. Among the architect's files, a proposal by the museum describes

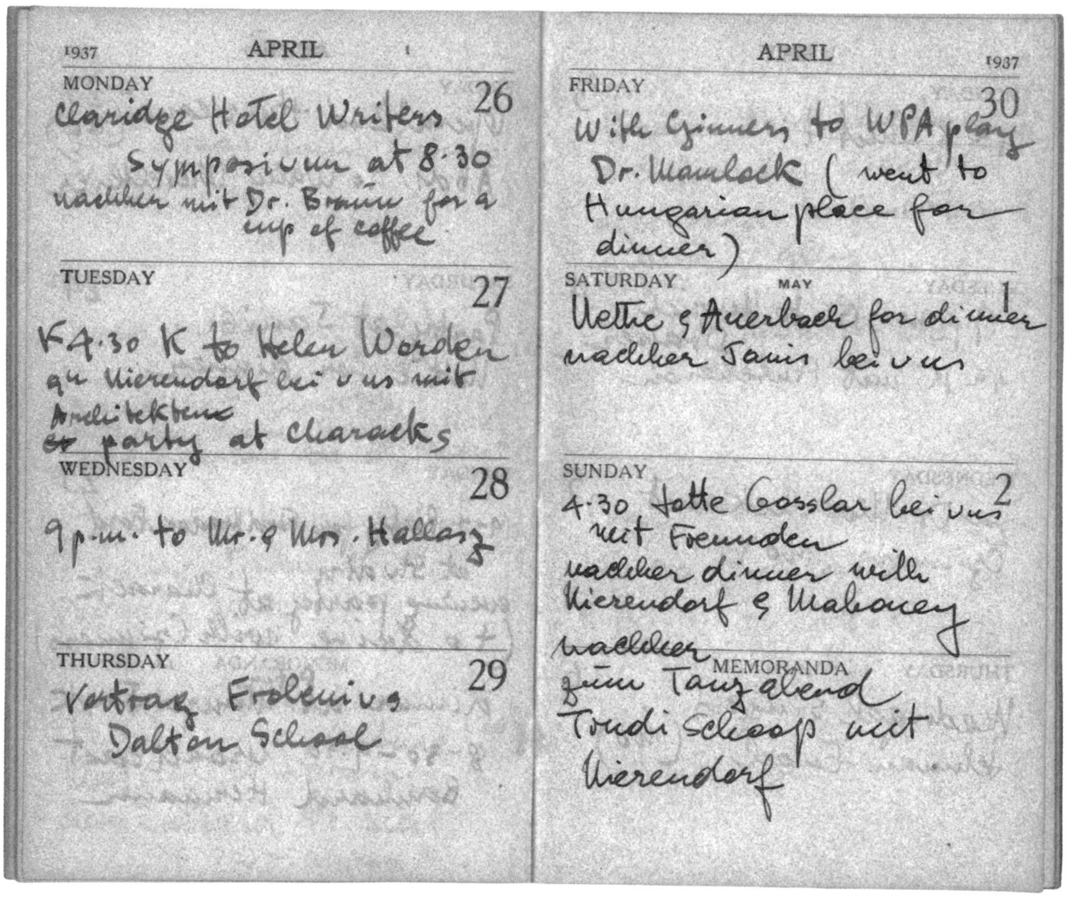

1937 APRIL

MONDAY 26
Claridge Hotel Writers
Symposium at 8.30
nachher mit Dr. Braun for a
cup of coffee

TUESDAY 27
K 4.30 K to Helen Worden
4[h] Kiesendorf bei uns mit
Architekten
~~et~~ party at Characks

WEDNESDAY 28
9 p.m. to Mr. & Mrs. Hallasz

THURSDAY 29
Vortrag Frolenius
Dalton School

APRIL 1937

FRIDAY 30
With Czinners to WPA play
Dr. Maulock (went to
Hungarian place for
dinner)

SATURDAY MAY 1
Nettie & Auerbach for dinner
nachher Janis bei uns

SUNDAY 2
4.30 Lotte Gosslar bei uns
mit Freunden
nachher dinner with
Kiesendorf & Mahoney
nachher
zum Tanzabend
Trudi Schoop mit
Kiesendorf

MEMORANDA

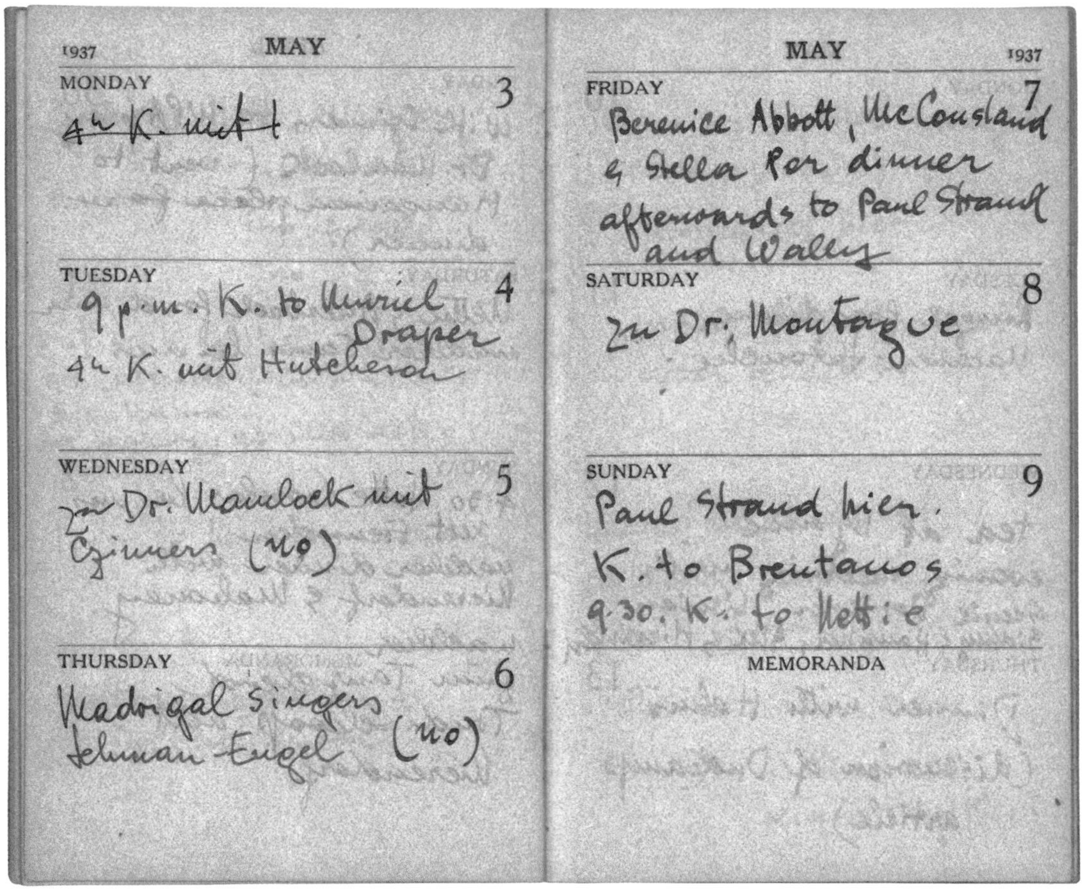

1937 MAY

MONDAY 3
~~4[h] K. mit~~

TUESDAY 4
9 p.m. K. to Muriel
Draper
4[h] K. mit Hutcheson

WEDNESDAY 5
zu Dr. Maulock mit
Czinners (no)

THURSDAY 6
Madrigal Singers
Lehman Engel (no)

MAY 1937

FRIDAY 7
Berenice Abbott, McCausland
& Stella for dinner
afterwards to Paul Strand
and Walley

SATURDAY 8
zu Dr. Montague

SUNDAY 9
Paul Strand hier.
K. to Brentanos
9.30. K. to Nettie

MEMORANDA

Stefi Kiesler, Calendar Yearbook, 1937: April 26–May 2 and May 3–9. ÖFLKS, MED_851/0

"Special Exhibits on Man Proposed for December, 1942," and outlines a number of displays, such as "A. From Ape to Man ... B. From Birth to Old Age ... C. Some Fundamentals in Behavior ... D. An Outline of Man's Achievements," reflecting some of the evolutionary themes probed by Kiesler in *Magic Architecture.* [24]

In 1944, Kiesler works on a "Hall of Ecology," also for the American Museum of Natural History, which does not advance beyond the stage of a preliminary proposal. Chart-like drawings illustrating the evolution of all living species on earth presage some of the evolutionary concepts developed in diagrams for *Magic Architecture.*[25]

1944–1945

Kiesler works on an exhibition on American architecture sent to the Soviet Union by the National Council of American-Soviet Friendship.[26] His daring design for display wall frames is rejected by the organizing committee and, ultimately, a heavily scaled-down and more sober panel system designed by the architect travels to Moscow.[27] References to current housing conditions in America and the USSR appear in the concluding chapters of *Magic Architecture.*[28]

Summer 1945
Stefi Kiesler's calendar marks a series of meetings with Doubleday editor Clara Claasen over the course of the summer: June 1, June 16, June 28, and August 2, 1945. The meetings continue in October.[29]

August 14, 1945
An entry in Stefi Kiesler's calendar notes a meeting with Helen and Kurt Wolff: "... eve. Mr & Mrs. Kurt Wolf [sic] here (to discuss dream anthology)."[30] Kurt Wolff was one of the most prominent publishers of European literature, including works by Franz Kafka and Viennese intellectuals like Franz Werfel and Karl Krauss. In 1942, the Wolffs arrived in New York and founded Pantheon Books. They were also interested in an extensive anthology of dreams in literature, compiled by Stefi Kiesler and titled *Dream Book.* (fig. C.16) There is a certain amount of overlap between the authors represented in Stefi's anthology and Frederick's literary sources for *Magic Architecture*, for example, Lucien Lévy-Bruhl, Leo Frobenius, Bronisław Malinowski, Franz Kafka, and Lafcadio Hearn. To some extent, this also applies to the structure of certain parts and chapters.[31] Similar to Stefi's work on *Magic Architecture*, Frederick suggested corrections or revisions to her typescript. Only a few of these comments were adopted by Stefi.

October 18, 1945
Stefi Kiesler notes another meeting with Kenneth McCormick from Doubleday publishing company: "lunch McCormick."[32]

October 30, 1945
In her calendar, Stefi notes a "Meeting about Exp[osition] on Magic" with artist friends Max Ernst, Dorothea Tanning, Marcel Duchamp, Kurt Seligmann, and Roberto Matta,[33] surrealists with whom Kiesler shared a strong interest in ethnography, anthropology, paleo-sciences, and psychoanalysis, as well as the study of myth and magic. On the following day, October 31, Stefi notes a dinner with André Breton.

Winter 1945
Kiesler works on André Breton's *Ode à Charles Fourier.* The book was published in 1947.[34]

1946

July 31 and August 1, 1946
Over these two days, an entry in Stefi's calendar notes meetings with Hugh Garvey from publishers Henry Holt & Co.: "Mr. Garvey (Holt Publ.) here with other editor (K. manuscript)."[35]

August 2–4, 1946
Entries in Stefi's calendar indicate that she was working on the manuscripts: "typed all day Mss."[36] (figs. C.17a–b) Stefi not only helped with researching and obtaining literature, image sources, and photostats, but also spent long hours transcribing book excerpts for her husband and typing his drafts. Many typescript pages show the hanging "s" typical of Stefi's typewriter and are marked with her handwritten comments and corrections.

August 5, 1946
An entry in Stefi's calendar notes a visit from book editors "Mr. Lindley, Allen Tate," and Hugh Garvey, as well as a foreign representative from Henry Holt.[37]

August 6, 1946
In a letter to Garvey, dated August 6, 1946, Kiesler includes an outline of *Magic Architecture* in three parts, as well as an estimated page and illustration count (totaling five hundred pages of text and one hundred illustrations), which corresponds with the tripartite division of the "Note to the Publisher," included with the *Magic Architecture* typescripts.[38] Kiesler mentions that the first part (on "the past history") is already finished, which explains the manuscript's emphasis on prehistoric and Indigenous cultures: "I have completed almost the writing of all the nine chapters of the first part [which] gave the outline an over-weight on the first section." Yet the architect insists that, despite its emphasis on "past history," his manuscript addresses contemporary problems.[39] Kiesler's acknowledgment that he has only completed the chapters of Part I suggests that the rest of the manuscript had not yet been written. The major shift in structure from three large, chronologically arranged sections mentioned in the earlier book proposals to the ten "parts" of the later manuscript, which has a very different thematic (and often anti-chronological) organization, also suggests that most of the later chapters were still not drafted and that major changes would take place over the following months.

August 26, 1946
In two separate letters Kiesler informs Clara Claasen and Kenneth McCormick of Doubleday on the progress of his book, with the invitation to "see the complete material of the extensive outline, including illustrations, of my script on architecture."[40] To McCormick, he notes that he would "hesitate to give it out without having first gone over it with you together undisturbed."[41]

August 28, 1946
Kiesler receives a letter from Henry Rago of Pellegrini & Cudahy dated August 28, 1946, politely refusing to publish *Magic Architecture.*[42]

August 30, 1946
Annoyed by Rago's brief and formal refusal, Kiesler asks for an explanation in a letter dated August 30, 1946. "Having sent you the manuscript ... may I ask you the favor, to tell me some of the professional considerations which guided you in your negative decision. Is the book too voluminous; has it too many illustrations and is, therefore, too expensive? Is the style not popular enough? ... You may be quite merciless and direct in your answer; I shall appreciate it very much."[43]

By September 3, he receives a response stating that, besides "the obvious business reasons," the company was "anxious to avoid being 'typed'" on either side of the "quality" versus popularity spectrum.[44] (fig. C.18)

September 5, 1946
Stefi's calendar notes a visit by Clara Claasen and Kenneth McCormick (Doubleday), following Kiesler's request to review the manuscript together before

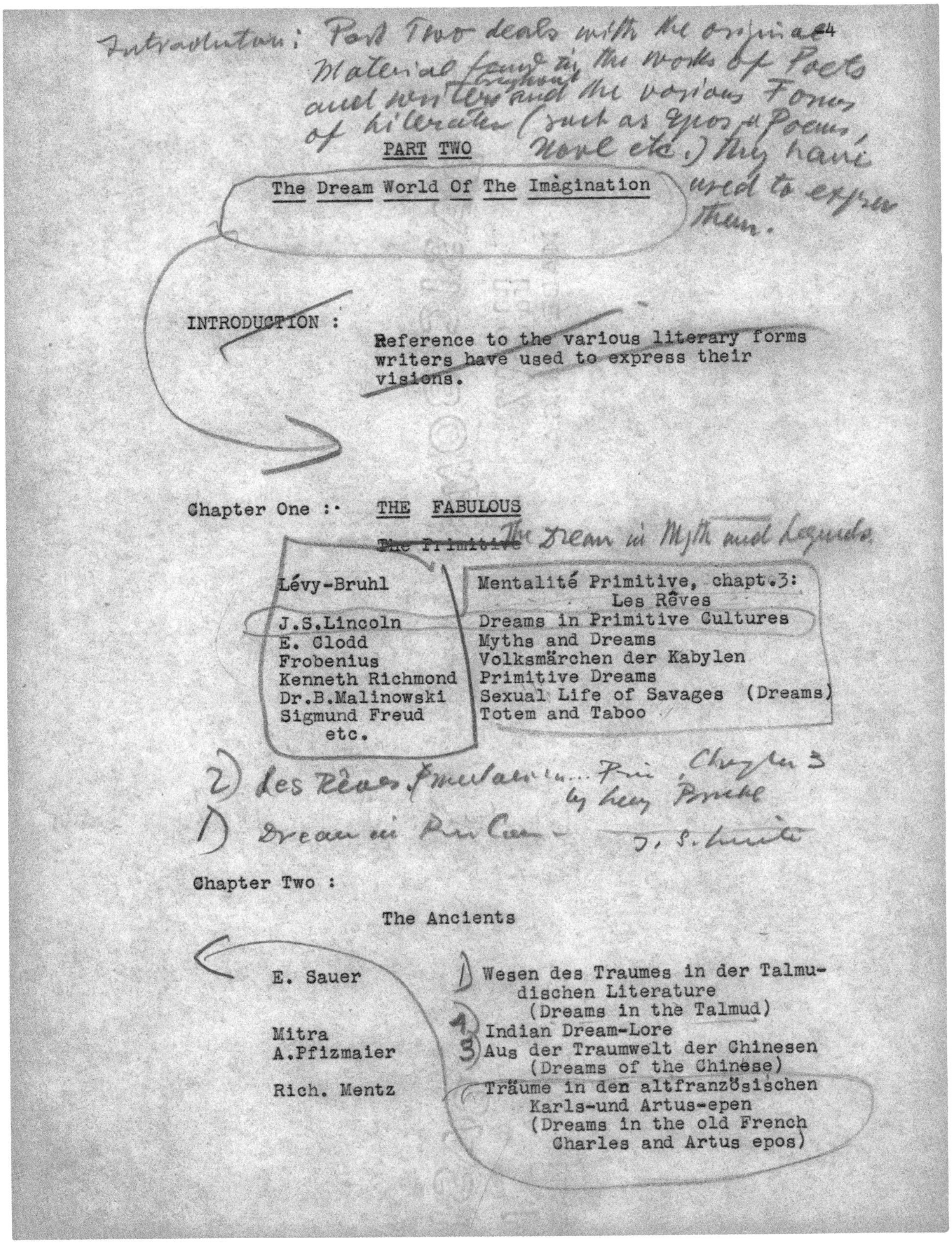

Introduction: Part Two deals with the original Material found in the works of Poets and writers throughout the various Forms of literature (such as Epos, Poems, Novel etc.) they have used to express them. 4

PART TWO

The Dream World Of The Imagination

INTRODUCTION : ~~Reference to the various literary forms writers have used to express their visions.~~

Chapter One : THE FABULOUS

~~The Primitive~~ The Dream in Myth and Legends

Lévy-Bruhl	Mentalité Primitive, chapt.3: Les Rêves
J.S.Lincoln	Dreams in Primitive Cultures
E. Clodd	Myths and Dreams
Frobenius	Volksmärchen der Kabylen
Kenneth Richmond	Primitive Dreams
Dr.B.Malinowski	Sexual Life of Savages (Dreams)
Sigmund Freud	Totem and Taboo
etc.	

2) Les Rêves (Mentalité Primi... Chapter 3 by Lévy Bruhl

1) Dream in Prim Cu— J. S. Lincoln

Chapter Two :

The Ancients

E. Sauer	1) Wesen des Traumes in der Talmudischen Literature (Dreams in the Talmud)
Mitra	4) Indian Dream-Lore
A.Pfizmaier	3) Aus der Traumwelt der Chinesen (Dreams of the Chinese)
Rich. Mentz	Träume in den altfranzösischen Karls-und Artus-epen (Dreams in the old French Charles and Artus epos)

Stefi Kiesler, *Dreambook*, Table of Contents with handwritten notes by Frederick Kiesler, mid 1940s. (TS, pencil) ÖFLKS, TXT_8000/0

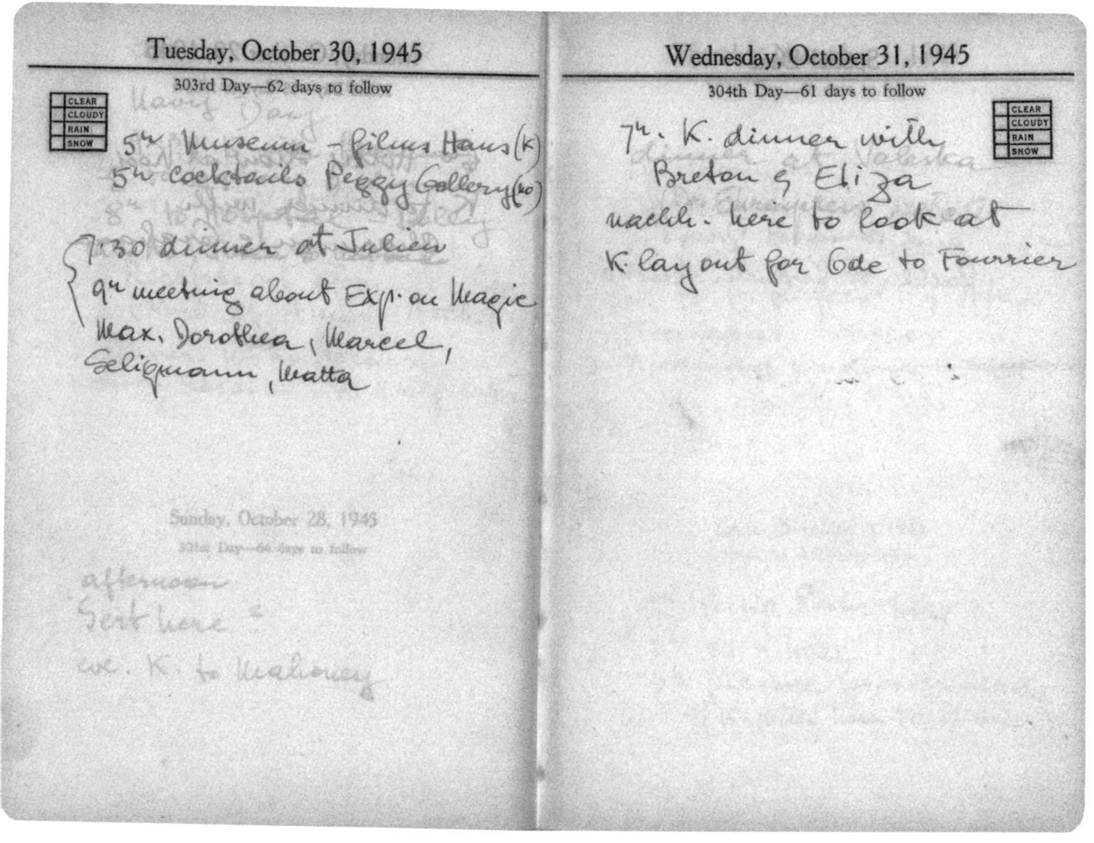

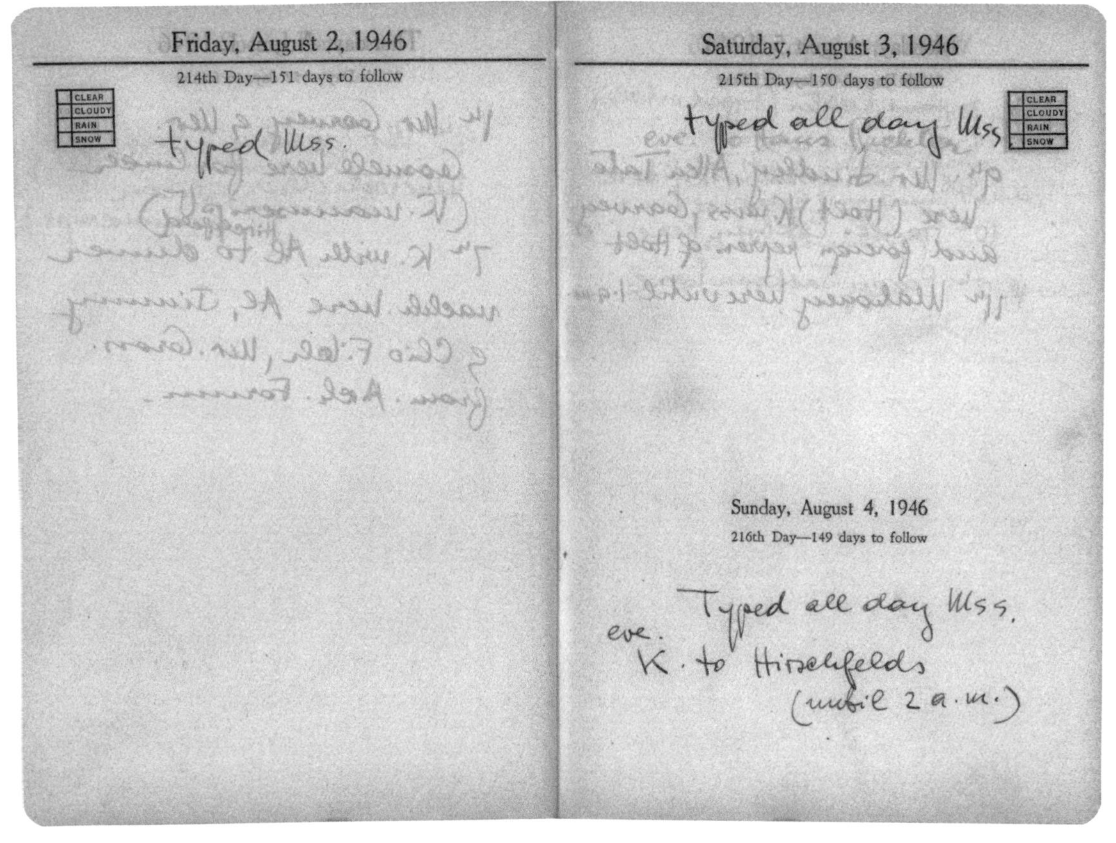

Stefi Kiesler, Calendar Yearbook, 1945, October 30–31, and Calendar Yearbook, 1946, August 2–3. ÖFLKS, MED_860/0 and MED_861/0.

PELLEGRINI & CUDAHY

ARIEL BOOKS
FRANKLIN 4992

75 EAST WACKER DRIVE
CHICAGO 1, ILLINOIS

September 3, 1946

Mr. Frederick J. Kiesler
56 Seventh Avenue
New York, New York

Dear Mr. Kiesler:

I do not know how relevant you would find our own reasons for being unable to place MAGIC ARCHITECTURE on our schedule. Our problems are, I suppose peculiar in so far as we are just starting, and we must give more than ordinary thought to the question of "balance" in our 1947 list. That list will be taken as the concrete example of the range of our interest and will of course have an obvious effect on the attitude of booksellers and potential authors toward our house-policy. We felt that we could not make room for MAGIC ARCHITECTURE, despite its indisputable soundness and quality, because we are fearful that perhaps our list is already overloaded on the side of "quality"--i.e., books which have genuine merit, much more so than others of wider interest, but which cannot be counted on for large sales. Aside from the obvious business reasons, we are anxious to avoid being "typed" on one side or the other. It is entirely possible that a book on the subject of architecture could sell extremely well if slanted for the popular market (Van Loon's book is an example in a broader field), but what is most moving and most important in your book would suffer fatally from over-simplification if you'd try to make it a ~~definite~~ different sort of book. That is not to say that there couldn't be a popular book on architecture in its relations to human culture, but you'd have to plan another book entirely rather than rewrite the one you have. But why rewrite the present book? I should suggest instead that you show it to some university press. Unfortunately, I have no way of knowing which one might be interested and so cannot make my suggestion any more concrete.

Sincerely,
PELLEGRINI & CUDAHY

Henry Rago

Henry Rago
Associate Editor

HR:jc

Letter from Henry Rago to Frederick Kiesler, September 3, 1946. (TS) ÖFLKS, LET_1745/0

officially submitting it to the press (see letter of August 26, 1946).[45]

September 19, 1946
An entry in Stefi's calendar notes "eve. Kurt Wolff here."[46] In addition to co-founding Pantheon Books, Wolff served as an editor for the Bollingen Series published by Princeton University Press. Kiesler would apply to the Bollingen Foundation the following year.

Winter 1946
Kiesler works on one of his most prominent stage designs, the American premiere of Jean-Paul Sartre's *No Exit (Huis clos)*, which opened at the Biltmore Theatre in New York on November 26, 1946.

1947

January 14, 1947
Stefi's calendar notes a photoshoot with photographer Ben Schnall. Two of Schnall's photographs show Kiesler lying on top of his "Metabolism Chart of Correalism." Also visible in the photographs, across from the architect and his cat, is a hard binder containing a manuscript with a few loose pages. These pages contain the "Table of Contents" for Part I of *Magic Architecture* and the second page of its "Synopsis."[47] One of these well-known photographs is used to illustrate the article on Kiesler, "Design's Bad Boy," published in *Architectural Forum* in February 1947.[48] (See Sources, Disciplines, and Objects fig. A.05)

January 30, 1947
An entry in Stefi's calendar refers to a meeting between Kiesler and the Bollingen Foundation or the Bollingen (book) Series.[49] In the following years, the Bollingen Foundation and the Bollingen Series appear repeatedly in Stefi's calendars and in Kiesler's own correspondence. Kiesler befriends the Foundation's staff: the editor, Jack (John D.) Barrett, his secretary, Vaun Gillmor, and the assistant editor, Hugh Chisholm. (He would later draw a portrait of Barrett probably in the early 1950s.) The architect also tried to secure a commission for Chisholm (who, in addition to being a book editor, was himself a writer and poet) at the Juilliard School of Music to record his *Atlantic City Cantata*.[50]

March 11, 1947
A letter from Vaun Gillmor informs Kiesler that the "text material and illustrations of the *Magic Architecture* have been sent from Florida to the Foundation office in Washington."[51] This implies that Kiesler sent an assembled manuscript version of *Magic Architecture*, including illustrations, to the editors of the Bollingen Series. Along with the Schnall photographs of 1947, Gillmor's letter provides the clearest indication that by early 1947 Kiesler assembled a book manuscript.

Stefi notes several meetings between Kiesler and the staff of the Bollingen Foundation in April and May.[52]

Summer 1947
Kiesler spends the summer of 1947 in Paris installing the *Exposition Internationale du Surrealisme* at the Galerie Maeght. He designs the "Hall of Superstition" and contributes an essay to the catalogue on "the magic architecture of the hall of superstitions."[53] (figs. C.19a–b) Kiesler left for Paris on May 27 and returned on September 21, 1947.

While in Paris, Kiesler also produces a series of pencil, ballpoint pen, and watercolor drawings. The series, labeled *Paris Endless*, depicts non-figurative shapes reminiscent of cavernous structures and Neolithic stone formations, similar to some of the illustrations for *Magic Architecture*. (figs. C.20a–d)

June 16, 1947
During Kiesler's absence, a letter of recommendation from the architect Edgar Irving Williams praising Kiesler as an author is sent to the Bollingen Series: "Frederick Kiesler is more than a philosopher. He is a creator–an inventor–and whether or not you like the things he does you may be certain that his notes will be of great interest because his thinking is stimulating and constructive."[54]

August 1, 1947
Kiesler receives a letter from the Bollingen Foundation, stating that his application for a grant is being deferred to the next jury meeting in 1948 because it was not submitted on time.[55]

September 22, 1947
A 169-page, typed manuscript titled *Kunst und Architektur vereint. Ein Manifest des Korrealismus* (*Art and Architecture United. A Manifesto of Correalism*) bears the handwritten date of September 22, 1947, on its last page, coinciding with Kiesler's fifty-seventh birthday.[56] An introductory note about the content and method of this text echoes the "Note to the Publisher" accompanying the book proposal for *Magic Architecture*. However, this new book project affirms a more pronounced geopolitical objective, which is to reunite the world via the unification of painting, sculpture, and architecture: "Just as in the political sphere, the tendency is becoming increasingly clear to create a world whole out of individually delimited states and countries, so also in the coming art and architecture a closer rapprochement of these two fields will inevitably take place."[57] In the following years, Kiesler's interest in publishing a book on "correalism" and this project on the unity of art and architecture will gradually upstage *Magic Architecture*.

October 8, 1947
Kiesler receives a letter from André Bloc, editor of *L'Architecture d'Aujourd'hui*, who he met during his summer stay in Paris.[58] Its content suggests that the two have discussed the publication of Kiesler's "Manifeste du Corréalisme" as well as *Magic Architecture*. With reference to the former, the editor expresses his hope that he will "receive around October 15th the dossier you are preparing for the presentation of your manifesto in *L'Architecture d'Aujourd'hui*." With reference to the latter, he mentions having frequently pondered "how to edit the grand project titled 'MAGIC ARCHITECTURE.'" Bloc notes that the "journal could possibly take care of the complete illustration section of this enormous work. However, the full text is too extensive for the faculties of our printing house to absorb."[59] He proposes contacting another publisher, namely Gallimard, through its editor, Henri Parisot. If this solution is not satisfactory to Kiesler, Bloc proposes to publish "only the illustration section, accompanied by a more condensed text."[60] The collaboration with Bloc would eventually result in the publication of Kiesler's "Manifeste du Corréalisme," but no version of *Magic Architecture*.

October 4, 1947
Henri Parisot informs Kiesler about the interest of Éditions Gallimard to publish his book, subject to economic circumstances. The amicable but very brief letter is followed by a postscript of almost equal length, containing Parisot's precise instructions to Kiesler about how to send him, from the US, a certain cowboy shirt "made of thick woolen cloth, with colors harmonious as well as discreet as possible, 39 centimeters neckline, long enough arms (for a man of six feet tall)," and "two or three packs of Pall Mall cigarettes."[61]

October 19, 1947
In a letter from October 19, Kiesler thanks André Bloc for his commitment: "I warmly welcome your desire to participate in the edition of my book 'Magic Architecture.' I am very grateful for your interest and support for my ideas." Kiesler informs Bloc that he has received a letter from Gallimard, "which is very favorable, but I have still not made any decisions. I'll contact you as soon as I have any news." (fig. C.21) He

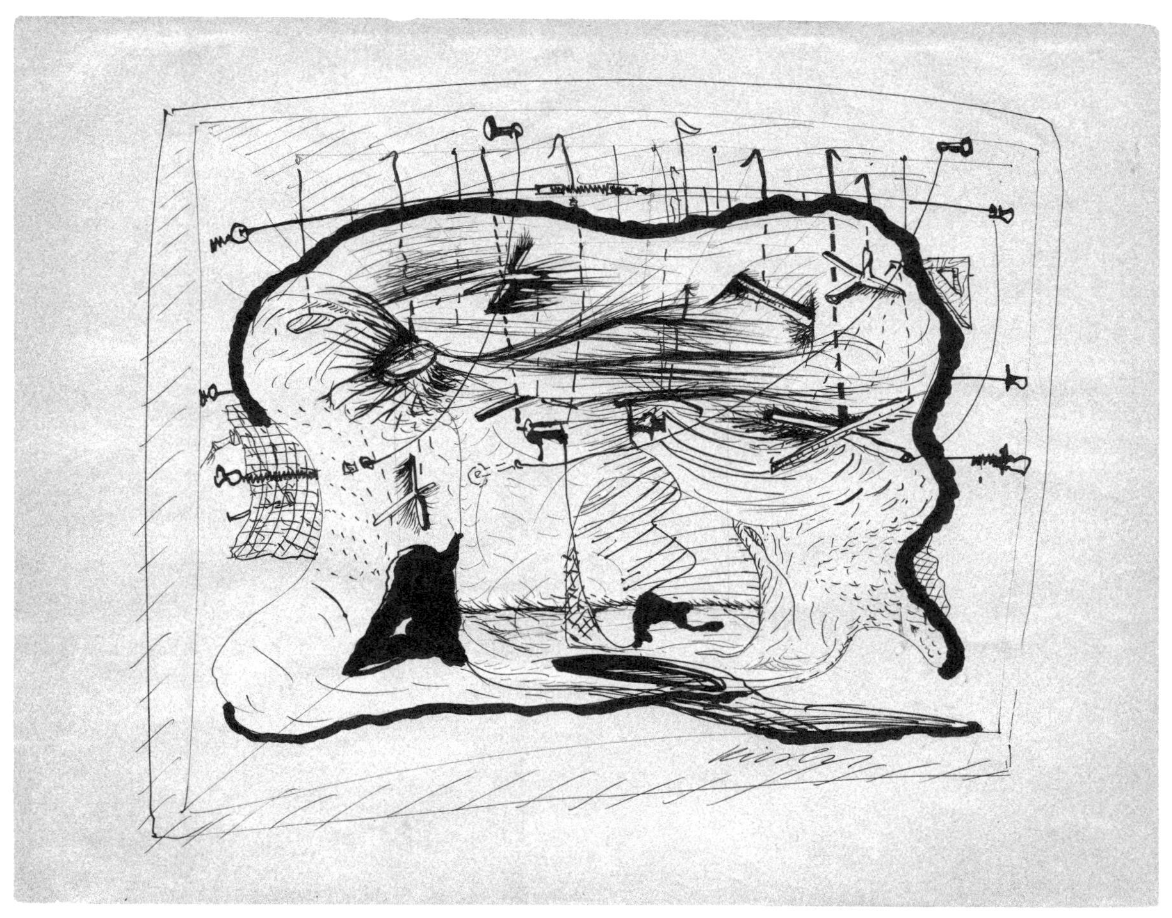

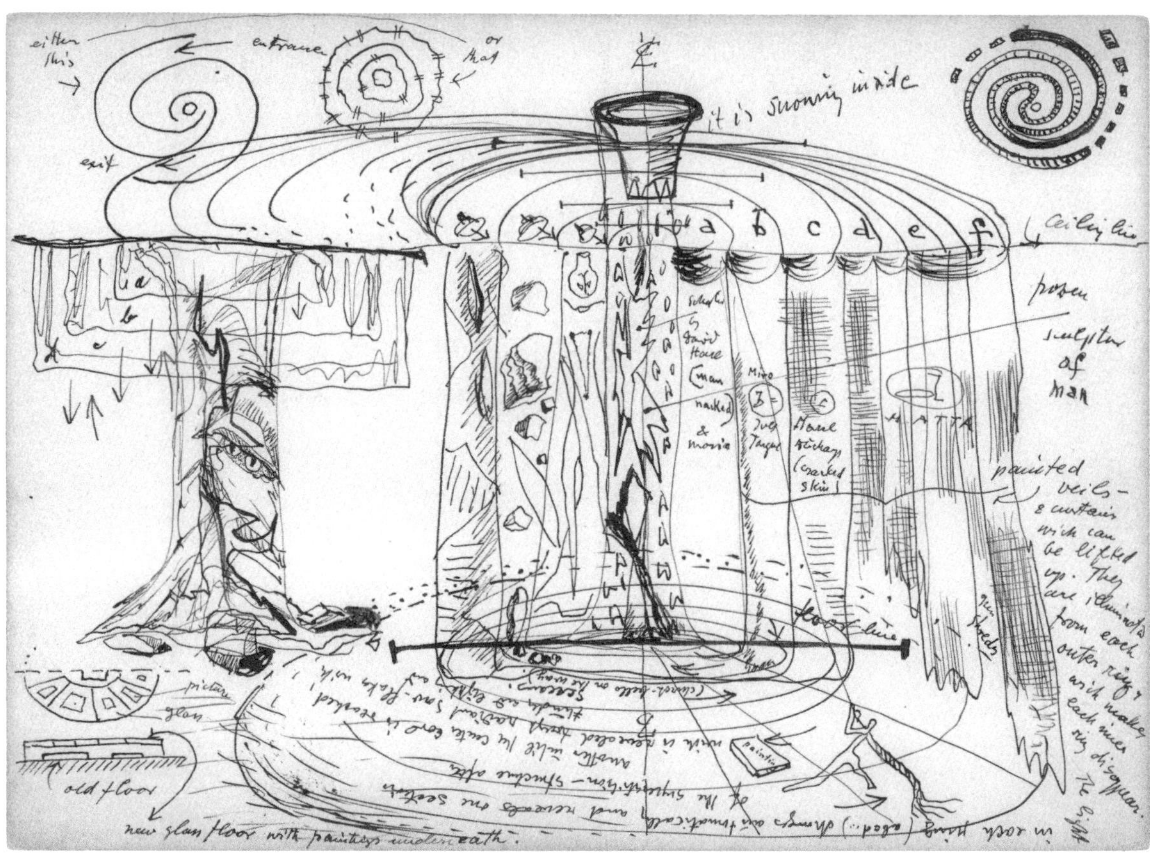

Frederick Kiesler, *Hall of Superstition*, conceptual drawings, 1947. (ink) ÖFLKS, MFP_1022/0 and SFP_1205/0

fig. C.20a

Frederick Kiesler, *Study for Endless House* [Paris Endless], 1947. ÖFLKS, SFP_505/0

fig. C.20b

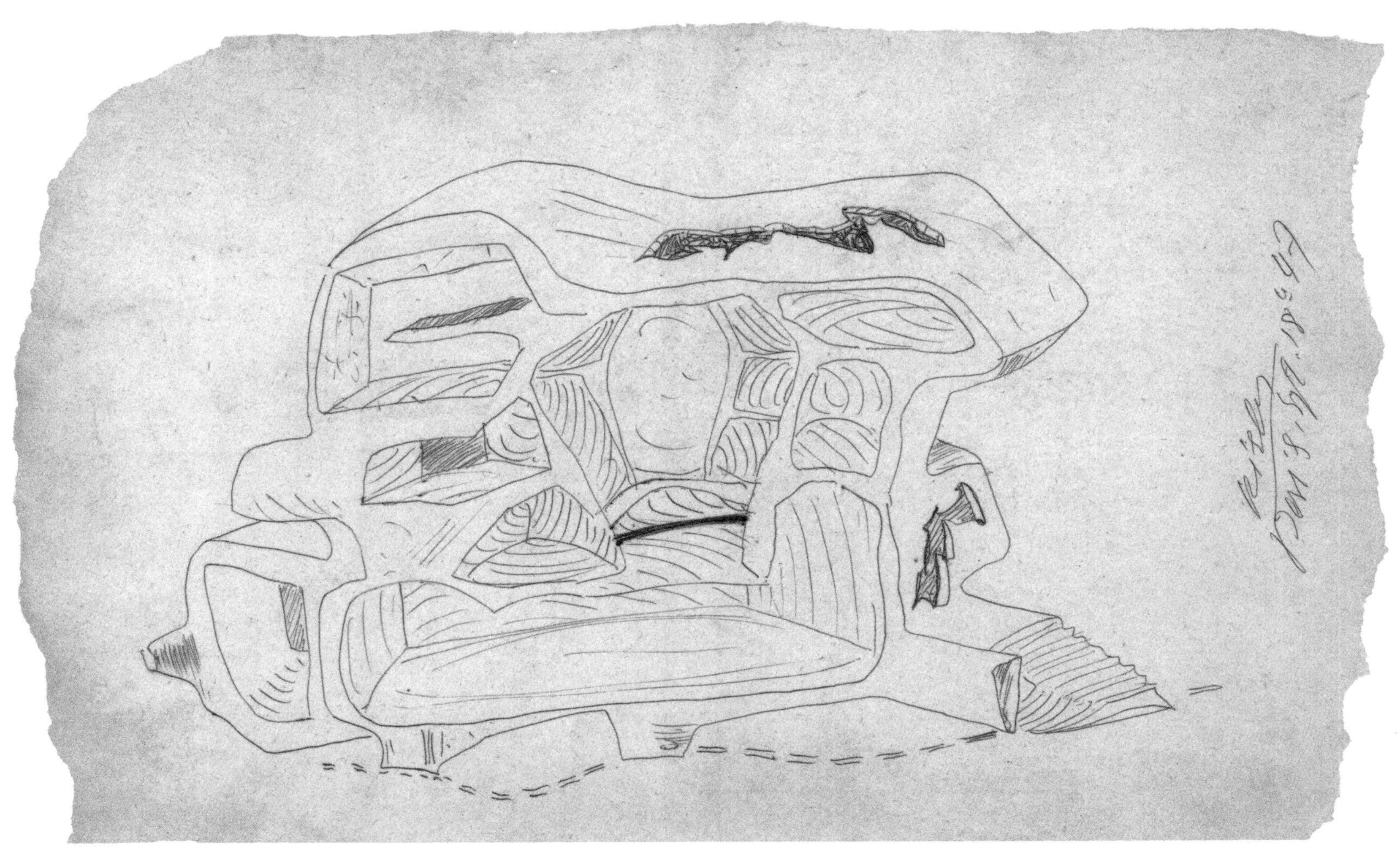

Frederick Kiesler, *Study for Endless House* [Paris Endless], 1947. (ink) ÖFLKS, SFP_507/0

fig. C.20c

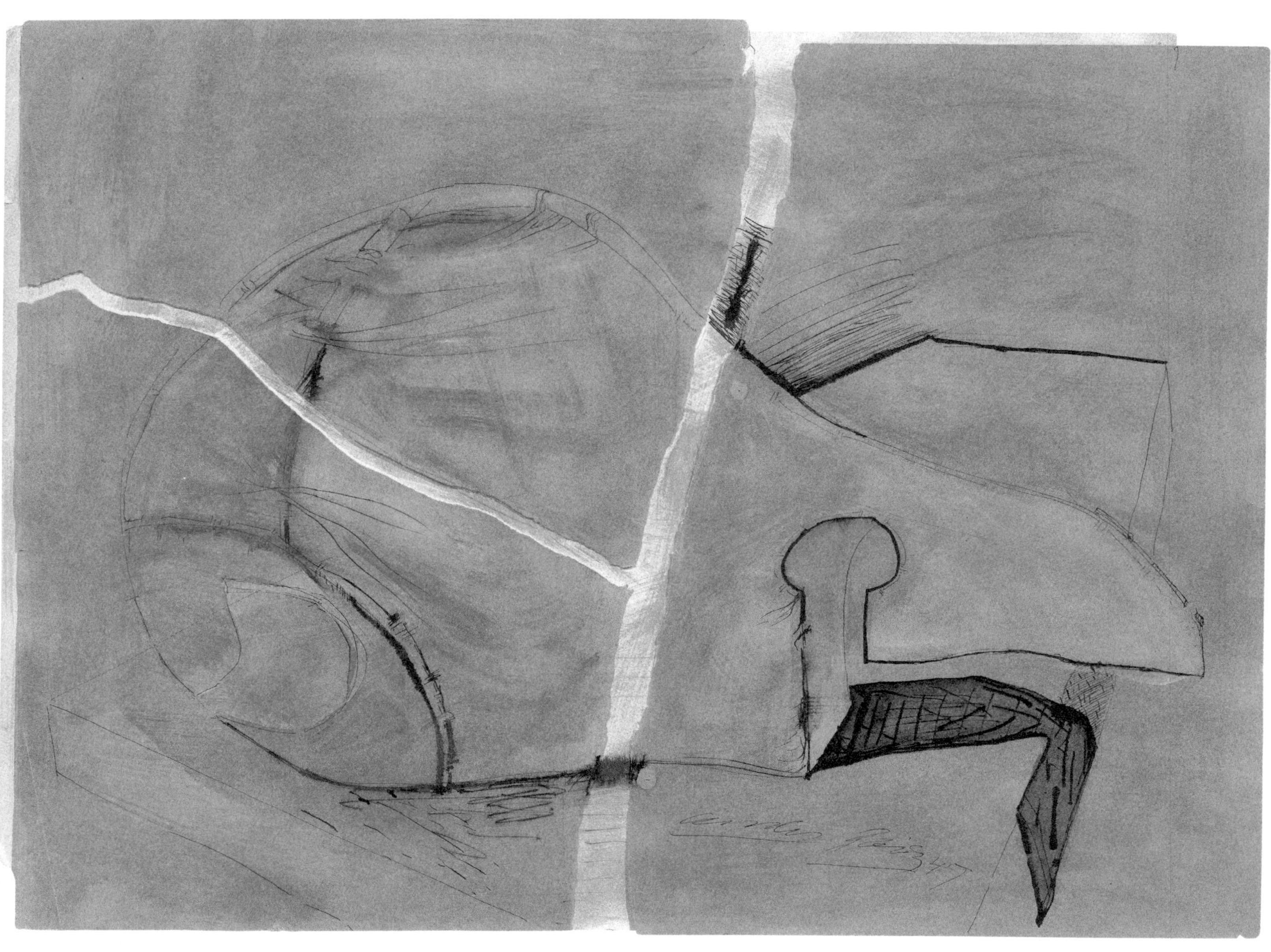

Frederick Kiesler, *Study for Endless House* [Paris Endless], 1947. (gouache and ink on paper mounted on cardboard) ÖFLKS, SFP_495/0

fig. C.20d

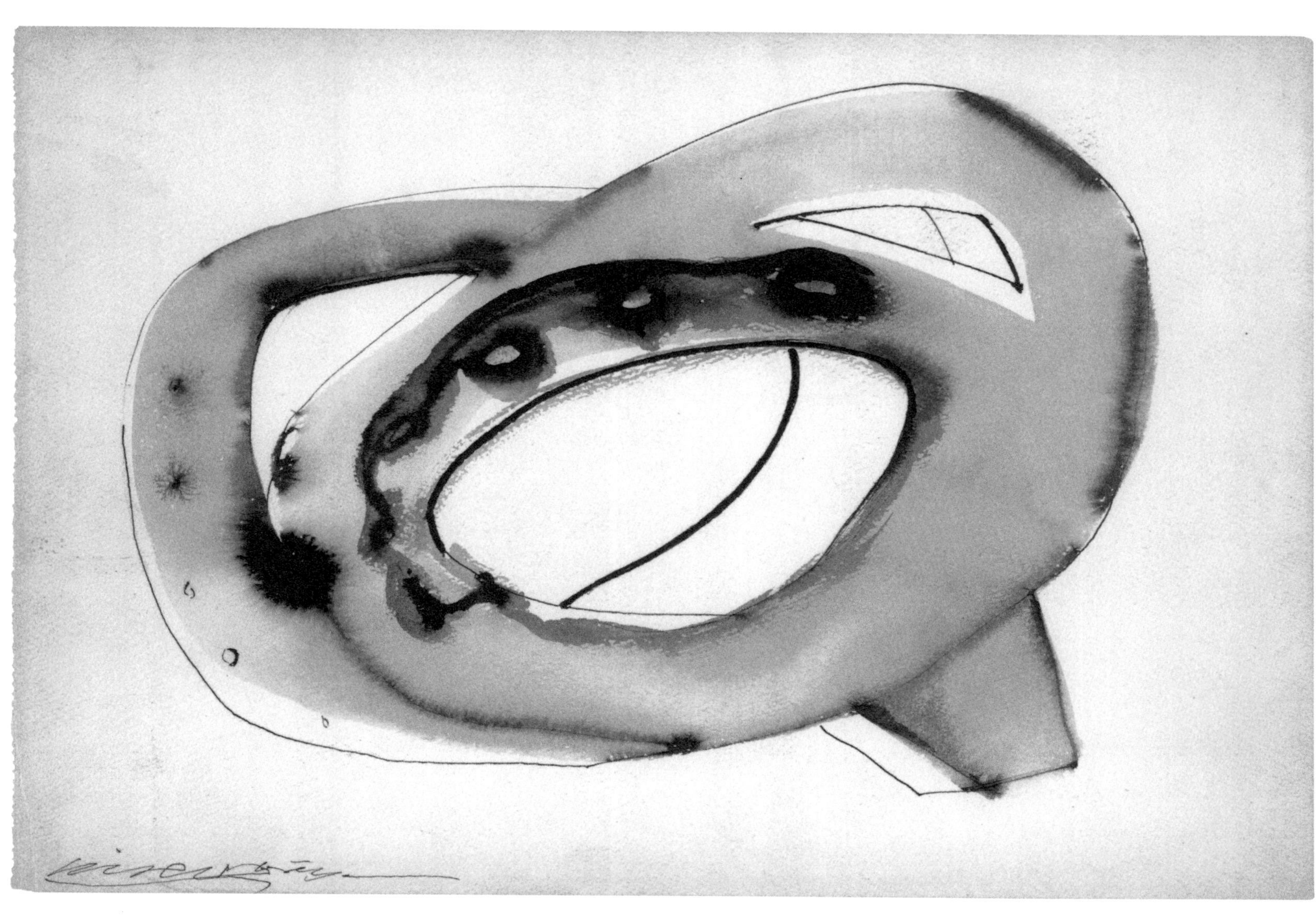

Frederick Kiesler, *Study for Endless House* [Paris Endless], 1947. (gouache, ink) ÖFLKS, SFP_497/0

L'ARCHITECTURE D'AUJOURD'HUI

REVUE MENSUELLE D'ARCHITECTURE CONTEMPORAINE ★ 5, RUE BARTHOLDI, BOULOGNE (SEINE) ★ TÉL. : MOLITOR 31-71

ANDRÉ BLOC, DIRECTEUR GÉNÉRAL
PIERRE VAGO, PRÉS. DU COMITÉ DE RÉDACTION ★ A. PERSITZ, RÉDACTEUR EN CHEF

4502/Y.C. Boulogne, le 8 Octobre 1947

Monsieur Frederic KIESLER
56, 7th Avenue
NEW-YORK CITY

U.S.A.

Cher Monsieur KIESLER,

J'espère que vous avez fait un bon voyage de retour aux U.S.A. et je me permets de vous rappeler que, comme convenu, j'espère recevoir vers le 15 Octobre le dossier que vous me préparez pour la présentation de votre manifeste dans l'Architecture d'Aujourd'Hui. Je suis persuadé que vous réunirez tous les éléments de la manière la plus précise de façon à ce que cette publication ait toute la portée que nous lui souhaitons.

D'autre part, j'ai pensé souvent aux conditions d'édition de votre grand ouvrage intitulé "L'ARCHITECTURE MAGIQUE". Notre Revue pourrait éventuellement se charger de toute la partie illustrationde cet énorme travail. Toutefois le texte complet est trop considérable pour les facultés d'absorption de notre imprimeur. Ne serait-il pas possible de demander ce travail à un autre éditeur, par exemple, GALLIMARD? Autrement dit, l'impression et la diffusion des ouvrages seraient faites en collaboration entre deux éditeurs. Si cette solution vous paraissait impossible, nous pourrions faire éditer seulement la partie illustration, en l'accompagnant d'un texte plus condensé.

Veuillez me faire connaître votre point de vue, et dans l'attente du plaisir de vous lire, je vous prie de croire, Cher Monsieur KIESLER, à mes sentiments cordiaux et dévoués.

A. BLOC

COMPTE CHEQUES POSTAUX PARIS 1519-97 ★ REGISTRE DU COMMERCE DE LA SEINE 485.930

André Bloc to Frederick Kiesler, October 8, 1947. (TS) ÖFLKS, LET_679/0

informs Bloc about the progress with his manifesto: "I worked a lot! The manifesto is ready and I will send it to you within a week at the latest." Kiesler proposes to contact Mme Gabrielle Picabia for the translation of his "Manifesto of Correalism" (referred to as "Manifeste du Corréalisme"), since the text was drafted in German.[62]

November 5, 1947
Stefi notes in her calendar that Kiesler has a lunch meeting with James Barrett and Hugh Chisholm from the Bollingen Series.[63]

November 6, 1947
Raymond Queneau, acquisitions editor at Gallimard, writes to Kiesler, informing him that he received the letter from Parisot, but that they cannot commit to publishing the book without having viewed the entire manuscript. "We are still willing to publish your History of Architecture, but unfortunately, we do not see the possibility of committing ourselves in a definitive way, before having the complete manuscript in our hands."[64]

December 31, 1947
A letter from Parisot explains how publishing houses communicate with prospective authors in France (suggesting Kiesler may have been caught off guard by the sober tone of Queneau's correspondence). "But the commitment of Gallimard to you nevertheless, appeared quasi-formal to me, according to what Queneau told me. Gallimard intends to publish your book provided that it is drafted according to the suggestions contained in your plan, which I do not doubt. Of course, as long as you have not signed a contract with them, you stay free to give your manuscript to another publisher."[65] (figs. C.22a–b)

1948

January 15, 1948
An entry in Stefi's calendar shows a meeting between Kiesler and staff from the Bollingen Series.[66]

January 30, 1948
A letter from the vice president of the Bollingen Foundation, D. D. Shepard, informs Kiesler that he has been granted a fellowship "of $200 per month for eighteen consecutive months, commencing in the month of February, 1948." The fellowship will enable him "to carry out the project referred to above, namely, the preparation and writing of a work on the basic problems of architectural design, or 'Magic Architecture.'" In return, Kiesler should present the manuscript upon its completion. The letter states that the Bollingen Foundation will have "an option to publish, or to arrange for the publication" of the work. Until then, Kiesler is not allowed to publish the work, neither in its entirety nor in parts.[67]

March 19, 1948
Stefi notes in her calendar a party at Kurt Seligmann's on the occasion of the completion of his book, *The History of Magic*, published by Kurt Wolff's Pantheon Books.[68]

June 30, 1948
Kiesler informs Queneau about the state of his book projects, writing that he appreciates the editor's "interest in my history of *Magic Architecture*; an American publisher has since ordered me to finish the manuscript for them"– an apparent reference to the Bollingen Series. "Hopefully I will have it ready within a year, and then I will send it to you for a French edition." Kiesler tries to convince Queneau to publish his more than 160-page "Manifeste du Corréalisme" and suggests Gabrielle Picabia as a French translator of the German manuscript. At the end of his letter, he states: "As you will read, the Manifesto of Correalism is more than a matter for the Artists. Surrealism and Existentialism have served the past and the present well. The Future will be correalistic."[69]

July 21, 1948
An entry in Stefi's calendar indicates "K. to Kurt Wolff."[70]

November to December, 1948
According to a series of entries in Stefi's calendar, Kiesler meets Hugh Chisholm almost weekly: "November 10, eve. Chisholm–[Frederic] Cohen"; "November 19, 8.30 Chisholm & lady friend and Cohen"; "December 1, dinner Marcel [Duchamp] Chisholm / French Fest. Pauvre Matelot / nach. [afterwards] to Julien Levy / Chisholm, [Leo] Castelli, / [I.B.] Neumanns"; "December 15, eve. Juilliard opening / 9h Chisholm meeting / James Human."[71]

During this time, Kiesler's interest gradually shifts from the publication of *Magic Architecture* to publishing his writings on correalism. However, the translation of his "Manifesto of Correalism" from German to French and later to English proves problematic, in spite of the large circle of friends who support the endeavor, including not only Hans Arp, Marcel Duchamp, and the composer Edgard Varèse, but also the diplomat, activist, and writer Stéphane Hessel.

December 15, 1948
During the winter of 1948, Kiesler is engaged with the set design for the opera *The Poor Sailor (Le Pauvre Matelot)*, with music by Darius Milhaud and libretto by Jean Cocteau, which premieres at the Juilliard Opera Theater in mid-December. He will eventually use parts of the set in a sculptural environment titled *Wooden Galaxy* that is later bought by Nelson Rockefeller.[72]

1949

January 29, 1949
In a letter, Kiesler informs Kurt Wolff, head of Pantheon Books, that *Partisan Review* will publish two chapters from his book and urges Wolff not to take any offence. "Meanwhile, I can also notify that *Partisan Review* has accepted two full chapters of my book for publication. I am still working on the final corrections. I do not want these, my lines to be misunderstood. Of course, I would be very happy if you would accept my book, on the other hand, I can assure you that my feeling of friendship for you would not be saddened in the opposite case." Kiesler does not mention which "book" he was discussing with Wolff at that point, yet his only article published in *Partisan Review* was a section of the "Manifesto of Correalism."[73]

February 28, 1949
Parisot notes in a letter that if Kiesler still wishes to publish the book, he should send the manuscript. Despite only a general reference to the "manuscript of your book," the context of the correspondence indicates that Parisot is referring to *Magic Architecture*.[74]

March 17, 1949
Stefi notes in her calendar that Kiesler is working with Philip Rahv, editor of *Partisan Review*, on the manuscript for the "Manifesto of Correalism." Kiesler and Rahv meet frequently in the course of the year and form a close working relationship.[75]

March 3, 1949
Kiesler contacts Paul Theobald, founder of Paul Theobald and Company, a fine art book publisher, following a phone call from Harriet Janis, wife of gallerist Sidney Janis and a longtime friend of the Kieslers. In a letter to the publisher dated March 9, Kiesler points to the problem of sending the illustrations and invites Theobald to visit his studio in New York. It is unclear which "new manuscript" Kiesler is referring to, but his mention of illustrated material points to *Magic Architecture*, since the book version of his "Manifesto of Correalism" did not contain a separate illustration section.[76] In the letter's concluding paragraph, Kiesler states that "it was only my friend Moholy-Nagy who saw the beginnings of my script, and hoped to include it in the

Juin 30, 48
New York, 56 -7th Avenue

Cher Monsieur Queneau:

J'ai vouly vous écrire il y a cinq mois, mais New York est une place où rien est plus rare -que le temps.

J'ai voulu vous dire que j'étais heureux de savoir que vous êtes interessé dans mon histoire de L'Architecture Magique; depuis un éditeur américain m'a donné l'ordre de finir le manuscrit pour eux. J'éspère d'être arrivé au but dans une année, et je vous l'enverrai alors pour une édition française.

Mais aujourd'hui une autre matière est pressante.
L'été dernier (à Paris) j'ai fini un manifeste concernant l'unité des arts plastiques et ce manifeste sera publié en octobre dans le numéro spécial de l'art de L'Architecture d'Aujourd'hui.
Il y aura beaucoup de photos et des planches en couleur, mais seulement 16 pages de texte, extrait de mon manuscrit qui a 160 pages.

Voilà ma proposition:
Je vous offre (confidentiellement) ce manuscrit complet, qui est dans les main de Mme Gabrielle Picabia, 11, rue Chateaubriand, qui traduit de l'allemand par excellence. Si vous êtes interessé, cher Monsieur Queneau, telephonez à elle, et elle vous rendera le manuscrit.

Peut-être on pourrait faire une combinaison avec M.Bloc de L'Architecture d'Aujourd'hui en usant les clichées,etc. pour l'édition d'un livre complet - ou, imprimer un petit livre sans photos (peut-être une seule feuille avec des photos comme frontis-pice). Le texte pourrait être illustré avec une douzaine des dessins en ligne noire, illustrations qui ne coûtent chères. (Ça ce qui sera souhaitable c'est de l'éditer si vite que possible.)

Il est bien possible que j'accepterai une invitation de faire ma première exposition en Novembre à Paris - comme peintre - et peut-être ça me donnera une opportunité de venir à Paris -- rien de plus désirable pour moi !

Cordialement,

P.S.
Comme vous liserez, le Manifeste du Correalisme est plus qu'une affaire des Artistes. Le surrealisme, l'existentialisme ont bien servi le passé et le présent. Le Future sera correaliste.

Frederick Kiesler to Raymond Queneau, June 30, 1948. (TS) ÖFLKS, LET_1740/0_recto-verso

series of his planned publications." Indeed as mentioned earlier, a book by Kiesler had been announced in a 1925 advertisement of future Bauhaus books edited by Gropius and Moholy-Nagy, although that publication was supposedly on "new forms of display" and "the city in space."[77] Still, Kiesler's reference to Moholy-Nagy is strategic, an aim to make his proposal more attractive to Theobald, who had recently published *Vision in Motion*, one year after the artist's death. In later correspondence with Theobald, the manuscript under discussion strongly suggests itself as Kiesler's book on "correalism."

March 18, 1949
Theobald replies that he is unable to visit Kiesler but that he will treat the manuscript discreetly. "It would, of course, simplify matters if I could come to New York to see the work. Unhappily this will not be possible for some time to come and I am compelled to impose on you to send it–even though only a small part of it."[78]

April 10, 1949
Kiesler informs Henri Parisot that his article will soon be published in the *Partisan Review* and begins to negotiate the publication of his manuscript on "correalism." In a postscript to the letter, he refers to *Magic Architecture:* "It will probably be of interest to Mr. Queneau to know that my plan for a History of Magic Architecture, which you so graciously referred to him and which he accepted in principle, has also been accepted here by the Bollingen Press. But I will not have finished the manuscript for another year."[79]

April–May 1949
Kiesler frequently corresponds with André Bloc on the publication of his "Manifeste du Corréalisme"; a comprehensive bundle of correspondence and other documents bears witness to their joint efforts.[80]

April 25, 1949
Stefi's calendar notes Kiesler's presence at a CIAM meeting, held at the office of Josep Lluís Sert.[81]

May 17, 1949
John D. Barrett from the Bollingen Foundation informs Kiesler that his requests for an extension of the grant by six months will be presented to the Board of Trustees at the next meeting.[82]

May 28, 1949
Parisot informs Kiesler that Raymond Queneau does not intend to publish his manuscript. "Queneau tells me that the text in question is not exactly what he expected. He was intending to publish … in principle, this architecture through the ages that you told him about."[83]

June 1949
Kiesler's "Manifeste du Corréalisme" finally appears in the special edition of *L'Architecture d'Aujourd'hui* on "Les Arts Plastiques."[84]

June 22, 1949
A letter from the Bollingen Foundation responds to a request by Kiesler for an extension of his fellowship for six months. The subject of Kiesler's project is generically described as "basic problems of architectural design." The extension is granted under the same terms of the original fellowship. Payments will start August 1949 and end January 1950.[85]

July 1949
Philip Rahv publishes an article based on a chapter from Kiesler's manuscript on "correalism" in the *Partisan Review* under the title "Pseudo-Functionalism in Modern Architecture."[86]

October 17, 1949
Kiesler writes to Paul Theobald saying he will be in Chicago to lecture at the Institute of Design and could meet to review the manuscript. Theobald accepts the invitation.[87]

November 16, 1949
Kiesler informs Kurt Wolff that he is offering his edited manuscript on correalism to the Bollingen Series. "As you can see, the matter is gaining ground. I have decided to submit the corrected manuscript to the Bollingen Series for publication and will talk to Barrett about it these days. …The content of this manuscript will be urgently requested by schools of architecture."[88]

November 22, 1949
After meeting Kiesler in Chicago to discuss his correalism manuscript, Paul Theobald sends Kiesler a letter of rejection. Four days later, Kiesler sends a letter asking for more details on the press's decision: "I think, I deserve a somewhat more detailed account of your reaction. … Please, be frank. I will appreciate that very much."[89] On December 6, Theobald replies: "There is more than one factor which led to our conclusion. There is the matter of a translation. If not well translated into English it may become a little hard to understand. Altogether it is a little too learned and would require quite a revision."[90]

1950

May 19, 1950
Lew Schwartz, editor at Abelard Press asks Kiesler for a meeting. According to Stefi's calendar, they meet each other frequently between May and July.[91]

June 28, 1950
Kiesler receives blank copies of a standard contract from Abelard Press, Inc.[92] Since only the press's letter has survived (with no reference to a book title), it is unclear whether Kiesler ever signed and returned the contract or for which book project this contract was intended.

July 10, 1950
In a letter to Margot Cutter from Princeton University Press negotiating the publication of his book on correalism, Kiesler praises the importance of his manuscript. The letter reveals that the text is still in German and needs to be translated into English. In his concluding paragraph, Kiesler makes a reference to his book project on *Magic Architecture*: "the Bollingen Foundation had given a grant three years ago to enable my research on a voluminous work 'The Story of Human Housing', which I will not be able to finish until 1952."[93]

July–September 1950
Kiesler corresponds with Swiss art historian, conductor, theater director, and contributor to *Zeitschrift für Bauen und Wohnen* Hans Curjel about publishing his "Manifesto of Correalism" in German. Curjel passes the manuscript to publisher Hans Girsberger.[94]

1950–1954

Kiesler shifts from writing to producing a highly prolific body of work as architect and artist. He exhibits his first *Endless House* at the Kootz Gallery (1950) and MoMA (1952), and creates *Galaxy* paintings and sculptures. There is no evidence of any work on *Magic Architecture* during this period.

MID-1950S

A bundle of research material includes letters from Kay Johnson, Kiesler's research assistant, to *LIFE* Magazine and the American Museum of Natural History in New York, asking for "diverse construction of the nests, homes, and burrows of various insects, birds, and animals. We are interested in the structural aspect." Library slips for books on bees demonstrate that Kiesler continues to research certain themes described in *Magic Architecture*.[95]

1955

January 2, 1955
Stefi records in her diary: "and [he asked whether] would I be good enough and let me dictate a report to the Bollingen Foundation. I asked how long it will take and he said about an hour. ... At 6.30 he came in ... dictated me a letter to Princeton University, and then started on his report. I sat quiet and only rarely did I point out a mistake of his by repeating himself. He just never thinks from one sentence to the next. That lasted until past eight."[96] (figs. C.23a–b)

January 9, 1955
In his response to a letter from Ernest Brooks, Jr., secretary to John D. Barrett at the Bollingen Foundation, Kiesler mentions updating his book project: "I take this opportunity to bring my project up to date. I enclose these details that I trust will clarify the theme of my proposed book."[97] Yet, instead of a detailed report, the attachments archived along with this letter include a single-page draft titled "Re: Magic Architecture, the Story of Human Housing," as well as a two-page addendum, "Re: Project–Frederick J. Kiesler," with a listing of Kiesler's projects of the late 1940s and early 1950s culminating in a proposal for funding an exhibition of his *Galaxy* paintings and sculptures. In his brief update "Re: Magic Architecture," Kiesler reiterates his "determination to complete the book," because "the problems" on which it touched "had grown more acute" since his previous applications to the Foundation (1947 and 1950). He mentions recent developments in the US, Central and South America as well as Italy and France, which "show a trend towards the goal described in my original outline." He also notes the "broadening" of societal needs from "immediate shelter" towards "the aesthetic and psychological aspects of human housing."[98]

September 28, 1955
Kiesler writes to John D. Barrett about his application for another fellowship from the Bollingen Foundation: "I do hope it will be feasible to get together on our book [*Magic Architecture*], which I am very eager to finish, because I feel it is now a very timely matter."[99]

December 5, 1955
Ernest Brooks, Jr., informs Kiesler, on behalf of the Bollingen Foundation, about "an extension of the fellowship, which you held in 1948–1949, to enable you to complete your manuscript entitled *Magic Architecture*." Brooks states that the Trustees have granted his request but "do not anticipate that it will be possible to grant any further extension of your fellowship."[100] In a separate letter addressed to Kiesler and written on the same day, John D. Barrett personally expresses that he is "so glad that it was found possible here to make this extension for you, and I know good work will be done."[101]

In a letter dated January 2, 1956, Kiesler thanks Barrett for "your grant of a fellowship of your Foundation. I have received the first payment, and would like to make an appointment with you to discuss the further procedure of my script. Your grant is most encouraging."[102]

1956–1965

In the last decade of his career, Kiesler becomes absorbed in architectural projects, such as the *Shrine of the Book* (1957–1965), the *Endless House* (1958–1959), and the *Grotto for Meditation* (1963–1964); artworks, such as his *Shell Sculptures* (1950s); and sculptural environments, such as *US-YOU-ME* (1963–1965) and *Bucephalus* (1964–1965).

He no longer pursues the completion or publication of *Magic Architecture*. Instead, in 1956, Kiesler starts writing a diary, describing his personal and professional life as an artist, architect, stage designer, and world traveler. This "journal" would eventually be published by Simon & Schuster one year after his death in 1965, in a large volume titled *Inside the Endless House* and illustrated with the architect's drawings.[103] While detailing the very activities that essentially prevented him from completing *Magic Architecture* or any other of the ambitious theoretical book projects he had planned in previous decades, this sprawling and somewhat anachronic diary also contains a few spolia from the investigations broached in Kiesler's "Story of Housing," such as his research on termite constructions, or the spatial structures of artists like Michelangelo.[104]

1966
Finally, an essay titled "Notes on Architecture as Sculpture," published posthumously in *Art in America*–and completed, according to the editor, "a week before [the author's] death"[105]–includes references to "cave dwellings," straw huts, and "branch woven" shelters,[106] as well as illustrations of building monuments, ranging from Neolithic dolmen, Egyptian pyramids, and the Machu Pichu Inca citadel, to Greek, Gothic, Indian, and Japanese temples, all of which echo *Magic Architecture*'s global architectural and "pre-architectural" examples.[107] (figs. C.24a–d)

January 2,1955, evening,Sunday.

Went to bed last night around midnight. The dizziness became better. Fell asleep exhausted around one, and he was not home yet.

This morning I woke up at 9, bathed my hand with salt, breakfasted and felt slightly better than yesterday. At 11 took my little rugs and went to the laundry, knowing that he will be up much later. Came back at 12, hung around, bather my flowers, cleaned my windows and could not settle to any real work knwoing that I will be interrupted. I just cannot let my creative mood go when I know that some duty, which is really not a duty of mine, is awaiting me. It became two and I phoned with Fritzi who wanted to go with me to a movie. Finally after three I heard his phone and him talking, so I went into his apt., already quite angry with myself and him. He began to tell me that after the concert he went with "the boys" to dinner, also Paul and Mimi Brach and then with them to a movie. I interrupted his tales by saying that I must pick up the dry laundry, and if he is finally ready for breakfast.

Fritzi told me he phoned with her last night at 8.30, but he did not call here. When I came back from downstairs and prepared his dinner he continued by saying that Mimi showed him her new painting and that she is a very good painter. They had to wait long in her studio until she was ready (exactly one block from us) and they went to Desirée on 14th Str. It became late because they came in the middle of the film and had to sit through a stupid Westerner and then Mimi insisted of seeing again the entire fil, so it became very late and then they went for a coffee and he came home after two. He could not fall asleep and took a sleeping powder at 6. I could have screamed listening to the blasted story over and over again - always the same - always complaining, always wondering about the same thing. I sat on my chair like on nails, trying to think of my own things but he hammered away whome he met at the concert, telling me the story of Napoleon (inspired by the stupid film). I gave short answers just here and there. He has a wonderful capacity to absolutely ignore the other person's feelings and desires. Finally, at 4.45 he said that he will dress and would I then be good enough and let me dictate a report to the Bollingen Foundation. I asked how long it will take, and he said about an hour. Went back to my room, fuming. Here it was past five and I haven't done a blessed thing. Now waiting again for his dictation.

At6.30 he came in (I heard him telephone a lot with people), dictated me a letter to Princeton University, and then started on his report. I sat quiet and only rarely did I point out a mistake of his by repeating himself. He just never thinks from one sentence to the

-798

next. That lasted until past eight, I got hungry and asked his plans for the evening. He said that he is going to Elfi. She is the Swedish girl he could not stand, then asked her to work for him, then did not see her, and now again they seem to be thick. His darling Stella. I guess, just visits him rarely and only when she needs something, so he has to look for other interests. And the way he talks about the Brachs, it seems that "Mimi" is his next occupation, but the husband Paul is not an easy guy, and he may have trouble with him.

He left at 8.45, and said that if he is not back until midnight he will not distrub me. Before he left he thanked me profusely and said that he hopes he did not disturb too much my Sunday. He disturbed it completely. I even didn8t bother to answer that. While in the door, he quickly said that we are invited to the Steinbergs for dinner, and he will call me tomorrow afternoon if I go or not. I asked if he had accepted for me, and he said yes, but I don't have to tell him now. What a slick operator he is for his own interests. Well, it will go so far and one day I will have the courage to go off for good. If Stella did not give me enough strength perhaps his dealings with Mimi, if it ever comes to something (and I have my doubts) will give me the strength; yet, funny enough, my desire to go does not at all come for these reasons, but existed before any of them ever came into the picture. Do I need this type of help for my decisions? Then, I am perhaps as weak as he is.

Tomorrow a hard work week begins. I had not seen Marianne and not phoned. He managed all his life to keep me off the things I want to do most - but, after all, it is I to blame really.

Began to copy my story and I am determined to send it off, to prove to myself that inspite of it all I must muster strength and will power enough to try my way in the literary field, to use the material I have and perhaps really can earn some extra money with it. Wrote a little short short in between but had no time to copy it from longhand to type. Will try to perhaps work at the library more for myself.

Stefi Kiesler, *Diary*, January 2, 1955. (TS) ÖFLKS, TXT_6888/2_N797-N798

Frederick J. Kiesler examining model of small horse sculpture he fashioned in his shell construction technique.

The Future: **NOTES ON ARCHITECTURE AS SCULPTURE**

The visionary architect Frederick J. Kiesler completed this text and the photo captions a week before his death at age seventy. He discusses contemporary buildings in relation to the past and the development of his own revolutionary projects—from his theater designs of the 1920s, which anticipated the needs of the most avant-garde groups performing today, to his "Endless House," a cornerless, curving construction in which floors, walls and ceilings merge in one continuous architectural flow

It is very difficult and it is quite easy to find historical and functional excuses for changes in styles of architecture. Of course most historians, you must not forget, come after, way after, soon after, after-after the changes in architecture have taken place. The archeologists, the tomb-robbers of building treasures, try to make a mosaic out of lost time even if half the stones of the image or more than half are missing. But we must not forget that quite some time before buildings of any period are erected and exposed to contemporaries and posterity, certain individuals have envisioned the buildings and fostered their realization through government sponsors, social or private agencies or religious institutions, believers and dreamers. Thus the two dreamers, the individual artist-architect and the individual Maecenas or the hypnotized group who believe in common goals, common social or economic goals, have created the work. Thus it stands as an outgrowth of vision plus necessity. So it has been since the beginning of time; and thus it will remain even through the space age. Two painters cannot paint one painting. But before we go any further, let us not forget the two laws which govern architecture and shelter-building:

Art in America May–June 1966

Architecture is the art of making the superfluous necessary—in time.

Rental buildings are the methods of making the necessary obsolete—in time.

With these two depth charges we should quite easily hit the targets in both cases.

I am very much afraid that the growing aim of our contemporary architects to create architecture as sculpture is not only an outcome of the new awareness of the time-space concept of our age, but also, if not chiefly, a pursuit of fashions, an insidious by-product of our madness for the ever-changing new, a direct outgrowth of novelties sponsored at least twice a year by industry, be they womens' fashions, industrial design products—automobiles, refrigerators, washing machines, television sets—the whole range of a profit mentality, which truly builds in obsolescence as deliberately as nature makes everyone ultimately die—except that these manufactured objects have a much shorter range of life, some from season to season, others from showroom to junkyard.

Where does the human being come in here? What is happening to him? He is bombarded hourly through newspapers, magazines, radio and television, to keep up with fashion. Otherwise he is apt to lose status and is made to believe that his very physical and psychic comfort is impaired by the lack of the latest or near-latest contemporary technological environment. To be—is to sell yourself in style.

Let us take in comparison with this attitude the architecture of the Parthenon in Athens, built about 447–432 B.C. A long time ago, yet it holds our full attention from adolescence to old age—and through all types of society, be they Greek, Latin, Slavic, Anglo-Saxon, primitive or sophisticated! Yet not even the kernel of the building, the functional *raison d'être* of the whole structure, is in

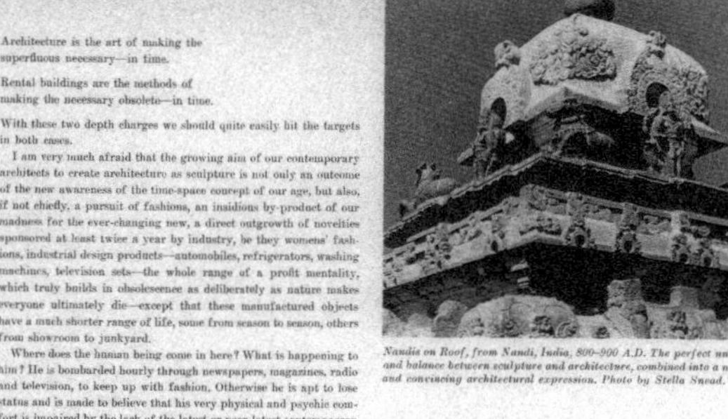

Nandis on Roof, from Nandi, India, 800–900 A.D. The perfect unity and balance between sculpture and architecture, combined into a new and convincing architectural expression. Photo by Stella Snead.

Parthenon, Acropolis, Greece, 448–432 B.C. The ultimate expression of post and lintel construction, a method on which our steel skyscrapers are also based and which the Endless House, through its continuous shell construction, has broken.

Corbusier are dedicated to art and to religion and not to everyday common life. They are abstractions of the highest order—an abstraction of art and death.

The weighty issue of Everyman's home is still to be achieved.

We want buildings solely dedicated to the meaning of everyday's life, life in all its aspects for the old, the young, the poet, the worker, the priest, jailbirds, thieves, money-changers, executives and truckers. To make it clear for all of us: *the guiding principle for our future relationship to all people is the new awareness throughout the world of time-space continuity.* Everyone and every part, nature and man-made objects, are subject to the interrelationship of a single continuum, whose beginning and whose end are unknown to man.

With regard to architecture the laws of continuity mean a space concept whose end returns to meet its beginning. Structurally the post and lintel construction of architecture has therefore become totally invalid; instead, continuity through shell construction is the new means to create the breathing indoor space of life.

A contradiction to this principle of continuity is Eero Saarinen's TWA terminal at Kennedy Airport in New York; it almost makes it. The sculptural roof develops from buttresses stuck into the ground. This nice comfortable compromise—the old post and lintel masqueraded into flowering bows of the ceilings—is deceiving. I don't understand how one and the same talented architect one year can build block after block of red brick buildings and a year or three afterward adopt the principle of the Endless House to flying buttresses and soon afterwards return to build adaptations of square towers in memory of Italian mountain villages, which he did at Yale.

The competitive spirit is thus very detrimental to the mental health and character of the architect. It has too often been stated (and by me, too) that any real talent has throughout his own life one—and only one—basic creative idea, not two (for example, think of William Blake, James Joyce, Edgar Varèse, Ledoux). And the pursuit of this one idea takes a lifetime, be it short or long. Whenever the thread of life is cut, it bleeds the same color of blood.

We must keep in mind:

a) that if a building looks sculptural, this by no means makes it architecture.

b) that in order to achieve the order of architecture there are four components which must be inter-related: 1) vision, 2) a structural concept, 3) the functional necessities in an evolution progression and 4) the most important ingredient: at the root of itself, a fundamental belief, a credent, growing out of man's relationship to the unknown (the universe).

Only the integration of these four could lead to architecture. The first three points may change, due to past or present environment, and therefore crystallize in diverse mutations—but the fourth point, that is, the content, must be as steadfast as the Greeks at Thermopylae.

It is outstanding to find that almost all prehistoric dwellings have a distinct sculptural look, a spherical or conical shape. All of these are based on the circular ground plan. For example:

a) The hut, covered with straw or leaves
b) Shieldings, branches woven together and covered with turf
c) Beehives
d) Dolmens (a large stone lifted up by three or more stone blocks as supports)
e) Cave dwellings
f) Tents
g) Stonehenge
h) Tumuli or burial mounds

But this still does not make them architecture. But the burial mounds and monuments come closer to it because they really have no practical purposes pertaining to life issues but are dedicated to the abstract idea of the departed spirit.

64

Dolmen, Carnac, Brittany, France, 1500 B.C. Pre-architectural sculpture building—the beginning of post and lintel construction.

This holds true of all great monuments, of all structures dedicated to the dead, not necessarily mausoleums, but buildings consecrated to the pacification of the invisible powers that rule over life and death, as expressed in the temples and cathedrals of the world: the Pyramids, the Pantheon, Chartres, Frank Lloyd Wright's synagogue in Philadelphia. But there is not one building dedicated to a truly architectural expression of life itself. Our houses are simply shelters, protection against heat, wind, rain and surprise attacks by animals and enemies, and the richer classes of a population put on ornaments, high or low reliefs or colors to break the monotony of a protective flat wall. This wall receives high or low window openings, frames, cornices, open staircases, higher ceilings inside, more servants' quarters—but these houses still remain one box after another, softened by fat or meager interior furnishings and equipped to disperse boredom with hi-fi, television with remote controls or telestar imagery with sound. Our contribution in the twentieth century was to shrink the Victorian appetite for richer and more abundant architectural food so that the modern dwellings are reduced to bones and skins, to flat walls and ceilings, to cubes and rectangles. In the industrial age we are still putting one box on top of the other until in a multi-cellular fashion we reach fifty or sixty floors or more. We did and still do the same thing with dwellings of so-called modern house design. The more glass the better, the more equipment and labor-saving devices, the more saleable. Banned (this was one of the credos of our De Stijl group of the Twenties) were decorative walls with paintings or sculptures; we advocated a purity and abstraction of interior and exterior, and finally replaced vertical windows with horizontal ones, sometimes with one long strip of glass. As we came into the Thirties under the influence of Mondrian, primary colors covering the squares of all walls were permitted besides white, but brown, green and purple were tabu. The only variations allowed were shades of gray, and not too many. It was a damn good education in learning how to hold the horses of one's imagination, in driving into nothingness and *that* in restricted space areas.

As I look back at my own work of that period, I see that the designs of several Endless Houses which I tried to promote from Vienna (1924) to Paris and to New York are the first to break entirely with the cube-prison tradition, to liberate space into galaxies of *disclosed* spaces for living, to invent a special construction system, *the shell in continuous tension, to eliminate the sharp division between floor, wall and ceiling of the box*, and to inject into the whole concept of a dwelling the psychological and emotional impact of the unexpected heights and widths of all living areas within a singular or multiple dwelling. The floor plan and the sections were neither squarish nor rectangular nor circular, *but the expression of a flow of life-forces, intensified to the point of intrinsic expansion.* What was necessary was a thorough investigation of the *basic needs* of man, his family and community. Luckily I was invited to form a Laboratory for Design-Correlation at Columbia University in 1936, which continued until the middle of World War II, that is, until 1943. This investigation had nothing to do with actual architecture, designing exteriors or interiors. It was clear to me that our research group must first of all investigate the function of life-forces at their roots and not just modify or modernize old habits of living.

I still firmly believe that the study of the forces which make and maintain life is more important for schools of architecture than studies of past or present styles of design. The trouble begins when people, in order to crawl into their huts, no longer want to duck through tent-slits or beehive huts and start to make high door entrances and then windows—until with the evolution of new habits through thousands of years the enclosed wall of a house becomes perforated with openings—rectangular, arched, stone, wood, brick or glass. This opening for getting into a house or out of it, these windows for letting in air and sunshine—create all the so-called

Sphinx of Giza and Pyramid, Egypt, about 2550 B.C. The monumental Sphinx contrasts so violently in its curvilinear form with the hard-edged Pyramid that an immediate unification takes place by heavy contrast. The perfect scale of each building in relation to the other is the deciding factor in wide areas of highly individual structures.

65

Frederick Kiesler, "The Future: Notes on Architecture as Sculpture," *Art in America*, 54/3, May-June 1966. ÖFLKS, KUN ZEIT_031

1 For such a chronology, see Matthias Boeckl, Dieter Bogner, "Friedrich Kiesler 1890–1965," in *Friedrich Kiesler. Architekt Maler Bildhauer 1890–1965*, ed. Dieter Bogner (Vienna: Loecker, 1988), 9–177. Although written thirty years ago, this is still the most comprehensive chronology of Kiesler's life and work. For two more recent biographic accounts, see Gerd Zillner, "Friedrich Kiesler: Biografie," in *Friedrich Kiesler. Architekt Künstler Visionär*, ed. Gerd Zillner, Peter Bogner, and Dieter Bogner (Munich: Prestel, 2017), 15–35; Jill Meißner, "Frederick Kiesler 1890–1965," in *Frederick Kiesler. Life Visions*, ed. Christoph Thun-Hohenstein et al. (Basel: Birkhäuser, 2016), 194–200.

2 Note that all translations from non-English texts have been undertaken by the author and appear in the Main Text.

3 Frederick Kiesler, "Note to the Publisher," transcribed in the main section of this book. TXT_6712/0_N1

4 Kiesler, "Vitalbau–Raumstadt–Funktionelle Architektur," *De Stijl* 6 (1925): 141–147.

5 Kiesler, *Contemporary Art Applied to the Store and its Display* (New York: Brentano's, 1930), 48.

6 Announcement by Albert Langen Verlag of "Bauhausbücher," in J. J. Oud, *Holländische Architektur*, ed. Walter Gropius and László Moholy-Nagy [Bauhaus-Bücher, vol. 10] (Munich: Albert Langen, 1926), page unnumbered, following 107.

7 Jill Meißner-Wolfbeisser, "Stefi Kiesler: eine Bibliothekarin als 'geistiger Refugee Service,'" in *Das Exil von Frauen. Historische Perspektive und Gegenwart*, ed. Ilse Korotin, Ursula Stern (Vienna: Praesens, 2020), 251–267; Meißner-Wolfbeisser, "Explorationen über Steffi Kiesler und die Rolle der öffentlichen Bibliothek im Exil," in *Grenzüberschreitungen. Migrantinnen und Migranten als Akteure im 20. Jahrhundert*, ed. Kristina Schulz, Wiebke von Bernstorff, and Heike Klapdor (Munich: edition text+kritik, 2020), 191–206.

8 The bookstore's label reads: "B. WESTERMANN Co. INC. / GENERAL & SCIENTIFIC BOOKS / IN ALL LANGUAGES / 13.W.46th St. NEW YORK."

9 In Kiesler's CV, cited in note 10, the Westermann bookstore refurbishment commission is added by hand: "1930. Rebuild [sic] Westermann Book-Store N.Y.C."

10 "Curriculum Vitae. Frederick Kiesler architect." Heavily annotated TS copied in other CVS. TXT_6869/0 Cf. TXT_7414/0; TXT_7425/0 Kiesler also references *From Architecture to Life* in a prefatory note to the last article of a series he published in *Architectural Record* in the 1930s. Frederick Kiesler, "On Correalism and Biotechnique. A Definition and Test of a New Approach to Building Design," *Architectural Record* 86 no. 3 (September 1939): 60–75 (here 60).

11 See TXT_892_0-4 as well as the chapter, "The Hygiene of Functional Architecture," MA X. 8.

12 Cf. documents and preparatory material for later published essays by Kiesler: "Notes on Architecture. The Space House. Annotations at Random," *Hound & Horn* 7, no. 2 (January-March 1934): 292–297; "One Living Space Convertible into Many Rooms," *Home Beautiful* 44, no. 1, January 1934, 32–33; "Space-House," *Architectural Record* 75, no. 14 (January 1934): 44–61.

13 The catalogue accompanying the MoMA exhibition, with Frobenius's text included, becomes an important source for *Magic Architecture*, as do other publications by Frobenius. On Frobenius, see also editor's introduction.

14 Montagu would repeatedly appear in Stefi Kiesler's calendar, albeit with varied spellings: "Dr. Montagu," "Montague," and later with his first name, "Ashley." On Montagu, see also Sources, Disciplines, and Objects, pp. 44, 88 and MA, I.4.

15 Some of Kiesler's research clippings and photostats are stored in folders with materials for both the *Vision Machine* and the *Magic Architecture* projects. However, among the same materials are images not connected with *Magic Architecture*. It is not clear whether the filing was done by Kiesler himself or by his long-time assistant, second wife, and widow, Lillian Kiesler (née Olinsky).

16 "The Architect in Search of… Design Correlation. A Column on Exhibits, the Theater and the Cinema," *Architectural Record* 81, no. 2 (February 1937): 7–15; "Design-Correlation," *Architectural Record* 81, no. 5 (May 1937): 53–59; "Design-Correlation. Animals and Architecture," *Architectural Record* 81, no. 4 (April 1937): 87–92; "Design-Correlation. Certain Data Pertaining to the Genesis of Design by Light. Part I," *Architectural Record* 82, no. 7 (July 1937): 89–92; "Design-Correlation. Certain Data Pertaining to the Genesis of Design by Light. Part II," *Architectural Record* 82, no. 8 (August 1937): 79–84; "Design-Correlation. Towards a Prefabrication of Folk Festival," *Architectural Record* 81, no. 6 (June 1937): 93–96; "On Correalism and Biotechnique. Definition and Test of a New Approach to Building Design," *Architectural Record* 86, no. 3 (September 1939): 60–75. In the contents of this last *AR* issue, Kiesler's article has a different subtitle: "'On Correalism and Biotechnique:' A Study on the Genetics of Building Design, *Architectural Record* (September 1939), 5, see also editor's preface titled "The Genetics of Design," 59.

17 Stefi Kiesler, calendar of 1939, week 12, March 25. MED 853/0

18 This is mainly due to family rifts on both Stefi's and Frederick's sides during the 1910s and 1920s, and the subsequent absence of correspondence with most of the family members of both partners. Parts of Frederick's family survived in Romania; his nephew, Karl Rudner, with whom he maintained contact, survived in Vaduz. Little to nothing is known about most of Stefi's family members. Only her brother, Karl Frischer, is known to have taken his own life, due to the hardships of the time and the fear of Nazi persecution.

19 See the bundle of correspondence with Caro & Jellinek (Vienna, Austria) and Danzas & Co. (Buchs, Switzerland), American Archives of Art, Smithsonian Institution, Frederick Kiesler Papers, Folder: Correspondence, Chronological 1940.

20 The importance of Frederick and Stefi Kiesler as networking contacts for the European architects, artists, and writers who sought exile from Nazi terror in New York cannot be understated. This is especially true of the surrealists, for whom Kiesler played an integrative role, until their community fell apart in the aftermath of Arshile Gorky's suicide. See Peter Bogner, Gerd Zillner, ed., *Frederick Kiesler: Face to Face with the Avant-Garde: Essays on Network and Impact* (Basel: Birkhäuser, 2019).

21 Kiesler to Kenneth Dale McCormick, June 27, 1941. LET_4314/0 Stefi Kiesler, calendar of 1941, week 27, July 7. MED_855/1

22 Kiesler, "Some Testimonial Drawings of Dream Images," *VVV* 1 (June 1942): 27–32.

23 Kiesler, "Note on Designing the Gallery," *MA*, Introduction. TXT_188/0

24 "Special Exhibits on Man Proposed for December, 1942," TS with three pages. TXT_3595/0

25 Drawings and documents. Box_mfp_17

26 Correspondence, notes, photographs, research material and sketches at the Frederick Kiesler Foundation. Cf: box_pho_12, box_rec_17, box_sfp_17 and 18, box_mfp_04 and 17

27 For a description of the several phases of Kiesler's design and reproductions of the photographic panels sent to Moscow, see Jean-Louis Cohen, "American Exhibits for Moscow," in *Building a New World: Amerikanizm in Modern Architecture* (New Haven: Yale University Press, 2020), 384–406.

28 Correspondence, drawings, documents. Box_pho_12, Box_rec_17, Box_txt/let_18

29 Stefi Kiesler, calendar of 1945, week 21, June 1; week 23, June 16; week 25, June 28; week 30, August 2. MED_860/0

30 Stefi Kiesler, calendar of 1945, week 32, August 14. MED_860/0

31 Documents related to Stefi Kiesler's *Dream Book* project, six boxes. Box_txt_64-69

32 Stefi Kiesler, calendar of 1945, week 41, October 18. MED_860/0

33 Stefi Kiesler, calendar of 1945, week 43, October 30. MED_860/0

34 André Breton, *Ode à Charles Fourier* (Paris: Éditions de la Revue Fontaine, 1947). Stefi Kiesler, calendar of 1945, week 43, October 31. MED_860

35 Stefi Kiesler, calendar of 1946, week 30, July 31, August 1. MED_861/0

36 Stefi Kiesler, calendar of 1946, week 30, August 2–3. MED_861/0

37 Stefi Kiesler, calendar of 1946, week 31, August 5. MED_861/0

38 Kiesler, "Note to the Publisher," *MA*, Main Text.

39 Kiesler to Hugh Garvey, August 6, 1946, American Archives of Art, Smithsonian Institution, Frederick Kiesler Papers, Folder: Correspondence, Chronological 1946. See also "Note to the Editor" in Addenda: Drafts.

40 Kiesler to Clara Claasen, August 26, 1946, American Archives of Art, Smithsonian Institution, Frederick Kiesler Papers, Folder: Correspondence, Chronological 1946.

41 Kiesler to Kenneth McCormick, August 26, 1946, American Archives of Art, Smithsonian Institution, Frederick Kiesler Papers, Folder: Correspondence, Chronological 1946.

42 Henry Rago to Kiesler, August 28, 1946, American Archives of Art, Smithsonian Institution, Frederick Kiesler Papers, Folder: Correspondence, Chronological 1946.

43 Kiesler to Henry Rago, August 30, 1946, American Archives of Art, Smithsonian Institution, Frederick Kiesler Papers, Folder: Correspondence, Chronological 1946.

44 Henry Rago to Kiesler, September 3, 1946. LET_1745/0

45 Stefi Kiesler, calendar of 1946, week 35, September 5. MED_861/0

46 Stefi Kiesler, calendar of 1946, week 37, September 19. MED_861/0

47 Ben Schnall, *Frederick Kiesler with his cat Sing Sing on the "Metabolism Chart of Correalism,"* New York 1947. Several prints from the same negative. PHO_4862/0-3 See also "Synopsis." TXT_6682/0_N2 And see "CONTENTS," transcribed in *MA*, Main Text TXT_6686/0_N4

48 "Design's Bad Boy: A Pint-Size Scrapper Who After Thirty Years Still Challenges All Comers," *Architectural Forum* 86, no. 2 (February 1947), 88–91.

49 Stefi Kiesler, calendar of 1947, week 4, January 30. MED_862/0

50 Hugh Chisholm, *Atlantic City Cantata* (New York: Farrar Straus & Young, 1951).

51 Vaun Gillmor to Kiesler, March 11, 1947. LET_1199/0

52 Stefi Kiesler, calendar of 1947, week 13, April 2; week 20, May 20–22. MED_862/0

53 Frederick Kiesler, "L'Architecture magique de la Salle de Superstition," in *Le Surréalisme en 1947*, ed. André Breton, Marcel Duchamp (Paris: Galerie Maeght, 1947), 131–134.

54 Edgard I. Williams to Bollingen Series, June 16, 1947, American Archives of Art, Smithsonian Institution, Frederick Kiesler Papers, Folder: Correspondence, Chronological 1947. Edgar Irving Williams was a prominent East Coast architect, who became president of the Architecture League of New York and served as consulting architect to the New York Public Library. Williams taught for a number of years at Massachusetts Institute of Technology and Columbia University. See the obituary by Farnsworth Fowle, "Edgar I. Williams, architect, dead," *New York Times*, January 3, 1974.

55 Ernest R. Feidler to Kiesler, August 1, 1947, American Archives of Art, Smithsonian Institution, Frederick Kiesler Papers, Folder: Correspondence, Chronological 1947.

56 Kiesler, *Kunst und Architektur vereint. Ein Manifest des Korrealismus*, unpublished typescript, New York, 1947. TXT_6192/0 The date is probably fictitious—it would be the day after Kiesler's return flight from Paris to New York, coinciding with his fifty-seventh birthday.

57 Kiesler, *Kunst und Architektur vereint.*

58 Kiesler received letters from Bloc at his hotel in Paris, providing a record of their meetings. André Bloc to Kiesler, August 13, 1947; September 11, 1947. LET_2989; LET_678/0

59 "J'ai pensé souvent aux conditions d'édition de votre grand ouvrage intitulé 'L'ARCHITECTURE MAGIQUE,'" André Bloc to Kiesler, October 8, 1947. LET_679/0

60 André Bloc to Kiesler, October 8, 1947. LET_679/0

61 Henri Parisot to Kiesler, October 4, 1947. LET_1847/0

62 Kiesler to André Bloc, October 19, 1947. LET_683/0

63 Stefi Kiesler, calendar of 1947, week 44, November 5. MED_862/0

64 Raymond Queneau to Kiesler, November 6, 1947. LET_1739/0

65 Henri Parisot to Kiesler, December 31, 1947. LET_1848/0

66 Stefi Kiesler, calendar of 1948, week 2, January 15. MED_866/0

67 Donald D. Shepard to Kiesler, January 30, 1948, American Archives of Art, Smithsonian Institution, Frederick Kiesler Papers, Folder: Correspondence, Chronological 1948.

68 Stefi Kiesler, calendar of 1948, week 11, March 19. MED_866/0 Kurt Seligmann, *The History of Magic* (New York: Pantheon Books, 1948). The Kieslers often met with Seligmann and his wife, and Kiesler even drew portraits of his fellow-artist. He paid tribute to Seligmann after the latter's tragic death in 1962.

69 "Le surrealisme [sic], l'existentialisme ont bien servi le passé et le présent. Le Future sera correaliste…," Kiesler to Raymond Queneau, June 30, 1948. LET_1740/0

70 Stefi Kiesler, calendar of 1948, week 29, July 21, 1948. MED_866/0

71 Stefi Kiesler, calendar of 1948, week 45, November 10; week 45, November 19; week 48, December 1; week 50, December 15. MED_866/0

72 Kiesler, *Galaxy [for Nelson Rockefeller]*, New York 1948–1949 (base remade 1951), wood and rope, MoMA, New York, Obj.-No. 32.1991.a-n (Gift of Nelson Rockefeller).

73 Kiesler to Kurt Wolff, January 29, 2949, American Archives of Art, Smithsonian Institution, Frederick Kiesler Papers, Folder: Correspondence, Chronological 1949.

74 Henri Parisot to Kiesler, February 28, 1949. LET_1849/0

75 Stefi Kiesler, calendar of 1949, week 11, March 17. MED_867/0 The calendars account for more than thirty meetings between Kiesler and Philip Rahv.

76 Kiesler to Paul Theobald, March 9, 1949, American Archives of Art, Smithsonian Institution, Frederick Kiesler Papers, Folder: Correspondence, Chronological 1949.

77 See note 6 in this chronology.

78 Paul Theobald to Kiesler, March 18, 1949, American Archives of Art, Smithsonian Institution, Frederick Kiesler Papers, Folder: Correspondence, Chronological 1949.

79 Kiesler to Henri Parisot, April 10, 1949, American Archives of Art, Smithsonian Institution, Frederick Kiesler Papers, Folder: Correspondence, Chronological 1949.

80 In 1949, approximately twenty letters crossed the Atlantic Ocean between Bloc and Kiesler to coordinate the publication of the *Manifeste du Corréalisme*. The major part of this correspondence is held at the American Archives of Art, Smithsonian Institution, Frederick Kiesler Papers, Folder: Correspondence, Chronological 1949.

81 Stefi Kiesler, calendar of 1949, week 17, April 25. MED_867/0

82 Jack [John D.] Barrett to Kiesler, May 17, 1949. LET_2989 Kiesler to John D. Barrett, May 14, 1949, American Archives of Art, Smithsonian Institution, Frederick Kiesler Papers, Folder: Correspondence, Chronological 1949.

83 "Queneau me dit que le texte en question n'est pas exactement celui qu'il attendait. Il comptait éditer, comme … en principe, cette architecture à travers les âges dont vous lui aviez parlé. Il doit vous écrire d'ailleurs à ce sujet," Henri Parisot to Kiesler, May 28, 1949. LET_1850/0

84 Frederick Kiesler, "Manifeste du Corréalisme," *L'Architecture d'Aujourd'hui* (June 1949): 79–105.

85 Ernest Brooks Jr. to Kiesler, June 22, 1949. LET_715/0

86 Kiesler, "Pseudo-Functionalism in Modern Architecture," *Partisan Review* 16, no. 7 (July 1949): 733–742.

87 Kiesler to Paul Theobald, October 17, 1949, and Paul Theobald to Kiesler, October 19, 1949, American Archives of Art, Smithsonian Institution, Frederick Kiesler Papers, Folder: Correspondence, Chronological 1949.

88 Kiesler to Kurt Wolff, November 16, 1949, American Archives of Art, Smithsonian Institution, Frederick Kiesler Papers, Folder: Correspondence, Chronological.

89 Paul Theobald to Kiesler, November 22, 1949, and Kiesler to Paul Theobald, November 26, 1949, American Archives of Art, Smithsonian Institution, Frederick Kiesler Papers, Correspondence, Chronological.
90 Paul Theobald to Kiesler, December 6, 1949, American Archives of Art, Smithsonian Institution, Frederick Kiesler Papers, Correspondence, Chronological.
91 Lew Schwartz to Kiesler, May 19, 1950. LET_2991/0 Stefi Kiesler, calendar of 1950, week 20, May 23; week 22, June; week 25, June 13; week 27, July 11. MED_863/0
92 Paule H. Flavin to Kiesler, June 23, 1950. LET_3182/0
93 Frederick to Margot Cutter, July 10, 1950. LET_921/0_N1-N2
94 Hans Curjel to Kiesler, September 21, 1950. LET_919/0 An annotated typescript copy of "Menschen Kunst und Architecture. Ein Manifest des Korrealismus" is held at the partial estate of Zürich publisher Hans Girsberger in the gta Archives of ETH Zürich, Hq 374.
95 Bundle of research material on "Animal Building." TXT_6885/0 New York Public Library, order slips. LD 6425/0 See Addenda: Bibliographies.
96 Stefi Kiesler, calendar of 1955, Part 1, January 2, 797f. TXT_6888/2
97 Kiesler to Ernest Brooks, Jr., January 9, 1955, American Archives of Art, Smithsonian Institution, Frederick Kiesler Papers, Correspondence, Chronological, 1955.
98 Kiesler concludes his project "update" with a reference to the social scope of his book described in his original outline: "As in my original outline, I claim that the gulf between 'pure' shelter and 'pure' religious architecture (of past and present) must be bridged if the social gains of our time are to find expression in our architecture." For the entire text of this "update," see "Re: Magic Architecture" in Kiesler's letter to Brooks, January 9, 1955, cited in previous note.
99 Kiesler to John D. Barrett, September 28, 1955, American Archives of Art, Smithsonian Institution, Frederick Kiesler Papers, Correspondence, Chronological, 1955.
100 Ernest Brooks, Jr. to Kiesler, December 5, 1955, American Archives of Art, Smithsonian Institution, Frederick Kiesler Papers, Correspondence, Chronological, 1955.
101 John D. Barrett to Kiesler, December 5, 1955, American Archives of Art, Smithsonian Institution, Frederick Kiesler Papers, Correspondence, Chronological, 1955.
102 Kiesler to John D. Barrett, January 2, 1956, American Archives of Art, Smithsonian Institution, Frederick Kiesler Papers, Correspondence, Chronological, 1955.
103 Frederick Kiesler, *Inside the Endless House: Art, People, and Architecture. A Journal* (New York: Simon & Schuster, 1966).
104 See journal entry of May 27, 1956, "Animal Rex," *Inside the Endless House*, 35–36; and October 17, 1959, "First Clash with the 'Last Judgment' of Michelangelo," *Inside the Endless House*, 130–32.
105 See editor's note in Kiesler, "Notes on Architecture as Sculpture," *Art in America* (May–June 1966): 57–68 (at 57).
106 Editor's note, "Notes on Architecture as Sculpture," 64
107 In a caption, Kiesler describes the Neolithic Dolmen structure in Carnac, Britany, as a "[p]re-architectural sculpture building." See "Notes on Architecture as Sculpture," 64, and Sources, Disciplines, and Objects, p. 48.

ACKNOWLEDGEMENTS

This book project has taken more than ten years for the editors to complete—perhaps longer than the time its author spent on researching and writing it. Rehearsing Kiesler's own career trajectory, our collaboration on *Magic Architecture* traversed Vienna and New York, and so our thank-yous are equally divided between the two sides of the Atlantic.

On the Austrian side, our first token of gratitude goes to former Director of the Kiesler Foundation Monika Pessler, who introduced the idea of publishing excerpts of *Magic Architecture* alongside Bernard Rudofsky's research on "brute" and vernacular architecture, and who, upon leaving the Foundation in December 2013 to assume the directorship of Vienna's Freud Museum, put the two editors in contact to complete this task. The Kiesler Foundation's inaugural President, Dieter Bogner, whose groundbreaking research on Kiesler remains a model for all later scholarship on the architect, including ours, offered unwavering support. We are also grateful to the Foundation's Board of Directors—former President Hani Rashid and current President Elke Delugan-Meissl, as well as Monika's successor as the Foundation's Director, Peter Bogner—for their generosity in supporting this publication over the years. We are especially grateful to the Foundation's archive and research specialist, Jill Meißner-Wolfbeisser for sharing her expert knowledge of Stefi Kiesler and helping us to clarify her seminal role in the production of Kiesler's book manuscript. We are also grateful to Kerstin Putz for recording and re-cataloguing all archival documents related to *Magic Architecture* and for producing the first transcription of Kiesler's assembled manuscript back in 2015. Kerstin returned to the project in the summer of 2020 to compile the quotations and transcriptions included in the Addenda. We also appreciate the contributions of Anna Fliri for the handling of copyrights, as well as Theresa Czerny, Nina Nemes, Julia Kapferer, Anna Sauer, and Katharina Zwinger for their assistance at the Kiesler Foundation.

On the American side, we gratefully acknowledge the institutional support for this publication from the Barr Ferree Publication Grant Fund at Princeton University and the Graham Foundation for Advanced Studies in the Fine Arts in Chicago—in particular Sarah Herda, James Pike, and Caroline Murphy, who awarded us both a research and a publication grant for this project. We are also grateful to Princeton's Humanities Council for a Magic Grant for Innovation that supported an exhibition and workshop on *Magic Architecture* during the first years of our research. Heartfelt thanks to all workshop participants, including Laura McGuire, Stephen Phillips, whose own published scholarship on Kiesler remains invaluable for all Kiesler scholars, as well as Romy Golan, Ara Merjan, Effie Rentzou, and Esther Choi. Additional funding from the Mellon Initiative on Architecture, Urbanism, and the Humanities at Princeton supported Carson Chan, Vajdon Sohaili, and Clemens Finkelstein to work on identifying the sources of Kiesler's research clippings. Vajdon Sohaili also copyedited parts of the main text and introductory essays. We are most grateful to Clemens Finkelstein for his extensive bibliographic research on the image sources for Kiesler's plates, as well as the compilation of Kiesler's bibliographies. We are also grateful to Shirley Chen for her expert handling of text and image copyrights.

During the ten years of preparation for this book, excerpts from *Magic Architecture* have appeared in exhibitions, such as the second Istanbul Design Biennale *Are We Human* curated by Beatriz Colomina and Mark Wigley in 2016, *Préhistoire: Une énigme moderne* curated by Maria Stavrinaki et al. at the Centre Pompidou in 2019, and more recently *Magic Architecture/Habitat* by Kerstin Stoll curated by Gerd Zillner at the Kiesler Foundation in Vienna in the summer of 2024, as well as *pre-architectures* curated by Nikolaus Hirsch, Silvia Franceschini, and Spyros Papapetros at CIVA in Brussels on view from November 2024 to March 2025. The lessons we learned from exhibiting Kiesler's manuscript had significant impact on the final stages of its production as a published book.

Additionally, the editors wrote articles and edited excerpts from *Magic Architecture* published in catalogues of exhibitions, such as the Kiesler retrospective *Life Visions/Lebenswelten* at MAK (Vienna) curated among others by Bärbel Vischer, as well as art and architecture journals, such as *Les Cahiers du Musée National d'Art Moderne* and *Arquine*. Feedback from lectures about the project at Princeton, Harvard GSD, MAK (Vienna), the Royal College of Art (London), University of Oslo, EPFL (Lausanne), University of Hamburg, CIVA (Brussels), and many other venues has been invaluable in shaping our project, and we thank the organizers for their invitations. We are also grateful to scholars with whom we consulted in various stages of our work, including Kiesler specialists Laura McGuire, Almut Grunewald, and Stephen Phillips, as well as Sebastian Hackenschmidt, Markus Kristan, and Bernadette Reinhold. We are also grateful to Dieter Bogner and Ralph Ubl for supporting the project with letters, as well as the late Kurt W. Forster and Jean-Louis Cohen for recommending our book for publication to the MIT Press.

At the MIT Press, we are immensely grateful to its former Art and Architecture editor Tom Weaver, who enthusiastically endorsed our project and stewarded it to completion, as well as his production team, Sarah Handelman for her expert copyediting of this incomparably complex manuscript, and Ben Fehrman-Lee with Julia Novitch, whose exquisite layout realized Kiesler's vision for his book as a design "tool" for both present and future.

Our final thanks turn to the people whom Kiesler himself would or ought to have thanked had his book been published in his lifetime. Such a list might have included institutions like the Bollingen and Graham Foundations, which offered Kiesler multiple grants allowing him to work on *Magic Architecture* and other projects. The same hypothetical account could include fellow artists, like Marcel Duchamp and André Breton, whose own publication projects overlapped with Kiesler's during the 1940s, as well as scholars from whose expertise the architect drew in the context of his directorship of the Laboratory for Design Correlation at Columbia, such as the anthropologist Ashley Montagu.

While we can only speculate who might be included in this list, the presence of one name is undisputed: Kiesler's first wife Stefi, to whom the architect also dedicated his final book published the year after he died. One of the editors' most gratifying discoveries was unearthing the extensive contribution of Stefi in *Magic Architecture* across all stages of its incomplete production: from her research notes at the New York Public Library, to her transcriptions and translations of German and other publications, to her photostat ordering for the illustrations, and her tireless typing of Kiesler's often chaotic manuscript in its several versions, as well as countless letters to publishing house editors and grant institutions. As voiced in the pages of her calendar excerpted in our book, these tasks took precious time from her own book and art projects that never materialized. The publication of *Magic Architecture* is a testament to the surviving legacy of not only Kiesler's but also Stefi's unpublished work production.

Last but not least, the editors would like to acknowledge the uncanny coincidence of the posthumous publication of *Magic Architecture*, a text deeply informed by war and disease, during the aftermath of a global pandemic, in the midst of which the bulk of the editors' collaborative work was completed, and the ongoing war in Ukraine, whose sovereign territory proudly includes Kiesler's birth city of Chernivtsi.

Magic Architecture
The Story of Human Housing

Edited by
Spyros Papapetros and Gerd Zillner

FREDERICK KIESLER (1890–1965) was an Austrian-born American artist, architect, set designer, and sculptor best known for his exhibition installations and visionary architectural projects, including an experimental model of human habitation titled *The Endless House*.

SPYROS PAPAPETROS is Associate Professor of Art and Architectural Theory and Historiography at Princeton University. His many publications include *On the Animation of the Inorganic: Art, Architecture, and the Extension of Life* and the edited volume *Retracing the Expanded Field: Encounters between Art and Architecture* (MIT Press, 2014).

GERD ZILLNER is Director of the Austrian Frederick and Lillian Kiesler Private Foundation, Vienna. He has curated numerous exhibitions on Kiesler and coedited the volumes *Frederick Kiesler: Face to Face with the Avant-Garde* and *Friedrich Kiesler: Architekt, Künstler, Visionär*.

Frontispiece:
Ben Schnall, Portrait of Frederick Kiesler with his cat Sing Sing on top of his "Metabolism Chart of Correalism" and across the binder with the manuscript of *Magic Architecture* (photo taken inside the architect's and Stefi Kiesler's apartment in New York). B/W Photograph. New York, 1947. ÖFLKS, PHO_4862/2

The MIT Press
Massachusetts Institute of Technology
77 Massachusetts Avenue
Cambridge, MA 02139
mitpress.mit.edu

The MIT Press would like to thank the anonymous peer reviewers who provided comments on drafts of this book. The generous work of academic experts is essential for establishing the authority and quality of our publications. We acknowledge with gratitude the contributions of these otherwise uncredited readers.

The Austrian Frederick and Lillian Kiesler Private Foundation owns the copyright of all works by Frederick Kiesler, including all drawings and unpublished manuscripts, correspondence and diaries by Frederick and Stefi Kiesler, as well as of all documents at the Foundation's archive.

The production of this book was supported by grants by the Barr Ferree Publication Fund and the University Committee for Research in the Humanities and Social Sciences at Princeton University and the Graham Foundation for Advanced Studies in the Fine Arts.

This publication was also supported by the the Kiesler Foundation, whose research is funded by The Austrian Federal Ministry for Arts, Culture, the Civil Service and Sport, The Austrian Federal Ministry for Education, Science and Research and the City of Vienna.

Commissioning Editor: Thomas Weaver
Text Editor: Sarah Handelman
Design: Studio Ben Fehrman-Lee with Julia Novitch
Lithography: DawkinsColour in London

Printed and bound by Musumeci, SpA in Italy
With consultation from Michele Abrigo

Library of Congress Cataloging-in-Publication Data

Names: Kiesler, Frederick, author.
Papapetros, Spyros, editor. Zillner, Gerd, editor.
Title: Magic architecture : the story of human housing / Frederick Kiesler ; edited by Spyros Papapetros and Gerd Zillner.
Description: Cambridge, Massachusetts : The MIT Press, [2025]
Includes bibliographical references and index.
Identifiers: LCCN 2024059863 | ISBN 9780262046749 (hardcover)
Subjects: LCSH: Architecture--Human factors. Architecture--Philosophy.
Classification: LCC NA2542.4 .K47 2025
DDC 720.1--dc23/eng/20250122
LC record available at https://lccn.loc.gov/2024059863

10 9 8 7 6 5 4 3 2 1